D1282953

PILLSBURY KITCHENS' FAMILY COOKBOOK

Library of Congress Catalog Number: 78-78-230

CONTENTS

Publisher:
Wm. Edgley
Managing Editor:
Christine Fossum
Marketing Coordinator:
Reneé Dignan
Copy Editor and Managing Home Economist:
JoAnn Cherry
Assistant Copy Editor:
Roseanne Johnson
Art Director:
Bob Frink
Designer:
Kevin Kuester
Production Supervision:
Charlene Marinan Bland
Project Administrator:
Dory Skartvedt
Contributing Editorial Writers:
Louis Gelfand, Heather Randall,
Verone Smith
Home Economists:
Karen Schiemo, Elaine Christiansen,
Ginny Hoeschen, Irene Tufvander,
Mary Gunderson, Roseanne Johnson
Food Stylists:
Donnie Flora, Judy Tills
Photography:
Jack Revoir
Production:
Beth Van Bergen, Susan Truesdale
Nutrition Coordinators:
Pat Godfrey, Catherine Hanley
Ann Kapan,R.D.

NUTRI-CODED SYSTEM

THE NUTRI-CODED SYSTEM

This edition of the Pillsbury Kitchens' Family Cookbook is the first recipe book of its kind to feature NUTRI-CODED recipes. These recipes have been analyzed by computer to list the caloric and nutrient content per serving of every recipe, including minerals and vitamins.

The NUTRI-CODED system is a computerized method designed by Pillsbury's research scientists to utilize information compiled by the U.S. Department of Agriculture* and Pillsbury research. It represents Pillsbury's strong, continuing commitment to nutrition education. (Pillsbury was the first major food processor to add nutrition information to its consumer product labels.)

Specifically, these NUTRI-CODED recipes inform you on a per serving basis of:

1) The amount of calories, protein, carbohydrates, fat, sodium and potassium in that particular recipe. Protein, carbohydrates and fats are expressed in grams, sodium and potassium in milligrams.

2) The percentage contained in each recipe of protein, vitamins A and C, thiamine, riboflavin, niacin, calcium and iron needed by the body on a daily basis (U.S. Recommended Daily Allowance).

NOTE: FOR PEOPLE WITH SPECIAL DIETARY NEEDS, CONSULT YOUR PHYSICIAN BEFORE ACTING IN RELIANCE ON THE NUTRITIONAL INFORMATION IN THIS BOOK. Every effort has been made to ensure that this information is as accurate as possible. However, The Pillsbury Company does not guarantee its accuracy or its suitability for any specific medically imposed diets.

*The values used in this program are based upon files from U.S. Department of Agriculture, and are only as correct and complete as the information supplied.

*Primary Source: Agriculture Handbook No. 456

USING THE NUTRITIONAL INFORMATION

Pillsbury's NUTRI-CODED system can help you in your daily food planning. Below are guidelines.

SERVING SIZE: This has been determined by our home economists as a typical and an adequate serving size for each particular recipe. If you eat more or less you will have to adjust the nutritional information accordingly.

CALORIES: The amount of calories a person needs is determined by his age, size and activity level. The recommended daily allowances generally given are: 1800-2400 for children 4 to 10 years of age and women; and 2400-2800 for men.

PROTEIN: The amount of protein needed daily is also determined by age and size; however, the general U.S.RDA given for adults and children of at least 4 years of age is 65 grams.

CARBOHYDRATE AND FAT: The amount of carbohydrates and fat needed in the daily diet has not been determined, however, these amounts should be adequate so the body does not have to burn protein for energy.

SODIUM: There is much controversy today over the amount of sodium necessary in the diet and the effects on the body of any excess of sodium. However, many nutritionists feel a healthy person can consume 3500 to 4000 mg. per day.

POTASSIUM: The minimum daily requirement for potassium has not yet been determined. However, a reasonable lower level of intake is thought to be 2500 mg. per day.

PERCENT U.S.RDA PER SERVING: Choose recipes which, when totalled together, will give 100% of the U.S.RDA for each nutrient.

SOME NUTRIENTS OF MAJOR IMPORTANCE

PROTEIN: Protein provides the principal building blocks for all muscles and organs in the body. It is essential to life and an adequate amount should be eaten daily. Excess protein, which cannot be stored, is converted to energy, carbohydrates or fat.

Protein consists of substances known as amino acids. Twelve of the 20 amino acids can be produced by the body, the other eight must come from the daily diet. Complete protein – containing all of the essential amino acids in the right proportion – is found in meats, poultry, fish, eggs, milk and cheese. Dried beans and peas, and certain nuts also are rich in protein although their quality is somewhat lower.

FATS: Fats are the most concentrated source of energy for the body. In the diet, they are carriers of the fat soluble vitamins A, D, E and K. The body stores excess calories as fat. Fat contains slightly more than twice as many calories per gram or per ounce as do pure proteins and carbohydrates.

Food fat is available in two forms. One form, saturated fat (usually solid at room temperature) generally comes from animal sources such as meat and milk. Some vegetable fats, such as coconut oil and cocoa butter, are also saturated.

The other form is unsaturated, monounsaturated and polyunsaturated fat (usually liquid at room temperature) which come mostly from vegetable sources such as corn, safflower seed, peanuts, olives, sunflower seeds and soybeans.

Many nutritionists believe that a diet in which fat furnishes about 40% of the calories would be less inclined to result in overweight.

CARBOHYDRATES: A principal source of energy, digestible carbohydrates consist primarily of starches and sugars, including those sugars present in most fruits. They also help the body use fats effectively.

The starches are found in cereals (wheat, rice, corn, oats), breads, macaroni, noodles, potatoes, beets, yams and turnips. Honey, syrup, table sugar and fruit are the chief sugar sources. The body specifically needs carbohydrates as energy for the brain. Carbohydrates in excess of that required for immediate energy needs is largely converted to fat and stored as such.

SODIUM AND POTASSIUM: A proper balance of sodium and potassium within the body is necessary for normal functioning of the nervous system. Sodium is needed to maintain normal body fluid volume. Potassium is found principally within cells and is essential to their function. Important sources of potassium are meat, fish, fowl, cereals, vegetables and fruits, especially bananas.

One average size banana has 440 mg of the U.S.RDA of potassium.

The most common sources of sodium are table salt (1 teaspoon = 2,132 mg of sodium), milk, cheese, leavenings, soy sauce and monosodium glutamate (MSG). Modest excesses are generally eliminated by healthy persons. It has been recommended by some authorities that excessive intake of sodium be avoided.

CALCIUM: Calcium is needed for proper development of bones and teeth, helps the blood to clot and contributes to muscle contraction, normal heart rhythm and normal function of the nervous system. It is found in milk, hard cheese, ice cream, green leafy vegetables, shrimp, salmon, and clams.

IRON: Iron is an essential component of hemoglobin, that part of red blood corpuscles which carries oxygen from the lungs to the body tissues and carbon dioxide from the tissues to the lungs. Foods containing iron include lean meats, liver, egg yolk, breads and cereals, peaches, apricots, prunes, raisins and dark leafy green vegetables.

VITAMINS

VITAMIN A: Vitamin A is needed for proper vision in the dark. Also prolonged deficiency can cause damage to the eyes and to the lining of the passages that lead to the lungs. Vitamin A also is important to the health of the skin. It is abundant in green and yellow vegetables (carrots, squash, broccoli and spinach), cantaloupe, eggs, milk and butter.

VITAMIN C: The function of vitamin C (ascorbic acid) is still not well understood, but it is known that it plays an important role in the manufacture of a fibrous material called collagen (which serves to cushion the body's joints and reinforces the body's soft tissues). Lack of vitamin C causes bleeding gums, skin changes and impaired wound healing. Best vitamin C sources are citrus fruits, strawberries and some vegetables such as cabbage, broccoli, tomatoes, potatoes, brussels sprouts, cauliflower, and green peppers.

THIAMINE: Thiamine aids in the metabolism of carbohydrates. A marked deficiency will result in beriberi, still found in some undeveloped parts of the world. Good sources of thiamine are enriched cereals, enriched breads, pork, liver, dried peas and beans.

RIBOFLAVIN: Without adequate riboflavin our eyes would burn and hurt in bright light, and our skin would develop local inflammation and become crusted. Fortunately, riboflavin is in good supply in milk, liver, almonds, egg whites, dry lentils and Cheddar cheese as well as enriched cereals and breads.

NIACIN: Niacin is an essential part of the body's machinery involved in conversion of food into energy, and the body's processing of carbohydrates. A deficiency results in a condition known as pellagra, now rare in the United States since the enrichment of breads and cereals in the 1940's. Niacin is abundant in lean meats, chicken and poultry, enriched breads and cereals, eggs, peanuts, almonds, and wild and brown rice.

A DAILY FOOD GUIDE

The simplest, most effective method of utilizing the U.S.RDA guidelines is to follow the so-called Basic Four plan. By giving your family the recommended servings of each of the four food groups every day you can almost be assured of supplying their daily needs for good nutrition.

Food Group	No. Of Servings Per Day	Good Sources	Typical Serving Size
Milk Group	2 (adult) 3 (child)	milk	8 oz.
		Cheddar-type cheese	1-inch cube
		yogurt	½ cup
		cottage cheese	½ cup
		ice cream	½ cup
Meat Group	2	meat, poultry, fish	2 to 3 oz. cooked
		eggs	2
		dry beans or peas	1 cup
		peanut butter	4 tablespoons
Fruit and Vegetable Group	2 vegetables 2 fruit	yellow or green	½ cup
		potato	1 medium
		orange, peach, apple, pear	1 medium
		fruit juice	6 oz.
		tomato juice	6 oz.
Cereal Group	4	bread	1 slice
		dry cereal	⅔ cup
		macaroni	½ cup
		cooked cereal	½ cup

PILLSBURY GUIDELINES FOR CALCULATING THE NUTRITIONAL INFORMATION

Because many of the recipes in this book were not specifically developed for nutritional analysis, we had to make some basic assumptions to complete the nutritional information.

- Anytime an ingredient listing gives one or more options, the first ingredient listed is the one analyzed.
  Example: 1 cup mayonnaise or salad dressing
  The recipe was analyzed with 1 cup of mayonnaise.
- When a measurement range or quantity range is given for an ingredient within a recipe, the smaller amount is analyzed.
  Example: 2½ to 3-lb. frying chicken, cut up
  The recipe was analyzed with 2½ lb. of chicken.
- In recipes where ingredients are listed as optional or "if desired," these ingredients are included in the nutritional information.
  Example: ½ cup chopped nuts, if desired
  The recipe was analyzed to include ½ cup chopped nuts.
- Serving suggestions are often given with the recipe. If the serving suggestion was felt to be of major importance to the recipe, it was listed in the ingredients and was calculated in the nutritional information. If the serving suggestion was made only at the end of the recipe directions, it was not analyzed in the nutritional information.
- Many ingredients are given generically. The following generic ingredients were analyzed as follows:

GENERIC INGREDIENT	USED FOR ANALYSIS
chives	dried
cottage cheese	creamed small curd
cream	whipping
eggs	large
fish fillets	whitefish
flour	all-purpose
ground beef	70% lean, 30% fat
ice cream	12% fat
milk	whole milk, 3.8% fat
nuts	walnuts
orange juice	reconstituted frozen concentrate
oysters	Eastern
parsley	fresh
rice	long grain
tomato paste	without salt
vinegar	cider
yogurt	regular natural culture

- When a recipe has a basting sauce, it is assumed that the entire amount of sauce is used.
- Occasionally foods, particularly fish, vegetables and pasta are cooked in salted water. The nutritional information does not include any extra sodium as a result of absorption that may occur from the salted water.
- The TIPS given at the end of many recipes are not included in the nutritional information.

In some instances it was not possible to accurately determine the nutrition information:

- Occasionally there was not enough nutritional information available on a particular ingredient.
- Because of the many variables in the marinading process, we were unable to supply nutritional information with regard to marinades and recipes in which marinading is a cooking step.

- Some recipes are actually not recipes but rather serving suggestions as they do not list specific ingredients or they give a very wide range of ingredient options.

A WORD ABOUT SERVING SIZES

The pan sizes listed below are used throughout the book. The serving size was determined as indicated in this chart.

Pan size	Number of slices of pieces
8x4 or 9x5-inch loaf pan	16
1½-quart casserole	16
round loaf	12
small "French" loaf	12
large "French" loaf	24
10-inch ring mold	12
8 or 9-inch square pan	9
13x9-inch cake pan	12
9-inch round cake pan	8

SYMBOL MEANINGS

The following symbols were used in relation to the nutrition data:

Symbol	Reference
*	Less than 2% of the nutrient
<1	Less than one gram (or milligram) of the nutrient
†	There is not enough information available to give the nutritional amount for that particular nutrient

Any questions with regard to the nutritional information contained within this book, should be addressed to:

The Pillsbury Company
Department 840 Pillsbury Building
Minneapolis, Minnesota 55402

GUIDE TO BETTER COOKING

HOW TO MEASURE

- To measure liquids, use a standard liquid measuring cup. Place cup on level surface and fill to the required amount. Check at eye level.
- There is no need to sift flour before measuring; lightly spoon flour into measuring cup and then level with the straight edge of a spatula or knife.
- To measure shortening, firmly press into measuring cup, level with knife or metal spatula. Remove from cup with rubber spatula. Margarine or butter is often packaged in 4 sticks; each measure ½ cup. Special adjustments should be made when using whipped butter or margarine in baking.

GREASING PANS

Use only solid shortening or margarine for greasing baking pans. Oils or spray-on coatings may cause sticking of breads and cakes.

PREHEATING OVENS

It is necessary to preheat an oven for foods that cook in less than 1 hour and it is recommended that you continue to preheat your oven for our products with short baking times. There is no need to preheat for foods requiring longer cooking or when broiling or roasting. Remember, an oven needs only about 10 minutes of preheating.

HIGH ALTITUDE BAKING

If you live at an altitude of 3500 feet or over, you may have to make adjustments in some of your recipes. We have provided specific adjustments for high altitude baking. If no high altitude directions are given, a recipe change is unnecessary.

STORAGE OF LEFTOVERS

All leftover high moisture foods or foods containing meat, fish, poultry, custard and cream cheese fillings, cream sauces or cheese should be refrigerated immediately as they are quite perishable at room temperature.

We wish to express our appreciation to The American Home Economics Association for the use of the HANDBOOK OF FOOD PREPARATION as a resource.

MEAL PLANNING

Serving meals to a family or casually entertaining friends all takes planning. The foods that you select to serve should please the eye as well as the palate. Flavor, color and texture should all be taken into consideration when foods are combined in a menu. The overall appearance of the table setting and the display of the food on the plate help make the meal interesting.

Children develop attitudes toward food and eating early in life and usually from their parents' example. If you enjoy a variety of foods and include them in meals, chances are your children will learn to enjoy them too.

SPECIAL OCCASION MEALS

Food somehow seems to taste better when you share it with friends. Even when you entertain casually (this is most popular due to working homemakers' and busier family schedules), you will want everything just right. Take time to carefully organize your plans and try to prepare as much in advance as you can. You will be more at ease with your guests and you can enjoy the relaxed atmosphere knowing the table looks attractive, the food will be ready on time and the recipes you have selected to serve make an interesting meal. You'll be a gracious, carefree host!

Birthday Buffet for the Relatives
Tater-Crisp Chicken, page 424
Potato Salad, page 468
Triple Bean Salad, page 466
Molded Waldorf Salad, page 480
Dinner Rolls, page 70
Cherry Chip Lane Cake, page 136

Birthday Party for the School Crowd
Pizza Burgers, page 531
Apple Wedges
Carrot Curls
Peanut Butter-Filled Celery
Gelatin Cubes
Delicious Devil's Food Cake, page 132
Orange Julius, page 57

Wedding Reception Buffet Supper
Champagne Rosé Punch, page 58
Cocktail Nuts, page 28
Company Turkey Salad, page 491
Cottage-Stuffed Celery, page 28
Assorted Raw Vegetable Nibblers and Pickles
Cloverleaf Dinner Rolls, page 71
Whole Wheat Dinner Rolls, page 72
Simply White Cake, page 123 with Butter Frosting, page 148

Anniversary Dinner
Tangy Cornish Hens, page 434
Rice Pilaf, page 256
Layered Vegetable Salad, page 465
Cheesy Creamed Spinach, page 610
Dilly Casserole Bread, page 106
Bananas Royale, page 200

"Come for Dinner and a Good Visit"
Pot Roast Milano, page 300
Noodles Alfredo, page 260
Sunny Sprouts, page 575
Crisp Overnight Slaw, page 470
Old-Fashioned Honey Wheat Bread, page 64
Chilled Lemon Soufflé, page 211

For a Quickie Gathering
Snappy Wieners, page 344
Zesty Pork and Beans, page 568
Tossed Salad, page 463
Refrigerated Biscuits
Fruit and Sour Cream, page 203

A Quick-to-Fix Ham Dinner
Broiled Ham and Fruit Kabobs, page 341
Creamed Garden Potatoes and Peas, page 604
Spinach and Mushroom Salad, page 464
Refrigerated Crescent Rolls
Baked Custard, page 204

BASIC INGREDIENTS

GRAINS AND FLOURS

PEARL BARLEY is a whole grain with hull and bran removed. It is usually added to soup broth.

BARLEY FLOUR is milled by a process similar to wheat flour milling.

BUCKWHEAT FLOUR is made by grinding buckwheat kernels to a fine powder. It adds a hearty flavor when combined with regular flour in pancakes and waffles.

CORNMEAL is made by grinding cleaned, white or yellow corn. It can be enriched with added vitamins and minerals.

GRITS OR HOMINY GRITS are prepared by coarsely grinding white or yellow corn after the bran and germ have been removed.

CORNSTARCH is refined starch from the endosperm of corn.

ROLLED OATS are oats that are rolled after the hull is removed. *QUICK-COOKING OATS* are rolled thinner, making smaller flakes that cook and rehydrate more quickly than *OLD-FASHIONED OATS.* Usually quick-cooking and old-fashioned oats can be used interchangeably although the finished products vary in appearance.

RYE FLOUR gives products structure as they bake but is often combined with wheat flour to decrease the rye flavor. A blend of rye and wheat flour is available in some markets.

SOY FLOUR is available in two types. Full-fat flour is made by grinding soybeans after the hulls are removed; low-fat flour is made after most of the oil has been removed from the bran. It can be substituted for part of regular flour in recipes to increase the protein level. It is not used alone in baking because it does not have the structural properties of wheat or rye flour.

RICE BRAN is made from the bran, germ and varying amounts of the hull which are ground to a fine powder.

BULGAR WHEAT is whole wheat that has been cooked, dried, partially debranned and cracked into coarse angular fragments. It is prepared and used like rice and is similar to whole wheat in nutritive value.

CRACKED WHEAT is prepared by cracking or cutting the wheat into angular fragments.

FARINA is ground to a granular form from wheat after the bran and most of the germ have been removed.

WHEAT GERM is the fat-containing portion of the wheat kernel which has a high concentration of nutrients. Because of the fat content, wheat germ should be refrigerated or it may become rancid.

ALL-PURPOSE FLOUR is made from the milling and combination of hard and soft wheat to give a product satisfactory for many uses. The bran and germ are removed; the creamy white endosperm center of the grain is milled into flour. Enriched flour has some of the nutrients added that were lost through the removal of the bran and germ. Bleached flour has gone through a bleaching process to whiten the flour.

UNBLEACHED ALL-PURPOSE FLOUR is the same as all-purpose flour but has not been treated with bleaching or maturing agents of any kind. It is enriched as required by law in many states. Bleached and unbleached flour can be used interchangeably in recipes.

WHOLE WHEAT FLOUR, sometimes called graham flour, is milled from the entire wheat kernel. Usually up to 50% whole wheat flour can be substituted for white flour without affecting recipes.

INSTANT BLENDING FLOUR is a granular flour that is formed by exposing hot water or steam with all-purpose flour to form granular pieces. It is ideal for sauces and gravies because it dissolves readily in cool liquid.

SELF-RISING FLOUR is all-purpose flour with baking powder and salt added in proportions that are ideal for making biscuits. If the leavening and salt are adjusted it can be substituted for all-purpose flour in some recipes.

FATS AND OILS

BUTTER is made from sweet or sour cream and contains at least 80% butterfat. The addition of coloring and salt is optional. Butter may be graded with U.S. Department of Agriculture grades determined by flavor, body, texture, color and salt. Butter adds a special flavor in sautéed or baked foods. It should not be used for deep-fat frying because it has a low smoke point and will start to smoke before reaching frying temperature.

HYDROGENATED SHORTENING is made of vegetable oils, animal fats or a combination of the two. Cottonseed, soybean, corn or peanut are normally the vegetable oils used. The refined oils are hydrogenated by adding hydrogen under controlled conditions to change the liquid to a solid. Usually small amounts of mono and di-glyceride fats are added to improve the overall baking qualities. This shortening has a high smoke point, making it ideal for deep-fat frying.

LARD is fat rendered from the fatty tissue of pork. It is often preferred for pie crusts because it makes an especially tender and flavorful crust. The pronounced flavor of lard does interfere with some delicate food flavors. The smoke point is fairly low, making it a poor choice for deep-fat frying.

MARGARINE is made from refined vegetable oils or a combination of animal and vegetable oils, emulsified with milk or nonfat dry milk solids. Color, salt, butter-flavoring or butter may be added. Usually margarine is fortified with vitamins for a food value equal to or greater than butter. Margarine must contain 80% fat unless it is labeled imitation or diet margarine.

OILS are usually extracted from the seeds or fruits of vegetables. Salad oils are further treated to remain clear at refrigerator temperature. Oils have a high smoke point, making them excellent for deep-fat frying.

LEAVENING

Leavening is a gas such as air, carbon dioxide or steam that is incorporated or formed in a batter or dough making it rise and become light and porous during preparation and heating.

AIR is commonly incorporated into batters through creamed shortenings and beaten egg whites. Angel food cakes and soufflés are examples.

STEAM forms in batters and doughs as they are heated. Popovers and cream puffs are examples where steam is trapped inside.

CARBON DIOXIDE is formed by combining baking soda and an acid or by the action of yeast or certain bacteria with sugar.

BAKING POWDER is a mixture of acid and baking soda combined with starch or flour. In the presence of moisture and heat, it produces carbon dioxide gas. Double-acting baking powder contains acids that react when liquid is added and also when heat is applied.

BAKING SODA forms carbon dioxide when combined with the acid of an ingredient such as sour milk, sour cream or molasses. The alkaline soda mixture also neutralizes the "sour" taste of these ingredients.

YEAST is a microscopic plant which reacts with sugar to form carbon dioxide. Active dry yeast is in granular form and can be combined with flour before adding liquid or first dissolved in liquid before adding to flour mixture.

Compressed yeast is a moist yeast-starch mixture that is kept inactive by refrigeration. Before adding to a dough mixture, it is first dissolved in warm water.

MILK

CULTURED BUTTERMILK is a skim or part skim milk soured by means of a suitable culture of lactic acid bacteria.

SOUR MILK is milk soured naturally or by the addition of vinegar or lemon juice. Buttermilk and sour milk can be used interchangeably in recipes.

DRY MILK is the powder that remains after the water is removed from milk. *NONFAT DRY MILK* has the fat as well as the water removed. *INSTANT NONFAT DRY MILK* is processed to a coarse free-flowing particle that dissolves readily in water. Reconstituted dry milk can be used as milk in cooking and drinking.

EVAPORATED MILK is whole milk from which about 60% of the water has been removed. It is homogenized to distribute the fat uniformly, then canned. The nutritional composition of evaporated milk when mixed with an equal amount of water is slightly above regular whole milk. Undiluted evaporated milk can be substituted for light cream. *EVAPORATED SKIM MILK* is made from skim rather than whole milk.

SWEETENED CONDENSED MILK is whole milk with about half the water evaporated out, and sugar added before canning. Because it has sugar added it cannot be substituted for evaporated milk.

WHOLE MILK is milk that has not had the butterfat removed and is usually *pasteurized* by exposing the milk to temperatures high enough to destroy undesirable bacteria.

HOMOGENIZED MILK has been mechanically treated to reduce the size of the fat globule so it will remain dispersed in the milk and not separate and rise to the top. *SKIM MILK* has most of the fat removed, it contains less than .5% fat. *LOW-FAT MILK* may contain .5 to 2% fat according to federal standards.

YOGURT is a creamy-thick mixture made by fermenting whole or skim milk with a special culture. It can usually be substituted for sour cream in sauces and toppings, but is often more tart in flavor.

CREAM

WHIPPING CREAM contains 36 to 40% butterfat. When cold it will thicken when whipped. *LIGHT* or *COFFEE CREAM* contains 18 to 30% butterfat. It will not whip, but can be used as a liquid when added richness is desired. *HALF AND HALF* is cream containing about 10% butterfat.

DAIRY SOUR CREAM is a creamy-thick mixture made by fermenting light cream (18 to 20% butterfat) with a special culture. *SOUR HALF AND HALF* is like sour cream but is made with half and half rather than light cream.

SALT

COARSE SALT is a coarse granulation of salt that is often used as a garnish on breads or snacks.

PICKLING SALT is an untreated salt that is recommended for canning and pickle making. Table salt has additives that may cause discoloration in pickle making and canning.

TABLE SALT is finely ground and used to enhance the flavor of foods. It may or may not be iodized which means that it has iodine added.

SEASONING SALTS are mixtures of salt and one or more herb or spice such as garlic, celery or onion.

SEA SALT AND KELP (powdered seaweed) are used as salt substitutes. They are rich in iodine.

SALT SUBSTITUTES are substances resembling table salt in appearance and taste, but do not contain sodium.

SUGAR AND SWEETENING AGENTS

BROWN SUGAR is produced by two methods. One method uses the syrup that remains after the removal of commercially extractable white sugar; the other method adds refined syrups to white sugar crystals. Depending on the amount of molasses, it is labeled golden brown, light brown and dark brown.

CUBE SUGAR is granulated sugar pressed into cubes and dried.

GRANULATED SUGAR is the standard product for general use, made from the white crystals that remain after the molasses is removed from sugar cane or sugar beets, 99.5% sucrose.

POWDERED SUGAR is a fine, powdery sugar made by grinding and sifting granulated sugar. Also referred to as confectioners' sugar.

CORN SYRUP is made from corn sugar. *Light corn syrup* has been clarified and discolorized. *Dark corn syrup* contains a mixture of corn syrup and refiners' syrup (obtained in the process of refining raw sugar).

HONEY is the nectar of plants, gathered, modified, stored and concentrated by honey bees. Flavored honey is named after the plant from which the nectar was derived.

MAPLE SYRUP is produced by boiling down the sap from maple trees. Pure maple syrup is made only from this liquid. Maple syrup blends are combinations of maple syrup, sugar and maple flavoring.

MOLASSES is the liquid from which raw cane sugar is crystalized. *Blackstrap molasses* is very dark in color. *Light and dark cooking molasses* are lighter in color and contain a higher percentage of sugars. Molasses and brown sugar can be used interchangeably in small quantities such as in yeast breads.

SORGUM is a liquid concentrate produced from the sweet juice of the sugar sorghum.

NONCALORIC SWEETENERS are made from chemical substances that give a sweet sensation on the tongue, but contain little food value or calories. These sweeteners act differently from sugar in batters and doughs so special recipes are needed.

HERBS, SPICES AND SEASONINGS

Herbs, spices and seasonings add their own unique touch to food through flavor and aroma. Experiment with the ancient art of seasoning and create your own favorite blend of flavors. It may be as exotic as curry or as pleasantly common as cinnamon in sugar. Through the use of herbs, spices and seasonings, you can develop a subtle and delicate blending of flavors that will please the taste. It's best not to combine too many herbs in one dish. Also don't include too many herb dishes in a meal.

Generally 1 teaspoon of dried herb equals 1 tablespoon fresh. When cooking, allow about ¼ teaspoon dried herb or a pinch of powdered herb to 4 servings. Keep all herbs, spices and seasonings tightly covered and away from heat to preserve their freshness. Some flavor will be lost after a year of storage so you may wish to increase the amount when cooking.

The following list identifies the different parts of plants that are used as flavoring ingredients.

HERBS:
The leaves of aromatic annual or perennial plants which grow in temperate climates.

Basil	Peppermint
Bay leaves	Rosemary
Chervil	Sage
Dill weed	Summer Savory
Marjoram	Spearmint
Oregano	Tarragon
Parsley	Thyme

TRUE SPICES:
Roots, bark, seeds or fruit of aromatic perennial plants normally grown in the tropics.

Allspice	Nutmeg
Black pepper	Paprika
Chili pepper	Red pepper
Cinnamon	Saffron
Cloves	Turmeric
Ginger	White pepper
Mace	Peppercorns

AROMATIC SEEDS:
Seeds of annual plants.

Anise	Dill
Caraway	Fennel
Cardamom	Mustard
Celery	Poppy
Coriander	Sesame
Cumin	

SEASONING SALTS AND BLENDS:
Blends of spices, herbs and/or seeds.

Celery salt	Chili powder
Garlic salt	Poultry seasoning
Onion salt	Pumpkin pie spice
Smoke salt	Curry powder

VEGETABLE SEASONINGS:

Garlic	Cayenne pepper
Onion	Horseradish
Bell pepper	Mushrooms
Chives	Leek, Scallion
Paprika	Shallots
Chili peppers	

CONDIMENTS:
Usually liquid or semi-liquid mixtures of spices and other ingredients.

Worcestershire sauce	Wine and herb vinegars
Tabasco sauce	Chili sauce
Prepared mustard	Catsup

GUIDE TO USING HERBS AND SPICES

Herbs, spices and seasonings are available in many sizes and shapes. Some of the spices are left whole for a specific use in flavoring or garnishing food, other times the spice is finely ground. Herbs are available in the leaf form and in the ground form. Unless otherwise stated our recipes use the ground form. In order to assure the best flavor you should use the type called for in the recipe. The list below also indicates what foods are most often flavored with specific spices and herbs.

ALLSPICE: Purchased whole or ground. Whole allspice for meat broth, pickles, beverages. Ground allspice for cakes, pies, cookies, relishes, preserves, ground beef, sweet potatoes, tomatoes, winter squash.

BASIL or SWEET BASIL: Purchased in leaf form. For pizza, spaghetti sauce and other tomato dishes, lamb, vegetable soup, peas, zucchini, green beans, cucumbers, tomato.

BAY LEAF (LAUREL): Purchased as whole leaves. For beef, lamb, veal, poultry, fish, stews, soups, sauces.

CARAWAY SEED: Purchased as the whole seed. For pork, stews, bread, cheese, coleslaw, sauerkraut, Indian curries.

CARDAMOM SEED: Purchased whole or ground. Use ground cardamom for pastries, breads, cookies, apple and pumpkin desserts.

CELERY SEED: Purchased as the whole seed. For eggs, fish, oyster stew, tomato juice, potato salad, salad dressings, sauerkraut.

CHERVIL: Purchased in the leaf form. For cream soups, egg dishes, fish dishes.

CHILI POWDER: Purchased ground. For chili con carne, egg dishes, beef, shellfish, cocktail sauce.

CINNAMON: Purchased ground or in sticks. Use ground cinnamon for breads, cakes, cookies, pies, beef stew, beverages. Use stick cinnamon in beverages.

CLOVES: Purchased whole or ground. Use whole cloves for ham, pork, pot roasts, stews, pickled fruits. Use ground cloves for cake, cookies, chocolate desserts, beets, sweet potatoes, onions, winter squash.

CORIANDER SEED: Purchased as whole seed or ground. Use coriander seed in pickles. Use ground coriander in stews, cookies, candy, cake, pastry.

CUMIN SEED: Purchased as whole seed or ground. For curried meat and seafood, cheese spreads, rice dishes, chili.

CURRY POWDER: Purchased ground. For shrimp, lamb, poultry, tomato soup, egg and cheese dishes, salad dressings.

DILL: Purchased as whole seed or as the leaves (dill weed). Use dill seed for pickles, fish, pork, veal, potatoes, macaroni, sauerkraut, cucumbers. Use dill weed when a more delicate flavor is desired in the foods above.

FENNEL: Purchased as whole seed or ground. For Italian sausage, fish, seafood, pork, poultry, breads, cakes, apple pie.

GINGER: Purchased ground, whole dried gingerroot, whole fresh gingerroot or crystallized ginger. For roast chicken, cake, cookies, gingerbread, pumpkin desserts, fruit desserts.

MACE: Purchased ground. Use for doughnuts, pound cake, custards, fruit desserts, fish sauces, sometimes used interchangeably with nutmeg.

MARJORAM or SWEET MARJORAM: Purchased in leaf form or ground. Use for lamb, poultry, stuffings, cottage cheese, tomato dishes, vegetables, orange marmalade.

MINT: Purchased fresh or as dried leaves. Use for lamb, veal, beans, carrots, peas, chocolate desserts, fruits, beverages.

MUSTARD: Purchased as whole seed or ground. Use mustard seed for pickles, relishes, salads, beets, cabbage, sauerkraut. Use ground mustard for salad dressings, sauces, cheese and egg dishes, baked beans.

NUTMEG: Purchased whole or ground. Use for fish, poultry, spice butters, candied sweet potatoes, apple and custard desserts, eggnog.

OREGANO: Purchased in leaf form or ground. Use for pizza and other tomato dishes, beef, poultry, zucchini, green beans, eggplant, onions.

PAPRIKA: Purchased ground. For beef, poultry, Hungarian goulash, fish, soups, salads, salad dressings, eggs, garnish for many foods.

PARSLEY: Purchased fresh or as dried leaves. For beef, pork, veal, poultry, fish and seafood, eggs, bouquet garni. Fresh is used as a garnish for many foods.

PEPPER (BLACK): Purchased whole (peppercorns), coarsely ground or ground. For most meat, poultry, egg or cheese dishes, a seasoning for vegetables.

POPPY SEED: Purchased as whole seed. For bread, rolls, cookies, pastry filling, butters, pasta.

ROSEMARY: Purchased in leaf form or ground. For lamb, beef, veal, poultry, fish, beans, peas, spinach, mushrooms.

SAFFRON: Purchased ground. For paella, bouillabaisse, saffron buns, rice dishes.

SAGE: May be purchased in leaf form (rubbed) or ground. For lamb, pork, poultry stuffing, fish, chowder, eggplant, tomatoes, brussels sprouts.

SAVORY: Purchased in leaf form or ground. For beef, poultry, egg dishes, lentils, peas, squash, beans.

SESAME SEED: Purchased as whole seed. For poultry, bread, rolls, candy.

TARRAGON: Purchase in leaf form. For veal, lamb, beef, poultry, seafood, mushrooms, beans, broccoli, egg dishes, salad and salad dressing, butters.

THYME: Purchased in leaf form or ground. For pork, poultry stuffings, clams, vegetable soup, tomato aspic.

TURMERIC: Purchased ground. For poultry, relishes and pickles, egg dishes, rice, spice butters, curries.

COOKING TERMS

ANCHOVY: A small fish, somewhat like herring; often used in appetizers, butters and sauces.

ANTIPASTO: An assortment of appetizers and/or relishes such as cheeses, sausages, anchovies, olives, marinated vegetables and other Italian specialties which may be served as an hors d'oeuvre, salad or main course.

ASCORBIC ACID: Vitamin C. Available commercially to keep fruit from turning color; often used in canning.

ASPIC: A jelly made by chilling concentrated meat stock. Also, a jelly made by adding gelatin to meat or vegetable stock or fruit juice.

AU GRATIN: A topping of browned crumbs or cheese.

AU JUS: Served in juice, usually obtained from roasting meat.

BASTE: To moisten food by spooning liquid or fat over it during cooking to prevent drying out and to add flavor.

BISQUE: A rich cream soup, usually of fish or shellfish. Also, a rich frozen dessert with nuts, fruit or crushed macaroons.

BLANCH: To immerse briefly in boiling water, usually followed by quick cooling in cold water, as for vegetables to be frozen. Also, to scald by pouring boiling water over a food, as almonds or tomatoes, to loosen the skin.

BOUILLABAISSE: A hearty fish soup made with many ingredients. It originated in Southern France.

BOUILLON: A clear soup, usually made from beef. Also, the liquid which results from dissolving a meat, vegetable or chicken bouillon cube in hot water.

BOURGUIGNONNE (a la): Method of cooking (most often meat) that includes red wine and usually the addition of mushrooms and small onions.

BRAISE: To simmer covered in a small amount of liquid on top of the range or in the oven. Meat may sometimes be browned first.

BREAD: To cover by dipping in diluted egg or in milk and then in fine crumbs.

BROTH: A thin soup made by simmering meat and/or meat bones in liquid. Also, the water in which meat or vegetables have been cooked.

BROWN: To make food brown either in a small amount of hot fat on top of the range or by exposing it to dry heat in the oven.

CARAMELIZE: Usually of sugar, to heat until it is melted and brown. Also, to heat food containing sugar until brown. Browning of the sugar achieves a distinctive flavor.

CAROB: A Mediterranean evergreen from which comes a pod that is dried, ground and used as a sweetener or as a substitute for chocolate. Also known as St. John's bread.

CHAFING DISH: A deep metal pan with a handle, a container for water and a heat source. Used at the table to cook foods or to keep them warm for serving.

CHUTNEY: A sweet-sour condiment of fruits, raisins, dates and onions seasoned with spices.

CLARIFY: To make a liquid clear. Often achieved by skimming or by adding egg white or shell to liquid, then straining to remove particles that adhere to white or shell.

COAT: To cover entire surface with a mixture such as seasoned flour, fine crumbs or batter.

COMPOTE: A dessert or side dish of fruit which has often been stewed in syrup.

CONDIMENT: A pungent food served with or added to other foods as a relish or seasoning.

CONSOMMÈ: A clear soup usually made from a combination of veal, chicken or other meat broths.

CREAM: Combining two or more ingredients until the mixture is light and completely blended, or to soften one or more foods.

CRÊPE: A thin delicate pancake about 6 inches in diameter. May be filled with fruit or custard for dessert or with meat, vegetables or cheese for main dishes.

CRISP-TENDER: Describes the doneness of vegetables when they are cooked only until tender and remain slightly crisp in texture. Often associated with Oriental stir-frying.

CUT-IN: To use two knives, pastry blender or fork to distribute shortening through dry ingredients, leaving the shortening in small particles.

DEEP-FAT FRY: To cook in deep fat which completely covers the food being prepared.

DRIPPINGS: The residue left in the pan after meat or poultry is cooked, usually including fat.

DUST: To sprinkle with flour or sugar.

DUTCH OVEN: A deep heavy pan with a tight fitting lid. Used for pot roasts, stews, or as an extra large saucepan.

ENTREE: The main course of a meal. Also, a single dish served before the main course of an elaborate meal.

ESPRESSO: Coffee brewed by forcing steam through finely ground darkly roasted coffee beans.

FOLD: To combine a solid ingredient with a delicate substance such as beaten egg white or whipped cream without loss of air. Insert the edge of a spatula or other utensil vertically down through the middle of the mixture, slide the spatula across the bottom of the bowl, bring it up with some of the mixture and fold over on top of the rest. Continue until all is evenly mixed.

FONDUE: Originated in Switzerland. Guests cook their own food by dunking in a fondue pot or chafing dish. Cheese or beef fondue are traditional.

FONDUE POT: A saucepan-like pot with its own stand and burner.

FRICASSEE: To cook serving-size pieces of meat or poultry covered with liquid which is thickened to make a gravy.

GLAZE: To coat with syrup, thin icing or jelly, either during cooking or after the food is cooked.

GRANOLA: A sweetened ready-to-eat cereal of toasted natural grains, nuts and seeds.

JULIENNE: Food cut into long, thin strips, usually for salads.

LEEK: A cultivated plant that looks somewhat like large green onions. Used most often to flavor soups, it can also be prepared as a vegetable.

LIQUEUR: An alcoholic beverage flavored with aromatic substances and often sweetened. Served as an after-dinner drink and used in cooking, usually desserts.

LOX: Smoked salmon.

MARINATE: To let stand in liquid (a marinade) to increase flavor and tenderness.

MERINGUE: A mixture of stiffly beaten egg whites and sugar baked on top of a pie, or as a shell, often filled with fruit or ice cream.

MONOSODIUM GLUTAMATE (MSG): A crystalline chemical product added to food to intensify natural flavor.

MOUSSE: A light spongy dish that can be a dessert or can be made with fish, shellfish or meat.

NESSELRODE (a la): Most often refers to a mixture of candied fruits and chopped nuts, used in desserts.

NEWBURG: A sauce made of cream, butter, wine and egg yolks that is usually served with seafood; for example, Lobster Newburg.

PAELLA: A Spanish dish of rice, seafood, poultry and other ingredients; usually flavored with saffron.

PAN BROIL: To cook meat uncovered in a skillet, turning frequently and pouring off excess fat as it accumulates.

PAN FRY: To cook in a skillet with a small amount of fat.

PARBOIL: To boil until partially cooked.

PÂTÉ: A highly seasoned meat spread, usually served as an appetizer.

PATTY SHELL: An individual pastry for serving a creamed mixture, usually chicken or fish.

POACH: To cook in simmering liquid.

POCKET BREAD OR PITA BREAD: Flat rounds of bread which are split to make a pocket to hold sandwich fillings.

PROSCUITTO: A fine Italian smoked ham, usually served sliced thinly as an appetizer.

PURÉE: To put food through a colander, sieve, food mill or blender. Also, the thick pulp with juice that results from this process.

QUICHE: There are many kinds of quiche but it is basically an unsweetened custard in a pie shell, usually served as an appetizer or main course of a light meal.

RAGOUT: A highly seasoned thick stew, made with meat, poultry or fish.

RAMEKIN: Individual baking dish.

ROSETTE IRON: A long-handled iron with the end shaped in the form of a star, flower or other decorative shape. It is heated in hot fat, then dipped into batter and returned to the hot fat. Sprinkled with powdered sugar, rossettes are served as a cookie. They can also be a base for creamed dishes.

RUMTOPF: A pot used for naturally fermenting a mixture of fruit and sugar. Also, the fruit mixture.

SAUTÉ: To cook in a skillet in a small amount of shortening, stirring until tender.

SCALD: To heat just below the boiling point. Also, to pour boiling water over food, or to dip food briefly into boiling water.

SCALLION: A mild green onion.

SCAMPI: A shellfish that looks like large shrimp and can be prepared in the same manner.

SCORE: To slash the surface of a food, usually in a diamond design, before cooking.

SEAR: A quick application of heat to brown the surface of foods.

SIMMER: To cook in liquid just below the boiling point so that tiny bubbles form on bottom or sides of pan.

SKEWER: A metal or wooden pin used for fastening meat or poultry while cooking.

SMORGASBORD: A buffet offering a variety of foods; often appetizers, smoked and pickled fish, hot and cold meats and cheese.

SOUFFLÉ: A light, spongy baked dish made with beaten egg whites, white sauce and other ingredients.

SPAETZLE: A small egg noodle used often in German cooking.

SPRINGERLE: Traditional German Christmas cookie, anise flavored with a raised design made by a block or rolling pin.

SPUMONI: A frozen dessert made of layers of various kinds of ice cream, usually containing fruit and nuts.

STEAM: To cook over, but not in, boiling water.

STEW: To cook long and slowly in liquid.

STIR-FRY: A method of cooking originating with the use of the Oriental wok in which vegetables are fried quickly to a crisp-tender stage while stirring or tossing them constantly.

STOCK: The liquid in which meat, fish or vegetables have been cooked.

STRUDEL: A filled pastry of extremely thin layers of crust rolled with fruit inside. Sometimes made with a vegetable such as mushroom or spinach strudel.

SUB GUM: A Chinese dish of mixed vegetables.

SUKIYAKI: A Japanese stew of thinly sliced meat and vegetables traditionally cooked at the table and served directly from the pan.

TART: A small pie or pastry shell usually containing jelly, custard or fruit. Sometimes contains a meat or vegetable filling. Also called a flan.

TEMPURA: A method of preparing Japanese dishes by dipping sliced vegetables or small pieces of meat or fish into batter and then into hot oil.

TORTE: A rich cake made with crumbs and eggs, containing fruit and nuts. Also, a cake layered with filling.

TORTILLA: "Little cake." A flat, unleavened cake made from coarse cornmeal and water, baked on a griddle or on a stone in coals. Used in Spanish and Latin American cooking.

WHISK: A wire instrument, somewhat balloon shaped at the end, used for hand beating.

WOK: An Oriental cooking pan with a small curved bottom and wide sloping sides.

MOVING TOWARD METRICS IN THE KITCHEN...

What about metrics in the kitchen? Do they mean a whole new process of cooking? Indeed not! First of all, you can certainly continue to depend upon cookbooks already in your library and your grandmother's favorite recipes. Just use your conventional measuring cups and spoons as you always have. There would be no reason for conversion, unless you want to give metrics a try. Of course, **the best way to learn the metric system is to use it.** New metric measuring devices plus metric recipe instructions are increasingly available. And, all the work has been done for you by professional home economists.

The *milliliter (mL)* unit replaces the conventional measurements for dry and liquid ingredients –cups, tablespoons, teaspoons and ounces. The milliliter is .001 liter and a liter (L) equals 1 quart plus ¼ cup. Dry metric measures are labeled 50 mL, 125 mL and 250 mL (to replace the conventional nesting measuring cup sets) and liquid measures are marked 250 mL, 500 mL and 1 L. To replace the usual measuring spoons, there is a set of five small scoop or spoon-type measures marked 1 mL, 2 mL, 5 mL, 15 mL and 25 mL.

Metric weight, shown in grams (g) is used for measuring solids up to 500. Over that figure, kilograms (kg) are used.

Another change which will occur is our present Fahrenheit scale of temperature. With the new Celsius scale, the difference between the freezing and boiling point of water is divided into 100 degrees. One Celsius degree equals 1.8°F. If a recipe required a baking temperature of 375°F., you would soon learn that this is 190°C. Although confusing at first, our exposure to weather reports given in Celsius hasten our familiarity.

WEIGHTS AND MEASURES

a few grains = less than ⅛ teaspoon
60 drops = 1 teaspoon
1½ teaspoons = ½ tablespoon
3 teaspoons = 1 tablespoon
2 tablespoons = ⅛ cup or 1 fluid ounce
4 tablespoons = ¼ cup
5⅓ tablespoons = ⅓ cup
8 tablespoons = ½ cup
10⅔ tablespoons = ⅔ cup
12 tablespoons = ¾ cup
16 tablespoons = 1 cup
⅜ cup = ¼ cup plus 2 tablespoons
⅝ cup = ½ cup plus 2 tablespoons
⅞ cup = ¾ cup plus 2 tablespoons
1 cup = 8 fluid ounces
2 cups = 1 pint or 16 fluid ounces
2 pints = 1 quart or 32 fluid ounces
4 cups = 1 quart
4 quarts = 1 gallon
8 quarts = 1 peck
4 pecks = 1 bushel
16 ounces = 1 pound

1 gram = 0.035 ounces
1 kilogram = 2.21 pounds
1 ounce = 28.35 grams
1 pound = 453.59 grams
1 teaspoon = 4.9 milliliters
1 tablespoon = 14.8 milliliters
1 cup = 236.6 milliliters
1 liter = 1.06 quarts or 1,000 milliliters

EMERGENCY SUBSTITUTIONS

1 teaspoon **Apple** or **Pumpkin Pie Spice** = ½ teaspoon cinnamon, ¼ teaspoon nutmeg, ⅛ teaspoon each allspice and cardamom

1 teaspoon **Baking Powder** = ¼ teaspoon soda plus ½ teaspoon cream of tartar

¼ cup **Dry Bread Crumbs** = ¼ cup cracker crumbs, 1 slice bread cubed or ⅔ cup rolled oats

1 cup **Buttermilk** = 1 tablespoon vinegar or lemon juice plus milk to make 1 cup

1 square (1 oz.) **Unsweetened Chocolate** = 3 tablespoons unsweetened cocoa plus 1 tablespoon shortening or margarine

2 oz. **Semi-sweet Chocolate** = ⅓ cup semi-sweet chocolate chips

½ cup **Corn Syrup** = ½ cup sugar plus 2 tablespoons liquid

1 tablespoon **Cornstarch** = 2 tablespoons flour or 1⅓ tablespoons quick-cooking tapioca (used as thickener)

1 cup **Heavy Cream** (for baking, not whipping) = ¾ cup whole milk plus ¼ cup butter

1 cup **Light Cream** = ⅞ cup milk plus 3 tablespoons butter

1 cup **Sweetened Whipped Cream** = 4½-oz. pkg. frozen whipped topping or 1 envelope whipped topping mix prepared as directed on package

1 **Egg** = 2 egg yolks (in baking, add 1 tablespoon water)

1 cup **Cake Flour** = ⅞ cup all-purpose flour plus 2 tablespoons cornstarch

1 **Garlic Glove** = ⅛ teaspoon instant minced garlic or garlic powder or ½ teaspoon garlic salt

2 tablespoons **Green** or **Red Pepper** = 1 tablespoon sweet pepper flakes

1 teaspoon **Dried Leaf Herbs** = ¼ teaspoon powdered herbs

1 tablespoon **Fresh Herbs** = 1 teaspoon dried herbs

1 cup **Honey** = 1¼ cups sugar plus ¼ cup liquid

1 teaspoon **Lemon or Orange Peel** = ½ teaspoon dried peel

1 cup **Whole Milk** = ½ cup evaporated milk plus ½ cup water

1 cup **Whole Milk** = 1 cup skim or reconstituted nonfat dry milk plus 2 teaspoons butter

1 small **Onion** (¼ cup) = 1 tablespoon instant minced onion or onion flakes, ¼ cup frozen chopped onion or 1 teaspoon onion powder

1 cup **Tomato Juice** = ½ cup tomato sauce plus ½ cup water

1 lb. **Cooked Seasoned Tomatoes** = 8 oz. can tomato sauce

1 package **Active Dry Yeast** = 1 tablespoon dry or 1 cake compressed yeast

APPETIZERS & BEVERAGES

APPETIZERS

SERVING

Mention appetizers and most people think of tasty morsels of food served at a cocktail party. Generally speaking appetizers are served two ways: before the meal to "tease the appetite", or as the main attraction of the event.

If you choose to serve appetizers before a meal keep in mind there is more to come – you don't want them filled up on the first course. Select one or two nibblers along with a cheese ball or dip. Or simply serve a first course appetizer.

When the appetizers become the main food as in a festive gathering or party, a variety of nibblers, spreads and dips should be available from which to choose.

BASIC PREPARATION

Many appetizers can be made ahead, some partially and others completely. Wherever possible MAKE AHEAD tips are given.

Some appetizers such as dips and marinated vegetables are best when made ahead so flavors have time to blend.

If desired, many appetizers can be made ahead and frozen. See Chapter 15 for specific freezing tips. Avoid freezing appetizers made with sour cream or mayonnaise as these tend to separate. Also crisp vegetables and cooked egg whites are not recommended for freezing.

Guests can cook many of the broiled nibblers themselves on small hibachis especially designed for this purpose.

When preparing fruits, dip pieces in lemon juice to prevent discoloration.

Store vegetables in tightly sealed containers and keep refrigerated until serving.

Hot appetizers should be prepared on the range or in the oven and then transferred to a warming device such as a chafing dish, fondue pot, electric fry pan or warming tray for serving.

ABOUT NIBBLERS AND HORS D'OEUVRES

These are perfect to serve to large crowds where seating is limited and finger foods are a necessity. All the following recipes may be doubled or tripled to serve larger quantities. Allow two to four of each appetizer per person depending on the number of appetizers available and when it is being served. People tend to eat more the longer the occasion lasts.

STUFFED SHRIMP

2 tablespoons Roquefort or blue cheese, softened
1 oz. cream cheese, softened
½ teaspoon thyme leaves, crushed
½ teaspoon paprika
1 tablespoon mayonnaise or salad dressing
½ teaspoon lemon juice
1 lb. cooked cleaned large shrimp
¼ cup minced parsley

In small bowl, combine all ingredients except shrimp and parsley; mix well. Cut shrimp in half lengthwise and place ½ teaspoon filling between halves. Dip edge in parsley. Chill about 30 minutes to set cheese.

About 15 appetizers

NUTRITION INFORMATION PER SERVING

Serving Size: 1 appetizer		Percent U.S. RDA Per Serving	
Calories	40	Protein	7%
Protein	5g	Vitamin A	3%
Carbohydrate	<1g	Vitamin C	6%
Fat	2g	Thiamin	*
Sodium	35mg	Riboflavin	*
Potassium	48mg	Niacin	3%
		Calcium	3%
		Iron	3%

TIPS: *For a petite and less costly appetizer, sandwich 2 small shrimp together with ½ teaspoon filling between them.* About 40 appetizers

To MAKE AHEAD, prepare and refrigerate up to 12 hours.

Seasoned cream cheese is spread between layers of sliced salami.

SALAMI STACK-UPS

2 teaspoons chopped chives
2 tablespoons mayonnaise or salad dressing
Dash Tabasco sauce
3-oz. pkg. cream cheese, softened
25 thin slices salami

In small bowl, combine all ingredients except salami; mix well. Make 5 stacks of 5 salami slices each, spreading cheese mixture between slices. Wrap and chill. Cut each stack into 6 wedges. Serve on cocktail picks.
30 appetizers

NUTRITION INFORMATION PER SERVING

Serving Size: 3 appetizers		Percent U.S. RDA Per Serving	
Calories	223	Protein	16%
Protein	10g	Vitamin A	3%
Carbohydrate	1g	Vitamin C	*
Fat	20g	Thiamin	9%
Sodium	755mg	Riboflavin	9%
Potassium	8mg	Niacin	11%
		Calcium	*
		Iron	8%

GARLIC TOAST

Small loaf French bread or day old buns
½ cup margarine or butter, softened
1 teaspoon garlic salt

Heat oven to 300°F. Slice French bread at an angle, about ½-inch thick. In small bowl, blend margarine and garlic salt. Spread generously on both sides of each slice. Place on 15x10-inch jelly roll pan or cookie sheet. Bake at 300°F. for 1 to 2 hours or until dry and crisp.
20 slices

NUTRITION INFORMATION PER SERVING

Serving Size: 1 slice		Percent U.S. RDA Per Serving	
Calories	55	Protein	*
Protein	<1g	Vitamin A	3%
Carbohydrate	3g	Vitamin C	0%
Fat	4g	Thiamin	*
Sodium	171mg	Riboflavin	*
Potassium	7mg	Niacin	*
		Calcium	*
		Iron	*

Fast and easy and guaranteed to be a real crowd pleaser.

SNAPPY GLAZED MEATBALLS

1 lb. ground beef
¼ cup dry bread crumbs
1 teaspoon salt
1 small onion, chopped
1 egg, slightly beaten
1 cup chili sauce
10-oz. jar (1 cup) grape jelly

In medium bowl, combine first 5 ingredients; mix well. Shape into 1-inch balls. In medium skillet, brown meatballs, turning occasionally; drain excess fat. Add remaining ingredients; simmer 15 minutes, stirring occasionally to coat meatballs with glaze. Serve warm in chafing dish or electric fry pan.
24 to 30 appetizers

NUTRITION INFORMATION PER SERVING

Serving Size: 4 appetizers		Percent U.S. RDA Per Serving	
Calories	354	Protein	24%
Protein	16g	Vitamin A	15%
Carbohydrate	46g	Vitamin C	8%
Fat	12g	Thiamin	7%
Sodium	1019mg	Riboflavin	11%
Potassium	473mg	Niacin	19%
		Calcium	4%
		Iron	17%

TIP: *For SNAPPY GLAZED WIENERS, substitute 1-lb. wieners, cut up, or cocktail franks for meatballs.*

BAKED TUNA BALLS

6½-oz. can tuna, drained
½ cup dry bread crumbs
2 tablespoons chopped onion
2 tablespoons chopped parsley
2 tablespoons chopped almonds
3 tablespoons mayonnaise or salad dressing
1 tablespoon lemon juice
1 teaspoon prepared mustard
1 egg
3 tablespoons margarine or butter, melted
½ cup crushed corn flakes cereal

Heat oven to 450°F. In small bowl, combine first 9 ingredients; mix well. Shape into 1-inch balls. Dip in melted margarine; roll in corn flakes. Place in shallow baking pan. Bake at 450°F. for 10 minutes or until light brown. Serve on cocktail picks.

25 to 30 appetizers

NUTRITION INFORMATION PER SERVING

Serving Size: 4 appetizers		Percent U.S. RDA Per Serving	
Calories	208	Protein	16%
Protein	11g	Vitamin A	10%
Carbohydrate	5g	Vitamin C	6%
Fat	16g	Thiamin	4%
Sodium	173mg	Riboflavin	6%
Potassium	61mg	Niacin	18%
		Calcium	2%
		Iron	6%

Dry olives thoroughly on paper towels for ease in wrapping.

HOT OLIVE-CHEESE BALLS

1 cup (4 oz.) shredded Cheddar cheese
3 tablespoons margarine or butter, softened
½ cup Pillsbury's Best® All Purpose or Unbleached Flour*
1 teaspoon paprika
½ teaspoon Worcestershire sauce
Dash cayenne pepper
Dash salt
24 medium olives (pitted ripe or stuffed green)

Heat oven to 400°F. Grease cookie sheet. In small bowl, combine cheese and margarine. Add remaining ingredients except olives; mix well. Mold a slightly rounded teaspoonful of dough around each olive, covering completely; shape into ball. Place on prepared cookie sheet. Bake at 400°F. for 12 minutes or until golden brown.

24 appetizers

NUTRITION INFORMATION PER SERVING

Serving Size: 4 appetizers		Percent U.S. RDA Per Serving	
Calories	199	Protein	9%
Protein	6g	Vitamin A	10%
Carbohydrate	9g	Vitamin C	*
Fat	16g	Thiamin	5%
Sodium	470mg	Riboflavin	8%
Potassium	36mg	Niacin	3%
		Calcium	17%
		Iron	5%

TIPS: *Dough may be refrigerated up to 3 days and used as needed.*

**Self-rising flour is not recommended.*

An appetizer can be as easy as wrapping bacon around a nibbler. Here are a few serving suggestions.

BACON-WRAPPED HORS D'OEUVRES

½ lb. (8 slices) bacon
Desired centers, see below

Heat oven to 375°F. Cut bacon slices into thirds; wrap around filling, securing with toothpicks. Arrange on broiler pan or on rack in shallow baking pan. Bake at 375°F. for 20 to 25 minutes or until bacon is crisp. Serve hot. 24 appetizers

TIPS: *For WATER CHESTNUT CENTERS, combine 24 whole or halved drained water chestnuts (8-oz. can), ¼ cup soy sauce and 1 tablespoon sugar. Marinate about 30 minutes. Drain and continue as directed.*

For SMOKED OYSTER CENTERS, use a 3¾-oz. can (about 12 oysters) smoked drained oysters. Reduce bacon to 4 slices. 12 appetizers

For OLIVE CENTERS, use 24 stuffed green olives.

For CHICKEN LIVER CENTERS, cut 8 oz. chicken livers into 24 pieces. Combine ½ cup French dressing and ¼ teaspoon garlic salt. Marinate livers in dressing about 15 minutes. Drain and continue as directed.

For PINEAPPLE CENTERS, use fresh, drained canned, or frozen pineapple chunks. Marinate pineapple in French dressing. Drain and continue as directed.

For SCALLOP CENTERS, use 8 oz. fresh or frozen, thawed, scallops (cut large ones in half).

About 24 appetizers

This is a perfect hors d'oeuvres for guests to broil themselves on a miniature hibachi.

TERIYAKI WRAP-UPS

1 tablespoon sugar
1 tablespoon chopped onion
¼ teaspoon ginger
1 garlic clove, minced
¼ cup soy sauce
½ lb. sirloin steak, cut into thin strips
8-oz. can (⅔ cup) water chestnuts, drained

In small bowl, combine first 5 ingredients; mix well. Add steak strips and water chestnuts, tossing to coat with soy mixture. Marinate at least 30 minutes, stirring occasionally. Drain steak strips and wrap around water chestnuts (cut large chestnuts in half); secure with toothpicks.* Arrange on broiler pan. Broil 4 to 5 inches from heat for 5 to 8 minutes or until desired doneness, turning once.

About 20 appetizers

NUTRITION INFORMATION PER SERVING

Serving Size: 2 appetizers		Percent U.S. RDA Per Serving	
Calories	79	Protein	7%
Protein	4g	Vitamin A	*
Carbohydrate	3g	Vitamin C	*
Fat	5g	Thiamin	*
Sodium	529mg	Riboflavin	3%
Potassium	46mg	Niacin	4%
		Calcium	*
		Iron	5%

TIPS: *If desired, ⅓ cup prepared teriyaki sauce may be substituted for the first 5 ingredients.*

*To MAKE AHEAD, prepare to *, cover and refrigerate up to 12 hours. To serve continue as directed.*

Low in calories but high in flavor.

COTTAGE-STUFFED CELERY

½ cup small curd creamed cottage cheese
2 to 3 teaspoons chopped green onion or chopped chives
⅛ teaspoon salt, onion salt or seasoned salt
⅛ teaspoon prepared horseradish, if desired
⅛ teaspoon Worcestershire sauce
3 to 4 stalks celery, cut into 3-inch pieces

In small bowl, combine all ingredients except celery; mix well. Spoon mixture into each celery piece, using about 2 teaspoons for each. Garnish with paprika, additional sliced onion or chopped chives.
12 to 15 appetizers

NUTRITION INFORMATION PER SERVING

Serving Size: 2 pieces		Percent U.S. RDA Per Serving	
Calories	22	Protein	4%
Protein	3g	Vitamin A	*
Carbohydrate	1g	Vitamin C	3%
Fat	<1g	Thiamin	*
Sodium	101mg	Riboflavin	3%
Potassium	85mg	Niacin	*
		Calcium	2%
		Iron	*

BROILED STUFFED MUSHROOMS

16 oz. large fresh mushrooms
2 tablespoons finely chopped onion
¼ cup margarine or butter
¾ to 1 cup cooked finely chopped chicken livers
¼ teaspoon salt
Dash pepper
1 tablespoon sherry or brandy, if desired
2 tablespoons lemon juice
Melted margarine or butter

Remove stems from mushrooms and set aside caps. Finely chop stems. In large skillet, cook chopped mushroom stems and onion in margarine until tender. Add chicken livers, salt, pepper and sherry; mix well. Dip mushroom caps in lemon juice and arrange hollow-side-up in shallow baking pan. Fill with chopped mixture; brush with melted margarine. Broil 4 to 5 inches from heat 4 to 5 minutes or until heated through and caps are lightly browned. Serve hot.
40 to 48 appetizers

NUTRITION INFORMATION PER SERVING

Serving Size: 4 appetizers		Percent U.S. RDA Per Serving	
Calories	130	Protein	5%
Protein	3g	Vitamin A	31%
Carbohydrate	2g	Vitamin C	4%
Fat	12g	Thiamin	4%
Sodium	197mg	Riboflavin	24%
Potassium	180mg	Niacin	13%
		Calcium	*
		Iron	6%

COCKTAIL NUTS

2 tablespoons margarine or butter
¼ teaspoon seasoned salt
¼ teaspoon garlic powder
Dash Tabasco sauce
1 lb. (3 to 4 cups) mixed nuts
3 tablespoons Worcestershire sauce

Heat oven to 300°F. In 15x10-inch jelly roll pan or 13x9-inch pan, melt margarine with salt, garlic powder and Tabasco sauce; mix well. Add nuts, tossing to coat. Bake at 300°F. for 15 minutes, stirring occasionally. Sprinkle with Worcestershire sauce and continue baking 15 minutes or until crisp.
3 to 4 cups

NUTRITION INFORMATION PER SERVING

Serving Size: 1/4 cup		Percent U.S. RDA Per Serving	
Calories	230	Protein	14%
Protein	9g	Vitamin A	*
Carbohydrate	7g	Vitamin C	*
Fat	20g	Thiamin	8%
Sodium	250mg	Riboflavin	3%
Potassium	244mg	Niacin	31%
		Calcium	3%
		Iron	4%

COCKTAIL NUTS

Ready-to-eat cereal, peanuts and pretzels team together to make this out-of-the-hand eating snack. Great for TV football games.

PARTY SNACK MIX

½ cup margarine or butter
1 tablespoon Worcestershire sauce
⅛ teaspoon Tabasco sauce
4 cups bite-size crispy corn squares
2 cups bite-size crispy wheat squares
2 cups pretzel sticks
2 cups Spanish peanuts or mixed nuts
1 teaspoon salt
¼ teaspoon garlic powder

Heat oven to 325°F. In 15x10-inch jelly roll pan or two 13x9-inch pans, melt margarine. Add Worcestershire and Tabasco sauces; mix well. Stir in cereals, pretzel sticks and peanuts. Sprinkle with salt and garlic powder. Toss well. Bake at 325°F. for 25 to 30 minutes or until lightly toasted, stirring occasionally.

12 cups

NUTRITION INFORMATION PER SERVING

Serving Size: 1/2 cup		Percent U.S. RDA Per Serving	
Calories	146	Protein	6%
Protein	4g	Vitamin A	3%
Carbohydrate	11g	Vitamin C	*
Fat	10g	Thiamin	4%
Sodium	320mg	Riboflavin	*
Potassium	87mg	Niacin	11%
		Calcium	*
		Iron	3%

TIP: *If desired, 1 teaspoon garlic salt may be substituted for the salt and garlic powder.*

PARTY SNACK MIX

GLAZED SALTED ALMONDS

1 egg white, slightly beaten
1 tablespoon margarine or butter, melted
2 cups blanched almonds
Salt
Grated Parmesan cheese

Heat oven to 375°F. In medium bowl, blend egg white and margarine; stir in nuts. Spread in shallow baking pan; sprinkle with salt and Parmesan cheese. Bake at 375°F. for 15 to 20 minutes or until heated and glazed; watch closely and stir often to prevent burning. 2 cups

NUTRITION INFORMATION PER SERVING

Serving Size: 1/4 cup		Percent U.S. RDA Per Serving	
Calories	239	Protein	13%
Protein	8g	Vitamin A	*
Carbohydrate	7g	Vitamin C	0%
Fat	21g	Thiamin	6%
Sodium	314mg	Riboflavin	21%
Potassium	285mg	Niacin	6%
		Calcium	12%
		Iron	9%

ABOUT FIRST COURSE APPETIZERS

It's a special meal indeed when it opens with a tantalizing first course. An appetizer of this nature should stimulate the appetite and set the stage for the rest of the menu. It should not be too filling or heavy, especially if there is a lot more food to come.

Some soups make a lovely first course; see Chapter 17 for suggestions.

Seafood and specialty fruit salads are also popular first course appetizers. Make sure they are well chilled when serving. If necessary put the salad plates in the refrigerator a few hours before serving.

OYSTERS or CLAMS ON THE HALF SHELL

Allow 6 to 8 very fresh oysters or clams per serving. (See How to Clean and Shuck Oysters and Clams) page 284). Chill oysters or clams. Serve each on deeper half of shell, arranging shells on bed of crushed ice. Serve with Seafood Cocktail Sauce, page 552, lemon wedges and crackers.

NUTRITION INFORMATION PER SERVING

Serving Size: 6 clams		Percent U.S. RDA Per Serving	
Calories	84	Protein	18%
Protein	12g	Vitamin A	+
Carbohydrate	6g	Vitamin C	+
Fat	1g	Thiamin	+
Sodium	215mg	Riboflavin	+
Potassium	327mg	Niacin	+
		Calcium	7%
		Iron	44%

NUTRITION INFORMATION PER SERVING

Serving Size: 6 oysters		Percent U.S. RDA Per Serving	
Calories	73	Protein	14%
Protein	9g	Vitamin A	7%
Carbohydrate	4g	Vitamin C	0%
Fat	2g	Thiamin	10%
Sodium	81mg	Riboflavin	12%
Potassium	134mg	Niacin	14%
		Calcium	10%
		Iron	34%

Serve in a lettuce cup on a well-chilled salad plate.

WINTER FRUIT COCKTAIL

2 cups grapefruit sections, cut into thirds
2 cups orange sections, halved
1 cup cooked pitted prunes
2 bananas, sliced
1 medium apple, unpeeled and sliced
¼ cup sugar or honey
¼ cup lemon juice

In large bowl, combine all ingredients. Cover and chill.

6 to 8 servings

NUTRITION INFORMATION PER SERVING

Serving Size: 1/8 of recipe		Percent U.S. RDA Per Serving	
Calories	130	Protein	2%
Protein	1g	Vitamin A	8%
Carbohydrate	34g	Vitamin C	81%
Fat	<1g	Thiamin	6%
Sodium	3mg	Riboflavin	4%
Potassium	362mg	Niacin	3%
		Calcium	4%
		Iron	6%

SPRINGTIME FRUIT COCKTAIL

1 cup pineapple chunks, drained
1 cup orange sections
1 cup fresh strawberries, whole or sliced
¾ cup fresh or frozen melon balls
2 bananas, sliced
2 to 4 tablespoons sugar or honey
¼ cup lemon juice

In large bowl, combine fruit. Blend sugar and lemon juice; spoon over fruit. Cover and chill. If desired, garnish with mint leaves.

4 to 6 servings

NUTRITION INFORMATION PER SERVING

Serving Size: 1/6 of recipe		Percent U.S. RDA Per Serving	
Calories	85	Protein	*
Protein	1g	Vitamin A	17%
Carbohydrate	22g	Vitamin C	76%
Fat	<1g	Thiamin	6%
Sodium	4mg	Riboflavin	4%
Potassium	308mg	Niacin	3%
		Calcium	3%
		Iron	4%

ANTIPASTO TRAY

ANTIPASTO TRAY

An antipasto tray can serve as a salad, main dish or appetizer, depending on the amount and kinds of vegetables and meats that are included. Usually the vegetables are marinated or chilled for about 8 hours before serving.

Vegetables can include: asparagus spears, cauliflowerets, sliced cucumber, beets, olives, mushroom caps, artichoke hearts and/or cherry tomatoes marinated in a dressing such as Italian, oil and vinegar or French. Drain and arrange artfully in separate sections on tray or platter.

Other foods to add: sliced salami or luncheon meats, cooked sliced and chilled roast or ham, hard-cooked or deviled eggs, sliced cheeses, chilled canned salmon, shrimp, crab meat or tuna and/or pickles or peppers.

SEAFOOD COCKTAIL

1 small avocado, peeled and cubed
1 teaspoon lemon juice
2 cans (6½ oz. each) crab meat, drained and flaked
4½-oz. can tiny shrimp, drained
Lettuce cups
Seafood cocktail sauce

In small bowl, sprinkle avocado with lemon juice; combine gently with seafood. Serve in lettuce cups with cocktail sauce. 8 servings

NUTRITION INFORMATION PER SERVING

Serving Size: 1/8 of recipe		Percent U.S. RDA Per Serving	
Calories	97	Protein	15%
Protein	10g	Vitamin A	*
Carbohydrate	2g	Vitamin C	5%
Fat	6g	Thiamin	4%
Sodium	314mg	Riboflavin	5%
Potassium	220mg	Niacin	7%
		Calcium	4%
		Iron	5%

TIP: *If desired, substitute cooked frozen crab meat, lobster and shrimp –½ to 1 cup of each.*

SEAFOOD COCKTAIL

ESCARGOT

½ cup margarine or butter, softened
1 tablespoon minced parsley
½ to 1 teaspoon garlic powder or instant minced garlic
Dash nutmeg
4½-oz. can snails (about 24)
24 snail shells

Heat oven to 400°F. In small bowl, combine margarine, parsley, garlic and nutmeg. Place 1 snail in each shell; top with about 1 teaspoon margarine mixture. Bake uncovered at 400°F. for 10 to 12 minutes or until snails are firm. Serve immediately with remaining margarine sauce for dipping. 4 to 6 servings

NUTRITION INFORMATION PER SERVING

Serving Size: 4 appetizers		Percent U.S. RDA Per Serving	
Calories	160	Protein	6%
Protein	4g	Vitamin A	14%
Carbohydrate	<1g	Vitamin C	*
Fat	16g	Thiamin	*
Sodium	188mg	Riboflavin	*
Potassium	14mg	Niacin	*
		Calcium	*
		Iron	5%

ESCARGOT

ABOUT PARTY SANDWICHES AND CANAPÉS

There is a little more work involved in the preparation of these appetizers but the visual appeal on the platter is worth the effort. This is where your artistic talents can flower as you individually prepare and decorate each appetizer. Because one of their functions is to decorate the appetizer table, the appearance of each is important.

Uniformity in slicing and cutting will give a professional appearance and best results are achieved with machine sliced breads. When you order bread from the baker specify exactly how you wish the breads to be sliced – whether horizontal or vertical and how thick you want the slices. Cookie cutters will produce uniformity in fancy shapes.

Look for color contrast when garnishing. Light colored spreads should have sparks of dark or bright garnishes. Some easy garnishes are:

- tiny leaves of parsley
- thin strips of pimiento
- carrot curls
- green pepper strips
- sliced olives, green or black
- red caviar
- red onion rings
- whole cloves
- slices of fresh strawberries
- tiny whole shrimp
- cherry tomato slices
- sliced hard cooked egg
- sprinkles of paprika
- mandarin orange segments
- jellied cranberry slices cut in fancy shapes
- small green onion leaves
- thin sliced cucumber
- grated Parmesan cheese
- crumbled blue cheese

Cream cheese spreads may be tinted with a few drops of food coloring. Keep the colors pastel for appetite appeal.

PARTY SANDWICHES

Freeze bread, then cut and spread while frozen. Spread bread with soft margarine or butter to edge before spreading filling to prevent sogginess (see pages 524 and 525 for Fillings). If desired, sandwiches can be made a day ahead, wrapped in plastic wrap, then in a damp towel and refrigerated. See page 455 for freezing information.

OPEN-FACE SANDWICHES. Use unsliced sandwich loaf. Slice bread lengthwise, remove crusts. Cut into desired shapes and spread with favorite fillings. Garnishes such as sliced pimiento, sliced olives, sliced mushrooms, parsley, sliced radishes and sliced pickles may be used to decorate each sandwich. Garnish line should follow shape of sandwich as well as accent or enhance its color. Chill until served.

PINWHEEL SANDWICHES: Use unsliced sandwich loaf. Cut lengthwise in ¼ to ½-inch slices, then cut each slice in half crosswise. Flatten slices slightly with rolling pin. Spread with margarine or butter and favorite sandwich filling. If desired, at one end lay small sweet pickles or stuffed olives. Beginning at this end roll as for jelly roll. Spread edge with softened margarine to seal edge. The outside may be frosted with softened cream cheese and rolled in chopped nuts. Chill several hours and cut into slices.

RIBBON LOAF: Trim crusts from 1 whole wheat and 1 white loaf unsliced sandwich bread. Cut 6 horizontal slices each of whole wheat bread and white bread ½-inch thick. Fill between 3 slices with 2 of favorite fillings. Assemble loaf, alternating white and whole wheat slices.* If desired, frost loaf with softened cream cheese. Chill. Cut loaf into slices, about ½-inch thick; cut each slice in half.

4 loaves (about 12 dozen sandwiches)

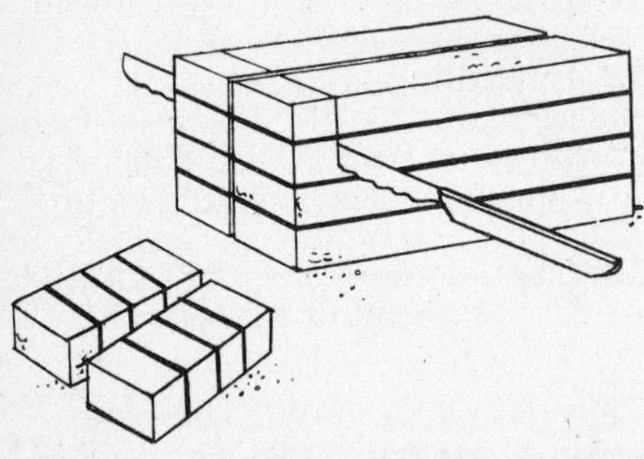

CHECKERBOARD SANDWICHES: Reserve two loaves RIBBON LOAF sandwiches; one loaf with a whole wheat slice on top, and the other loaf with a white slice on top. Do not frost with cream cheese. Chill. Cut each loaf into slices. Spread slices with margarine and place 3 or 4 in a stack so a white block will alternate with a whole wheat one. Chill and slice ½ inch thick.

About 3 dozen sandwiches

PARTY SANDWICH LOAF

1 loaf white or whole wheat sandwich bread, unsliced
½ cup margarine or butter, softened
3 sandwich fillings*
2 pkg. (8 oz. each) cream cheese, softened
½ cup light cream
Cucumber or olive slices

Trim crusts from bread. Cut lengthwise into 4 slices. Spread 3 slices with margarine; then spread each with a different filling. Stack slices, placing unspread slice on top. In large bowl, blend cream cheese and cream until fluffy and soft enough to spread; frost sides and top of loaf. Garnish with cucumber or olive slices.
For ease in slicing, chill at least 2 hours. Refrigerate leftovers.

1 loaf

Because of the variety of fillings which may be used, the nutrition information cannot accurately be determined.

TIPS: **About 1½ cups filling is needed for each layer. Filling combinations that go well together:*
chicken salad, pineapple cheese filling and ham salad; deviled ham filling, peanut butter-honey and egg salad.

Sandwich loaf may be made with alternating white and whole wheat slices. Use remaining slices for second sandwich loaf or other party sandwiches.

A few drops of food coloring may be added to cream cheese frosting.

HOT CRAB MEAT CANAPÉS

6½-oz. can crab meat, drained and flaked
½ cup mayonnaise or salad dressing
1 teaspoon prepared horseradish
½ teaspoon prepared mustard
½ teaspoon Worcestershire sauce
6 slices bread or 24 crackers
¼ cup grated Parmesan cheese

In small bowl, combine first 5 ingredients; mix well. Toast bread; trim crusts. Cut each slice into 4 squares; arrange on cookie sheet. Top each with about 1 tablespoon crab mixture; spread evenly. Sprinkle with Parmesan cheese. Broil 5 to 6 inches from heat for 2 to 3 minutes or until filling is bubbly.

24 canapés

NUTRITION INFORMATION PER SERVING

Serving Size: 2 appetizers		Percent U.S. RDA Per Serving	
Calories	129	Protein	6%
Protein	4g	Vitamin A	*
Carbohydrate	9g	Vitamin C	0%
Fat	9g	Thiamin	3%
Sodium	263mg	Riboflavin	4%
Potassium	36mg	Niacin	3%
		Calcium	4%
		Iron	3%

SNACK CREAM PUFFS

Heat oven to 425°F. Prepare Cream Puffs, page 211. Drop by teaspoonfuls onto ungreased cookie sheet. Bake at 425°F. for 13 to 17 minutes or until golden brown and crisp. Cool and split. Fill with Chicken Filling, page 524, Seafood Filling, page 524, or other desired filling. Refrigerate leftovers.

About 20 appetizers

NUTRITION INFORMATION PER SERVING

Serving Size: 1 cream puff without filling		Percent U.S. RDA Per Serving	
Calories	41	Protein	*
Protein	1g	Vitamin A	3%
Carbohydrate	2g	Vitamin C	0%
Fat	3g	Thiamin	*
Sodium	62mg	Riboflavin	*
Potassium	11mg	Niacin	*
		Calcium	*
		Iron	*

TIPS: *Cream puffs and filling may be prepared ahead; fill shortly before serving.*

About 1½ cups of filling are needed to fill 20 puffs.

TOASTED HAM CANAPÉS

1 cup cooked finely chopped ham
½ cup (2 oz.) shredded American cheese
3 tablespoons mayonnaise or salad dressing
2 tablespoons margarine or butter, melted
1 tablespoon prepared mustard
1 teaspoon prepared horseradish
6 slices bread, toasted
24 pickle slices

In small bowl, combine first 6 ingredients; mix well. Remove crusts from toast; cut each slice into 4 squares. Arrange on cookie sheet. Spread ham mixture on toast; top each with a pickle slice. Broil 3 to 4 inches from heat for 3 to 4 minutes or until hot and bubbly.

24 canapés

NUTRITION INFORMATION PER SERVING

Serving Size: 2 appetizers		Percent U.S. RDA Per Serving	
Calories	140	Protein	7%
Protein	5g	Vitamin A	3%
Carbohydrate	12g	Vitamin C	*
Fat	8g	Thiamin	7%
Sodium	313mg	Riboflavin	4%
Potassium	63mg	Niacin	4%
		Calcium	5%
		Iron	5%

ABOUT DIPS AND SPREADS

The smoothness of a dip is a very pleasant contrast to the crunchy dunkers generally used. Most dips are best prepared ahead so the flavors are allowed to mix. Cover and refrigerate. For the most flavorful dips take them out an hour or two ahead so they may be served at room temperature. Hot dips should be served hot.

EASY SOUR CREAM OR CREAM CHEESE DIPS

Turn sour cream or cream cheese into an easy dip by adding one of the following flavor additions. Use 1 cup dairy sour cream or yogurt or an 8-oz. package of cream cheese, softened and mixed with 2 tablespoons milk.

DEVILED HAM: add 4½-oz. can deviled ham, 2 tablespoons pickle relish and ¼ teaspoon Worcestershire sauce. 1½ cups

CHEESE: add 5-oz. jar processed cheese spread and ¼ teaspoon garlic salt. 1½ cups

ITALIAN: add 3 tablespoons (1-oz. pkg.) spaghetti sauce seasoning mix. 1 cup

NUTRITION INFORMATION PER SERVING

Serving Size: 1 tablespoon		Percent U.S. RDA Per Serving	
Calories	32	Protein	*
Protein	<1g	Vitamin A	2%
Carbohydrate	1g	Vitamin C	0%
Fat	3g	Thiamin	*
Sodium	167mg	Riboflavin	*
Potassium	6mg	Niacin	0%
		Calcium	*
		Iron	0%

ONION: add 1 envelope onion salad dressing mix or ½ envelope dry onion soup mix. Try with other flavors of dressing mix, too. 1¼ cups

NUTRITION INFORMATION PER SERVING

Serving Size: 1 tablespoon		Percent U.S. RDA Per Serving	
Calories	27	Protein	*
Protein	<1g	Vitamin A	*
Carbohydrate	<1g	Vitamin C	*
Fat	2g	Thiamin	*
Sodium	77mg	Riboflavin	*
Potassium	6mg	Niacin	*
		Calcium	*
		Iron	*

ZIPPY SEAFOOD DIP

½ cup dairy sour cream
1 teaspoon crushed chervil, if desired
½ teaspoon salt
2 green onions, chopped
Dash pepper
2 teaspoons prepared horseradish
1 teaspoon Worcestershire sauce
8-oz. pkg. cream cheese, softened
6½-oz. can tuna, shrimp, crab or clams, drained and flaked

In small bowl, combine all ingredients; mix well. Cover and chill. If desired, garnish with parsley.

2 cups

NUTRITION INFORMATION PER SERVING

Serving Size: 1 tablespoon		Percent U.S. RDA Per Serving	
Calories	44	Protein	3%
Protein	2g	Vitamin A	3%
Carbohydrate	<1g	Vitamin C	*
Fat	4g	Thiamin	*
Sodium	55mg	Riboflavin	*
Potassium	8mg	Niacin	3%
		Calcium	*
		Iron	*

COLD CLAM DIP

8-oz. pkg. cream cheese, softened
6½-oz. or 8-oz. can minced clams, drained (reserve liquor)
1 tablespoon grated onion
1 teaspoon minced parsley
¼ teaspoon salt
1 tablespoon lemon juice
1 teaspoon Worcestershire sauce
3 drops Tabasco sauce

In small bowl, combine all ingredients except reserved liquor; mix well. Cover and chill. If necessary to thin dip, add clam liquor a few drops at a time until desired consistency. Serve with chips, crackers or raw vegetables. 1⅓ cups

NUTRITION INFORMATION PER SERVING

Serving Size: 1 tablespoon		Percent U.S. RDA Per Serving	
Calories	46	Protein	3%
Protein	2g	Vitamin A	3%
Carbohydrate	<1g	Vitamin C	*
Fat	4g	Thiamin	*
Sodium	56mg	Riboflavin	*
Potassium	11mg	Niacin	*
		Calcium	*
		Iron	*

HOT CHIPPED BEEF DIP

2 pkg. (8 oz. each) cream cheese, softened
1 cup dairy sour cream
2 tablespoons milk
1 tablespoon Worcestershire sauce
¼ cup instant minced onion or ¾ cup finely chopped onion
¼ cup finely chopped green pepper
2 pkg. (3 oz. each) dried chipped beef, finely chopped

Heat oven to 350°F. In large bowl, combine cream cheese, sour cream, milk and Worcestershire sauce. Beat until fluffy. Stir in onion, green pepper and dried beef. Bake at 350°F. for 30 minutes. Serve hot in fondue pot or chafing dish. 4 cups

NUTRITION INFORMATION PER SERVING

Serving Size: 1 tablespoon		Percent U.S. RDA Per Serving	
Calories	41	Protein	2%
Protein	2g	Vitamin A	3%
Carbohydrate	<1g	Vitamin C	*
Fat	4g	Thiamin	*
Sodium	136mg	Riboflavin	*
Potassium	18mg	Niacin	*
		Calcium	*
		Iron	*

GUACAMOLE DIP

GUACAMOLE DIP

1 cup (1 medium) peeled, mashed avocado
2 tablespoons finely chopped onion
¼ teaspoon chili powder
¼ teaspoon garlic salt
2 tablespoons mayonnaise or salad dressing
5 to 6 drops Tabasco sauce
2 slices bacon, fried, drained and crumbled or 2 teaspoons imitation bacon bits

In small bowl, combine all ingredients except bacon; mix well. Cover and chill 30 minutes or until served. Before serving, stir in bacon or use as a garnish. Serve with tortilla or corn chips. 1⅓ cups

NUTRITION INFORMATION PER SERVING

Serving Size: 1 tablespoon		Percent U.S. RDA Per Serving	
Calories	33	Protein	*
Protein	<1g	Vitamin A	*
Carbohydrate	<1g	Vitamin C	3%
Fat	3g	Thiamin	*
Sodium	38mg	Riboflavin	*
Potassium	70mg	Niacin	*
		Calcium	*
		Iron	*

TIPS: *To prepare in blender, cut avocado into large pieces and process at medium speed. Add remaining ingredients except bacon; process just until onion is in small pieces.*

To use avocado shells for serving, cut unpeeled avocado in half lengthwise. Remove pit and scoop fruit out of shell with spoon. Continue with directions above. Fill shells with dip and refrigerate until serving.

BEAN AND BACON DIP

1 cup dairy sour cream
½ cup (2 oz.) shredded Cheddar or American cheese
½ teaspoon instant minced onion
11½-oz. can condensed bean with bacon soup

Heat oven to 375°F. In ovenproof dish, combine all ingredients. Bake at 375°F. for about 10 minutes or until heated through. Serve with corn or taco chips. 2½ cups

NUTRITION INFORMATION PER SERVING

Serving Size: 1 tablespoon		Percent U.S. RDA Per Serving	
Calories	28	Protein	*
Protein	1g	Vitamin A	2%
Carbohydrate	2g	Vitamin C	*
Fat	2g	Thiamin	*
Sodium	78mg	Riboflavin	*
Potassium	27mg	Niacin	*
		Calcium	2%
		Iron	*

TIP: *For TACO-BEAN DIP, add 2 tablespoons dry taco seasoning mix with onion.*

LO-CALORIE VEGETABLE DIP

1 cup (8 oz.) plain yogurt
¼ teaspoon salt
¼ teaspoon dill weed
⅛ teaspoon garlic salt
3 green onions, finely chopped
Dash pepper
1 teaspoon honey

In small bowl or blender, combine all ingredients; mix well. Refrigerate several hours to blend flavors. 1 cup

NUTRITION INFORMATION PER SERVING

Serving Size: 1 tablespoon		Percent U.S. RDA Per Serving	
Calories	10	Protein	*
Protein	<1g	Vitamin A	*
Carbohydrate	1g	Vitamin C	*
Fat	<1g	Thiamin	*
Sodium	55mg	Riboflavin	*
Potassium	28mg	Niacin	*
		Calcium	*
		Iron	*

The serving bowl for this cheese dip is a round loaf of bread. When the dip is gone, eat the "bowl." Great fun for casual parties.

BEER-CHEESE FONDUE DIP

1 round loaf unsliced limpa or cottage rye bread
3 rolls (6 oz. each) sharp pasteurized process cheese spread
1¼ oz. Roquefort cheese
¾ cup warm beer
3 tablespoons margarine or butter, melted
1 teaspoon Worcestershire sauce
Dash Tabasco sauce
¼ cup finely chopped onion
1 garlic clove, minced

Tear out inside of bread to make bowl, leaving at least ½ inch all around side and bottom. Tear bread from inside the loaf into bite-size pieces and place in plastic bag until ready to serve. Combine remaining ingredients except onion and garlic in blender until well blended. Add onion and garlic; blend. Pour cheese mixture into bread bowl; refrigerate at least 1 hour before serving. Serve bread bowl on platter surrounded by bread pieces; serve with toothpicks.

10 to 20 servings

NUTRITION INFORMATION PER SERVING

Serving Size: 1/10 of recipe		Percent U.S. RDA Per Serving	
Calories	329	Protein	23%
Protein	15g	Vitamin A	14%
Carbohydrate	29g	Vitamin C	*
Fat	17g	Thiamin	6%
Sodium	303mg	Riboflavin	21%
Potassium	80mg	Niacin	4%
		Calcium	34%
		Iron	7%

TIPS: *Three jars (5 oz. each) sharp pasteurized process cheese spread may be substituted for cheese roll.*

Cheese mixture freezes well for future use.

DILLY DIP

1 cup mayonnaise
1 cup dairy sour cream
1 tablespoon parsley flakes
1 tablespoon instant minced onion
1 teaspoon dill weed
1 teaspoon beau monde

In small bowl, combine all ingredients; mix well. Cover and refrigerate several hours to blend flavors. Serve with raw vegetables or chips.

2 cups

NUTRITION INFORMATION PER SERVING

Serving Size: 1 tablespoon		Percent U.S. RDA Per Serving	
Calories	64	Protein	*
Protein	<1g	Vitamin A	*
Carbohydrate	<1g	Vitamin C	*
Fat	7g	Thiamin	*
Sodium	44mg	Riboflavin	*
Potassium	6mg	Niacin	*
		Calcium	*
		Iron	*

CURRIED VEGETABLE DIP

1 cup mayonnaise or salad dressing
1 teaspoon grated onion
¼ teaspoon curry powder
1 teaspoon vinegar
1 teaspoon prepared horseradish

In small bowl, combine all ingredients; mix well. Cover and chill several hours to blend flavors. Serve with raw vegetables.

1 cup

NUTRITION INFORMATION PER SERVING

Serving Size: 1 tablespoon		Percent U.S. RDA Per Serving	
Calories	99	Protein	*
Protein	<1g	Vitamin A	*
Carbohydrate	<1g	Vitamin C	*
Fat	11g	Thiamin	*
Sodium	82mg	Riboflavin	*
Potassium	7mg	Niacin	*
		Calcium	*
		Iron	*

SALMON BALL

16-oz. can (2 cups) salmon, drained
1 tablespoon finely chopped onion
1 teaspoon prepared horseradish
¼ teaspoon salt
1 tablespoon lemon juice
8-oz. pkg. cream cheese
Minced parsley

In medium bowl, flake salmon, removing bones and skin. Add remaining ingredients except parsley; mix well. Refrigerate about 4 hours or until firm enough to shape into ball. Shape into ball; roll in parsley. Chill at least 1 hour before serving. Serve with assorted crackers or small slices of rye bread.

5-inch ball

NUTRITION INFORMATION PER SERVING

Serving Size: 1/15 of ball		Percent U.S. RDA Per Serving	
Calories	113	Protein	9%
Protein	6g	Vitamin A	10%
Carbohydrate	<1g	Vitamin C	7%
Fat	10g	Thiamin	2%
Sodium	86mg	Riboflavin	6%
Potassium	127mg	Niacin	*
		Calcium	*
		Iron	*

SALMON BALL

TASTY BRAUNSCHWEIGER SPREAD

TASTY BRAUNSCHWEIGER SPREAD

⅓ cup (2 oz.) braunschweiger or liver sausage
1 to 2 tablespoons drained pickle relish
¼ teaspoon garlic salt
½ to 1 teaspoon Worcestershire sauce
8-oz. pkg. cream cheese, softened
½ cup (3 oz.) chopped peanuts or pecans

In small bowl, combine all ingredients except peanuts; mix well. Chill about 15 minutes for easier handling. Shape into ball; roll in nuts. Cover and refrigerate 2 hours or until firm and flavors have blended. Serve with assorted crackers or small slices of rye bread. 3-inch ball

NUTRITION INFORMATION PER SERVING

Serving Size: 1/10 of ball		Percent U.S. RDA Per Serving	
Calories	147	Protein	7%
Protein	5g	Vitamin A	14%
Carbohydrate	3g	Vitamin C	0%
Fat	14g	Thiamin	2%
Sodium	190mg	Riboflavin	9%
Potassium	67mg	Niacin	9%
		Calcium	2%
		Iron	3%

TIPS: *For ONION-FLAVORED BRAUNSCHWEIGER SPREAD, combine 3 tablespoons dry onion soup mix with ¼ cup sour cream; add to cheese mixture. Mix well.*

For BRAUNSCHWEIGER DIP, thin mixture with cream or milk. Use nuts as a garnish.

For BRAUNSCHWEIGER LOAF, double recipe, omitting peanuts. Cut a loaf of French bread in half lengthwise. Hollow out center portion of bread leaving a 1-inch (crust) shell. Fill hollowed-out loaf with spread. Wrap and refrigerate several hours. To serve, cut into slices.

OLIVE CREAM CHEESE BALL

OLIVE CREAM CHEESE BALL

⅓ cup chopped stuffed green olives
¼ cup chopped ripe olives
¼ cup finely chopped onion
¼ teaspoon Tabasco sauce
8-oz. pkg. cream cheese, softened
½ cup minced parsley

In medium bowl, combine all ingredients except parsley; mix well. Chill about 15 minutes for easier handling. Shape into ball; roll in parsley. Chill about 20 minutes or until served. Serve with assorted crackers or chips. 4-inch ball

NUTRITION INFORMATION PER SERVING

Serving Size: 1/12 of ball		Percent U.S. RDA Per Serving	
Calories	81	Protein	3%
Protein	2g	Vitamin A	11%
Carbohydrate	1g	Vitamin C	8%
Fat	8g	Thiamin	*
Sodium	160mg	Riboflavin	3%
Potassium	40mg	Niacin	*
		Calcium	2%
		Iron	*

CHICKEN LIVER PÂTÉ

1 lb. chicken livers
1½ cups water
⅓ cup margarine or butter, melted
1 medium apple, peeled and chopped
1 medium onion, chopped
1 garlic clove, crushed
Dash thyme
Dash marjoram
⅓ cup cooking sherry
¼ teaspoon salt
Dash pepper

In medium saucepan, simmer chicken livers in water 2 to 3 minutes. Drain and reserve ¾ to 1 cup liquid. In medium skillet, cook livers in margarine until brown. Add apple, onion, garlic, thyme, marjoram, sherry and cooking liquid. Simmer uncovered, 15 minutes or until liquid is absorbed, stirring occasionally. Grind finely in food chopper or puree in blender. Add salt and pepper. Chill. Serve with melba toast or crackers. 2 cups

NUTRITION INFORMATION PER SERVING

Serving Size: 1 tablespoon		Percent U.S. RDA Per Serving	
Calories	49	Protein	6%
Protein	4g	Vitamin A	37%
Carbohydrate	2g	Vitamin C	5%
Fat	3g	Thiamin	*
Sodium	50mg	Riboflavin	23%
Potassium	37mg	Niacin	8%
		Calcium	*
		Iron	7%

FESTIVE CHEESE BALL

2 cups (8 oz.) shredded Cheddar cheese
3 tablespoons mayonnaise or salad dressing
½ teaspoon Worcestershire sauce
Dash onion, garlic and celery salt
3-oz. pkg. cream cheese, softened
¼ cup chopped ripe olives

In medium bowl, combine all ingredients except olives. Mix well; stir in olives. Cover and chill until firm. Shape into ball. If desired, roll in finely chopped parsley, chopped nuts, chopped olives or minced dried beef. Cover and refrigerate 2 hours or until firm. Serve with assorted crackers. 4-inch ball

NUTRITION INFORMATION PER SERVING

Serving Size: 1/12 of ball		Percent U.S. RDA Per Serving	
Calories	130	Protein	8%
Protein	5g	Vitamin A	7%
Carbohydrate	*	Vitamin C	0%
Fat	12g	Thiamin	*
Sodium	252mg	Riboflavin	6%
Potassium	23mg	Niacin	*
		Calcium	15%
		Iron	*

WINE AND CHEESE BALL

2 cups (8 oz.) shredded Cheddar cheese
1 tablespoon finely chopped onion
1½ teaspoons prepared mustard
1½ tablespoons port wine or dessert sherry
4 oz. cream cheese, softened
¼ cup sunflower nuts or chopped nuts

In medium bowl, combine all ingredients except nuts; mix well. Shape into ball. Cover and refrigerate 2 hours or until firm. Before serving, roll in nuts. Serve with assorted crackers. 3-inch ball

NUTRITION INFORMATION PER SERVING

Serving Size: 1/10 of ball		Percent U.S. RDA Per Serving	
Calories	156	Protein	11%
Protein	7g	Vitamin A	9%
Carbohydrate	2g	Vitamin C	*
Fat	13g	Thiamin	5%
Sodium	197mg	Riboflavin	8%
Potassium	64mg	Niacin	*
		Calcium	18%
		Iron	3%

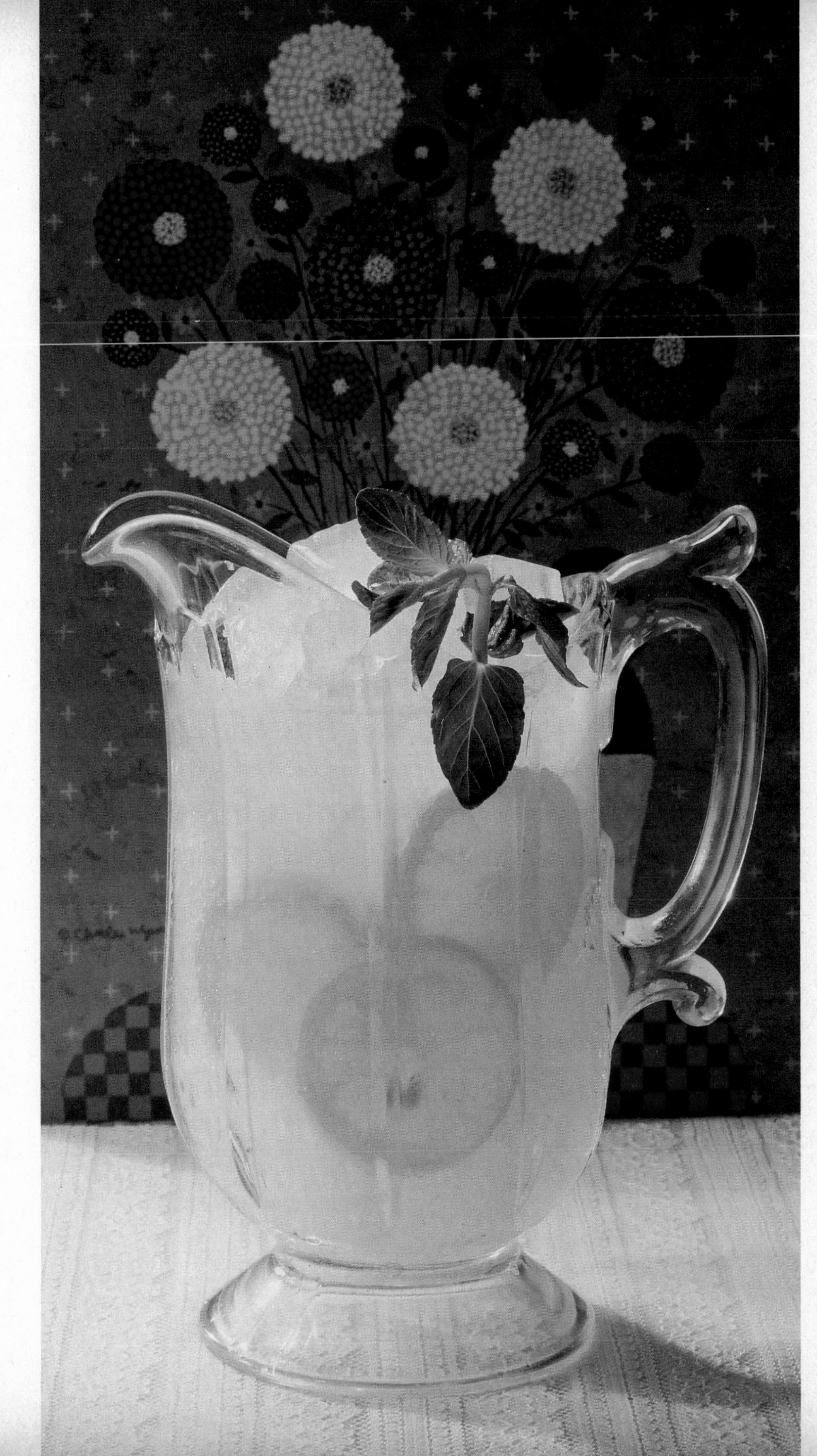

BEVERAGES

SERVING

Beverages are a must for everyday living, whether it is simply a glass of water, a cup of coffee, a healthful milkshake or a fancy champagne punch. Amost anytime is an occasion to serve a beverage.

Before the Meal: Beverages make a very good appetizer as they can stimulate the appetite without being filling. Choose a beverage which will be flavorful without overpowering the food to come. Sweeter drinks are not usually served as appetizers as they tend to dull the appetite.

With the Meal: Beverages that accompany a meal should be planned with the menu. Choose one which does not detract from the main course and steal the show but simply refreshes.

After the Meal: Beverages are often served as an accompaniment to dessert. The general rule to follow is: the sweeter and richer the dessert the less sweet the beverage. Coffee and tea are most popular.

Sometimes the beverage is the dessert. In this case sweeter, richer beverages are chosen. Ice cream drinks and chocolate beverages are popular; so are sweet sherries, liqueurs and sweeter coffees and teas.

Between Meals: Anything goes! It's all personal preference.

FLAVORED MILK BEVERAGES

In blender, combine 1 cup milk with one of the following:

BANANA: ½ medium-sized ripe banana.

BERRY: ½ cup fresh berries, 2 tablespoons sugar and 1 tablespoon lemon or orange juice; or ½ cup sweetened fruit.

CHOCOLATE: 2 to 3 tablespoons instant cocoa mix or 2 tablespoons chocolate ice cream topping.

COFFEE: 1 teaspoon instant coffee and 2 teaspoons sugar.

PEACH: ½ cup fresh peaches, 2 tablespoons sugar and 1 tablespoon lemon juice.

PEANUT BUTTER: 1 to 2 tablespoons peanut butter.

STRAWBERRY: 1 to 2 tablespoons strawberry preserves.

VANILLA: ½ teaspoon vanilla.

ENERGY SHAKE

In bowl or blender, combine 1 envelope Pillsbury Instant Breakfast, 1 cup milk and 1 to 2 scoops ice cream. Blend until smooth.

MILK SHAKE

In blender or mixer, combine 1 cup milk and ½ cup ice cream. Flavor with one of Flavored Milk suggestions, above.

YOGURT SHAKE

In blender or mixer, combine equal amounts of yogurt, milk and sweetened fruit. Blend until frothy. (For added nutrition, add 2 tablespoons wheat germ for each cup of milk.)

EGGNOG MILKSHAKE

1 tablespoon sugar
Dash salt
1 cup milk
½ teaspoon vanilla
½ teaspoon rum extract, if desired
1 scoop vanilla ice cream, if desired
Nutmeg

In blender or small bowl, combine first 5 ingredients; mix until frothy. Top serving with scoop of ice cream; sprinkle with nutmeg.

1 (1¼ cups) serving

NUTRITION INFORMATION PER SERVING

Serving Size: 1 1/4 cups		Percent U.S. RDA Per Serving	
Calories	335	Protein	18%
Protein	12g	Vitamin A	13%
Carbohydrate	38g	Vitamin C	5%
Fat	16g	Thiamin	7%
Sodium	435mg	Riboflavin	33%
Potassium	473mg	Niacin	*
		Calcium	39%
		Iron	*

HOT COCOA

⅓ cup sugar
3 tablespoons unsweetened cocoa
Dash salt
½ cup hot water
3 cups milk

In medium saucepan, combine first 4 ingredients; simmer 2 minutes. Add milk; heat. Before serving, beat until frothy. If desired, top with marshmallows or whipped cream.

4 servings

NUTRITION INFORMATION PER SERVING

Serving Size: 1/4 of recipe		Percent U.S. RDA Per Serving	
Calories	194	Protein	11%
Protein	7g	Vitamin A	5%
Carbohydrate	28g	Vitamin C	3%
Fat	7g	Thiamin	4%
Sodium	160mg	Riboflavin	19%
Potassium	326mg	Niacin	*
		Calcium	22%
		Iron	2%

TIP: *To make in mugs, combine 2 tablespoons sugar, 1 tablespoon cocoa, dash salt and 2 tablespoons hot water in each mug. Heat milk; pour into mugs; mix well.*

HOT CHOCOLATE

3-oz. (3 squares) unsweetened chocolate
½ cup water
½ cup sugar
Dash salt
5 cups hot milk
½ cup whipping cream, whipped
Nutmeg

In large saucepan, combine chocolate and water over low heat, stirring constantly until chocolate melts. Blend in sugar and salt; simmer 4 minutes, stirring occasionally. Add milk and stir to blend. Heat through, but do not boil. Top each cup with a dollop of whipped cream and sprinkle with nutmeg.

6 servings

NUTRITION INFORMATION PER SERVING

Serving Size: 1/6 of recipe		Percent U.S. RDA Per Serving	
Calories	337	Protein	14%
Protein	9g	Vitamin A	12%
Carbohydrate	31g	Vitamin C	2%
Fat	22g	Thiamin	5%
Sodium	154mg	Riboflavin	24%
Potassium	427mg	Niacin	2%
		Calcium	27%
		Iron	5%

HOT CHOCOLATE MIX

1 cup powdered sugar
¼ teaspoon salt
25.6-oz. pkg. (8 quarts) instant nonfat dry milk
1 lb. instant cocoa mix
6-oz. jar nondairy powdered creamer

In large container, combine all ingredients. Store tightly covered. For each serving, mix ¼ cup mix with 1 cup boiling water.

About 50 servings

NUTRITION INFORMATION PER SERVING

Serving Size: 1/4 cup mix plus 1 cup water		Percent U.S. RDA Per Serving	
Calories	113	Protein	11%
Protein	7g	Vitamin A	*
Carbohydrate	18g	Vitamin C	*
Fat	2g	Thiamin	4%
Sodium	135mg	Riboflavin	19%
Potassium	351mg	Niacin	*
		Calcium	24%
		Iron	*

A non-alcoholic treat to delight young and old.

CREAMY HOLIDAY EGGNOG

6 eggs, separated
⅓ cup honey or sugar
5 cups milk
1 tablespoon rum extract
1 teaspoon vanilla
1 cup (½ pint) whipping cream, whipped
Nutmeg

In large bowl, beat egg whites until soft peaks form. Add yolks and honey; beat well. Stir in milk, rum extract and vanilla. Chill. Just before serving, fold in whipped cream and pour into punch bowl. Sprinkle with nutmeg. 16 (½ cup) servings

NUTRITION INFORMATION PER SERVING

Serving Size: 1/2 cup		Percent U.S. RDA Per Serving	
Calories	157	Protein	9%
Protein	6g	Vitamin A	12%
Carbohydrate	10g	Vitamin C	*
Fat	11g	Thiamin	3%
Sodium	68mg	Riboflavin	12%
Potassium	153mg	Niacin	*
		Calcium	11%
		Iron	3%

MAKING COFFEE

There are several methods of making coffee and special grinds of coffee for each. Coffee varies in flavor depending on the blends of coffee bean types. With any method or blend of coffee, remember:

- Coffee pot should be clean so there are no carry-over "off" flavors. Wash pot with soap and water; rinse thoroughly.
- Use freshly drawn cold water and fresh coffee. The air present in freshly drawn water gives the coffee a special flavor. Cold water is necessary with most percolator-type coffeemakers because the perking time is based on temperature.
- As coffee is exposed to air, it loses some of its flavor, so keep coffee tightly covered and use as soon as possible. Storing coffee in refrigerator or freezer will help increase its shelf life.
- Allow 1 to 3 level tablespoonfuls of coffee for each cup of water, depending on the strength desired.
- Serve coffee as soon as possible after brewing. If necessary to hold, keep over very low heat. Never allow coffee to boil as it will become bitter.

METHODS OF MAKING COFFEE

PERCOLATOR: Many automatic coffeemakers are of this type. With this method, use a regular grind coffee. The water is forced up and down through the basket of coffee near the top of the pot. The coffee should perk slowly for about 6 to 8 minutes.

DRIP: Place a fine grind (drip) coffee in the filter section. Pour boiling water into the filter and allow to drip through the grounds and filter. When water has dripped through, the coffee is ready to serve.

VACUUM: Place cold water in lower bowl of pot and a filter and fine or drip grind coffee in the top. Heat water until it rises to the top bowl. Remove pot from heat. The coffee filters back into the bottom bowl as it cools slightly.

STEEPED OR BOILED COFFEE: Place cold water in enamel pot. Add regular grind coffee. Heat just to boiling; let steep 2 minutes. Add a small amount of cold water to cause grounds to settle to bottom.

EGG COFFEE: Prepare as for steeped coffee, but mix 1 uncooked egg with grounds before adding to the water. The egg absorbs some of the particles that can make coffee bitter.

INSTANT COFFEE: Follow manufacturer's instructions, remembering that freeze-dried coffee is more concentrated than regular instant coffee.

INTERNATIONAL BREWS

SWEDISH

¼ cup firmly packed brown sugar
¼ teaspoon cinnamon
¼ teaspoon cloves
¼ teaspoon nutmeg
Orange peel, cut into strips
Strong hot coffee
Whipped cream

Combine first 4 ingredients; mix well. Place 1 teaspoon spice mixture in each serving cup. Add strip of orange peel. Fill cup with coffee; stir. Top with whipped cream.

8 to 10 servings

BRAZILIAN

Place 2 tablespoons instant cocoa mix in each serving cup. Fill cup with strong hot coffee. Stir with cinnamon stick. Top with whipped cream.

TURKISH

Place 1 tablespoon honey or sugar and 1 crushed cardamom seed in each serving cup. Fill cup with strong hot coffee; stir. Top with whipped cream.

VIENNESE

Fill each serving cup with strong hot coffee. Stir in 1 teaspoon sugar. Top with whipped cream; sprinkle with nutmeg.

ARABIAN

Place 1 crushed cardamom seed in each serving cup. Fill cup with strong hot coffee. Stir with cinnamon stick.

ITALIAN

Fill each serving cup with strong hot coffee. Serve with a twist of lemon.

FRENCH

To prepare café au lait, 2 pots are needed – one for strong hot coffee and one for an equal amount of hot milk or cream. Pour from both pots at the same time into each serving cup.

ABOUT TEAS

Tea always has been the traditional beverage for receptions and formal occasions, and much fuss has been made in regard to the proper method of brewing. There are three rules to remember when preparing tea:

- Water should be cold and freshly drawn. Never let it stand in the pot while you go about other preparations.
- Heat the water just to boiling. To release the full tea flavor, the water must be boiling when it is poured on the leaves. However, water that boils too long or has been reheated becomes flat tasting.
- Steep the tea no less than 3 minutes and no longer than 5 minutes. Follow the clock rather than the color since different teas produce different colors.

TYPES OF TEA

There are many commercial varieties of teas which vary among the locality, age of tea, manufacture, blending and addition of spices and herbs. We have listed a few of the more popular varieties.

BLACK: The most popular tea in this country. Has a rich aroma and mild flavor. Through a special treatment, the leaves oxidize and turn black.

ORANGE PEKOE: Perhaps the most familiar example of black tea. Pekoe refers to the size of the tea leaf.

OOLONG: Has a delicate flavor and light color. The leaves are allowed to partially oxidize, making them a greenish-brown color.

GREEN: Gives a brew pale green in color with a pungent flavor. Green tea is not oxidized.

DARJEELING: An Indian Black tea.

EARL GREY BLEND: A tea from China with a hint of orange flavor.

ENGLISH BREAKFAST: A delicately-flavored black tea from China, also called Keemun.

FORMOSA OOLONG: Has a strong bouquet and flavor.

LAPSANG SOUCHONG: A Chinese tea with a heavy smoky flavor.

CHAMOMILE: A somewhat bitter tea, often sweetened with honey or sugar.

JASMINE: Fragrant blossoms are added to this pungent, scented brew.

ROSE-HIP: A strongly-flavored tea made from the dried fruit of the rose; a source of vitamin C.

BASIC TEA RECIPE
(One serving)

Boiling water
1 teaspoon tea leaves or 1 tea bag
5 to 6 oz. water, cold

Preheat a clean pottery or heat-resistant serving pot by filling with boiling water; let stand to warm pot. Meanwhile, heat cold water just to boiling. (Do not use a copper, brass or iron pot.) Pour out water in serving pot, add tea leaves and cover with freshly-boiled water. Steep 3 to 5 minutes. Remove tea bags or strain tea leaves. Serve immediately. Do not reheat tea or reuse tea leaves or bags.

TEA FOR MANY GUESTS
(25 servings)

½ cup tea leaves or 20 tea bags
4½ qt. water, cold

Follow directions for Basic Tea Recipe. Keep tea warm on low heat if not serving immediately. Do not reheat to boiling.

ICED TEA

Follow Basic Tea Recipe, steeping the full 5 minutes. Strain and pour over ice cubes. If a weaker tea is desired, add additional water.

TIP: *When tea is steeped or cooled too long, it sometimes becomes cloudy when added to ice. Just add a small amount of boiling water to make it clear again.*

PLANTATION ALMOND TEA

- **¾ cup sugar**
- **¼ cup lemon juice**
- **2 tea bags or 2 teaspoons tea leaves**
- **2 cups boiling water**
- **2 cups cold water**
- **½ teaspoon almond extract**
- **½ teaspoon vanilla**
- **Ice cubes**

In teapot, add sugar, lemon juice and tea bags. Pour boiling water over tea mixture. Cover; let steep about 10 minutes. Remove tea bags. Add remaining ingredients, except ice, to tea; stir. Serve over ice cubes. If desired, garnish with lemon slices.

4 (1 cup) servings

NUTRITION INFORMATION PER SERVING

Serving Size: 1 cup		Percent U.S. RDA Per Serving	
Calories	150	Protein	*
Protein	<1g	Vitamin A	*
Carbohydrate	39g	Vitamin C	12%
Fat	<1g	Thiamin	*
Sodium	<1mg	Riboflavin	*
Potassium	23mg	Niacin	*
		Calcium	*
		Iron	*

A homemade dry mix to use anytime. Cool and serve over ice in the summertime.

RUSSIAN TEA

- **3 cups sugar**
- **2 cups orange-flavored instant breakfast drink**
- **1 cup instant tea**
- **1 teaspoon cloves**
- **1 teaspoon cinnamon**

In medium bowl, combine all ingredients; mix well. Place 2 rounded tablespoonfuls of mix in each cup. Fill with boiling water; stir well. Dry mix may be kept in covered storage container.

32 servings

NUTRITION INFORMATION PER SERVING

Serving Size: 2 tablespoons mix plus water		Percent U.S. RDA Per Serving	
Calories	127	Protein	*
Protein	1g	Vitamin A	17%
Carbohydrate	32g	Vitamin C	51%
Fat	<1g	Thiamin	*
Sodium	1mg	Riboflavin	2%
Potassium	283mg	Niacin	*
		Calcium	*
		Iron	*

COCKTAIL PLANNING GUIDE

Number of People You're Having	For Pre-Dinner Cocktails (You'll Average 2-3 drinks per person)	For a Party (You'll Average 3-4 drinks per person)
4	8-12 drinks (4/5 qt. req.)	12-16 drinks (4/5 qt. req.)
6	12-18 drinks (Two 4/5 qts. req.)	18-24 drinks (Two 4/5 qts. req.)
8	16-24 drinks (Two 4/5 qts. req.)	24-32 drinks (Two 4/5 qts. req.)
12	24-36 drinks (Three 4/5 qts. req.)	36-48 drinks (Three 4/5 qts. req.)
20	40-60 drinks (4 qts. req.)	60-80 drinks (4 qts. req.)
40	80-120 drinks (6 qts. req.)	120-160 drinks (8 qts. req.)

A lovely springtime beverage to serve as an appetizer.

SPARKLING STRAWBERRIES

1 pint fresh strawberries, washed and hulled
4/5-qt. bottle (3¼ cups) champagne or sparkling Burgundy, chilled

Spoon berries into 6 wine, champagne or sherbet glasses. Chill. Just before serving, pour champagne over strawberries. Eat the berries with a spoon; then drink the wine from the glass.

6 servings

NUTRITION INFORMATION PER SERVING

Serving Size: 1/6 of recipe		Percent U.S. RDA Per Serving	
Calories	125	Protein	*
Protein	<1g	Vitamin A	*
Carbohydrate	10g	Vitamin C	53%
Fat	<1g	Thiamin	*
Sodium	7mg	Riboflavin	3%
Potassium	203mg	Niacin	2%
		Calcium	2%
		Iron	6%

WINE PLANNING GUIDE

Wine	Champagne	Table Wine	Dessert Wine
Bottle Size	Fifth	Fifth	Fifth
Amount Per Drink	3 oz.	3 oz.	2 oz.
No. of Drinks In Bottle	7	8	10
Average No. Drinks Per Person	3	2	2

A useful rule for wine punches is: Count one gallon (4 qts.) of the finished punch as enough for about 15 guests.

This is a traditional holiday favorite.

TOM AND JERRY BATTER

6 eggs, separated
2 tablespoons milk
6 cups powdered sugar
Dash salt
½ teaspoon vanilla
1 drop oil of cloves
1 drop oil of cinnamon
Brandy
Boiling water

In medium bowl, beat egg yolks until thick and lemon-colored; add milk and powdered sugar. Beat on low speed for 1 minute; beat on high for 2 minutes or until mixture is quite stiff. In large bowl, beat egg whites until stiff peaks form. Fold in yolk mixture and remaining ingredients. For each drink, use ¼ cup brandy, ¼ cup boiling water and ¼ cup batter floating on top.

About 24 servings

NUTRITION INFORMATION PER SERVING

Serving Size: 1/24 of recipe		Percent U.S. RDA Per Serving	
Calories	268	Protein	3%
Protein	2g	Vitamin A	3%
Carbohydrate	30g	Vitamin C	*
Fat	2g	Thiamin	*
Sodium	30mg	Riboflavin	3%
Potassium	22mg	Niacin	*
		Calcium	*
		Iron	*

TIP: *Refrigerate leftover batter for up to 2 days.*

PARTY PUNCHES

For serving large groups with little fuss or bother, nothing beats punch (either alcoholic or nonalcoholic). One thing to serve...one kind of glass ...and almost everything is do-ahead. It's especially good for budget-minded entertaining. A lot will go a long way.

In the good old summertime, serve up frosty tinkling glasses of something colorful and refreshing. On chilly winter days, a steaming cup of something hot and vigorous warms the body and the heart.

Keep in mind the conditions of the room as well as the outdoor temperature when selecting your beverages. No matter how cold it is outside, if the room will be fairly crowded with people for a long period of time, a thoughtful hostess will provide a cooler drink.

Punch will lose its "punch" if not served very cold or very hot. When serving cold punches, chill all the ingredients before mixing and keep the punch cold before and during serving. Add carbonated beverages just before serving; mix only enough to blend, so the carbonation is not lost.

Any form of ice – cubed, cracked, crushed, or molded – will make your beverage look cool and refreshing and help it stay that way. Ice trays and shaped gelatin molds may be used to freeze flavored cubes or "chunks" of ice. Try fruit juices, carbonated beverages, or make decorative ice cubes that have citrus fruit sections, strawberries, cherries or mint leaves frozen in them. Distilled water gives better clarity.

To mold fruit in ice, fill mold or ice cube tray with about ½ inch of water. Arrange fruits on top; freeze. Add more water to cover; freeze again. Use the cubes in glasses; invert and float molds in punch bowl.

For hot punches, float lemon or orange slices with cinnamon sticks in centers or wedges studded with cloves. To help keep the punch hot, serve in large chafing dish or crock pot. If you use a punch bowl make sure it is heat resistant before adding the hot punch. It will help to warm the bowl with hot water before you add the punch.

AMOUNT TO SERVE
How much to serve depends on the kind of party and the number of people. If the party precedes a dinner, two or three punch cups per person is sufficient. If the party is to take the larger part of the afternoon or evening, you had better plan on 4 or 5 punch cups per person. Plan on ½-cup servings for "punch bowl" punches.

PUNCH PLANNING GUIDE

No. of People	Before Dinner	Party
4	1-1½ qt.	2-2½ qt.
6	1½-2 qt.	3-4 qt.
8	2-3 qt.	1-1½ gal.
12	1-1½ gal.	1½-2 gal.
20	1½-2 gal.	2½-3 gal.
50	3-4½ gal.	6-7½ gal.

DRESS-UPS FOR PUNCHES

SUGAR-FROSTED GLASSES: Dip rim of each glass in lemon, lime or orange juice, then in sugar. Chill to harden sugar.

DECORATIVE ICE CUBES OR MOLDS: Fill ice cube trays or mold half full of water or fruit juice. Arrange fruit or mint leaves on top and freeze. Add more liquid and freeze again. (Remember, sweetened fruits usually sink and unsweetened fresh fruits float. Keep this in mind when adding fruit to molds to be sure it will freeze where you want it.) For multicolored molds, fill and freeze different layers using various colored juices. Ring molds work exceptionally well.

A hot punch—delicious and easy for small gatherings or large groups.

ROSY GLOW CRANBERRY PUNCH

	14 servings	28 servings	42 servings
Sugar	⅓ cup	⅔ cup	1 cup
Nutmeg	¼ tsp.	½ tsp.	¾ tsp.
Cinnamon	¼ tsp.	½ tsp.	¾ tsp.
Salt	¼ tsp.	½ tsp.	¾ tsp.
Water	2½ cups	5 cups	7½ cups
Lemon juice	½ cup	1 cup	1½ cups
Cranberry juice cocktail	4 cups (1 qt.)	8 cups (2 qts.)	12 cups (3 qts.)

In large saucepan, combine all ingredients; mix well. Simmer 10 to 15 minutes. Serve hot in mugs with orange slices floating on top or with cinnamon sticks as stirrers.

½ cup servings

NUTRITION INFORMATION PER SERVING

Serving Size: 1/2 cup		Percent U.S. RDA Per Serving	
Calories	69	Protein	*
Protein	<1g	Vitamin A	*
Carbohydrate	18g	Vitamin C	4%
Fat	<1g	Thiamin	*
Sodium	40mg	Riboflavin	*
Potassium	20mg	Niacin	*
		Calcium	*
		Iron	*

CLARET PUNCH

2 quarts (8 cups) claret wine, chilled
1 cup cointreau
1 cup brandy
6-oz. can frozen concentrated lemonade, thawed
1 quart (4 cups) club soda, chilled
Ice cubes or ice mold
1 orange, sliced

In large punch bowl (5 quart), combine first 5 ingredients. Add ice. Float orange slices on top.

30 (½ cup) servings

NUTRITION INFORMATION PER SERVING

Serving Size: 1/2 cup		Percent U.S. RDA Per Serving	
Calories	98	Protein	*
Protein	<1g	Vitamin A	*
Carbohydrate	7g	Vitamin C	9%
Fat	<1g	Thiamin	*
Sodium	4mg	Riboflavin	*
Potassium	81mg	Niacin	*
		Calcium	*
		Iron	*

Served in a cut glass bowl, this makes a lovely wedding reception punch.

FROSTY FRUIT COOLER

3 cups apricot nectar, chilled
3 cups pineapple or orange juice, chilled
1 quart (4 cups) ginger ale, chilled
1 pint (2 cups) pineapple or orange sherbet

In punch bowl (4 quart), combine apricot nectar and pineapple juice. Just before serving, add ginger ale. Float scoops of sherbet on top. Serve immediately. 16 (½ cup) servings

NUTRITION INFORMATION PER SERVING

Serving Size: 1/2 cup		Percent U.S. RDA Per Serving	
Calories	104	Protein	*
Protein	<1g	Vitamin A	10%
Carbohydrate	26g	Vitamin C	10%
Fat	<1g	Thiamin	2%
Sodium	3mg	Riboflavin	*
Potassium	146mg	Niacin	*
		Calcium	*
		Iron	*

TIP: *For individual servings, place a small scoop of sherbet in each glass. Fill glasses with punch.*

10 (1 cup) servings

Hot and spicy, this makes a great drink after wintertime sports.

WASSAIL BOWL

Whole cloves
1 large orange
2 quarts (8 cups) apple juice or cider
3 tablespoons lemon juice
4 cinnamon sticks

Heat oven to 350°F. Insert cloves, about ½ inch apart, into orange. Place in shallow baking pan; bake at 350°F. for 30 minutes. Pierce orange in several places with 2-pronged fork. In large saucepan, combine apple juice, lemon juice, cinnamon sticks and baked orange. Simmer covered for 30 minutes. Remove cinnamon sticks and orange. Pour into heatproof punch bowl. Float clove-studded orange in punch bowl. Serve hot.

16 (½ cup) servings

NUTRITION INFORMATION PER SERVING

Serving Size: 1/2 cup		Percent U.S. RDA Per Serving	
Calories	59	Protein	*
Protein	<1g	Vitamin A	*
Carbohydrate	15g	Vitamin C	3%
Fat	<1g	Thiamin	*
Sodium	1mg	Riboflavin	*
Potassium	129mg	Niacin	*
		Calcium	*
		Iron	4%

ORANGE JULIUS

¼ cup sugar
6-oz. can frozen concentrated orange juice
1 cup milk
1 cup water
1 teaspoon vanilla
10 ice cubes

In blender, combine all ingredients; blend for ½ minute or until ice cubes are crushed.

4 servings

NUTRITION INFORMATION PER SERVING

Serving Size: 1/4 of recipe		Percent U.S. RDA Per Serving	
Calories	172	Protein	5%
Protein	3g	Vitamin A	9%
Carbohydrate	36g	Vitamin C	141%
Fat	2g	Thiamin	12%
Sodium	32mg	Riboflavin	8%
Potassium	438mg	Niacin	3%
		Calcium	9%
		Iron	*

TIP: *If desired, top with scoop of vanilla ice cream.*

OLD-FASHIONED LEMONADE

4 lemons
¾ cup sugar
1 quart (4 cups) water
Ice cubes

Cut lemons into thin slices; remove seeds. Place in large bowl and sprinkle with sugar. Let stand about 10 minutes. Press fruit with a potato masher or back of spoon to extract juice. Add water, pressing fruit until well flavored. Remove fruit slices. Serve over ice cubes. If desired, garnish with lemon slices.

5 (1 cup) servings

NUTRITION INFORMATION PER SERVING

Serving Size: 1 cup		Percent U.S. RDA Per Serving	
Calories	131	Protein	*
Protein	<1g	Vitamin A	*
Carbohydrate	35g	Vitamin C	52%
Fat	<1g	Thiamin	*
Sodium	1mg	Riboflavin	*
Potassium	82mg	Niacin	*
		Calcium	*
		Iron	2%

TIPS: *For LIMEADE, substitute 2 limes for 2 of the lemons. Prepare as directed, increasing sugar to 1 cup.*

For ORANGEADE, use 2 oranges and 3 lemons. Prepare as directed, decreasing sugar to ½ cup.

Tangy and refreshing—great for the backyard barbecue.

LUAU REFRESHER

5 cups cold water
46-oz. can (5¾ cups) pineapple juice, chilled
12-oz. can frozen concentrated orange juice, partially thawed
12-oz. can frozen concentrated lemonade, partially thawed
12-oz. can frozen concentrated limeade, partially thawed
1 quart (4 cups) club soda, chilled
Ice cubes or ice mold

In large punch bowl (5 quart), combine all ingredients except club soda and ice; mix well.* Just before serving, add club soda and ice, mixing well. 31 (½ cup) servings

NUTRITION INFORMATION PER SERVING

Serving Size: 1/2 cup		Percent U.S. RDA Per Serving	
Calories	101	Protein	*
Protein	<1g	Vitamin A	2%
Carbohydrate	26g	Vitamin C	53%
Fat	<1g	Thiamin	5%
Sodium	1mg	Riboflavin	*
Potassium	178mg	Niacin	*
		Calcium	*
		Iron	*

TIPS: *If desired, about 1 cup rum, vodka, gin or dry sherry may be added.*

*To MAKE AHEAD, prepare to *. Refrigerate in covered container. To serve, add club soda and ice.*

A warm punch that's a little different.

MULLED APRICOT NECTAR

46-oz. can (5¾ cups) apricot nectar
1 cup orange juice
4 cinnamon sticks
¼ teaspoon allspice
⅛ to ¼ teaspoon whole cloves
1 lemon, sliced, if desired

In large saucepan, combine apricot nectar and orange juice; mix well. Tie spices in a piece of cheesecloth (break cinnamon sticks if necessary); add to juices. Simmer covered, 20 to 25 minutes. Remove spice bag. Serve hot in mugs with lemon slice in each. 14 (½ cup) servings

NUTRITION INFORMATION PER SERVING

Serving Size: 1/2 cup		Percent U.S. RDA Per Serving	
Calories	69	Protein	*
Protein	<1g	Vitamin A	20%
Carbohydrate	18g	Vitamin C	19%
Fat	<1g	Thiamin	*
Sodium	<1mg	Riboflavin	*
Potassium	202mg	Niacin	*
		Calcium	*
		Iron	*

TIPS: *May be made in electric percolator with spices tied in cheesecloth.*

Rum may be added to brewed nectar. Fill cups almost full with mulled nectar; add 1 to 2 tablespoons rum, mixing well.

CHAMPAGNE ROSÉ PUNCH

2 pkg. (10 oz. each) frozen sweetened strawberries, thawed
2 bottles (4/5 qt. each) rosé wine, chilled
6-oz. can frozen concentrated lemonade, thawed
4/5-qt. bottle (3¼ cups) champagne, chilled
Ice cubes or ice mold

In large bowl, combine strawberries and one 4/5 quart rosé wine. Cover; let stand at room temperature 1 hour. Press strawberry mixture through strainer into punch bowl or 3-quart container; add lemonade, remaining rosé wine, champagne and ice; mix well. Serve immediately. 26 (½ cup) servings

NUTRITION INFORMATION PER SERVING

Serving Size: ½ cup		Percent U.S. RDA Per Serving	
Calories	89	Protein	*
Protein	<1g	Vitamin A	*
Carbohydrate	13g	Vitamin C	24%
Fat	<1g	Thiamin	*
Sodium	3mg	Riboflavin	*
Potassium	83mg	Niacin	*
		Calcium	*
		Iron	2%

TIP: *Wines vary in sweetness so taste punch and add sugar if necessary.*

BREADS

BREADS

YEAST BREADS

The aroma of bread baking in the oven is probably one of everyone's favorites. And there is something about a freshly baked homemade loaf of bread that says you are an accomplished baker.

Today, it is even easier than before to make all the wonderful yeast breads so reminiscent of what Grandma used to make. Today's recipes have been developed with many time saving factors – no-knead and one-rise breads for example. The results are just as delicious with a little less work and time on your part.

TYPES OF YEAST DOUGH RECIPES

Kneaded Dough produces breads with a fine even light texture. It has better keeping qualities.

One-rise Dough has a little less flour than the traditional two-rise yeast breads so that the second rise can be done in the oven while it is baking.

No-knead Dough produces breads that are a little more open textured. The dough is mixed and allowed to rise. If further shaping is required the dough is turned out onto a floured surface for easier handling.

Batter Doughs also are not kneaded which results in a more porous bread. The dough is allowed to rise, stirred down, turned into the pans, and let rise again before baking.

Hot Roll Mix simplifies preparation by premeasuring all the ingredients except the liquid. The kneading times are often shorter, too.

Are you wondering exactly what we mean in a particular step of bread making? Below are helpful hints for the beginning bread maker.

THE ART OF MAKING BREAD – STEP BY STEP

1. *In saucepan, heat milk and margarine until very warm (120° to 130°F.).* In most of the recipes in this book we have used the method of adding the yeast with other dry ingredients to the warm liquid without first being dissolved in warm water. This method is easier and more foolproof, but this does require warmer liquid temperatures to activate the yeast. The liquid should be as hot as feels comfortable to you without being scalding. We suggest purchasing a thermometer to take away the guesswork. Although margarine or butter need not melt, if using chilled margarine or butter cut into pieces to allow it to soften while milk is warming.

2. *In large bowl, blend warm liquid, part of flour, sugar, salt, dry yeast and egg at low speed until moistened; beat at medium speed.* An amount of flour is added approximately equal to the liquid. This gives a consistency which allows the yeast particles to dissolve. Blending at low speed and beating at medium speed with a mixer is necessary to develop the flour structural framework, eliminating or decreasing the kneading time.

3. *By hand, stir in remaining flour to form a stiff dough.* A range of flour is given to accommodate various flour conditions. Flour can lose or gain moisture depending on weather conditions and how it is stored. If your flour is dry, you will need less as it will absorb more of the liquid. Flour that has been in a more humid environment will probably be added in the larger amount.

In any case, *just* enough flour should be added to make the dough soft and pliable. Doughs that will be kneaded or shaped need enough flour to make them easy to handle.

4. *Knead on floured surface until smooth and elastic.* Rub enough flour into the surface so that the dough will not stick and can be handled easily. It may be necessary to add more flour as you knead. To knead, fold edges of dough in toward you. Push dough down and away from you with heels of both hands. Give dough a quarter turn, then repeat folding, pushing and turning until dough is smooth, elastic and small blisters appear on the surface.

5. *Place dough in greased bowl; turn greased-side-up.* Use a bowl large enough for dough to double in size. The greased-side-up helps prevent any crust formations that could make hard lumps in the finished bread. Covering the bowl with plastic wrap or towel helps to further prevent this.

6. *Let rise in warm place until light and doubled in size.* Yeast dough needs a warm place (80° to 85°F.) for rising. To provide a warm place you may turn on oven at 400°F. for 1 minute, turn off oven and place the bowl of bread dough on the center rack, oven door closed. Or, place a pan of very hot water on lower rack of unheated oven and place dough on center rack. When dough is doubled in size, a dent will remain in the dough when poked lightly and quickly with 2 fingers. If the dent fills up rapidly, let rise a little longer.

7. *Punch down dough.* Punch down center of dough with fist. Pull the edges of dough to the center and turn out of bowl onto floured surface. This step removes large air bubbles so that bread will be fine textured.

SHAPING A LOAF

1. Divide dough into number of loaves specified in recipe.

2. Roll dough on lightly floured surface to a 14x7-inch rectangle.

3. Starting with 7-inch side, roll up, sealing well with heel of hand after each turn. This sealing prevents any open pockets in the interior of finished bread. (a)

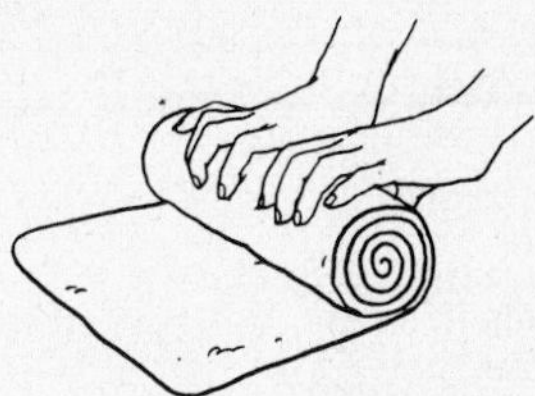

4. Pinch ends and edges to seal. (b)

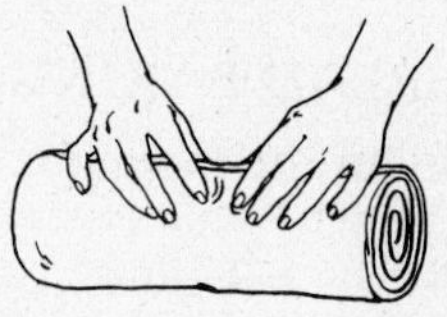

5. Place loaf, seam-side-down, in greased loaf pan. (c)

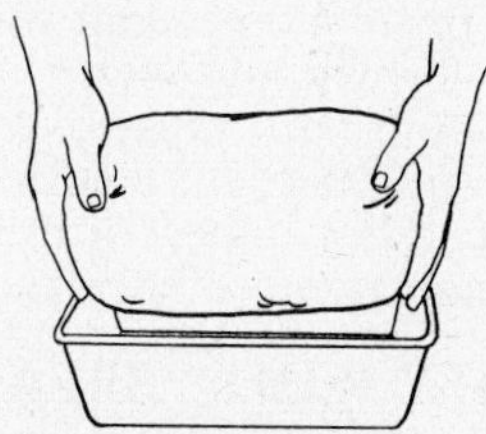

SHAPING A ROUND LOAF

1. Divide dough into number of loaves specified in recipe.

2. Knead dough several times to form a smooth, even ball.

3. Bring edges together and seal well.

4. Place loaf on cookie sheet, seam-side-down; lightly flatten edges to form a rounded shape.

A WORD ABOUT SERVING SIZES

When each of these bread recipes was analyzed for nutritional information, 1 slice of bread was considered the serving size. But since a slice of bread is not uniform in size, we have determined the number of slices per loaf to be as follows:

Bread pan size	Number of slices or pieces
8x4 or 9x5-inch loaf pan	16
1½-quart casserole	16
round loaf	12
small "French" loaf	12
large "French" loaf	24
10-inch ring mold	12
8 or 9-inch square pan	9
13x9-inch cake pan	12
9-inch round cake pan	8

BREAD BAKING

Bake bread on the lower shelf of the oven. The top of each pan should be at about the middle of the oven. Arrange loaf pans so that they do not touch each other or the sides of the oven when baking. Bread is done if the loaf sounds hollow when lightly tapped. Top of loaf should be golden brown and well-rounded. Remove from pan immediately; cool on wire rack. For a softer crust, brush hot loaves or rolls with melted margarine or butter.

EASY WHITE BREAD

2¼ cups milk
¼ cup oil
6 to 7 cups Pillsbury's Best® All Purpose or Unbleached Flour*
¼ cup sugar
3 teaspoons salt
2 pkg. active dry yeast
1 egg

In small saucepan, heat milk and oil until very warm (120° to 130°F.). In large bowl, blend warm liquid, 2 cups flour, sugar, salt, yeast and egg at low speed until moistened. Beat 3 minutes at medium speed. By hand, stir in remaining flour to form a soft dough. On well-floured surface, knead until smooth and elastic, about 1 minute. Place dough in greased bowl; turn greased-side-up. Cover; let rise in warm place until light and doubled in size, 45 to 60 minutes.

Generously grease (not oil) two 9x5 or 8x4-inch loaf pans. Punch down dough; divide and shape into 2 loaves. Place in prepared pans. Cover; let rise in warm place until light, 30 to 45 minutes. Heat oven to 350°F. Bake 40 to 45 minutes or until golden brown and loaves sound hollow when lightly tapped. Immediately remove from pans; cool. If desired, brush warm loaves with melted margarine or butter.

2 loaves

NUTRITION INFORMATION PER SERVING

Serving Size: 1 slice		Percent U.S. RDA Per Serving	
Calories	122	Protein	5%
Protein	3g	Vitamin A	*
Carbohydrate	20g	Vitamin C	*
Fat	3g	Thiamin	11%
Sodium	211mg	Riboflavin	9%
Potassium	58mg	Niacin	7%
		Calcium	3%
		Iron	4%

TIPS: *For RAISIN BREAD, add 1 cup raisins and ½ teaspoon cinnamon after beating step.*

For CINNAMON SWIRL BREAD, shape each loaf by pressing into 15x7-inch rectangle. Brush with margarine or butter and sprinkle each with mixture of ¼ cup sugar and 1 teaspoon cinnamon. Starting with 7-inch side, roll up. Seal edges and place seam-side-down in greased loaf pan. Proof and bake as directed.

**Self-rising flour is not recommended.*

HIGH ALTITUDE—Above 3500 Feet: Bake at 375°F. for 35 to 40 minutes.

French bread has the typical crunchy crust because it is baked over a pan of water.

FRENCH BREAD

2¼ cups water
5½ to 6½ cups Pillsbury's Best® All Purpose or Unbleached Flour*
1 tablespoon sugar
1 tablespoon salt
2 pkg. active dry yeast

In small saucepan, heat water until very warm (120° to 130°F.). In large bowl, blend warm liquid, 2 cups flour, sugar, salt and yeast at low speed until moistened. Beat 2 minutes at medium speed. By hand, stir in remaining flour to form a stiff dough. Knead on floured surface until smooth and elastic, about 8 minutes. Place dough in greased bowl; turn greased-side-up. Cover; let rise in warm place until light and doubled in size, about 1 hour.

Generously grease (not oil) cookie sheet; sprinkle with cornmeal. Punch down dough; divide and shape into 2 long loaves, tapering ends. Place on prepared cookie sheet. Cut diagonal slashes in dough, about ¼ inch deep. Cover; let rise in warm place until light and doubled in size, 30 to 45 minutes. Brush loaves with water. Place a shallow pan of boiling water in bottom of 400°F. oven. Place bread on rack above water and bake at 400°F. for 25 to 30 minutes or until golden brown. Immediately remove from cookie sheet; cool. 2 loaves

NUTRITION INFORMATION PER SERVING

Serving Size: 1 slice		Percent U.S. RDA Per Serving	
Calories	108	Protein	5%
Protein	3g	Vitamin A	0%
Carbohydrate	23g	Vitamin C	0%
Fat	<1g	Thiamin	13%
Sodium	267mg	Riboflavin	9%
Potassium	39mg	Niacin	9%
		Calcium	*
		Iron	5%

TIP: **Self-rising flour is not recommended.*

WHOLE WHEAT BREAD

2 cups water
¼ cup margarine or oil
¼ cup molasses or honey
2 cups Pillsbury's Best® All Purpose or Unbleached Flour*
2 teaspoons salt
2 pkg. active dry yeast
4 to 4½ cups Pillsbury's Best® Whole Wheat Flour

In small saucepan, heat first 3 ingredients until very warm (120° to 130°F.). In large bowl, blend warm liquid, all-purpose flour, salt and yeast at low speed until moistened. Beat 3 minutes at medium speed. By hand, stir in whole wheat flour to form a stiff dough. Knead on floured surface until smooth and elastic, about 5 minutes. Place dough in greased bowl; turn greased-side-up. Cover; let rise in warm place until light and doubled in size, 45 to 60 minutes.

Generously grease (not oil) two 9x5 or 8x4-inch loaf pans. Punch down dough; divide and shape into 2 loaves. Cover; let rise in warm place until light and doubled in size, 45 to 60 minutes. Bake at 350°F. for 35 to 45 minutes or until deep golden brown and loaves sound hollow when lightly tapped. Immediately remove from pans; cool. If desired, brush warm loaves with melted margarine or butter. 2 loaves

NUTRITION INFORMATION PER SERVING

Serving Size: 1 slice		Percent U.S. RDA Per Serving	
Calories	98	Protein	5%
Protein	3g	Vitamin A	*
Carbohydrate	18g	Vitamin C	0%
Fat	2g	Thiamin	10%
Sodium	153mg	Riboflavin	4%
Potassium	99mg	Niacin	6%
		Calcium	*
		Iron	5%

TIPS: *One-half cup firmly packed brown sugar may be substituted for the molasses.*

**Self-rising flour is not recommended.*

Cottage cheese is added to make the bread more moist.

OLD-FASHIONED HONEY WHEAT BREAD

1½ cups water
1 cup creamed cottage cheese
½ cup honey
¼ cup margarine or butter
5½ to 6 cups Pillsbury's Best® All Purpose or Unbleached Flour*
1 cup Pillsbury's Best® Whole Wheat Flour
2 tablespoons sugar
3 teaspoons salt
2 pkg. active dry yeast
1 egg

In medium saucepan, heat first 4 ingredients until very warm (120° to 130°F.). In large bowl, blend warm liquid, 2 cups all-purpose flour, whole wheat flour, sugar, salt, yeast and egg at low speed until moistened. Beat 2 minutes at medium speed. By hand, stir in remaining flour to form a stiff dough. Knead on floured surface until smooth and elastic, about 2 minutes. Place dough in greased bowl; turn greased-side-up. Cover; let rise in warm place until light and doubled in size, 45 to 60 minutes.

Grease (not oil) two 9x5 or 8x4-inch loaf pans. Punch down dough; divide and shape into 2 loaves. Place in prepared pans. Cover; let rise in warm place until light and doubled in size, 45 to 60 minutes. Heat oven to 350°F. Bake 40 to 50 minutes or until deep golden brown and loaves sound hollow when lightly tapped. Immediately remove from pans; cool. If desired, brush warm loaves with melted margarine or butter.

2 loaves

NUTRITION INFORMATION PER SERVING

Serving Size: 1 slice		Percent U.S. RDA Per Serving	
Calories	134	Protein	6%
Protein	4g	Vitamin A	*
Carbohydrate	25g	Vitamin C	*
Fat	2g	Thiamin	11%
Sodium	236mg	Riboflavin	8%
Potassium	54mg	Niacin	7%
		Calcium	*
		Iron	5%

TIP: **If using Pillsbury's Best® Self Rising Flour, omit salt.*

HIGH ALTITUDE–Above 3500 Feet: Bake at 375°F. for 40 to 50 minutes.

Chunks of cheese add interest to this flavorful bread.

CHEESE AND BEER WHEAT BREAD

⅔ cup water
½ cup oil
12-oz. can (1½ cups) beer
1½ cups Pillsbury's Best® Whole Wheat Flour
4½ to 5 cups Pillsbury's Best® All Purpose or Unbleached Flour*
½ cup sugar
½ cup wheat germ
2 teaspoons salt
2 pkg. active dry yeast
1 egg
8-oz. (2 cups) Cheddar or American cheese, cut into ½-inch cubes

In medium saucepan, heat first 3 ingredients until very warm (120° to 130°F.). In large bowl, blend warm liquid, whole wheat flour, 1 cup all-purpose flour, sugar, wheat germ, salt, yeast and egg at low speed until moistened. Beat 2 minutes at medium speed. By hand, stir in remaining all-purpose flour to form a stiff dough. Knead dough on floured surface until smooth and elastic, about 5 minutes. Place in greased bowl; turn greased-side-up. Cover; let rise in warm place until light and doubled in size, about 1 hour.

Line two 9x5-inch loaf pans with foil; generously grease. Punch down dough. On well-floured surface, work cheese cubes into dough, half at a time, until evenly distributed. Divide; shape into 2 loaves, covering cheese cubes. Place in prepared pans. Cover; let rise in warm place until light and doubled in size, 45 to 60 minutes. Heat oven to 350°F. Bake 40 to 50 minutes or until loaf sounds hollow when lightly tapped. Immediately remove from pans; cool.

2 loaves

NUTRITION INFORMATION PER SERVING

Serving Size: 1 slice		Percent U.S. RDA Per Serving	
Calories	168	Protein	8%
Protein	5g	Vitamin A	2%
Carbohydrate	22g	Vitamin C	*
Fat	6g	Thiamin	12%
Sodium	187mg	Riboflavin	9%
Potassium	71mg	Niacin	7%
		Calcium	6%
		Iron	6%

TIPS: *If desired, two 1-qt. casseroles may be used. Line with foil; generously grease.* 2 round loaves

**If using Pillsbury's Best® Self Rising Flour, omit salt.*

The flavor is just like the muffins but easier to slice and toast.

ENGLISH MUFFIN BREAD

1¼ cups water
½ cup oil
4 to 4½ cups Pillsbury's Best® All Purpose or Unbleached Flour*
¼ cup sugar
2 teaspoons salt
2 pkg. active dry yeast
2 eggs
Cornmeal

In small saucepan, heat water and oil until very warm (120° to 130°F.). In large bowl, blend warm liquid, 1½ cups flour, sugar, salt, yeast and eggs at low speed until moistened. Beat 2 minutes at medium speed. By hand, stir in enough remaining flour to make a stiff batter. Cover; let rise in warm place until light and doubled in size, 45 to 60 minutes.

Grease (not oil) and sprinkle with cornmeal two 8x4-inch loaf pans or 3 one-pound coffee cans. Stir down dough (beat vigorously 30 seconds); spoon into prepared pans. Cover; let rise in warm place until doubled in size, 30 to 45 minutes. Heat oven to 375°F. Bake 15 to 20 minutes or until loaf sounds hollow when lightly tapped. If baked in loaf pans, immediately remove bread; cool. If baked in coffee cans, cool bread in cans for 10 minutes; remove and cool completely.

2 loaves or 3 round loaves

NUTRITION INFORMATION PER SERVING

Serving Size: 1 slice		Percent U.S. RDA Per Serving	
Calories	102	Protein	4%
Protein	2g	Vitamin A	*
Carbohydrate	14g	Vitamin C	0%
Fat	4g	Thiamin	8%
Sodium	138mg	Riboflavin	6%
Potassium	29mg	Niacin	5%
		Calcium	*
		Iron	3%

TIP: **Self-rising flour is not recommended.*

HIGH ALTITUDE–Above 3500 feet: Decrease flour to 3½ to 4 cups.

Heavy, dark and robust in flavor.

RUSSIAN BLACK BREAD

2½ cups water
½ cup molasses
¼ cup oil
1 oz. (1 square) unsweetened chocolate or 1 envelope unsweetened baking chocolate flavor
2½ cups Pillsbury's Best® All Purpose or Unbleached Flour*
2 cups whole bran cereal (shredded type)
1 tablespoon sugar
1 tablespoon instant coffee
3 teaspoons salt
2 teaspoons onion powder
1 teaspoon crushed fennel seed, if desired
2 pkg. active dry yeast
4 cups Pillsbury's Best® Medium Rye Flour

In medium saucepan, heat first 4 ingredients until very warm (120° to 130°F.). (Chocolate does not need to melt completely.) In large bowl, blend warm liquid, all-purpose flour, bran, sugar, coffee, salt, onion powder, fennel seed and yeast at low speed until moistened. Beat 3 minutes at medium speed. By hand, stir in rye flour. On well-floured surface, knead adding ½ to 1½ cups additional all-purpose flour until dough is smooth and elastic, about 5 minutes. (Dough will be slightly sticky.) Place in greased bowl; turn greased-side-up. Cover; let rise in warm place until not quite doubled in size, 45 to 60 minutes.

Generously grease (not oil) two 8 or 9-inch round cake pans or cookie sheets. Punch down dough. For rolls, divide dough into 24 pieces; shape each into a ball. Place in prepared round cake pans. For loaves; divide dough; shape into 2 round pans. Place in prepared pans. Cover; let rise in warm place until not quite doubled in size, 30 to 45 minutes. Heat oven to 375°F. If desired, brush rolls or loaves with mixture of 1 egg white and 1 tablespoon water. Bake rolls at 375°F. for 35 to 40 minutes or loaves 45 to 55 minutes or until crust is dark brown and loaves sound hollow when lightly tapped. Immediately remove from pans; cool.

24 rolls or 2 round loaves

NUTRITION INFORMATION PER SERVING

Serving Size: 1 slice		Percent U.S. RDA Per Serving	
Calories	153	Protein	6%
Protein	4g	Vitamin A	*
Carbohydrate	28g	Vitamin C	*
Fat	3g	Thiamin	10%
Sodium	301mg	Riboflavin	7%
Potassium	142mg	Niacin	9%
		Calcium	3%
		Iron	9%

TIP: **If using Pillsbury's Best® Self Rising Flour, omit salt.*

HIGH ALTITUDE–Above 3500 feet: Decrease rising times about 15 minutes; bake rolls at 400°F. for 35 to 40 minutes or loaves for 45 to 55 minutes.

RUSSIAN BLACK BREAD

Light in color and texture.

SCANDINAVIAN RYE BREAD

1 cup water
1 cup buttermilk
¼ cup shortening or oil
¼ cup molasses
2 cups Pillsbury's Best® All Purpose or Unbleached Flour*
⅓ cup firmly packed brown sugar or honey
1 tablespoon grated orange peel
3 teaspoons salt
1 teaspoon anise or caraway seed
½ teaspoon soda
2 pkg. active dry yeast
4 to 4½ cups Pillsbury's Best® Medium Rye Flour

In small saucepan, heat first 4 ingredients until very warm (120° to 130°F.). In large bowl, blend warm liquid, all-purpose flour, brown sugar, peel, salt, anise, soda and yeast at low speed until moistened. Beat 3 minutes at medium speed. By hand, stir in rye flour to make a stiff dough. On well-floured surface, knead until smooth and elastic, about 5 minutes. Place dough in greased bowl, turn greased-side-up. Cover; let rise in warm place until light and doubled in size, 45 to 60 minutes.

Grease (not oil) cookie sheet. Punch down dough; divide. Shape into 2 round loaves; place on opposite corners of prepared cookie sheet. Cover; let rise in warm place until light and doubled in size, 45 to 60 minutes. Heat oven to 350°F. Bake 45 to 50 minutes or until deep golden brown and loaves sound hollow when lightly tapped. Immediately remove from cookie sheet; cool. If desired, brush warm loaves with melted margarine or butter.

2 round loaves

NUTRITION INFORMATION PER SERVING

Serving Size: 1 slice		Percent U.S. RDA Per Serving	
Calories	133	Protein	5%
Protein	3g	Vitamin A	*
Carbohydrate	25g	Vitamin C	*
Fat	2g	Thiamin	9%
Sodium	305mg	Riboflavin	7%
Potassium	113mg	Niacin	6%
		Calcium	3%
		Iron	6%

TIP: **Self-rising flour is not recommended.*

A beautiful golden bread with a rich flavor.

BRAIDED EGG BREAD

1¼ cups milk
½ cup margarine or butter
4½ to 5 cups Pillsbury's Best® All Purpose or Unbleached Flour*
2 tablespoons sugar
2 teaspoons salt
1 pkg. active dry yeast
2 eggs

In small saucepan, heat milk and margarine until very warm (120° to 130°F.). In large bowl, blend warm liquid, 1½ cups flour, sugar, salt, yeast and eggs at low speed until moistened. Beat 2 minutes at medium speed. By hand, stir in remaining flour to form a stiff dough. Knead on floured surface until smooth and elastic, about 5 minutes. Place dough in greased bowl; turn greased-side-up. Cover; let rise in warm place until light and doubled in size, about 1½ to 2 hours.

Grease (not oil) cookie sheet. Punch down dough; divide into 4 equal parts. Shape each part into a strip about 20 inches long. Place the 4 strips side-by-side on prepared cookie sheet, pinching together at one end to seal. Braid by weaving far right strip over and under other strips to far left, then weave next far right strip, etc. When braided, pinch ends together to seal. Cover; let rise in warm place until light and doubled in size, 45 to 60 minutes. Brush with beaten egg or egg yolk. Heat oven to 375°F. Bake 35 to 40 minutes or until deep golden brown and loaf sounds hollow when lightly tapped. Immediately remove from cookie sheet; cool.

1 large loaf

NUTRITION INFORMATION PER SERVING

Serving Size: 1 slice		Percent U.S. RDA Per Serving	
Calories	140	Protein	6%
Protein	4g	Vitamin A	5%
Carbohydrate	20g	Vitamin C	*
Fat	5g	Thiamin	11%
Sodium	237mg	Riboflavin	9%
Potassium	53mg	Niacin	7%
		Calcium	2%
		Iron	5%

TIP: *If using Pillsbury's Best® Self Rising Flour, omit salt.*

Great fun to eat for lunch or supper, savory buttery pieces pull off the loaf.

ONE-RISE MONKEY BREAD

Dill weed, if desired
3 to 3½ cups Pillsbury's Best® All Purpose or Unbleached Flour*
2 tablespoons sugar
1 teaspoon salt
1 pkg. active dry yeast
1 cup very warm water (120°F. to 130°F.)
2 tablespoons margarine or butter, softened
1 egg
⅓ cup margarine or butter

ONE-RISE MONKEY BREAD

Grease (not oil) 12-cup fluted tube pan. Sprinkle with ½ teaspoon dill weed. In large bowl, blend 1½ cups flour, sugar, salt, yeast, water, margarine and egg at low speed until moistened. Beat 3 minutes at medium speed. By hand, stir in remaining flour. Knead dough on floured surface until smooth, about 1 minute. Press or roll dough to 15x12-inch rectangle. Using pastry wheel or sharp knife, cut dough into diamond-shaped pieces by cutting into 1½ to 2-inch strips diagonally across dough. In shallow pan, melt ⅓ cup margarine. Dip each piece in melted margarine and layer prepared pan, overlapping pieces. Sprinkle each layer with about ½ teaspoon dill weed. Cover; let rise in warm place until light and doubled in size, 45 to 60 minutes. Heat oven to 400°F. Bake 20 to 25 minutes or until deep golden brown. Cool 2 minutes; invert onto serving plate. Serve warm.

10-inch ring pull-apart loaf

NUTRITION INFORMATION PER SERVING

Serving Size: 1 slice		Percent U.S. RDA Per Serving	
Calories	194	Protein	6%
Protein	4g	Vitamin A	7%
Carbohydrate	26g	Vitamin C	*
Fat	8g	Thiamin	15%
Sodium	270mg	Riboflavin	10%
Potassium	51mg	Niacin	9%
		Calcium	*
		Iron	6%

TIP: **If using Pillsbury's Best® Self Rising Flour, omit salt.*

HIGH ALTITUDE—Above 3500 feet: Bake at 400°F. for 25 to 30 minutes.

Versatility is the subtitle for this recipe! It can take on many shapes and additional flavors.

BASIC ROLL DOUGH

1 cup milk
3 tablespoons margarine or butter
2¾ to 3¼ cups Pillsbury's Best® All Purpose or Unbleached Flour*
¼ cup sugar
1 teaspoon salt
1 pkg. active dry yeast
1 egg

In small saucepan, heat milk and margarine until very warm (120° to 130°F.). In large bowl, blend warm liquid, 1 cup flour, sugar, salt, yeast and egg at low speed until moistened. Beat 2 minutes at medium speed. By hand, stir in remaining flour to form a soft dough. On well-floured surface, knead until smooth and elastic, about 2 minutes. Place dough in greased bowl; turn greased-side-up. Cover; let rise in warm place until light and doubled in size, 45 to 60 minutes.

Punch down dough. On well-floured surface, toss dough lightly until no longer sticky. Make into rolls, coffee cake or sweet rolls. See specific recipes for shaping, baking directions and yield. 16 rolls

NUTRITION INFORMATION PER SERVING

Serving Size: 1 roll		Percent U.S. RDA Per Serving	
Calories	126	Protein	5%
Protein	3g	Vitamin A	3%
Carbohydrate	20g	Vitamin C	*
Fat	3g	Thiamin	10%
Sodium	172mg	Riboflavin	9%
Potassium	56mg	Niacin	7%
		Calcium	2%
		Iron	4%

TIPS: *If desired, substitute up to 2 cups Pillsbury's Best® Whole Wheat Flour.*

If desired, substitute 1 pkg. Pillsbury Hot Roll Mix for Basic Roll Dough. Prepare as directed on pkg.; let rise and use as Basic Roll Dough in any of the recipes that follow.

For REFRIGERATOR ROLL DOUGH, substitute warm water for milk. After mixing dough, cover and refrigerate up to 5 days. Use as directed for the basic dough. If desired, to double recipe, double the ingredient amounts; bake part of dough immediately, and refrigerate remaining dough for later use.

For POTATO ROLL DOUGH, add up to ¾ cup mashed potatoes, sweet potatoes or pumpkin; increase flour addition to 3½ to 3¾ cups.

**Self-rising flour is not recommended.*

The same basic roll dough is used to make every type of dinner roll—the only difference is in the shaping.

DINNER ROLLS

Prepare 1 recipe Basic Roll Dough, this page. Shape as desired (see Tips). Cover; let rise in warm place until light and doubled in size, about 30 to 45 minutes. Heat oven to 400°F. Bake 15 to 20 minutes or until golden brown and rolls sound hollow when lightly tapped. Immediately remove from pans; cool.

About 16 rolls

TIPS: *For BROWN 'N SERVE DINNER ROLLS, prepare as directed, but bake at 300°F. for 10 to 20 minutes or until rolls are set, but not brown. Remove from pan; cool completely. Store in refrigerator up to 2 days or in freezer 2 to 3 months. Bake refrigerated or frozen rolls on cookie sheet at 400°F. for 10 minutes or until golden brown.*

For PAN ROLLS, divide dough into 15 equal parts; shape into balls. Place smooth-side-up in greased 13x9-inch pan.

For FINGER ROLLS, divide dough into 16 equal parts; shape each piece into a roll about 4-inches long. Place in greased 8-inch square pan, forming 2 rows in pan. Cover; let rise in warm place until light and doubled in size. Bake at 375°F. for 20 to 25 minutes or until golden brown and rolls sound hollow when lightly tapped.

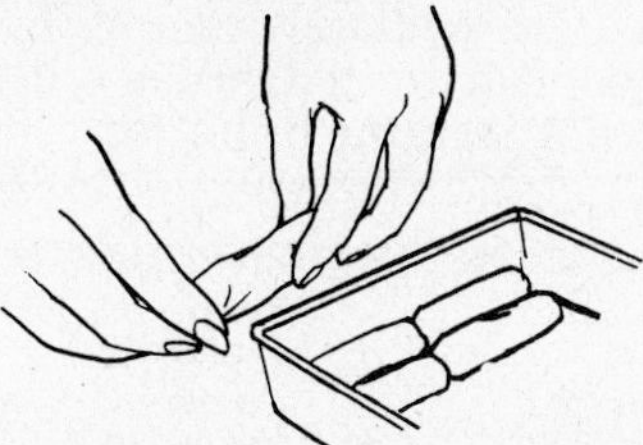

For CLOVERLEAF ROLLS, divide dough into 16 equal parts; divide each part into thirds. Shape each piece into a ball. Place 3 balls in each greased muffin cup.

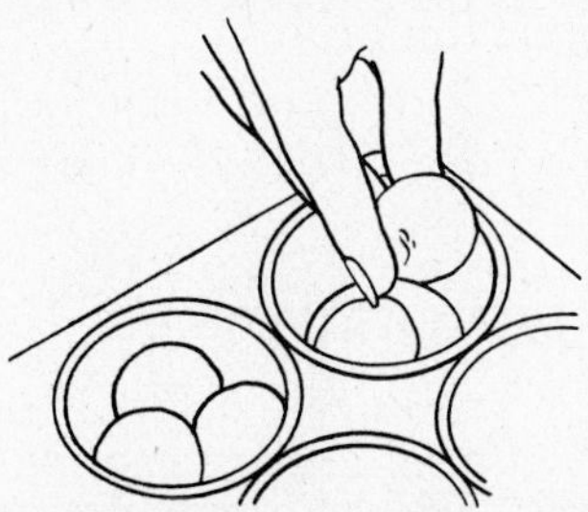

For QUICK CLOVERLEAF ROLLS, divide dough into 16 equal parts; form into balls. Place in greased muffin cups. With kitchen shears, cut balls of dough in half almost to bottom, then cut each half into quarters.

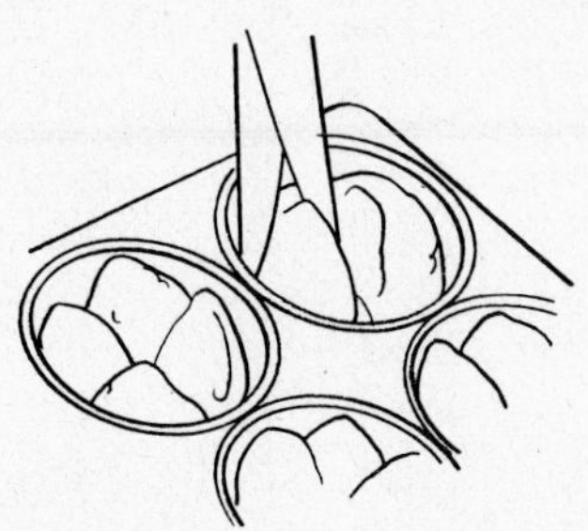

For PARKERHOUSE ROLLS, on floured surface roll dough until about ¼-inch thick. Cut into 2½ to 3-inch circles; brush with melted margarine or butter. Use the handle of a knife to make a deep crease across each circle. Fold on crease line, slightly overlapping the top half. Press edges together lightly. Place rolls close together in rows on greased cookie sheet.

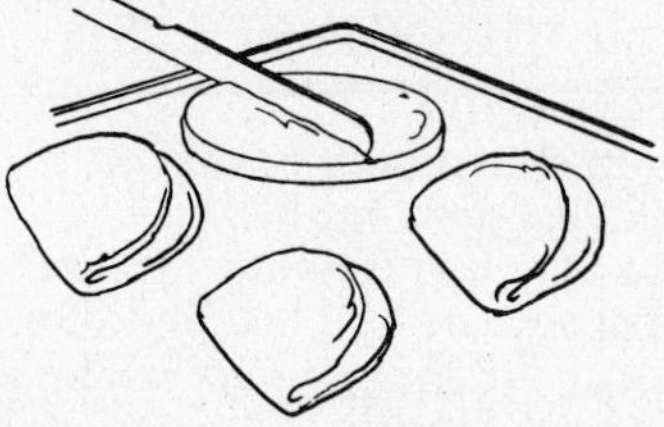

For BOW KNOTS, divide dough into 16 equal parts. Shape each into a strip about 9-inches long by rolling between hands. Tie in loose knot being careful not to stretch dough. Place on greased cookie sheets.

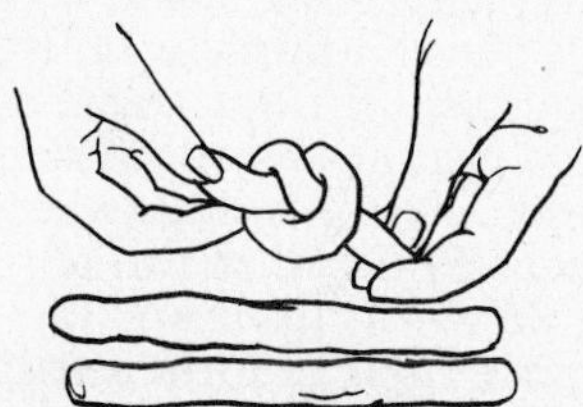

For CRESCENT ROLLS, roll dough to 15-inch circle; brush with melted margarine or butter. Cut into 16 wedges. Starting with wide end, roll up each wedge toward point. Place point underneath on greased cookie sheet, curving ends to form a crescent shape.

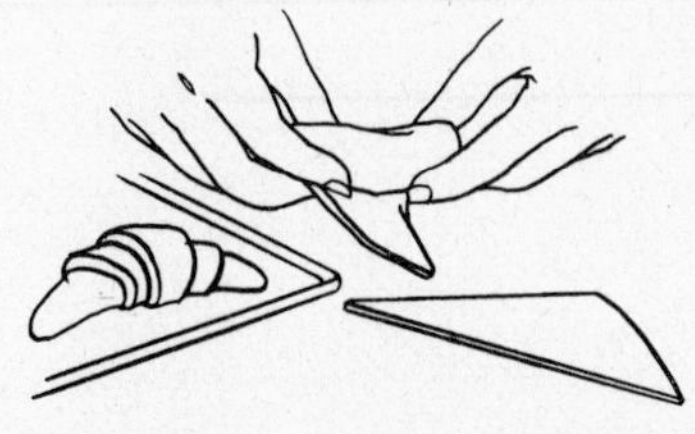

WHOLE WHEAT DINNER ROLLS

2 cups water
¾ cup shortening or oil
2 tablespoons molasses
3¾ to 4¼ cups Pillsbury's Best® All Purpose or Unbleached Flour*
3 cups Pillsbury's Best® Whole Wheat Flour
½ cup sugar
2 teaspoons salt
2 pkg. active dry yeast
2 eggs

In small saucepan, heat first 3 ingredients until very warm (120° to 130°F.). In large bowl, blend warm liquid, 2 cups all-purpose flour, 1 cup whole wheat flour, sugar, salt, yeast and eggs at low speed until moistened. Beat 4 minutes at medium speed. By hand, stir in remaining whole wheat flour and enough all-purpose flour to form a stiff dough. Knead on floured surface until smooth and elastic, about 5 minutes. Place dough in greased bowl; turn greased-side-up. Cover; let rise in warm place until light and doubled in size, 45 to 60 minutes.

Generously grease (not oil) one 13x9-inch pan and one 8-inch square pan. Punch down dough. Divide dough into 36 pieces; shape into balls. Place in prepared pans. Cover; let rise in warm place until light and doubled in size, 30 to 45 minutes. Heat oven to 375°F. Bake 15 to 20 minutes or until golden brown and rolls sound hollow when lightly tapped. Immediately remove from pan; cool. If desired, brush with melted margarine or butter.

36 rolls

NUTRITION INFORMATION PER SERVING

Serving Size: 1 roll		Percent U.S. RDA Per Serving	
Calories	137	Protein	5%
Protein	3g	Vitamin A	*
Carbohydrate	21g	Vitamin C	0%
Fat	5g	Thiamin	10%
Sodium	123mg	Riboflavin	6%
Potassium	73mg	Niacin	6%
		Calcium	*
		Iron	5%

TIP: **If using Pillsbury's Best® Self Rising Flour, omit salt.*

For savory SEASONED BUTTERS, see page 102.

FRUIT BUTTER

Cream ½ cup softened margarine or butter and 2 tablespoons honey or sugar until light and fluffy. Blend in ½ cup fresh fruit (blueberries, raspberries, strawberries, peaches or chopped banana).

1½ cups

NUTRITION INFORMATION PER SERVING

Serving Size: 1 tablespoon		Percent U.S. RDA Per Serving	
Calories	41	Protein	*
Protein	<1g	Vitamin A	3%
Carbohydrate	2g	Vitamin C	*
Fat	4g	Thiamin	*
Sodium	47mg	Riboflavin	*
Potassium	4mg	Niacin	*
		Calcium	*
		Iron	*

Delicious rolls in record time with no kneading involved.

BATTER ROLLS

1¼ cups milk
¼ cup margarine or butter
3¼ cups Pillsbury's Best® All Purpose or Unbleached Flour*
¼ cup sugar
1 teaspoon salt
1 pkg. active dry yeast
1 egg

In small saucepan, heat milk and margarine until very warm (120° to 130°F.). In large bowl, blend warm liquid, 1¼ cups flour, sugar, salt, yeast and egg at low speed until moistened. Beat 2 minutes at medium speed. By hand, stir in remaining flour to form a stiff batter. Cover; let rise in warm place until light and doubled in size, 45 to 60 minutes.

Grease (not oil) 16 muffin cups. Stir down batter. Spoon into prepared muffin cups, filling each about half full. Cover; let rise in warm place until light and doubled in size, about 45 minutes. Heat oven to 400°F. Bake 15 to 20 minutes or until golden brown. Immediately remove from pan; cool. 16 rolls

NUTRITION INFORMATION PER SERVING

Serving Size: 1 roll		Percent U.S. RDA Per Serving	
Calories	149	Protein	6%
Protein	4g	Vitamin A	4%
Carbohydrate	24g	Vitamin C	*
Fat	4g	Thiamin	12%
Sodium	183mg	Riboflavin	10%
Potassium	66mg	Niacin	8%
		Calcium	3%
		Iron	5%

TIPS: *For POTATO ROLLS, add up to ½ cup mashed potatoes when adding egg.*

For CHEESE ROLLS, stir in 1 cup shredded cheese with remaining flour.

**Self-rising flour is not recommended.*

ORANGE STICKY ROLLS

1 recipe Basic Roll Dough, page 70
3 tablespoons margarine or butter
½ cup orange juice
¾ cup sugar
1½ tablespoons grated orange peel
2 tablespoons margarine or butter, melted

Prepare Basic Roll Dough. In small saucepan, heat 3 tablespoons margarine, orange juice, sugar and orange peel until boiling. Boil 5 minutes, stirring occasionally. Place scant tablespoonful of sauce in each of 24 muffin cups. On floured surface, roll dough to 18x15-inch rectangle. Brush with melted margarine, leaving ½ inch on one 18-inch side free of margarine for ease in sealing edges. Starting with 18-inch side, roll up (jelly-roll fashion) toward side with ½-inch ungreased edge. Pinch edges to seal. Cut into 24 slices. Place cut-side down on orange sauce in muffin cup. Cover; let rise until light and doubled in size, about 45 minutes. Heat oven to 375°F. Bake 15 to 20 minutes or until golden brown. Cool 1 minute; invert onto aluminum foil. Let stand 1 minute; remove from pan.
24 rolls

NUTRITION INFORMATION PER SERVING

Serving Size: 1 roll		Percent U.S. RDA Per Serving	
Calories	136	Protein	4%
Protein	2g	Vitamin A	5%
Carbohydrate	20g	Vitamin C	5%
Fat	5g	Thiamin	7%
Sodium	150mg	Riboflavin	6%
Potassium	49mg	Niacin	4%
		Calcium	*
		Iron	3%

TIP: *If desired, sprinkle dough with 1 cup toasted coconut before rolling up.*

Very popular among our tasters! We guarantee this to be a favorite of yours, too.

ONE-RISE CARAMEL ROLLS

TOPPING

1 cup firmly packed brown sugar
1 cup (½ pint) heavy whipping cream (do not substitute)

ROLLS

1 cup very warm water (120° to 130°F.)
2 tablespoons margarine or butter, softened
3 to 3½ cups Pillsbury's Best® All Purpose or Unbleached Flour*
¼ cup sugar
1 teaspoon salt
1 pkg. active dry yeast
1 egg

FILLING

½ cup sugar
½ cup chopped nuts
½ cup margarine or butter, softened
2 teaspoons cinnamon

In 13x9-inch pan, combine brown sugar and heavy cream; mix well. In large bowl, blend warm water, margarine, 1½ cups flour, sugar, salt, yeast and egg at low speed until moistened. Beat 3 minutes at medium speed. By hand, stir in remaining flour. Knead on floured surface 1 minute. Press or roll dough to 15x7-inch rectangle. In small bowl, combine Filling ingredients and spread over dough. Starting with 15-inch side, roll up (jelly-roll fashion) tightly. Pinch edges to seal. Cut into 20 rolls. Place rolls cut-side-down in cream mixture. Cover; let rise in warm place until light and doubled in size, 35 to 45 minutes.

Heat oven to 400°F. Bake 20 to 25 minutes or until golden brown and rolls sound hollow when lightly tapped. Cool 5 minutes; invert onto foil. 20 rolls

NUTRITION INFORMATION PER SERVING

Serving Size: 1 roll		Percent U.S. RDA Per Serving	
Calories	257	Protein	5%
Protein	3g	Vitamin A	9%
Carbohydrate	33g	Vitamin C	*
Fat	13g	Thiamin	10%
Sodium	188mg	Riboflavin	7%
Potassium	92mg	Niacin	6%
		Calcium	3%
		Iron	6%

TIP: **If using Pillsbury's Best® Self Rising Flour, omit salt.*

DATE TWISTS

1 recipe Basic Roll Dough, page 70

DATE FILLING

1 cup chopped dates
¼ cup firmly packed brown sugar
¼ cup chopped nuts
¼ teaspoon cinnamon or nutmeg, if desired
¼ cup water
1 tablespoon lemon juice

Prepare Basic Roll Dough. Combine all Filling ingredients in small saucepan. Cook over medium heat until thickened, about 5 minutes, stirring occasionally. Cool.
Grease (not oil) cookie sheet. On floured surface, roll dough to 18x12-inch rectangle. Spread with cooled Date Filling. Starting with 18-inch side, fold dough in thirds to make 3 layers. Pinch edges to seal. Cut into eighteen 1-inch strips. Twist each strip twice and place 2 inches apart on prepared cookie sheet. Cover; let rise in warm place until light and doubled in size, 30 to 45 minutes.
Heat oven to 375°F. Bake 10 to 15 minutes or until golden brown. Immediately remove from cookie sheet; cool. If desired, glaze with Orange or Lemon Glaze, page *149* while still warm. 18 twists

NUTRITION INFORMATION PER SERVING

Serving Size: 1 twist		Percent U.S. RDA Per Serving	
Calories	163	Protein	5%
Protein	3g	Vitamin A	3%
Carbohydrate	29g	Vitamin C	*
Fat	4g	Thiamin	10%
Sodium	154mg	Riboflavin	8%
Potassium	133mg	Niacin	7%
		Calcium	3%
		Iron	6%

See the TIPS for additional ideas.

CINNAMON ROLLS

1 recipe Basic Roll Dough, page 70
¼ cup margarine or butter, melted
½ cup firmly packed brown sugar or sugar
2 teaspoons cinnamon

Prepare Basic Roll Dough. Grease (not oil) 13x9-inch pan. On floured surface, roll dough to 18x15-inch rectangle. Brush dough with margarine, leaving ½ inch on one 18-inch side free of margarine for ease in sealing edges. Combine sugar and cinnamon; sprinkle over dough. Starting with 18-inch side, roll up (jelly-roll fashion) toward side with ½-inch ungreased edge. Pinch edges to seal.* Cut into 15 slices. Place in prepared pan. Cover; let rise until light and doubled in size, 30 to 45 minutes. Heat oven to 375°F. Bake 20 to 25 minutes or until golden brown. Immediately remove from pan. Serve warm. 15 rolls

NUTRITION INFORMATION PER SERVING

Serving Size: 1 roll		Percent U.S. RDA Per Serving	
Calories	190	Protein	6%
Protein	4g	Vitamin A	6%
Carbohydrate	29g	Vitamin C	*
Fat	7g	Thiamin	11%
Sodium	223mg	Riboflavin	9%
Potassium	86mg	Niacin	7%
		Calcium	3%
		Iron	6%

TIPS: *If desired, two 8-inch square pans or 18 individual muffin cups may be used. Cut roll into 18 slices; continue as directed.*

If desired, add ½ cup raisins and/or chopped nuts with the brown sugar.

For CARAMEL PECAN ROLLS, combine ½ cup firmly packed brown sugar, ½ cup chopped pecans, ¼ cup margarine or butter and 2 tablespoons corn syrup in 13x9-inch pan. Heat until margarine melts. Blend well. Arrange cinnamon rolls on mixture. Let rise and bake as directed. Cool 1 minute; invert onto cookie sheet or serving plate. Let stand 1 minute more; remove baking pan. To make in muffin cups; combine sugar mixture; divide evenly between 18 muffin cups and continue as directed.

For CARAMEL PINEAPPLE ROLLS, prepare Caramel Pecan Rolls, substituting ¾ cup (8-oz. can) drained crushed pineapple, for pecans.

For CINNAMON RING, arrange cinnamon rolls in greased 12-inch fluted tube pan. Cover; let rise in warm place until light and doubled in size, 30 to 45 minutes. Heat oven to 350°F. Bake for 35 to 40 minutes or until golden brown and rolls sound hollow when lightly tapped. Cool 5 minutes; remove from pan. If desired, drizzle warm ring with ½ recipe of Basic Powdered Sugar Glaze, page 149. Serve warm.
1 ring

For BROWN 'N SERVE CINNAMON ROLLS, prepare as directed, but bake at 275°F. for 25 to 30 minutes or until rolls are set but not brown. Remove from pan and cool completely. Store in refrigerator up to 2 days or in freezer 2 to 3 months. Place refrigerated or frozen rolls on lightly greased cookie sheet. Heat oven to 375°F. Bake for 15 to 20 minutes or until golden brown.

*For SWEDISH TEA RING, prepare to *, place roll seam-side-down on greased cookie sheet, joining ends to form a circle (pinch to seal). With scissors, make cuts at 1-inch intervals to within ½ inch of inside of ring. Turn each slice on its side, cut-side-up. Cover; let rise until doubled in size, about 45 minutes. Bake at 350°F. for 25 to 30 minutes. If desired, glaze with ½ recipe of Basic Powdered Sugar Glaze, page 149.*

HOT CROSS BUNS

1 recipe Basic Roll Dough, page 70
½ cup currants or raisins
3 tablespoons chopped citron, if desired
1 teaspoon cinnamon
1 tablespoon margarine or butter, melted

FROSTING
½ cup powdered sugar
1½ teaspoons margarine or butter, softened
1 teaspoon milk or light cream
¼ teaspoon vanilla

Prepare Basic Roll Dough as directed, adding currants, citron and cinnamon when the remaining flour is stirred in.

Grease (not oil) 9-inch square pan. After dough rises once, divide dough into 16 equal portions and shape into round balls. Place in prepared pan. Cover; let rise until light and doubled in size, 30 to 45 minutes. Heat oven to 375°F. Bake 20 to 25 minutes or until golden brown and buns sound hollow when lightly tapped. Brush with melted margarine. Remove from pan to cool.

In small bowl, blend all Frosting ingredients until smooth. Form frosting cross on top of each bun with decorating tube. 16 buns

NUTRITION INFORMATION PER SERVING

Serving Size: 1 bun		Percent U.S. RDA Per Serving	
Calories	215	Protein	6%
Protein	4g	Vitamin A	8%
Carbohydrate	29g	Vitamin C	*
Fat	9g	Thiamin	11%
Sodium	253mg	Riboflavin	9%
Potassium	96mg	Niacin	7%
		Calcium	3%
		Iron	5%

TIP: *See directions for making a decorating tube, page 147.*

HOT CROSS BUNS

A tender yeast coffee cake is split and filled with a creamy filling—almonds give the crunch on top.

CRUNCHY CREAM-FILLED KUCHEN

½ cup milk
2 tablespoons margarine or butter
2 to 2¼ cups Pillsbury's Best® All Purpose or Unbleached Flour*
2 tablespoons sugar
1 teaspoon salt
¼ teaspoon nutmeg
1 pkg. active dry yeast
1 egg

TOPPING

½ cup sugar
¼ cup margarine or butter
1 tablespoon milk
¾ cup sliced almonds

CREAM FILLING

3⅛-oz. pkg. vanilla-flavored pudding and pie filling
2 cups milk
¼ teaspoon almond extract

Grease (not oil) two 8-inch round cake pans. In small saucepan, heat milk and margarine until very warm (120° to 130°F.). In large bowl, blend warm liquid, 1 cup flour, sugar, salt, nutmeg, yeast and egg at low speed until moistened. Beat 3 minutes at medium speed. By hand, stir in remaining flour to form a stiff dough. Knead on floured surface until smooth and elastic, about 3 minutes. Divide dough in half. Press dough into prepared pans. Cover; let rise in warm place until light and doubled in size, 45 to 60 minutes.

In small saucepan, combine first 3 Topping ingredients. Heat until sugar dissolves. Add almonds; cool. Heat oven to 375°F. Spread half of Topping on each coffee cake. Bake at 375°F. for 20 to 25 minutes or until golden brown. Immediately remove from pans; cool.

Prepare pudding as directed on package; after cooking stir in almond extract; cool. Split the 2 coffee cakes in half horizontally and spread half of filling on bottom layer of each. Place top layers over filling. Chill. Cut in wedges. Refrigerate leftovers.

Two 8-inch coffee cakes

NUTRITION INFORMATION PER SERVING

Serving Size: 1/18 of recipe		Percent U.S. RDA Per Serving	
Calories	181	Protein	6%
Protein	4g	Vitamin A	5%
Carbohydrate	25g	Vitamin C	*
Fat	8g	Thiamin	8%
Sodium	209mg	Riboflavin	11%
Potassium	111mg	Niacin	5%
		Calcium	6%
		Iron	4%

TIPS: *Cream Filling may be omitted. Do not split cakes. Serve warm, cut in wedges.*

**If using Pillsbury's Best® Self Rising Flour, omit salt.*

MAPLE-NUT COFFEE TWIST

Although a 12-inch pizza pan is a must to make this recipe, one taste will assure you it was well worth the investment.

MAPLE-NUT COFFEE TWIST

COFFEE CAKE

¾ cup milk
¼ cup margarine or butter
2¾ to 3 cups Pillsbury's Best® All Purpose or Unbleached Flour*
3 tablespoons sugar
½ teaspoon salt
1 pkg. active dry yeast
1 teaspoon maple extract
1 egg
¼ cup margarine or butter, melted

FILLING

½ cup sugar
⅓ cup chopped nuts
1 teaspoon cinnamon
1 teaspoon maple extract

GLAZE

1 cup powdered sugar
2 tablespoons margarine or butter, melted
1 to 2 tablespoons milk or water
½ teaspoon maple extract

In small saucepan, heat milk and margarine until very warm (120° to 130°F.). In large bowl, blend warm liquid, 1 cup flour, sugar, salt, yeast, extract and egg at low speed until moistened. Beat 2 minutes at medium speed. By hand, stir in remaining flour to form a soft dough. Knead on floured surface until smooth and elastic, about 2 minutes. Place dough in greased bowl; turn greased-side-up. Cover; let rise in warm place until light and doubled in size, 45 to 60 minutes. In small bowl, combine Filling ingredients; set aside.

Grease (not oil) 12-inch pizza pan. Punch down dough; divide and shape into 3 balls. On floured surface, roll or press 1 ball of dough to cover bottom of prepared pizza pan. Place in prepared pan. Brush dough with about ⅓ of melted margarine; sprinkle with ⅓ Filling. Repeat layers of dough, melted margarine and Filling. To shape, place a glass about 2 inches in diameter in center of dough. With scissors, cut from outside edge to the glass, forming 16 pie-shaped wedges. Twist each wedge 5 times. Remove glass. Cover; let rise until light and doubled in size, 30 to 45 minutes. Heat oven to 375°F. Bake 18 to 22 minutes or until golden brown. Cool 5 minutes; remove from pan. In small bowl, blend Glaze ingredients until smooth. Drizzle over warm coffee cake.

One 12-inch coffee cake

NUTRITION INFORMATION PER SERVING

Serving Size: 1/16 of recipe		Percent U.S. RDA Per Serving	
Calories	235	Protein	6%
Protein	4g	Vitamin A	7%
Carbohydrate	34g	Vitamin C	*
Fat	10g	Thiamin	11%
Sodium	167mg	Riboflavin	8%
Potassium	65mg	Niacin	7%
		Calcium	2%
		Iron	5%

TIP: **Self-rising flour is not recommended.*

STREUSEL COFFEE CAKE

½ cup milk
⅓ cup margarine or butter
2 to 2¼ cups Pillsbury's Best® All Purpose or Unbleached Flour*
⅓ cup sugar
½ teaspoon salt
1 pkg. active dry yeast
1 egg

TOPPING

½ cup Pillsbury's Best® All Purpose or Unbleached Flour*
⅓ cup firmly packed brown sugar
1 teaspoon cinnamon
¼ cup margarine or butter
½ cup chopped nuts

Grease (not oil) 13x9-inch pan. In small saucepan, heat milk and margarine until very warm (120° to 130°F.). In large bowl, blend warm liquid, 1 cup flour, sugar, salt, yeast and egg at low speed until moistened. Beat 3 minutes at medium speed. By hand, stir in remaining flour to make a stiff batter. Press onto bottom of prepared 13x9-inch pan. Cover; let rise in warm place until light and doubled in size, 45 to 60 minutes. In small bowl, combine ½ cup flour, brown sugar, cinnamon and ¼ cup margarine until crumbly. Stir in nuts. Sprinkle Topping over dough. Heat oven to 375°F. Bake 20 to 25 minutes or until golden brown. Serve warm.

13x9-inch coffee cake

NUTRITION INFORMATION PER SERVING

Serving Size: 1/12 of recipe		Percent U.S. RDA Per Serving	
Calories	267	Protein	7%
Protein	5g	Vitamin A	9%
Carbohydrate	33g	Vitamin C	*
Fat	13g	Thiamin	14%
Sodium	213mg	Riboflavin	10%
Potassium	103mg	Niacin	8%
		Calcium	3%
		Iron	7%

TIPS: *For APPLE STREUSEL COFFEE CAKE, arrange 3 cups peeled, sliced apples over dough before sprinkling with Topping. Increase sugar in Topping to ½ cup (white or brown sugar may be used).*

For RHUBARB STREUSEL COFFEE CAKE, arrange 2 cups finely chopped, fresh rhubarb over dough before sprinkling with Topping. Increase sugar in Topping to ½ cup (white or brown sugar may be used).

For ALMOND CRUNCH COFFEE CAKE, combine in saucepan ⅓ cup margarine or butter, 1 cup sugar and 2 tablespoons milk; heat to boiling. Remove from heat, stir in 1 cup sliced almonds and ½ teaspoon almond flavoring or 1 teaspoon vanilla. Spread over dough. If desired, serve as dessert topped with whipped cream.

**Self-rising flour is not recommended.*

A must for the holiday breakfast or brunch.

CHRISTMAS STOLLEN

1 cup milk
½ cup water
⅔ cup margarine or butter
5½ to 6½ cups Pillsbury's Best® All Purpose or Unbleached Flour*
½ cup sugar
1½ teaspoons salt
1 teaspoon cardamom
2 pkg. active dry yeast
3 eggs
¾ cup mixed candied fruits
½ cup candied red cherries, cut in half
½ cup golden raisins

ALMOND GLAZE
1½ cups powdered sugar
2 to 3 tablespoons light cream
¼ teaspoon almond extract

In small saucepan, heat first 3 ingredients until very warm (120° to 130°F.). In large bowl, blend warm liquid, 2½ cups flour, sugar, salt, cardamom, yeast and eggs at low speed until moistened. Beat 3 minutes at medium speed. By hand, stir in remaining flour and fruits to form a soft dough. On well-floured surface, knead until smooth and elastic, about 8 minutes. Place dough in greased bowl; turn greased-side-up. Cover; let rise in warm place until light and doubled in size, about 1½ hours.

Grease (not oil) 3 cookie sheets. Punch down dough; divide in thirds. On lightly-floured surface, press or roll one portion of dough to a 12x7-inch oval. Fold in half lengthwise. Place on prepared cookie sheet. Repeat with 2 remaining sections of dough. Cover; let rise in warm place until light and doubled in size, about 45 minutes. Heat oven to 350°F. Bake 30 to 35 minutes or until golden brown. Immediately remove from cookie sheet; cool. In small bowl, blend Glaze ingredients until smooth; drizzle over stollens.

3 loaves

NUTRITION INFORMATION PER SERVING

Serving Size: 1/24 of recipe (1 slice)		Percent U.S. RDA Per Serving	
Calories	251	Protein	7%
Protein	5g	Vitamin A	6%
Carbohydrate	44g	Vitamin C	*
Fat	7g	Thiamin	14%
Sodium	223mg	Riboflavin	11%
Potassium	94mg	Niacin	9%
		Calcium	3%
		Iron	7%

TIP: **If using Pillsbury's Best® Self Rising Flour, omit salt.*

WHIPPED CREAM CHEESE

In small bowl, cream 1 pkg. (8 oz.) cream cheese until soft. Gradually beat in 3 to 4 tablespoons milk until light and fluffy.

1½ cups

NUTRITION INFORMATION PER SERVING

Serving Size: 1 tablespoon		Percent U.S. RDA Per Serving	
Calories	37	Protein	*
Protein	<1g	Vitamin A	3%
Carbohydrate	<1g	Vitamin C	*
Fat	4g	Thiamin	*
Sodium	25mg	Riboflavin	*
Potassium	10mg	Niacin	*
		Calcium	*
		Iron	*

TIPS: *For CHERRY CREAM CHEESE, substitute cherry liquid for milk. After beating, fold in ¼ cup chopped maraschino cherries and if desired, 2 tablespoons chopped nuts.*

For HONEY, MARMALADE, MAPLE OR ORANGE CREAM CHEESE, follow Tips on Whipped Butter, page 102.

QUICK BREADS

As their name implies, these breads can be made quickly and easily. Because the leavening agent is either baking powder, soda or steam, there is not any rising time. Due to this convenience, quick breads are popular to serve and give as gifts. Although most often served as a meal accompaniment, special quick breads such as pancakes and waffles are served as main dishes.

PREPARATION

Probably the mistake made most often is overbeating. With most quick breads, much of the mixing is done by hand just until dry ingredients are moistened; in many cases there will still be lumps remaining–this is okay. Overbeating will often cause the bread to peak sharply; the bread will be coarse in texture with tunnels.

A nicely baked quick bread will have a gently rounded top that is slightly bumpy. Don't worry about a crack on top of the quick bread loaves–it is typical.

Take care not to overbake quick breads, as they dry out quickly and will form hard crusts.

SERVING

Muffins and biscuits may be served warm or cool. Quick bread loaves are easiest to slice if allowed to cool completely and often their flavors improve if made a day or two ahead; thus they make delightful gifts.

Popovers should be served piping hot so make them just before serving.

Although pancakes and waffles are generally served hot, leftovers are almost as good cold topped with jam or jelly.

For savory BREAD BUTTERS, see page 102.

OLD-FASHIONED BAKING POWDER BISCUITS

2 cups Pillsbury's Best® All Purpose or Unbleached Flour*
3 teaspoons baking powder
½ teaspoon salt
½ cup shortening or margarine
⅔ to ¾ cup milk

Heat oven to 450°F. In large bowl, combine flour, baking powder and salt. Using pastry blender or fork, cut in shortening until consistency of coarse meal. Add milk; stir with fork *just* until a soft dough forms. Turn dough onto floured surface; sprinkle lightly with flour. Knead gently 10 to 12 times until no longer sticky. Roll or press dough to ½-inch thickness; cut with 2-inch floured cutter. Place biscuits ½ inch apart for soft sides or 1 inch apart for crusty sides on ungreased cookie sheet. Bake at 450°F. for 8 to 12 minutes or until golden brown. Serve immediately.

12 to 15 biscuits

NUTRITION INFORMATION PER SERVING

Serving Size: 1 biscuit		Percent U.S. RDA Per Serving	
Calories	159	Protein	4%
Protein	3g	Vitamin A	*
Carbohydrate	17g	Vitamin C	*
Fat	9g	Thiamin	9%
Sodium	180mg	Riboflavin	6%
Potassium	40mg	Niacin	6%
		Calcium	3%
		Iron	3%

TIPS: *For BUTTERMILK BISCUITS, decrease baking powder to 2 teaspoons, add ¼ teaspoon soda and substitute buttermilk for the milk.*

For DROP BISCUITS, increase milk to 1 cup. Drop by tablespoonfuls onto greased cookie sheet. If desired, sprinkle with sesame or poppy seed.

For CHEESE BISCUITS, add ½ cup shredded cheese with flour.

**If using Pillsbury's Best® Self Rising Flour, omit baking powder and salt.*

Here is a simple recipe with enough variations to suit anyone's taste.

BASIC MUFFINS

2 cups Pillsbury's Best® All Purpose or Unbleached Flour*
¼ cup sugar
3 teaspoons baking powder
½ teaspoon salt
1 egg, well-beaten
1 cup milk
¼ cup oil or melted shortening

Heat oven to 400°F. Line with paper baking cups or grease (not oil) bottoms only of 12 muffin cups. In medium bowl, combine first 4 ingredients. Stir in remaining ingredients *just* until dry ingredients are moistened. (Batter will be lumpy.) Spoon batter into prepared muffin cups, filling ⅔ full. Bake at 400°F. for 20 to 25 minutes or until golden brown. Run knife around edge to loosen; immediately remove from pan. Serve warm.

12 muffins

NUTRITION INFORMATION PER SERVING

Serving Size: 1 muffin		Percent U.S. RDA Per Serving	
Calories	154	Protein	5%
Protein	3g	Vitamin A	*
Carbohydrate	21g	Vitamin C	*
Fat	6g	Thiamin	10%
Sodium	189mg	Riboflavin	8%
Potassium	56mg	Niacin	6%
		Calcium	4%
		Iron	4%

TIPS: *For RICH BASIC MUFFINS, increase sugar to ½ cup, oil to ⅓ cup and decrease milk to ⅔ cup. Bake at 400°F. for 15 to 20 minutes.*

BLUEBERRY MUFFINS

For BLUEBERRY MUFFINS, gently stir in 1 cup fresh or ¾ cup (thawed and drained) frozen blueberries into RICH BASIC MUFFIN batter (first Tip).

For JAM MUFFINS, place ½ teaspoon favorite jam on each muffin before baking; press into batter. If desired, sprinkle with finely chopped nuts.

For APPLE MUFFINS, add ½ teaspoon cinnamon with flour. Add 1 peeled and grated apple with oil.

For CHEESE MUFFINS, add ½ to 1 cup shredded cheese to flour mixture.

For ORANGE MUFFINS, add 1 tablespoon grated orange peel with flour and substitute orange juice for milk. Bake as directed. Brush tops of hot muffins with 2 tablespoons melted margarine or butter; dip in mixture of ¼ cup sugar, 1 tablespoon grated orange peel and ¼ teaspoon cinnamon.

For SUGAR-COATED MUFFINS, brush tops of hot muffins with 2 tablespoons melted margarine or butter; dip in mixture of ¼ cup sugar and ½ teaspoon cinnamon.

For STREUSEL-TOPPED MUFFINS, combine ¼ cup firmly packed brown sugar, 1 tablespoon softened margarine or butter, ½ teaspoon cinnamon and ¼ cup chopped nuts or flaked coconut. Sprinkle over muffins before baking.

**If using Pillsbury's Best® Self Rising Flour, omit baking powder and salt.*

HIGH ALTITUDE—Above 3500 Feet: Decrease baking powder to 1 teaspoon.

BANANA MUFFINS

2 cups Pillsbury's Best® All Purpose or Unbleached Flour*
½ cup sugar
2 teaspoons baking powder
½ teaspoon soda
½ teaspoon salt
¼ teaspoon nutmeg or cinnamon
½ cup (1 medium) mashed banana
½ cup milk
⅓ cup oil
1 egg, slightly beaten

Heat oven to 375°F. Line with paper baking cups or grease (not oil) 12 muffin cups. In medium bowl, combine first 6 ingredients. Stir in remaining ingredients *just* until dry ingredients are moistened. Spoon batter into prepared muffin cups, filling ⅔ full. Bake at 375°F. for 15 to 20 minutes or until golden brown. Immediately remove from pan. Serve warm. 12 muffins

NUTRITION INFORMATION PER SERVING

Serving Size: 1 muffin		Percent U.S. RDA Per Serving	
Calories	184	Protein	5%
Protein	3g	Vitamin A	*
Carbohydrate	27g	Vitamin C	*
Fat	7g	Thiamin	10%
Sodium	202mg	Riboflavin	7%
Potassium	76mg	Niacin	6%
		Calcium	3%
		Iron	4%

TIP: **Self-rising flour is not recommended.*

HIGH ALTITUDE–Above 3500 Feet: Decrease baking powder and soda to ¼ teaspoon each. Bake at 375°F. for 15 to 20 minutes.

The batter may be kept in the refrigerator for several weeks so this recipe makes a perfect hurry-up breakfast addition.

BRAN MUFFINS

3 cups whole-bran wheat cereal
1 cup boiling water
½ cup shortening or oil
2 eggs
2½ cups Pillsbury's Best® All Purpose or Unbleached Flour*
1½ cups sugar
2½ teaspoons soda
2 cups buttermilk

Heat oven to 400°F. Line with paper baking cups or grease (not oil) desired number of muffin cups. In large bowl, combine cereal and boiling water. Stir in shortening and eggs. Add remaining ingredients; blend well. Spoon batter into prepared muffin cups, filling ¾ full. (Remaining batter may be stored in tightly covered container in refrigerator up to 6 weeks.) Bake at 400°F. for 18 to 22 minutes or until golden brown. Immediately remove from pan. Serve warm.

24 to 30 muffins

NUTRITION INFORMATION PER SERVING

Serving Size: 1 muffin		Percent U.S. RDA Per Serving	
Calories	137	Protein	4%
Protein	3g	Vitamin A	*
Carbohydrate	23g	Vitamin C	*
Fat	4g	Thiamin	7%
Sodium	191mg	Riboflavin	6%
Potassium	38mg	Niacin	8%
		Calcium	3%
		Iron	5%

TIPS: *One cup chopped dates, raisins or chopped nuts may be added to batter.*

**Self-rising flour is not recommended.*

HIGH ALTITUDE–Above 3500 Feet: Bake at 400°F. for 20 to 25 minutes.

Our "British experts" proclaimed this authentically delicious.

SCOTCH SCONES

2 cups Pillsbury's Best® All Purpose or Unbleached Flour*
½ cup raisins or currants, if desired
2 tablespoons sugar
3 teaspoons baking powder
1 teaspoon salt
¼ teaspoon soda
½ cup dairy sour cream
¼ cup oil
3 tablespoons milk
1 egg, slightly beaten

Heat oven to 425°F. In large bowl, combine first 6 ingredients. Add remaining ingredients, stirring until dough clings together. On well-floured surface, toss dough lightly until no longer sticky. Knead 12 to 15 times. Divide dough in half. Pat each ball of dough to a 6-inch circle with top slightly rounded. Brush surface with milk; sprinkle with sugar. Cut each circle into 6 wedges. Place 2 inches apart on cookie sheet. Bake at 425°F. for 10 to 12 minutes or until golden brown. Serve hot with margarine or butter, honey, raspberry or strawberry jam.

12 scones

NUTRITION INFORMATION PER SERVING

Serving Size: 1 scone		Percent U.S. RDA Per Serving	
Calories	171	Protein	5%
Protein	3g	Vitamin A	3%
Carbohydrate	23g	Vitamin C	*
Fat	7g	Thiamin	10%
Sodium	296mg	Riboflavin	7%
Potassium	78mg	Niacin	6%
		Calcium	4%
		Iron	5%

TIP: **If using Pillsbury's Best® Self Rising Flour, omit baking powder and salt.*

Don't peek when these are baking or they might fall!

POPOVERS

2 eggs
1 cup Pillsbury's Best® All Purpose or Unbleached Flour*
½ teaspoon salt
1 cup milk

Heat oven to 450°F. Generously grease (not oil) popover pans or deep custard cups. In small bowl, beat eggs slightly. Add remaining ingredients and beat *just* until blended. (Do not overbeat.) Fill prepared cups half full (about ⅓ cup) of batter. Bake at 450°F. for 15 minutes; reduce oven temperature to 325°F. and bake 25 to 30 minutes or until deep golden brown. Serve immediately. If desired, serve from baking cups.

6 or 7 large popovers

NUTRITION INFORMATION PER SERVING

Serving Size: 1 popover		Percent U.S. RDA Per Serving	
Calories	132	Protein	9%
Protein	6g	Vitamin A	5%
Carbohydrate	18g	Vitamin C	*
Fat	4g	Thiamin	11%
Sodium	224mg	Riboflavin	12%
Potassium	102mg	Niacin	6%
		Calcium	6%
		Iron	6%

TIPS: *Greased muffin cups may be substituted for popover pans.*

8 to 10 popovers

**Self-rising flour is not recommended.*

POPOVERS

An easier way to get steamed bread flavor.

OVEN BROWN BREAD

1 cup Pillsbury's Best® All Purpose* or Medium Rye Flour
1 cup Pillsbury's Best® Whole Wheat Flour
1 cup cornmeal
1 cup raisins
1½ teaspoons soda
1 teaspoon salt
2 cups buttermilk
¾ cup dark molasses
2 tablespoons oil or melted shortening

Heat oven to 350°F. Grease (not oil) three one-pound fruit or vegetable cans or 6-cup ring mold. In large bowl, combine first 6 ingredients. Add remaining ingredients; blend well. Spoon batter into prepared cans, filling ⅔ full. Cover tightly with foil. (Place cans on foil or cookie sheet during baking to guard against spillage.) Bake at 350°F. for 50 to 60 minutes or until toothpick inserted in center comes out clean. Cool 15 minutes; remove from cans, slice and serve warm.

3 small loaves

NUTRITION INFORMATION PER SERVING

Serving Size: 1 slice		Percent U.S. RDA Per Serving	
Calories	154	Protein	5%
Protein	3g	Vitamin A	*
Carbohydrate	32g	Vitamin C	*
Fat	2g	Thiamin	9%
Sodium	253mg	Riboflavin	7%
Potassium	285mg	Niacin	6%
		Calcium	8%
		Iron	10%

TIPS: *For STEAMED BROWN BREAD, place covered cans on rack in large saucepan or steamer. Add boiling water to a depth of 2 inches; cover and steam 3 hours or until toothpick inserted in center comes out clean (if necessary, add additional boiling water during last half hour of cooking). Cool 15 minutes and remove from cans.*

**Self-rising flour is not recommended.*

HIGH ALTITUDE–Above 3500 Feet: Reduce soda to 1¼ teaspoons, use four 1-lb. cans, three 1 lb. 5-oz. cans or 8-cup ring mold; bake at 350°F. for 50 to 60 minutes or steam 3 to 3½ hours.

Tastes like a popover but serve in wedges.

YORKSHIRE PUDDING

¼ cup roast beef drippings
2 eggs
1 cup Pillsbury's Best® All Purpose or Unbleached Flour*
½ teaspoon salt
1 cup milk

Heat oven to 425°F. Pour drippings into 9-inch square or round cake pan; tilt pan to grease sides. Place pan in oven to heat about 2 minutes. In small bowl, beat eggs slightly. Add remaining ingredients and beat *just* until blended. (Do not overbeat.) Pour batter into hot pan. Bake at 425°F. for 15 minutes. Reduce oven temperature to 350°F. Bake 10 to 15 minutes longer or until golden brown. Serve immediately.

6 servings

NUTRITION INFORMATION PER SERVING

Serving Size: 1/6 of recipe		Percent U.S. RDA Per Serving	
Calories	151	Protein	9%
Protein	6g	Vitamin A	5%
Carbohydrate	18g	Vitamin C	*
Fat	6g	Thiamin	11%
Sodium	241mg	Riboflavin	12%
Potassium	105mg	Niacin	6%
		Calcium	6%
		Iron	6%

TIPS: *For CHEESE YORKSHIRE PUDDING, stir ½ cup shredded American or Cheddar cheese into batter; sprinkle additional ½ cup shredded cheese over batter. Bake as directed.*

**Self-rising flour is not recommended.*

CORN BREAD

1 cup Pillsbury's Best® All Purpose or Unbleached Flour*
1 cup cornmeal
2 tablespoons sugar
4 teaspoons baking powder
1 teaspoon salt
1 cup milk
¼ cup oil or melted shortening
1 egg, slightly beaten

Heat oven to 425°F. Grease (not oil) 8 or 9-inch square pan. In medium bowl, combine first 5 ingredients. Stir in remaining ingredients beating by hand *just* until smooth. Pour batter into prepared pan. Bake at 425°F. for 20 to 25 minutes or until toothpick inserted in center comes out clean.

8 or 9-inch bread

NUTRITION INFORMATION PER SERVING

Serving Size: 1/9 of recipe		Percent U.S. RDA Per Serving	
Calories	199	Protein	7%
Protein	4g	Vitamin A	4%
Carbohydrate	27g	Vitamin C	*
Fat	8g	Thiamin	11%
Sodium	404mg	Riboflavin	9%
Potassium	81mg	Niacin	7%
		Calcium	7%
		Iron	6%

TIPS: *If desired, fry 4 to 5 slices bacon until crisp; drain on paper towel. Substitute bacon drippings for oil. Sprinkle batter with crumbled bacon before baking.*

For MEXICAN CORN BREAD, prepare batter using 2 eggs, slightly beaten. Stir in ½ cup shredded Cheddar cheese, ¼ cup chopped green chilies and ¼ cup finely chopped onion. Bake 22 to 28 minutes.

For CORN MUFFINS, spoon batter into greased muffin cups and bake 15 to 20 minutes; makes 12 muffins. Immediately remove from pan. To halve recipe, use half the ingredient amounts.

For CORN STICKS, bake in well-greased, hot (place in oven to heat) corn stick pans, filling ⅔ full. Bake 12 to 15 minutes. Immediately remove from pan. 18 corn sticks

For CORN BREAD RING, bake in greased 1½-quart (6 cup) ring mold 15 to 20 minutes. Immediately remove from mold and fill center with a creamed meat or seafood mixture.

**If using Pillsbury's Best® Self Rising Flour, omit baking powder and salt.*

HIGH ALTITUDE–Above 3500 Feet: Decrease baking powder to 1½ teaspoons.

SPOON BREAD

½ cup cornmeal
½ teaspoon salt
2 cups milk
2 tablespoons margarine or butter
2 eggs

Heat oven to 375°F. Grease (not oil) 1-quart casserole. In medium saucepan, combine cornmeal, salt and milk. Heat until boiling, stirring constantly. Remove from heat and stir in margarine. Add eggs, 1 at a time, beating by hand after each addition. Pour batter into prepared casserole. Bake uncovered at 375°F. for 30 to 35 minutes or until golden brown. Serve hot, spooned from casserole; top with additional margarine or butter.

5 servings

NUTRITION INFORMATION PER SERVING

Serving Size: 1/5 of recipe		Percent U.S. RDA Per Serving	
Calories	190	Protein	11%
Protein	7g	Vitamin A	13%
Carbohydrate	16g	Vitamin C	*
Fat	11g	Thiamin	8%
Sodium	349mg	Riboflavin	16%
Potassium	187mg	Niacin	3%
		Calcium	13%
		Iron	5%

To get tender flaky dumplings be sure the stew is boiling and keep the lid on.

FLUFFY DUMPLINGS

1½ cups Pillsbury's Best® All Purpose or Unbleached Flour*
1 tablespoon minced parsley
2 teaspoons baking powder
½ teaspoon salt
⅛ teaspoon nutmeg or mace, if desired
⅔ cup milk
2 tablespoons oil or melted shortening
1 egg, slightly beaten

In medium bowl, combine first 5 ingredients. Stir in remaining ingredients *just* until dry ingredients are moistened. Drop dough by tablespoonfuls onto hot chicken or meat in boiling stew. Cook covered, 12 to 15 minutes or until dumplings are fluffy and no longer doughy underneath.

8 to 10 dumplings

NUTRITION INFORMATION PER SERVING

Serving Size: 1/10 of recipe		Percent U.S. RDA Per Serving	
Calories	113	Protein	5%
Protein	3g	Vitamin A	2%
Carbohydrate	15g	Vitamin C	*
Fat	4g	Thiamin	9%
Sodium	190mg	Riboflavin	7%
Potassium	52mg	Niacin	5%
		Calcium	4%
		Iron	4%

TIP: **If using Pillsbury's Best® Self Rising Flour, omit baking powder and salt.*

NUT BREAD

¾ cup sugar
½ cup margarine or butter, softened
2 eggs
1 cup buttermilk
2 cups Pillsbury's Best® All Purpose or Unbleached Flour*
½ teaspoon soda
½ teaspoon baking powder
½ teaspoon salt
1 cup chopped nuts

Heat oven to 350°F. Grease (not oil) bottom only of 8x4 or 9x5-inch loaf pan. In large bowl, cream sugar and margarine. Beat in eggs; blend in buttermilk. Stir in remaining ingredients *just* until dry ingredients are moistened. Pour batter into prepared pan. Bake at 350°F. for 50 to 55 minutes or until toothpick inserted in center comes out clean. Cool 10 minutes; remove from pan. Cool completely.

1 loaf

NUTRITION INFORMATION PER SERVING

Serving Size: 1 slice		Percent U.S. RDA Per Serving	
Calories	210	Protein	7%
Protein	4g	Vitamin A	6%
Carbohydrate	23g	Vitamin C	*
Fat	11g	Thiamin	9%
Sodium	211mg	Riboflavin	7%
Potassium	81mg	Niacin	5%
		Calcium	4%
		Iron	5%

TIP: **Self-rising flour is not recommended.*

HIGH ALTITUDE–Above 3500 Feet: Bake at 375°F. for 50 to 55 minutes.

BANANA BREAD

1 cup sugar
1 cup (2 medium) mashed bananas
½ cup margarine or butter, softened
¼ cup milk
1 teaspoon vanilla
2 eggs
2 cups Pillsbury's Best® All Purpose or Unbleached Flour*
½ cup chopped nuts
1 teaspoon soda
½ teaspoon salt

Heat oven to 350°F. Grease (not oil) bottom only of 9x5 or 8x4-inch loaf pan. In large bowl, blend first 6 ingredients; beat 1 minute at medium speed. Stir in remaining ingredients *just* until dry ingredients are moistened. Pour batter into prepared pan. Bake at 350°F. for 50 to 60 minutes or until toothpick inserted in center comes out clean. Cool 5 minutes; remove from pan. Cool completely. 1 loaf

NUTRITION INFORMATION PER SERVING

Serving Size: 1 slice		Percent U.S. RDA Per Serving	
Calories	206	Protein	5%
Protein	3g	Vitamin A	7%
Carbohydrate	28g	Vitamin C	3%
Fat	9g	Thiamin	9%
Sodium	217mg	Riboflavin	6%
Potassium	100mg	Niacin	5%
		Calcium	*
		Iron	5%

TIPS: *If desired, add 1 tablespoon grated orange peel or ½ cup flaked coconut.*

For HONEY-BANANA BREAD, substitute ½ cup honey for all of sugar and decrease milk to 2 tablespoons.

For APPLESAUCE BREAD, decrease sugar to ¾ cup, substitute 1 cup applesauce for mashed banana, omit milk and add 1 teaspoon cinnamon or nutmeg with flour. If desired, add 1 cup (4 oz.) shredded cheese with nuts.

NUTRITION INFORMATION PER SERVING

Serving Size: 1 slice		Percent U.S. RDA Per Serving	
Calories	223	Protein	8%
Protein	5g	Vitamin A	8%
Carbohydrate	26g	Vitamin C	*
Fat	11g	Thiamin	8%
Sodium	265mg	Riboflavin	7%
Potassium	59mg	Niacin	4%
		Calcium	7%
		Iron	5%

**Self-rising flour is not recommended.*

BLONDE DATE-NUT BREAD

⅓ cup margarine or butter
¾ cup sugar
2 eggs
¾ cup buttermilk
2 cups Pillsbury's Best® All Purpose or Unbleached Flour*
1 cup chopped dates
½ cup nuts
½ teaspoon soda
½ teaspoon baking powder
½ teaspoon salt

Heat oven to 350°F. Grease (not oil) bottom only of 9x5-inch loaf pan. In medium bowl, cream margarine and sugar. Beat in eggs; blend in buttermilk. Stir in remaining ingredients *just* until dry ingredients are moistened. Pour batter into prepared pan. Bake at 350°F. for 50 to 55 minutes or until toothpick inserted in center comes out clean. Cool 10 minutes; remove from pan. Cool completely. 1 loaf

NUTRITION INFORMATION PER SERVING

Serving Size: 1 slice		Percent U.S. RDA Per Serving	
Calories	197	Protein	6%
Protein	4g	Vitamin A	5%
Carbohydrate	31g	Vitamin C	*
Fat	7g	Thiamin	9%
Sodium	183mg	Riboflavin	7%
Potassium	130mg	Niacin	6%
		Calcium	3%
		Iron	6%

TIP: **Self-rising flour is not recommended.*

HIGH ALTITUDE—Above 3500 Feet: Bake at 375°F. for 50 to 55 minutes.

PUMPKIN BREAD

15 or 16-oz. can (2 cups) pumpkin
3 cups sugar
1 cup oil
⅔ cup water
4 eggs
3½ cups Pillsbury's Best® All Purpose or Unbleached Flour*
2 teaspoons soda
1½ teaspoons salt
1 teaspoon cinnamon
1 teaspoon nutmeg
½ teaspoon ginger

Heat oven to 350°F. Grease (not oil) and flour bottoms only of two 9x5 or 8x4-inch loaf pans. In large bowl, blend first 5 ingredients. Beat 1 minute at medium speed. Add remaining ingredients; blend at low speed until moistened. Beat 1 minute at medium speed. Pour batter into prepared pans. Bake at 350°F. for 60 to 75 minutes or until toothpick inserted in center comes out clean. Cool 5 minutes; remove from pans. Cool completely.

2 loaves

NUTRITION INFORMATION PER SERVING

Serving Size: 1 slice		Percent U.S. RDA Per Serving	
Calories	199	Protein	4%
Protein	2g	Vitamin A	20%
Carbohydrate	30g	Vitamin C	*
Fat	8g	Thiamin	7%
Sodium	177mg	Riboflavin	5%
Potassium	57mg	Niacin	4%
		Calcium	*
		Iron	4%

TIP: **Self-rising flour is not recommended.*

The traditional holiday bread with a hint of orange.

CRANBERRY NUT BREAD

2 cups Pillsbury's Best® All Purpose or Unbleached Flour*
1 cup sugar
1½ teaspoons baking powder
1 teaspoon salt
½ teaspoon soda
¼ cup shortening or margarine
1 teaspoon grated orange peel
¾ cup orange juice
1 egg, slightly beaten
1 cup fresh or frozen cranberries, coarsely chopped
½ cup chopped nuts

Heat oven to 350°F. Grease (not oil) bottom only of 9x5 or 8x4-inch loaf pan. In large bowl, combine first 5 ingredients. Using pastry blender, cut in shortening until particles are size of coarse meal. Stir in peel, juice and egg *just* until dry ingredients are moistened. Fold in cranberries and nuts. Pour batter into prepared pan. Bake at 350°F. for 50 to 60 minutes or until toothpick inserted in center comes out clean. Cool 10 minutes; remove from pan. Cool completely. 1 loaf

NUTRITION INFORMATION PER SERVING

Serving Size: 1 slice		Percent U.S. RDA Per Serving	
Calories	171	Protein	4%
Protein	3g	Vitamin A	*
Carbohydrate	27g	Vitamin C	11%
Fat	6g	Thiamin	9%
Sodium	203mg	Riboflavin	5%
Potassium	65mg	Niacin	5%
		Calcium	*
		Iron	4%

TIPS: *A well-greased (not oiled) 12-cup fluted tube pan, may be substituted for the loaf pan. Bake at 350°F. for 30 to 40 minutes or until toothpick inserted in center comes out clean.*

**Self-rising flour is not recommended.*

HIGH ALTITUDE—Above 3500 Feet: Bake at 375°F. for 50 to 60 minutes.

ZUCCHINI BREAD

3 eggs
2 cups sugar
2 cups (3 medium) shredded zucchini*
1 cup oil
2 teaspoons vanilla
3 cups Pillsbury's Best® All Purpose or Unbleached Flour**
½ cup chopped nuts
1 teaspoon salt
1 teaspoon soda
1 teaspoon baking powder
2 teaspoons cinnamon
½ teaspoon nutmeg
¼ teaspoon cloves

Heat oven to 325°F. Grease (not oil) bottoms only of two 9x5 or 8x4-inch pans. In large bowl, beat eggs until foamy. Stir in sugar, zucchini, oil and vanilla. Add remaining ingredients; by hand, blend well. Pour batter into prepared pans. Bake at 325°F. for 50 to 60 minutes or until toothpick inserted in center comes out clean. Cool 10 minutes; remove from pans. Cool completely.

2 loaves

NUTRITION INFORMATION PER SERVING

Serving Size: 1 slice		Percent U.S. RDA Per Serving	
Calories	174	Protein	4%
Protein	2g	Vitamin A	*
Carbohydrate	22g	Vitamin C	3%
Fat	9g	Thiamin	6%
Sodium	118mg	Riboflavin	4%
Potassium	43mg	Niacin	4%
		Calcium	*
		Iron	3%
		Phosphorus	3%

TIPS: **Young tender zucchini need not be peeled or seeded.*

***Self-rising flour is not recommended.*

HIGH ALTITUDE—Above 3500 Feet: Decrease soda to ¾ teaspoon; bake at 325°F. for 50 to 60 minutes.

Perfect with a chicken salad or a light luncheon.

LEMON CAKE BREAD

1½ cups sugar
¼ cup fresh grated lemon peel
1 cup oil
6 eggs
1⅔ cups Pillsbury's Best® All Purpose or Unbleached Flour*
2 teaspoons baking powder
¼ teaspoon salt

Heat oven to 325°F. Grease (not oil) and lightly flour two 8x4-inch loaf pans. In large bowl, blend first 3 ingredients. Beat 1 minute at medium speed. Add eggs 1 at a time, beating well after each addition. Stir in remaining ingredients *just* until dry ingredients are moistened. Pour batter into prepared pans. Bake at 325°F. for 50 to 65 minutes or until toothpick inserted in center comes out clean. Cool 10 minutes; remove from pan. Cool completely. If desired, glaze with Lemon Glaze, page *149*

2 loaves

NUTRITION INFORMATION PER SERVING

Serving Size: 1 slice		Percent U.S. RDA Per Serving	
Calories	274	Protein	6%
Protein	4g	Vitamin A	5%
Carbohydrate	29g	Vitamin C	3%
Fat	16g	Thiamin	7%
Sodium	101mg	Riboflavin	7%
Potassium	42mg	Niacin	4%
		Calcium	2%
		Iron	5%

TIP: **If using Pillsbury's Best® Self Rising Flour, omit baking powder and salt.*

HIGH ALTITUDE—Above 3500 Feet: Decrease sugar to 1¼ cups plus 1 tablespoon and baking powder to 1¼ teaspoon. Bake at 350°F. for 50 minutes.

STREUSEL SPICE COFFEE CAKE

1 cup Pillsbury's Best® All Purpose or Unbleached Flour*
1 cup firmly packed brown sugar
½ cup rolled oats
½ cup margarine or butter
1 teaspoon baking powder
½ teaspoon cinnamon
¼ teaspoon salt
¼ teaspoon soda
¼ teaspoon nutmeg
½ cup buttermilk
2 eggs
½ cup chopped nuts
½ cup flaked coconut, if desired

Heat oven to 375°F. Grease (not oil) and lightly flour 8-inch square or 9-inch round pan. In large bowl, combine first 3 ingredients. Using pastry blender, cut in margarine until particles are size of small peas. Reserve ½ cup crumb mixture; set aside. To crumb mixture in bowl, add remaining ingredients, except nuts and coconut; blend well. Pour batter into prepared pan. Sprinkle with reserved crumbs, nuts and coconut. Bake at 375°F. for 25 to 30 minutes or until toothpick inserted in center comes out clean. Serve warm or cool.

8 or 9-inch coffee cake

NUTRITION INFORMATION PER SERVING

Serving Size: 1/9 of recipe		Percent U.S. RDA Per Serving	
Calories	392	Protein	10%
Protein	6g	Vitamin A	13%
Carbohydrate	45g	Vitamin C	*
Fat	22g	Thiamin	12%
Sodium	329mg	Riboflavin	9%
Potassium	233mg	Niacin	5%
		Calcium	7%
		Iron	13%

TIP: **Self-rising flour is not recommended.*

HIGH ALTITUDE–Above 3500 Feet: Reduce sugar to ¾ cup plus 2 tablespoons and baking powder to ¾ teaspoon. Bake at 400°F. for 25 to 30 minutes.

Need something quick in the morning? Make batter the night before and just pop it in the oven for a fresh warm breakfast bread.

OVERNIGHT COFFEE CAKE

CAKE

2 cups Pillsbury's Best® All Purpose or Unbleached Flour*
1 cup sugar
½ cup firmly packed brown sugar
1 teaspoon soda
1 teaspoon baking powder
1 teaspoon cinnamon
½ teaspoon salt
1 cup buttermilk
⅔ cup shortening
2 eggs

TOPPING

½ cup firmly packed brown sugar
½ cup chopped nuts
1 teaspoon cinnamon
½ teaspoon nutmeg, if desired

Grease (not oil) and lightly flour bottom only of 13x9-inch pan. In large bowl, blend all Cake ingredients at low speed until moistened. Beat 3 minutes at medium speed. Pour batter into prepared pan. In small bowl, blend Topping ingredients; sprinkle over batter. Cover; refrigerate overnight. Heat oven to 350°F. Bake 30 to 40 minutes or until golden brown. Serve warm.

13x9-inch coffee cake

NUTRITION INFORMATION PER SERVING

Serving Size: 1/12 of recipe		Percent U.S. RDA Per Serving	
Calories	362	Protein	7%
Protein	5g	Vitamin A	2%
Carbohydrate	52g	Vitamin C	*
Fat	16g	Thiamin	11%
Sodium	253mg	Riboflavin	9%
Potassium	147mg	Niacin	6%
		Calcium	6%
		Iron	9%

TIP: **Self-rising flour is not recommended.*

HIGH ALTITUDE–Above 3500 Feet: Decrease baking powder to ½ teaspoon.

Yogurt adds moistness and flavor variety.

ONE-STEP TROPICAL COFFEE CAKE

CAKE

1½ cups Pillsbury's Best® All Purpose or Unbleached Flour*
1 cup sugar
2 teaspoons baking powder
½ teaspoon salt
½ cup oil
2 eggs
8-oz. carton pineapple, apricot or orange yogurt or 1 cup dairy sour cream

TOPPING

1 cup coconut or chopped nuts
⅓ cup sugar
1 teaspoon cinnamon

Heat oven to 350°F. Grease (not oil) 9-inch square pan or 11x7-inch pan. In large bowl, add all Cake ingredients; stir *just* until dry ingredients are moistened. Pour batter into prepared pan. In small bowl, combine Topping ingredients; sprinkle over batter. Bake at 350°F. for 35 to 45 minutes or until toothpick inserted in center comes out clean. 9-inch coffee cake

NUTRITION INFORMATION PER SERVING

Serving Size: 1/9 of recipe		Percent U.S. RDA Per Serving	
Calories	456	Protein	10%
Protein	6g	Vitamin A	4%
Carbohydrate	60g	Vitamin C	*
Fat	22g	Thiamin	13%
Sodium	250mg	Riboflavin	12%
Potassium	141mg	Niacin	7%
		Calcium	6%
		Iron	8%

TIP: **If using Pillsbury's Best® Self Rising Flour, omit baking powder and salt.*

HIGH ALTITUDE–Above 3500 Feet: Bake at 375°F. for 30 to 40 minutes.

A cookie like crust gives this cake an unusual texture. Spicy and not too sweet.

SYRIAN NUTMEG COFFEE CAKE

2 cups Pillsbury's Best® All Purpose or Unbleached Flour*
2 cups firmly packed brown sugar
½ cup shortening or margarine, softened
¾ cup chopped nuts (reserve ¼ cup for topping)
1 teaspoon soda
1 teaspoon nutmeg
1 cup dairy sour cream
1 egg

Heat oven to 350°F. In large bowl, combine first 3 ingredients; blend at low speed until crumbly. Press 2 cups crumb mixture into ungreased 9-inch square pan. To remaining crumb mixture, add ½ cup nuts, soda, nutmeg, sour cream and egg; blend well. Pour batter over crumb mixture. Sprinkle with remaining ¼ cup nuts. Bake at 350°F. for 35 to 40 minutes or until toothpick inserted in center comes out clean. Serve warm.

9-inch coffee cake

NUTRITION INFORMATION PER SERVING

Serving Size: 1/9 of recipe		Percent U.S. RDA Per Serving	
Calories	509	Protein	9%
Protein	6g	Vitamin A	6%
Carbohydrate	71g	Vitamin C	*
Fat	23g	Thiamin	15%
Sodium	155mg	Riboflavin	11%
Potassium	248mg	Niacin	8%
		Calcium	9%
		Iron	16%

TIP: **Self-rising flour is not recommended.*

HIGH ALTITUDE–Above 3500 Feet: Add 2 tablespoons flour and 1 teaspoon baking powder. Reduce sugar to 1½ cups and soda to ½ teaspoon. Bake at 375°F. for 35 to 40 minutes.

A holiday favorite that makes a delicious breakfast treat or midnight dessert.

SCANDINAVIAN KRINGLER

CRUST

1 cup Pillsbury's Best® All Purpose or Unbleached Flour*
½ cup margarine or butter, chilled
2 tablespoons ice water

PUFF TOPPING

1 cup water
½ cup margarine or butter
1 cup Pillsbury's Best® All Purpose or Unbleached Flour*
3 eggs
½ teaspoon almond extract

FROSTING

1 cup powdered sugar
1 tablespoon margarine or butter, softened
½ teaspoon almond extract
2 to 3 tablespoons milk or cream
Sliced almonds or chopped nuts, if desired

Heat oven to 350°F. In small bowl, add flour and margarine. Using a pastry blender, cut margarine into flour until particles are size of small peas. Sprinkle with water, 1 tablespoon at a time. Stir with fork just until soft dough forms. Divide dough in half. On ungreased cookie sheet, press each half into 12x3-inch strip.

In medium saucepan, heat water and ½ cup margarine to boiling. Remove from heat; immediately stir in 1 cup flour until smooth. Add eggs, 1 at a time, beating until smooth after each addition. Stir in ½ teaspoon almond extract. Spoon ½ of batter over each crust, spreading to ¾ inch from edges. Bake at 350°F. for 50 to 60 minutes or until golden brown and puffy. Immediately remove from pan; cool. Topping will shrink and fall. In small bowl, blend all Frosting ingredients except nuts, until smooth. Spread on cooled kringler. Sprinkle with nuts. Cut each into 8 to 10 slices. 16 to 20 slices

NUTRITION INFORMATION PER SERVING

Serving Size: 1/16 of recipe		Percent U.S. RDA Per Serving	
Calories	230	Protein	6%
Protein	4g	Vitamin A	12%
Carbohydrate	20g	Vitamin C	*
Fat	15g	Thiamin	8%
Sodium	163mg	Riboflavin	7%
Potassium	58mg	Niacin	5%
		Calcium	2%
		Iron	5%

TIP: **Self-rising flour is not recommended.*

HIGH ALTITUDE—Above 3500 Feet: Bake at 375°F. for 50 to 60 minutes.

SCANDINAVIAN KRINGLER

CAKE DOUGHNUTS

4½ cups Pillsbury's Best® All Purpose or Unbleached Flour*
1 cup sugar
3 teaspoons baking powder
1 teaspoon soda
1 teaspoon salt
½ teaspoon nutmeg
1 cup buttermilk
¼ cup margarine or butter, melted or ¼ cup oil
1 teaspoon vanilla
2 eggs, slightly beaten

In large bowl, combine first 6 ingredients. Stir in remaining ingredients *just* until dry ingredients are moistened. If desired, chill dough for easier handling. In electric skillet or large saucepan, heat 2 to 3 inches oil to 375°F. On well-floured surface, toss dough lightly until no longer sticky. Roll half the dough at a time to a ⅜-inch thickness. Cut with floured doughnut cutter. With pancake turner, slip doughnuts into hot oil (375°F.). Fry doughnuts 1 to 1½ minutes on each side or until deep golden brown. Drain on paper towel. Shake a few doughnuts at a time in a bag with powdered, granulated or cinnamon-sugar, or dip each in favorite glaze.

30 doughnuts

NUTRITION INFORMATION PER SERVING

Serving Size: 1 doughnut		Percent U.S. RDA Per Serving	
Calories	117	Protein	4%
Protein	3g	Vitamin A	2%
Carbohydrate	21g	Vitamin C	*
Fat	2g	Thiamin	8%
Sodium	175mg	Riboflavin	6%
Potassium	35mg	Niacin	5%
		Calcium	2%
		Iron	4%
		Phosphorus	4%

TIPS: *For CHOCOLATE DOUGHNUTS, omit nutmeg, increase sugar to 1¼ cups and add 1 oz. (1 square) melted unsweetened chocolate or 1 envelope premelted chocolate baking flavor with eggs. Dip in Chocolate Glaze, page 149, and roll in chopped nuts.*

For ORANGE DOUGHNUTS, omit nutmeg, add 2 tablespoons grated orange peel. Decrease buttermilk to ½ cup; add ½ cup orange juice. Dip in Orange Glaze, page 149, and roll in flaked coconut.

For APPLESAUCE DOUGHNUTS, add ½ teaspoon cinnamon with nutmeg. Decrease buttermilk to ⅔ cup; add ½ cup applesauce.

**Self-rising flour is not recommended.*

No rolling or cutting—these are super quick and easy.

CINNAMON-SUGARED DOUGHNUT DROPS

1½ cups Pillsbury's Best® All Purpose or Unbleached Flour*
⅓ cup sugar
2 teaspoons baking powder
½ teaspoon salt
¼ teaspoon cinnamon
¼ teaspoon nutmeg
½ cup milk
2 tablespoons oil
½ teaspoon vanilla
1 egg
½ cup sugar
1 teaspoon cinnamon

In large saucepan, heat 2 to 3 inches oil to 375°F. In large bowl, combine first 6 ingredients. Stir in milk, oil, vanilla and egg with a fork *just* until dry ingredients are moistened. Drop by teaspoonfuls into hot oil (375°F.), 5 to 6 at a time. Fry doughnut drops 1 to 1½ minutes on each side until deep golden brown. Drain on paper towel. Mix ½ cup sugar and 1 teaspoon cinnamon; roll warm doughnut balls in sugar-cinnamon mixture.

30 to 36 doughnut balls

NUTRITION INFORMATION PER SERVING

Serving Size: 2 doughnut balls		Percent U.S. RDA Per Serving	
Calories	117	Protein	3%
Protein	2g	Vitamin A	*
Carbohydrate	21g	Vitamin C	*
Fat	3g	Thiamin	6%
Sodium	125mg	Riboflavin	4%
Potassium	29mg	Niacin	3%
		Calcium	2%
		Iron	3%

TIPS: *PUMPKIN DOUGHNUT DROPS, decrease milk to ¼ cup and add ½ cup canned pumpkin and ¼ teaspoon ginger.*

Up to ¾ cup Pillsbury's Best® Whole Wheat Flour may be substituted.

**Self-rising flour is not recommended.*

HIGH ALTITUDE—Above 3500 Feet: Decrease baking powder to 1½ teaspoons; increase milk to ½ cup plus 2 tablespoons. Reduce oil temperature to 360°F.

YEAST DOUGHNUTS

3 to 3½ cups Pillsbury's Best® All Purpose or Unbleached Flour*
¼ cup sugar
1 teaspoon salt
½ teaspoon nutmeg, cinnamon or vanilla
1 pkg. active dry yeast
1 cup milk
¼ cup margarine or butter
1 egg

In large bowl, combine 1 cup flour, sugar, salt, nutmeg and yeast. In small saucepan, heat milk and margarine until very warm (120° to 130°F.). Add warm liquid and egg to flour mixture. Blend at low speed until moistened; beat 3 minutes at medium speed. Stir in remaining flour to form a stiff dough. Cover; let rise in warm place until light and doubled in size, 60 to 75 minutes.

On floured surface, knead dough a few times until no longer sticky. Roll dough to ½-inch thickness. Cut with floured doughnut cutter. Cover; let rise on cookie sheet in warm place until light and doubled in size, 30 to 45 minutes. In electric skillet or large saucepan, heat 2 to 3 inches oil to 375°F. With pancake turner, slip doughnuts into hot oil. Fry doughnuts about 1 minute on each side or until deep golden brown. Drain on paper towel. While warm, coat with sugar or dip in favorite glaze. 24 doughnuts

NUTRITION INFORMATION PER SERVING

Serving Size: 1 doughnut		Percent U.S. RDA Per Serving	
Calories	93	Protein	4%
Protein	2g	Vitamin A	2%
Carbohydrate	15g	Vitamin C	*
Fat	3g	Thiamin	7%
Sodium	121mg	Riboflavin	6%
Potassium	39mg	Niacin	5%
		Calcium	*
		Iron	3%

TIPS: *For POTATO YEAST DOUGHNUTS, add ¾ cup mashed white or sweet potato or canned pumpkin with milk. (The 2-serving recipe of Hungry Jack® Mashed Potato Flakes, prepared as directed on package, makes 1 cup potatoes.)*

For LONG JOHNS, roll dough to ½-inch thick square. Cut into oblong pieces, about 1½x4 inches. Let rise and fry as directed. Glaze with Vanilla, Chocolate or Maple Glaze, page 149.

For BISMARKS, roll dough ¼-inch thick; cut rounds with 2 to 3-inch cutter. Place ½ teaspoon favorite jam, jelly or applesauce in center of half the rounds. Moisten edge of these rounds with slightly beaten egg white. Top with remaining rounds; seal well. Let rise and fry as for doughnuts.

**Self-rising flour is not recommended.*

HIGH ALTITUDE—Above 3500 Feet: Increase oil temperature to 400°F.

BASIC PANCAKES

2 eggs
2 cups buttermilk
¼ cup oil
1¾ cups Pillsbury's Best® All Purpose or Unbleached Flour*
2 tablespoons sugar
2 teaspoons baking powder
1 teaspoon soda
1 teaspoon salt

Heat griddle to medium-high heat (400°F.). In large bowl, beat eggs; stir in buttermilk and oil. Add remaining ingredients; beat (or stir) *just* until large lumps disappear. For thicker pancakes, thicken with additional flour; for thinner pancakes, thin with additional milk. Lightly grease heated griddle. A few drops of water sprinkled on griddle sizzle and bounce when heat is just right. Pour batter, about ¼ cup at a time, onto hot griddle. Bake until bubbles form and edges start to dry; turn and bake other side.

Sixteen 4-inch pancakes

NUTRITION INFORMATION PER SERVING

Serving Size: 4 pancakes		Percent U.S. RDA Per Serving	
Calories	433	Protein	21%
Protein	14g	Vitamin A	6%
Carbohydrate	55g	Vitamin C	2%
Fat	17g	Thiamin	29%
Sodium	1165mg	Riboflavin	31%
Potassium	261mg	Niacin	15%
		Calcium	20%
		Iron	12%

TIPS: *To halve recipe, use half the ingredient amounts.*

If using sweet milk, decrease milk to 1¾ cups, increase baking powder to 4 teaspoons and omit soda.

Part or all Pillsbury's Best® Whole Wheat Flour may be substituted.

For APPLE PANCAKES, add ½ cup peeled shredded apple and ½ teaspoon cinnamon to batter.

For BLUEBERRY PANCAKES, add 1 cup drained fresh or frozen blueberries (thawed and drained) to batter.

For CHEESE PANCAKES, add ½ cup shredded cheese to batter.

For NUT PANCAKES, add ½ cup chopped nuts to batter.

**If using Pillsbury's Best® Self Rising Flour, omit baking powder; decrease soda and salt to ½ teaspoon.*

WHOLE WHEAT PANCAKES

2 cups Pillsbury's Best® Whole Wheat Flour
2 tablespoons sugar
3 teaspoons baking powder
1 teaspoon salt
½ teaspoon soda
2 cups milk
¼ cup oil
2 eggs

Heat griddle to medium-high heat (400°F.). In large bowl, combine first 5 ingredients. Add remaining ingredients; beat (or stir) *just* until large lumps disappear. Lightly grease heated griddle. A few drops of water sprinkled on griddle sizzle and bounce when heat is just right. Pour batter, about ¼ cup at a time, onto hot griddle. Bake until bubbles form and edges start to dry; turn and bake other side.

Sixteen 4-inch pancakes

NUTRITION INFORMATION PER SERVING

Serving Size: 4 pancakes		Percent U.S. RDA Per Serving	
Calories	470	Protein	24%
Protein	16g	Vitamin A	10%
Carbohydrate	55g	Vitamin C	2%
Fat	22g	Thiamin	26%
Sodium	1013mg	Riboflavin	21%
Potassium	437mg	Niacin	14%
		Calcium	23%
		Iron	15%

These have a slightly "sour dough" flavor.

MAKE AHEAD PANCAKE AND WAFFLE BATTER

2¼ cups Pillsbury's Best® All Purpose or Unbleached Flour*
2 tablespoons sugar
1 teaspoon salt
1 pkg. active dry yeast
2 cups milk
¼ cup margarine, butter or oil
3 eggs

In large bowl, combine first 4 ingredients. In small saucepan, heat milk and margarine until very warm (120° to 130°F.). Add to flour mixture along with eggs. Beat at medium speed until smooth. Cover and refrigerate up to 4 days, adding 2 additional tablespoons sugar after second day. Bake as directed in Basic Pancakes, page 99 or Basic Waffles, page *100*.

Twenty 4-inch pancakes or 4 waffles

MAKE AHEAD PANCAKE NUTRITION INFORMATION PER SERVING

Serving Size: 4 pancakes		Percent U.S. RDA Per Serving	
Calories	426	Protein	22%
Protein	14g	Vitamin A	18%
Carbohydrate	53g	Vitamin C	*
Fat	17g	Thiamin	31%
Sodium	629mg	Riboflavin	33%
Potassium	267mg	Niacin	18%
		Calcium	15%
		Iron	15%

MAKE AHEAD WAFFLE NUTRITION INFORMATION PER SERVING

Serving Size: 1 waffle		Percent U.S. RDA Per Serving	
Calories	532	Protein	27%
Protein	18g	Vitamin A	23%
Carbohydrate	67g	Vitamin C	2%
Fat	21g	Thiamin	38%
Sodium	787mg	Riboflavin	42%
Potassium	334mg	Niacin	23%
		Calcium	18%
		Iron	18%

TIPS: *Store batter in large container. Yeast "works" as it is stored and volume of batter increases.*

If desired, use up to ½ Pillsbury's Best® Whole Wheat Flour.

**If using Pillsbury's Best® Self Rising Flour, omit salt.*

WAFFLES

2 eggs, separated
2 cups buttermilk
2 cups Pillsbury's Best® All Purpose or Unbleached Flour*
2 teaspoons baking powder
1 teaspoon soda
1 teaspoon salt
½ cup margarine or butter, melted or oil

Heat waffle iron. Place egg yolks in large bowl; whites in small bowl. To yolks add buttermilk; beat well. Add flour, baking powder, soda and salt; beat until smooth. Stir in melted margarine. Beat egg whites until soft peaks form; fold into batter. Bake in hot waffle iron until steaming stops and waffle is golden brown.

About 4 waffles

NUTRITION INFORMATION PER SERVING

Serving Size: 1 waffle		Percent U.S. RDA Per Serving	
Calories	524	Protein	23%
Protein	15g	Vitamin A	25%
Carbohydrate	55g	Vitamin C	2%
Fat	27g	Thiamin	32%
Sodium	1447mg	Riboflavin	33%
Potassium	275mg	Niacin	17%
		Calcium	21%
		Iron	14%

TIPS: *Refrigerate or freeze leftover waffles. Reheat or thaw in toaster.*

For APPLE WAFFLES, add 1 peeled shredded apple and ½ teaspoon cinnamon.

For BANANA WAFFLES, brush waffle iron with oil before heating it. Place banana slices on batter before closing lid of waffle iron.

For BLUEBERRY WAFFLES, add 1 cup fresh or frozen drained blueberries to batter.

Up to ½ Pillsbury's Best® Whole Wheat Flour may be substituted.

**If using Pillsbury's Best® Self Rising Flour, omit baking powder and decrease soda to ½ teaspoon.*

HIGH ALTITUDE–Above 3500 Feet: Decrease baking powder to 1 teaspoon.

BASIC CRÊPES

4 eggs
1⅓ cups milk
2 tablespoons oil, margarine or butter, melted
1 cup Pillsbury's Best® All Purpose or Unbleached Flour*
½ teaspoon salt, if desired

In medium bowl, beat eggs slightly. Add remaining ingredients and beat until smooth. Batter may be covered and refrigerated up to 2 hours or cooked immediately. Heat crêpe pan or 7 or 8-inch skillet over medium-high heat (375°F.). A few drops of water sprinkled on the pan sizzle and bounce when heat is just right. Grease pan lightly. Pour about 3 tablespoons batter into pan, tilting pan to spread evenly. When crêpe is light brown and set, turn to brown other side. Remove from pan. Repeat with remaining batter to make about 14 crêpes; stack cooked crêpes. Fill crêpes with desired filling or cool, wrap and refrigerate up to 2 days.

About 14 crêpes

NUTRITION INFORMATION PER SERVING

Serving Size: 1 crêpe		Percent U.S. RDA Per Serving	
Calories	90	Protein	6%
Protein	4g	Vitamin A	4%
Carbohydrate	8g	Vitamin C	*
Fat	5g	Thiamin	5%
Sodium	108mg	Riboflavin	7%
Potassium	62mg	Niacin	3%
		Calcium	4%
		Iron	3%

TIPS: *For DESSERT CRÊPES, add 2 tablespoons sugar. Fill crêpes with desired fillings.*

To freeze, layer crêpes with 2 sheets of waxed paper; wrap and store up to 3 months.

**Self-rising flour is not recommended.*

FRENCH TOAST

2 eggs, slightly beaten
1 tablespoon sugar
½ teaspoon salt
¼ teaspoon cinnamon, if desired
½ cup milk
2 tablespoons margarine or butter
4 to 6 slices bread or 6 to 8 slices French bread, cut diagonally about 1-inch thick

Heat griddle to medium heat (340°F.). In shallow bowl or pie pan, combine all ingredients except margarine and bread; mix well. Melt margarine on griddle. Dip bread in egg mixture, turning to coat both sides. Cook on griddle over medium heat, about 4 minutes on each side or until golden brown. If desired, sprinkle with powdered sugar.

4 to 6 slices toast

NUTRITION INFORMATION PER SERVING

Serving Size: ¼ of recipe		Percent U.S. RDA Per Serving	
Calories	191	Protein	10%
Protein	7g	Vitamin A	12
Carbohydrate	16g	Vitamin C	*
Fat	11g	Thiamin	7%
Sodium	504mg	Riboflavin	11%
Potassium	109mg	Niacin	3%
		Calcium	8%
		Iron	7%

TIPS: *For OVEN FRENCH TOAST, melt margarine in jelly roll or broiler pan. Place egg-coated slices in margarine and broil 3 to 4 inches from heat about 3 minutes or until golden brown. Turn and broil other side.*

To MAKE AHEAD, dip bread in egg mixture, place in 13x9-inch glass baking dish. Pour any remaining egg mixture over bread. Cover; refrigerate 8 to 12 hours. Use a pancake turner to remove bread slices to hot griddle; continue as directed.

To double or triple recipe, double or triple the ingredient amounts.

BREAD BUTTERS

The following butters may be spread over any type of cut bread such as French, pumpernickel or rye slices, sliced hamburger or hot dog buns, toasted English muffins, bagels or leftover sliced dinner rolls.

Combine ½ cup soft margarine or butter for the following seasoned butters.

GARLIC BUTTER: 1 teaspoon garlic salt or 1 garlic clove, minced.

ONION BUTTER: 2 tablespoons instant minced onion, 1 teaspoon onion salt or 2 tablespoons dry onion soup mix.

CHEESE BUTTER: 1 cup (4 oz.) shredded cheese and ½ teaspoon each garlic salt, prepared mustard and Worcestershire sauce.

SAVORY BUTTER: 1½ tablespoons dry salad dressing mix. (Italian, blue cheese, garlic cheese, etc.)

HERB BUTTER: ½ teaspoon thyme leaves.

PARMESAN BUTTER: ½ cup grated Parmesan cheese and 1 tablespoon sesame or poppy seed.

WHIPPED BUTTER

In small bowl, cream ½ cup margarine or butter until soft. Slowly beat in 2 tablespoons milk or cream. Beat on high speed until light and fluffy. 1 cup

NUTRITION INFORMATION PER SERVING

Serving Size: 1 tablespoon		Percent U.S. RDA Per Serving	
Calories	52	Protein	*
Protein	<1g	Vitamin A	5%
Carbohydrate	<1g	Vitamin C	*
Fat	6g	Thiamin	*
Sodium	71mg	Riboflavin	*
Potassium	4mg	Niacin	*
		Calcium	*
		Iron	0%

Variations: *For HONEY BUTTER, omit milk; gradually add ¼ cup honey; beat until light.*

NUTRITION INFORMATION PER SERVING

Serving Size: 1 tablespoon		Percent U.S. RDA Per Serving	
Calories	67	Protein	*
Protein	<1g	Vitamin A	5%
Carbohydrate	4g	Vitamin C	*
Fat	6g	Thiamin	*
Sodium	70mg	Riboflavin	*
Potassium	4mg	Niacin	*
		Calcium	*
		Iron	*

For MARMALADE BUTTER, omit milk; gradually add ¼ cup marmalade; beat until light.

For MAPLE BUTTER, substitute maple-flavored syrup for milk.

For ORANGE BUTTER, substitute orange juice for milk and add 1 tablespoon grated orange peel.

For PEANUT-HONEY BUTTER, decrease margarine to ¼ cup and add ¼ cup peanut butter. Omit milk; beat in ¼ cup honey.

NUTRITION INFORMATION PER SERVING

Serving Size: 1 tablespoon		Percent U.S. RDA Per Serving	
Calories	65	Protein	*
Protein	1g	Vitamin A	2%
Carbohydrate	5g	Vitamin C	*
Fat	5g	Thiamin	*
Sodium	60mg	Riboflavin	*
Potassium	29mg	Niacin	3%
		Calcium	*
		Iron	*

BAKE-OFF CLASSICS

BAKE-OFF CLASSICS

In 1949 the first BAKE-OFF® contest was held. Needless to say it was a resounding success and today, over 28 years later it is the granddaddy of cooking contests.

All over America these BAKE-OFF® recipes have been shared by millions. They have become "tried and true", classics to be treasured.

And every day Pillsbury receives requests for these recipes...a favorite one has been lost...my daughter borrowed the book...the neighbor next door served it with coffee...the reasons are many. So we at Pillsbury felt the time has come to gather into a collection these most often requested recipes, those which have withstood the test of time, remaining popular year after year.

Inside this chapter are 21 of these BAKE-OFF® classics. Each recipe has been retested to ensure perfect results with today's products, equipment and cooking methods. Every attempt was made to remain as close to the original recipe as possible but keeping in mind today's cooking needs.

We hope you will be pleased with this classic collection – that you will find many old favorites and delight in some new ones. Each recipe is a winner – yesterday and today.

SPICY APPLE TWISTS

4 medium apples
1½ cups Pillsbury's Best® All Purpose or Unbleached Flour*
½ teaspoon salt
½ cup shortening
4 to 5 tablespoons cold water
2 tablespoons margarine or butter, softened

TOPPING
⅓ cup margarine or butter, melted
½ cup sugar
1 to 1½ teaspoons cinnamon
¾ cup water

Heat oven to 425°F. Peel, core and cut each apple into 4 wedges. In medium bowl, combine flour and salt. Using pastry blender or mixer at low speed, cut in shortening until particles are size of small peas. Sprinkle flour mixture with water, one tablespoon at a time, while tossing and mixing lightly with a fork. Add water until dough is just moist enough to hold together.

Form dough into ball; place on floured surface. Flatten ball slightly; smooth edges. Roll dough to a 12-inch square. Spread with 2 tablespoons margarine. Fold both sides to center. Roll to 16x10-inch rectangle. Cut into sixteen 10-inch strips. Wrap one strip around each apple wedge. Arrange in ungreased 13x9-inch pan, sides not touching. Brush each twist, using all of melted margarine. Combine sugar and cinnamon; sprinkle over twists. Pour water into pan. Bake at 425°F. for 30 to 35 minutes or until golden brown. Serve warm or cool, plain or with whipped cream. 16 twists

NUTRITION INFORMATION PER SERVING

Serving Size: 1 twist		Percent U.S. RDA Per Serving	
Calories	186	Protein	2%
Protein	1g	Vitamin A	5%
Carbohydrate	20g	Vitamin C	*
Fat	12g	Thiamin	6%
Sodium	133mg	Riboflavin	3%
Potassium	48mg	Niacin	3%
		Calcium	*
		Iron	2%

TIP: **If using Pillsbury's Best® Self Rising Flour, omit salt.*

A creamy peach filling that oozes with good taste when you bite into these warm little pastries. When you start with biscuit dough, preparation time is quick.

CREAMY PEACH BISCUIT PUFFS

⅓ cup sugar
¼ to ½ teaspoon pumpkin pie spice
8-oz. pkg. cream cheese, softened
⅓ cup canned peaches, well-drained and chopped (reserve syrup)
10-oz. can Hungry Jack® Refrigerated Big Flaky Biscuits
1 to 2 tablespoons peach syrup

GLAZE
¾ cup powdered sugar
1 to 2 tablespoons peach syrup

Heat oven to 375°F. In medium bowl, combine sugar and spice; reserve 1 tablespoon. Add cream cheese to remaining sugar mixture; blend well. Stir in peaches.

Separate biscuit dough into 10 biscuits; press or roll each between waxed paper to a 5-inch circle. Spoon about 2 tablespoons peach mixture onto center of each biscuit. Pull edges of dough to top center; twist firmly and pinch to seal. Place on ungreased cookie sheet. Brush top of each with peach syrup; sprinkle with reserved sugar mixture.

Bake at 375°F. for 10 to 15 minutes or until tops are golden brown. Combine Glaze ingredients until smooth; drizzle over warm rolls. Remove from cookie sheet while warm. Serve warm or cool.

10 pastries

NUTRITION INFORMATION PER SERVING

Serving Size: 1 pastry		Percent U.S. RDA Per Serving	
Calories	232	Protein	6%
Protein	4g	Vitamin A	8%
Carbohydrate	32g	Vitamin C	*
Fat	10g	Thiamin	7%
Sodium	349mg	Riboflavin	7%
Potassium	55mg	Niacin	5%
		Calcium	*
		Iron	3%

A departure from traditional banana bread. Whole wheat flour adds something extra special to the flavor of this moist bread.

BANANA-WHEAT QUICK BREAD

1¼ cups Pillsbury's Best® All Purpose or Unbleached Flour*
½ cup Pillsbury's Best® Whole Wheat Flour
1 cup sugar
1 teaspoon soda
1 teaspoon salt
1½ cups (3 medium) mashed bananas
¼ cup margarine or butter, softened
2 tablespoons orange juice
¼ teaspoon lemon juice, if desired
1 egg
¼ to ½ cup raisins

Heat oven to 325°F. Grease (not oil) and flour bottom only of 9x5 or 8x4-inch loaf pan. In large bowl, blend all ingredients. Beat 3 minutes at medium speed. Pour batter into prepared pan. Bake at 325°F. for 60 to 70 minutes or until toothpick inserted in center comes out clean. Immediately remove from pan; cool.

1 loaf

NUTRITION INFORMATION PER SERVING

Serving Size: 1 slice		Percent U.S. RDA Per Serving	
Calories	155	Protein	4%
Protein	2g	Vitamin A	4%
Carbohydrate	30g	Vitamin C	5%
Fat	4g	Thiamin	7%
Sodium	242mg	Riboflavin	4%
Potassium	132mg	Niacin	4%
		Calcium	*
		Iron	4%

TIPS: *Make 4 miniature loaves using 5x2½x1½-inch pans or soup cans. Bake 35 to 40 minutes.*

**If using Pillsbury's Best® Self Rising Flour, omit salt.*

HIGH ALTITUDE–Above 3500 Feet: Bake at 350°F. for 55 to 65 minutes.

Even though this is truly a Bake-Off® classic, its popularity for everyday baking made us put it in this chapter.

DILLY CASSEROLE BREAD

1 cup creamed cottage cheese
¼ cup water
1 tablespoon margarine or butter
2½ cups Pillsbury's Best® All Purpose or Unbleached Flour*
2 tablespoons sugar
2 to 3 teaspoons instant minced onion
2 teaspoons dill seed
1¼ teaspoons salt
¼ teaspoon soda
1 pkg. active dry yeast
1 egg
Margarine or butter, softened
Coarse salt, if desired

In small saucepan, heat first 3 ingredients until very warm (120° to 130°F.). In large bowl, blend warm liquid, 1 cup flour, sugar, onion, dill seed, salt, soda, yeast and egg at low speed until moistened. Beat 3 minutes at medium speed. By hand, stir in remaining flour to form a stiff batter. Cover; let rise in warm place until light and doubled in size, 45 to 65 minutes.

Generously grease (not oil) 1½ or 2-quart casserole. Stir down dough. Place in prepared casserole. Cover; let rise in warm place until light and doubled in size, 30 to 45 minutes. Heat oven to 350°F. Bake 35 to 40 minutes or until golden brown and loaf sounds hollow when lightly tapped. Immediately remove from casserole; cool. Brush warm loaf with melted margarine or butter and sprinkle with coarse salt. 1 round loaf

NUTRITION INFORMATION PER SERVING

Serving Size: 1 slice		Percent U.S. RDA Per Serving	
Calories	112	Protein	7%
Protein	5g	Vitamin A	2%
Carbohydrate	17g	Vitamin C	*
Fat	3g	Thiamin	10%
Sodium	305mg	Riboflavin	9%
Potassium	49mg	Niacin	6%
		Calcium	2%
		Iron	4%

TIP: **If using Pillsbury's Best® Self Rising Flour, omit salt and soda.*

HIGH ALTITUDE—Above 3500 feet: Bake at 375°F. for 35 to 40 minutes.

RING-A-LINGS

Well worth the time it takes to make these lovely yeast rolls…top winner in the 7th BAKE-OFF® contest. They'll draw a crowd in your home just like they do in our test kitchens.

RING-A-LINGS

⅓ cup margarine or butter
1 cup milk
4 to 4½ cups Pillsbury's Best® All Purpose or Unbleached Flour*
⅓ cup sugar
2 teaspoons salt
2 teaspoons grated orange peel
2 pkg. active dry yeast
2 eggs

NUT FILLING

1 cup powdered sugar
⅓ cup margarine or butter, softened
1 cup filberts or other nuts, ground

GLAZE

3 tablespoons sugar
¼ cup orange juice

In small saucepan, heat margarine and milk until very warm (120° to 130°F.). In large bowl, combine 2 cups flour, sugar, salt, orange peel and yeast. Add warm liquid and eggs. Beat 3 minutes at medium speed until smooth. By hand, stir in remaining 2 to 2½ cups flour to form a stiff dough. Mix thoroughly. Cover; let rise in warm place until light, 30 to 45 minutes. Grease 2 cookie sheets.

In small bowl, blend powdered sugar and ⅓ cup margarine until smooth. Stir in ground nuts; set aside. Combine Glaze ingredients; set aside.

On floured surface, roll or press dough to 22x12-inch rectangle. Spread Filling over half of dough on long side. Fold dough over Filling. Cut into 1-inch strips; twist each strip 4 to 5 times. Holding one end of each strip down on prepared cookie sheet, curl strip around center; tuck end under. Cover; let rise in warm place until light and doubled in size 30 to 45 minutes. Heat oven to 375°F. Bake 9 to 12 minutes or until very lightly browned. Brush tops of rolls with Glaze. Bake 3 to 5 minutes longer or until golden brown. Immediately remove from cookie sheets.

18 to 24 rolls

NUTRITION INFORMATION PER SERVING

Serving Size: 1/18 of recipe		Percent U.S. RDA Per Serving	
Calories	272	Protein	8%
Protein	5g	Vitamin A	7%
Carbohydrate	36g	Vitamin C	2%
Fat	12g	Thiamin	16%
Sodium	335mg	Riboflavin	12%
Potassium	124mg	Niacin	9%
		Calcium	4%
		Iron	7%

TIPS: *A blender works well to grind nuts if grinder is unavailable.*

**If using Pillsbury's Best® Self Rising Flour, omit salt.*

Snacks became an important part of the BAKE-OFF® contest in the 70's and this recipe has turned into one of the favorites because of its ease and good taste.

CRESCENTS 'N SAUSAGE SNACKS ITALIANO

8-oz. can Pillsbury Refrigerated Quick Crescent Dinner Rolls
2 tablespoons margarine or butter, melted
¼ cup grated Parmesan cheese
1 to 2 teaspoons oregano leaves
8 brown and serve sausage links

Heat oven to 375°F. Separate crescent dough into 4 rectangles; press perforations to seal. Brush each with margarine. Combine cheese and oregano; sprinkle over dough. Cut each rectangle crosswise to form 2 squares. Place a sausage link on each square; roll up. Cut each roll into 3 or 4 pieces; secure each with toothpick. Place cut-side-down on ungreased cookie sheet. Bake at 375°F. for 12 to 15 minutes or until golden brown. 24 snacks

NUTRITION INFORMATION PER SERVING

Serving Size: 1 snack		Percent U.S. RDA Per Serving	
Calories	65	Protein	3%
Protein	2g	Vitamin A	*
Carbohydrate	4g	Vitamin C	0%
Fat	5g	Thiamin	4%
Sodium	172mg	Riboflavin	2%
Potassium	21mg	Niacin	*
		Calcium	*
		Iron	*

TIP: *To MAKE AHEAD, prepare, cover and refrigerate up to 2 hours; bake as directed.*

MAGIC MARSHMALLOW CRESCENT PUFFS

ROLLS
¼ cup sugar
1 teaspoon cinnamon
2 cans (8 oz. each) Pillsbury Refrigerated Quick Crescent Dinner Rolls
16 marshmallows
¼ cup margarine or butter, melted

GLAZE
½ cup powdered sugar
½ teaspoon vanilla
2 to 3 teaspoons milk
¼ cup chopped nuts, if desired

Heat oven to 375°F. In small bowl, combine sugar and cinnamon. Separate crescent dough into 16 triangles. Dip a marshmallow in melted margarine; roll in sugar-cinnamon mixture. Wrap a triangle around marshmallow, completely covering marshmallow and squeezing edges of dough tightly to seal. Dip in melted margarine and place margarine-side-down in deep muffin cups. Repeat with remaining marshmallows. (Place pans on foil or cookie sheet during baking to guard against spillage.) Bake at 375°F. for 10 to 15 minutes or until golden brown. Immediately remove from pans. In small bowl, blend first 3 Glaze ingredients until smooth; drizzle over warm rolls. Sprinkle with nuts. Serve warm. 16 rolls

NUTRITION INFORMATION PER SERVING

Serving Size: 1 roll		Percent U.S. RDA Per Serving	
Calories	178	Protein	3%
Protein	2g	Vitamin A	2%
Carbohydrate	25g	Vitamin C	*
Fat	8g	Thiamin	6%
Sodium	371mg	Riboflavin	3%
Potassium	35mg	Niacin	4%
		Calcium	*
		Iron	4%

This recipe is an easy way to prepare a quiche. It's no-fail with its crescent dough crust and cheesy topping. Serve with a salad and a light dessert for an elegant yet easy meal.

CHEESE BACON CRESCENT SQUARES

8-oz. can Pillsbury Refrigerated Quick Crescent Dinner Rolls
¾ cup (3 oz.) shredded Swiss cheese
¾ cup (3 oz.) shredded Mozzarella or Monterey Jack cheese
1 egg, beaten
1 tablespoon instant minced onion or ¼ cup chopped onion
¾ cup milk
¼ to ½ cup sliced, stuffed green olives, if desired
4-oz. can (½ cup) mushroom stems and pieces, drained
6 slices bacon, fried, drained and crumbled
1 tablespoon minced parsley, if desired

Heat oven to 375°F. Separate crescent dough into 2 rectangles. Place in ungreased 13x9-inch pan; press over bottom and ½ inch up sides to form crust, sealing perforations. Sprinkle cheeses over dough. Combine egg, onion, milk, olives and mushrooms; pour over cheeses. Sprinkle with bacon and parsley. Bake at 375°F. for 22 to 28 minutes or until crust is deep golden brown and filling is set. Cool 5 minutes; cut into squares. 4 to 6 servings

NUTRITION INFORMATION PER SERVING

Serving Size: 1/4 of recipe		Percent U.S. RDA Per Serving	
Calories	590	Protein	36%
Protein	24g	Vitamin A	15%
Carbohydrate	31g	Vitamin C	2%
Fat	41g	Thiamin	23%
Sodium	1404mg	Riboflavin	36%
Potassium	253mg	Niacin	16%
		Calcium	50%
		Iron	16%

TIP: *To MAKE AHEAD, prepare, cover and refrigerate up to 2 hours; bake as directed.*

CHEESE BACON CRESCENT SQUARES

It takes only 4 ingredients to make the flavorful filling for these biscuit cups and they'll be poppin' from your oven in just minutes.

POPPIN' FRESH BARBECUPS

¾ lb. ground beef
½ cup barbecue sauce
1 tablespoon instant minced onion or ¼ cup chopped onion
2 tablespoons firmly packed brown sugar
10-oz. can Hungry Jack® Refrigerated Big Flaky Biscuits
¾ cup (3 oz.) shredded Cheddar or American cheese

Heat oven to 400°F. Grease 10 muffin cups. Brown ground beef; drain. Add barbecue sauce, onion and brown sugar. Separate biscuit dough into 10 biscuits. Place each biscuit in prepared muffin cup, pressing dough to cover bottom and sides. Spoon meat mixture into each cup. Sprinkle each with cheese. Bake at 400°F. for 10 to 12 minutes or until golden brown. Loosen with spatula; remove from pans. Serve immediately.

10 barbecups

NUTRITION INFORMATION PER SERVING

Serving Size: 1 barbecup		Percent U.S. RDA Per Serving	
Calories	202	Protein	16%
Protein	10g	Vitamin A	3%
Carbohydrate	17g	Vitamin C	*
Fat	10g	Thiamin	9%
Sodium	465mg	Riboflavin	9%
Potassium	172mg	Niacin	11%
		Calcium	8%
		Iron	9%

TIP: *To MAKE AHEAD, prepare, cover and refrigerate up to 2 hours; bake as directed.*

It tastes like lasagna; it tastes like pizza! A young man came up with this delicious recipe idea that you'll soon be adding to your weekly menu plans because it's so good.

CHEESY LASAGNA PIZZA

1 lb. ground beef
¼ cup water
8-oz. can (1 cup) tomato sauce
1 envelope spaghetti sauce mix (reserve 1 tablespoon for crust)
1 pkg. Pillsbury Hot Roll Mix
1 cup very warm water (105° to 115°F.)
12-oz. carton (1½ cups) creamed cottage cheese
¼ cup grated Parmesan cheese
1 cup (4 oz.) shredded Mozzarella cheese

Heat oven to 400°F. Grease (not oil) 14-inch pizza pan or 15x10-inch jelly roll pan. In medium skillet, brown ground beef; drain excess fat. Stir in ¼ cup water, tomato sauce and seasoning mix (reserve 1 tablespoon for crust); simmer while preparing crust.

In large bowl, dissolve yeast from hot roll mix in warm water. Add reserved sauce mix and hot roll flour mixture; blend well. Press dough in prepared pan forming a high rim around edge. Spread cottage cheese over dough; spoon meat mixture over cottage cheese. Sprinkle with Parmesan cheese. Place on low rack in oven. Bake at 400°F. for 25 to 35 minutes or until deep golden brown. Sprinkle with Mozzarella cheese; bake 2 to 3 minutes or until cheese melts. Let stand 5 minutes before serving; cut into wedges.

14-inch pizza

NUTRITION INFORMATION PER SERVING

Serving Size: 1/4 of recipe		Percent U.S. RDA Per Serving	
Calories	957	Protein	74%
Protein	48g	Vitamin A	27%
Carbohydrate	80g	Vitamin C	5%
Fat	48g	Thiamin	47%
Sodium	1804mg	Riboflavin	65%
Potassium	616mg	Niacin	50%
		Calcium	43%
		Iron	34%

This recipe makes a big hearty casserole that will be enjoyed by the whole family as well as those hungry boys. It was a $25,000 winner in the 15th BAKE-OFF® contest.

HUNGRY BOYS' CASSEROLE

1½ lb. ground beef
1 cup chopped celery
½ cup chopped onion or 2 tablespoons instant minced onion
½ cup chopped green pepper
1 garlic clove, minced
6-oz. can tomato paste
¾ cup water
½ teaspoon monosodium glutamate
1 teaspoon salt
1 teaspoon paprika
16-oz. can pork and beans, undrained
16-oz. can chick peas or lima beans, drained

BISCUITS

1½ cups Pillsbury's Best® All Purpose or Unbleached Flour*
2 teaspoons baking powder
½ teaspoon salt
¼ cup margarine or butter
½ cup milk
2 tablespoons sliced, stuffed green olives
1 tablespoon slivered almonds

In large skillet, combine first 5 ingredients. Cook until meat is browned and vegetables are tender; drain. Add tomato paste, water, monosodium glutamate, salt and paprika. Add pork and beans and peas; simmer.

Heat oven to 425°F. In large bowl, combine flour, baking powder and salt. Using pastry blender or mixer at low speed, cut in shortening. Add milk; stir until dough clings together. Knead on floured surface 8 times. Roll dough to ¼-inch thickness. Cut with 2½-inch doughnut cutter, saving holes.

Pour all but 1 cup meat mixture into 12x8 or 13x9-inch (2½ to 3 qt.) baking dish. Arrange Biscuits without centers on casserole. Stir olives and almonds into reserved 1 cup meat mixture; spoon in hole of each Biscuit. Top with the biscuit holes. Bake at 425°F. for 15 to 20 minutes or until golden brown.

6 to 8 servings

NUTRITION INFORMATION PER SERVING

Serving Size: 1/6 of recipe		Percent U.S. RDA Per Serving	
Calories	612	Protein	50%
Protein	33g	Vitamin A	32%
Carbohydrate	57g	Vitamin C	38%
Fat	28g	Thiamin	29%
Sodium	1522mg	Riboflavin	26%
Potassium	1077mg	Niacin	39%
		Calcium	20%
		Iron	41%

TIPS: *To halve recipe, use half the ingredient amounts; bake in 1½ to 2-quart casserole.*
**If using Pillsbury's Best Self Rising Flour, omit baking powder and salt in biscuits.*

DEEP DISH BISCUIT PIZZA

Don't send out for pizza–try this instead! Biscuit dough makes a quick and easy crust.

DEEP DISH BISCUIT PIZZA

1½ lb. ground beef
¼ to ½ cup chopped onion or 2 tablespoons instant minced onion
⅓ cup tomato sauce or 6-oz. can tomato paste
2 tablespoons grated Parmesan cheese
1 to 1½ teaspoons oregano leaves
1 teaspoon salt
¼ teaspoon pepper
8-oz. can Pillsbury Refrigerated Buttermilk or Country Style Biscuits
2-oz. can (¼ cup) mushroom stems and pieces, drained
1 tomato, sliced
1 cup (4 oz.) shredded Mozzarella cheese

Heat oven to 350°F. Grease 9-inch pie pan. Brown ground beef and onion; drain. Stir in tomato sauce, 1 tablespoon Parmesan cheese, oregano, salt and pepper. Simmer while preparing crust.

Separate biscuit dough into 10 biscuits. Arrange biscuits in prepared pan; press over bottom and up sides to form crust. Spoon hot meat mixture into crust. Place mushrooms over meat mixture. Arrange tomato slices over pie; sprinkle with Mozzarella cheese and remaining Parmesan cheese. Bake at 350°F. for 20 to 25 minutes or until crust is deep golden brown. Cool 5 minutes before serving.

9-inch pizza

NUTRITION INFORMATION PER SERVING

Serving Size: 1/4 of recipe		Percent U.S. RDA Per Serving	
Calories	533	Protein	42%
Protein	27g	Vitamin A	15%
Carbohydrate	32g	Vitamin C	5%
Fat	33g	Thiamin	22%
Sodium	1302mg	Riboflavin	34%
Potassium	502mg	Niacin	34%
		Calcium	28%
		Iron	25%

WESTERN BEEF AND CORN PIE

FILLING

1 lb. ground beef
½ teaspoon salt
½ teaspoon chili powder
1 cup (4 oz.) shredded Cheddar or American cheese
¼ to ¾ cup barbecue sauce
12-oz. can (1½ cups) Mexicorn Brand Golden Whole Kernel Corn with Sweet Peppers
6-oz. can tomato paste

CRUST

1 cup Pillsbury's Best® All Purpose or Unbleached Flour*
½ cup yellow cornmeal
2 tablespoons sugar
1 teaspoon baking powder
1 teaspoon salt
½ cup milk
¼ cup margarine or butter, softened
1 egg
1 cup (4 oz.) shredded Cheddar or American cheese

Heat oven to 400°F. In large skillet, brown ground beef; drain excess fat. Stir in remaining Filling ingredients.

Grease (not oil) 9-inch deep dish or 10-inch pie pan. In large bowl, blend all Crust ingredients except ½ cup cheese; mix well. Spread over bottom and sides of prepared pie pan. Pour filling into crust. Sprinkle with remaining ½ cup cheese. Bake at 400°F. for 25 to 30 minutes.

9 or 10-inch pie

NUTRITION INFORMATION PER SERVING

Serving Size: 1/8 of recipe		Percent U.S. RDA Per Serving	
Calories	463	Protein	35%
Protein	23g	Vitamin A	36%
Carbohydrate	35g	Vitamin C	14%
Fat	26g	Thiamin	18%
Sodium	885mg	Riboflavin	24%
Potassium	559mg	Niacin	22%
		Calcium	26%
		Iron	20%

TIP: **If using Pillsbury's Best® Self Rising Flour, omit baking powder and salt.*

FUDGE RIBBON CAKE

FUDGE RIBBON CAKE

FILLING

¼ cup sugar
1 tablespoon cornstarch
2 tablespoons milk
½ teaspoon vanilla
1 egg
8-oz. pkg. cream cheese, softened

CAKE

2 cups Pillsbury's Best® All Purpose or Unbleached Flour*
2 cups sugar
1 teaspoon salt
1 teaspoon baking powder
½ teaspoon soda
1⅓ cups milk
½ cup margarine or butter, softened
1 teaspoon vanilla
4 oz. (4 squares) unsweetened chocolate, melted or 4 envelopes premelted unsweetened baking chocolate flavor
2 eggs

FROSTING

¼ cup margarine or butter
¼ cup milk
1 teaspoon vanilla
6-oz. pkg. (1 cup) semi-sweet chocolate chips
2 cups powdered sugar

Heat oven to 350°F. Grease (not oil) and lightly flour bottom of 13x9-inch pan. In small bowl, blend all Filling ingredients 1 minute at low speed; beat at high speed until smooth. Set aside. In large bowl, blend all Cake ingredients at low speed until moistened. Beat 3 minutes at medium speed. Pour half of batter (about 2½ cups) into prepared pan. Spoon Filling over batter; spread carefully to cover. Spoon remaining batter by teaspoonfuls uniformly over Filling; spread to edges as evenly as possible. Bake at 350°F. for 50 to 60 minutes or until toothpick inserted in center comes out clean. Cool. In small saucepan, heat margarine and milk to boiling; remove from heat. Stir in vanilla and chocolate chips. Blend in powdered sugar until smooth. If necessary, thin with milk to spreading consistency. Spread over cooled cake.

13x9-inch cake

NUTRITION INFORMATION PER SERVING

Serving Size: 1/12 of recipe		Percent U.S. RDA Per Serving	
Calories	637	Protein	13%
Protein	8g	Vitamin A	20%
Carbohydrate	87g	Vitamin C	*
Fat	32g	Thiamin	11%
Sodium	474mg	Riboflavin	15%
Potassium	230mg	Niacin	6%
		Calcium	8%
		Iron	11%

TIP: **Self-rising flour is not recommended.*

CHOCOLATE MACAROON CAKE

FILLING

1 egg white (reserve yolk for cake)
¼ cup sugar
1 cup coconut
1 tablespoon flour
1 teaspoon vanilla

CAKE

1¾ cups Pillsbury's Best® All Purpose or Unbleached Flour*
1¾ cups sugar
½ cup unsweetened cocoa
1 teaspoon salt
1 teaspoon soda
¾ cup water
½ cup shortening
½ cup dairy sour cream
2 teaspoons vanilla
3 eggs, plus reserved yolk

GLAZE

1 cup powdered sugar
1 tablespoon margarine or butter, softened
2 to 3 tablespoons milk

Heat oven to 350°F. Generously grease, (using 1 tablespoon solid shortening) and lightly flour 12-cup fluted tube pan. In small bowl, beat egg white at high speed until soft peaks form. *Gradually* add sugar, beating continuously until stiff peaks form. By hand, stir in remaining Filling ingredients; set aside.

In large bowl, blend all Cake ingredients at low speed until moistened. Beat 3 minutes at medium speed. Pour chocolate batter into prepared pan. Drop teaspoonfuls of Filling over chocolate batter. Bake at 350°F. for 50 to 60 minutes or until toothpick inserted in center comes out clean. Cool until lukewarm; invert onto serving plate. Cool completely. In small bowl, blend Glaze ingredients until smooth. Spoon over cake. If desired, sprinkle cake with powdered sugar or serve with whipped cream. 10-inch ring cake

NUTRITION INFORMATION PER SERVING

Serving Size: 1/12 of recipe		Percent U.S. RDA Per Serving	
Calories	420	Protein	10%
Protein	6g	Vitamin A	8%
Carbohydrate	61g	Vitamin C	*
Fat	18g	Thiamin	10%
Sodium	251mg	Riboflavin	11%
Potassium	138mg	Niacin	6%
		Calcium	4%
		Iron	9%

TIPS: *For 13x9-inch cake, grease and lightly flour 13x9-inch pan. Prepare Filling and Cake as directed. Pour 3 cups chocolate batter into prepared pan. Drop teaspoonfuls of Filling over batter. Spoon remaining batter over Filling. Bake at 350°F. for 35 to 40 minutes or until toothpick inserted in center comes out clean. Cool. Drizzle Glaze over top of cake.*

**Self-rising flour is not recommended.*

HIGH ALTITUDE–Above 3500 Feet: Increase cake batter flour to 1¾ cups plus 2½ tablespoons and water to 1 cup. Bake at 375°F for 50 minutes.

ORANGE KISS ME CAKE

ORANGE KISS ME CAKE

CAKE

2 cups Pillsbury's Best® All Purpose or Unbleached Flour*
1 cup sugar
1 cup raisins
⅓ cup chopped nuts
1 teaspoon soda
1 teaspoon salt
1 teaspoon baking powder
½ cup milk
½ cup shortening
½ cup (from 6-oz. can) frozen concentrated orange juice (reserve remaining concentrate)
2 eggs

TOPPING

Reserved concentrated orange juice
⅓ cup sugar
¼ cup chopped nuts
1 teaspoon cinnamon

Heat oven to 350°F. Grease (not oil) and lightly flour 13x9-inch pan. In large bowl, blend all Cake ingredients at low speed until moistened. Beat 3 minutes at medium speed. Pour batter into prepared pan. Bake at 350°F. for 40 to 45 minutes or until toothpick inserted in center comes out clean. Drizzle reserved orange juice over warm cake. In small bowl, mix sugar, nuts and cinnamon; sprinkle over cake.

13x9-inch cake

NUTRITION INFORMATION PER SERVING

Serving Size: 1/12 of recipe		Percent U.S. RDA Per Serving	
Calories	358	Protein	8%
Protein	5g	Vitamin A	5%
Carbohydrate	56g	Vitamin C	28%
Fat	14g	Thiamin	16%
Sodium	317mg	Riboflavin	9%
Potassium	282mg	Niacin	7%
		Calcium	5%
		Iron	8%

TIP: **Self-rising flour is not recommended.*

HIGH ALTITUDE–Above 3500 Feet: Add 2 tablespoons flour; bake at 375°F. (350°F. for glass baking dish) for 35 to 40 minutes.

SOUR CREAM APPLE SQUARES

2 cups Pillsbury's Best® All Purpose or Unbleached Flour*
2 cups firmly packed brown sugar
½ cup margarine or butter, softened
1 cup chopped nuts
1 to 2 teaspoons cinnamon
1 teaspoon soda
½ teaspoon salt
1 cup dairy sour cream
1 teaspoon vanilla
1 egg
2 cups (2 medium) peeled and finely chopped apples

Heat oven to 350°F. In large bowl, combine first 3 ingredients; blend at low speed until crumbly. Stir in nuts. Press 2¾ cups crumb mixture into ungreased 13x9-inch pan. To remaining mixture, add cinnamon, soda, salt, sour cream, vanilla and egg; blend well. Stir in apples. Spoon evenly over base. Bake at 350°F. for 25 to 35 minutes or until toothpick inserted in center comes out clean. Cut into squares. If desired, serve with whipped cream or ice cream.

12 to 15 squares

NUTRITION INFORMATION PER SERVING

Serving Size: 1/12 of recipe		Percent U.S. RDA Per Serving	
Calories	403	Protein	8%
Protein	5g	Vitamin A	11%
Carbohydrate	57g	Vitamin C	*
Fat	18g	Thiamin	12%
Sodium	301mg	Riboflavin	9%
Potassium	222mg	Niacin	6%
		Calcium	7%
		Iron	13%

TIP: **If using Pillsbury's Best® Self Rising Flour, omit soda and salt.*
HIGH ALTITUDE–Above 3500 Feet: Bake at 375°F. for 25 to 35 minutes.

CHOCOLATE CHERRY BARS

1 pkg. Pillsbury Plus Devil's Food Cake Mix
21-oz. can (2 cups) cherry fruit filling
1 teaspoon almond extract
2 eggs, beaten

FROSTING

1 cup sugar
5 tablespoons margarine or butter
⅓ cup milk
6-oz. pkg. (1 cup) semi-sweet chocolate chips

Heat oven to 350°F. Grease (not oil) and flour 15x10-inch jelly roll or 13x9-inch pan. In large bowl, combine first 4 ingredients. By hand, stir until well mixed. Pour into prepared pan. Bake (350°F.) jelly roll pan for 20 to 30 minutes; 13x9-inch pan for 25 to 30 minutes or until toothpick inserted in center comes out clean. In small saucepan, combine sugar, margarine and milk. Heat to boiling; boil 1 minute, stirring constantly. Remove from heat; stir in chocolate chips until smooth. Pour over warm bars.

36 bars

NUTRITION INFORMATION PER SERVING

Serving Size: 2 bars		Percent U.S. RDA Per Serving	
Calories	311	Protein	4%
Protein	3g	Vitamin A	6%
Carbohydrate	53g	Vitamin C	2%
Fat	11g	Thiamin	6%
Sodium	288mg	Riboflavin	5%
Potassium	123mg	Niacin	3%
		Calcium	8%
		Iron	6%

HIGH ALTITUDE–Above 3500 Feet: Bake (375°F.) 15x10-inch pan for 20 to 30 minutes; 13x9-inch pan for 25 to 35 minutes.

CHOCOLATE CHERRY BARS

TUNNEL OF FUDGE CAKE

1½ cups margarine or butter, softened
6 eggs
1½ cups sugar
2 cups Pillsbury's Best® All Purpose or Unbleached Flour*
3⅓ cups Pillsbury Rich 'N Easy® Double Dutch Frosting Mix (save remaining mix for glaze, if desired)**
2 cups chopped walnuts or pecans

Heat oven to 350°F. Generously grease (using 1 tablespoon solid shortening) 12-cup fluted tube pan or 10-inch tube pan. In large bowl, cream margarine. Add eggs, one at a time, beating well after each. Gradually add sugar, creaming until light and fluffy. By hand, stir in flour, dry frosting mix and walnuts until well blended. Pour batter into prepared pan. Bake at 350°F. for 55 to 60 minutes. Cool to lukewarm; invert onto serving plate. Cool completely. For glaze, blend remaining frosting mix and 4 teaspoons water until smooth. If necessary add a few drops of water to make a glaze consistency. Spoon over cake.

10-inch ring cake

NUTRITION INFORMATION PER SERVING

Serving Size: 1/12 of recipe		Percent U.S. RDA Per Serving	
Calories	711	Protein	15%
Protein	10g	Vitamin A	25%
Carbohydrate	74g	Vitamin C	*
Fat	44g	Thiamin	16%
Sodium	404mg	Riboflavin	12%
Potassium	179mg	Niacin	7%
		Calcium	5%
		Iron	13%

TIPS: ***Rich 'N Easy® Double Dutch Frosting Mix or Rich 'N Easy® Fudge Frosting Mix and walnuts or pecans are essential to the success of this recipe.*

**Self-rising flour is not recommended.*

HIGH ALTITUDE–Above 3500 Feet: Bake at 375°F. for 60 to 65 minutes.

FRENCH SILK CHOCOLATE PIE

FRENCH SILK CHOCOLATE PIE

8 or 9-inch Baked Pie Shell, page 221
½ cup margarine or butter, softened
¾ cup sugar
2 eggs*
2 oz. (2 squares) unsweetened chocolate, melted
1 teaspoon vanilla
Whipped cream
Chopped nuts

Bake pie shell. In medium bowl, cream margarine and sugar until fluffy. Add eggs, one at a time, beating at medium speed 2 minutes after each addition. Blend in chocolate and vanilla. Spoon into cooled pie shell. Chill 2 hours or until served. Serve with whipped cream and nuts. 8 or 9-inch pie

NUTRITION INFORMATION PER SERVING

Serving Size: 1/8 of recipe		Percent U.S. RDA Per Serving	
Calories	432	Protein	8%
Protein	5g	Vitamin A	17%
Carbohydrate	34g	Vitamin C	*
Fat	33g	Thiamin	9%
Sodium	298mg	Riboflavin	8%
Potassium	119mg	Niacin	5%
		Calcium	3%
		Iron	7%

TIPS: **For this recipe, use only Grade A fresh whole shell eggs. Be sure they have clean, uncracked shells to ensure against contamination.*

For a cheesecake-like flavor, substitute an 8-oz. pkg. cream cheese for the margarine. Serve very small servings. 8 servings

For PEANUT BUTTER CHOCOLATE PIE, decrease margarine to ¼ cup and add ¼ cup peanut butter.

SPICE 'N EASY APPLE CRUNCH PIE

1½ cups Pillsbury's Best® All Purpose or Unbleached Flour*
2 teaspoons sugar
1 teaspoon salt
½ cup oil
2 tablespoons milk

FILLING
⅔ cup sugar
¼ cup flour
1 teaspoon cinnamon
3 to 4 cups (4 medium) peeled sliced apples
½ cup dairy sour cream

TOPPING
½ cup grapenut cereal or 1 cup crispy rice or corn flakes cereal
⅓ cup flour
⅓ cup firmly packed brown sugar
½ teaspoon cinnamon
¼ to ½ teaspoon nutmeg
⅛ teaspoon grated lemon peel, if desired
¼ cup margarine or butter, softened

Heat oven to 375°F. In ungreased 9-inch pie pan, combine flour, sugar and salt. Stir in oil and milk; mix well. Pat in pan. Flute edge if desired.

In large bowl, combine Filling ingredients. Turn into crust. In small bowl, combine Topping ingredients. Sprinkle over pie. Bake at 375°F. for 35 to 45 minutes or until Topping is golden brown and apples are tender. 9-inch pie

NUTRITION INFORMATION PER SERVING

Serving Size: 1/8 of recipe		Percent U.S. RDA Per Serving	
Calories	454	Protein	6%
Protein	4g	Vitamin A	7%
Carbohydrate	60g	Vitamin C	2%
Fat	23g	Thiamin	16%
Sodium	367mg	Riboflavin	10%
Potassium	119mg	Niacin	9%
		Calcium	4%
		Iron	8%

TIP: **If using Pillsbury's Best® Self Rising Flour, omit salt.*

CAKES, FROSTINGS & FILLINGS

CAKES, FROSTINGS & FILLINGS

Cake is a favorite dessert in almost any household, whether served warm from the oven with a scoop of ice cream or prettily frosted for the birthday star-attraction.

Most cakes belong in one of two categories – shortening or foam. The shortening cake contains shortening, margarine or butter which gives the cakes their classic moist rich texture and flavor.

Foam cakes depend mainly on air beaten into egg whites as a leavening agent. There is no shortening added so the cakes are very light. Angel food and sponge cakes are the most familiar examples.

Chiffon cake is actually a combination of the two types of cake – a shortening cake batter is folded into beaten egg whites.

BASIC PREPARATION

Cake baking is an exacting art. For the most perfect cake possible follow these tips in preparation.

Ingredients should be used as specified. Each recipe has been specially formulated to give the best results with the given ingredients – do not substitute unless the recipe gives an alternative. Every recipe uses all-purpose flour; cake flour is not necessary.

Cake pan size is important. Too large a pan will cause the cake to bake too fast; the result is a dark bottom, pale top and tough coarse texture. A pan too small may result in the cake spilling over, a sunken middle and a sticky center layer. Measure pans across the top from inside edge to inside edge. If you wish to use an odd size pan fill with water and measure. The amount of batter used should be half the amount of water. Make cupcakes out of any extra batter.

Prepare pans according to recipe directions. Use solid shortening. Using oil or aerosol cooking sprays may cause cake to stick to pan.

Combine ingredients in order listed. For best results do not skip or alter steps.

Do not sift or scoop flour. Lightly spoon flour into measuring cup, level off with knife.

Beat cake for the exact time given. Over or underbeating will result in a cake with low volume and coarse texture.

Spread batter evenly in pans.

Bake at the specified temperature. If you are unsure of the accuracy of your oven, check it with an oven thermometer.

Use the doneness test specified in the recipe. That is the most accurate method for that particular cake.

Allow layers to cool slightly before removing from pan. If the cake is removed from the pan too soon, the cake may crack and break. However, do remove while still warm or the cake may stick. If the cake pan has been properly prepared, the cake should come out easily. In some cases, it may be necessary to run a knife along the edge first before removing from pan.

CUPCAKES

Most cake batters may also be baked in paper-lined muffin cups for cupcakes. Fill cups ⅔ full and bake at 350°F. for 15 to 20 minutes or until top springs back when lightly touched. A one-layer cake recipe yields 12 to 15 cupcakes; a 2-layer cake recipe yields 24 to 30 cupcakes.

COMMON CAKE BAKING PROBLEMS

Low Volume	Under or overbeaten, too much liquid, pan too large, not enough leavening, oven too cool.
"Wet" Layer	Under or overbeaten, too much liquid, oven too cool.
Dry, crumbly	Not enough liquid or shortening, oven too hot, overbaked, too much flour.
Coarse texture	Under or overbeaten, oven too hot, too much sugar or leavening.
Fallen cake	Underbaked, pan too small, oven too hot or cool, opening oven door too soon, too much leavening, liquid or sugar, oven not sealed tight.
Extreme shrinkage	Too much water, overbeaten.
Peaked cake	Pan too small, oven too hot.
Sticky top	High humidity, cake stored before completely cool, underbaked, too much liquid or sugar.
Sticking in pan	Not enough grease, in pan too long.
Cracked top	Pan too deep, oven too hot.

A WORD ABOUT FOAM CAKES

- Do not underbeat.
- Never grease pans.
- Fold gently. Do not over fold.
- Before baking, cut through batter with a knife to help eliminate air pockets.
- Do not underbake.

STORAGE

Store one-layer cakes in the baking pan, tightly sealed with the pan's cover, foil or plastic wrap.

Store two or three-layer cakes under a "cake saver."

Cakes with whipped cream frostings or cream fillings should be stored in the refrigerator.

See Chapter 15 for tips on freezing cakes.

BASIC YELLOW CAKE

2½ cups Pillsbury's Best® All Purpose or Unbleached Flour*
1½ cups sugar
3 teaspoons baking powder
1 teaspoon salt
1¼ cups milk
⅔ cup shortening
2 teaspoons vanilla
2 egg yolks
2 eggs

Heat oven to 350°F. Generously grease (not oil) and lightly flour bottom only of 13x9-inch pan. In large bowl, blend all ingredients except vanilla and eggs, at low speed until moistened. Beat 2 minutes at medium speed. Add vanilla, egg yolks and eggs; beat 2 more minutes at medium speed. Pour batter into prepared pan. Bake at 350°F. for 40 to 45 minutes or until toothpick inserted in center comes out clean. Cool completely. Frost as desired.

13x9-inch cake

NUTRITION INFORMATION PER SERVING

Serving Size: 1/12 of recipe		Percent U.S. RDA Per Serving	
Calories	332	Protein	8%
Protein	5g	Vitamin A	5%
Carbohydrate	46g	Vitamin C	*
Fat	14g	Thiamin	13%
Sodium	286mg	Riboflavin	11%
Potassium	78mg	Niacin	7%
		Calcium	6%
		Iron	6%

TIPS: *Cake may be baked in 2 well-greased and lightly floured 9-inch or three 8-inch round cake pans. Bake 35 to 40 minutes. Cool 10 minutes; remove from pans. Cool completely.* 2 or 3 layer cake

**If using Pillsbury's Best® Self Rising Flour, omit baking powder and salt.*

HIGH ALTITUDE–Above 3500 Feet: Increase flour 2 tablespoons and milk to 1½ cups; use 3 whole eggs. Bake at 375°F. for 30 to 40 minutes.

SIMPLY WHITE CAKE
CHERRY NUT CAKE
COCONUT CAKE
POPPY SEED CAKE

Delicious enough for a wedding, but easy enough for everyday.

SIMPLY WHITE CAKE

- **2 cups Pillsbury's Best® All Purpose or Unbleached Flour***
- **1½ cups sugar**
- **3 teaspoons baking powder**
- **1 teaspoon salt**
- **1 cup milk**
- **½ cup shortening**
- **4 egg whites**
- **2 teaspoons vanilla or ½ teaspoon almond extract**

Heat oven to 350°F. Generously grease (not oil) and lightly flour bottom only of 13x9-inch pan. In large bowl, blend all ingredients except egg whites and vanilla, at low speed until moistened. Beat 2 minutes at medium speed. Add egg whites and vanilla; beat 2 more minutes at medium speed. Pour batter into prepared pan. Bake at 350°F. for 35 to 40 minutes or until toothpick inserted in center comes out clean. Cool completely. If desired, frost with White Cloud Frosting, page 151. 13x9-inch cake

NUTRITION INFORMATION PER SERVING

Serving Size: 1/12 of recipe		Percent U.S. RDA Per Serving	
Calories	266	Protein	7%
Protein	4g	Vitamin A	*
Carbohydrate	42g	Vitamin C	*
Fat	9g	Thiamin	9%
Sodium	289mg	Riboflavin	9%
Potassium	68mg	Niacin	6%
		Calcium	4%
		Iron	4%

TIPS: *For CHERRY NUT CAKE, stir in ½ cup each chopped maraschino cherries and nuts into batter before pouring into pans.*

For COCONUT CAKE, stir 1 cup flaked coconut into batter before pouring into pans. Sprinkle additional coconut over frosting.

For POPPY SEED CAKE, combine ¼ cup poppy seed with ¼ cup milk; allow to stand 30 minutes. Add to batter with egg whites and vanilla. Frost with Caramel Frosting, page 148.

Cake may be baked in two 8 or 9-inch round cake pans; generously grease and lightly flour bottoms only. Bake 30 to 35 minutes. Cool 10 minutes; remove from pans. Cool completely.

**Self-rising flour is not recommended.*

HIGH ALTITUDE–Above 3500 Feet: Decrease sugar to 1¼ cups plus 1 tablespoon and baking powder to 2½ teaspoons. Bake at 375°F. for 35 to 40 minutes.

PETITS FOURS

Heat oven to 350°F. Grease (not oil) and lightly flour 15x10-inch jelly roll pan. Prepare Simply White Cake as directed, page 123. Pour into prepared pan. Bake at 350°F. for 25 to 30 minutes or until toothpick inserted in center comes out clean. Cut into desired shapes using heart, diamond, round and square cutters. To avoid cake crumbs, freeze before cutting; return cake to freezer while icing is prepared.

Working with cake pieces, dip in icing or spoon icing over as directed below.

TO DIP CAKE PIECES: Cakes can be dipped by spearing with fork and dipping into icing until coated. (This process is easier if cakes are frozen.) Set iced cakes on wire rack over pan or cookie sheet.

TO SPOON ICING: Set cake pieces on wire rack over pan. Spoon icing evenly over top and sides of cake pieces. Icing which drips off can be reused.

PETIT FOUR ICING

6 cups (about 1½ lb.) powdered sugar
½ cup water
⅓ cup white corn syrup
3 tablespoons margarine or butter, melted
1 teaspoon vanilla
½ to 1 teaspoon rum, lemon or almond extract, if desired
Food coloring, if desired

In large bowl, combine all ingredients. Blend on low speed until powdered sugar is moistened; beat on high speed until smooth. Add 1 to 2 tablespoons additional water if icing is too thick. In small bowls, tint small portions of icing to desired colors.

Frosts 24 to 30 small cakes

NUTRITION INFORMATION PER SERVING

Serving Size: 1/24 of recipe with cake		Percent U.S. RDA Per Serving	
Calories	275	Protein	3%
Protein	2g	Vitamin A	*
Carbohydrate	54g	Vitamin C	*
Fat	6g	Thiamin	5%
Sodium	165mg	Riboflavin	4%
Potassium	36mg	Niacin	3%
		Calcium	2%
		Iron	3%

TIP: *For chocolate icing, stir in 2 oz. (2 squares) melted unsweetened chocolate or 2 envelopes premelted unsweetened baking chocolate flavor.*

EASY ONE-EGG CAKE

1¼ cups Pillsbury's Best® All Purpose or Unbleached Flour*
¾ cup sugar
2 teaspoons baking powder
½ teaspoon salt
⅔ cup milk
¼ cup shortening
1 teaspoon vanilla
1 egg

Heat oven to 350°F. Grease (not oil) and lightly flour bottom only of 8 or 9-inch square pan. In medium bowl, blend all ingredients at low speed until moistened. Beat 2 minutes at medium speed. Pour batter into prepared pan. Bake at 350°F. for 35 to 40 minutes or until toothpick inserted in center comes out clean.

8 or 9-inch square cake

NUTRITION INFORMATION PER SERVING

Serving Size: 1/9 of recipe		Percent U.S. RDA Per Serving	
Calories	199	Protein	5%
Protein	3g	Vitamin A	*
Carbohydrate	31g	Vitamin C	*
Fat	7g	Thiamin	8%
Sodium	206mg	Riboflavin	7%
Potassium	52mg	Niacin	5%
		Calcium	4%
		Iron	4%

TIP: **If using Pillsbury's Best® Self Rising Flour, omit baking powder and salt.*

HIGH ALTITUDE–Above 3500 Feet: Use 1 tablespoon less sugar and decrease baking powder to 1½ teaspoons; increase milk to ¾ cup. Bake at 375°F. for 35 to 40 minutes.

CRUMB-TOPPED BUTTER CAKE

CAKE

- **2 cups Pillsbury's Best® All Purpose or Unbleached Flour***
- **1¼ cups sugar**
- **2 teaspoons baking powder**
- **½ teaspoon salt**
- **½ teaspoon soda**
- **½ cup milk**
- **½ cup margarine or butter, softened**
- **1 teaspoon vanilla**
- **2 eggs**
- **8-oz. pkg. cream cheese, softened**

TOPPING

- **½ cup Pillsbury's Best® All Purpose or Unbleached Flour**
- **½ cup firmly packed brown sugar**
- **¼ cup margarine or butter**

Heat oven to 350°F. Grease (not oil) bottom only of 13x9-inch pan. In large bowl, blend all Cake ingredients at low speed until moistened. Beat 3 minutes at medium speed. Pour batter into prepared pan. In small bowl, combine Topping ingredients until crumbly; sprinkle over batter. Bake at 350°F. for 30 to 35 minutes or until toothpick inserted in center comes out clean. Serve warm or cooled. 13x9-inch cake

NUTRITION INFORMATION PER SERVING

Serving Size: 1/12 of recipe		Percent U.S. RDA Per Serving	
Calories	404	Protein	9%
Protein	6g	Vitamin A	18%
Carbohydrate	51g	Vitamin C	*
Fat	20g	Thiamin	12%
Sodium	398mg	Riboflavin	12%
Potassium	101mg	Niacin	7%
		Calcium	5%
		Iron	7%

TIPS: *To halve recipe, use half the ingredient amounts; bake in 8-inch square pan 25 to 30 minutes.*

**Self-rising flour is not recommended.*

HIGH ALTITUDE–Above 3500 Feet: Decrease sugar to 1 cup and baking powder to 1½ teaspoons; increase milk to ⅔ cup.

An easy to do basic cake. Omit Glaze and top with whipped cream or fruit.

ONE-STEP POUND CAKE

CAKE

- **2¼ cups Pillsbury's Best® All Purpose or Unbleached Flour***
- **2 cups sugar**
- **1 teaspoon grated lemon or orange peel**
- **½ teaspoon salt**
- **½ teaspoon baking soda**
- **1 cup dairy sour cream**
- **1 cup margarine or butter, softened**
- **1 teaspoon vanilla**
- **3 eggs**

GLAZE

- **1 cup powdered sugar**
- **1 to 2 tablespoons lemon juice**

Heat oven to 325°F. Generously grease (using 1 tablespoon solid shortening) and lightly flour 12-cup fluted tube pan. In large bowl, blend all Cake ingredients at low speed until moistened. Beat 3 minutes at medium speed. Pour batter into prepared pan. Bake at 325°F. for 55 to 60 minutes or until toothpick inserted in center comes out clean. Cool to lukewarm; invert onto serving plate. Cool completely. In small bowl, blend Glaze ingredients until smooth. Spoon over cake. 10-inch ring cake

NUTRITION INFORMATION PER SERVING

Serving Size: 1/12 of recipe		Percent U.S. RDA Per Serving	
Calories	448	Protein	8%
Protein	5g	Vitamin A	19%
Carbohydrate	62g	Vitamin C	*
Fat	21g	Thiamin	11%
Sodium	345mg	Riboflavin	9%
Potassium	48mg	Niacin	6%
		Calcium	4%
		Iron	6%

TIP: **Self-rising flour is not recommended.*

HIGH ALTITUDE–Above 3500 Feet: Increase flour to 2⅓ cups; decrease margarine to ¾ cup. Bake at 350°F. for 35 to 40 minutes.

A hot butter sauce is poured over the cake. Let stand overnight—this one gets better with age.

KENTUCKY BUTTER CAKE

CAKE

- **3 cups Pillsbury's Best® All Purpose or Unbleached Flour***
- **2 cups sugar**
- **1 teaspoon salt**
- **1 teaspoon baking powder**
- **½ teaspoon soda**
- **1 cup buttermilk**
- **1 cup margarine or butter, softened**
- **2 teaspoons vanilla or rum extract**
- **4 eggs**

BUTTER SAUCE

- **¾ cup sugar**
- **⅓ cup margarine or butter**
- **3 tablespoons water**
- **1 to 2 teaspoons vanilla or rum extract**

Heat oven to 325°F. Generously grease (using 1 tablespoon solid shortening) and lightly flour 12-cup fluted tube pan or 10-inch tube pan. In large bowl, blend all Cake ingredients at low speed until moistened. Beat 3 minutes at medium speed. Pour batter into prepared pan. Bake at 325°F. for 55 to 70 minutes or until toothpick inserted in center comes out clean. In small saucepan, combine sugar, margarine and water; heat until margarine melts. Remove from heat; add vanilla. Leaving cake in pan, prick hot cake deeply every inch with long-tined fork. For fluted tube cake; pour ¾ cup hot Butter Sauce over hot cake. Cool upright in pan 5 minutes; invert onto serving plate. Spoon or carefully brush remaining Sauce over cake. For 10-inch tube cake: pour all of hot Butter Sauce over hot cake. Cool upright in pan 30 minutes; remove from pan.

10-inch ring cake

NUTRITION INFORMATION PER SERVING

Serving Size: 1/12 of recipe		Percent U.S. RDA Per Serving	
Calories	508	Protein	10%
Protein	7g	Vitamin A	21%
Carbohydrate	71g	Vitamin C	*
Fat	23g	Thiamin	15%
Sodium	550mg	Riboflavin	13%
Potassium	89mg	Niacin	8%
		Calcium	5%
		Iron	8%

TIP: **Self-rising flour is not recommended.*

HIGH ALTITUDE—Above 3500 Feet: Decrease sugar to 1¾ cups; increase buttermilk to 1 cup plus 2 tablespoons. Bake at 350°F. for 60 to 70 minutes.

LEMON DELIGHT POUND CAKE

CAKE

2½ cups Pillsbury's Best® All Purpose or Unbleached Flour*
1½ cups sugar
3 teaspoons baking powder
½ teaspoon salt
¾ cup orange juice or apricot nectar
¾ cup oil
2 teaspoons lemon extract
4 eggs

GLAZE

1½ cups powdered sugar
½ cup lemon juice

Heat oven to 325°F. Generously grease (using 1 tablespoon solid shortening) and lightly flour 12-cup fluted tube pan. In large bowl, blend all Cake ingredients at low speed until moistened. Beat 3 minutes at medium speed. Pour batter into prepared pan. Bake at 325°F. for 40 to 50 minutes or until toothpick inserted in center comes out clean. Prick deeply every inch with long-tined fork. In small bowl, blend Glaze ingredients until smooth. Spoon half of Glaze over hot cake in pan. Let stand 10 minutes; invert onto serving plate. Spoon remaining Glaze over cake.

10-inch ring cake

NUTRITION INFORMATION PER SERVING

Serving Size: 1/12 of recipe		Percent U.S. RDA Per Serving	
Calories	410	Protein	8%
Protein	5g	Vitamin A	5%
Carbohydrate	62g	Vitamin C	19%
Fat	16g	Thiamin	14%
Sodium	193mg	Riboflavin	10%
Potassium	94mg	Niacin	7%
		Calcium	3%
		Iron	7%

TIP: **Self-rising flour is not recommended.*

HIGH ALTITUDE–Above 3500 Feet: Decrease baking powder to 2½ teaspoons. Bake at 350°F for 40 to 50 minutes.

LEMON DELIGHT POUND CAKE

CARROT CAKE

CAKE
2¼ cups Pillsbury's Best® All Purpose or Unbleached Flour*
2 cups sugar
2 teaspoons soda
1 teaspoon cinnamon
½ teaspoon salt
2 cups (4 medium) shredded carrots
1½ cups oil
4 eggs
1 cup chopped nuts

FROSTING
3 cups powdered sugar
2 tablespoons margarine or butter, softened
1 teaspoon vanilla
8-oz. pkg. cream cheese

Heat oven to 350°F. Grease (not oil) and lightly flour two 9-inch round cake pans. In large bowl, blend all Cake ingredients except nuts, at low speed until moistened. Beat 3 minutes at high speed. Stir in nuts; pour batter into prepared pans. Bake at 350°F. for 35 to 45 minutes or until toothpick inserted in center comes out clean. Cool 10 minutes; remove from pans. Cool completely. In medium bowl, blend Frosting ingredients; beat until smooth. Spread over cake. 9-inch layer cake

NUTRITION INFORMATION PER SERVING

Serving Size: 1/12 of recipe		Percent U.S. RDA Per Serving	
Calories	761	Protein	12%
Protein	8g	Vitamin A	52%
Carbohydrate	85g	Vitamin C	3%
Fat	45g	Thiamin	15%
Sodium	373mg	Riboflavin	13%
Potassium	170mg	Niacin	7%
		Calcium	4%
		Iron	9%

TIPS: *Cake may be baked in 13x9-inch pan; grease on bottom only. Bake 40 to 45 minutes.*

**Self-rising flour is not recommended.*

HIGH ALTITUDE–Above 3500 Feet: Decrease sugar to 1¾ cups and soda to 1½ teaspoons; use 5 eggs. Bake at 350°F. for 40 minutes.

A great little cake for an after school snack.

APPLESAUCE SNACK CAKE

CAKE
½ cup margarine or butter
¾ cup Pillsbury's Best® All Purpose or Unbleached Flour*
¾ cup Pillsbury's Best® Medium Rye or Whole Wheat Flour
¾ cup firmly packed brown sugar
½ cup raisins or chopped dates
1 teaspoon soda
2 teaspoons cinnamon
½ teaspoon salt
1 cup applesauce
1 egg

TOPPING
½ cup firmly packed brown sugar
½ cup chopped nuts
¼ cup Pillsbury's Best® Medium Rye or Whole Wheat Flour
¼ cup margarine or butter, softened

Heat oven to 350°F. Generously grease (not oil) and lightly flour 9-inch square pan. In medium saucepan, melt margarine; remove from heat. Stir in remaining Cake ingredients; blend well. Pour batter into prepared pan. In small bowl, combine Topping ingredients until crumbly; sprinkle over batter. Bake at 350°F. for 30 to 35 minutes or until toothpick inserted in center comes out clean. 9-inch square cake

NUTRITION INFORMATION PER SERVING

Serving Size: 1/9 of recipe		Percent U.S. RDA Per Serving	
Calories	390	Protein	6%
Protein	4g	Vitamin A	14%
Carbohydrate	55g	Vitamin C	*
Fat	19g	Thiamin	9%
Sodium	445mg	Riboflavin	6%
Potassium	245mg	Niacin	5%
		Calcium	5%
		Iron	13%

TIP: **If using Pillsbury's Best® Self Rising Flour, decrease soda to ½ teaspoon and omit salt.*

HIGH ALTITUDE–Above 3500 Feet: Decrease soda to ¾ teaspoon. Bake at 375°F. for 25 to 30 minutes.

Probably one of the all time favorites with our tasters. The very best ginger cake ever!

POKE 'N POUR GINGER CAKE

CAKE

2¼ cups Pillsbury's Best® All Purpose or Unbleached Flour*
¾ cup firmly packed brown sugar
1 teaspoon baking powder
2 teaspoons cinnamon
1 teaspoon ginger
½ teaspoon soda
½ teaspoon salt
½ teaspoon mace or nutmeg
¼ teaspoon cloves
¾ cup water
¾ cup oil
¾ cup molasses or sorghum
2 eggs

BUTTER SAUCE

1 cup firmly packed brown sugar
½ cup margarine or butter
⅓ cup water

Heat oven to 350°F. Generously grease (using 1 tablespoon solid shortening) and lightly flour 12-cup fluted tube pan. In large bowl, blend all Cake ingredients at low speed until moistened. Beat 3 minutes at medium speed. Pour into prepared pan. Bake at 350°F. for 45 to 55 minutes or until toothpick inserted in center comes out clean. In small saucepan, combine Sauce ingredients; heat until margarine melts. Prick hot cake deeply every inch with long-tined fork. Spoon hot Sauce over hot cake in pan. Let stand 30 minutes; invert onto serving plate. Serve warm or cool. If desired, top with whipped cream.

10-inch ring cake

NUTRITION INFORMATION PER SERVING

Serving Size: 1/12 of recipe		Percent U.S. RDA Per Serving	
Calories	458	Protein	6%
Protein	4g	Vitamin A	8%
Carbohydrate	62g	Vitamin C	*
Fat	23g	Thiamin	11%
Sodium	283mg	Riboflavin	9%
Potassium	368mg	Niacin	8%
		Calcium	10%
		Iron	18%

**Self-rising flour is not recommended.*

HIGH ALTITUDE–Above 3500 Feet: Decrease baking powder to ¾ teaspoon. Bake at 375°F. for 45 to 55 minutes.

AUNT LOU'S DIXIE SPICE CAKE

2½ cups Pillsbury's Best® All Purpose or Unbleached Flour*
1½ cups firmly packed brown sugar
½ cup sugar
1 teaspoon salt
1 teaspoon soda
½ teaspoon nutmeg
½ teaspoon allspice
1¼ cups buttermilk
1 cup shortening
1 teaspoon vanilla
3 eggs
1 cup chopped black walnuts

Heat oven to 350°F. Generously grease (not oil) bottom only of 13x9-inch pan. In large bowl, blend all ingredients except black walnuts, at low speed until moistened. Beat 3 minutes at medium speed. Stir in black walnuts. Pour batter into prepared pan. Bake at 350°F. for 40 to 45 minutes or until toothpick inserted in center comes out clean. Cool completely. Frost as desired or serve with Cinnamon Whipped Cream, page 235. 13x9-inch cake

NUTRITION INFORMATION PER SERVING

Serving Size: 1/12 of recipe		Percent U.S. RDA Per Serving	
Calories	475	Protein	12%
Protein	8g	Vitamin A	4%
Carbohydrate	58g	Vitamin C	*
Fat	25g	Thiamin	15%
Sodium	328mg	Riboflavin	12%
Potassium	222mg	Niacin	8%
		Calcium	7%
		Iron	15%

TIP: **Self-rising flour is not recommended.*

HIGH ALTITUDE–Above 3500 Feet: Increase flour to 2½ cups plus 3 tablespoons and add ¼ cup water along with buttermilk; use 4 eggs. Bake at 375°F. for 40 minutes.

A holiday classic that keeps!

DARK FRUITCAKE

3 cups Pillsbury's Best® All Purpose or Unbleached Flour*
1¾ cups firmly packed brown sugar
2 teaspoons baking powder
1 teaspoon salt
2 teaspoons cinnamon
½ teaspoon nutmeg
½ teaspoon allspice
1 cup liquid (fruit juice, water or milk)
¾ cup shortening, melted or oil
¼ cup molasses
4 eggs
3 cups (1 lb.) raisins
2 cups (1 lb.) mixed candied fruit
2 cups (½ lb.) pecan halves
1 cup (½ lb.) whole candied cherries
½ cup chopped candied pineapple
8-oz. pkg. (1¼ cups) pitted dates, cut into large pieces

Heat oven to 275°F. Grease (not oil) two 9x5-inch loaf pans and line with waxed paper or foil. In large bowl, blend all ingredients except fruits and nuts at low speed until moistened. Beat 3 minutes at high speed. Stir in fruits and nuts. Spoon batter into prepared pans. Bake at 275°F. for 2½ to 3 hours or until toothpick inserted in center comes out clean. Remove from pans; cool. Peel off paper; wrap cooled cakes tightly in plastic wrap or foil to keep moist. If wrapped tightly, fruitcake will keep in refrigerator up to a year. 2 loaf cakes

NUTRITION INFORMATION PER SERVING

Serving Size: 1 slice		Percent U.S. RDA Per Serving	
Calories	302	Protein	5%
Protein	3g	Vitamin A	2%
Carbohydrate	54g	Vitamin C	3%
Fat	10g	Thiamin	10%
Sodium	130mg	Riboflavin	5%
Potassium	282mg	Niacin	4%
		Calcium	5%
		Iron	10%

TIPS: *If desired, use up to half Pillsbury's Best® Whole Wheat or Rye Flour.*

**Self-rising flour is not recommended.*

HIGH ALTITUDE–Above 3500 Feet: Decrease brown sugar to 1½ cups and baking powder to 1½ teaspoons. Bake at 300°F. for 2½ to 3 hours.

FRUITCAKE TIPS

Candied fruitcake mix may be substituted for candied cherries and pineapple.

For brandy or rum fruitcake, use ¼ cup brandy or rum for part of liquid. Wrap cooled fruitcake in cheesecloth or other porous cloth that has been soaked in brandy or rum. Then wrap in foil or plastic. If desired, resoak cloth about once or twice a month.

To glaze fruitcake, brush with warm corn syrup or melted apple or other light-colored jelly.

Fruitcake makes a nice holiday gift wrapped attractively in plastic or foil. Bake a variety of sizes for your various gift needs.

OTHER FRUITCAKE PAN SIZES

(For Dark Fruitcake recipe filling container ⅔ to ¾ full.)

COFFEE CANS (1 lb. size): 4 cans; bake 1½ to 2 hours.

SOUP CANS (10½-oz. size): 12 cans; bake 1 to 1½ hours.

MINIATURE LOAF PANS: 6 pans; bake about 1½ hours.

MUFFIN PANS: about 48 muffin cups lined with paper baking cups; bake 50 to 60 minutes.

A little lighter and sweeter than the traditional.

DELICIOUS WHITE FRUITCAKE

- **1¾ cups Pillsbury's Best® All Purpose or Unbleached Flour***
- **1 cup sugar**
- **½ teaspoon salt**
- **½ teaspoon baking powder**
- **1½ cups margarine or butter, softened**
- **1 tablespoon vanilla**
- **1 tablespoon lemon extract**
- **5 eggs**
- **4 cups (1 lb.) pecan halves**
- **2 cups (1 lb.) candied pineapple, cut up**
- **1½ cups (¾ lb.) candied cherries, whole or cut up**

Heat oven to 300°F. Generously grease (not oil) and lightly flour 10-inch tube pan.** In large bowl, blend all ingredients except nuts and fruit at low speed until moistened. Beat 2 minutes at medium speed. Stir in nuts and fruit. Spoon batter into prepared pan. Bake at 300°F. for 1½ to 2 hours or until toothpick inserted in center comes out clean. Cool; remove from pan. Wrap tightly in plastic wrap or foil and refrigerate up to 6 months.

5-lb. ring fruitcake

NUTRITION INFORMATION PER SERVING

Serving Size: 1/36 of recipe		Percent U.S. RDA Per Serving	
Calories	272	Protein	5%
Protein	3g	Vitamin A	8%
Carbohydrate	28g	Vitamin C	*
Fat	18g	Thiamin	10%
Sodium	138mg	Riboflavin	4%
Potassium	94mg	Niacin	2%
		Calcium	*
		Iron	4%

TIPS: **Self-rising flour is not recommended.*

***Cake may be baked in 2 greased and floured 8x4-inch loaf pans for 65 to 75 minutes. Smaller loaves for gifts may also be baked. See "Other Fruitcake Pan Sizes."*

DELICIOUS WHITE FRUIT CAKE

DELICIOUS DEVIL'S FOOD CAKE

DELICIOUS DEVIL'S FOOD CAKE

1½ cups Pillsbury's Best® All Purpose or Unbleached Flour*
1¼ cups sugar
½ cup unsweetened cocoa
1¼ teaspoons soda
1 teaspoon salt
1 cup buttermilk
⅔ cup oil
1 teaspoon vanilla
2 eggs

Heat oven to 350°F. Grease (not oil) and lightly flour bottoms only of two 8-inch round cake pans. In large bowl, blend all ingredients at low speed until moistened. Beat 3 minutes at medium speed. Pour batter into prepared pans. Bake at 350°F. for 25 to 30 minutes or until toothpick inserted in center comes out clean. Cool 5 minutes; remove from pans. Cool completely. Frost with White Cloud Frosting, page 151.

8-inch layer cake

NUTRITION INFORMATION PER SERVING

Serving Size: 1/12 of recipe		Percent U.S. RDA Per Serving	
Calories	276	Protein	6%
Protein	4g	Vitamin A	2%
Carbohydrate	36g	Vitamin C	*
Fat	14g	Thiamin	8%
Sodium	330mg	Riboflavin	8%
Potassium	110mg	Niacin	5%
		Calcium	4%
		Iron	6%

TIPS: *Cake may be baked in greased and lightly floured 13x9-inch pan. Bake 30 to 35 minutes.*

**Self-rising flour is not recommended.*

Simple cake for a smaller family.

DUTCH SUPPER CAKE

1 cup Pillsbury's Best® All Purpose or Unbleached Flour*
1 cup sugar
½ cup chopped nuts
½ teaspoon salt
½ teaspoon soda
2 oz. (2 squares) unsweetened chocolate, melted or 2 envelopes premelted unsweetened baking chocolate flavor
½ cup oil
½ cup applesauce
1 teaspoon vanilla
2 eggs

Heat oven to 350°F. Generously grease (not oil) bottom only of 8 or 9-inch square pan. In medium bowl, combine all ingredients. Stir until well blended. Pour batter into prepared pan. Bake at 350°F. for 35 to 40 minutes or until toothpick inserted in center comes out clean. Serve warm or cold, plain or with whipped cream.

8 or 9-inch square cake

NUTRITION INFORMATION PER SERVING

Serving Size: 1/9 of recipe		Percent U.S. RDA Per Serving	
Calories	375	Protein	8%
Protein	5g	Vitamin A	3%
Carbohydrate	39g	Vitamin C	*
Fat	25g	Thiamin	9%
Sodium	193mg	Riboflavin	8%
Potassium	174mg	Niacin	5%
		Calcium	3%
		Iron	10%

TIP: **If using Pillsbury's Best® Self Rising Flour, omit salt and soda.*

HIGH ALTITUDE–Above 3500 Feet: Decrease sugar to ¾ cup. Bake at 375°F. for 25 to 30 minutes.

GERMAN CHOCOLATE CAKE

- ½ cup hot water
- 4-oz. bar sweet cooking chocolate
- 1 cup margarine or butter, softened
- 2 cups sugar
- 4 eggs
- 2¼ cups Pillsbury's Best® All Purpose or Unbleached Flour*
- 1 teaspoon soda
- ½ teaspoon salt
- 1 cup buttermilk
- 1 teaspoon vanilla
- Coconut Pecan Frosting, page 152

Heat oven to 350°F. Grease (not oil) and lightly flour two or three 9-inch round cake pans. In small saucepan over low heat, melt chocolate with water. Set aside. In large bowl, cream margarine and sugar until light and fluffy. Add eggs, one at a time, beating well after each. Add remaining ingredients except Frosting; blend at low speed just until combined. Pour batter into prepared pans. Bake at 350°F. for 35 to 45 minutes or until toothpick inserted in center comes out clean. Cool 5 minutes; remove from pans. Cool completely. Spread frosting between layers and on top leaving sides plain or spreading with whipped cream. 9-inch 2 or 3-layer cake

NUTRITION INFORMATION PER SERVING

Serving Size: 1/12 of recipe with frosting		Percent U.S. RDA Per Serving	
Calories	733	Protein	17%
Protein	11g	Vitamin A	28%
Carbohydrate	79g	Vitamin C	*
Fat	43g	Thiamin	19%
Sodium	553mg	Riboflavin	19%
Potassium	289mg	Niacin	7%
		Calcium	12%
		Iron	12%

TIPS: *Do not use 13x9-inch pan unless part of batter is used for cupcakes.*

**Self-rising flour is not recommended.*

HIGH ALTITUDE–Above 3500 Feet: Decrease sugar to 1¾ cups and soda to ¾ teaspoon. Bake at 375°F. for 25 to 30 minutes.

A sprinkling of cinnamon and sugar tops this cake so no frosting is needed–quick, easy and flavorful!

CHOCOLATE CHIP CAKE

- 2 cups Pillsbury's Best® All Purpose or Unbleached Flour*
- 1½ cups sugar
- 2 teaspoons baking powder
- ½ teaspoon soda
- ½ teaspoon salt
- 1⅓ cups dairy sour cream
- ⅔ cup margarine or butter, softened
- 1 teaspoon vanilla
- 3 eggs
- ½ cup sugar
- 1 teaspoon cinnamon
- 6-oz. pkg. (1 cup) semi-sweet chocolate chips

Heat oven to 350°F. Grease (not oil) 13x9-inch pan. In large bowl, blend first 9 ingredients at low speed until moistened. Beat 3 minutes at medium speed. Pour half of batter (about 2½ cups) into prepared pan. In small bowl, combine ½ cup sugar and cinnamon. Sprinkle half of sugar mixture and chocolate chips over batter. Repeat with remaining batter, sugar mixture and chocolate chips. Bake at 350°F. for 35 to 40 minutes or until toothpick inserted in center comes out clean.

13x9-inch cake

NUTRITION INFORMATION PER SERVING

Serving Size: 1/12 of recipe		Percent U.S. RDA Per Serving	
Calories	441	Protein	8%
Protein	5g	Vitamin A	16%
Carbohydrate	58g	Vitamin C	*
Fat	22g	Thiamin	11%
Sodium	344mg	Riboflavin	10%
Potassium	88mg	Niacin	6%
		Calcium	6%
		Iron	7%

TIP: **Self-rising flour is not recommended.*

HIGH ALTITUDE–Above 3500 Feet: Decrease baking powder to 1 teaspoon. Bake at 375°F. for 30 to 35 minutes.

Sliced peaches and streusel topping bake atop this brown sugar cake.

POCKET PEACH CAKE

CAKE

1 cup Pillsbury's Best® All Purpose or Unbleached Flour*
⅔ cup firmly packed brown sugar
1 teaspoon cinnamon
½ teaspoon salt
½ teaspoon soda
½ cup dairy sour cream
1 teaspoon vanilla
1 egg
16-oz. can (1½ cups) sliced peaches, well-drained

TOPPING

½ cup chopped nuts
½ cup coconut
⅓ cup firmly packed brown sugar
2 tablespoons margarine or butter

Heat oven to 375°F. Generously grease (not oil) bottom only of 8 or 9-inch square pan. In small bowl, blend all Cake ingredients except peaches, at low speed until moistened. Beat 1 minute at medium speed. Pour batter into prepared pan. Arrange peaches over batter. In small bowl, combine Topping ingredients until crumbly; sprinkle over peaches. Bake at 375°F. for 35 to 45 minutes or until golden brown and toothpick inserted in center comes out clean. Cool 30 minutes; cut into squares. Serve warm with whipped cream or ice cream.

8 or 9-inch cake

NUTRITION INFORMATION PER SERVING

Serving Size: 1/9 of recipe		Percent U.S. RDA Per Serving	
Calories	294	Protein	6%
Protein	4g	Vitamin A	9%
Carbohydrate	44g	Vitamin C	2%
Fat	12g	Thiamin	9%
Sodium	230mg	Riboflavin	7%
Potassium	201mg	Niacin	5%
		Calcium	5%
		Iron	10%

TIP: **Self-rising flour is not recommended.*

PINEAPPLE UPSIDE-DOWN CAKE

¼ cup margarine or butter
½ cup firmly packed brown sugar
8¼-oz. can (4 slices) pineapple, drained
4 maraschino cherries, drained
Easy One-Egg Cake, page 124

Heat oven to 350°F. In 8 or 9-inch square pan, melt margarine. Stir in brown sugar. Arrange pineapple slices and cherries on top of sugar mixture. Prepare cake batter as directed; pour evenly over fruit in pan. Bake at 350°F. for 40 to 45 minutes or until toothpick inserted in center comes out clean. Invert onto plate. Leave pan over cake a few minutes. Serve warm or cold, plain or with whipped cream.

8 or 9-inch square cake

NUTRITION INFORMATION PER SERVING

Serving Size: 1/9 of recipe		Percent U.S. RDA Per Serving	
Calories	309	Protein	5%
Protein	3g	Vitamin A	6%
Carbohydrate	48g	Vitamin C	3%
Fat	12g	Thiamin	9%
Sodium	272mg	Riboflavin	7%
Potassium	117mg	Niacin	5%
		Calcium	6%
		Iron	6%

TIP: *For ORANGE-COCONUT UPSIDE-DOWN CAKE, omit brown sugar and pineapple; add ¾ cup orange marmalade and ½ cup coconut to margarine.*

STREUSEL RHUBARB CAKE

CAKE

2 cups Pillsbury's Best® All Purpose or Unbleached Flour*
½ cup sugar
2 teaspoons baking powder
1 teaspoon salt
1 cup milk
¼ cup margarine or shortening
1 egg
4 cups sliced fresh rhubarb
½ pkg. (3 tablespoons) strawberry or raspberry-flavored gelatin

STREUSEL TOPPING

¾ cup sugar
½ cup Pillsbury's Best® All Purpose or Unbleached Flour
½ cup quick-cooking rolled oats
½ teaspoon cinnamon, if desired
¼ cup margarine or butter

Heat oven to 375°F. Grease (not oil) bottom only of 13x9-inch or 12x8-inch pan. In large bowl, blend all Cake ingredients except rhubarb and gelatin at low speed until moistened. Beat 2 minutes at medium speed. Pour batter into prepared pan; top with rhubarb and sprinkle with gelatin. In small bowl, combine first 4 Topping ingredients; cut in margarine until crumbly. Sprinkle Topping over rhubarb mixture. Bake at 375°F. for 35 to 40 minutes or until toothpick inserted in several places comes out clean. Serve warm or cool, topped with whipped cream, if desired.

13x9-inch cake

NUTRITION INFORMATION PER SERVING

Serving Size: 1/12 of recipe		Percent U.S. RDA Per Serving	
Calories	297	Protein	8%
Protein	5g	Vitamin A	9%
Carbohydrate	49g	Vitamin C	4%
Fat	9g	Thiamin	14%
Sodium	354mg	Riboflavin	11%
Potassium	177mg	Niacin	8%
		Calcium	8%
		Iron	8%

TIP: **Self-rising flour is not recommended.*

Moist and flavorful, a perfect banana cake.

BANANA NUT CAKE

2¼ cups Pillsbury's Best® All Purpose or Unbleached Flour*
1⅔ cups sugar
1¼ teaspoons baking powder
1 teaspoon salt
1 teaspoon soda
1¼ cups (2 medium) mashed ripe bananas
⅔ cup buttermilk
⅔ cup margarine or butter, softened
2 eggs
⅔ cup chopped nuts

Heat oven to 350°F. Grease (not oil) and lightly flour bottom only of 13x9-inch pan. In large bowl, blend all ingredients except eggs and nuts at low speed until moistened. Beat 2 minutes at medium speed. Add eggs; beat 2 more minutes at medium speed. Stir in nuts. Pour batter into prepared pan. Bake at 350°F. for 35 to 45 minutes or until toothpick inserted in center comes out clean. Cool completely. Frost with Butter Frosting, page 148.

13x9-inch cake

NUTRITION INFORMATION PER SERVING

Serving Size: 1/12 of recipe		Percent U.S. RDA Per Serving	
Calories	367	Protein	8%
Protein	5g	Vitamin A	11%
Carbohydrate	53g	Vitamin C	2%
Fat	16g	Thiamin	13%
Sodium	457mg	Riboflavin	10%
Potassium	174mg	Niacin	7%
		Calcium	4%
		Iron	7%

TIP: **If using Pillsbury's Best® Self Rising Flour, omit baking powder, salt and soda.*

HIGH ALTUTIDE–Above 3500 Feet: Increase flour to 2½ cups and buttermilk to 1 cup. Bake at 375°F. for 35 minutes.

A 3⅛-oz. pkg. vanilla-flavored pudding and pie filling, prepared according to package directions may be substituted for the canned pudding.

CHERRY CHIP LANE CAKE

CAKE

- **3 cups Pillsbury's Best® All Purpose or Unbleached Flour***
- **1½ cups sugar**
- **4 teaspoons baking powder**
- **1 teaspoon salt**
- **1 cup milk**
- **¾ cup margarine or butter, softened**
- **1½ teaspoons almond extract**
- **1 teaspoon vanilla**
- **2 eggs**
- **10-oz. jar (1¼ cups) maraschino cherries, drained and finely chopped (reserve some whole for garnish, if desired)**

FILLING

- **1 cup coconut**
- **½ cup chopped nuts**
- **17½-oz. can (2 cups) prepared vanilla pudding**
- **Powdered sugar**

Heat oven to 350°F. Generously grease (using 1 tablespoon solid shortening) and lightly flour 12-cup fluted tube pan. In large bowl, blend all Cake ingredients except cherries, at low speed until moistened. Beat 3 minutes at medium speed. Stir in cherries. Spoon batter into prepared pan. Bake at 350°F. for 40 to 50 minutes or until toothpick inserted in center comes out clean. Cool to lukewarm; invert onto serving plate. Cool completely. In small bowl, combine coconut, nuts and pudding. Cut cake into 3 layers; fill layers with pudding mixture. Sprinkle top with powdered sugar, garnish with whole cherries. Store covered in refrigerator.

10-inch ring cake

NUTRITION INFORMATION PER SERVING

Serving Size: 1/12 of recipe		Percent U.S. RDA Per Serving	
Calories	493	Protein	11%
Protein	7g	Vitamin A	12%
Carbohydrate	67g	Vitamin C	*
Fat	22g	Thiamin	16%
Sodium	705mg	Riboflavin	14%
Potassium	127mg	Niacin	9%
		Calcium	8%
		Iron	8%

TIP: **Self-rising flour is not recommended.*

CHERRY CHIP LANE CAKE

A graham cake topped with caramel ice cream topping, pecans and chocolate chips–sweet and gooey but so heavenly.

TURTLE SUNDAE CAKE

CAKE

1¼ cups Pillsbury's Best® All Purpose or Unbleached Flour*
1 cup (14 squares) graham cracker crumbs
⅔ cup sugar
1 tablespoon baking powder
½ teaspoon salt
½ cup margarine or butter, softened
2 eggs
1 pint (2 cups) vanilla ice cream, softened

TOPPING

½ cup dairy sour cream
12-oz. jar (1 cup) caramel ice cream topping
½ cup chopped pecans
¼ cup semi-sweet chocolate chips
2 to 3 tablespoons milk

Heat oven to 350°F. Grease (not oil) bottom only of 13x9-inch pan. In large bowl, blend all Cake ingredients at low speed until moistened. Beat 2 minutes at medium speed. Pour batter into prepared pan. Bake at 350°F. for 25 to 30 minutes or until toothpick inserted in center comes out clean. Cool completely. In small saucepan, combine sour cream and ice cream topping. Heat just until it starts to bubble, stirring occasionally; cool slightly. Pour over cooled cake; spread evenly. Sprinkle pecans over cake. In small saucepan, melt chocolate chips with milk over low heat; stirring constantly. If necessary thin with additional milk to drizzling consistency. Drizzle chocolate over frosted cake. 13x9-inch cake

NUTRITION INFORMATION PER SERVING

Serving Size: 1/12 of recipe		Percent U.S. RDA Per Serving	
Calories	403	Protein	8%
Protein	5g	Vitamin A	12%
Carbohydrate	60g	Vitamin C	*
Fat	20g	Thiamin	10%
Sodium	439mg	Riboflavin	10%
Potassium	140mg	Niacin	4%
		Calcium	8%
		Iron	5%

TIP: **Self-rising flour is not recommended.*

HIGH ALTITUDE–Above 3500 Feet: Increase flour to 1¼ cups plus 2 tablespoons and add ¼ cup water along with ice cream. Bake at 375°F. for 30 minutes.

LAZY SUMMER SPONGE CAKE

LAZY SUMMER SPONGE CAKE

CAKE

1 cup milk, scalded
¼ cup margarine or butter
1¾ cups sugar
1 teaspoon vanilla
4 eggs
1¾ cups Pillsbury's Best® All Purpose or Unbleached Flour*
3 teaspoons baking powder
¾ teaspoon salt

TOPPING

⅔ cup firmly packed brown sugar
½ cup light cream or evaporated milk
1 cup coconut
½ cup chopped nuts

Heat oven to 350°F. Grease (not oil) 13x9-inch pan. In small saucepan, heat milk to scalding. Add margarine to hot milk; set aside. In large bowl, blend sugar, vanilla and eggs; beat 2 minutes at high speed until thick and lemon colored. Add remaining ingredients; beat 1 minute at low speed. Add milk mixture; beat 1 minute more at low speed. Pour batter into prepared pan. Bake at 350°F. for 30 to 35 minutes or until toothpick inserted in center comes out clean. Cool slightly. In medium saucepan, combine brown sugar and cream. Heat to boiling; cook over medium heat 3 minutes. Stir in coconut and nuts. Spread Topping over cake.

13x9-inch cake

NUTRITION INFORMATION PER SERVING

Serving Size: 1/12 of recipe		Percent U.S. RDA Per Serving	
Calories	400	Protein	10%
Protein	7g	Vitamin A	10%
Carbohydrate	59g	Vitamin C	*
Fat	16g	Thiamin	11%
Sodium	302mg	Riboflavin	11%
Potassium	189mg	Niacin	6%
		Calcium	8%
		Iron	10%

TIP: **Self-rising flour is not recommended.*

HIGH ALTITUDE—Above 3500 Feet: Not recommended.

SPONGE CAKE

6 eggs, separated
¾ teaspoon cream of tartar
1½ cups sugar
1½ cups Pillsbury's Best® All Purpose or Unbleached Flour*
1 tablespoon grated orange peel
1 teaspoon baking powder
½ teaspoon salt
½ cup apricot nectar or water
1 teaspoon rum extract or vanilla

Heat oven to 350°F. Separate eggs, placing whites in large bowl, yolks in small bowl. Add cream of tartar to egg whites; beat until mixture forms soft peaks. *Gradually* add ¾ cup sugar, 2 tablespoons at a time, beating on high speed until stiff peaks form. To egg yolks, add flour, remaining ¾ cup sugar, orange peel, baking powder, salt, apricot nectar and rum extract. Blend at low speed until moistened; beat 1 minute at medium speed. Pour over egg whites; fold in gently *just* until blended. Pour batter into ungreased 10-inch tube pan. Bake at 350°F. for 40 to 45 minutes or until top springs back when lightly touched. Invert tube pan on funnel or soft drink bottle; let hang until completely cool. Remove cooled cake from pan. Serve with fruit, sherbet, whipped cream or soft custard or split cake into 3 layers and fill with Lemon Filling, page 153.

10-inch ring cake

NUTRITION INFORMATION PER SERVING

Serving Size: 1/12 of recipe		Percent U.S. RDA Per Serving	
Calories	204	Protein	8%
Protein	5g	Vitamin A	9%
Carbohydrate	39g	Vitamin C	*
Fat	3g	Thiamin	9%
Sodium	149mg	Riboflavin	9%
Potassium	68mg	Niacin	4%
		Calcium	2%
		Iron	6%

TIP: **Self-rising flour is not recommended.*

HIGH ALTITUDE—Above 3500 Feet: Decrease sugar to 1¼ cups (using ½ cup plus 2 tablespoons for first addition). Bake at 375°F. for 35 to 40 minutes.

An easy chiffon cake that was equally popular with our bakers and tasters.

LAYER CHIFFON CAKE

2 eggs, separated
1½ cups sugar
2 cups Pillsbury's Best® All Purpose or Unbleached Flour*
2 tablespoons cornstarch
3 teaspoons baking powder
1 teaspoon salt
1 cup milk
⅓ cup oil
1½ teaspoons vanilla

Heat oven to 350°F. Grease (not oil) and lightly flour two 8 or 9-inch round cake pans. In small bowl, beat egg whites until foamy. *Gradually* add ½ cup sugar, beating until stiff peaks form; set aside. In large bowl, blend remaining 1 cup sugar with flour, cornstarch, baking powder, salt, oil and half of milk at low speed until moistened. Beat 1 minute at medium speed. Add remaining milk, vanilla and egg yolks; beat 1 minute more at medium speed. Fold in beaten egg whites. Pour batter into prepared pans. Bake at 350°F. for 30 to 35 minutes or until toothpick inserted in center comes out clean. Cool 10 minutes; remove from pans. Cool completely. Frost as desired. 8 or 9-inch layer cake

NUTRITION INFORMATION PER SERVING

Serving Size: 1/12 of recipe		Percent U.S. RDA Per Serving	
Calories	260	Protein	6%
Protein	4g	Vitamin A	3%
Carbohydrate	43g	Vitamin C	*
Fat	8g	Thiamin	10%
Sodium	282mg	Riboflavin	9%
Potassium	63mg	Niacin	6%
		Calcium	5%
		Iron	5%

TIP: **If using Pillsbury's Best® Self Rising Flour, omit baking powder and salt.*

HIGH ALTITUDE–Above 3500 Feet: Decrease sugar to 1¼ cups plus 1 tablespoon; add 1 additional tablespoon milk and bake at 375°F. for 25 to 30 minutes.

LEMON CHIFFON CAKE

2 cups Pillsbury's Best® All Purpose or Unbleached Flour*
1½ cups sugar
1 tablespoon baking powder
1 tablespoon grated lemon peel
1 teaspoon salt
½ cup oil
7 egg yolks
⅔ cup water
2 tablespoons lemon juice
1 cup egg whites (7 egg whites room temperature)
½ teaspoon cream of tartar

Heat oven to 325°F. In large bowl, combine first 5 ingredients. Make well in center; add in order oil, egg yolks, water and lemon juice. Stir or beat until smooth. In large bowl, beat egg whites with cream of tartar until very stiff peaks form (do not underbeat). *Gradually* pour egg yolk mixture over beaten whites; fold gently *just* until blended. Pour batter into ungreased 10-inch tube pan. Bake at 325°F. for 70 to 75 minutes or until top springs back when lightly touched in center. Invert tube pan on funnel or soft drink bottle; let hang until completely cool. Remove cooled cake from pan. Glaze with Lemon Glaze, page 149 or serve with sweetened fruit and ice cream or whipped cream. 10-inch ring cake

NUTRITION INFORMATION PER SERVING

Serving Size: 1/12 of recipe		Percent U.S. RDA Per Serving	
Calories	302	Protein	9%
Protein	6g	Vitamin A	6%
Carbohydrate	41g	Vitamin C	3%
Fat	13g	Thiamin	10%
Sodium	295mg	Riboflavin	10%
Potassium	63mg	Niacin	6%
		Calcium	3%
		Iron	6%

TIP: *For ORANGE CHIFFON CAKE, substitute 2 tablespoons grated orange peel for the lemon peel and ¾ cup orange juice for the liquid.*

**Self-rising flour is not recommended.*

HIGH ALTITUDE–Above 3500 Feet: Decrease sugar to 1¼ cups plus 1 tablespoon and baking powder to 2¼ teaspoons; add 1 additional tablespoon lemon juice. Bake at 350°F. for 70 to 75 minutes.

Very tender with a delicious flavor. But don't expect a homemade angelfood to have quite the volume as the boxed mix version.

ANGEL FOOD CAKE

- **¾ cup Pillsbury's Best® All Purpose or Unbleached Flour***
- **1½ cups sugar**
- **1½ cups egg whites (12 egg whites room temperature)**
- **1½ teaspoons cream of tartar**
- **¼ teaspoon salt**
- **1½ teaspoons vanilla**
- **½ teaspoon almond extract**

Heat oven to 375°F. In small bowl, combine flour with ¾ cup sugar. In large bowl, beat egg whites with cream of tartar and salt until mixture forms soft peaks. *Gradually* add remaining ¾ cup sugar, 2 tablespoons at a time, beating on high speed until stiff peaks form. Fold in vanilla and almond extract. Spoon flour mixture, ¼ cup at a time, over beaten egg whites; fold in gently *just* until blended. Pour batter into ungreased 10-inch tube pan. Cut gently through batter to remove large air bubbles. Bake at 375°F. for 30 to 35 minutes or until crust is golden brown and cracks are very dry. Immediately invert pan on funnel or soft drink bottle; let hang until completely cool. Remove cooled cake from pan.

10-inch ring cake

NUTRITION INFORMATION PER SERVING

Serving Size: 1/12 of recipe		Percent U.S. RDA Per Serving	
Calories	139	Protein	6%
Protein	4g	Vitamin A	0%
Carbohydrate	31g	Vitamin C	0%
Fat	<1g	Thiamin	3%
Sodium	88mg	Riboflavin	6%
Potassium	49mg	Niacin	2%
		Calcium	*
		Iron	*

TIPS: *If desired, fold ½ cup well-drained chopped maraschino cherries, 1 cup shredded coconut or 2 squares grated semi-sweet chocolate, into batter.*

To halve recipe, use half the ingredient amounts; bake in 9x5-inch loaf pan for 25 to 30 minutes.

Bake cake in tube pan on bottom rack in oven.

**Self-rising flour is not recommended.*

HIGH ALTITUDE–Above 3500 Feet: Decrease sugar to 1¼ cups plus 1 tablespoon and bake at 375°F. for 35 to 45 minutes.

CHOCOLATE DESSERT ROLL

CHOCOLATE DESSERT ROLL

CAKE

½ cup Pillsbury's Best® All Purpose or Unbleached Flour*
¼ cup unsweetened cocoa
1 teaspoon baking powder
¼ teaspoon salt
4 eggs, separated
¾ cup sugar
1 teaspoon vanilla
2 tablespoons water

FILLING

1 envelope unflavored gelatin
½ cup cold water
1 cup (½ pint) whipping cream
2 tablespoons sugar
1 to 2 teaspoons mint or rum extract
Few drops of green food coloring, if desired

Heat oven to 350°F. Generously grease (not oil) bottom only of 15x10-inch jelly roll pan; line with waxed paper and grease again. Combine first 4 ingredients; set aside. In small bowl, beat egg whites until foamy. *Gradually* add ½ of sugar, beating continuously until stiff peaks form. Set aside. In large bowl, beat egg yolks until thick and lemon-colored. Add remaining sugar and vanilla; beat until very thick. Stir in water. Add flour mixture gradually, folding into egg yolk mixture after each addition. Gently fold in beaten egg whites. Spread batter into prepared pan. Bake at 350°F. for 18 to 22 minutes or until top springs back when lightly touched in center. Loosen edges; immediately turn onto towel dusted with powdered sugar. Starting at narrow end, roll up cake in towel; place on rack to cool completely.

To make Filling, soften gelatin in cold water then heat over hot water until dissolved. In small bowl, beat whipping cream until slightly thickened. Add sugar and mint extract; beat until thickened. Stir in dissolved gelatin. Chill until firm. Beat Filling until smooth. When cake is cooled, unroll; remove towel. Spread cake with ¾ of Filling; roll up again, rolling loosely to incorporate Filling. Wrap in foil or waxed paper; refrigerate. To serve, top roll with remaining cream mixture; sprinkle with shaved chocolate, if desired. 8 to 10 slices

NUTRITION INFORMATION PER SERVING

Serving Size: 1/10 of recipe with Filling		Percent U.S. RDA Per Serving	
Calories	218	Protein	8%
Protein	5g	Vitamin A	13%
Carbohydrate	24g	Vitamin C	*
Fat	12g	Thiamin	5%
Sodium	122mg	Riboflavin	7%
Potassium	89mg	Niacin	2%
		Calcium	4%
		Iron	5%

TIP: **Self-rising flour is not recommended.*

HIGH ALTITUDE—Above 3500 Feet: Decrease baking powder to ½ teaspoon. Bake at 375°F. for 12 to 15 minutes.

JELLY ROLL

3 eggs
1 cup sugar
¼ cup cold water
1 teaspoon vanilla
1 cup Pillsbury's Best® All Purpose or Unbleached Flour*
2 teaspoons baking powder
½ teaspoon salt

Heat oven to 375°F. Generously grease (not oil) and lightly flour 15x10-inch jelly roll pan. In large bowl, beat eggs at high speed until thick and lemon-colored, about 5 minutes. *Gradually* add sugar, beating until light and fluffy. Stir in water and vanilla. Add flour, baking powder and salt; blend at low speed *just* until dry ingredients are moistened. Pour batter into prepared pan; spread evenly. Bake at 375°F. for 10 to 12 minutes or until top springs back when lightly touched in center. Loosen edges; immediately turn onto towel dusted with powdered sugar. Starting at narrow end, roll up cake in towel; place on rack to cool completely. When cake is cooled, unroll; remove towel. Spread cake with desired filling; roll up again, rolling loosely to incorporate filling. Wrap in foil or waxed paper; refrigerate. If desired, sprinkle with powdered sugar to serve.

8 to 10 slices

NUTRITION INFORMATION PER SERVING

Serving Size: 1/10 of recipe		Percent U.S. RDA Per Serving	
Calories	150	Protein	5%
Protein	3g	Vitamin A	4%
Carbohydrate	30g	Vitamin C	0%
Fat	2g	Thiamin	7%
Sodium	191mg	Riboflavin	6%
Potassium	35mg	Niacin	3%
		Calcium	2%
		Iron	4%

TIPS: *For filling try Lemon Filling, page 153, or Pineapple Filling, page 154.*

For variety, spread cake with ¾ cup raspberry preserves or favorite jelly before rolling up.

**Self-rising flour is not recommended.*

HIGH ALTITUDE–Above 3500 Feet: Decrease baking powder to 1 teaspoon. Bake at 375°F. for 10 to 12 minutes.

FROSTINGS AND FILLINGS

The saying "it's the frosting on the cake," is very true. When you top your cake with a frosting or glaze, you have truly added that final touch which says you care to make the very best.

Many of our cake recipes have suggestions for a complementary frosting. However, there are no strict rules–just what is commonly done. So, feel free to experiment with different flavor and texture combinations.

CAKE GLAZING TIPS

Cakes baked in fluted or plain tube pans are usually glazed instead of frosted (cakes are always inverted). To glaze, brush off crumbs, spoon small amount of glaze at a time on top of cake and spread, allowing some to run unevenly down the sides. A glaze should be thin enough to pour or drizzle but not so thin that it runs off the cake.

CAKE FROSTING TIPS

- Be sure cake is cool before frosting. Brush loose crumbs from sides of cake.
- Place first layer, top-side-down, on a plate. Pile about ⅓ to ½ cup frosting or filling lightly in the center of layer and spread evenly to the edge using spatula.

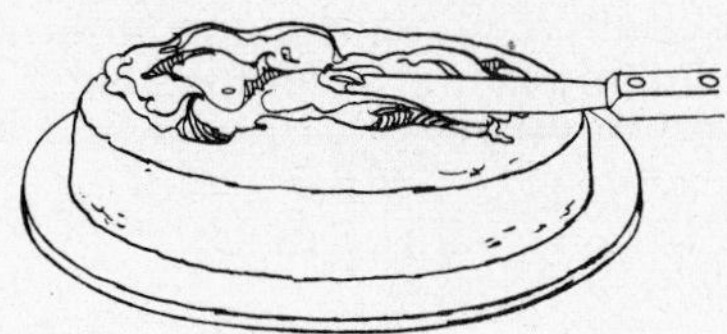

- Place top layer, bottom-side-down, on bottom layer. Frost sides with very light "base coat" of frosting to seal in crumbs. Apply more frosting using free, easy strokes. Spread with upward strokes, leaving a ridge of frosting around top of cake.

- Spread remaining frosting on top, making swirls with spatula or back of spoon.

- When frosting angel food cake, place cake up-side-down on plate. If you are using a thin frosting or glaze, spread it over top of cake, allowing it to "drip" down the sides. If you are using a fluffy or creamy frosting, spread sides with thin layer of frosting to seal crumbs. Apply another layer to sides, then frost top.
- Cupcakes may be frosted (use fluffy or soft whipped type frosting) by dipping top of each cupcake in frosting; turn slightly and remove.

QUICK DECORATING TECHNIQUES WITHOUT A DECORATING TUBE

There are many ways to achieve a decorative effect on a cake besides the fancy roses and writing you often see on "bakery cakes."

- Use the back side of a spoon to swirl S's or deep circles in the frosting.
- To make a spiral design on the top of a frosted cake, hold the spatula in the center of the cake; rotate cake while drawing spatula outward.
- With an inverted teaspoon, press tip in frosted cake. Make any type of pattern you wish.
- For a feather design, frost cake with vanilla frosting. Carefully drizzle chocolate glaze in narrow lines across the top about 1 inch apart. Lightly draw a toothpick or knife edge across chocolate lines at similar intervals. For a variation alternate directions of toothpick lines.
- Sprinkle or sift powdered sugar onto an unfrosted cake. For an interesting design first place a paper doily on cake; sprinkle powdered sugar over entire doily. Carefully remove doily by pulling straight up.

OTHER DECORATING GARNISHES

- Chocolate chips or butterscotch morsels
- Candied fruit—whole or cut up
- Grated chocolate
- Chocolate shot
- Coconut—flaked, grated or shredded
- Colored nonpareils and sugars
- Small nosegays of fresh flowers
- Grated lemon or orange peel
- Marshmallows
- Mint leaves
- Nuts—whole or chopped
- Peppermint candy—whole or crushed
- Fresh fruit—strawberries, sliced peaches, orange slices, cherries
- Sugared grapes
- Maraschino cherries
- Chocolate curls
- Banana slices dipped in lemon juice
- Candles
- Holly sprigs
- Animal crackers

CUTTING 13x9-INCH OR SHEET CAKES

Make diamonds, squares or triangles. Cut cake lengthwise into thirds. Then cut diagonally into triangles or diamonds or cut at right angles into squares or rectangles. Perfect for small party cakes. Just add a decorative touch on top of each piece. (30 to 36 servings.)

CUTTING LAYER CAKES

Method A: Cut layer cake in half. Cut slices parallel to first, continuing through one half of cake. Begin cutting at right angles into long thin slices—the size you desire. Continue with second half.

Method B: About 2 inches from outside of cake, cut a circle all the way around cake. Cut slices from outer circle first; continue with inner circle. This is a good method of cutting round wedding cakes. (36 to 40 servings.)

A.

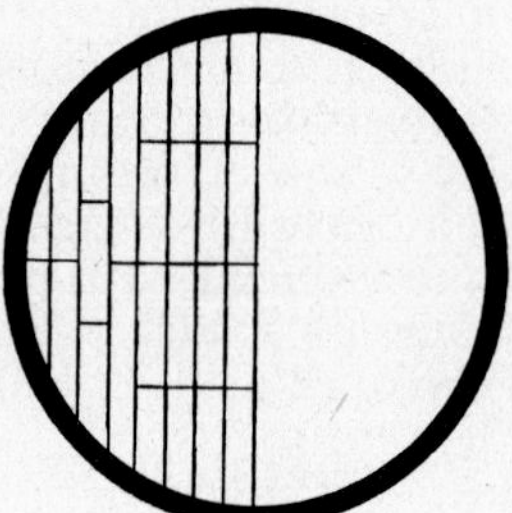

B.

MAKING AND USING A DECORATING CONE OR PASTRY TUBE

To make a "throw-away" cone, fold a 12-inch square sheet of heavy waxed paper or freezer-type paper in half diagonally, to form a triangle. Roll a cone, having a sharp point at one end and leaving other end open. Tape to hold. For a writing and outlining design, cut off pointed end, being careful that opening is right size. For a leaf design, cut W-shape from cone tip. For a scallop or shell design, cut several V's at tip. Decorating tips purchased at the store may be used with paper cones. Cut off about 1½ inches of pointed end; drop tip into cone having about ¾ of tip protruding on outside. Fill cone about ¾ full with Decorator Frosting; fold paper over several times and squeeze end shut above frosting. Make designs as you wish.

A purchased pastry tube and tips may be used similarly. Whipped cream designs may be made with the larger cone and tips.

TIPS FOR DECORATING WITH DECORATOR FROSTING

We suggest sifted powdered sugar; small lumps present in some unsifted sugar may clog pastry tip or show in the design.

Always keep bowl of frosting covered with a damp cloth to prevent frosting from drying.

If necessary, thin frosting if it becomes too stiff upon standing.

For writing, use a softer frosting than for border work. Roses and some other flowers require a stiffer consistency.

If frosting is too thin and is already in the pastry tube, chill it for a few minutes.

An uncolored shortening works best as food colorings give a more natural tint to uncolored frosting. Margarine or butter may also be used, but the yellow color may affect the tinted colors.

Draw design with a toothpick on cake before beginning to decorate.

Practice on waxed paper if uncertain what to do. (You can scrape off frosting and reuse it.)

DECORATOR FROSTING

⅔ cup shortening
4 cups (1 lb.) powdered sugar
1 teaspoon vanilla or ½ teaspoon almond extract
2 to 3 tablespoons milk
Food coloring, if desired

In medium bowl, cream shortening. Add powdered sugar, vanilla and enough milk for decorating consistency; beat until smooth and well blended. If necessary, thin with a few drops milk. Divide into small bowls, coloring as desired.

About 3 cups frosting

NUTRITION INFORMATION PER SERVING

Serving Size: 1 tablespoon		Percent U.S. RDA Per Serving	
Calories	63	Protein	*
Protein	<1g	Vitamin A	*
Carbohydrate	10g	Vitamin C	*
Fat	3g	Thiamin	*
Sodium	<1mg	Riboflavin	*
Potassium	1mg	Niacin	*
		Calcium	*
		Iron	*

The traditional basic frosting—creamy and easy to spread, with variations to suit any taste.

BUTTER FROSTING

⅓ cup margarine or butter, softened
4 cups (1 lb.) powdered sugar
¼ teaspoon salt
2 to 3 tablespoons milk
1 teaspoon vanilla

In large bowl, cream margarine. Add remaining ingredients. Beat until frosting is smooth and of spreading consistency. If necessary, thin with additional milk.

Frosts 13x9-inch cake or 2-layer cake

NUTRITION INFORMATION PER SERVING

Serving Size: 1/12 of recipe		Percent U.S. RDA Per Serving	
Calories	201	Protein	*
Protein	<1g	Vitamin A	4%
Carbohydrate	40g	Vitamin C	*
Fat	5g	Thiamin	*
Sodium	151mg	Riboflavin	*
Potassium	6mg	Niacin	*
		Calcium	*
		Iron	*

TIPS: *For BROWN BUTTER FROSTING, brown margarine in large saucepan over medium heat until light golden brown. Blend in remaining ingredients; beat until smooth.*

For CHOCOLATE BUTTER FROSTING, blend ⅓ cup unsweetened cocoa or 2 envelopes premelted unsweetened baking chocolate flavor or 2 oz. (2 squares) melted unsweetened chocolate into creamed margarine.

For CHOCOLATE-CHERRY BUTTER FROSTING, blend 3 tablespoons drained chopped maraschino cherries into Chocolate Butter Frosting.

For COFFEE BUTTER FROSTING, add 1½ teaspoons instant coffee with the sugar. (The coffee may be dissolved in the milk for a smooth, no fleck appearance.)

For CREAM CHEESE FROSTING, substitute 3-oz. pkg. cream cheese for margarine.

For MOCHA BUTTER FROSTING, blend 3 tablespoons unsweetened cocoa and 1 teaspoon instant coffee into creamed margarine.

For NUT BUTTER FROSTING, blend ¼ cup chopped nuts into frosting.

For ORANGE or LEMON BUTTER FROSTING, substitute 1 teaspoon grated orange or lemon peel for the vanilla and 2 to 3 tablespoons orange or lemon juice for the milk.

For PEANUT BUTTER FROSTING, cream 3 tablespoons peanut butter with the margarine.

Spread while still warm since the frosting cools to a very stiff consistency.

CARAMEL FROSTING

½ cup margarine or butter
1 cup firmly packed brown sugar
¼ cup milk
3 cups powdered sugar
½ teaspoon vanilla

In medium saucepan, melt margarine. Add brown sugar, cook over low heat 2 minutes, stirring constantly. Add milk; continue cooking until mixture boils. Remove from heat; gradually add powdered sugar. Add vanilla; mix well. If necessary, thin with a few drops milk.

Frosts 13x9-inch or 2-layer cake

NUTRITION INFORMATION PER SERVING

Serving Size: 1/12 of recipe		Percent U.S. RDA Per Serving	
Calories	255	Protein	*
Protein	<1g	Vitamin A	6%
Carbohydrate	48g	Vitamin C	*
Fat	8g	Thiamin	*
Sodium	102mg	Riboflavin	*
Potassium	73mg	Niacin	*
		Calcium	2%
		Iron	4%

Just like candy!

FUDGE FROSTING

2 cups sugar
¾ cup light cream
2 oz. (2 squares) unsweetened chocolate or 2 envelopes premelted unsweetened baking chocolate flavor
2 tablespoons light corn syrup
⅛ teaspoon salt
2 tablespoons margarine or butter
1 teaspoon vanilla

In heavy saucepan, combine first 5 ingredients. Heat slowly, stirring just until dissolved. Cook covered over medium heat for 2 minutes. Uncover and cook to soft-ball stage (234°F.); do not stir while cooking. Remove from heat; add margarine. Cool to lukewarm (110°F.). Additional cooling may cause frosting to harden too soon. Add vanilla; beat until frosting begins to thicken and loses its gloss. If necessary, thin with a few drops cream.

Frosts 2-layer or 13x9-inch cake

NUTRITION INFORMATION PER SERVING

Serving Size: 1/12 of recipe		Percent U.S. RDA Per Serving	
Calories	210	Protein	*
Protein	<1g	Vitamin A	4%
Carbohydrate	38g	Vitamin C	*
Fat	7g	Thiamin	*
Sodium	55mg	Riboflavin	*
Potassium	59mg	Niacin	*
		Calcium	2%
		Iron	3%

TIPS: *For MARSHMALLOW NUT-FUDGE FROSTING, add 1 cup miniature marshmallows and ½ cup chopped nuts to frosting just before spreading.*

For PEANUT BUTTER FUDGE FROSTING, add ¼ cup creamy peanut butter with margarine.

For best results add milk a teaspoon at a time until glaze is desired consistency.

BASIC POWDERED SUGAR GLAZE

2 cups powdered sugar
1 teaspoon vanilla
2 tablespoons margarine or butter, softened
3 to 4 tablespoons milk or light cream

In medium bowl, combine powdered sugar, vanilla, margarine and milk until mixture has consistency of a glaze. Use to glaze cakes, coffee cakes or pastries. 1½ cups glaze

NUTRITION INFORMATION PER SERVING

Serving Size: 1/12 of recipe		Percent U.S. RDA Per Serving	
Calories	96	Protein	*
Protein	<1g	Vitamin A	*
Carbohydrate	20g	Vitamin C	*
Fat	2g	Thiamin	*
Sodium	25mg	Riboflavin	*
Potassium	7mg	Niacin	*
		Calcium	*
		Iron	*

TIPS: *For CHOCOLATE GLAZE, add 2 oz. (2 squares) melted unsweetened chocolate or 2 envelopes premelted unsweetened baking chocolate flavor.*

For COFFEE GLAZE, substitute hot water for milk. Dissolve 1 teaspoon instant coffee in the hot water.

For LEMON GLAZE, substitute 2 tablespoons lemon juice for milk and add 1 teaspoon grated lemon peel.

For MAPLE GLAZE, add ½ teaspoon maple extract.

For ORANGE GLAZE, substitute orange juice for milk and add 1 teaspoon grated orange peel.

For SPICE GLAZE, combine ¼ teaspoon cinnamon and ⅛ teaspoon nutmeg with powdered sugar.

A creamy frosting that tastes like pudding but spreads like frosting. Be sure to allow time to refrigerate frosting before beating.

CREAMY WHIPPED FROSTING

¾ cup sugar
¼ cup flour
Dash salt
¾ cup milk
½ cup margarine or butter
1 teaspoon vanilla
Grated chocolate

In small saucepan, combine first 3 ingredients. Blend in milk. Cook over medium heat until mixture boils and thickens, stirring constantly. Stir in margarine (does not need to melt). Chill about ½ hour or until cool. Stir in vanilla and beat at high speed until light and fluffy. Sprinkle top of frosted cake with grated chocolate.

Frosts 13x9-inch cake

NUTRITION INFORMATION PER SERVING

Serving Size: 1/12 of recipe		Percent U.S. RDA Per Serving	
Calories	160	Protein	*
Protein	1g	Vitamin A	7%
Carbohydrate	18g	Vitamin C	*
Fat	10g	Thiamin	*
Sodium	125mg	Riboflavin	3%
Potassium	40mg	Niacin	*
		Calcium	2%
		Iron	*

TIPS: *For an eggnog flavor, add ½ teaspoon nutmeg and 1 tablespoon rum with vanilla.*

For CHOCOLATE CREAMY WHIPPED FROSTING, add 1 additional tablespoon flour and 1 envelope premelted unsweetened baking chocolate flavor or 1 square (1 oz.) melted unsweetened chocolate before cooking.

Cool whipped cream with crushed toffee. Delicious on a yellow or chiffon cake.

ENGLISH TOFFEE TOPPING

1½ cups whipping cream
¼ teaspoon instant coffee
3 tablespoons firmly packed brown sugar
1 tablespoon white creme de cacao, if desired
1 or 2 (1⅛ oz. each) Heath Candy Bars, crushed

In medium bowl, beat cream and coffee until slightly thickened. Beat in brown sugar and continue beating until thickened. Fold in creme de cacao. Spread Toffee Topping on cake or spoon dollops on individual servings. Sprinkle with crushed candy. Chill until served.

Frosts 13x9-inch cake

NUTRITION INFORMATION PER SERVING

Serving Size: 1/12 of recipe		Percent U.S. RDA Per Serving	
Calories	138	Protein	*
Protein	1g	Vitamin A	9%
Carbohydrate	6g	Vitamin C	*
Fat	13g	Thiamin	*
Sodium	11mg	Riboflavin	2%
Potassium	62mg	Niacin	*
		Calcium	3%
		Iron	*

TIPS: *To crush Heath bars, place between pieces of waxed paper. Roll or pound until pieces are of desired size.*

One teaspoon vanilla may be substituted for creme de cacao.

An easy frosting to spread on a cake —get creative with plenty of peaks and swirls.

SEVEN MINUTE FROSTING

1½ cups sugar
¼ teaspoon cream of tartar
¼ teaspoon salt
⅓ cup water
2 teaspoons light corn syrup
2 egg whites
1 teaspoon vanilla

In top of double boiler, combine all ingredients except vanilla. Place over rapidly boiling water (water should not touch bottom of pan), beating on high speed until mixture stands in peaks, about 7 minutes (don't overcook). Remove from heat; add vanilla. Continue beating until frosting holds deep swirls (about 2 minutes).

Frosts 13x9-inch cake or 2-layer cake

NUTRITION INFORMATION PER SERVING

Serving Size: 1/12 of recipe		Percent U.S. RDA Per Serving	
Calories	102	Protein	*
Protein	<1g	Vitamin A	0%
Carbohydrate	26g	Vitamin C	0%
Fat	0g	Thiamin	*
Sodium	54mg	Riboflavin	*
Potassium	8mg	Niacin	*
		Calcium	*
		Iron	*

TIPS: *For SEVEN MINUTE CHERRY FROSTING, substitute ⅓ cup maraschino cherry juice for water. Fold ⅓ cup drained chopped maraschino cherries into finished frosting.*

For SEVEN MINUTE CHOCOLATE REVEL FROSTING, add ⅓ cup semi-sweet chocolate chips to finished frosting. Let stand 1 to 2 minutes. Chocolate will swirl through frosting when spread on cake.

For SEVEN MINUTE LEMON FROSTING, fold in 3 teaspoons grated lemon peel.

For SEVEN MINUTE MAPLE FROSTING, substitute ½ to 1 teaspoon maple extract for vanilla.

For SEVEN MINUTE NESSELRODE FROSTING, substitute 1 teaspoon rum extract for vanilla. Remove 1 cup frosting to small bowl; stir in ½ cup chopped candied fruit and ½ cup toasted coconut. Spread between layers. Frost top and sides with remaining frosting.

For SEVEN MINUTE PEPPERMINT FROSTING, substitute 3 to 5 drops peppermint extract for vanilla. Fold ½ cup crushed hard peppermint candy into finished frosting.

An easy to make version of the Seven Minute Frosting.

WHITE CLOUD FROSTING

2 egg whites
¼ teaspoon salt
¼ cup sugar
¾ cup light corn syrup
1½ teaspoons vanilla

In small bowl, beat egg whites and salt until foamy. Gradually add sugar, continuously beating until soft peaks form. In small saucepan, heat corn syrup just to boiling. Pour in thin stream over egg whites, continuing to beat until frosting is stiff. Beat in vanilla. Spread on cooled cake.

Frosts 13x9-inch or 2-layer cake

NUTRITION INFORMATION PER SERVING

Serving Size: 1/12 of recipe		Percent U.S. RDA Per Serving	
Calories	78	Protein	*
Protein	<1g	Vitamin A	0%
Carbohydrate	20g	Vitamin C	0%
Fat	0g	Thiamin	0%
Sodium	67mg	Riboflavin	*
Potassium	9mg	Niacin	*
		Calcium	*
		Iron	5%

TIP: *For 8 or 9-inch square or 1-layer cake, use half ingredient amounts.*

This is the traditional German Chocolate Cake frosting.

COCONUT PECAN FROSTING

1 cup sugar
1 cup evaporated milk
½ cup margarine or butter
3 eggs, beaten
1⅓ cups flaked coconut
1 cup chopped pecans or almonds
1 teaspoon vanilla

In medium saucepan, combine sugar, milk, margarine and eggs. Cook over medium heat until mixture starts to bubble, stirring constantly. Stir in remaining ingredients. Cool until of spreading consistency. Frosts 13x9-inch cake or tops of 3 layers

NUTRITION INFORMATION PER SERVING

Serving Size: 1/12 of recipe		Percent U.S. RDA Per Serving	
Calories	317	Protein	8%
Protein	5g	Vitamin A	11%
Carbohydrate	23g	Vitamin C	*
Fat	24g	Thiamin	8%
Sodium	135mg	Riboflavin	8%
Potassium	202mg	Niacin	*
		Calcium	7%
		Iron	5%

BROILED COCONUT TOPPING

¼ cup margarine or butter
1 cup flaked or shredded coconut
⅔ cup firmly packed brown sugar
½ cup chopped nuts
3 tablespoons cream or milk

In small saucepan, melt margarine. Stir in remaining ingredients. Spread on warm cake. Broil about 5 inches from heat for 1 to 2 minutes or until bubbly and light golden brown. (Watch carefully, mixture burns easily.) Frosts 13x9-inch cake

NUTRITION INFORMATION PER SERVING

Serving Size: 1/12 of recipe		Percent U.S. RDA Per Serving	
Calories	146	Protein	*
Protein	1g	Vitamin A	3%
Carbohydrate	14g	Vitamin C	*
Fat	10g	Thiamin	*
Sodium	50mg	Riboflavin	*
Potassium	96mg	Niacin	*
		Calcium	*
		Iron	4%

TIPS: *Half a recipe will frost one 8 or 9-inch cake.*

For ORANGE-COCONUT TOPPING, substitute orange juice for cream and add 1 tablespoon grated orange peel.

BROILED ALMOND TOPPING

¼ cup sugar
1 tablespoon flour
¼ cup margarine or butter
1 tablespoon milk
½ cup slivered almonds

In small saucepan, combine all ingredients except almonds. Heat to boiling, stirring occasionally. Add almonds. Spread on warm cake. Broil about 5 inches from heat for 2 to 3 minutes or until bubbly and golden brown. (Watch carefully, mixture burns easily.) Frosts 8 or 9-inch square cake

NUTRITION INFORMATION PER SERVING

Serving Size: 1/9 of recipe		Percent U.S. RDA Per Serving	
Calories	109	Protein	2%
Protein	1g	Vitamin A	4%
Carbohydrate	8g	Vitamin C	*
Fat	9g	Thiamin	*
Sodium	63mg	Riboflavin	4%
Potassium	54mg	Niacin	*
		Calcium	*
		Iron	*

TIP: *If desired, add ½ cup coconut with almonds.*

Cakes and desserts that use this filling should be refrigerated to preserve freshness.

BASIC CREAM FILLING

½ cup sugar
3 tablespoons flour
¼ teaspoon salt
1¼ cups milk
2 egg yolks or 1 egg, slightly beaten
1 tablespoon margarine or butter
1 teaspoon vanilla

In small saucepan, combine sugar, flour and salt. Gradually add milk; mix well. Cook over medium heat until mixture boils, stirring constantly; boil 1 minute. Blend small amount (¼ cup) hot mixture into egg. Return egg mixture to saucepan; mix well. Cook until mixture starts to bubble, stirring constantly. Stir in margarine and vanilla. Cover and cool. Fills 1 layer or 1 jelly roll

NUTRITION INFORMATION PER SERVING

Serving Size: 1/12 of recipe		Percent U.S. RDA Per Serving	
Calories	73	Protein	2%
Protein	1g	Vitamin A	3%
Carbohydrate	11g	Vitamin C	*
Fat	3g	Thiamin	*
Sodium	71mg	Riboflavin	4%
Potassium	41mg	Niacin	*
		Calcium	3%
		Iron	*

TIPS: *For CHOCOLATE CREAM FILLING, increase sugar to ¾ cup and add 1 square (1 oz.) unsweetened chocolate or 1 envelope premelted unsweetened baking chocolate flavor with the sugar.*

For COCONUT CREAM FILLING, stir in ⅓ cup flaked coconut with vanilla.

For BUTTERSCOTCH CREAM FILLING, substitute ⅔ cup firmly packed brown sugar for granulated sugar.

LEMON FILLING

¾ cup sugar
3 tablespoons cornstarch
¼ teaspoon salt
¾ cup water
2 egg yolks, slightly beaten
3 tablespoons lemon juice
2 teaspoons grated lemon peel
1 tablespoon margarine or butter

In small saucepan, combine sugar, cornstarch and salt; blend in water. Cook over medium heat until mixture boils, stirring constantly; boil 1 minute. Blend a small amount of hot mixture into egg yolks. Return yolk mixture to saucepan; mix well. Gradually stir in lemon juice, lemon peel and margarine. Cook just until mixture starts to bubble, stirring constantly. Cool.

Fills 1 jelly roll or 2 layers

NUTRITION INFORMATION PER SERVING

Serving Size: 1/12 of recipe		Percent U.S. RDA Per Serving	
Calories	74	Protein	*
Protein	<1g	Vitamin A	3%
Carbohydrate	15g	Vitamin C	3%
Fat	2g	Thiamin	*
Sodium	58mg	Riboflavin	*
Potassium	9mg	Niacin	*
		Calcium	*
		Iron	*

TIP: *For ORANGE FILLING, omit lemon peel and juice; substitute orange juice for water and add 1 tablespoon grated orange peel with margarine.*

DATE FILLING

¼ cup sugar
1 tablespoon flour
1 cup milk
¾ cup chopped dates
1 egg, slightly beaten
½ teaspoon vanilla

In small saucepan, combine sugar and flour. Gradually stir in milk; add dates. Cook over medium heat until mixture boils, stirring constantly; boil 1 minute. Blend a small amount of hot mixture into egg. Return egg mixture to saucepan; mix well. Cook until mixture starts to bubble, stirring constantly. Stir in vanilla and cool. Fills 1 layer

NUTRITION INFORMATION PER SERVING

Serving Size: 1/12 of recipe		Percent U.S. RDA Per Serving	
Calories	70	Protein	2%
Protein	2g	Vitamin A	*
Carbohydrate	14g	Vitamin C	*
Fat	1g	Thiamin	*
Sodium	16mg	Riboflavin	4%
Potassium	108mg	Niacin	*
		Calcium	3%
		Iron	2%

PINEAPPLE FILLING

¾ cup sugar
3 tablespoons cornstarch
¼ teaspoon salt
8-oz. can (1 cup) crushed pineapple, drained (reserve liquid)
¾ cup liquid (reserved liquid plus water)
2 egg yolks, slightly beaten
1 tablespoon margarine or butter

In small saucepan, combine sugar, cornstarch and salt; blend in liquid. Cook over medium heat until mixture boils, stirring constantly; boil 1 minute. Blend a small amount of hot mixture into egg yolks. Return yolk mixture to saucepan; mix well. Gradually stir in pineapple and margarine. Cook just until mixture starts to bubble, stirring constantly. Cool. Fills 2 layers or 1 jelly roll

NUTRITION INFORMATION PER SERVING

Serving Size: 1/12 of recipe		Percent U.S. RDA Per Serving	
Calories	89	Protein	*
Protein	<1g	Vitamin A	3%
Carbohydrate	18g	Vitamin C	2%
Fat	2g	Thiamin	*
Sodium	59mg	Riboflavin	*
Potassium	22mg	Niacin	*
		Calcium	*
		Iron	*

APRICOT FILLING

½ cup sugar
¼ cup cornstarch
⅛ teaspoon salt
1½ cups apricot nectar
½ cup orange juice
1 tablespoon grated orange peel
2 tablespoons margarine or butter
½ teaspoon rum extract

In medium saucepan, combine sugar with cornstarch and salt. Gradually blend in apricot nectar and orange juice. Cook over medium heat until mixture boils and thickens, stirring occasionally. Stir in orange peel, margarine and rum extract. Cool thoroughly. Fill split cake layers or spread on 13x9-inch cake; top with whipped cream. Fills 3 layers

NUTRITION INFORMATION PER SERVING

Serving Size: 1/12 of recipe		Percent U.S. RDA Per Serving	
Calories	81	Protein	*
Protein	<1g	Vitamin A	8%
Carbohydrate	16g	Vitamin C	10%
Fat	2g	Thiamin	*
Sodium	46mg	Riboflavin	*
Potassium	69mg	Niacin	*
		Calcium	*
		Iron	*

COOKIES & CANDIES

COOKIES & CANDY

COOKIES

The first historic record of cookies was their use as test cakes. A small amount of cake batter was baked to test the oven temperature. The name cookie is derived from the Dutch word "koekje" meaning "little cake."

BASIC PREPARATION

It is best to heat your oven a few minutes before you begin baking your cookies. Because cookies need such a relatively short baking time, the oven temperature shoud be uniform when they start to bake or you may have some difficulty with uneven baking.

An electric mixer is of great help in creaming butter and sugar and in the blending of soft doughs. However, if you are making a stiffer cookie dough, you will have to make the last flour additions by hand.

Cookie sheets with little or no sides will allow the cookies to bake quickly and evenly. To allow for best circulation of heat, do not allow the pans to touch the oven sides.

Pans need to be greased only when stated in the recipe.

Avoid placing one sheet above another in the oven as this causes uneven baking. Cookies should be baked in the center of the oven.

Cool cookies on a wire rack immediately after baking. Warm cookies should never be stacked on top of each other. Drop, rolled, molded and pressed cookies are best removed from the cookie sheet with a wide spatula. If they stick they may have been cooled too much. In this case return to the oven for a few seconds until they can be easily removed.

STORAGE

Store cookies after they have completely cooled. Soft cookies should be stored in a tightly covered container. Crisp cookies are best stored in a container with a loosely fitting lid. If they soften in storage, they may be made crisp again by placing in a 300°F. oven for about 5 minutes.

ABOUT DROP COOKIES

Drop cookies are the quickest and easiest to make. The dough is usually mixed in one bowl and dropped by spoonfuls onto a cookie sheet. Use 2 teaspoons (not measuring spoons), spooning up the dough with one and pushing it onto the cookie sheet with the tip of the second. The size of each spoonful should be uniform with the others.

APRICOT JEWELS

¼ cup sugar
½ cup margarine or butter, softened
3-oz. pkg. cream cheese, softened
1¼ cups Pillsbury's Best® All Purpose or Unbleached Flour*
½ cup flaked coconut
1½ teaspoons baking powder
¼ teaspoon salt
½ cup apricot preserves

Heat oven to 350°F. In large bowl, combine first 3 ingredients; blend well. Stir in remaining ingredients until well blended. Drop by rounded teaspoonfuls, 2 inches apart onto ungreased cookie sheet. Bake at 350°F. for 15 to 20 minutes or until lightly browned. Immediately remove from cookie sheet.

36 cookies

NUTRITION INFORMATION PER SERVING

Serving Size: 2 cookies		Percent U.S. RDA Per Serving	
Calories	146	Protein	2%
Protein	2g	Vitamin A	6%
Carbohydrate	16g	Vitamin C	*
Fat	9g	Thiamin	4%
Sodium	133mg	Riboflavin	3%
Potassium	36mg	Niacin	2%
		Calcium	*
		Iron	2%

TIPS: *Drop by half-teaspoonfuls for 60 to 72 dainty, tea-size cookies.*

**If using Pillsbury's Best® Self Rising Flour, omit baking powder and salt.*

HIGH ALTITUDE–Above 3500 Feet: Decrease baking powder to 1 teaspoon. Bake at 350°F. for 15 to 20 minutes.

DROP BUTTER COOKIES

1 cup sugar or firmly packed brown sugar
¾ cup margarine or butter, softened
¼ cup milk
1 teaspoon vanilla
1 egg
2 cups Pillsbury's Best® All Purpose or Unbleached Flour*
1 teaspoon baking powder
¾ teaspoon salt

Heat oven to 375°F. In large bowl, combine first 5 ingredients; blend well. Stir in remaining ingredients; blend well. Drop by rounded teaspoonfuls, 1 inch apart onto ungreased cookie sheet. Bake at 375°F. for 9 to 12 minutes or until lightly browned. Immediately remove from cookie sheet. 48 cookies

NUTRITION INFORMATION PER SERVING

Serving Size: 2 cookies		Percent U.S. RDA Per Serving	
Calories	127	Protein	2%
Protein	2g	Vitamin A	5%
Carbohydrate	16g	Vitamin C	*
Fat	6g	Thiamin	5%
Sodium	154mg	Riboflavin	3%
Potassium	19mg	Niacin	3%
		Calcium	*
		Iron	2%

TIPS: *For COCONUT COOKIES, add 1½ cups flaked coconut with flour.*

For ORANGE-PECAN COOKIES, add ½ cup chopped pecans and 2 tablespoons grated orange peel with flour.

For LEMON-NUT COOKIES, add ½ cup chopped nuts and 2 teaspoons grated lemon peel with flour.

For GUMDROP COOKIES, add ¾ cup finely cut gumdrops and ½ cup chopped nuts with flour.

For CHOCOLATE-NUT COOKIES, add ¼ cup unsweetened cocoa and ½ cup chopped nuts with flour.

**Self-rising flour is not recommended.*

HIGH ALTITUDE–Above 3500 Feet: Bake at 400°F. for about 12 minutes.

A soft, tender cookie that is delicious frosted as an extra special treat.

SOUR CREAM COOKIES

1 cup sugar
½ cup shortening or margarine, softened
½ cup dairy sour cream
1 teaspoon vanilla
2 eggs
2¼ cups Pillsbury's Best® All Purpose or Unbleached Flour*
1 teaspoon soda
½ teaspoon nutmeg, if desired
¼ teaspoon salt

Heat oven to 350°F. Lightly grease (not oil) cookie sheets. In large bowl, combine first 5 ingredients; blend well. Stir in remaining ingredients. Drop by rounded teaspoonfuls, 2 inches apart onto prepared cookie sheet. Bake at 350°F. for 10 to 12 minutes or until golden brown. Immediately remove from cookie sheet. 42 to 48 cookies

NUTRITION INFORMATION PER SERVING

Serving Size: 2 cookies		Percent U.S. RDA Per Serving	
Calories	147	Protein	3%
Protein	2g	Vitamin A	2%
Carbohydrate	20g	Vitamin C	0%
Fat	7g	Thiamin	6%
Sodium	87mg	Riboflavin	5%
Potassium	20mg	Niacin	4%
		Calcium	*
		Iron	3%

TIPS: *If desired, add 1 cup chopped dates, chopped apricots or flaked coconut or ½ cup raisins or chopped nuts.*

For CHOCOLATE SOUR CREAM DROPS, omit nutmeg and add ¼ cup unsweetened cocoa with flour or 1 envelope premelted unsweetened baking chocolate flavor with vanilla.

**Self-rising flour is not recommended.*

HIGH ALTITUDE–Above 3500 Feet: Decrease soda to ¾ teaspoon. Bake at 375°F. for about 12 minutes.

The old-fashioned version that is everyone's favorite.

CHOCOLATE CHIP COOKIES

¾ cup firmly packed brown sugar
½ cup sugar
½ cup margarine or butter, softened
½ cup shortening
1½ teaspoons vanilla
1 egg
1¾ cups Pillsbury's Best® All Purpose or Unbleached Flour*
1 teaspoon soda
½ teaspoon salt
6-oz. pkg. (1 cup) semi-sweet chocolate chips
½ cup chopped nuts or sunflower nuts

Heat oven to 375°F. In large bowl, combine first 6 ingredients; blend well. Stir in flour, soda and salt; blend well. Stir in chocolate chips and nuts; mix well. Drop by rounded teaspoonfuls, 2 inches apart onto ungreased cookie sheet. Bake at 375°F. for 8 to 10 minutes or until light golden brown. Immediately remove from cookie sheet.
48 cookies

NUTRITION INFORMATION PER SERVING

Serving Size: 2 cookies		Percent U.S. RDA Per Serving	
Calories	202	Protein	3%
Protein	2g	Vitamin A	4%
Carbohydrate	22g	Vitamin C	*
Fat	12g	Thiamin	5%
Sodium	143mg	Riboflavin	3%
Potassium	71mg	Niacin	3%
		Calcium	*
		Iron	5%

TIPS: *For OATMEAL-CHOCOLATE CHIP COOKIES, decrease flour to 1¼ cups and add 1 cup quick-cooking rolled oats. Bake at 375°F. for 10 to 12 minutes.*

For PEANUT BUTTER-CHOCOLATE CHIP COOKIES, decrease margarine to ¼ cup, add ½ cup peanut butter and 2 tablespoons milk; increase eggs to 2.

Rising Flour, omit soda and salt.

CHOCOLATE CHIP COOKIES

A soft cake-like cookie with lots of spice.

PUMPKIN COOKIES

½ cup sugar
½ cup margarine or butter, softened
½ cup cooked pumpkin
1 teaspoon vanilla
1 egg
1 cup Pillsbury's Best® All Purpose or Unbleached Flour*
½ teaspoon baking powder
1½ teaspoons pumpkin pie spice
¼ teaspoon salt
½ cup raisins
½ cup chopped nuts

Heat oven to 350°F. In large bowl, combine first 5 ingredients; blend well. Stir in flour, baking powder, spice and salt; blend well. Stir in raisins and nuts. Drop by rounded teaspoonfuls, 2 inches apart onto ungreased cookie sheet. Bake at 350°F. for 12 to 15 minutes or until lightly browned. Immediately remove from cookie sheet; cool. If desired, frost with Brown Butter Frosting, page 148. 24 cookies

NUTRITION INFORMATION PER SERVING

Serving Size: 2 cookies (without frosting)		Percent U.S. RDA Per Serving	
Calories	200	Protein	4%
Protein	3g	Vitamin A	20%
Carbohydrate	23g	Vitamin C	*
Fat	12g	Thiamin	7%
Sodium	160mg	Riboflavin	4%
Potassium	113mg	Niacin	3%
		Calcium	2%
		Iron	5%

TIPS: *To double recipe, double the ingredient amounts.*

Cinnamon may be substituted for pumpkin pie spice; decrease to 1 teaspoon.

Whole wheat flour may be substituted for all-purpose flour.

For APPLESAUCE COOKIES, substitute applesauce for pumpkin. Increase flour to 1¼ cups and substitute cinnamon for pumpkin pie spice.

**Self-rising flour is not recommended.*

HIGH ALTITUDE–Above 3500 Feet: Bake at 375°F. about 15 minutes.

COCONUT MERINGUE MACAROONS

2 egg whites
⅛ teaspoon salt
¾ cup sugar
1 teaspoon vanilla or ½ teaspoon almond extract
1½ cups flaked coconut

Heat oven to 350°F. Grease (not oil) cookie sheets. In medium bowl, beat egg whites and salt until frothy. *Gradually* add sugar, beating continuously until stiff peaks form. By hand, fold in remaining ingredients. Drop by teaspoonfuls, 2 inches apart onto prepared cookie sheet. Bake at 350°F. for 12 to 15 minutes or until lightly browned. Cool 1 minute; remove from cookie sheet. 24 cookies

NUTRITION INFORMATION PER SERVING

Serving Size: 2 cookies		Percent U.S. RDA Per Serving	
Calories	101	Protein	*
Protein	1g	Vitamin A	0%
Carbohydrate	14g	Vitamin C	0%
Fat	5g	Thiamin	*
Sodium	32mg	Riboflavin	*
Potassium	53mg	Niacin	*
		Calcium	*
		Iron	*

This frosted cake cookie was a real favorite with our tasters.

GINGER CREAMS

½ cup sugar
½ cup hot water
½ cup molasses
¼ cup shortening
1 egg
2 cups Pillsbury's Best® All Purpose or Unbleached Flour*
1 teaspoon soda
½ teaspoon salt
½ teaspoon ginger
½ teaspoon cinnamon
½ teaspoon nutmeg
½ teaspoon cloves

FROSTING
2 cups powdered sugar
Dash salt
2 tablespoons margarine or butter, softened
2 to 3 tablespoons milk
½ teaspoon vanilla

Heat oven to 375°F. Grease (not oil) cookie sheets. In large bowl, combine first 5 ingredients; blend well. Stir in remaining cookie ingredients. Drop by rounded teaspoonfuls, 2 inches apart onto prepared cookie sheet. Bake at 375°F. for 10 to 15 minutes or until golden brown. Immediately remove from cookie sheet; cool. In small bowl, combine all Frosting ingredients; beat until light and fluffy. Spread over cooled cookies. 36 cookies

TIP: **Self-rising flour is not recommended.*

NUTRITION INFORMATION PER SERVING

Serving Size: 2 cookies		Percent U.S. RDA Per Serving	
Calories	187	Protein	3%
Protein	2g	Vitamin A	*
Carbohydrate	35g	Vitamin C	*
Fat	5g	Thiamin	6%
Sodium	160mg	Riboflavin	5%
Potassium	119mg	Niacin	4%
		Calcium	3%
		Iron	6%

PEANUT BUTTER-OATMEAL COOKIES

1 cup firmly packed brown sugar
¾ cup sugar
1 cup margarine or butter, softened or solid shortening
1 cup peanut butter
2 eggs
2 cups Pillsbury's Best® All Purpose or Unbleached Flour*
1 cup rolled oats
2 teaspoons soda
½ teaspoon salt

Heat oven to 350°F. In large bowl, combine first 5 ingredients; blend well. Stir in remaining ingredients. Drop by teaspoonfuls, 2 inches apart onto ungreased cookie sheet. Press each with a fork. Bake at 350°F. for 8 to 12 minutes or until golden brown. Immediately remove from cookie sheet. 60 to 72 cookies

NUTRITION INFORMATION PER SERVING

Serving Size: 2 cookies		Percent U.S. RDA Per Serving	
Calories	198	Protein	6%
Protein	4g	Vitamin A	6%
Carbohydrate	22g	Vitamin C	0%
Fat	11g	Thiamin	6%
Sodium	243mg	Riboflavin	4%
Potassium	103mg	Niacin	9%
		Calcium	*
		Iron	5%

TIP: **Self-rising flour is not recommended.*

HIGH ALTITUDE–Above 3500 Feet: Decrease soda to 1½ teaspoons. Bake at 375°F. for 8 to 12 minutes.

ABOUT MOLDED COOKIES

Molded cookies are made with a stiff dough and shaped by hand, generally into balls. The dough is more easily handled if it is well chilled and your hands are dusted with flour.

A favorite cookie for the holidays. Fill with green and red jam or jelly—frosting is nice also.

THUMBPRINT COOKIES

½ cup firmly packed brown sugar
¾ cup margarine or butter, softened
½ teaspoon vanilla
1 egg, separated
1⅓ cups Pillsbury's Best® All Purpose or Unbleached Flour*
¼ teaspoon salt
1 cup finely chopped nuts
Jam or jelly

Heat oven to 375°F. In large bowl, combine first 3 ingredients and egg yolk (reserve white); blend well. Stir in flour and salt; blend well. Shape into 1-inch balls. Slightly beat egg white. Dip balls in egg white, then roll in nuts. Place 1 inch apart on ungreased cookie sheet; press deep indention in center of each cookie with thumb. Bake at 375°F. for 8 to 10 minutes or until lightly browned. Immediately remove from cookie sheet; cool. Fill centers with jam or jelly.

30 to 36 cookies

NUTRITION INFORMATION PER SERVING

Serving Size: 2 cookies		Percent U.S. RDA Per Serving	
Calories	243	Protein	5%
Protein	3g	Vitamin A	8%
Carbohydrate	26g	Vitamin C	*
Fat	15g	Thiamin	7%
Sodium	157mg	Riboflavin	4%
Potassium	91mg	Niacin	3%
		Calcium	2%
		Iron	6%

TIP: **Self-rising flour is not recommended.*

Everybody's favorite! They keep well if you can manage to save a few.

PEANUT BUTTER COOKIES

½ cup sugar
½ cup firmly packed brown sugar
½ cup shortening or margarine, softened
½ cup peanut butter
2 tablespoons milk
1 teaspoon vanilla
1 egg
1¾ cups Pillsbury's Best® All Purpose or Unbleached Flour*
1 teaspoon soda
½ teaspoon salt

Heat oven to 375°F. In large bowl, combine first 7 ingredients; blend well. Stir in remaining ingredients; blend well. Shape into 1-inch balls. Place 2 inches apart on ungreased cookie sheet. Flatten in crisscross pattern with fork dipped in sugar. Bake at 375°F. for 10 to 12 minutes or until golden brown. Immediately remove from cookie sheet.

36 to 48 cookies

NUTRITION INFORMATION PER SERVING

Serving Size: 2 cookies		Percent U.S. RDA Per Serving	
Calories	186	Protein	5%
Protein	4g	Vitamin A	*
Carbohydrate	22g	Vitamin C	*
Fat	10g	Thiamin	6%
Sodium	171mg	Riboflavin	4%
Potassium	84mg	Niacin	9%
		Calcium	*
		Iron	4%

TIPS: *If desired, substitute whole wheat flour.*

For PEANUT BLOSSOMS, roll balls of dough in sugar. Place on cookie sheet, but do not flatten. Bake at 375°F. for 10 to 12 minutes or until golden brown. Immediately top each cookie with a candy kiss, pressing down firmly so cookie cracks around edge.

**Self-rising flour is not recommended.*

Crispy, light and spicy describes these homey cookies.

GINGERSNAPS

1 cup sugar
¾ cup shortening or margarine, softened
¼ cup molasses
1 egg
2 cups Pillsbury's Best® All Purpose or Unbleached Flour*
2 teaspoons soda
½ teaspoon salt
½ teaspoon cinnamon
½ teaspoon ginger
¼ teaspoon cloves

Lightly grease (not oil) cookie sheets. In large bowl, combine first 4 ingredients; blend well. Stir in remaining ingredients; blend well. Chill dough for easier handling. Heat oven to 375°F. Shape dough into 1-inch balls; roll balls in sugar. Place 2 inches apart on prepared cookie sheet. Bake at 375°F. for 8 to 10 minutes or until edges are set. Cool 1 to 2 minutes before removing from cookie sheet. 48 cookies

NUTRITION INFORMATION PER SERVING

Serving Size: 2 cookies		Percent U.S. RDA Per Serving	
Calories	137	Protein	2%
Protein	1g	Vitamin A	*
Carbohydrate	18g	Vitamin C	*
Fat	7g	Thiamin	5%
Sodium	141mg	Riboflavin	3%
Potassium	50mg	Niacin	3%
		Calcium	*
		Iron	3%

TIPS: *If desired, use whole wheat flour; decrease to 1¾ cups.*

**Self-rising flour is not recommended.*

A very buttery cookie with a tangy lemon filling. Perfect for a wedding or anniversary reception.

LEMON TEA COOKIES

1⅔ cups Pillsbury's Best® All Purpose or Unbleached Flour*
⅓ cup powdered sugar
1 cup margarine or butter, softened
1 teaspoon vanilla

FILLING
1 egg, beaten
⅔ cup sugar
2 to 3 teaspoons grated lemon peel
1 teaspoon cornstarch
¼ teaspoon salt
3 tablespoons lemon juice
1 tablespoon margarine or butter
Coconut or powdered sugar

In medium bowl, combine first 4 ingredients; blend well. Chill dough. Heat oven to 350°F. Shape dough into 1-inch balls. Place 2 inches apart on ungreased cookie sheet. With thumb or forefinger, make imprint in center of each cookie. Bake at 350°F. for 8 to 10 minutes or until lightly browned. Immediately remove from cookie sheet; cool. In medium saucepan, combine Filling ingredients except coconut or powdered sugar; cook over low heat, stirring constantly until smooth and thickened. Cool. Top each cookie with about ¼ teaspoon Filling; sprinkle with coconut or powdered sugar. 36 cookies

NUTRITION INFORMATION PER SERVING

Serving Size: 3 cookies		Percent U.S. RDA Per Serving	
Calories	311	Protein	5%
Protein	3g	Vitamin A	14%
Carbohydrate	30g	Vitamin C	4%
Fat	21g	Thiamin	8%
Sodium	250mg	Riboflavin	5%
Potassium	67mg	Niacin	5%
		Calcium	*
		Iron	5%

TIP: **Self-rising flour is not recommended.*

Also known as Mexican Wedding Cakes or Russian Tea Cakes, these are round butter-nut cookies rolled in powdered sugar.

SWEDISH TEA CAKES

½ cup powdered sugar
1 cup margarine or butter, softened
2 teaspoons vanilla
2 cups Pillsbury's Best® All Purpose or Unbleached Flour*
1 cup finely chopped or ground almonds or pecans
¼ teaspoon salt

Heat oven to 325°F. In large bowl, combine first 3 ingredients; blend well. Stir in remaining ingredients until dough holds together. Shape into 1-inch balls. Place 1 inch apart on ungreased cookie sheet. Bake at 325°F. for 15 to 20 minutes or until set but not brown. Immediately remove from cookie sheet. Cool slightly; roll in powdered sugar. Cool completely; roll again in powdered sugar. 60 cookies

NUTRITION INFORMATION PER SERVING

Serving Size: 3 cookies		Percent U.S. RDA Per Serving	
Calories	178	Protein	4%
Protein	3g	Vitamin A	7%
Carbohydrate	14g	Vitamin C	0%
Fat	13g	Thiamin	6%
Sodium	140mg	Riboflavin	6%
Potassium	65mg	Niacin	4%
		Calcium	*
		Iron	4%

TIP: **Self-rising flour is not recommended.*

A chocolate cookie that is rolled in powdered sugar before baking.

CHOCOLATE PIXIES

¼ cup margarine or butter
4 oz. (4 squares) unsweetened chocolate or 4 envelopes pre-melted unsweetened baking chocolate flavor
2 cups Pillsbury's Best® All Purpose or Unbleached Flour*
2 cups sugar
½ cup chopped walnuts
2 teaspoons baking powder
½ teaspoon salt
3 eggs
Powdered sugar

In large saucepan, melt margarine and chocolate over low heat, stirring constantly. Remove from heat; cool slightly. Stir in remaining ingredients, except powdered sugar; blend well. Chill dough for 30 minutes. Heat oven to 300°F. Shape into 1-inch balls. Roll in powdered sugar (coat heavily). Place 2 inches apart on ungreased cookie sheet. Bake at 300°F. for 15 to 18 minutes or until edges are set. Immediately remove from cookie sheet. 48 cookies

NUTRITION INFORMATION PER SERVING

Serving Size: 2 cookies		Percent U.S. RDA Per Serving	
Calories	190	Protein	4%
Protein	3g	Vitamin A	3%
Carbohydrate	31g	Vitamin C	*
Fat	7g	Thiamin	6%
Sodium	105mg	Riboflavin	5%
Potassium	70mg	Niacin	3%
		Calcium	*
		Iron	5%

TIP: **If using Pillsbury's Best® Self Rising Flour, omit baking powder and salt.*

Tender sugar cookie with a cinnamon-sugar topping.

SNICKERDOODLES

1½ cups sugar
½ cup margarine or butter, softened
1 teaspoon vanilla
2 eggs
2¾ cups Pillsbury's Best® All Purpose or Unbleached Flour*
1 teaspoon cream of tartar
½ teaspoon soda
¼ teaspoon salt
2 tablespoons sugar
2 teaspoons cinnamon

Heat oven to 400°F. In large bowl, combine first 4 ingredients; blend well. Stir in flour, cream of tartar, soda and salt; blend well. Shape dough into 1-inch balls. Combine 2 tablespoons sugar and cinnamon; roll balls in sugar mixture. Place 2 inches apart on ungreased cookie sheet. Bake at 400°F. for 8 to 10 minutes or until set. Immediately remove from cookie sheet.

48 cookies

NUTRITION INFORMATION PER SERVING

Serving Size: 2 cookies		Percent U.S. RDA Per Serving	
Calories	146	Protein	3%
Protein	2g	Vitamin A	4%
Carbohydrate	25g	Vitamin C	*
Fat	5g	Thiamin	6%
Sodium	98mg	Riboflavin	4%
Potassium	21mg	Niacin	4%
		Calcium	*
		Iron	3%

TIP: **Self-rising flour is not recommended.*

ABOUT ROLLED COOKIES

Rolled cookies are made from a stiff dough which is rolled and cut with sharp cookie cutters, a knife or pastry wheel. The cookies should be thin and crisp.

It is usually best to work with a small amount of dough at a time. Chill the dough if it is too soft to handle easily. A floured stockinette cover on the rolling pin will also help keep the dough from sticking. Dip cookie cutters in flour each time before cutting.

For the most tender cookies, use as little flour as possible. Save all the trimmings and roll at one time as these cookies will be less tender.

Be sure to roll dough as evenly as possible to a uniform thickness.

A wide spatula will help in transferring cookies from cutting surface to cookie sheet.

Lovely any time of the year. These are an easy cookie to roll; not too dry to break and not too wet to stick.

ROLLED SUGAR COOKIES

1 cup sugar
1 cup margarine or butter, softened
3 tablespoons cream or milk
1 teaspoon vanilla
1 egg
3 cups Pillsbury's Best® All Purpose or Unbleached Flour*
1½ teaspoons baking powder
½ teaspoon salt

In large bowl, combine first 5 ingredients; blend well. Stir in remaining ingredients; blend well. Chill dough for easier handling. Heat oven to 400°F. Roll dough, ⅓ at a time, on floured surface to ⅛-inch thickness. Cut with floured cookie cutter. Place 1 inch apart on ungreased cookie sheet. If desired, sprinkle with sugar. Bake at 400°F. for 5 to 8 minutes or until edges are light brown. Immediately remove from cookie sheet. 60 to 72 cookies

NUTRITION INFORMATION PER SERVING

Serving Size: 2 cookies		Percent U.S. RDA Per Serving	
Calories	132	Protein	3%
Protein	2g	Vitamin A	6%
Carbohydrate	16g	Vitamin C	*
Fat	7g	Thiamin	5%
Sodium	130mg	Riboflavin	3%
Potassium	18mg	Niacin	3%
		Calcium	*
		Iron	2%

TIPS: *For FILLED SUGAR COOKIES, prepare one of fillings suggested for Date-Filled Bars, page 177 or use jam or marmalade. Cut rolled dough with 2 to 2½-inch floured cookie cutter. Place half of cookies on cookie sheet. Place teaspoonful of filling on each. Top with another cookie; press edges to seal with floured tines of fork or tip of finger. Prick tops once with fork. Bake at 400°F. for 8 to 10 minutes or until edges are light brown.*

**Self-rising flour is not recommended.*

A child's holiday delight. Before baking make a small hole in the top for hanging on the Christmas tree.

ROLLED MOLASSES COOKIES

¾ cup sugar
½ cup margarine, softened or shortening
¾ cup molasses
½ cup buttermilk
4 cups Pillsbury's Best® All Purpose or Unbleached Flour*
1 teaspoon soda
2 teaspoons ginger
¾ teaspoon salt
½ teaspoon baking powder

In large bowl, combine first 4 ingredients; blend well. Stir in remaining ingredients; blend well. Chill several hours or overnight. Lightly grease (not oil) cookie sheets. Heat oven to 400°F. Roll dough, ½ at a time, on floured surface to ⅛-inch thickness. Cut with floured cookie cutter. Place 1 inch apart on prepared cookie sheet. Bake at 400°F. for 5 to 7 minutes or until edges are set. Immediately remove from cookie sheet. 84 cookies

NUTRITION INFORMATION PER SERVING

Serving Size: 2 cookies		Percent U.S. RDA Per Serving	
Calories	92	Protein	2%
Protein	1g	Vitamin A	*
Carbohydrate	16g	Vitamin C	*
Fat	2g	Thiamin	5%
Sodium	101mg	Riboflavin	4%
Potassium	80mg	Niacin	4%
		Calcium	2%
		Iron	4%

TIPS: *For GINGERBREAD MEN, roll dough ¼ inch thick for soft cookies or ⅛ inch thick for crisp cookies. Bake at 375°F. for 7 to 10 minutes.* 48 cookies

NUTRITION INFORMATION PER SERVING

Serving Size: 1 gingerbread man		Percent U.S. RDA Per Serving	
Calories	80	Protein	*
Protein	1g	Vitamin A	*
Carbohydrate	14g	Vitamin C	*
Fat	2g	Thiamin	5%
Sodium	88mg	Riboflavin	3%
Potassium	70mg	Niacin	3%
		Calcium	2%
		Iron	3%

If desired, substitute up to 2 cups whole wheat flour.

**If using Pillsbury's Best® Self Rising Flour, decrease soda to ¼ teaspoon and omit salt.*

We found this to be one of the easier Pepparkahar doughs to roll. A spicy crisp cookie that keeps for weeks.

PEPPARKAHAR

1½ cups sugar
1 cup margarine or butter, softened
2 tablespoons water or milk
3 tablespoons molasses
1 egg
3¼ cups Pillsbury's Best® All Purpose or Unbleached Flour*
2 teaspoons soda
2 teaspoons cinnamon
½ teaspoon salt
1½ teaspoons ginger
1 teaspoon cloves
½ teaspoon cardamom, if desired

Heat oven to 350°F. In large bowl, combine first 5 ingredients; blend well. Stir in remaining ingredients; blend well. Roll dough, ⅓ at a time, on floured surface to ⅛-inch thickness. Cut with floured cookie cutter. Place 1 inch apart on ungreased cookie sheet. Bake at 350°F. for 7 to 10 minutes or until cookies are set. Immediately remove from cookie sheet. 84 to 96 cookies

NUTRITION INFORMATION PER SERVING

Serving Size: 2 cookies		Percent U.S. RDA Per Serving	
Calories	108	Protein	*
Protein	1g	Vitamin A	4%
Carbohydrate	15g	Vitamin C	*
Fat	5g	Thiamin	4%
Sodium	134mg	Riboflavin	3%
Potassium	29mg	Niacin	3%
		Calcium	*
		Iron	2%

TIP: **Self-rising flour is not recommended.*

ABOUT VARIETY COOKIES

Variety cookies are cookies which have been developed as unique specialty items. We suggest you read through each recipe carefully before beginning, as they may contain special ingredients, utensils and/or unusual baking techniques.

SPRITZ

1 cup powdered sugar
1 cup margarine or butter, softened
1 egg or 2 egg yolks
1 teaspoon vanilla
½ teaspoon almond extract
2⅓ cups Pillsbury's Best® All Purpose or Unbleached Flour*
½ teaspoon salt

Heat oven to 400°F. In large bowl, combine powdered sugar and margarine; blend well. Stir in remaining ingredients; blend well. Fill cookie press with small amount of dough at a time; press dough into desired shapes onto ungreased cookie sheet. Bake at 400°F. for 6 to 8 minutes or until set but not browned. Immediately remove from cookie sheet.

72 cookies

NUTRITION INFORMATION PER SERVING

Serving Size: 3 cookies		Percent U.S. RDA Per Serving	
Calories	135	Protein	2%
Protein	2g	Vitamin A	7%
Carbohydrate	14g	Vitamin C	0%
Fat	8g	Thiamin	5%
Sodium	142mg	Riboflavin	3%
Potassium	17mg	Niacin	3%
		Calcium	*
		Iron	2%

TIP: **Self-rising flour is not recommended.*

HIGH ALTITUDE–Above 3500 Feet: Bake at 400°F. for 8 to 10 minutes.

SPRINGERLE

4 eggs
2 cups sugar
4 to 6 drops anise oil or ½ to 1 teaspoon anise extract
¼ teaspoon vanilla
3¾ cups Pillsbury's Best® All Purpose or Unbleached Flour*
1 teaspoon baking powder
¼ teaspoon salt

Lightly grease (not oil) cookie sheets or flour waxed paper sheets. In large bowl, beat eggs until very thick, about 15 minutes. *Gradually* add sugar, beating well after each addition. Continue beating 10 minutes. Beat in anise and vanilla. Stir in remaining ingredients. On floured surface, roll dough to ½-inch thickness; with Springerle rolling pin, roll designs in dough. Cut cookies along design lines and place on prepared cookie sheet or floured waxed paper. Cover with a cloth and let stand 8 hours or overnight. Heat oven to 375°F. Place cookies in oven and immediately decrease temperature to 300°F. Bake 10 to 15 minutes or until set. Immediately remove from cookie sheet. Store in tightly covered containers several weeks before using.

48 cookies

NUTRITION INFORMATION PER SERVING

Serving Size: 1 cookie		Percent U.S. RDA Per Serving	
Calories	75	Protein	2%
Protein	1g	Vitamin A	*
Carbohydrate	16g	Vitamin C	0%
Fat	1g	Thiamin	4%
Sodium	24mg	Riboflavin	3%
Potassium	16mg	Niacin	3%
		Calcium	*
		Iron	2%

TIPS: *If Springerle mold is used, roll dough ¼-inch thick and press a floured mold into dough; lift out and cut along design lines with a knife.*

**Self-rising flour is not recommended.*

FATTIGMAN

6 egg yolks, slightly beaten
4 tablespoons sugar
⅛ teaspoon salt
⅛ teaspoon cardamom
6 tablespoons whipping cream
1 tablespoon margarine or butter, melted
1¾ to 2 cups Pillsbury's Best® All Purpose or Unbleached Flour*

In large saucepan, heat 2 inches oil to 375°F. In large bowl, combine all ingredients except flour; blend well. Mix in enough flour to make a stiff dough. Divide dough in half. On well-floured surface, roll each half until very thin (about ⅛-inch thick). Cut dough into 1½x4-inch diamonds. Cut a slit in center of each diamond; pull 1 corner through slit. Fry in hot oil (375°F.) for about 1 minute or until light golden brown. Drain on paper towel. Dust with powdered sugar when served.

24 to 30 cookies

NUTRITION INFORMATION PER SERVING

Serving Size: 2 cookies		Percent U.S. RDA Per Serving	
Calories	148	Protein	5%
Protein	4g	Vitamin A	9%
Carbohydrate	18g	Vitamin C	*
Fat	7g	Thiamin	9%
Sodium	42mg	Riboflavin	7%
Potassium	33mg	Niacin	5%
		Calcium	2%
		Iron	6%

TIP: **Self-rising flour is not recommended.*

BUTTERY LACE COOKIES

½ cup margarine or butter
¾ cup quick-cooking rolled oats
½ cup sugar
¼ cup flour
2 tablespoons milk

Heat oven to 375°F. In medium saucepan, melt margarine. Stir in remaining ingredients. Cook, stirring constantly, just until mixture begins to bubble. Drop by level teaspoonfuls into ungreased muffin cups. Bake at 375°F. for 5 to 6 minutes or until light golden brown. Cool 2 minutes; while still warm, remove from muffin cups.

36 cookies

NUTRITION INFORMATION PER SERVING

Serving Size: 2 cookies		Percent U.S. RDA Per Serving	
Calories	87	Protein	*
Protein	<1g	Vitamin A	4%
Carbohydrate	9g	Vitamin C	*
Fat	5g	Thiamin	2%
Sodium	63mg	Riboflavin	*
Potassium	17mg	Niacin	*
		Calcium	*
		Iron	*

HIGH ALTITUDE–Above 3500 Feet: Bake at 400°F. for 5 to 6 minutes. Cool 1 minute; remove from muffin cups.

SANDBAKELS

½ cup sugar
½ cup margarine or butter, softened
1 teaspoon vanilla
¼ teaspoon almond extract
1 egg white
1¼ cups Pillsbury's Best® All Purpose or Unbleached Flour*

In large bowl, combine all ingredients except flour; blend thoroughly. Stir in flour; blend well. Chill dough 2 to 3 hours for easier handling.

Heat oven to 350°F. With floured fingers press dough about ⅛-inch thick into 36 sandbakel molds. Place molds on cookie sheet. Bake at 350°F. for 10 to 13 minutes or until lightly browned. Cool 3 minutes; remove from molds, pressing edge of mold lightly to loosen cookie. 36 cookies

NUTRITION INFORMATION PER SERVING

Serving Size: 2 cookies		Percent U.S. RDA Per Serving	
Calories	99	Protein	*
Protein	1g	Vitamin A	4%
Carbohydrate	12g	Vitamin C	0%
Fat	5g	Thiamin	4%
Sodium	65mg	Riboflavin	2%
Potassium	13mg	Niacin	2%
		Calcium	*
		Iron	*

TIP: **Self-rising flour is not recommended.*

ROSETTES

2 eggs, slightly beaten
1 cup milk
1 tablespoon lemon extract
2 teaspoons sugar
1 cup Pillsbury's Best® All Purpose or Unbleached Flour*
¼ teaspoon salt

In medium saucepan, heat 2 to 3 inches oil to 375°F. Place rosette iron in oil to heat. In small bowl, combine first 4 ingredients; blend well. Stir in flour and salt; beat until smooth. Remove iron, allowing excess oil to drip off. Dip hot iron into batter, *just* to depth of the form (not over the top); then in hot oil (375°F.). Hold iron in oil until rosette is a delicate brown, about ½ minute. Immediately slide rosette off iron (if necessary tap top of form with wooden spoon to release cookie); drain on paper towel. Repeat with remaining batter, reheating iron each time. If iron or fat is not the correct temperature (too hot or too cold), the batter will not stick to the forms. Cool; sprinkle with powdered sugar. 30 to 36 rosettes

NUTRITION INFORMATION PER SERVING

Serving Size: 1 rosette		Percent U.S. RDA Per Serving	
Calories	54	Protein	*
Protein	1g	Vitamin A	*
Carbohydrate	4g	Vitamin C	*
Fat	4g	Thiamin	2%
Sodium	27mg	Riboflavin	2%
Potassium	20mg	Niacin	*
		Calcium	*
		Iron	*

TIPS: *If rosettes are not crisp the batter is too thick. Thin with small amount of milk.*

**Self-rising flour is not recommended.*

COCOA BUTTER STICKS

¾ cup sugar
¾ cup margarine or butter, softened
1 egg, slightly beaten (reserve 1 tablespoon)
1½ cups Pillsbury's Best® All Purpose or Unbleached Flour*
2 tablespoons unsweetened cocoa
1 teaspoon baking powder
½ teaspoon salt
1 tablespoon water
3 tablespoons finely chopped almonds or other nuts
2 tablespoons sugar

In large bowl, combine first 3 ingredients; blend well. Stir in flour, cocoa, baking powder and salt; blend well. Chill dough for easier handling. Heat oven to 400°F. Divide dough into 4 parts. Shape each into roll ¾ inches in diameter. Place 4 inches apart on ungreased cookie sheet (use 2 cookie sheets). With fork dipped in flour, flatten each roll to ¼-inch thickness. Combine water with reserved egg; brush over dough. Combine almonds with sugar; sprinkle over dough. Bake at 400°F. for 9 to 12 minutes or until set but not brown. Cool about 1 minute. Cut strips crosswise into 1-inch "sticks"; remove from cookie sheet.

60 cookies

NUTRITION INFORMATION PER SERVING

Serving Size: 2 cookies		Percent U.S. RDA Per Serving	
Calories	95	Protein	*
Protein	1g	Vitamin A	4%
Carbohydrate	11g	Vitamin C	0%
Fat	5g	Thiamin	3%
Sodium	106mg	Riboflavin	2%
Potassium	22mg	Niacin	*
		Calcium	*
		Iron	*

TIPS: *For individual cookies, shape dough into 1-inch balls. Place on cookie sheet 2 inches apart, flatten and brush with egg and sprinkle with sugar mixture. Bake as directed.* About 36 cookies

If desired, substitute up to half whole wheat flour.

**Self-rising flour is not recommended.*

SWEDISH SHORTBREAD

1 cup margarine or butter, softened
½ cup plus 2 tablespoons sugar
2 to 2½ cups Pillsbury's Best® All Purpose, Unbleached or Self Rising Flour
⅓ cup raspberry jam
1 cup powdered sugar
1 teaspoon almond extract
2 to 3 teaspoons water

Heat oven to 350°F. In large bowl, blend margarine and sugar; add flour and mix well. Divide dough into 6 parts. On ungreased cookie sheet, roll or pat each part into a strip about 1½ inches wide and 12 inches long. Using knife handle, make slight indention lengthwise down center of each strip. (Do not make indention too deep or cookies will break.) Fill indention with jam. Bake at 350°F. for 10 to 12 minutes or until edges are lightly browned. In small bowl, mix powdered sugar, almond extract and water to make thin glaze. While still warm, drizzle glaze across strips and cut diagonally into 1-inch slices.

60 cookies

NUTRITION INFORMATION PER SERVING

Serving Size: 2 cookies		Percent U.S. RDA Per Serving	
Calories	119	Protein	*
Protein	<1g	Vitamin A	5%
Carbohydrate	15g	Vitamin C	*
Fat	6g	Thiamin	4%
Sodium	75mg	Riboflavin	2%
Potassium	13mg	Niacin	2%
		Calcium	*
		Iron	*

REFRIGERATOR COOKIES

Refrigerator cookies are the answer to having fresh cookies on a moment's notice. They are usually made with a rich dough which is very stiff and shaped into long rolls 1 or 2 inches in diameter. Because they are refrigerated before baking, they can be sliced quite thin for a very tender cookie.

For a festive touch, roll the entire roll in finely chopped nuts or colored sugar.

Cookie dough may be stored in the refrigerator for several days, or carefully wrapped and stored in the freezer for several months.

CHERRY-NUT SLICES

1 cup powdered sugar
1 cup margarine or butter, softened
1 teaspoon vanilla
1 egg
2 cups Pillsbury's Best® All Purpose or Unbleached Flour*
2 cups candied cherries, halved
1 cup chopped pecans

In large bowl, combine first 4 ingredients; blend well. Stir in flour, cherries and pecans. If desired, chill dough for easier handling. Divide dough into thirds on 3 sheets of waxed paper; shape each third into roll 1½ inches in diameter. Wrap; refrigerate until firm, about 3 hours. Heat oven to 325°F. Cut dough into ¼-inch slices. Place 1 inch apart on ungreased cookie sheet. Bake at 325°F. for 15 minutes or until edges are lightly browned. Immediately remove from cookie sheet.

72 to 96 cookies

NUTRITION INFORMATION PER SERVING

Serving Size: 2 cookies		Percent U.S. RDA Per Serving	
Calories	125	Protein	*
Protein	1g	Vitamin A	5%
Carbohydrate	13g	Vitamin C	*
Fat	8g	Thiamin	5%
Sodium	64mg	Riboflavin	2%
Potassium	30mg	Niacin	2%
		Calcium	*
		Iron	*

TIP: **Self-rising flour is not recommended.*

BASIC REFRIGERATOR COOKIES

½ cup sugar
½ cup firmly packed brown sugar
⅔ cup margarine or butter, softened
1 teaspoon vanilla
1 egg
2 cups Pillsbury's Best® All Purpose or Unbleached Flour*
1 teaspoon baking powder
½ teaspoon salt
¾ cup finely chopped nuts

In large bowl, combine first 5 ingredients; blend well. Stir in flour, baking powder and salt; blend well. Stir in nuts. Divide dough in half on 2 sheets of waxed paper; shape each half into roll 1½ inches in diameter. Wrap; chill until firm, about 2 hours. Heat oven to 425°F. Cut dough into ¼-inch slices. Place 1 inch apart on ungreased cookie sheet. Bake at 425°F. for 5 to 7 minutes or until light brown. Immediately remove from cookie sheet.

60 to 72 cookies

NUTRITION INFORMATION PER SERVING

Serving Size: 2 cookies		Percent U.S. RDA Per Serving	
Calories	116	Protein	2%
Protein	2g	Vitamin A	4%
Carbohydrate	14g	Vitamin C	*
Fat	6g	Thiamin	4%
Sodium	100mg	Riboflavin	3%
Potassium	38mg	Niacin	2%
		Calcium	*
		Iron	3%

TIPS: *For ORANGE or LEMON REFRIGERATOR COOKIES, add 1 tablespoon grated peel with flour.*

For SPICE REFRIGERATOR COOKIES, add 1 teaspoon cinnamon, ½ teaspoon nutmeg and ¼ to ½ teaspoon cloves with flour.

For COCONUT REFRIGERATOR COOKIES, add 1 cup coconut with nuts.

Cookie dough keeps up to 2 weeks in refrigerator and up to 6 weeks in freezer. Slice and bake frozen dough as directed above.

**Self-rising flour is not recommended.*

Oatmeal makes these extra crispy—nuts give it crunch!

OATMEAL REFRIGERATOR COOKIES

1 cup sugar
1 cup firmly packed brown sugar
1 cup margarine, butter or shortening
2 eggs
2 cups Pillsbury's Best® All Purpose or Unbleached Flour*
1 teaspoon soda
1 teaspoon baking powder
1 teaspoon salt
2 cups quick-cooking rolled oats
1 cup coconut
½ to 1 cup chopped nuts

In large bowl, combine first 4 ingredients; blend well. Stir in flour, soda, baking powder and salt; blend well. Add remaining ingredients; mix well. Divide dough in half on 2 sheets of waxed paper; shape each half into a roll 2 inches in diameter. Wrap; chill until firm, about 2 hours. Heat oven to 375°F. Cut dough into ¼-inch slices. Place 2 inches apart on ungreased cookie sheet. Bake at 375°F. for 10 to 12 minutes or until golden brown. Immediately remove from cookie sheet. 60 to 72 cookies

NUTRITION INFORMATION PER SERVING

Serving Size: 2 cookies		Percent U.S. RDA Per Serving	
Calories	198	Protein	4%
Protein	3g	Vitamin A	6%
Carbohydrate	25g	Vitamin C	*
Fat	10g	Thiamin	7%
Sodium	200mg	Riboflavin	3%
Potassium	86mg	Niacin	3%
		Calcium	*
		Iron	5%

TIP: **Self-rising flour is not recommended.*

CHOCOLATE-NUT WAFERS

1 cup sugar
¾ cup margarine or butter, softened
2 oz. (2 squares) unsweetened chocolate, melted or 2 envelopes premelted unsweetened baking chocolate flavor
1 teaspoon vanilla
1 egg
2¼ cups Pillsbury's Best® All Purpose or Unbleached Flour*
¼ teaspoon soda
¼ teaspoon salt
¼ teaspoon cinnamon
½ cup chopped nuts

In large bowl, combine first 5 ingredients; blend well. Stir in remaining ingredients. Divide dough in half on 2 sheets of waxed paper; shape each half into a roll 2 inches in diameter. Wrap; refrigerate until firm, about 3 hours. Heat oven to 400°F. Cut dough into ¼-inch slices. Place 1 inch apart on ungreased cookie sheet. Bake at 400°F. for 6 to 8 minutes or until lightly browned; do not overbake. Immediately remove from cookie sheet.
60 to 72 cookies

NUTRITION INFORMATION PER SERVING

Serving Size: 2 cookies		Percent U.S. RDA Per Serving	
Calories	126	Protein	3%
Protein	2g	Vitamin A	4%
Carbohydrate	15g	Vitamin C	*
Fat	7g	Thiamin	5%
Sodium	86mg	Riboflavin	3%
Potassium	37mg	Niacin	3%
		Calcium	*
		Iron	3%

TIP: **Self-rising flour is not recommended.*

A pretty swirl of chocolate in a coffee flavored cookie.

PINWHEEL BUTTERFLIES

¾ cup sugar
½ cup margarine or butter, softened
1 teaspoon vanilla
1 egg
1¾ cup Pillsbury's Best® All Purpose or Unbleached Flour*
½ teaspoon baking powder
¼ teaspoon salt
⅓ cup chopped pecans
1 teaspoon instant coffee
1 envelope premelted unsweetened baking chocolate flavor or 1 oz. (1 square) unsweetened chocolate, melted

In large bowl, combine first 4 ingredients; blend well. Stir in flour, baking powder and salt; blend well. Divide dough in half. Blend pecans and coffee into ½ of dough. Add chocolate to remaining dough. Chill for easier handling.

Roll light dough on waxed paper to a 16x8-inch rectangle. Repeat with chocolate dough. Place light dough on top of chocolate dough. Roll up jelly-roll fashion, starting with 16-inch side. Wrap roll in waxed paper; chill until firm, about 2 hours. Heat oven to 350°F. Cut dough into ¼-inch slices. Place 1 inch apart on ungreased cookie sheet. Bake at 350°F. for 9 to 12 minutes or until set. Immediately remove from cookie sheet.

60 cookies

NUTRITION INFORMATION PER SERVING

Serving Size: 2 cookies		Percent U.S. RDA Per Serving	
Calories	90	Protein	*
Protein	1g	Vitamin A	3%
Carbohydrate	11g	Vitamin C	*
Fat	5g	Thiamin	4%
Sodium	63mg	Riboflavin	2%
Potassium	26mg	Niacin	2%
		Calcium	*
		Iron	*

TIP: **Self-rising flour is not recommended.*

ABOUT BAR COOKIES

Bar cookies are probably the most varied—from cake-like brownies to candy-type confections.

For ease in removal from pan, be sure to follow the specific recipe directions for pan preparation.

Be careful not to overbake (or underbake) so use the specified doneness test given in the recipe.

Very little to mix—easy for a child to make.

SIX-LAYER BARS

½ cup margarine or butter
1½ cups (24 squares) graham cracker crumbs
1 cup chopped nuts
6-oz. pkg. (1 cup) semi-sweet chocolate chips
1½ cups flaked coconut
14-oz. can sweetened condensed milk (not evaporated)

Heat oven to 350°F. In 13x9-inch pan, melt margarine while heating oven. Combine graham cracker crumbs with margarine; press on bottom of pan. Sprinkle with layer of nuts, chocolate chips and coconut. Pour sweetened condensed milk over coconut. Bake at 350°F. for 20 to 30 minutes or until lightly browned. Cool; cut into bars.

36 bars

NUTRITION INFORMATION PER SERVING

Serving Size: 2 bars		Percent U.S. RDA Per Serving	
Calories	314	Protein	8%
Protein	5g	Vitamin A	6%
Carbohydrate	31g	Vitamin C	*
Fat	21g	Thiamin	4%
Sodium	154mg	Riboflavin	9%
Potassium	232mg	Niacin	*
		Calcium	9%
		Iron	5%

These all-time favorites may be topped with fudge frosting, mint frosting, cherry frosting or simply dusted with powdered sugar.

BROWNIES

- ½ cup margarine or butter
- 2 oz. (2 squares) unsweetened chocolate or 2 envelopes pre-melted unsweetened baking chocolate flavor
- 1 cup sugar
- 2 eggs
- 1 teaspoon vanilla
- ⅔ cup Pillsbury's Best® All Purpose or Unbleached Flour*
- ½ cup chopped nuts, if desired
- ½ teaspoon baking powder
- ¼ teaspoon salt

Heat oven to 350°F. Grease (not oil) and lightly flour bottom only of 8 or 9-inch square pan. In large saucepan, melt margarine and chocolate over low heat, stirring constantly. Remove from heat; cool slightly. Blend in sugar. Beat in eggs, one at a time. Stir in remaining ingredients. Spread in prepared pan. Bake at 350°F. for 25 to 30 minutes or until set in center. Cool; cut into bars.
24 bars

NUTRITION INFORMATION PER SERVING

Serving Size: 2 bars		Percent U.S. RDA Per Serving	
Calories	229	Protein	5%
Protein	3g	Vitamin A	8%
Carbohydrate	24g	Vitamin C	*
Fat	14g	Thiamin	5%
Sodium	164mg	Riboflavin	4%
Potassium	83mg	Niacin	2%
		Calcium	*
		Iron	5%

TIPS: *To double recipe, double the ingredient amounts; bake in 13x9-inch pan for 30 to 35 minutes.*

**If using Pillsbury's Best® Self Rising Flour, omit baking powder and salt.*

HIGH ALTITUDE–Above 3500 Feet: Decrease baking powder to ¼ teaspoon.

PUMPKIN BARS

- 4 eggs
- 2 cups sugar
- 1 cup oil
- 15-oz. can (2 cups) pumpkin
- 2 cups Pillsbury's Best® All Purpose or Unbleached Flour*
- 2 teaspoons baking powder
- 1 teaspoon soda
- ¾ teaspoon salt
- 2 teaspoons cinnamon
- 1 cup raisins or chopped nuts

FROSTING

- 3-oz. pkg. cream cheese, softened
- ⅓ cup margarine or butter, softened
- 1 tablespoon milk
- 1 teaspoon vanilla
- 2 cups powdered sugar

Heat oven to 350°F. Grease (not oil) 15x10-inch jelly roll pan. In large bowl, beat eggs until foamy. Add sugar, oil and pumpkin; beat 2 minutes at medium speed. Add flour, baking powder, soda, salt and cinnamon; beat 1 minute at low speed. Stir in raisins. Pour into prepared pan. Bake at 350°F. for 25 to 30 minutes or until toothpick inserted in center comes out clean. Cool. In small bowl, beat cream cheese, margarine, milk and vanilla until fluffy. Add powdered sugar; blend until smooth. Spread Frosting over cooled bars. Cut into bars. 48 bars

NUTRITION INFORMATION PER SERVING

Serving Size: 2 bars		Percent U.S. RDA Per Serving	
Calories	296	Protein	5%
Protein	3g	Vitamin A	28%
Carbohydrate	41g	Vitamin C	*
Fat	14g	Thiamin	6%
Sodium	193mg	Riboflavin	5%
Potassium	115mg	Niacin	4%
		Calcium	2%
		Iron	5%

TIP: **Self-rising flour is not recommended.*

HIGH ALTITUDE–Above 3500 Feet: Decrease soda to ½ teaspoon; bake at 375°F. for 30 to 35 minutes.

Chocolate and peanut butter with the crunch of corn flakes.

CHOCODILES

1¼ cups firmly packed brown sugar
½ cup margarine or butter, softened
½ cup shortening
⅓ cup crunchy peanut butter
1 teaspoon vanilla
1 egg
2¼ cups Pillsbury's Best® All Purpose or Unbleached Flour*
½ teaspoon salt

CHOCOLATE CRUNCH TOPPING

6-oz. pkg. (1 cup) semi-sweet chocolate chips
½ cup crunchy peanut butter
1½ cups slightly crushed corn flakes cereal

Heat oven to 350°F. In large bowl, combine first 6 ingredients; blend well. Stir in flour and salt; mix well. Press dough into ungreased 15x10-inch jelly roll pan. Bake at 350°F. for 15 to 20 minutes or until light golden brown. Cool slightly. In medium saucepan over low heat, melt chocolate chips. Stir in ½ cup peanut butter and corn flakes. Spread over slightly cooled crust. Cool slightly; cut into bars. Cool completely. 48 bars

NUTRITION INFORMATION PER SERVING

Serving Size: 2 cookies		Percent U.S. RDA Per Serving	
Calories	269	Protein	7%
Protein	5g	Vitamin A	4%
Carbohydrate	30g	Vitamin C	0%
Fat	15g	Thiamin	8%
Sodium	206mg	Riboflavin	5%
Potassium	140mg	Niacin	11%
		Calcium	2%
		Iron	7%

TIP: **If using Pillsbury's Best® Self Rising Flour, omit salt.*

CRISPY DATE BARS

1 cup Pillsbury's Best® All Purpose or Unbleached Flour*
½ cup firmly packed brown sugar
½ cup margarine or butter, softened

FILLING

1 cup chopped dates
½ cup sugar
½ cup margarine or butter
1 egg, well-beaten
2 cups crisp rice cereal
1 cup chopped nuts
1 teaspoon vanilla

FROSTING

2 cups powdered sugar
½ teaspoon vanilla
3-oz. pkg. cream cheese, softened

Heat oven to 375°F. In small bowl, combine first 3 ingredients; mix until crumbly. Press into ungreased 11x7 or 9-inch square pan. Bake at 375°F. for 10 to 12 minutes or until golden brown.

In medium saucepan, combine first 3 Filling ingredients. Cook over medium heat to boiling, stirring constantly; simmer 3 minutes. Blend about ¼ cup hot mixture into beaten egg; return to saucepan. Cook until mixture bubbles, stirring constantly. Remove from heat; stir in rice cereal, nuts and vanilla. Spread over baked crust; cool.

In small bowl, combine Frosting ingredients; beat at low speed until smooth. Spread over Filling. Cut into bars. 24 bars

NUTRITION INFORMATION PER SERVING

Serving Size: 2 bars		Percent U.S. RDA Per Serving	
Calories	477	Protein	7%
Protein	4g	Vitamin A	16%
Carbohydrate	62g	Vitamin C	*
Fat	25g	Thiamin	9%
Sodium	263mg	Riboflavin	6%
Potassium	208mg	Niacin	6%
		Calcium	4%
		Iron	9%

TIP: **Self-rising flour is not recommended.*

HIGH ALTITUDE–Above 3500 Feet: Add 1 tablespoon water to Filling. Add 1 tablespoon milk to Frosting.

DATE-FILLED BARS

2 cups chopped dates
⅔ cup water
1 tablespoon lemon juice
½ cup chopped nuts
¾ cup firmly packed brown sugar
½ cup margarine or butter, softened
1 cup Pillsbury's Best® All Purpose or Unbleached Flour*
1 cup rolled oats
1 teaspoon cinnamon, if desired
¼ teaspoon salt
¼ teaspoon nutmeg, if desired

Heat oven to 350°F. Grease (not oil) 9-inch square pan. In medium saucepan, combine first 3 ingredients. Cook over medium heat until thickened, stirring occasionally. Stir in nuts; cool. In large bowl, combine sugar and margarine; blend well. Stir in remaining ingredients until crumbly. Pat ⅔ of mixture in prepared pan; spread with date mixture. Top with remaining crumb mixture, pressing lightly. Bake at 350°F. for 35 to 40 minutes or until golden brown. Cool and cut into bars. 24 bars

NUTRITION INFORMATION PER SERVING

Serving Size: 2 bars		Percent U.S. RDA Per Serving	
Calories	298	Protein	5%
Protein	4g	Vitamin A	7%
Carbohydrate	48g	Vitamin C	*
Fat	12g	Thiamin	10%
Sodium	143mg	Riboflavin	5%
Potassium	300mg	Niacin	7%
		Calcium	4%
		Iron	12%

TIPS: *For APRICOT-FILLED BARS, make filling by combining 1½ cups dried cut-up apricots and ⅔ cup orange juice. Cook 10 minutes or until apricots are tender and mixture is thickened. Stir in ¼ cup sugar, ¼ cup honey and ¼ cup chopped nuts or dates. Continue as directed.*

For MINCEMEAT-FILLED BARS, substitute 1½ cups prepared mincemeat for date filling. Continue as directed.

**If using Pillsbury's Best® Self Rising Flour, omit salt.*

DREAM BARS

CRUST
½ cup firmly packed brown sugar
½ cup margarine or butter, softened
1¼ cups Pillsbury's Best® All Purpose or Unbleached Flour*

TOPPING
3 eggs
1½ cups firmly packed brown sugar
¼ cup flour
1 teaspoon baking powder
¼ teaspoon salt
1 teaspoon vanilla
1½ cups flaked coconut
1 cup chopped nuts

Heat oven to 350°F. In large bowl, blend ½ cup brown sugar and margarine. Stir in 1¼ cups flour until crumbly. Press into bottom of ungreased 13x9-inch pan. Bake at 350°F. for 10 minutes. In large bowl, beat eggs until foamy. *Gradually* add brown sugar, beating continuously until thick. Blend in flour, baking powder, salt and vanilla. Fold in coconut and nuts. Spread over partially baked crust. Bake at 350°F. for 20 to 25 minutes or until golden brown. Cool; cut into bars. 36 bars

NUTRITION INFORMATION PER SERVING

Serving Size: 2 bars		Percent U.S. RDA Per Serving	
Calories	266	Protein	6%
Protein	4g	Vitamin A	6%
Carbohydrate	34g	Vitamin C	*
Fat	14g	Thiamin	7%
Sodium	129mg	Riboflavin	5%
Potassium	167mg	Niacin	3%
		Calcium	4%
		Iron	10%

TIPS: *For CHOCOLATE CHIP DREAM BARS, sprinkle 1 cup chocolate chips over partially baked crust before spreading on topping.*

For LEMON DREAM BARS, add 2 teaspoons lemon peel and 2 tablespoons lemon juice with coconut.

**Self-rising flour is not recommended.*

CHOCOLATE TOFFEE BARS

1 cup Pillsbury's Best® All Purpose or Unbleached Flour*
½ cup firmly packed brown sugar
½ cup margarine or butter, softened

TOPPING

1 cup firmly packed brown sugar
2 tablespoons flour
1 teaspoon baking powder
2 eggs
6-oz. pkg. (1 cup) semi-sweet chocolate chips
½ cup chopped nuts

Heat oven to 350°F. In small bowl, combine first 3 ingredients; blend well. Press into ungreased 13x9-inch pan. Bake at 350°F. for 8 to 10 minutes; cool slightly. In medium bowl, combine first 4 Topping ingredients; blend well. Stir in chocolate chips and nuts; pour over crust. Bake at 350°F. for 15 to 20 minutes or until golden brown. Cool; cut into bars. 36 bars

NUTRITION INFORMATION PER SERVING

Serving Size: 2 bars		Percent U.S. RDA Per Serving	
Calories	222	Protein	4%
Protein	3g	Vitamin A	6%
Carbohydrate	30g	Vitamin C	*
Fat	11g	Thiamin	5%
Sodium	77mg	Riboflavin	4%
Potassium	126mg	Niacin	3%
		Calcium	3%
		Iron	7%

TIP: **If using Pillsbury's Best® Self Rising Flour, decrease baking powder to ½ teaspoon.*

MARASCHINO CHERRY BARS

MARASCHINO CHERRY BARS

CRUST
2 cups Pillsbury's Best® All Purpose or Unbleached Flour*
⅓ cup sugar
¾ cup margarine or butter, softened

FILLING
2 eggs, slightly beaten
1 cup firmly packed brown sugar
⅓ cup flour
1½ teaspoons baking powder
½ teaspoon salt
½ teaspoon vanilla
10-oz. jar maraschino cherries, drained and chopped (reserve juice)
½ cup chopped walnuts

FROSTING
2 tablespoons margarine or butter, softened
2½ cups powdered sugar
3 to 4 tablespoons reserved cherry juice
3 to 4 tablespoons flaked coconut

Heat oven to 350°F. In large bowl, combine first 3 ingredients; blend until crumbly. Press mixture into ungreased 13x9-inch pan. Bake at 350°F. for 12 to 15 minutes or until lightly browned. In small bowl, combine all Filling ingredients; mix well. Pour over Crust. Bake at 350°F. for 20 to 25 minutes or until toothpick inserted in center comes out clean. Cool. In small bowl, combine all Frosting ingredients except coconut; beat until light and fluffy. Spread Frosting over cooled bars; sprinkle with coconut. Cut into bars. 36 bars

NUTRITION INFORMATION PER SERVING

Serving Size: 2 bars		Percent U.S. RDA Per Serving	
Calories	325	Protein	5%
Protein	3g	Vitamin A	9%
Carbohydrate	52g	Vitamin C	*
Fat	13g	Thiamin	8%
Sodium	208mg	Riboflavin	5%
Potassium	89mg	Niacin	5%
		Calcium	3%
		Iron	7%

TIP: **Self-rising flour is not recommended.*

HIGH ALTITUDE—Above 3500 Feet: Bake at 375°F. for 20 to 25 minutes.

Similar in looks and texture to a brownie. Great for the lunch box.

BUTTERSCOTCH BARS

¼ cup margarine or butter
1 cup firmly packed brown sugar
1 teaspoon vanilla
1 egg
1 cup Pillsbury's Best® All Purpose or Unbleached Flour*
1 teaspoon baking powder
½ teaspoon salt
½ cup chopped nuts
Powdered sugar, if desired

Heat oven to 350°F. In medium saucepan, melt margarine; remove from heat. Stir in brown sugar, vanilla and egg; beat well. Add flour, baking powder and salt; blend well. Stir in nuts. Spread into ungreased 9-inch square pan. Bake at 350°F. for 15 to 20 minutes or until golden brown. Cool completely; cut into bars. Sprinkle with powdered sugar. 24 bars

NUTRITION INFORMATION PER SERVING

Serving Size: 2 bars		Percent U.S. RDA Per Serving	
Calories	190	Protein	4%
Protein	2g	Vitamin A	4%
Carbohydrate	29g	Vitamin C	*
Fat	8g	Thiamin	6%
Sodium	176mg	Riboflavin	4%
Potassium	103mg	Niacin	3%
		Calcium	3%
		Iron	7%

TIP: **Self-rising flour is not recommended.*

HIGH ALTITUDE—Above 3500 Feet: Decrease baking powder to ¾ teaspoon. Add 1 tablespoon water to sugar and egg mixture.

Always a favorite for luncheons and teas.

ALL-TIME FAVORITE LEMON BARS

1 cup Pillsbury's Best® All Purpose or Unbleached Flour*
¼ cup powdered sugar
½ cup margarine or butter
2 eggs
1 cup sugar
2 tablespoons flour
1 tablespoon grated lemon peel
½ teaspoon baking powder
2 tablespoons lemon juice

Heat oven to 350°F. In large bowl, combine flour and powdered sugar; cut in margarine until crumbly. Press flour mixture into ungreased 8 or 9-inch square pan. Bake at 350°F. for 15 minutes. In small bowl, beat eggs and sugar until light colored; stir in remaining ingredients. Pour egg mixture over partially baked crust. Return to oven and bake 18 to 25 minutes or until light golden brown. Cool completely. If desired, sprinkle with powdered sugar. Cut into bars.

24 bars

NUTRITION INFORMATION PER SERVING

Serving Size: 2 bars		Percent U.S. RDA Per Serving	
Calories	200	Protein	4%
Protein	2g	Vitamin A	8%
Carbohydrate	28g	Vitamin C	3%
Fat	9g	Thiamin	6%
Sodium	119mg	Riboflavin	4%
Potassium	30mg	Niacin	3%
		Calcium	*
		Iron	3%

ALL-LIME FAVORITE LEMON BARS

TIPS: *To double recipe, double the ingredient amounts; bake in 13x9-inch pan 25 to 28 minutes.*

**Self-rising flour is not recommended.*

OATMEAL CARMELITAS

CRUST

2 cups Pillsbury's Best® All Purpose or Unbleached Flour*
2 cups quick-cooking rolled oats
1½ cups firmly packed brown sugar
1 teaspoon soda
½ teaspoon salt
1¼ cups margarine or butter, softened

FILLING

6-oz. pkg. (1 cup) semi-sweet chocolate chips
½ cup chopped nuts
12-oz. jar (1 cup) caramel ice cream topping
3 tablespoons flour

Heat oven to 350°F. Grease (not oil) 13x9-inch pan. In large bowl, combine Crust ingredients; blend to form crumbs. Press half of crumbs (about 3 cups) into prepared pan. Bake at 350°F. for 10 minutes; remove from oven. Sprinkle with chocolate chips and nuts. Blend caramel topping and flour; drizzle over chocolate and nuts. Sprinkle with remaining crumbs. Return to oven, bake 18 to 22 minutes or until golden brown. Cool completely; cut into bars. (Chill for easier cutting.)

36 bars

NUTRITION INFORMATION PER SERVING

Serving Size: 2 bars		Percent U.S. RDA Per Serving	
Calories	399	Protein	7%
Protein	5g	Vitamin A	10%
Carbohydrate	54g	Vitamin C	*
Fat	19g	Thiamin	11%
Sodium	324mg	Riboflavin	5%
Potassium	158mg	Niacin	5%
		Calcium	3%
		Iron	10%

TIP: **Self-rising flour is not recommended.*

ALL ABOUT CANDY MAKING

- Use a saucepan large enough to allow space for candy to bubble up when boiling. Too large or too small a saucepan may also affect the cooking time.
- A good candy thermometer is almost a necessity. The investment is small and the rewards are great. When using the thermometer make sure that the ball of your thermometer does not touch the bottom of the pan.
- The cold water test may be used if you do not have a thermometer. Drop a small amount of hot syrup into a cup of ice-cold water. Test with your fingers to determine the desired consistency (see Candy Chart).
- During humid weather or rainy days, cook candy 1 or 2 degrees higher than you would on a normal day.
- To prevent sugaring, follow directions in recipes about stirring and covering. Also use moderate heat so candy does not come to the boiling point too rapidly.

TEMPERATURE TESTS FOR CANDY

TEMPERATURE OF SYRUP	TEST	DESCRIPTION OF SYRUP WHEN DROPPED INTO VERY COLD WATER:
234° to 240°F.	Soft ball	Forms a soft ball which flattens on removal from water.
244° to 248°F.	Firm ball	Forms a firm ball which does not flatten on removal from water.
250° to 266°F.	Hard ball	Forms a ball which is hard enough to hold its shape, yet pliable.
270° to 290°F.	Soft crack	Separates into threads which are hard but not brittle.
300° to 310°F.	Hard crack	Separates into threads which are hard and brittle.

The thick old-fashioned kind that's worth the effort.

FUDGE

2 oz. (2 squares) unsweetened chocolate
1 cup milk
2 cups sugar
Dash salt
1 tablespoon light corn syrup
2 tablespoons margarine or butter
1 teaspoon vanilla
½ cup chopped nuts

Butter 9x5-inch loaf pan. In medium saucepan, combine chocolate and milk. Cook over low heat until smooth and chocolate is melted, stirring constantly. Add sugar, salt and syrup. Stir until mixture boils; do not stir again. Cover and cook 1 minute. Uncover and cook to soft-ball stage (236°F.). Add margarine; place saucepan in pan of cold water to quickly cool to lukewarm (120°F.). Add vanilla; beat with wooden spoon until thick and creamy and candy loses gloss. Quickly stir in nuts; pour into prepared pan. When fudge is firm, cut into squares. 1 pound

NUTRITION INFORMATION PER SERVING

Serving Size: 1 ounce		Percent U.S. RDA Per Serving	
Calories	165	Protein	2%
Protein	1g	Vitamin A	*
Carbohydrate	28g	Vitamin C	*
Fat	6g	Thiamin	*
Sodium	43mg	Riboflavin	2%
Potassium	69mg	Niacin	*
		Calcium	3%
		Iron	2%

TIP: *If desired, 8-inch square pan may be substituted.*

Guaranteed not to be sugary—just creamy rich.

NO-FAIL FUDGE

3 cups sugar
¾ cup margarine or butter
5-oz. can (⅔ cup) evaporated milk
7-oz. jar (2 cups) marshmallow creme
12-oz. pkg. (2 cups) semi-sweet chocolate chips
¾ cup chopped nuts
1 teaspoon vanilla

Butter 13x9-inch pan. In large saucepan, combine first 3 ingredients. Heat to boiling, stirring frequently. Reduce heat; simmer 5 minutes, stirring constantly. Remove from heat; add marshmallow creme and chocolate chips; blend well. Stir in nuts and vanilla. Pour into prepared pan. Chill until firm. Cut into squares. 2 pounds

Insufficient data on marshmallow creme to give nutritional information.

SUGARED NUTS

1 cup firmly packed brown sugar
½ cup water
2 cups pecan or walnut halves

Butter cookie sheet. In medium saucepan, combine sugar and water. Cook to firm-ball stage (244°F.). Remove from heat; add nuts. Stir until coating on nuts begins to sugar. Spread nuts on prepared cookie sheet; cool. ¾ pound

NUTRITION INFORMATION PER SERVING

Serving Size: 1/2 ounce		Percent U.S. RDA Per Serving	
Calories	96	Protein	*
Protein	<1g	Vitamin A	*
Carbohydrate	10g	Vitamin C	*
Fat	6g	Thiamin	5%
Sodium	3mg	Riboflavin	*
Potassium	86mg	Niacin	*
		Calcium	*
		Iron	3%

TIP: *For SPICED NUTS, add ½ teaspoon cinnamon with nuts.*

ORANGE-LEMON WALNUTS

1 cup sugar
2 tablespoons water
2 tablespoons orange juice
2 tablespoons grated orange peel
2 tablespoons grated lemon peel
2 cups walnut halves

Butter cookie sheet. In medium saucepan, combine first 3 ingredients. Cook to firm-ball stage (244°F.), stirring constantly. Remove from heat. Add orange peel, lemon peel and walnuts. Stir until creamy. Spread on prepared cookie sheet, separating nuts; cool. ¾ pound

NUTRITION INFORMATION PER SERVING

Serving Size: 1/2 ounce		Percent U.S. RDA Per Serving	
Calories	72	Protein	3%
Protein	2g	Vitamin A	*
Carbohydrate	7g	Vitamin C	3%
Fat	5g	Thiamin	*
Sodium	<1mg	Riboflavin	*
Potassium	43mg	Niacin	*
		Calcium	*
		Iron	3%

TIP: *For SPICED NUTS, add 1 teaspoon cinnamon with nuts. If desired, omit peels.*

MALLOW-NUT SQUARES

3 tablespoons margarine or butter
40 large or 3 cups miniature marshmallows
4 cups crisp rice cereal
½ cup chopped nuts
½ cup flaked coconut

Butter 13x9-inch pan. In saucepan, melt margarine and marshmallows over low heat. Stir in remaining ingredients. Press into prepared pan; chill until set. Cut into squares. 36 pieces

NUTRITION INFORMATION PER SERVING

Serving Size: 2 bars		Percent U.S. RDA Per Serving	
Calories	116	Protein	*
Protein	1g	Vitamin A	*
Carbohydrate	17g	Vitamin C	*
Fat	5g	Thiamin	2%
Sodium	95mg	Riboflavin	*
Potassium	35mg	Niacin	2%
		Calcium	*
		Iron	3%

ENGLISH TOFFEE

1 cup sugar
½ teaspoon salt
1 cup margarine or butter
¼ cup water
3 oz. (3 squares) semi-sweet chocolate or ½ cup semi-sweet chocolate chips
1 cup chopped pecans

In medium saucepan, combine first 4 ingredients. Cook to hard-crack stage (300°F.), stirring constantly and watching temperature carefully. Immediately pour onto ungreased cookie sheet. Cool until hard. Melt chocolate over hot, but not boiling water. Spread over toffee; sprinkle and press nuts into chocolate. Let set 2 to 3 hours or chill 30 minutes. Break into bite-size pieces.

1 pound

NUTRITION INFORMATION PER SERVING

Serving Size: 1 ounce		Percent U.S. RDA Per Serving	
Calories	228	Protein	*
Protein	<1g	Vitamin A	10%
Carbohydrate	17g	Vitamin C	*
Fat	19g	Thiamin	4%
Sodium	208mg	Riboflavin	*
Potassium	65mg	Niacin	*
		Calcium	*
		Iron	*

PEANUT BRITTLE

2 cups sugar
1 cup light corn syrup
1 cup water
2 cups raw Spanish peanuts
½ teaspoon salt
1 teaspoon soda
1 tablespoon margarine or butter
1 teaspoon vanilla

Butter 2 cookie sheets. In large saucepan, combine first 3 ingredients. Cook until sugar dissolves, stirring constantly. Add peanuts and salt. Cook to hard-crack stage (300°F.), stirring occasionally. Add soda, margarine and vanilla; mix well. Pour onto prepared cookie sheets; while warm pull to desired thickness. When cool, crack into pieces.

2 pounds

NUTRITION INFORMATION PER SERVING

Serving Size: 1 ounce		Percent U.S. RDA Per Serving	
Calories	107	Protein	*
Protein	1g	Vitamin A	*
Carbohydrate	21g	Vitamin C	0%
Fat	3g	Thiamin	*
Sodium	80mg	Riboflavin	*
Potassium	32mg	Niacin	4%
		Calcium	*
		Iron	3%

Light and fluffy—deliciously sweet.

DIVINITY

2 cups sugar
¼ teaspoon salt
½ cup hot water
⅓ cup light corn syrup
2 egg whites
1 teaspoon vanilla
½ to 1 cup chopped nuts

In medium saucepan, combine first 4 ingredients. Cook until mixture boils, stirring constantly. Cook uncovered, without stirring to hard-ball stage (255°F.). In large bowl, beat egg whites until stiff peaks form. Pour syrup over egg whites in steady fine stream and continue beating until mixture holds its shape and loses gloss. Stir in vanilla and nuts. Drop by teaspoonfuls onto waxed paper.

1¼ pounds

NUTRITION INFORMATION PER SERVING

Serving Size: 1 ounce		Percent U.S. RDA Per Serving	
Calories	111	Protein	*
Protein	<1g	Vitamin A	*
Carbohydrate	24g	Vitamin C	*
Fat	2g	Thiamin	*
Sodium	36mg	Riboflavin	*
Potassium	17mg	Niacin	*
		Calcium	*
		Iron	*

CARAMEL APPLES
POPCORN BALLS

CARAMEL APPLES

14-oz. pkg. (49) caramels
2 tablespoons water
4 or 5 medium apples
4 or 5 wooden sticks

In top of double boiler or saucepan, combine caramels and water. Cook until melted, stirring occasionally. Insert wooden sticks into stem end of each apple. Keep caramel mixture over low heat. Dip apples into caramel mixture, turning to coat. Scrape off excess caramel mixture when removing apple from pan. Place on greased waxed paper and chill until set. 4 to 5 apples

NUTRITION INFORMATION PER SERVING

Serving Size: 1/4 of recipe		Percent U.S. RDA Per Serving	
Calories	478	Protein	6%
Protein	4g	Vitamin A	3%
Carbohydrate	97g	Vitamin C	10%
Fat	11g	Thiamin	5%
Sodium	223mg	Riboflavin	12%
Potassium	353mg	Niacin	*
		Calcium	16%
		Iron	10%

TOFFEE PIECES

12 graham cracker squares
¾ cup firmly packed brown sugar
½ cup margarine or butter
¼ cup chopped nuts
6-oz. pkg. (1 cup) semi-sweet chocolate chips

Place graham crackers in buttered 13x9-inch pan. In small saucepan, cook brown sugar and margarine until bubbly. Boil 2 minutes, stirring constantly. Stir in nuts. Pour syrup over crackers. Sprinkle with chocolate chips. When chocolate is soft, spread over top. Chill until set. Break into pieces. 22 to 24 pieces

NUTRITION INFORMATION PER SERVING

Serving Size: 1/22 of recipe		Percent U.S. RDA Per Serving	
Calories	128	Protein	*
Protein	<1g	Vitamin A	3%
Carbohydrate	15g	Vitamin C	*
Fat	8g	Thiamin	*
Sodium	79mg	Riboflavin	*
Potassium	73mg	Niacin	*
		Calcium	*
		Iron	3%

POPCORN BALLS

12 cups popped popcorn
1 cup sugar
½ teaspoon salt
⅔ cup water
⅔ cup light corn syrup
½ cup margarine or butter
1 teaspoon vinegar
½ teaspoon vanilla

Place popcorn in very large bowl. In medium saucepan, combine remaining ingredients, except vanilla. Cook uncovered, stirring occasionally, until soft-crack stage (270°F.). Remove from heat; stir in vanilla. Slowly pour syrup over popcorn, tossing until coated. With buttered fingers, quickly shape into balls. 16 balls

NUTRITION INFORMATION PER SERVING

Serving Size: 1 ball		Percent U.S. RDA Per Serving	
Calories	155	Protein	*
Protein	<1g	Vitamin A	5%
Carbohydrate	26g	Vitamin C	0%
Fat	6g	Thiamin	0%
Sodium	146mg	Riboflavin	*
Potassium	3mg	Niacin	*
		Calcium	*
		Iron	4%

FRUIT CHEWS

1½ cups raisins
1 cup dried apricots or figs, cut up
1 cup dates, cut up
1 cup flaked coconut
½ cup chopped nuts
¼ cup sesame seed

Grind first 3 ingredients using food grinder or blender. In medium bowl, mix with coconut and nuts. Form into 1-inch balls. Roll each in sesame seed, pressing seeds firmly into chews. 30 pieces

NUTRITION INFORMATION PER SERVING

Serving Size: 1 piece		Percent U.S. RDA Per Serving	
Calories	79	Protein	*
Protein	1g	Vitamin A	10%
Carbohydrate	14g	Vitamin C	*
Fat	3g	Thiamin	*
Sodium	3mg	Riboflavin	*
Potassium	155mg	Niacin	2%
		Calcium	*
		Iron	5%

TAFFY

1½ cups sugar
⅛ teaspoon salt
½ cup light corn syrup
¼ cup water
2 tablespoons margarine or butter
½ teaspoon vanilla

Butter large platter. In medium saucepan, combine all ingredients except vanilla. Cook, stirring constantly, until mixture reaches hard-ball stage (255°F.). Remove from heat; stir in vanilla. Pour onto prepared platter. As candy cools, lift edges toward center. When cool enough to handle, pull candy with buttered fingertips until it becomes white and stiff. Pull into a long rope, about ½-inch wide. Cut with scissors into about 1-inch pieces while soft and twist, if desired, or crack into pieces after it hardens.

¾ pound

NUTRITION INFORMATION PER SERVING

Serving Size: 1 ounce		Percent U.S. RDA Per Serving	
Calories	193	Protein	*
Protein	<1g	Vitamin A	*
Carbohydrate	45g	Vitamin C	0%
Fat	2g	Thiamin	0%
Sodium	65mg	Riboflavin	0%
Potassium	2mg	Niacin	0%
		Calcium	*
		Iron	6%

TIPS: *For PEPPERMINT TAFFY, substitute peppermint extract for vanilla.*

If candy becomes too cool to work with, warm briefly in oven at 350°F.

DESSERTS, SAUCES & PIES

DESSERTS

FRUIT

Fruits are a natural in anyone's diet anytime! Their bright colors and wide variety of flavors and textures can complement any meal. With today's modern methods of transportation, storage, canning and freezing no one has an excuse not to include fruit in their daily diet.

BUYING

The best way to select fruit is by sight. If the fruit looks good, it should be good to eat. With a little practice, selecting good fruit should be easy.

GRADING

Grading of fresh fruits is done primarily at the wholesale level. However, consumers do make use of the federal grading standards in the selection of apples, oranges, grapefruit and peaches. There are two general factors influencing the grading of fruit: *quality* (maturity, color, surface blemishes, insect damage) and *condition* (internal or external decay and shipping conditions).

The following are the grading levels set by the federal government:

U.S. Extra Fancy
U.S. Fancy
U.S. Extra No. 1
U.S. No. 1
U.S. No. 2

In general you will pay a higher price for Extra Fancy, Fancy and Extra No. 1. These are best when appearance is of prime importance such as for gifts, fruit arrangements or recipes where the fruit is to be used whole.

U.S. No. 1 are the most readily available and are perfectly suitable for everyday usage.

U.S. No. 2 can be a very good buy. Often, fruits are rated No. 2 because they are smaller or have external blemishes which in no way alter the quality of the fruit. However, damage can lead to rapid decay so plan to use within a short time.

CANNED, FRESH OR FROZEN

In general, the best buy will be fresh fruit in its peak season. Canned and frozen fruit are very acceptable alternatives when fresh fruit is limited.

U.S. grades are available for canned and frozen fruits although it is not compulsory. U.S. Grade A or U.S. Fancy is excellent quality, products are uniform in size and color, practically free from blemishes, and are mature and tender. U.S. Grade B or U.S. Choice are not as perfect but are acceptable for everyday use. U.S. Grade C fruits are just as wholesome and as nutritious as the higher grades, but appearance and tenderness rate lower.

The label indicates the sweetening used if any, the number of servings and cooking instructions.

Frozen fruits offer as much food value as fresh (any loss of vitamin C is negligible). It depends on preference and cost as to which you buy.

Frozen or canned fruit and fruit juices, once opened, should be refrigerated to preserve nutrients. Store in the refrigerator no longer than three days for maximum freshness.

DRIED FRUITS

In drying fruits, the water content is reduced to the point where bacteria and mold are unable to grow under ordinary storage conditions. Usually dried fruits can be stored in a closed container at room temperature; in hot and humid weather it may be best to store in the refrigerator. Dried fruits are not a reliable source of Vitamin C. Although there is no marked difference in the nutritive value of first and second grade fruits, there can be a difference in appearance and taste.

WAXED FRUITS

Nature naturally protects most fruits with a shield of wax to minimize the loss of moisture and nutrients. Mechanical harvesting often includes a bath to rid the fruit of dust or dirt and the natural wax is often removed. So a man-made wax is applied; without it fruits would dehydrate and spoil very quickly. The amount of wax needed is very small and there is no harm in eating it. However, if you wish to remove the wax, do so just before serving.

APPLES

There are over 7,000 varieties of apples grown in the U.S. Listed below are some of those most available.

BUYING

Apples are best when they are well-colored, free from bruises, fresh and firm. The best quality apple is soon after harvest. Peak season is October through February.

STORAGE

Apples will store several months in a cool (40°F.) place or refrigerator.

1 MEDIUM APPLE WITH SKIN—RAW

NUTRITION INFORMATION PER SERVING

Serving Size: 1 medium apple with skin		Percent U.S. RDA Per Serving	
Calories	87	Protein	*
Protein	<1g	Vitamin A	3%
Carbohydrate	22g	Vitamin C	10%
Fat	<1g	Thiamin	3%
Sodium	1mg	Riboflavin	*
Potassium	165mg	Niacin	*
		Calcium	*
		Iron	2%

APPLES, 1/4 CUP DRIED

NUTRITION INFORMATION PER SERVING

Serving Size: 1/4 cup dried apples		Percent U.S. RDA Per Serving	
Calories	58	Protein	*
Protein	<1g	Vitamin A	0%
Carbohydrate	15g	Vitamin C	3%
Fat	<1g	Thiamin	*
Sodium	1mg	Riboflavin	*
Potassium	119mg	Niacin	*
		Calcium	*
		Iron	*

VARIETY	CHARACTERISTICS	USAGE
Red Delicious	dark red, sweet, mild, tender	fresh, salads
Golden Delicious	yellow, sweet, semi-firm	fresh, all-purpose cooking, freezing
McIntosh	red striped green, slightly tart, tender	fresh, salads, pies, sauces
Rome	red and yellow, slightly tart, firm	all-purpose cooking, freezing
Jonathan	deep red, tart, crisp-tender	fresh, all-purpose cooking, freezing
Winesap	bright red, slightly tart, firm	fresh, salads, freezing
Newtown Pippin	green, slightly tart, firm	fresh, all-purpose cooking, freezing
Northern Spy	striped red, slightly tart, firm	fresh, pies, sauces, freezing
Cortland	red, mild, tender	fresh, pies, sauces

APRICOTS

Available fresh, canned or dried. Fresh have an entirely different flavor than dried or canned.

2 MEDIUM APRICOTS—RAW

NUTRITION INFORMATION PER SERVING

Serving Size: 2 medium apricots		Percent U.S. RDA Per Serving	
Calories	36	Protein	*
Protein	<1g	Vitamin A	38%
Carbohydrate	9g	Vitamin C	12%
Fat	<1g	Thiamin	*
Sodium	<1mg	Riboflavin	*
Potassium	200mg	Niacin	2%
		Calcium	*
		Iron	*

APRICOTS, CANNED 1/2 CUP

NUTRITION INFORMATION PER SERVING

Serving Size: 1/2 cup canned apricots		Percent U.S. RDA Per Serving	
Calories	47	Protein	*
Protein	<1g	Vitamin A	45%
Carbohydrate	12g	Vitamin C	8%
Fat	<1g	Thiamin	*
Sodium	1mg	Riboflavin	*
Potassium	303mg	Niacin	2%
		Calcium	*
		Iron	2%

APRICOTS, DRIED 1/4 CUP

NUTRITION INFORMATION PER SERVING

Serving Size: 1/4 cup dried apricots		Percent U.S. RDA Per Serving	
Calories	84	Protein	2%
Protein	2g	Vitamin A	71%
Carbohydrate	22g	Vitamin C	6%
Fat	<1g	Thiamin	*
Sodium	8mg	Riboflavin	3%
Potassium	318mg	Niacin	5%
		Calcium	2%
		Iron	10%

BUYING

Apricots should develop their flavor and sweetness on the tree. Select plump juicy fruits, golden orange in color. Avoid soft mushy fruits or very firm yellow or green fruit. Peak season is June or July.

STORAGE

Store fully ripe fruit in refrigerator 3 to 5 days.

BANANAS

Bananas, popular with all ages, are one of the biggest sellers. It is one fruit that tastes better when it is not tree ripened, and thus it is shipped in the green state. Bananas contain only a trace of fat and it is highly unsaturated. They have a very low sodium content.

NUTRITION INFORMATION PER SERVING

Serving Size: 1 medium banana		Percent U.S. RDA Per Serving	
Calories	101	Protein	2%
Protein	1g	Vitamin A	5%
Carbohydrate	26g	Vitamin C	20%
Fat	<1g	Thiamin	4%
Sodium	<1mg	Riboflavin	4%
Potassium	440mg	Niacin	4%
		Calcium	*
		Iron	5%

BUYING

Select bananas which are firm and not fully yellow, so have less chance of bruising. Available all year.

STORAGE

Leave at room temperature until ripe. Ripe bananas may be stored for 3 to 4 days in the refrigerator; the peel will turn dark but the edible portion will remain unchanged.

BERRIES

STRAWBERRIES

The most popular berry and the only one marketed with the stem on. Do not remove the hull until ready to use as the berry will lose nutrients quickly. Although available year around, the peak months are mid-April to mid-July. Look for berries which are fully red but not soft.

NUTRITION INFORMATION PER SERVING

Serving Size: 1/2 cup strawberries		Percent U.S. RDA Per Serving	
Calories	28	Protein	*
Protein	<1g	Vitamin A	*
Carbohydrate	6g	Vitamin C	74%
Fat	<1g	Thiamin	*
Sodium	<1mg	Riboflavin	3%
Potassium	123mg	Niacin	2%
		Calcium	*
		Iron	4%

BLACKBERRIES, DEWBERRIES, LOGANBERRIES, BOYSENBERRIES, and **YOUNGBERRIES** are harvested locally from June to August. Similar to the raspberry, they are used in much the same manner.

GOOSEBERRIES

They are marketed as fully developed but unripened fruit. Gooseberries have a soft yellow-green color and are available only through local suppliers. June and July are peak months. Gooseberries are most often used in jams and pies.

NUTRITION INFORMATION PER SERVING

Serving Size: 1 cup gooseberries		Percent U.S. RDA Per Serving	
Calories	59	Protein	*
Protein	1g	Vitamin A	9%
Carbohydrate	15g	Vitamin C	83%
Fat	<1g	Thiamin	†
Sodium	2mg	Riboflavin	†
Potassium	233mg	Niacin	†
		Calcium	3%
		Iron	4%

BLUEBERRIES

These are a natural convenience food as they do not need to be pitted or peeled–just wash and serve. Peak season is May to August. Select berries that are firm but plump with a dark silver-blue color.

NUTRITION INFORMATION PER SERVING

Serving Size: 1 cup blueberries		Percent U.S. RDA Per Serving	
Calories	90	Protein	*
Protein	1g	Vitamin A	3%
Carbohydrate	22g	Vitamin C	33%
Fat	<1g	Thiamin	3%
Sodium	1mg	Riboflavin	5%
Potassium	117mg	Niacin	3%
		Calcium	2%
		Iron	8%

RASPBERRIES

These come in a variety of colors; red and black are the most popular. Because of the many varieties, raspberries are available from April to November. Buy berries which are uniform in color and shape. Berries should be plump but not soft.

NUTRITION INFORMATION PER SERVING

Serving Size: 1/2 cup red raspberries		Percent U.S. RDA Per Serving	
Calories	35	Protein	*
Protein	<1g	Vitamin A	*
Carbohydrate	8g	Vitamin C	26%
Fat	<1g	Thiamin	*
Sodium	<1mg	Riboflavin	3%
Potassium	103mg	Niacin	3%
		Calcium	*
		Iron	3%

NUTRITION INFORMATION PER SERVING

Serving Size: 1/2 cup black raspberries		Percent U.S. RDA Per Serving	
Calories	49	Protein	*
Protein	1g	Vitamin A	0%
Carbohydrate	11g	Vitamin C	20%
Fat	<1g	Thiamin	*
Sodium	<1mg	Riboflavin	4%
Potassium	133mg	Niacin	3%
		Calcium	2%
		Iron	3%

CRANBERRIES

The best keeper of the berry family, these bright red berries are a winter holiday favorite. Marketed from September to January. They are very popular in cakes, breads, pies and sauces. Purchase very firm plump berries. Store in the refrigerator. Cranberries may be frozen by placing the unopened package in the freezer. No need to thaw before using. One pound of fruit measures 4 cups.

NUTRITION INFORMATION PER SERVING

Serving Size: 1/2 cup raw whole cranberries		Percent U.S. RDA Per Serving	
Calories	22	Protein	*
Protein	<1g	Vitamin A	*
Carbohydrate	5g	Vitamin C	9%
Fat	<1g	Thiamin	*
Sodium	<1mg	Riboflavin	*
Potassium	39mg	Niacin	*
		Calcium	*
		Iron	*

CHERRIES

Cherries are available both sweet and sour. Probably the most popular sweet cherry is the Bing, characterized by its dark maroon-red color. There are varieties of white or golden sweet cherries, however they bruise easily so they are generally found canned. Sour cherries are most often used for canning, sauces, pies and desserts where sugar is added.

NUTRITION INFORMATION PER SERVING

Serving Size: 1/2 cup sweet cherries		Percent U.S. RDA Per Serving	
Calories	42	Protein	*
Protein	<1g	Vitamin A	*
Carbohydrate	10g	Vitamin C	10%
Fat	<1g	Thiamin	2%
Sodium	1mg	Riboflavin	2%
Potassium	115mg	Niacin	*
		Calcium	*
		Iron	*

BUYING

The most reliable test for a good cherry is taste. Also look for fresh, firm, plump, well-colored cherries. Peak season is May through July.

STORAGE

Keep in refrigerator for 3 to 5 days.

CITRUS FRUITS

These include **GRAPEFRUIT, LEMONS, LIMES, ORANGES** and **TANGERINES** (or **MANDARINS**). The most common varieties of oranges are Navel and Florida Temple which are easily peeled and separated for eating; and Valencia which are excellent for juicing and slicing for salads. Grapefruit varieties vary in color from white to red.

1/2 MEDIUM GRAPEFRUIT

NUTRITION INFORMATION PER SERVING

Serving Size: 1/2 medium grapefruit		Percent U.S. RDA Per Serving	
Calories	40	Protein	*
Protein	<1g	Vitamin A	*
Carbohydrate	10g	Vitamin C	62%
Fat	<1g	Thiamin	3%
Sodium	<1mg	Riboflavin	*
Potassium	132mg	Niacin	*
		Calcium	*
		Iron	2%

LEMON 1 MEDIUM

NUTRITION INFORMATION PER SERVING

Serving Size: 1 medium lemon		Percent U.S. RDA Per Serving	
Calories	23	Protein	*
Protein	<1g	Vitamin A	*
Carbohydrate	7g	Vitamin C	77%
Fat	<1g	Thiamin	2%
Sodium	2mg	Riboflavin	*
Potassium	120mg	Niacin	*
		Calcium	2%
		Iron	3%

LIME 1 MEDIUM

NUTRITION INFORMATION PER SERVING

Serving Size: 1 medium lime		Percent U.S. RDA Per Serving	
Calories	19	Protein	*
Protein	<1g	Vitamin A	*
Carbohydrate	6g	Vitamin C	41%
Fat	<1g	Thiamin	*
Sodium	1mg	Riboflavin	*
Potassium	68mg	Niacin	*
		Calcium	2%
		Iron	*

ORANGE 1 MEDIUM

NUTRITION INFORMATION PER SERVING

Serving Size: 1 medium orange		Percent U.S. RDA Per Serving	
Calories	64	Protein	2%
Protein	1g	Vitamin A	5%
Carbohydrate	16g	Vitamin C	109%
Fat	<1g	Thiamin	9%
Sodium	1mg	Riboflavin	3%
Potassium	262mg	Niacin	3%
		Calcium	5%
		Iron	3%

TANGERINE 1 MEDIUM

NUTRITION INFORMATION PER SERVING

Serving Size: 1 medium tangerine		Percent U.S. RDA Per Serving	
Calories	40	Protein	*
Protein	<1g	Vitamin A	7%
Carbohydrate	10g	Vitamin C	45%
Fat	<1g	Thiamin	3%
Sodium	2mg	Riboflavin	*
Potassium	110mg	Niacin	*
		Calcium	3%
		Iron	*

BUYING

Look for firm heavy fruit with a bright color. Citrus fruits are generally picked ripe so are ready to eat when purchased. Available year round, the peak season is November to May (except Valencia oranges which peak April to October).

STORAGE

Can be left at room temperature several days. For longer storage refrigerate.

COCONUTS

Not a nut but a fruit in the same classification as a peach! Americans are more familiar with the dried packaged coconut, however you may find fresh coconut to be a delightful treat.

COCONUT-FRESH 1 SLICE 2 X 2

NUTRITION INFORMATION PER SERVING

Serving Size: 1 slice (2″ x 2″)		Percent U.S. RDA Per Serving	
Calories	156	Protein	2%
Protein	2g	Vitamin A	0%
Carbohydrate	4g	Vitamin C	*
Fat	16g	Thiamin	*
Sodium	10mg	Riboflavin	*
Potassium	115mg	Niacin	*
		Calcium	*
		Iron	4%

COCONUT WATER 1 CUP

NUTRITION INFORMATION PER SERVING

Serving Size: 1 cup		Percent U.S. RDA Per Serving	
Calories	53	Protein	*
Protein	<1g	Vitamin A	0%
Carbohydrate	11g	Vitamin C	5%
Fat	<1g	Thiamin	0%
Sodium	60mg	Riboflavin	0%
Potassium	353mg	Niacin	*
		Calcium	5%
		Iron	4%

BUYING

Look for those which are heavy for their size. Avoid those without milk or moldy or wet "eyes".

STORAGE

They can be held 4 to 6 weeks in the refrigerator.

PREPARATION

With an ice pick, pierce the 3 soft spots at the top of the shell; drain the milk. Then tap all over the coconut with a hammer until the shell cracks.

DATES

Referred to as the candy that grows on trees. When fully ripe, dates are plump, golden brown with a smooth skin. Sold pitted or unpitted. Dates are an excellent addition to breakfast cereals, breads, cakes, puddings, or tossed in salads. They are a natural appetizer stuffed with cream cheese.

NUTRITION INFORMATION PER SERVING

Serving Size: 1/4 cup dates		Percent U.S. RDA Per Serving	
Calories	122	Protein	*
Protein	<1g	Vitamin A	*
Carbohydrate	32g	Vitamin C	0%
Fat	<1g	Thiamin	3%
Sodium	<1mg	Riboflavin	3%
Potassium	288mg	Niacin	5%
		Calcium	3%
		Iron	7%

BUYING

Select fresh dates which are plump, of good color and not too dry. Available year round with top abundance September through May.

STORAGE

Stored in the refrigerator in a tightly sealed container, dates should keep almost indefinitely.

FIGS

Although not a fruit in the strict sense of the word, figs are a sweet edible pod which range in color from green to brown to almost black. They are most often pear shaped. Fresh or dried, figs are popular additions to salads, cakes, sweet fillings and candy.

NUTRITION INFORMATION PER SERVING

Serving Size: 1 medium fig		Percent U.S. RDA Per Serving	
Calories	40	Protein	*
Protein	<1g	Vitamin A	*
Carbohydrate	10g	Vitamin C	*
Fat	<1g	Thiamin	2%
Sodium	1mg	Riboflavin	*
Potassium	97mg	Niacin	*
		Calcium	*
		Iron	*

BUYING

The fig should be fully mature and tree ripened. Choose those which are soft to the touch and have no sour odor.

STORAGE

Refrigerate and use fresh figs immediately; they are highly perishable.

GRAPES

Some of the most important varieties include Thompson Seedless, an early green grape; Cardinal, early bright red grapes; Emperor, a late, deep red grape and Concord, a juicy blue-black grape with soft flesh. Use as a fresh fruit, in salads or fruit cups and in jelly making.

NUTRITION INFORMATION PER SERVING

Serving Size: 1/2 cup green grapes		Percent U.S. RDA Per Serving	
Calories	54	Protein	*
Protein	<1g	Vitamin A	*
Carbohydrate	14g	Vitamin C	5%
Fat	<1g	Thiamin	3%
Sodium	2mg	Riboflavin	*
Potassium	138mg	Niacin	*
		Calcium	*
		Iron	*

BUYING

Select well-colored, plump grapes that are firmly attached to the stem. Stems should still be green and pliable. Avoid soft or wrinkled grapes.

STORAGE

Grapes are highly perishable. Store in refrigerator 3 to 5 days.

GUAVAS

Use firm guavas for cooking; use slightly soft guavas for eating fresh or pureeing for juice. To prepare, wash, peel carefully and remove seeds.

KIWI FRUIT

Also known as Chinese gooseberry, this fruit is a New Zealand export. The fruit is slightly softened when ripe. Fuzzy brownish skin is peeled, revealing green, sweet-flavored fruit with edible dark seeds. Cut in slices, quarters or halves and use in salads or as garnishes in punch.

KUMQUATS

Native to China, these miniature oranges are available in the States. The sweet skin and tart interior add an interesting flavor to salads and compotes. If using raw, be sure kumquats are very ripe. Prepare by washing, slicing and removing seeds.

NUTRITION INFORMATION PER SERVING

Serving Size: 1 raw kumquat		Percent U.S. RDA Per Serving	
Calories	12	Protein	*
Protein	<1g	Vitamin A	2%
Carbohydrate	3g	Vitamin C	11%
Fat	<1g	Thiamin	*
Sodium	1mg	Riboflavin	*
Potassium	44mg	Niacin	0%
		Calcium	*
		Iron	*

MANGOES

Buy firm fruit and allow to ripen at room temperature until skin feels slightly soft. The fruit is very juicy and will be easier to peel if refrigerated before peeling. To prepare, make 3 or 4 lengthwise cuts through to seed and pull off peel like the peel of a banana. The fruit clings to the seed so pull fruit away from seed or pry away with a knife.

NUTRITION INFORMATION PER SERVING

Serving Size: 1 mango		Percent U.S. RDA Per Serving	
Calories	132	Protein	2%
Protein	1g	Vitamin A	192%
Carbohydrate	34g	Vitamin C	117%
Fat	<1g	Thiamin	7%
Sodium	14mg	Riboflavin	6%
Potassium	378mg	Niacin	11%
		Calcium	2%
		Iron	4%

MELONS

CANTALOUPES, also known as muskmelons, have orange-colored flesh. Select cantaloupe without any stem and a smooth symmetrical shape. The rind should be thick, coarse and have a corky netting with bold relief over part of surface. Base color of rind should be somewhat yellow. If further ripening is needed, leave at room temperature 2 to 3 days. Melons will not ripen after cutting.

NUTRITION INFORMATION PER SERVING

Serving Size: 1/4 of cantaloupe		Percent U.S. RDA Per Serving	
Calories	40	Protein	*
Protein	<1g	Vitamin A	90%
Carbohydrate	10g	Vitamin C	73%
Fat	<1g	Thiamin	4%
Sodium	16mg	Riboflavin	2%
Potassium	334mg	Niacin	4%
		Calcium	*
		Iron	3%

HONEYDEW MELONS are known for their sweet taste that makes them a dessert favorite. This large, oval-shaped melon has a very smooth rind ranging in color from creamy white to creamy yellow. The interior is a pale green. They are often imported, making them available year around. To ripen, leave at room temperature, do not cut until ripe.

NUTRITION INFORMATION PER SERVING

Serving Size: 1/4 of honeydew melon		Percent U.S. RDA Per Serving	
Calories	124	Protein	5%
Protein	3g	Vitamin A	3%
Carbohydrate	29g	Vitamin C	144%
Fat	1g	Thiamin	10%
Sodium	45mg	Riboflavin	7%
Potassium	941mg	Niacin	11%
		Calcium	5%
		Iron	8%

WATERMELON are available whole; retailers may also cut them so they are more desirable for small family purchasing. The rind should be smooth and a rich green color with a yellowish underside. Cut melons should have firm juicy red flesh (free from white streaks) with black seeds. Store watermelon in the refrigerator and use within 3 to 5 days.

NUTRITION INFORMATION PER SERVING

Serving Size: 1 cup watermelon		Percent U.S. RDA Per Serving	
Calories	42	Protein	*
Protein	<1g	Vitamin A	19%
Carbohydrate	10g	Vitamin C	19%
Fat	<1g	Thiamin	3%
Sodium	2mg	Riboflavin	3%
Potassium	160mg	Niacin	*
		Calcium	*
		Iron	4%

NECTARINES

This fruit has both the characteristics of a peach and plum. May be used the same as a peach, not necessary to remove peel.

NUTRITION INFORMATION PER SERVING

Serving Size: 1 nectarine		Percent U.S. RDA Per Serving	
Calories	88	Protein	*
Protein	<1g	Vitamin A	46%
Carbohydrate	24g	Vitamin C	30%
Fat	0g	Thiamin	0%
Sodium	8mg	Riboflavin	0%
Potassium	406mg	Niacin	0%
		Calcium	*
		Iron	4%

BUYING

Most varieties have a rich orange-yellow color with red highlights. Ripe nectarines are slightly soft along the "seam" of the fruit. Avoid shriveled or soft fruit. Bright looking fruit, still firm, will ripen in a few days at room temperature.

STORAGE

Ripe fruit should be refrigerated and used within 3 to 5 days.

PAPAYA

Select fruit greenish-yellow to yellow in color. The fruit should give slightly when ripe. Ripe papaya will keep several weeks in the refrigerator. Peel fruit, cut in half, remove seeds, slice; use in salads or compotes. The flavor and texture is similar to a melon.

NUTRITION INFORMATION PER SERVING

Serving Size: 1 papaya		Percent U.S. RDA Per Serving	
Calories	119	Protein	3%
Protein	2g	Vitamin A	106%
Carbohydrate	30g	Vitamin C	284%
Fat	<1g	Thiamin	8%
Sodium	9mg	Riboflavin	7%
Potassium	711mg	Niacin	5%
		Calcium	6%
		Iron	5%

PEACHES

Many varieties of peaches are available, but they all fall into two categories, Freestone (the pit easily separates from the peach) and Clingstone (pit clings to the peach). Freestones are usually preferred for eating fresh and for freezing while Clingstones are used mainly for canning. Dip cut fruit in lemon juice to prevent darkening.

PEACH 1

NUTRITION INFORMATION PER SERVING

Serving Size: 1 peach		Percent U.S. RDA Per Serving	
Calories	38	Protein	*
Protein	<1g	Vitamin A	27%
Carbohydrate	10g	Vitamin C	12%
Fat	<1g	Thiamin	*
Sodium	1mg	Riboflavin	3%
Potassium	202mg	Niacin	5%
		Calcium	*
		Iron	3%

PEACHES, CANNED 1/2 CUP

NUTRITION INFORMATION PER SERVING

Serving Size: 1/2 cup canned peaches		Percent U.S. RDA Per Serving	
Calories	100	Protein	*
Protein	<1g	Vitamin A	11%
Carbohydrate	26g	Vitamin C	6%
Fat	<1g	Thiamin	*
Sodium	3mg	Riboflavin	*
Potassium	166mg	Niacin	4%
		Calcium	*
		Iron	2%

BUYING

Select fairly firm peaches or ones just beginning to soften. Color should be yellow or orange with red highlights. Avoid firm, hard peaches with green background color as they were probably picked too early and will not ripen properly. Also avoid peaches with tan or brown bruised spots.

STORAGE

Underripe fruit will ripen at room temperature in a few days. Store ripe fruit in refrigerator and use within 3 to 5 days.

PEARS

Pears are picked green in late summer or fall and allowed to ripen. They are available August through April. Bartlett, the most common variety, is available in the fall and is used for canning as well as eating fresh. Anjou, Bosc and Comice are late varieties that keep well in cold storage and are available throughout the winter months.

PEAR 1

NUTRITION INFORMATION PER SERVING

Serving Size: 1 pear		Percent U.S. RDA Per Serving	
Calories	100	Protein	*
Protein	1g	Vitamin A	*
Carbohydrate	25g	Vitamin C	11%
Fat	<1g	Thiamin	2%
Sodium	3mg	Riboflavin	4%
Potassium	213mg	Niacin	*
		Calcium	*
		Iron	3%

PEARS, CANNED 1/2 CUP

NUTRITION INFORMATION PER SERVING

Serving Size: 1/2 cup canned pears		Percent U.S. RDA Per Serving	
Calories	97	Protein	*
Protein	<1g	Vitamin A	0%
Carbohydrate	25g	Vitamin C	2%
Fat	<1g	Thiamin	*
Sodium	1mg	Riboflavin	*
Potassium	108mg	Niacin	*
		Calcium	*
		Iron	*

PEARS, 1/4 CUP DRIED

NUTRITION INFORMATION PER SERVING

Serving Size: 1/4 cup dried pears		Percent U.S. RDA Per Serving	
Calories	121	Protein	2%
Protein	1g	Vitamin A	*
Carbohydrate	30g	Vitamin C	5%
Fat	<1g	Thiamin	*
Sodium	3mg	Riboflavin	5%
Potassium	258mg	Niacin	*
		Calcium	*
		Iron	3%

BUYING

Select firm pears, free of brown, bruised spots. Bartlett pears should be light to rich yellow in color; Anjou and Comice, light to yellowish green; Bosc, greenish yellow to brownish yellow.

STORAGE

Let ripen at room temperature. Ripe pears may be stored in refrigerator up to 5 days.

PINEAPPLE

Pineapples are picked when still firm but mature and then allowed to ripen. To prepare, cut off top and peel. With tip of knife, cut out "eyes". Discard core if tough. Slice or chop fruit. Use raw or in cooked foods. Do not add fresh pineapple to gelatin unless you first boil it 1 minute to destroy an enzyme which prevents gelatin from setting.

PINEAPPLE, 1/2 CUP RAW

NUTRITION INFORMATION PER SERVING

Serving Size: 1/2 cup pineapple		Percent U.S. RDA Per Serving	
Calories	41	Protein	*
Protein	<1g	Vitamin A	*
Carbohydrate	11g	Vitamin C	22%
Fat	<1g	Thiamin	5%
Sodium	<1mg	Riboflavin	*
Potassium	114mg	Niacin	*
		Calcium	*
		Iron	2%

PINEAPPLE, CANNED 1/2 CUP

NUTRITION INFORMATION PER SERVING

Serving Size: 1/2 cup canned pineapple		Percent U.S. RDA Per Serving	
Calories	95	Protein	*
Protein	<1g	Vitamin A	*
Carbohydrate	25g	Vitamin C	15%
Fat	<1g	Thiamin	7%
Sodium	1mg	Riboflavin	*
Potassium	123mg	Niacin	*
		Calcium	*
		Iron	2%

BUYING

Select plump, firm pineapples that are heavy for their size and bright in color with glossy "eyes". Most varieties of pineapple turn from green to golden yellow, orange-yellow or reddish-brown as they ripen.

STORAGE

To ripen, leave at room temperature several days. Ripe pineapple can be refrigerated 1 to 3 days.

PLANTAINS

Members of the banana family, but larger, firmer, starchier and less sweet than the banana. The greenish-looking rough skin may have many blemishes. Plantains are usually used for baking, boiling or frying and are served as a vegetable rather than a fruit. If used as fruit, they should be fully ripe and the skin yellowish in color.

PLUMS and PRUNES

A wide variety of plums are marketed. Flavor and appearance vary widely. Prunes are purplish or blue-black with a moderately firm yellowish flesh that separates freely from the pit.

PLUMS

NUTRITION INFORMATION PER SERVING

Serving Size: 2 plums		Percent U.S. RDA Per Serving	
Calories	13	Protein	*
Protein	<1g	Vitamin A	*
Carbohydrate	4g	Vitamin C	†
Fat	<1g	Thiamin	*
Sodium	0mg	Riboflavin	*
Potassium	60mg	Niacin	*
		Calcium	*
		Iron	*

PRUNES, 1/4 CUP DRIED

NUTRITION INFORMATION PER SERVING

Serving Size: 1/4 cup dried prunes		Percent U.S. RDA Per Serving	
Calories	86	Protein	*
Protein	<1g	Vitamin A	11%
Carbohydrate	23g	Vitamin C	*
Fat	<1g	Thiamin	2%
Sodium	3mg	Riboflavin	3%
Potassium	235mg	Niacin	3%
		Calcium	2%
		Iron	6%

BUYING

Select prunes or plums with good color for the variety and fairly firm to slightly soft in texture. Avoid fruits with brown discoloration, shriveled fruit or other indications of spoilage.

STORAGE

Ripe plums and prunes can be refrigerated 3 to 5 days.

POMEGRANATES

Range in color from light yellow to purplish red. They keep very well and are marketed throughout the winter months. Select fruit with thick, tough skin and red in color. The seeds and ruby-red portions are the edible parts. Cut into quarters, remove seeds with a spoon and discard connecting pulp. Eat seeds plain, add to salads and fruit plates or use as a garnish for desserts. Pomegranates can also be juiced by cutting in half and squeezing on an orange juicer. Grenadine syrup is made from pomegranates.

NUTRITION INFORMATION PER SERVING

Serving Size: 1 pomegranate		Percent U.S. RDA Per Serving	
Calories	97	Protein	*
Protein	<1g	Vitamin A	0%
Carbohydrate	25g	Vitamin C	10%
Fat	<1g	Thiamin	3%
Sodium	5mg	Riboflavin	3%
Potassium	399mg	Niacin	2%
		Calcium	*
		Iron	3%

RAISINS

The term refers to a special kind of grape which has been sun-dried or artificially dried. Raisins should be plump and soft – not hard or dry. They may be stored on the shelf in a cool place or in the refrigerator. Raisins are used in all types of baking–puddings, pies, cakes, sauces, breads, preserves and stuffings.

NUTRITION INFORMATION PER SERVING

Serving Size: 1/4 cup raisins		Percent U.S. RDA Per Serving	
Calories	104	Protein	*
Protein	<1g	Vitamin A	*
Carbohydrate	28g	Vitamin C	*
Fat	<1g	Thiamin	3%
Sodium	10mg	Riboflavin	*
Potassium	275mg	Niacin	*
		Calcium	2%
		Iron	7%

APPLESAUCE

6 to 8 medium apples, peeled and quartered
½ cup water
½ to ¾ cup sugar or firmly packed brown sugar

In large saucepan, combine apples and water. Heat to boiling. Simmer covered over low heat, 15 to 20 minutes or until tender, stirring occasionally. Stir in sugar and heat through. 6 servings

NUTRITION INFORMATION PER SERVING

Serving Size: 1/6 of recipe		Percent U.S. RDA Per Serving	
Calories	138	Protein	*
Protein	<1g	Vitamin A	*
Carbohydrate	36g	Vitamin C	4%
Fat	<1g	Thiamin	3%
Sodium	7mg	Riboflavin	*
Potassium	205mg	Niacin	*
		Calcium	2%
		Iron	6%

TIPS: *If desired, add 1 teaspoon cinnamon.*

To retain the apple pieces, combine sugar and water. Add sliced apples; simmer covered 15 to 20 minutes or until tender. (Most fruits keep their shape when cooked in a sugar-water mixture, but become sauce-like when cooked without sugar.)

BAKED APPLES

BAKED APPLES

6 baking apples, cored
3 tablespoons sugar
6 teaspoons margarine or butter
⅓ cup firmly packed brown sugar
1 tablespoon flour
½ teaspoon cinnamon
1 tablespoon water

Heat oven to 375°F. Place baking apples in 12x8 or 9-inch baking dish. Place ½ tablespoon sugar and 1 teaspoon margarine in cavity of each apple. Bake at 375°F. for 45 to 50 minutes or until apples are tender. In small bowl, combine brown sugar, flour, cinnamon and water. Spoon over baked apples; continue baking 10 minutes. Serve warm or cool. 6 servings

NUTRITION INFORMATION PER SERVING

Serving Size: 1 apple		Percent U.S. RDA Per Serving	
Calories	188	Protein	*
Protein	<1g	Vitamin A	6%
Carbohydrate	39g	Vitamin C	6%
Fat	5g	Thiamin	3%
Sodium	52mg	Riboflavin	2%
Potassium	196mg	Niacin	*
		Calcium	2%
		Iron	5%

TIP: *For variety, add 1 tablespoon raisins or mincemeat to each apple when adding sugar.*

The old-fashioned apple wrapped in pastry.

APPLE DUMPLINGS

9-inch Double-Crust Pastry, page 220
6 baking apples, peeled and cored
6 tablespoons sugar
½ teaspoon cinnamon
¼ teaspoon nutmeg
Raisins, if desired
1 cup firmly packed brown sugar
1½ cups water
2 tablespoons margarine or butter

Heat oven to 425°F. Prepare pastry as directed except form into 1 large ball. Roll pastry to 18x12-inch rectangle. Cut into six 6-inch squares. Place apples on pastry squares. In small bowl, combine 6 tablespoons sugar, cinnamon and nutmeg; spoon about 1 tablespoon in the cavity of each apple. Spoon a few raisins on top. Moisten edges of pastry. Bring up corners to top of apple; pinch edges together. Place dumplings in ungreased 13x9-inch pan. In small saucepan, heat brown sugar, water and margarine to boiling; pour over dumplings. Bake at 425°F. for 30 to 40 minutes or until apples are tender. Serve warm with cream. 6 servings

NUTRITION INFORMATION PER SERVING

Serving Size: 1/6 of recipe		Percent U.S. RDA Per Serving	
Calories	675	Protein	7%
Protein	5g	Vitamin A	4%
Carbohydrate	101g	Vitamin C	4%
Fat	30g	Thiamin	21%
Sodium	416mg	Riboflavin	12%
Potassium	344mg	Niacin	12%
		Calcium	5%
		Iron	17%

TIPS: *For PEACH DUMPLINGS, substitute 2 fresh peeled and pitted peach halves for each apple.*

To halve recipe, use half the ingredient amounts. Roll pastry to 18x6-inch rectangle. Bake at 425°F. in 8 or 9-inch round cake pans.

See the TIP for a delicious caramel variation.

APPLE CRISP

6 cups (6 medium) peeled, sliced cooking apples
1 tablespoon lemon juice
1 tablespoon water
¾ cup firmly packed brown sugar
½ cup Pillsbury's Best® All Purpose, Unbleached or Self Rising Flour
½ cup rolled oats
1 teaspoon cinnamon, if desired
½ cup margarine or butter

Heat oven to 375°F. Place apples in 8 or 9-inch square pan. Sprinkle with lemon juice and water. In small bowl, combine remaining ingredients until crumbly; sprinkle over apples. Bake at 375°F. for 40 to 45 minutes or until apples are tender. 6 servings

NUTRITION INFORMATION PER SERVING

Serving Size: 1/6 of recipe		Percent U.S. RDA Per Serving	
Calories	351	Protein	3%
Protein	2g	Vitamin A	13%
Carbohydrate	53g	Vitamin C	6%
Fat	16g	Thiamin	8%
Sodium	253mg	Riboflavin	5%
Potassium	249mg	Niacin	4%
		Calcium	4%
		Iron	10%

TIP: *For APPLESCOTCH CRISP, prepare apples, place in pan and sprinkle with lemon juice and water as directed. Combine ¼ cup brown sugar, flour, rolled oats, cinnamon and one 3¼-oz. pkg. butterscotch pudding and pie filling (not instant). Melt ½ cup margarine and mix with pudding mixture until crumbly. Sprinkle over apples and bake as directed.*

NUTRITION INFORMATION PER SERVING

Serving Size: 1/6 of recipe		Percent U.S. RDA Per Serving	
Calories	342	Protein	4%
Protein	2g	Vitamin A	13%
Carbohydrate	50g	Vitamin C	6%
Fat	16g	Thiamin	8%
Sodium	320mg	Riboflavin	5%
Potassium	202mg	Niacin	4%
		Calcium	3%
		Iron	8%

BANANAS ROYALE

4 medium bananas, peeled
⅓ cup margarine or butter
⅓ cup firmly packed brown sugar
¼ teaspoon cinnamon
¼ teaspoon nutmeg
¼ cup light cream
¼ cup brandy*
1 qt. (4 cups) vanilla ice cream

Slice bananas in half crosswise, then lengthwise. In chafing dish, melt margarine. Stir in brown sugar, cinnamon and nutmeg. Add bananas; cook 3 minutes over low heat. Bananas should be slightly firm. (Do not overcook.) Stir in cream, cooking until thickened, about 2 minutes. Just before serving, heat brandy in small saucepan or ladle until vapors begin to rise. Ignite and quickly pour over bananas in chafing dish. Serve flaming over ice cream. 8 servings

NUTRITION INFORMATION PER SERVING

Serving Size: 1/8 of recipe		Percent U.S. RDA Per Serving	
Calories	319	Protein	6%
Protein	4g	Vitamin A	16%
Carbohydrate	36g	Vitamin C	11%
Fat	16g	Thiamin	4%
Sodium	142mg	Riboflavin	11%
Potassium	384mg	Niacin	3%
		Calcium	12%
		Iron	4%

TIPS: **Two teaspoons brandy or rum extract may be substituted for the brandy. Add cream and omit flaming.*

To halve recipe, use 3 tablespoons each, margarine, firmly packed brown sugar and brandy; use half the remaining ingredient amounts.

If chafing dish is not available, a large heavy saucepan or skillet may be substituted.

Warm from the oven—it's a family favorite.

CHERRY CRUMBLE

2½ cups Pillsbury's Best® All Purpose or Unbleached Flour*
1¼ cups sugar
½ teaspoon salt
¾ cup margarine or butter, softened
2 cans (16 oz. each) red sour pitted cherries, well-drained (reserve juice for Sauce)

SAUCE
½ cup sugar
2 tablespoons cornstarch
¼ teaspoon salt
Reserved cherry juice
1 tablespoon margarine or butter
3 drops red food coloring, if desired
¼ teaspoon almond extract

Heat oven to 375°F. In large bowl, combine first 4 ingredients; blend until crumbly. Press 2½ cups crumb mixture into ungreased 13x9-inch pan. Spoon cherries evenly over crumbs; sprinkle with remaining crumb mixture. Bake at 375°F. for 30 to 35 minutes or until golden brown. In small saucepan, combine first 3 Sauce ingredients. Stir in reserved cherry juice, margarine and food coloring. Cook until thickened and clear, stirring constantly; stir in extract. Top each serving with warm Sauce.

12 to 15 servings

NUTRITION INFORMATION PER SERVING

Serving Size: 1/15 of recipe		Percent U.S. RDA Per Serving	
Calories	284	Protein	4%
Protein	3g	Vitamin A	16%
Carbohydrate	47g	Vitamin C	5%
Fat	10g	Thiamin	10%
Sodium	232mg	Riboflavin	6%
Potassium	102mg	Niacin	6%
		Calcium	*
		Iron	4%

TIP: **Self-rising flour is not recommended.*

The answer to a simple but elegant dessert.

CHERRIES JUBILEE

1 tablespoon cornstarch
16-oz. can (2 cups) pitted dark sweet cherries, undrained
¼ cup brandy
1 qt. (4 cups) French vanilla or vanilla ice cream

In chafing dish or skillet, combine cornstarch and cherries. Heat until mixture boils and thickens, stirring occasionally. Flame with brandy as directed in Bananas Royale, page *200*. Serve over ice cream.

6 to 8 servings

NUTRITION INFORMATION PER SERVING

Serving Size: 1/8 of recipe		Percent U.S. RDA Per Serving	
Calories	199	Protein	5%
Protein	4g	Vitamin A	7%
Carbohydrate	26g	Vitamin C	4%
Fat	7g	Thiamin	3%
Sodium	43mg	Riboflavin	9%
Potassium	192mg	Niacin	*
		Calcium	11%
		Iron	*

SPICY PRUNES

1½ cups dried prunes
¼ cup firmly packed brown sugar
10 whole allspice or ¼ teaspoon ground allspice
1 stick cinnamon or 1 teaspoon ground cinnamon
2 cups water

In medium saucepan, combine all ingredients. Heat to boiling. Remove from heat; cool. Remove cinnamon stick and allspice. Chill prunes until served. 6 servings

NUTRITION INFORMATION PER SERVING

Serving Size: 1/6 of recipe		Percent U.S. RDA Per Serving	
Calories	149	Protein	*
Protein	<1g	Vitamin A	14%
Carbohydrate	39g	Vitamin C	2%
Fat	<1g	Thiamin	3%
Sodium	6mg	Riboflavin	5%
Potassium	345mg	Niacin	4%
		Calcium	3%
		Iron	12%

TIP: *For variety, add ½ cup port wine just before serving.*

Serve as a first course or salad, too.

FRUIT COMPOTE

¼ cup margarine or butter
¾ cup powdered sugar or ½ cup honey
2 teaspoons grated orange peel
1 teaspoon cornstarch
⅓ cup orange juice
2 tablespoons lemon juice
4 cups fresh fruits, cut into bite-size pieces (bananas, pineapple, peaches, pears, oranges, dark sweet cherries, blueberries)

In chafing dish or large skillet, melt margarine. Add remaining ingredients except fruit. Cook until slightly thickened, stirring constantly. Fold in fruit. Simmer *just* until fruit is warm. Serve immediately with Cream Cheese Topping, page *235*, ice cream or whipped cream. 6 to 8 servings

NUTRITION INFORMATION PER SERVING

Serving Size: 1/8 of recipe		Percent U.S. RDA Per Serving	
Calories	147	Protein	*
Protein	<1g	Vitamin A	12%
Carbohydrate	25g	Vitamin C	22%
Fat	6g	Thiamin	3%
Sodium	71mg	Riboflavin	2%
Potassium	189mg	Niacin	2%
		Calcium	*
		Iron	2%

TIPS: *If strawberries are used, add just before serving; do not cook.*

For WINTER FRUIT COMPOTE, substitute canned drained fruits—pineapple, mandarin oranges, peach slices, pear slices and maraschino cherries.

AMBROSIA MEDLEY

2 cups (1 pint) fresh strawberries, halved
2 cups fresh pineapple or drained canned pineapple chunks
2 bananas, sliced
¼ cup chopped dates, if desired
1 cup flaked coconut or shredded coconut
Powdered sugar
¾ cup orange juice

In large bowl, combine first 4 ingredients. Arrange fruit and coconut in layers in serving dish or individual serving dishes; sprinkle each layer with powdered sugar. Sprinkle coconut on top; drizzle with orange juice. Chill. 6 to 8 servings

NUTRITION INFORMATION PER SERVING

Serving Size: 1/8 of recipe		Percent U.S. RDA Per Serving	
Calories	167	Protein	3%
Protein	2g	Vitamin A	3%
Carbohydrate	28g	Vitamin C	74%
Fat	7g	Thiamin	6%
Sodium	1mg	Riboflavin	4%
Potassium	372mg	Niacin	4%
		Calcium	3%
		Iron	7%

RHUBARB SAUCE

4 cups rhubarb, cut into 1-inch pieces
¼ cup water
1 cup sugar

In large saucepan, combine rhubarb and water; heat to boiling. Simmer covered, 15 to 20 minutes or until tender, stirring occasionally. Stir in sugar and heat through. 6 servings

NUTRITION INFORMATION PER SERVING

Serving Size: 1/6 of recipe		Percent U.S. RDA Per Serving	
Calories	141	Protein	*
Protein	<1g	Vitamin A	*
Carbohydrate	36g	Vitamin C	7%
Fat	<1g	Thiamin	*
Sodium	2mg	Riboflavin	3%
Potassium	205mg	Niacin	*
		Calcium	8%
		Iron	4%

TIP: *If desired, use ⅓ cup honey and ½ cup sugar.*

PEACH MELBA

2 teaspoons cornstarch
½ cup currant jelly
10-oz. pkg. (1¼ cups) frozen sweetened raspberries, thawed and drained
29-oz. can peach halves, drained or 6 fresh peach halves
1 qt. (4 cups) vanilla ice cream

In medium saucepan, combine first 3 ingredients. Cook over medium heat until mixture boils and thickens, stirring frequently. If desired, strain to remove seeds; cool. Place peach half in each serving dish. Top with ice cream; spoon cooled berry sauce over ice cream. 6 servings

NUTRITION INFORMATION PER SERVING

Serving Size: 1/6 of recipe		Percent U.S. RDA Per Serving	
Calories	349	Protein	7%
Protein	5g	Vitamin A	15%
Carbohydrate	64g	Vitamin C	16%
Fat	10g	Thiamin	4%
Sodium	62mg	Riboflavin	14%
Potassium	327mg	Niacin	4%
		Calcium	14%
		Iron	5%

FRUIT AND SOUR CREAM

Arrange fruit in serving dishes. (If fruit darkens easily, dip in orange or lemon juice.) Top with spoonfuls of dairy sour cream or yogurt. Sprinkle with brown sugar or drizzle with honey. Chill about ½ hour before serving.

TIPS: *Fruits which go well with sour cream: peaches, seedless green grapes, blueberries, strawberries, raspberries, pineapple, pears and bananas.*

Fruits may also be tossed lightly with the sour cream, adding brown sugar to taste. Chill; sprinkle with additional brown sugar just before serving.

See page 519, for the original Fruit Soup recipe.

MOCK FRUIT SOUP

½ cup raisins
1½ tablespoons cornstarch
⅛ teaspoon nutmeg
1 cup orange juice
16-oz. can (2 cups) fruit cocktail, undrained
2 tablespoons orange-flavored liqueur, if desired

In medium saucepan, combine all ingredients except liqueur; mix well. Cook over medium heat until mixture boils; simmer 1 to 2 minutes, stirring occasionally. Stir in liqueur. Serve warm or chilled.

4 to 5 servings

NUTRITION INFORMATION PER SERVING

Serving Size: 1/4 of recipe		Percent U.S. RDA Per Serving	
Calories	207	Protein	2%
Protein	1g	Vitamin A	6%
Carbohydrate	49g	Vitamin C	31%
Fat	<1g	Thiamin	7%
Sodium	12mg	Riboflavin	*
Potassium	461mg	Niacin	4%
		Calcium	3%
		Iron	7%

BAKED CUSTARD

½ cup sugar
¼ teaspoon salt
1 teaspoon vanilla
3 eggs, slightly beaten
2½ cups milk
Nutmeg

Heat oven to 350°F. In large bowl, blend together first 4 ingredients. Gradually stir in milk. Pour into six 6-oz. custard cups. Sprinkle with nutmeg. Place in 13x9-inch pan with about 1-inch hot water. Bake at 350°F. for 45 to 50 minutes or until knife inserted near center comes out clean. Serve warm or chilled.

6 servings

NUTRITION INFORMATION PER SERVING

Serving Size: 1/6 of recipe		Percent U.S. RDA Per Serving	
Calories	183	Protein	11%
Protein	7g	Vitamin A	9%
Carbohydrate	24g	Vitamin C	*
Fat	7g	Thiamin	4%
Sodium	175mg	Riboflavin	15%
Potassium	183mg	Niacin	*
		Calcium	14%
		Iron	4%

TIPS: *If desired, bake in 1 to 1½-quart casserole. Bake at 350°F. for 50 to 60 minutes.*

For BAKED CUSTARD WITH CARAMEL SAUCE, heat ½ cup sugar in small heavy saucepan over low heat until sugar melts and browns, stirring constantly. Evenly divide syrup into 6 custard cups; rotate to coat bottom of cups. Let stand to harden while preparing custard as directed above. Pour custard over syrup. Bake at 350°F. for 45 to 50 minutes or until knife inserted near center comes out clean. Invert custard cups to unmold.

SOFT CUSTARD

6 egg yolks or 3 eggs, well beaten
⅓ cup sugar
¼ teaspoon salt
1½ cups milk or light cream
½ teaspoon vanilla

In heavy saucepan*, combine first 3 ingredients. Gradually stir in milk. Cook over medium heat until mixture coats a metal spoon, stirring constantly. (Do not let mixture boil or it will have a curdled texture.) Remove from heat; stir in vanilla. If necessary, beat with a rotary beater until smooth. Chill. Pour into serving dishes or serve as a sauce over cake or fruits.

4 servings

NUTRITION INFORMATION PER SERVING

Serving Size: 1/4 of recipe		Percent U.S. RDA Per Serving	
Calories	218	Protein	12%
Protein	8g	Vitamin A	21%
Carbohydrate	21g	Vitamin C	*
Fat	11g	Thiamin	6%
Sodium	196mg	Riboflavin	16%
Potassium	159mg	Niacin	*
		Calcium	15%
		Iron	8%

TIPS: **If desired, a double boiler may be used. Place enough hot water in bottom of double boiler so that top part does not touch water. Heat mixture over medium-high heat, stirring constantly for 20 minutes or until mixture coats a metal spoon. (Water should not boil in double boiler.)*

For FLOATING ISLAND CUSTARD, pour soft custard into 4 individual baking dishes or custard cups. Beat 2 egg whites and ⅛ teaspoon salt until frothy. Gradually add ¼ cup sugar, beating continuously until stiff peaks form. Float spoonfuls of meringue on each custard. Broil 1 to 2 minutes or until tips of meringue are golden brown.

NUTRITION INFORMATION PER SERVING

Serving Size: 1/4 of recipe		Percent U.S. RDA Per Serving	
Calories	270	Protein	14%
Protein	9g	Vitamin A	20%
Carbohydrate	34g	Vitamin C	*
Fat	11g	Thiamin	6%
Sodium	290mg	Riboflavin	19%
Potassium	183mg	Niacin	*
		Calcium	15%
		Iron	8%

For CRÈME BRÛLÉE, pour cooked custard into 1-quart casserole. Chill at least 1 hour. Sprinkle with 1 tablespoon firmly packed brown sugar. Broil 2 to 5 minutes or until sugar is carmelized. Serve plain or as a sauce over fruit or cake.

TAPIOCA PUDDING

¼ cup sugar
2 tablespoons quick-cooking tapioca
¼ teaspoon salt
2 cups milk
2 eggs, separated
1 teaspoon vanilla
2 tablespoons sugar

In medium saucepan, combine first 4 ingredients and egg yolks (reserve whites in small bowl). Cook over medium heat until mixture comes to full boil, stirring constantly. Remove from heat; blend in vanilla. Beat egg whites until frothy. *Gradually* add 2 tablespoons sugar, beating continuously until stiff peaks form. Fold into tapioca mixture. Spoon into serving dishes; cool.

6 servings

NUTRITION INFORMATION PER SERVING

Serving Size: 1/6 of recipe		Percent U.S. RDA Per Serving	
Calories	140	Protein	8%
Protein	5g	Vitamin A	7%
Carbohydrate	19g	Vitamin C	*
Fat	5g	Thiamin	3%
Sodium	154mg	Riboflavin	11%
Potassium	142mg	Niacin	*
		Calcium	11%
		Iron	2%

TIP: *If desired, fold in ½ cup finely chopped dates, peaches, apricots, strawberries, raspberries or other desired fruit.*

VANILLA PUDDING

⅓ cup sugar
2 tablespoons cornstarch
⅛ teaspoon salt
2 cups milk
2 egg yolks, slightly beaten
1 tablespoon margarine or butter
1 teaspoon vanilla

In medium saucepan, combine first 3 ingredients. Gradually add milk. Cook over medium heat until mixture boils and thickens, stirring constantly. Boil 1 minute. In small bowl, blend about ⅓ of hot mixture into egg yolks. Return to saucepan; blend well. Cook until mixture bubbles, stirring constantly. Remove from heat; add margarine and vanilla. Cool slightly; spoon into serving dishes. 4 servings

NUTRITION INFORMATION PER SERVING

Serving Size: 1/4 of recipe		Percent U.S. RDA Per Serving	
Calories	215	Protein	9%
Protein	6g	Vitamin A	12%
Carbohydrate	26g	Vitamin C	2%
Fat	10g	Thiamin	4%
Sodium	169mg	Riboflavin	15%
Potassium	186mg	Niacin	*
		Calcium	16%
		Iron	3%

TIPS: *For CHOCOLATE PUDDING, increase sugar to ½ cup and cornstarch to 3 tablespoons. Add 1 oz. (1 square) unsweetened chocolate with milk. After cooking pudding, beat with rotary beater until smooth. Omit margarine.*

NUTRITION INFORMATION PER SERVING

Serving Size: 1/4 of recipe		Percent U.S. RDA Per Serving	
Calories	264	Protein	10%
Protein	6g	Vitamin A	10%
Carbohydrate	38g	Vitamin C	2%
Fat	11g	Thiamin	4%
Sodium	134mg	Riboflavin	16%
Potassium	243mg	Niacin	*
		Calcium	16%
		Iron	5%

For BUTTERSCOTCH PUDDING, substitute ½ cup firmly packed brown sugar for granulated sugar.

NUTRITION INFORMATION PER SERVING

Serving Size: 1/4 of recipe		Percent U.S. RDA Per Serving	
Calories	253	Protein	9%
Protein	6g	Vitamin A	12%
Carbohydrate	36g	Vitamin C	2%
Fat	10g	Thiamin	4%
Sodium	177mg	Riboflavin	15%
Potassium	280mg	Niacin	*
		Calcium	18%
		Iron	8%

RICE PUDDING

1½ cups cooked rice
½ cup raisins, if desired
⅓ cup sugar
¼ teaspoon cinnamon
2 cups milk, scalded
1 teaspoon vanilla
2 eggs, beaten

Heat oven to 350°F. In 1½-quart ungreased casserole, combine all ingredients; mix well. Place casserole in baking pan with about 1-inch hot water. Bake at 350°F. for 45 to 55 minutes or until knife inserted near center comes out clean. Serve warm or chilled, with cream if desired. 6 servings

NUTRITION INFORMATION PER SERVING

Serving Size: 1/6 of recipe		Percent U.S. RDA Per Serving	
Calories	198	Protein	10%
Protein	6g	Vitamin A	7%
Carbohydrate	33g	Vitamin C	*
Fat	5g	Thiamin	6%
Sodium	194mg	Riboflavin	12%
Potassium	243mg	Niacin	3%
		Calcium	12%
		Iron	6%

TIPS: *Pudding will bake with a custard layer on bottom. For a more even distribution of rice and raisins, stir pudding carefully after 30 minutes of baking.*

If desired, omit scalding milk; increase baking time to 50 to 65 minutes.

STEAMED CHRISTMAS PUDDING

1 cup Pillsbury's Best® All Purpose or Unbleached Flour*
3 tablespoons firmly packed brown sugar
½ teaspoon salt
½ teaspoon baking powder
½ teaspoon cinnamon
¼ teaspoon soda
⅛ teaspoon nutmeg
⅛ teaspoon ginger
Dash cloves
3 tablespoons oil
½ cup raisins or chopped dates
¼ cup chopped nuts
½ cup milk
3 tablespoons molasses

Generously grease (not oil) 1-quart mold or casserole. In medium bowl, combine all ingredients. Mix until dry ingredients are moistened. Spoon into prepared mold. Cover with lid or foil. Place on rack in large steamer or kettle. Pour boiling water into steamer until 2 inches deep; cover. Keep water boiling gently over low heat. If necessary, add water to maintain steam. Steam 1½ to 2 hours or until pudding springs back when lightly touched in center. Cut in slices. Serve hot with Hard or Lemon Sauce, page 236.

6 to 8 servings

NUTRITION INFORMATION PER SERVING

Serving Size: 1/8 of recipe		Percent U.S. RDA Per Serving	
Calories	200	Protein	5%
Protein	3g	Vitamin A	*
Carbohydrate	30g	Vitamin C	*
Fat	8g	Thiamin	9%
Sodium	205mg	Riboflavin	7%
Potassium	221mg	Niacin	5%
		Calcium	6%
		Iron	8%

TIPS: *For BAKED CHRISTMAS PUDDING, prepare as directed. Bake covered at 325°F. for 55 to 60 minutes: place pan of water on lower rack of oven.*

If desired, a well-greased 6-cup fluted tube pan may be substituted for mold.

**If using Pillsbury's Best® Self Rising Flour, omit baking powder, soda and salt.*

BREAD PUDDING

2 cups (about 2 slices) soft or dry bread cubes
½ cup raisins
2 eggs, slightly beaten
⅓ cup sugar
¼ teaspoon cinnamon
⅛ teaspoon salt
2 cups milk
1 teaspoon vanilla

Heat oven to 350°F. Lightly grease (not oil) 1-quart casserole. Place bread cubes in casserole; sprinkle with raisins. In small bowl, add remaining ingredients; beat well. Pour over bread cubes. Place casserole in baking pan with about 1-inch hot water. Bake at 350°F. for 55 to 65 minutes or until knife inserted near center comes out clean. Serve warm.

4 to 5 servings

NUTRITION INFORMATION PER SERVING

Serving Size: 1/5 of recipe		Percent U.S. RDA Per Serving	
Calories	226	Protein	12%
Protein	8g	Vitamin A	8%
Carbohydrate	36g	Vitamin C	*
Fat	6g	Thiamin	7%
Sodium	193mg	Riboflavin	16%
Potassium	295mg	Niacin	2%
		Calcium	15%
		Iron	7%

A light cake sparked with cranberries is topped with a rich sauce.

SAUCY CRANBERRY DESSERT

2 cups Pillsbury's Best® All Purpose or Unbleached Flour*
1 cup sugar
3 teaspoons baking powder
½ teaspoon salt
1 cup milk
3 tablespoons margarine or butter, softened
1 teaspoon vanilla
2 cups raw whole cranberries, washed and drained

BUTTER SAUCE
1 cup sugar
¾ cup light cream or evaporated milk
½ cup margarine or butter

Heat oven to 350°F. Grease (not oil) 9-inch square or 11x7-inch pan. In large bowl, blend first 7 ingredients at low speed until moistened. Beat 3 minutes at medium speed. Stir in cranberries. Pour into prepared pan. Bake at 350°F. for 25 to 30 minutes or until toothpick inserted in center comes out clean. In small saucepan, combine Butter Sauce ingredients; heat just to boiling. To serve, spoon hot Butter Sauce over dessert squares; if desired, pass additional Sauce. 9 servings

NUTRITION INFORMATION PER SERVING

Serving Size: 1/9 of recipe		Percent U.S. RDA Per Serving	
Calories	468	Protein	7%
Protein	5g	Vitamin A	16%
Carbohydrate	70g	Vitamin C	5%
Fat	20g	Thiamin	13%
Sodium	425mg	Riboflavin	11%
Potassium	114mg	Niacin	8%
		Calcium	8%
		Iron	5%

TIP: **Self-rising flour is not recommended.*

A sometimes forgotten, but much loved, warm-from-the-oven dessert.

CHOCOLATE PUDDING CAKE

1 cup Pillsbury's Best® All Purpose or Unbleached Flour*
¾ cup sugar
½ cup chopped nuts, if desired
2 tablespoons unsweetened cocoa
2 teaspoons baking powder
½ teaspoon salt
½ cup milk
2 tablespoons melted shortening or oil
1 teaspoon vanilla
¾ cup firmly packed brown sugar
¼ cup unsweetened cocoa
1¾ cups hot water

Heat oven to 350°F. In large bowl, combine first 9 ingredients. Mix at medium speed until well blended. Spread in ungreased 8 or 9-inch square pan. In small bowl, combine brown sugar, ¼ cup cocoa and hot water; pour over batter. Bake at 350°F. for 40 to 45 minutes or until cake is set. Serve warm or cool, topped with cream or whipped cream. 6 to 8 servings

NUTRITION INFORMATION PER SERVING

Serving Size: 1/8 of recipe		Percent U.S. RDA Per Serving	
Calories	302	Protein	6%
Protein	4g	Vitamin A	3%
Carbohydrate	55g	Vitamin C	*
Fat	9g	Thiamin	9%
Sodium	268mg	Riboflavin	7%
Potassium	206mg	Niacin	5%
		Calcium	7%
		Iron	10%

TIP: **If using Pillsbury's Best® Self Rising Flour, omit baking powder and salt.*

LEMON PUDDING CAKE

3 eggs, separated
1 teaspoon grated lemon peel
½ cup milk
¼ cup lemon juice
½ cup sugar
⅓ cup flour
⅛ teaspoon salt

Heat oven to 325°F. Grease (not oil) 1-quart casserole. In small bowl, beat egg yolks (reserve whites in small bowl). Blend in lemon peel, milk and lemon juice. Add sugar, flour and salt; beat until smooth. Beat egg whites until stiff. Fold in yolk mixture gently but thoroughly. Pour into prepared casserole. Set in another pan with ½-inch hot water. Bake at 325°F. for 30 to 35 minutes or until golden brown. Serve warm or cool. 5 to 6 servings

NUTRITION INFORMATION PER SERVING

Serving Size: 1/6 of recipe		Percent U.S. RDA Per Serving	
Calories	150	Protein	8%
Protein	5g	Vitamin A	7%
Carbohydrate	24g	Vitamin C	5%
Fat	4g	Thiamin	6%
Sodium	89mg	Riboflavin	9%
Potassium	87mg	Niacin	2%
		Calcium	4%
		Iron	5%

HIGH ALTITUDE–Above 3500 Feet: Bake at 350°F.

LEMON PUDDING CAKE

Strawberries are traditionally served but fresh peaches, blueberries or raspberries are equally as nice.

SHORTCAKE

2 cups Pillsbury's Best® All Purpose or Unbleached Flour*
½ cup sugar
3 teaspoons baking powder
½ teaspoon salt
½ cup margarine, butter or shortening
¾ cup milk
2 eggs, slightly beaten

Heat oven to 375°F. Grease (not oil) 9-inch round cake or 8-inch square pan. In large bowl, combine first 4 ingredients. Using pastry blender, cut in margarine until consistency of coarse meal. Add milk and eggs; stir *just* until dry ingredients are moistened. Spread dough in prepared pan. Bake at 375°F. for 25 to 30 minutes or until golden brown. Serve warm. Split and fill whole shortcake with sweetened fruit and whipped cream. 8 servings

NUTRITION INFORMATION PER SERVING

Serving Size: 1/8 of recipe		Percent U.S. RDA Per Serving	
Calories	303	Protein	9%
Protein	6g	Vitamin A	13%
Carbohydrate	38g	Vitamin C	*
Fat	14g	Thiamin	15%
Sodium	428mg	Riboflavin	12%
Potassium	86mg	Niacin	8%
		Calcium	6%
		Iron	7%

TIPS: *Shortcake may be cut into wedges or squares before splitting. Fill each individual piece with sweetened fruit and whipped cream.*

For individual shortcakes, drop dough by rounded tablespoonfuls, 2 inches apart, onto greased cookie sheet. Bake at 450°F. for 10 to 12 minutes or until golden brown.

**Self-rising flour is not recommended.*

GINGERBREAD

1⅓ cups Pillsbury's Best® All Purpose or Unbleached Flour*
¾ teaspoon cinnamon
¾ teaspoon ginger
½ teaspoon salt
½ teaspoon baking powder
½ teaspoon soda
½ teaspoon allspice
½ cup firmly packed brown sugar
½ cup shortening or margarine
½ cup boiling water
½ cup molasses
1 egg, slightly beaten

Heat oven to 350°F. Grease (not oil) bottom only of 8 or 9-inch square pan. In large bowl, combine first 7 ingredients. Add remaining ingredients; blend well. Pour batter into prepared pan. Bake at 350°F. for 30 to 40 minutes or until toothpick inserted in center comes out clean. Serve slightly warm with whipped cream, whipped cream cheese, lemon sauce or applesauce. 9 servings

NUTRITION INFORMATION PER SERVING

Serving Size: 1/9 of recipe		Percent U.S. RDA Per Serving	
Calories	256	Protein	4%
Protein	3g	Vitamin A	10%
Carbohydrate	37g	Vitamin C	*
Fat	11g	Thiamin	8%
Sodium	343mg	Riboflavin	7%
Potassium	267mg	Niacin	6%
		Calcium	8%
		Iron	12%

TIPS: *If desired, use ⅔ cup Pillsbury's Best® Whole Wheat Flour and ½ cup all-purpose flour.*

If desired, 11x7-inch pan or 12 muffin cups (use paper baking cups) may be substituted. Bake at 350°F. for 25 to 30 minutes.

**If using Pillsbury's Best® Self Rising Flour, omit salt and baking powder; decrease soda to ¼ teaspoon.*

HIGH ALTITUDE–Above 3500 Feet: Decrease baking powder to ¼ teaspoon. Bake at 375°F. for about 35 minutes.

CREAM PUFFS

½ cup hot water
¼ cup margarine or butter
½ cup Pillsbury's Best® All Purpose or Unbleached Flour*
¼ teaspoon salt
2 eggs

Heat oven to 425°F. In medium saucepan, heat water and margarine to boiling. Stir in flour and salt. Cook over medium heat, stirring vigorously until mixture leaves sides of pan in smooth compact ball, about 2 minutes. Remove from heat. Add eggs, one at a time, beating vigorously after each until mixture is smooth and glossy. Spoon 6 mounds of dough about 3 inches apart onto ungreased cookie sheet. Bake at 425°F. for 30 to 40 minutes or until puffed and golden brown. Cool completely. Split; remove any filaments of soft dough. Fill with ice cream, whipped cream or pudding. If desired, top with chocolate sauce.

6 cream puffs

NUTRITION INFORMATION PER SERVING

Serving Size: 1 cream puff		Percent U.S. RDA Per Serving	
Calories	136	Protein	5%
Protein	4g	Vitamin A	11%
Carbohydrate	8g	Vitamin C	0%
Fat	10g	Thiamin	6%
Sodium	206mg	Riboflavin	6%
Potassium	36mg	Niacin	3%
		Calcium	*
		Iron	4%

TIPS: *For ECLAIRS, drop cream puff dough into 12 long ovals about 1-inch wide. When cool fill with Vanilla Pudding, page 206 and glaze with Chocolate Glaze, page 149.*

To double recipe, double the ingredient amounts.

**If using Pillsbury's Best® Self Rising Flour, omit salt.*

CHILLED LEMON SOUFFLÉ

½ cup sugar
1 envelope unflavored gelatin
¼ teaspoon salt
1 cup water
3 eggs, separated*
1 tablespoon grated fresh lemon peel or ½ tablespoon prepared lemon peel
3 to 4 tablespoons lemon juice
⅓ cup sugar
1 cup (½ pint) whipping cream, whipped

Prepare 3 to 4-cup soufflé dish or 5 to 6 individual soufflé dishes by forming a collar of waxed paper around top of dish that extends about 3 inches above dish. (Greasing inside upper edge of dish holds paper in place.) In medium saucepan, combine ½ cup sugar with gelatin and salt. Stir in water. Beat egg yolks (reserve whites in small bowl); add to gelatin mixture. Cook over medium heat just until mixture begins to bubble, stirring constantly. Remove from heat. If mixture is not smooth, beat with rotary beater. Stir in lemon peel and juice. Cool until mixture is thickened but not set. Beat egg whites until frothy. *Gradually* add ⅓ cup sugar, beating continuously until stiff peaks form. Fold into gelatin mixture along with whipped cream. Pour into prepared dish. Refrigerate 4 hours or until set. Carefully remove waxed paper before serving.

5 to 6 servings

NUTRITION INFORMATION PER SERVING

Serving Size: 1/6 of recipe		Percent U.S. RDA Per Serving	
Calories	297	Protein	8%
Protein	5g	Vitamin A	19%
Carbohydrate	30g	Vitamin C	5%
Fat	18g	Thiamin	3%
Sodium	137mg	Riboflavin	8%
Potassium	84mg	Niacin	*
		Calcium	5%
		Iron	4%

TIP: **For this recipe, use only Grade A fresh whole shell eggs. Be sure they have clean, uncracked shells to ensure against contamination.*

CHOCOLATE SOUFFLÉ

2 tablespoons cornstarch
½ cup sugar
¼ teaspoon salt
¾ cup milk
2 oz. (2 squares) unsweetened chocolate or 2 envelopes pre-melted unsweetened baking chocolate flavor
3 tablespoons margarine or butter
1 teaspoon vanilla
4 eggs, separated
¼ teaspoon cream of tartar

Heat oven to 350°F. Prepare a 4 or 5-cup soufflé dish or casserole with foil band by cutting 3-inch strip of foil to go around dish. Lightly grease dish and strip of foil. With greased side toward inside of dish, place foil strip around top of dish letting it extend 2 inches above top of dish. In small saucepan, combine cornstarch, sugar and salt. Stir in milk. Cook over medium heat until mixture boils and thickens, stirring constantly. Remove from heat and stir in chocolate and margarine until melted. Stir in vanilla. Add egg yolks (reserve whites in medium bowl) one at a time, beating well after each. Beat egg whites with cream of tartar until soft peaks form. Fold in chocolate mixture. Pour into prepared soufflé dish (soufflé can stand at room temperature, loosely covered, up to 1 hour before baking). Bake at 350°F. for 45 to 50 minutes or until knife inserted near center comes out clean. Remove band; immediately serve soufflé with ice cream or whipped cream. 4 to 5 servings

NUTRITION INFORMATION PER SERVING

Serving Size: 1/4 of recipe		Percent U.S. RDA Per Serving	
Calories	377	Protein	16%
Protein	10g	Vitamin A	21%
Carbohydrate	35g	Vitamin C	*
Fat	24g	Thiamin	5%
Sodium	332mg	Riboflavin	16%
Potassium	256mg	Niacin	*
		Calcium	10%
		Iron	12%

TIP: *For MOCHA SOUFFLÉ, add 1 teaspoon instant coffee with cornstarch.*

CHOCOLATE MOUSSE

1 cup milk
1 envelope unflavored gelatin
2 oz. (2 squares) semi-sweet chocolate or ⅓ cup semi-sweet chocolate chips
⅓ cup sugar
2 eggs, separated*
⅛ teaspoon salt
1 teaspoon vanilla
⅓ cup sugar
1 cup (½ pint) whipping cream

Combine milk and gelatin; let stand while melting chocolate in medium saucepan over low heat. Stir ⅓ cup sugar and milk mixture into chocolate. Beat in egg yolks (reserve whites in small bowl) and salt. Cook over medium heat, stirring constantly, until mixture thickens slightly and coats a metal spoon. Add vanilla; cool. Beat egg whites until frothy. *Gradually* add ⅓ cup sugar beating continuously until stiff peaks form. Fold into cooled chocolate mixture. In large bowl, beat chilled cream until thickened. Fold chocolate mixture into whipped cream. Spoon into 6 to 8 individual serving dishes or 1 large serving dish. Refrigerate 2 to 3 hours or until set.

6 to 8 servings

NUTRITION INFORMATION PER SERVING

Serving Size: 1/8 of recipe		Percent U.S. RDA Per Serving	
Calories	250	Protein	7%
Protein	5g	Vitamin A	13%
Carbohydrate	23g	Vitamin C	*
Fat	16g	Thiamin	2%
Sodium	76mg	Riboflavin	8%
Potassium	111mg	Niacin	*
		Calcium	7%
		Iron	3%

TIP: **For this recipe, use only Grade A fresh whole shell eggs. Be sure they have clean, uncracked shells to ensure against contamination.*

CHEESECAKE

1 cup Pillsbury's Best® All Purpose or Unbleached Flour*
2 tablespoons sugar
½ teaspoon baking powder
¼ teaspoon salt
⅓ cup margarine or butter
2 to 3 tablespoons milk

FILLING

5 pkg. (8 oz. each) cream cheese, softened
1¾ cups sugar
3 tablespoons flour
1 teaspoon grated lemon peel
¼ teaspoon salt
1 teaspoon vanilla
6 eggs
¼ cup light cream or milk

Heat oven to 450°F. In large bowl, combine first 5 ingredients; blend until crumbly. Sprinkle milk over mixture, stirring until dough is just moist enough to hold together. Form into ball. Press mixture evenly over bottom and 2½ inches up sides of ungreased 9-inch springform pan. Chill. In large bowl, beat cream cheese until creamy. Add sugar, flour, lemon peel, salt and vanilla; beat well. Add eggs, one at a time, beating well after each. Blend in cream. Pour Filling into prepared pan. Bake at 450°F. for 10 minutes; reduce heat to 200°F. and bake 65 to 70 minutes or until Filling is almost set and golden brown. Cool. Refrigerate several hours or overnight before serving. Serve plain or with sweetened fresh fruit. 14 to 16 servings

NUTRITION INFORMATION PER SERVING

Serving Size: 1/16 of recipe		Percent U.S. RDA Per Serving	
Calories	466	Protein	15%
Protein	10g	Vitamin A	31%
Carbohydrate	32g	Vitamin C	*
Fat	34g	Thiamin	7%
Sodium	330mg	Riboflavin	16%
Potassium	97mg	Niacin	3%
		Calcium	7%
		Iron	5%

TIPS: *To halve recipe, use half the ingredient amounts. Press crust on bottom of 8-inch square pan. Bake at 450°F. for 10 minutes; at 200°F. for 35 to 40 minutes.*

Cheesecake may be baked in 13x9-inch pan. Press crust only on bottom of pan. Bake at 450°F. for 10 minutes; 200°F. for 55 to 60 minutes.

**Self-rising flour is not recommended.*

CRUNCHY CREAM DESSERT SQUARES

1 cup Pillsbury's Best® All Purpose or Unbleached Flour*
1 cup flaked coconut or finely chopped nuts
¼ cup sugar
½ cup margarine or butter, softened
3¼-oz. pkg. vanilla pudding and pie filling
1¾ cups milk
1 cup (½ pint) whipping cream
2 tablespoons sugar
½ teaspoon vanilla

Heat oven to 350°F. In ungreased 9-inch square pan, combine first 4 ingredients; blend until crumbly. Bake at 350°F. for 18 to 22 minutes or until golden brown, stirring occasionally. Cool. Prepare pudding as directed, using 1¾ cup milk; cool. In small bowl, whip cream until slightly thickened. Blend in sugar and vanilla; beat until thickened. Reserve 1 cup crumb mixture; press remaining crumbs over bottom of pan. Spoon pudding evenly over crumbs. Top with whipped cream. Sprinkle with reserved crumbs. Refrigerate 2 to 3 hours before serving. 8 to 9 servings

NUTRITION INFORMATION PER SERVING

Serving Size: 1/9 of recipe		Percent U.S. RDA Per Serving	
Calories	503	Protein	9%
Protein	6g	Vitamin A	18%
Carbohydrate	38g	Vitamin C	*
Fat	38g	Thiamin	8%
Sodium	206mg	Riboflavin	11%
Potassium	265mg	Niacin	5%
		Calcium	9%
		Iron	8%

TIP: **Self-rising flour is not recommended.*

CRÊPES SUZETTE

CRÊPES

½ cup (4 oz.) creamed cottage cheese
½ cup Pillsbury's Best® All Purpose or Unbleached Flour*
1½ teaspoons sugar
1½ teaspoons grated orange peel
½ teaspoon salt
½ cup dairy sour cream
1½ tablespoons orange juice
2 eggs

ORANGE HONEY SAUCE

½ cup honey
⅓ cup margarine or butter
2 teaspoons grated orange peel
¼ teaspoon cinnamon
2 tablespoons orange juice

BRANDY (to flame)

2 tablespoons, if desired

In blender, blend cottage cheese until fine. Add remaining ingredients; blend at high speed until well mixed. Heat 6-inch crêpe pan or skillet over medium-high heat (375°F.) A few drops of water sprinkled on the pan sizzle and bounce when heat is just right. Grease pan lightly. Pour 3 tablespoons batter into pan, tilting pan to spread evenly. When crêpe is light brown and set, turn to brown other side. Fold warm crêpes in quarters; arrange in chafing dish or oblong serving dish.

In small saucepan, blend all Orange Honey Sauce ingredients. Heat until hot, stirring occasionally. Pour hot Orange Honey Sauce over crêpes. To flame, warm brandy in small saucepan just until small bubbles form; ignite with match. Immediately pour over crêpes. If desired, serve with whipped cream.
5 to 6 servings

NUTRITION INFORMATION PER SERVING

Serving Size: 1/5 of recipe		Percent U.S. RDA Per Serving	
Calories	389	Protein	12%
Protein	8g	Vitamin A	20%
Carbohydrate	42g	Vitamin C	7%
Fat	20g	Thiamin	9%
Sodium	454mg	Riboflavin	13%
Potassium	104mg	Niacin	4%
		Calcium	7%
		Iron	6%

TIPS: *To MAKE AHEAD, prepare crêpes; stack between paper towels. Wrap and store in refrigerator or freezer.*

For EASY CRÊPES, beat together 2 eggs, 1 cup milk and 3 tablespoons melted margarine or butter. Add ¾ cup Hungry Jack® Buttermilk Pancake and Waffle Mix and beat until smooth. Bake as directed above.

**If using Pillsbury's Best® Self Rising Flour, omit salt.*

STRAWBERRY CREAM CRÊPES

12 cooked Dessert Crêpes, page 101
2 cups (1 pint) fresh strawberries, washed and sliced
¼ cup sugar
8-oz. pkg. cream cheese, softened
¼ cup powdered sugar

Prepare crêpes. Reserve 1 cup strawberries. In small bowl, combine remaining strawberries and ¼ cup sugar; chill. In medium bowl, blend cream cheese and powdered sugar until smooth. Stir in reserved strawberries. Spread about 1 tablespoon strawberry-cheese mixture over each crêpe. Roll up. Serve topped with sweetened chilled strawberries.
12 crêpes

NUTRITION INFORMATION PER SERVING

Serving Size: 1/12 of recipe		Percent U.S. RDA Per Serving	
Calories	219	Protein	9%
Protein	6g	Vitamin A	11%
Carbohydrate	21g	Vitamin C	27%
Fat	13g	Thiamin	7%
Sodium	174mg	Riboflavin	12%
Potassium	131mg	Niacin	4%
		Calcium	6%
		Iron	6%

CRÊPES SUZETTE

CHERRY-TOPPED BLINTZES

12 cooked Dessert Crêpes, page 101
1 cup creamed cottage cheese, drained
2 tablespoons sugar
¼ teaspoon cinnamon
2 tablespoons margarine or butter, softened
½ teaspoon vanilla
1 egg, slightly beaten
2 tablespoons margarine or butter, melted, if desired
21-oz. can (2 cups) prepared cherry fruit filling
1 teaspoon almond extract
Powdered sugar

Prepare crêpes. Heat oven to 350°F. In small bowl, combine cottage cheese, sugar, cinnamon, 2 tablespoons margarine, vanilla and egg; blend well. Spoon about 2 tablespoons cheese mixture onto center of each crêpe. Fold opposite edges over filling. Fold remaining edges to center, forming a square packet. Place seam-side-down in 13x9 or 12x8-inch baking dish. Brush crêpes with melted margarine. Cover loosely with foil. Bake at 350°F. for 15 to 20 minutes or until heated through. While crêpes are baking, in medium saucepan, heat cherry filling until bubbly; stir in almond extract. Serve warm crêpes sprinkled with powdered sugar and topped with cherry sauce.

12 blintzes

NUTRITION INFORMATION PER SERVING

Serving Size: 1 blintz		Percent U.S. RDA Per Serving	
Calories	262	Protein	12%
Protein	8g	Vitamin A	13%
Carbohydrate	34g	Vitamin C	9%
Fat	11g	Thiamin	8%
Sodium	275mg	Riboflavin	13%
Potassium	143mg	Niacin	4%
		Calcium	7%
		Iron	6%

TIP: *Additional garnishes of dairy sour cream or whipped cream may be used.*

CHERRY-TOPPED BLINTZES

ANGEL PIE

ANGEL PIE

3 eggs, separated
⅛ teaspoon cream of tartar
¾ cup sugar

FILLING
½ cup sugar
1 tablespoon grated lemon peel
3 tablespoons lemon juice
3 reserved egg yolks
1 cup (½ pint) whipping cream, whipped

Heat oven to 275°F. Grease (not oil) 9-inch pie pan. In small bowl, beat egg whites (reserve yolks) with cream of tartar until frothy. *Gradually* add ¾ cup sugar, beating continuously until stiff peaks form. Spread over bottom and sides of prepared pie pan. Meringue puffs up during baking, so spread only to top edge of pan. Bake at 275°F. for 60 minutes. Turn oven off. Leave crust in oven to cool and dry. In small saucepan, combine Filling ingredients except whipped cream. Cook over low heat until thickened, stirring constantly. Cool. Fold into whipped cream. Pour into meringue shell. Refrigerate overnight. If desired, garnish with thin lemon slices or grated lemon peel.

9-inch pie

NUTRITION INFORMATION PER SERVING

Serving Size: 1/8 of recipe		Percent U.S. RDA Per Serving	
Calories	260	Protein	5%
Protein	3g	Vitamin A	14%
Carbohydrate	33g	Vitamin C	4%
Fat	14g	Thiamin	2%
Sodium	35mg	Riboflavin	6%
Potassium	63mg	Niacin	*
		Calcium	3%
		Iron	3%

TIP: *For CHOCOLATE ANGEL PIE, prepare Filling by combining 6-oz. pkg. (1 cup) semi-sweet chocolate chips and ¼ cup water in small saucepan. Heat over low heat until chocolate is soft; blend well. Beat in 3 egg yolks, 3 tablespoons sugar and ½ teaspoon vanilla or 2 tablespoons rum or brandy; cool. Beat 1 cup chilled whipping cream until thickened; fold into chocolate mixture. Pour into cooled meringue shell and refrigerate overnight.*

MERINGUE SHELLS

2 egg whites
⅛ teaspoon cream of tartar
¼ teaspoon salt
1 teaspoon vanilla
⅔ cup sugar

Heat oven to 275°F. Line cookie sheet with brown paper. In small bowl, beat egg whites, cream of tartar, salt and vanilla until frothy. *Gradually* add sugar, beating continuously, until stiff peaks form. Do not underbeat. Using a heaping tablespoonful for each shell, spoon onto prepared pan. Form individual meringue shells. Make a deep well in center of each, spreading meringues to 3-inch circles. Bake at 275°F. about 1 hour or until crisp and very lightly browned. Turn off oven; leave in oven with door closed 1½ hours. Remove from oven. Cool completely. 8 shells

NUTRITION INFORMATION PER SERVING

Serving Size: 1 shell		Percent U.S. RDA Per Serving	
Calories	69	Protein	*
Protein	1g	Vitamin A	0%
Carbohydrate	17g	Vitamin C	0%
Fat	0g	Thiamin	0%
Sodium	81mg	Riboflavin	*
Potassium	13mg	Niacin	*
		Calcium	*
		Iron	*

TIP: *Fill with ice cream, fresh fruit, prepared fruit filling or custard.*

Designed to be made in the crank-type freezer. A terrific idea for a family reunion.

VANILLA CUSTARD ICE CREAM

2 eggs, beaten
2 cups milk
¾ cup sugar
⅛ teaspoon salt
1 tablespoon vanilla
2 cups (1 pint) light cream or whipping cream

Prepare ice cream freezer according to manufacturer's directions. In large saucepan, combine eggs, milk, sugar and salt. Cook over low heat until mixture *just* begins to bubble, stirring constantly. Cool*. Add vanilla and cream. Pour into freezer can. Freeze as directed. Any leftover ice cream may be stored in freezer in covered container. If ice cream is frozen solid, allow to stand in refrigerator 10 to 20 minutes to soften slightly before serving.

2 quarts (about 8 servings)

NUTRITION INFORMATION PER SERVING

Serving Size: 1 cup		Percent U.S. RDA Per Serving	
Calories	261	Protein	9%
Protein	6g	Vitamin A	15%
Carbohydrate	24g	Vitamin C	2%
Fat	16g	Thiamin	3%
Sodium	107mg	Riboflavin	14%
Potassium	179mg	Niacin	*
		Calcium	14%
		Iron	*

TIPS: *For CHOCOLATE CUSTARD ICE CREAM, increase sugar to 1 cup and add 2 oz. (2 squares) melted unsweetened chocolate or 2 envelopes premelted unsweetened baking chocolate flavor before cooking. Beat with rotary beater until smooth before adding cream.*

For STRAWBERRY ICE CREAM, wash, hull and crush 2 cups (1 pint) fresh strawberries. Stir in ¼ cup sugar with cream; omit vanilla. Also try peaches, raspberries and blackberries or other favorite fruits.

*To MAKE AHEAD, prepare to *, cover and refrigerate up to 2 days. When ready to freeze, continue from *.*

*To prepare without ice cream freezer, use whipping cream not light cream. Prepare to * and pour into 2 ice cube trays or loaf pans. Freeze until edges are set. In small bowl, beat whipping cream until thickened. In large bowl, beat partially frozen custard mixture until smooth and light. Fold whipped cream into custard mixture. Return to trays and freeze until firm. (Store covered with foil.)*

YOGURT SHERBET

1 cup unsweetened fruit (peaches, raspberries or strawberries)
1 ripe banana, sliced
1 cup plain yogurt
¾ cup orange juice
½ cup crushed pineapple, drained
⅓ cup honey

In blender, combine all ingredients. Process at medium speed until smooth and creamy. Pour into ice cube tray or 9x5-inch loaf pan. Freeze until firm but not solid. Place in bowl and beat until creamy. Return to freezer container, cover and freeze until firm, 5 to 6 hours. Allow to soften slightly before serving.

1½ pints

NUTRITION INFORMATION PER SERVING

Serving Size: 1 cup		Percent U.S. RDA Per Serving	
Calories	263	Protein	6%
Protein	4g	Vitamin A	22%
Carbohydrate	63g	Vitamin C	66%
Fat	2g	Thiamin	10%
Sodium	45mg	Riboflavin	13%
Potassium	531mg	Niacin	6%
		Calcium	12%
		Iron	5%

TIPS: *Sherbet can be mixed with mixer or egg beater, but mash banana and fruit before adding remaining ingredients.*

To make in ice cream freezer, combine all ingredients, place in ice cream freezer and freeze according to manufacturer's directions.

If desired, use fruit-flavored yogurt and decrease honey to 2 tablespoons.

FROZEN LEMON TORTE

Be creative with your combinations—chocolate cake and peppermint ice cream, caramel cake and chocolate ice cream, or yellow cake and strawberry ice cream are favorites.

BAKED ALASKA

One baked 8 or 9-inch square cake or brownie
1 qt. brick ice cream
4 egg whites
½ teaspoon cream of tartar
½ cup sugar

Heat oven to 450°F. Place cooled cake on cookie sheet. Place brick of ice cream in center, trimming side of cake to within 1 inch of ice cream. Place in freezer while preparing meringue. In small bowl, beat egg whites and cream of tartar until frothy. *Gradually* add sugar, beating continuously until stiff peaks form. Completely cover ice cream and cake with meringue, sealing meringue to cookie sheet.* Bake at 450°F. on lowest rack in oven for 3 to 5 minutes or until delicately browned. Transfer to serving plate; serve immediately. 10 to 12 servings

NUTRITION INFORMATION PER SERVING

Serving Size: 1/12 of recipe		Percent U.S. RDA Per Serving	
Calories	229	Protein	7%
Protein	4g	Vitamin A	5%
Carbohydrate	33g	Vitamin C	*
Fat	10g	Thiamin	*
Sodium	128mg	Riboflavin	9%
Potassium	135mg	Niacin	*
		Calcium	9%
		Iron	*

TIP: *TO MAKE AHEAD, prepare to*, leave in freezer up to 24 hours. Just before serving, heat oven to 450°F. and continue from*.*

FROZEN LEMON TORTE

¾ cup (18 cookies) vanilla wafer crumbs or graham cracker crumbs (12 squares)
¼ cup sugar
1 tablespoon grated lemon peel
⅛ teaspoon salt
¼ cup lemon juice
3 eggs, separated
¼ cup sugar
1 cup (½ pint) whipping cream, whipped or 4½-oz. carton (2 cups) frozen whipped topping, thawed

Line ice cube tray or 8-inch square pan with half the vanilla wafer crumbs. In medium saucepan, blend ¼ cup sugar, lemon peel, salt, lemon juice and egg yolks (reserve whites in small bowl.) Cook over medium heat until mixture just begins to bubble, stirring constantly. Cool. Beat egg whites until frothy. *Gradually* add ¼ cup sugar, beating continuously until stiff peaks form. Fold beaten egg whites and whipped cream into cooled lemon mixture. Pour into prepared pan; top with remaining crumbs. Freeze about 4 hours or until set. (For longer storage wrap in foil.) 6 servings

NUTRITION INFORMATION PER SERVING

Serving Size: 1/6 of recipe		Percent U.S. RDA Per Serving	
Calories	297	Protein	8%
Protein	5g	Vitamin A	19%
Carbohydrate	26g	Vitamin C	8%
Fat	20g	Thiamin	3%
Sodium	117mg	Riboflavin	8%
Potassium	94mg	Niacin	*
		Calcium	5%
		Iron	4%

PASTRY

8 or 9-INCH SINGLE-CRUST PIE

1 cup Pillsbury's Best® All Purpose or Unbleached Flour*
½ teaspoon salt
⅓ cup shortening
3 to 4 tablespoons cold water

8 or 9-INCH DOUBLE-CRUST PIE

2 cups Pillsbury's Best® All Purpose or Unbleached Flour*
1 teaspoon salt
⅔ cup shortening
5 to 7 tablespoons cold water

In medium bowl, combine flour and salt. Using pastry blender, cut in shortening until particles are size of small peas. Sprinkle flour mixture with water, 1 tablespoon at a time, while tossing and mixing lightly with a fork. Add water until dough is just moist enough to hold together. (Too much water causes dough to be sticky and tough; too little water causes edges to crack and pastry to tear easily while rolling.)

Form dough into ball (2 balls for double crust); place on well-floured pastry cloth or surface. Flatten ball slightly; smooth edges. With stockinette-covered rolling pin, roll dough to a circle 1 inch larger than inverted 8 or 9-inch pie pan. Fold pastry into quarters; place in pan and unfold, easing into pan. Press in place.

For SINGLE-CRUST PIE, fold edge of pastry under, even with rim and flute. Pour in filling and bake as directed in recipe.

For DOUBLE-CRUST PIE, trim bottom crust even with edge of pan. Pour filling into bottom crust. Roll out top crust; cut slits for escape of steam. Cover filling with top crust. Fold top crust under bottom crust. Seal; flute edge.

8 OR 9-INCH SINGLE-CRUST PIE

NUTRITION INFORMATION PER SERVING

Serving Size: 1/6 of recipe		Percent U.S. RDA Per Serving	
Calories	174	Protein	3%
Protein	2g	Vitamin A	0%
Carbohydrate	16g	Vitamin C	0%
Fat	11g	Thiamin	9%
Sodium	181mg	Riboflavin	5%
Potassium	20mg	Niacin	6%
		Calcium	*
		Iron	3%

8 OR 9-INCH DOUBLE-CRUST PIE

NUTRITION INFORMATION PER SERVING

Serving Size: 1/6 of recipe		Percent U.S. RDA Per Serving	
Calories	348	Protein	7%
Protein	4g	Vitamin A	0%
Carbohydrate	32g	Vitamin C	0%
Fat	23g	Thiamin	18%
Sodium	356mg	Riboflavin	10%
Potassium	40mg	Niacin	11%
		Calcium	*
		Iron	7%

TIPS: *For an attractive shiny top crust, brush with milk or slightly beaten egg white; sprinkle with sugar.*

If desired, use up to half Pillsbury's Best® Whole Wheat Flour.

For DOUBLE-CRUST OIL PASTRY, substitute ½ cup oil for ⅔ cup shortening; decrease water to ¼ cup. Add oil and water all at once. Roll dough between 2 sheets of waxed paper.

For LATTICE CRUST, prepare pastry for Double-Crust Pie, leaving ½ inch of bottom crust extending beyond edge of pan. Roll out remainder of dough. Cut strips ½-inch wide (for decorative edge, use pastry wheel). Lay part of strips across filling in parallel rows about 1 inch apart, twisting if desired. Place more strips at right angles forming a crisscross pattern. (For a woven lattice top, lift every other strip as the cross strips are added.) Trim ends even with edge of pastry. Fold extension up over strips to form standing rim; flute.

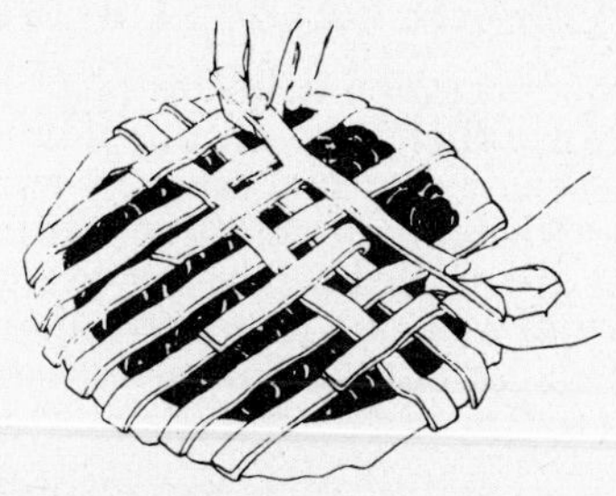

For BAKED PIE SHELL, heat oven to 450°F. Prepare as directed for Single-Crust Pie. Prick bottom and sides of pastry generously with fork. Bake at 450°F. for 9 to 12 mintues or until light golden brown; cool.

For BAKED TART SHELLS, heat oven to 450°F. Prepare Double-Crust Pastry; divide into 10 parts. Roll each to a 4 to 5-inch round. Turn muffin pan upside down or turn custard cups upside down on cookie sheet. Fit pastry rounds over cups, pleating sides so pastry fits cups. Prick generously with fork. Bake at 450°F. for 9 to 12 minutes or until light golden brown; cool.

For CHEESE PASTRY, add shredded Cheddar cheese along with flour. Use ½ cup for single crust, 1 cup for double crust.

**If using Pillsbury's Best Self Rising Flour, omit salt.*

PASTRY TIPS

Sprinkle water over mixture, a tablespoon at a time, while tossing and stirring. If water is added too fast, there will be wet spots in pastry that may stick when rolling.

Flatten each ball to ½-inch thickness; smooth edges. Smoothing edges before rolling helps prevent cracked, broken edges. If cracks appear, press together and smooth out – they just get bigger if you keep rolling.

Roll on floured surface. A cloth-covered surface and a stockinette-covered rolling pin are best. There is much less chance of pastry sticking or of too much flour on pastry.

When making pie shells, be sure to *ease* (not stretch) pastry into pan. As it bakes, it shrinks slightly. If it has been stretched, it will shrink excessively.

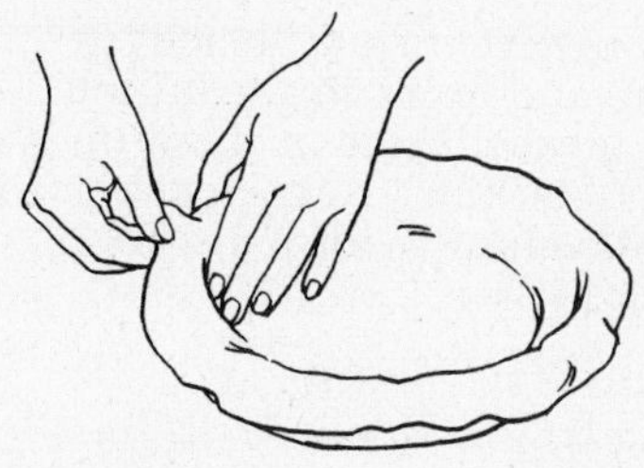

Add a special touch to your pie by fluting. First make edge stand up, then try a fluted edge.

FLUTED EDGE: Place left index finger inside stand-up rim. Make flutes about ½ inch apart by pushing pastry into the "V" shaped by the right thumb and index finger on the outside of the rim. Pinch points to make definite edges.

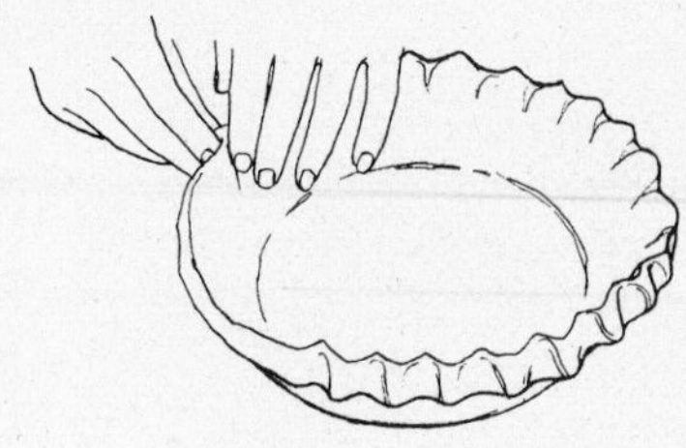

FORK EDGE: Dip fork tines in flour; press firmly around edge on rim of pie pan.

ROPE EDGE: Place thumb on stand-up rim at an angle; press pastry against thumb with knuckle of index finger.

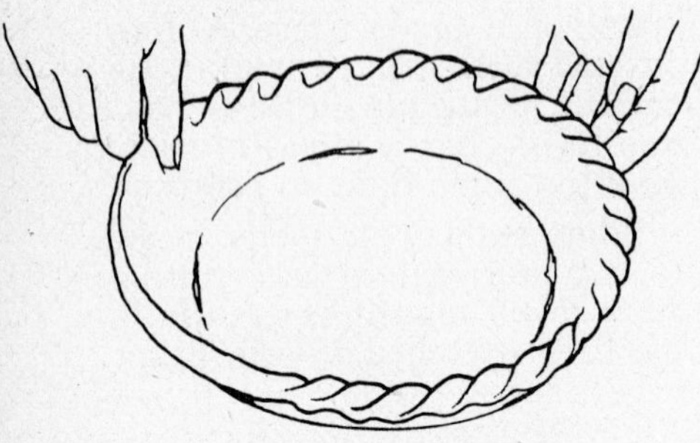

SCALLOPED EDGE: Place left thumb and index finger ¾ inch apart on the inside of stand-up rim. With right index finger, push pastry toward center to form a scallop shape.

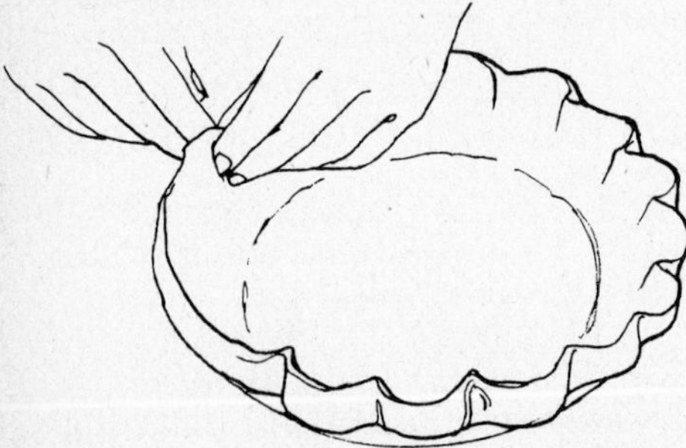

To prevent shrinking of pastry shell during baking, hook edge of fluted pastry over side of pan. This little "hook" helps hold it on pie pan rim.

COOKIE CRUMB CRUSTS

Cookie crumb crusts are easy because there's no rolling of dough. These add a special crunchy goodness to cream or gelatin pie fillings that are chilled before serving. Choose a cookie flavor to enhance the flavor of the filling.

TYPE OF CRUST	AMOUNT	SUGAR	MARGARINE OR BUTTER MELTED
Graham Cracker (crushed)	1½ cups (21 squares)	¼ cup	⅓ cup
Vanilla Wafer (crushed)	1½ cups (36 wafers)	Omit	¼ cup
Gingersnap (crushed)	1½ cups (30 cookies)	Omit	⅓ cup
Chocolate Creme-filled Cookie (crushed)	1½ cups (20 cookies)	Omit	¼ cup
Flaked or Shredded Coconut	2 cups	Omit	¼ cup

Heat oven to 375°F. In medium bowl, combine crumbs, sugar and melted margarine; blend well. Press firmly into bottom and up sides of 9-inch pie pan. Bake at 375°F. for 8 to 10 minutes or until golden brown. Cool.

NUTRITION INFORMATION PER SERVING

Serving Size: 1/6 of recipe		Percent U.S. RDA Per Serving	
Calories	224	Protein	3%
Protein	2g	Vitamin A	8%
Carbohydrate	28g	Vitamin C	0%
Fat	13g	Thiamin	*
Sodium	302mg	Riboflavin	3%
Potassium	104mg	Niacin	*
		Calcium	*
		Iron	2%

TIP: *The graham cracker, vanilla wafer, gingersnap and chocolate cookie crusts may be chilled without baking, if desired.*

MERINGUE

8 INCH PIE

2 egg whites
¼ teaspoon cream of tartar
¼ cup sugar

9 INCH PIE

3 egg whites
¼ teaspoon cream of tartar
6 tablespoons sugar

Heat oven to 400°F. In small bowl, beat egg whites and cream of tartar until frothy. *Gradually* add sugar, beating continuously, until stiff peaks form. Do not underbeat. Spread meringue over hot filling; seal to edge of crust. Bake at 400°F. For 8 to 10 minutes or until lightly browned.

NUTRITION INFORMATION PER SERVING

Serving Size: 1/6 of recipe		Percent U.S. RDA Per Serving	
Calories	56	Protein	3%
Protein	2g	Vitamin A	0%
Carbohydrate	12g	Vitamin C	0%
Fat	0g	Thiamin	0%
Sodium	27mg	Riboflavin	3%
Potassium	26mg	Niacin	*
		Calcium	*
		Iron	*

TIPS: *Separate eggs when they are cold. However, allow egg whites to reach room temperature before beating–the volume will be higher.*

An easy way to make a tender crust.

PAT-IN-PAN CRUST

1½ cups Pillsbury's Best® All Purpose or Unbleached Flour*
2 teaspoons sugar
1 teaspoon salt
½ cup oil
2 tablespoons milk

In medium bowl, combine first 3 ingredients. Add oil and milk; blend well and pat in 9-inch pie pan, fluting edge, if desired. Fill with desired filling. If top crust is needed, use Streusel Topping, this page. Bake as directed in filling recipe. For baked pie shell, bake at 425°F. for 10 to 12 minutes. 9-inch crust

NUTRITION INFORMATION PER SERVING

Serving Size: 1/6 of recipe		Percent U.S. RDA Per Serving	
Calories	283	Protein	5%
Protein	3g	Vitamin A	*
Carbohydrate	25g	Vitamin C	*
Fat	19g	Thiamin	13%
Sodium	358mg	Riboflavin	8%
Potassium	37mg	Niacin	8%
		Calcium	*
		Iron	5%

TIPS: *If desired, use half whole wheat flour and substitute honey for sugar.*

**If using Pillsbury's Best® Self Rising Flour, omit salt.*

STREUSEL TOPPING FOR FRUIT PIE

¾ cup Pillsbury's Best® All Purpose, Unbleached or Self Rising Flour
½ cup firmly packed brown sugar
½ teaspoon cinnamon
½ cup margarine or butter

In small bowl, combine all ingredients until crumbly. Sprinkle over fruit filling. Bake as directed in fruit filling recipe. Cover topping with foil last 10 minutes of baking time if top browns too quickly.

NUTRITION INFORMATION PER SERVING

Serving Size: 1/6 of recipe		Percent U.S. RDA Per Serving	
Calories	262	Protein	3%
Protein	2g	Vitamin A	12%
Carbohydrate	30g	Vitamin C	*
Fat	15g	Thiamin	7%
Sodium	193mg	Riboflavin	4%
Potassium	82mg	Niacin	4%
		Calcium	2%
		Iron	6%

TIP: *If desired, stir ¼ cup chopped nuts or coconut into streusel mixture.*

CHERRY PIE

8 or 9-inch Double-Crust Pastry, page 220
2 cans (16 oz. each) pitted red tart cherries, drained
1¼ cups sugar
¼ cup flour
2 tablespoons margarine or butter

Heat oven to 425°F. Prepare pastry. In large bowl, combine cherries, sugar and flour; toss lightly to mix. Turn into pastry-lined pie pan. Dot with margarine. Cover with top crust (cut slits for escape of steam); seal and flute edge. Bake at 425°F. for 35 to 45 minutes or until juice begins to bubble through slits in crust. 8 or 9-inch pie

NUTRITION INFORMATION PER SERVING

Serving Size: 1/6 of recipe		Percent U.S. RDA Per Serving	
Calories	614	Protein	9%
Protein	6g	Vitamin A	20%
Carbohydrate	90g	Vitamin C	10%
Fat	27g	Thiamin	22%
Sodium	406mg	Riboflavin	12%
Potassium	205mg	Niacin	14%
		Calcium	3%
		Iron	10%

TIPS: *Four cups fresh red tart pitted cherries may be substituted for the canned cherries.* 9-inch pie

If desired, sprinkle cherries with ¼ teaspoon almond extract before dotting with margarine.

APPLE PIE

8 INCH

8-inch Double-Crust Pastry, page 220
5 cups peeled sliced apples
½ to ⅔ cup sugar
2 tablespoons flour
½ teaspoon cinnamon or nutmeg
Dash salt
1 tablespoon margarine or butter

9 INCH

9-inch Double-Crust Pastry, page 220
6 cups peeled sliced apples
¾ to 1 cup sugar
3 tablespoons flour
½ to ¾ teaspoon cinnamon or nutmeg
Dash salt
1 tablespoon margarine or butter

Heat oven to 425°F. Prepare pastry. In large bowl, combine apples, sugar, flour, cinnamon and salt; toss lightly to mix. Turn into pastry-lined pie pan. Dot with margarine. Cover with top crust (cut slits for escape of steam); seal and flute edge. Bake at 425°F. for 40 to 45 minutes or until juice begins to bubble through slits in crust. 8 or 9-inch pie

NUTRITION INFORMATION PER SERVING

Serving Size: 1/6 of recipe		Percent U.S. RDA Per Serving	
Calories	527	Protein	8%
Protein	5g	Vitamin A	2%
Carbohydrate	73g	Vitamin C	3%
Fat	25g	Thiamin	21%
Sodium	426mg	Riboflavin	12%
Potassium	149mg	Niacin	13%
		Calcium	*
		Iron	9%

TIPS: *For FRENCH APPLE PIE, prepare Single-Crust Pastry, page 220; omit margarine and top with Streusel Topping for Fruit Pie, page 223. Bake at 425°F. for about 45 minutes.*

For GREEN APPLE PIE, increase sugar for 8-INCH pie to 1 cup; for 9-INCH pie to 1¼ cups.

For variety, use CHEESE PASTRY, page 221.

FRESH PEACH PIE

8 INCH

8-inch Double-Crust Pastry, page 220
4 cups peeled sliced fresh peaches
1½ teaspoons lemon juice
⅔ cup sugar
3 tablespoons flour
¼ teaspoon cinnamon
1 tablespoon margarine or butter

9 INCH

9-inch Double-Crust Pastry, page 220
5 cups peeled sliced fresh peaches
2 teaspoons lemon juice
¾ cup sugar
¼ cup flour
¼ teaspoon cinnamon
2 tablespoons margarine or butter

Heat oven to 425°F. Prepare pastry. In large bowl, combine peaches and lemon juice. Add sugar, flour and cinnamon; toss lightly to mix. Turn into pastry-lined pie pan. Dot with margarine. Cover with top crust (cut slits for escape of steam); seal and flute edge. Bake at 425°F. for 35 to 40 minutes or until juice begins to bubble through slits in crust. 8 or 9-inch pie

NUTRITION INFORMATION PER SERVING

Serving Size: 1/6 of recipe		Percent U.S. RDA Per Serving	
Calories	552	Protein	9%
Protein	6g	Vitamin A	41%
Carbohydrate	74g	Vitamin C	13%
Fat	27g	Thiamin	22%
Sodium	405mg	Riboflavin	15%
Potassium	335mg	Niacin	20%
		Calcium	2%
		Iron	12%

TIP: *For FRESH APRICOT PIE, substitute 5 cups apricot halves for the peaches.* 9-inch pie

NUTRITION INFORMATION PER SERVING

Serving Size: 1/6 of recipe		Percent U.S. RDA Per Serving	
Calories	560	Protein	9%
Protein	6g	Vitamin A	69%
Carbohydrate	76g	Vitamin C	15%
Fat	27g	Thiamin	22%
Sodium	404mg	Riboflavin	14%
Potassium	390mg	Niacin	16%
		Calcium	3%
		Iron	11%

FRESH BLUEBERRY PIE

8 INCH

8-inch Double-Crust Pastry, page 220
3 cups fresh blueberries
½ cup sugar
3 tablespoons flour
⅛ teaspoon cinnamon, if desired
1½ teaspoons lemon juice
1 tablespoon margarine or butter

9 INCH

9-inch Double-Crust Pastry, page 220
4 cups fresh blueberries
¾ cup sugar
¼ cup flour
¼ teaspoon cinnamon, if desired
2 teaspoons lemon juice
2 tablespoons margarine or butter

Heat oven to 425°F. Prepare pastry. In large bowl, combine blueberries, sugar, flour and cinnamon; toss lightly to mix. Turn into pastry-lined pie pan. Sprinkle with lemon juice; dot with margarine. Cover with top crust (cut slits for escape of steam); seal and flute edge. Bake at 425°F. for 35 to 45 minutes or until juice begins to bubble through slits in crust. 8 or 9-inch pie

NUTRITION INFORMATION PER SERVING

Serving Size: 1/6 of recipe		Percent U.S. RDA Per Serving	
Calories	558	Protein	9%
Protein	6g	Vitamin A	5%
Carbohydrate	76g	Vitamin C	17%
Fat	27g	Thiamin	22%
Sodium	404mg	Riboflavin	14%
Potassium	127mg	Niacin	15%
		Calcium	3%
		Iron	13%

TIP: *Drained canned blueberries or unsweetened frozen blueberries, partially thawed, may be substituted for the fresh blueberries.*

Canned pears with sour cream, covered with a crunchy streusel top.

FRENCH PEAR PIE

9-inch Single-Crust Pastry, page 220
29-oz. can pear halves, drained
⅓ cup sugar
⅛ teaspoon ginger
1 cup dairy sour cream
1 egg
Streusel Topping, page 223

Heat oven to 400°F. Prepare pastry. Arrange pear halves, cut-side-up, in pastry-lined pan. In small bowl, combine sugar, ginger, sour cream and egg; blend well. Pour over pears. Sprinkle with Streusel Topping. Bake at 400°F. for 25 to 30 minutes or until golden brown. Cool.

9-inch pie

NUTRITION INFORMATION PER SERVING

Serving Size: 1/6 of recipe		Percent U.S. RDA Per Serving	
Calories	640	Protein	10%
Protein	6g	Vitamin A	21%
Carbohydrate	76g	Vitamin C	*
Fat	35g	Thiamin	18%
Sodium	402mg	Riboflavin	15%
Potassium	192mg	Niacin	10%
		Calcium	8%
		Iron	12%

RHUBARB-STRAWBERRY PIE

9-inch Double-Crust Pastry, page 220
3 cups sliced rhubarb (½-inch pieces)
¾ cup sugar
¼ cup cornstarch
10-oz. pkg. (1¼ cups) frozen strawberries, thawed and undrained

Heat oven to 425°F. Prepare pastry. In large bowl, combine rhubarb, sugar and cornstarch; mix well. Stir in strawberries. Pour into pastry-lined pie pan. Cover with top crust (cut slits for escape of steam); seal and flute edge. Bake at 425°F. for 35 to 40 minutes or until juice begins to bubble through slits in crust. Serve warm or cool.

9-inch pie

NUTRITION INFORMATION PER SERVING

Serving Size: 1/6 of recipe		Percent U.S. RDA Per Serving	
Calories	525	Protein	8%
Protein	5g	Vitamin A	*
Carbohydrate	77g	Vitamin C	36%
Fat	23g	Thiamin	20%
Sodium	358mg	Riboflavin	14%
Potassium	246mg	Niacin	13%
		Calcium	7%
		Iron	11%

TIP: *If desired, use Single-Crust Pastry and top with Streusel Topping, page 223.*

FRESH STRAWBERRY PIE

9-inch Baked Pie Shell, page 221
3 pints (6 cups) strawberries, hulled, washed and drained
1 cup sugar
3 tablespoons cornstarch
½ cup water
4 to 5 drops red food coloring, if desired
Whipped cream

Bake pie shell. In small bowl, crush enough strawberries to make 1 cup. In medium saucepan, combine sugar and cornstarch. Add crushed strawberries and water. Cook until mixture boils and thickens, stirring constantly; stir in food coloring. Cool. Spoon remaining whole or sliced strawberries into cooled pie shell; pour cooked strawberry mixture over top. Refrigerate 3 hours or until set. To serve top with whipped cream.

9-inch pie

NUTRITION INFORMATION PER SERVING

Serving Size: 1/6 of recipe		Percent U.S. RDA Per Serving	
Calories	424	Protein	5%
Protein	4g	Vitamin A	6%
Carbohydrate	65g	Vitamin C	147%
Fat	18g	Thiamin	12%
Sodium	188mg	Riboflavin	12%
Potassium	278mg	Niacin	10%
		Calcium	5%
		Iron	12%

FRESH STRAWBERRY PIE

PUMPKIN PIE

Deliciously old-fashioned!

PUMPKIN PIE

8 INCH

8-inch Single-Crust Pastry, page 220
2 eggs
⅔ cup sugar
¾ teaspoon cinnamon
¼ teaspoon salt
¼ teaspoon ginger
⅛ teaspoon cloves
1½ cups canned or cooked pumpkin
1 cup evaporated milk or light cream

9 INCH

9-inch Single-Crust Pastry, page 220
2 eggs
¾ cup sugar
1 teaspoon cinnamon
½ teaspoon salt
½ teaspoon ginger
¼ teaspoon cloves
16-oz. can (2 cups) canned or cooked pumpkin
13-oz. can (1⅔ cups) evaporated milk or light cream

Heat oven to 425°F. Prepare pastry. In large bowl, beat eggs slightly. Add remaining ingredients; blend well. Pour into pastry-lined pie pan. Bake at 425°F. for 15 minutes. Reduce oven temperature to 350°F. and continue baking 8-inch pie for 35 minutes and 9-inch pie for 45 minutes or until knife inserted near center comes out clean. Cool. Serve plain or with whipped cream.

8 or 9-inch pie

NUTRITION INFORMATION PER SERVING

Serving Size: 1/6 of recipe		Percent U.S. RDA Per Serving	
Calories	367	Protein	12%
Protein	8g	Vitamin A	83%
Carbohydrate	47g	Vitamin C	3%
Fat	17g	Thiamin	13%
Sodium	345mg	Riboflavin	18%
Potassium	316mg	Niacin	8%
		Calcium	14%
		Iron	7%

TIPS: *If desired, pumpkin pie spice may be substituted for the cinnamon, ginger and cloves. Use 2 teaspoons pumpkin pie spice for the 8-inch pie and 2½ teaspoons for the 9-inch pie.*

For PUMPKIN-EGGNOG PIE, substitute prepared eggnog for evaporated milk.

CUSTARD PIE

8 INCH

8-inch Single-Crust Pastry, page 220
2 eggs
½ cup sugar
⅛ teaspoon salt
⅛ teaspoon nutmeg or cinnamon
¾ teaspoon vanilla
1¾ cups milk, scalded

9 INCH

9-inch Single-Crust Pastry, page 220
3 eggs
¾ cup sugar
¼ teaspoon salt
¼ teaspoon nutmeg or cinnamon
1 teaspoon vanilla
2½ cups milk, scalded

Heat oven to 400°F. Prepare pastry. In large bowl, beat eggs. Add sugar, salt, nutmeg and vanilla; mix well. Blend in hot milk. Pour into pastry-lined pie pan. Bake at 400°F. for 25 to 30 minutes or until knife inserted near center comes out clean. Cool. Serve slightly warm or chilled.

8 or 9-inch pie

NUTRITION INFORMATION PER SERVING

Serving Size: 1/6 of recipe		Percent U.S. RDA Per Serving	
Calories	382	Protein	14%
Protein	9g	Vitamin A	9%
Carbohydrate	46g	Vitamin C	*
Fat	18g	Thiamin	13%
Sodium	356mg	Riboflavin	20%
Potassium	203mg	Niacin	6%
		Calcium	14%
		Iron	7%

RHUBARB CUSTARD PIE

- **9-inch Double-Crust Pastry, page 220**
- **3 eggs**
- **2 tablespoons milk**
- **1½ to 1¾ cups sugar**
- **¼ cup flour**
- **½ to ¾ teaspoon nutmeg**
- **4 cups sliced rhubarb (½-inch pieces)**
- **1 tablespoon margarine or butter**

Heat oven to 400°F. Prepare pastry. In large bowl, beat eggs slightly; add milk. Stir in sugar, flour and nutmeg; mix well. Stir in rhubarb. Pour into pastry-lined pan. Dot with margarine. Cover top with Lattice Crust, page *220*; seal and flute edge. Bake at 400°F. for 50 to 60 minutes or until golden brown. Serve warm.

9-inch pie

NUTRITION INFORMATION PER SERVING

Serving Size: 1/6 of recipe		Percent U.S. RDA Per Serving	
Calories	639	Protein	14%
Protein	9g	Vitamin A	10%
Carbohydrate	89g	Vitamin C	8%
Fat	28g	Thiamin	24%
Sodium	418mg	Riboflavin	20%
Potassium	294mg	Niacin	14%
		Calcium	11%
		Iron	15%

PECAN PIE

- **9-inch Single-Crust Pastry, page 220**
- **⅓ cup firmly packed brown sugar**
- **1½ teaspoons flour**
- **1¼ cups dark corn syrup**
- **4 eggs**
- **1¼ teaspoons vanilla**
- **¼ cup margarine or butter, melted**
- **1 cup pecan halves or broken pecans**

Heat oven to 375°F. Prepare pastry. In large bowl, combine brown sugar, flour, corn syrup, eggs and vanilla; beat well. Stir in margarine and pecans. Pour into pastry-lined pie pan. Bake at 375°F. for 35 to 45 minutes or until center of pie is puffed and golden brown. Cool. Serve plain or with whipped cream.

9-inch pie

NUTRITION INFORMATION PER SERVING

Serving Size: 1/6 of recipe		Percent U.S. RDA Per Serving	
Calories	672	Protein	13%
Protein	9g	Vitamin A	15%
Carbohydrate	82g	Vitamin C	*
Fat	36g	Thiamin	22%
Sodium	369mg	Riboflavin	13%
Potassium	223mg	Niacin	7%
		Calcium	8%
		Iron	28%

TIP: *Light corn syrup may be substituted for dark corn syrup, but the flavor will be milder and less rich.*

MINCEMEAT PIE

8 INCH

- **8-inch Double-Crust Pastry, page 220**
- **22-oz. jar (2 cups) mincemeat**
- **1¼ cups chopped apple**
- **¼ cup chopped nuts, if desired**
- **1 teaspoon grated orange peel**

9 INCH

- **9-inch Double-Crust Pastry, page 220**
- **28-oz. jar (3 cups) mincemeat**
- **1½ cups chopped apple**
- **⅓ cup chopped nuts, if desired**
- **2 teaspoons grated orange peel**

Heat oven to 425°F. Prepare pastry. In large bowl, combine mincemeat and remaining ingredients. Pour into pastry-lined pie pan. Cover with top crust (cut slits for escape of steam); seal and flute edge. For variety, use Lattice Crust, page *220*. Bake at 425°F. for 25 to 30 minutes or until golden brown. Serve warm.

8 or 9-inch pie

NUTRITION INFORMATION PER SERVING

Serving Size: 1/6 of recipe		Percent U.S. RDA Per Serving	
Calories	738	Protein	11%
Protein	7g	Vitamin A	*
Carbohydrate	109g	Vitamin C	5%
Fat	30g	Thiamin	20%
Sodium	357mg	Riboflavin	17%
Potassium	103mg	Niacin	12%
		Calcium	8%
		Iron	23%

TIP: *If desired, add 1 to 2 tablespoons rum or brandy to mincemeat filling; blend well.*

Can be easily made any time of the year with frozen strawberries.

FROZEN STRAWBERRY CREAM PIE

9-inch baked Pat-In-Pan Crust, page 223
2 egg whites
1 tablespoon lemon juice
1 cup sugar
10-oz. pkg. (1¼ cups) frozen strawberries, thawed and undrained
1 cup (½ pint) whipping cream, whipped

Bake pie shell. In medium bowl, beat egg whites until frothy; add lemon juice. *Gradually* add sugar continuously beating until mixture forms stiff peaks. Blend in strawberries. Fold in whipped cream. Pour filling into cooled pie shell; freeze. Serve frozen. If desired, top with whipped cream. 9-inch pie

NUTRITION INFORMATION PER SERVING

Serving Size: 1/6 of recipe		Percent U.S. RDA Per Serving	
Calories	601	Protein	9%
Protein	6g	Vitamin A	13%
Carbohydrate	71g	Vitamin C	38%
Fat	34g	Thiamin	15%
Sodium	396mg	Riboflavin	14%
Potassium	139mg	Niacin	9%
		Calcium	5%
		Iron	7%

LIME CHIFFON PIE

9-inch baked Coconut or Graham Cracker Crust, page 222
¾ cup sugar
1 envelope unflavored gelatin
½ cup water
⅓ cup lime juice (2 limes)
2 eggs, separated*
1 teaspoon grated lime peel, if desired
4 to 5 drops green food coloring
2 tablespoons sugar
1 cup (½ pint) whipping cream, whipped or 4½-oz. carton (2 cups) frozen whipped topping, thawed

Bake crust. In medium saucepan, combine ¾ cup sugar with gelatin. Stir in water and lime juice. Beat egg yolks (reserve whites in small bowl) and add to gelatin mixture; mix well. Cook over medium heat until mixture just begins to bubble, stirring constantly. Remove from heat. If mixture is not smooth, beat with rotary beater. Stir in lime peel and food coloring. Chill until mixture is thickened, but not set. Beat egg whites until frothy. *Gradually* add 2 tablespoons sugar, beating continuously until stiff peaks form. Fold into gelatin mixture along with whipped cream. Pour into cooled crust. Refrigerate 3 hours or until set. 9-inch pie

NUTRITION INFORMATION PER SERVING

Serving Size: 1/6 of recipe		Percent U.S. RDA Per Serving	
Calories	489	Protein	9%
Protein	6g	Vitamin A	23%
Carbohydrate	36g	Vitamin C	9%
Fat	38g	Thiamin	3%
Sodium	129mg	Riboflavin	6%
Potassium	194mg	Niacin	*
		Calcium	5%
		Iron	6%

TIPS: **For this recipe, use only Grade A fresh whole shell eggs. Be sure they have clean, uncracked shells to ensure against contamination.*

For LEMON CHIFFON PIE, substitute lemon peel and juice for lime; omit green food coloring.

LEMON MERINGUE PIE

8 INCH

8-inch Baked Pie Shell, page 221
¾ cup sugar
3 tablespoons cornstarch
¼ teaspoon salt
1¼ cups water
2 egg yolks, slightly beaten
1 tablespoon margarine or butter
1 teaspoon grated lemon peel
¼ cup lemon juice

9 INCH

9-inch Baked Pie Shell, page 221
1 cup sugar
¼ cup cornstarch
½ teaspoon salt
1⅔ cups water
3 egg yolks, slightly beaten
2 tablespoons margarine or butter
1½ teaspoons grated lemon peel
⅓ cup lemon juice

Bake pie shell. Heat oven to 400°F. In medium saucepan, combine sugar, cornstarch and salt. Stir in water; blend until smooth. Cook over medium heat until mixture boils and thickens, stirring constantly. Boil 1 minute. Remove from heat. Blend a small amount of hot mixture into egg yolks (reserve whites in small bowl). Return to saucepan, blend well. Cook just until mixture begins to bubble, stirring constantly. Remove from heat; stir in margarine, lemon peel and lemon juice. Pour into cooled pie shell. Prepare Meringue, page 223. Spoon meringue onto hot pie filling, sealing to edge of crust to prevent shrinking or weeping. Bake at 400°F. for 8 to 10 minutes or until lightly browned. Cool away from drafts, 3 to 4 hours or until set. 8 or 9-inch pie

NUTRITION INFORMATION PER SERVING

Serving Size: 1/6 of recipe		Percent U.S. RDA Per Serving	
Calories	387	Protein	6%
Protein	4g	Vitamin A	9%
Carbohydrate	55g	Vitamin C	11%
Fat	18g	Thiamin	10%
Sodium	414mg	Riboflavin	7%
Potassium	50mg	Niacin	6%
		Calcium	*
		Iron	6%

TIP: *For PINEAPPLE-LEMON PIE, prepare as directed, add 8-oz. can (1 cup) crushed pineapple (drain and use part of syrup for water); stir in crushed pineapple with lemon juice.*

Green and minty filling in a crunchy chocolate crust.

GRASSHOPPER PIE

9-inch baked Chocolate Cookie Crust, page 222
30 large or 3 cups miniature marshmallows
½ cup milk
¼ cup green creme de menthe
3 tablespoons white creme de cacao
1½ cups whipping cream, whipped or 4½- oz. carton (2 cups) frozen whipped topping, thawed

Bake pie crust. In medium saucepan, combine marshmallows and milk. Heat until marshmallows are melted, stirring constantly. Stir in creme de menthe and creme de cacao. Chill until thickened but not set. Fold in whipped cream. Pour into cooled crust. Refrigerate 3 hours or until set. Serve garnished with whipped cream, chocolate curls or pistachio nuts. 9-inch pie

NUTRITION INFORMATION PER SERVING

Serving Size: 1/6 of recipe		Percent U.S. RDA Per Serving	
Calories	619	Protein	7%
Protein	4g	Vitamin A	25%
Carbohydrate	55g	Vitamin C	*
Fat	38g	Thiamin	2%
Sodium	298mg	Riboflavin	7%
Potassium	100mg	Niacin	*
		Calcium	9%
		Iron	4%

Variations galore for a create your own dessert.

VANILLA CREAM PIE

8 INCH

8-inch Baked Pie Shell, page 221
½ cup sugar
3 tablespoons cornstarch
¼ teaspoon salt
2 cups milk
2 egg yolks, slightly beaten
1 tablespoon margarine or butter
1½ teaspoons vanilla

9 INCH

9-inch Baked Pie Shell, page 221
¾ cup sugar
¼ cup cornstarch
¼ teaspoon salt
3 cups milk
3 egg yolks, slightly beaten
2 tablespoons margarine or butter
2 teaspoons vanilla

Bake pie shell. In medium saucepan, combine sugar, cornstarch and salt. Stir in milk, blending until smooth. Cook over medium heat until mixture boils and thickens, stirring constantly. Boil 2 minutes. Remove from heat. Blend a small amount of hot mixture into egg yolks (reserve whites in small bowl). Return to saucepan, blending well. Cook until mixture just begins to bubble, stirring constantly. Remove from heat; stir in margarine and vanilla. Pour into cooled pie shell. Refrigerate 3 hours or until set. Serve with whipped cream.

NUTRITION INFORMATION PER SERVING

Serving Size: 1/6 of recipe		Percent U.S. RDA Per Serving	
Calories	434	Protein	12%
Protein	8g	Vitamin A	13%
Carbohydrate	51g	Vitamin C	2%
Fat	22g	Thiamin	13%
Sodium	384mg	Riboflavin	19%
Potassium	206mg	Niacin	6%
		Calcium	16%
		Iron	6%

TIPS: *If desired, prepare Meringue, page 223 with reserved egg whites. Spoon onto hot filling, sealing to edge of crust to prevent shrinking or weeping. Bake at 400°F. for 8 to 10 minutes or until lightly browned. Cool; refrigerate until set.*

For BANANA CREAM PIE, cool filling in saucepan to lukewarm. Slice 2 or 3 bananas into pie shell; pour filling over bananas. Refrigerate until set. To serve, top with whipped cream.

For BUTTERSCOTCH CREAM PIE, substitute firmly packed brown sugar for granulated sugar.

For CHOCOLATE CREAM PIE, add ¼ cup additional sugar and unsweetened chocolate. Use 1½ oz. (1½ squares) of chocolate for 8-inch pie, 2 oz. (2 squares) for 9-inch pie.

For COCONUT CREAM PIE, add flaked coconut to cooked pudding. Use ¾ cup coconut for 8-inch pie, 1 cup for 9-inch pie.

Like a chiffon pie with a little cream cheese blended in for richness.

LEMON CLOUD PIE

CRUST

1 cup Pillsbury's Best® All Purpose or Unbleached Flour*
½ teaspoon salt
⅓ cup shortening
1 egg, slightly beaten
1 teaspoon grated lemon peel
1 tablespoon lemon juice
1 to 2 tablespoons water

FILLING

¾ cup sugar
¼ cup cornstarch
1 cup water
2 egg yolks, slightly beaten (reserve whites)**
1 teaspoon grated lemon peel
⅓ cup lemon juice
3-oz. pkg. cream cheese
Reserved egg whites
¼ cup sugar

Heat oven to 400°F. In medium bowl, combine flour and salt. Using pastry blender, cut in shortening until mixture is size of small peas. Combine slightly beaten egg, lemon peel and lemon juice; sprinkle over flour while tossing lightly with a fork. Add water until dough is just moist enough to hold together. (Too much water causes dough to be sticky and tough; too little water causes edges to crack and pastry to tear easily while rolling out.) Form dough into ball; place on well-floured pastry cloth or surface. Flatten ball slightly; smooth edges. With stockinette-covered rolling pin, roll dough to a circle 1 inch larger than inverted 8 or 9-inch pie pan. Fold pastry in half; place in pan and unfold, easing into pan. Trim edge of pastry 1 inch from rim of pan; fold pastry under even with rim and flute. Prick bottom and sides of pastry generously with fork. Bake at 400°F. for 12 to 15 minutes or until light golden brown; cool.

In medium saucepan, combine sugar and cornstarch; stir in water. Cook over medium heat until mixture boils and thickens, stirring constantly. Remove from heat. In small bowl, combine egg yolks (reserve whites in small bowl), lemon peel and juice; add small amount of hot mixture and blend well. Return lemon mixture to saucepan; blend well. Cook *just* until mixture starts to bubble, stirring constantly. Remove from heat. Add cream cheese, beat until smooth; cool. Beat reserved egg whites until frothy. *Gradually* add ¼ cup sugar, beating continuously until stiff peaks form. Fold into cooled lemon mixture. Pour into cooled pastry shell. Chill 2 hours or until set.

9-inch pie

NUTRITION INFORMATION PER SERVING

Serving Size: 1/6 of recipe		Percent U.S. RDA Per Serving	
Calories	424	Protein	11%
Protein	7g	Vitamin A	11%
Carbohydrate	56g	Vitamin C	14%
Fat	20g	Thiamin	11%
Sodium	251mg	Riboflavin	12%
Potassium	91mg	Niacin	6%
		Calcium	3%
		Iron	7%

TIPS: **If using Pillsbury's Best® Self Rising Flour, omit salt.*

***For this recipe, use only Grade A fresh whole shell eggs. Be sure they have clean, uncracked shells to ensure against contamination.*

ALL ABOUT WHIPPING CREAM

A dollop of this heavenly fluff dresses up just about any dessert. For success every time, make sure the whipping cream has at least a 35% butterfat content and is thoroughly chilled. Also, chill bowl and beaters. Beat until it thickens and forms soft firm mounds. If you overbeat it begins to separate and you will eventually have butter! Cream doubles in volume when it is whipped, so plan accordingly.

WHIPPED CREAM

1 cup (½ pint) whipping cream
2 to 4 tablespoons sugar
½ teaspoon vanilla

In small bowl, beat cream until slightly thickened. Blend in sugar and vanilla; beat until thickened.
2 cups

NUTRITION INFORMATION PER SERVING

Serving Size: 1 tablespoon		Percent U.S. RDA Per Serving	
Calories	29	Protein	*
Protein	<1g	Vitamin A	2%
Carbohydrate	<1g	Vitamin C	*
Fat	3g	Thiamin	*
Sodium	2mg	Riboflavin	*
Potassium	7mg	Niacin	0%
		Calcium	*
		Iron	*

TIPS: *For CHOCOLATE WHIPPED CREAM, add 1 to 2 tablespoons unsweetened cocoa to whipping cream before beating; use 4 tablespoons sugar.*

For CINNAMON WHIPPED CREAM, add ¼ teaspoon cinnamon with sugar and vanilla.

For COFFEE WHIPPED CREAM, add ½ to 1 teaspoon instant coffee with sugar and vanilla.

For LEMONADE WHIPPED CREAM, fold 2 tablespoons frozen concentrated lemonade thawed with 2 tablespoons sugar; omit vanilla.

For SPICY WHIPPED CREAM, add ½ teaspoon each nutmeg and cinnamon with sugar and vanilla.

For STRAWBERRY CREAM TOPPING, fold ½ cup strawberry preserves, sweetened sliced fresh strawberries or thawed and drained frozen strawberries into whipped cream. Omit sugar and vanilla.

LEMON WHIPPED TOPPING

Beat 1 cup (½ pint) whipping cream until slightly thickened. Add ½ to 1 cup canned lemon pudding, continuing to beat until thickened.
2½ to 3 cups

NUTRITION INFORMATION PER SERVING

Serving Size: 1 tablespoon		Percent U.S. RDA Per Serving	
Calories	12	Protein	*
Protein	<1g	Vitamin A	*
Carbohydrate	<1g	Vitamin C	*
Fat	<1g	Thiamin	*
Sodium	5mg	Riboflavin	*
Potassium	12mg	Niacin	*
		Calcium	*
		Iron	0%

Serve over puddings, warm gingerbread or other cake or on top of pancakes or waffles.

CREAM CHEESE TOPPING

8-oz. pkg. cream cheese, softened
½ cup powdered sugar
2 tablespoons light cream or milk
1 teaspoon vanilla

In small bowl, beat cream cheese until fluffy. Add remaining ingredients; beat well.
1½ cups

NUTRITION INFORMATION PER SERVING

Serving Size: 1 tablespoon		Percent U.S. RDA Per Serving	
Calories	48	Protein	*
Protein	<1g	Vitamin A	3%
Carbohydrate	3g	Vitamin C	*
Fat	4g	Thiamin	*
Sodium	24mg	Riboflavin	*
Potassium	9mg	Niacin	*
		Calcium	*
		Iron	*

Traditionally served over the Christmas pudding.

HARD SAUCE

2 cups powdered sugar
⅛ teaspoon salt
½ cup margarine or butter, softened
1 tablespoon hot water
2 teaspoons rum or brandy extract or 2 tablespoons rum or brandy
1 teaspoon vanilla

In small bowl, combine all ingredients. Beat at high speed until well blended. Chill until served. Serve on warm steamed pudding, cake or gingerbread. 2 cups

NUTRITION INFORMATION PER SERVING

Serving Size: 1 tablespoon		Percent U.S. RDA Per Serving	
Calories	54	Protein	*
Protein	<1g	Vitamin A	2%
Carbohydrate	7g	Vitamin C	0%
Fat	3g	Thiamin	0%
Sodium	44mg	Riboflavin	0%
Potassium	1mg	Niacin	0%
		Calcium	*
		Iron	*

TIP: *Hard sauce may be shaped before refrigerating by pressing through cookie press onto cookie sheet using decorating tips for desired shapes. Sauce may be pressed into frozen juice cans (6 oz. size); refrigerate. Open end of can with opener and push out sauce. Cut into slices to serve.*

For an easy but elegant dessert, serve over crêpes filled with ice cream or cream cheese.

GRAND MARNIER SAUCE

¼ cup sugar
1 tablespoon cornstarch
¾ cup orange juice
2 to 4 tablespoons Grand Marnier or other orange liqueur

In small saucepan, combine sugar and cornstarch. Stir in orange juice. Cook over medium heat until mixture boils, stirring constantly. Stir in liqueur. Serve warm or cool. 1 cup

NUTRITION INFORMATION PER SERVING

Serving Size: 1 tablespoon		Percent U.S. RDA Per Serving	
Calories	24	Protein	*
Protein	<1g	Vitamin A	*
Carbohydrate	5g	Vitamin C	6%
Fat	<1g	Thiamin	*
Sodium	<1mg	Riboflavin	*
Potassium	22mg	Niacin	*
		Calcium	*
		Iron	*

TIP: *For KAHLUA SAUCE, substitute strong coffee for orange juice and kahlua or coffee-flavored brandy for Grand Marnier.*

The perfect topping for warm gingerbread or bread pudding.

LEMON SAUCE

½ cup sugar
2 tablespoons cornstarch
Dash salt
1 cup hot water
2 teaspoons grated lemon peel
2 tablespoons lemon juice
2 tablespoons margarine or butter

In medium saucepan, combine sugar with cornstarch and salt; blend in water. Cook over medium heat until mixture boils and is clear and slightly thickened, stirring constantly. Stir in lemon peel, lemon juice and margarine. Serve warm or cool. 1½ cups

NUTRITION INFORMATION PER SERVING

Serving Size: 1 tablespoon		Percent U.S. RDA Per Serving	
Calories	27	Protein	*
Protein	<1g	Vitamin A	*
Carbohydrate	5g	Vitamin C	*
Fat	<1g	Thiamin	*
Sodium	23mg	Riboflavin	*
Potassium	2mg	Niacin	*
		Calcium	*
		Iron	*

TIP: *For ORANGE SAUCE, substitute orange juice for water and orange peel for lemon peel; omit lemon juice.*

Lovely cold over fresh fruit or warm over ice cream.

APRICOT NECTAR SAUCE

1 teaspoon cornstarch
½ cup apricot nectar
1 tablespoon brandy

In small saucepan, combine all ingredients. Cook over medium heat until mixture boils, stirring constantly. 1/2 cup

NUTRITION INFORMATION PER SERVING

Serving Size: 1 tablespoon		Percent U.S. RDA Per Serving	
Calories	15	Protein	*
Protein	<1g	Vitamin A	3%
Carbohydrate	3g	Vitamin C	*
Fat	<1g	Thiamin	*
Sodium	<1mg	Riboflavin	*
Potassium	24mg	Niacin	*
		Calcium	*
		Iron	*

Instead of the traditional hard sauce, try serving this sauce over the Christmas pudding.

NUTMEG SAUCE

½ cup sugar
1 tablespoon cornstarch
½ teaspoon nutmeg
1 cup water or milk
¼ cup margarine or butter
1 teaspoon vanilla or 1 tablespoon rum or brandy

In small saucepan, combine first 3 ingredients. Stir in water and margarine. Cook over medium heat until mixture boils and is slightly thickened, stirring occasionally. Stir in vanilla. Serve warm over steamed pudding. 1⅓ cups

NUTRITION INFORMATION PER SERVING

Serving Size: 1 tablespoon		Percent U.S. RDA Per Serving	
Calories	39	Protein	*
Protein	<1g	Vitamin A	*
Carbohydrate	5g	Vitamin C	0%
Fat	2g	Thiamin	*
Sodium	27mg	Riboflavin	*
Potassium	<1mg	Niacin	*
		Calcium	*
		Iron	*

Serve thickened fruit as a sauce over ice cream, cake or pudding.

HOW TO THICKEN FRUITS

Drain sweetened canned or frozen fruit, reserving ⅓ cup fruit syrup. In saucepan, stir syrup and 1½ teaspoons cornstarch until smooth. Cook over medium heat until sauce boils and thickens, stirring occasionally. Cool; fold in fruit.

TIPS: *If additional thickened fruit syrup is desired, allow 1½ teaspoons cornstarch for each ⅓ cup syrup.*

For fresh fruit, sugar fruit and allow to stand several hours for syrup to form. Drain and thicken as directed.

For a delicious change try serving over chocolate ice cream.

BUTTERSCOTCH SAUCE

1½ cups firmly packed brown sugar
½ cup light corn syrup
⅓ cup margarine or butter
⅔ cup light cream
1 teaspoon vanilla

In medium saucepan, combine first 3 ingredients. Cook over medium heat, stirring occasionally, to soft ball stage (234°F.). Cool 5 minutes. Blend in cream and vanilla. Serve warm or cool. 2¼ cups

NUTRITION INFORMATION PER SERVING

Serving Size: 1 tablespoon		Percent U.S. RDA Per Serving	
Calories	72	Protein	*
Protein	<1g	Vitamin A	2%
Carbohydrate	12g	Vitamin C	*
Fat	3g	Thiamin	*
Sodium	29mg	Riboflavin	*
Potassium	38mg	Niacin	*
		Calcium	*
		Iron	3%

A good ice cream sauce, too.

CHOCOLATE FONDUE SAUCE

2 oz. (2 squares) unsweetened chocolate
1 tablespoons margarine or butter
1 cup sugar
5⅜-oz. can (⅔ cup) evaporated milk

In small saucepan, melt chocolate and margarine over low heat. Stir in sugar; gradually stir in milk. Continue heating, stirring constantly, until sugar is dissolved. Serve in fondue pot over candlewarmer.

1¼ cups

NUTRITION INFORMATION PER SERVING

Serving Size: 1 tablespoon		Percent U.S. RDA Per Serving	
Calories	69	Protein	*
Protein	<1g	Vitamin A	*
Carbohydrate	12g	Vitamin C	*
Fat	3g	Thiamin	*
Sodium	17mg	Riboflavin	2%
Potassium	49mg	Niacin	*
		Calcium	2%
		Iron	*

TIP: *See Dippers for Dessert Fondues, this page.*

A caramel rum sauce that is equally as good over cake, ice cream or puddings.

FRUIT FONDUE AU RUM

3 tablespoons margarine or butter
1½ cups firmly packed brown sugar
½ cup evaporated milk
2 tablespoons rum or 1 teaspoon rum extract

In medium saucepan, melt margarine over low heat. Stir in brown sugar; gradually stir in milk. Continue heating, stirring constantly until sugar is dissolved. Remove from heat. Let stand about 3 minutes; stir in rum. Serve warm in fondue pot over candlewarmer.

1½ cups

NUTRITION INFORMATION PER SERVING

Serving Size: 1 tablespoon		Percent U.S. RDA Per Serving	
Calories	74	Protein	*
Protein	<1g	Vitamin A	*
Carbohydrate	14g	Vitamin C	*
Fat	2g	Thiamin	*
Sodium	28mg	Riboflavin	*
Potassium	64mg	Niacin	*
		Calcium	3%
		Iron	3%

TIP: *Dippers for Dessert Fondues:*
Cubes of angel food or sponge cake
Vanilla wafers
Banana slices
Orange or tangarine sections
Pineapple chunks
Strawberries
Apple or pear pieces
Mandarin oranges
Cherries
Large marshmallows

To MAKE AHEAD, prepare, cover and refrigerate. Serve cold or reheat.

EGGS, CHEESE, RICE & PASTA

EGGS, CHEESE, RICE & PASTA

EGGS

The recipes in this book have all been tested using large eggs, however, in general the recipe should perform satisfactorily with any of the other 3 sizes available. When the size of the egg is critical to the recipe the cup measurement will also be given.

STORAGE

Egg shells are porous and therefore are susceptible to moisture loss and spoilage. Eggs should be refrigerated to reduce spoilage. If refrigerated at temperatures close to 45°F., they should keep for several weeks. There is no significant nutritional loss.

It is best to store eggs with the large end up to avoid movement of the air cell and yolk.

BASIC PREPARATION

For best results when making egg dishes, here are a few tips:

- Cook eggs on low heat for best flavor and texture–high heat toughens eggs and makes them rubbery.
- When combining beaten eggs with a hot mixture, add just a small amount of the hot mixture to the beaten eggs, then gradually add the warmed eggs to the remainder of the hot mixture.
- To prevent the greenish color on the surface of hard-cooked egg yolks, cook eggs for the minimum time required to make them hard and then cool in cold running water.

BEATING EGG WHITES

- Egg whites that have been allowed to come to room temperature (70°F.) give the best volume.
- Cream of tartar, added to egg whites while beating, increases the beating time but also increases the stability.
- Sugar beaten into egg whites increases their stability, but decreases the volume and therefore should be added gradually during the final beating stage.
- Fat inhibits the foaming action of egg white. Therefore, carefully separate the fat containing yolk from the white. Also use bowls that contain no trace of oil or fat. Avoid using a plastic bowl because it tends to retain fat.

BUYING

GRADING: Although ungraded eggs are sold in some areas, most states have laws requiring eggs to be graded before they are sold at retail.

The grading of an egg takes into account the quality and appearance of the egg. The highest rating of AA is given to eggs with clean, unbroken, normal-shaped shells. The yolks are high and centered and the whites clear and firm. Grade AA and A eggs are best for poached, fried and deviled eggs where the appearance of the egg is important. Also when making a recipe in which the egg is not cooked, such as chiffon pies or eggnog, it is important to use clean, uncracked eggs to insure against contamination. Grade B eggs are more economical and are fine to use when the appearance of the egg is not important and the eggs are thoroughly cooked. The grade of egg does not affect the nutritional value.

SCRAMBLED EGGS

For each egg, allow 1 tablespoon milk, cream or water, ⅛ teaspoon salt and 1 teaspoon margarine. In bowl, break eggs; add milk and salt. Beat slightly with a fork until uniform yellow in color. In skillet, melt margarine over medium heat; tilt pan to coat. Add egg mixture, reduce heat; cook slowly. Occasionally stir from outside edge of pan to center to allow uncooked egg to flow to bottom of pan. Cook until set but still moist as eggs continue to cook after being removed from heat.

NUTRITION INFORMATION PER SERVING

Serving Size: 1 egg		Percent U.S. RDA Per Serving	
Calories	137	Protein	12%
Protein	8g	Vitamin A	17%
Carbohydrate	1g	Vitamin C	*
Fat	11g	Thiamin	4%
Sodium	395mg	Riboflavin	12%
Potassium	97mg	Niacin	*
		Calcium	5%
		Iron	7%

TIPS: *Dress up scrambled eggs by adding one of the following toward end of cooking: chopped chives, parsley or pimiento, Tabasco sauce, shredded or cubed cheese, diced ham, cooked crumbled bacon, cut-up cooked sausage links, drained seafood (flaked crab meat, tuna, salmon or shrimp), drained canned mushrooms, cubed cream cheese or chive cream cheese, chopped tomato or green pepper, chopped green chilies, catsup.*

For EGGS FOO YONG SCRAMBLE, use 6 eggs, 16-oz. can (2 cups) drained bean sprouts, 1 small chopped onion, ¼ cup chopped green pepper and 2 tablespoons soy sauce. Cook onion and green pepper in 2 tablespoons margarine or butter until tender. Beat eggs; add bean sprouts and soy sauce. Omit milk and salt. Add egg mixture to onions; cook as directed. 4 to 5 servings

BAKED EGGS

Heat oven to 325°F. Butter 5 or 6-oz. custard cups. Break an egg into each. If desired, add 1 tablespoon cream or milk to each. Sprinkle with salt and pepper; dot with margarine. Bake uncovered at 325°F. for 12 to 15 minutes or until eggs are set. Serve from baking dishes.

NUTRITION INFORMATION PER SERVING

Serving Size: 1 egg		Percent U.S. RDA Per Serving	
Calories	158	Protein	12%
Protein	8g	Vitamin A	19%
Carbohydrate	1g	Vitamin C	*
Fat	13g	Thiamin	4%
Sodium	394mg	Riboflavin	11%
Potassium	90mg	Niacin	*
		Calcium	5%
		Iron	7%

TIPS: *For BAKED BACON AND EGGS, partially cook slices of bacon and place a slice of bacon around inside edge of each dish before adding egg.*

For BAKED EGGS SUISSE, sprinkle about 2 tablespoons shredded Swiss cheese on each egg after baking; return to oven a few minutes to melt cheese.

For BAKED EGGS IN TOAST CUPS, line dishes with bread which has the crusts removed and is buttered on both sides and cut in half. Fit into dishes. Top with eggs and continue as directed. If desired, serve with Cheese Sauce, page 540 or condensed cheese soup heated with ¼ cup milk.

For BAKED EGGS AND HASH, line each dish with about ¼ cup corned beef hash, making a well in the center. Top with egg and continue as directed.

HARD AND SOFT-COOKED EGGS

Place eggs in saucepan; cover with cold water. Heat to boiling; reduce heat and allow to barely simmer about 15 minutes for hard-cooked; 2 to 3 minutes (depending on desired doneness) for soft-cooked. Cool eggs under cold water a few seconds to stop cooking. Cut eggs in half, spoon out of shell. Serve in egg cups. Peel hard-cooked eggs and use in casseroles, etc.

NUTRITION INFORMATION PER SERVING

Serving Size: 1 egg		Percent U.S. RDA Per Serving	
Calories	93	Protein	11%
Protein	7g	Vitamin A	13%
Carbohydrate	<1g	Vitamin C	0%
Fat	7g	Thiamin	3%
Sodium	70mg	Riboflavin	9%
Potassium	74mg	Niacin	*
		Calcium	3%
		Iron	7%

TIPS: *For a tender egg white, allow the water to barely simmer; if it boils hard, the white will toughen.*

Eggs a few days old are easier to remove from the shell than the very fresh; the white does not separate easily from the shell. For ease in shelling, crack and peel under running cold water, beginning at larger end.

POACHED EGGS

Use a saucepan or skillet at least 1½ inches deep so eggs can be covered with water. Grease pan lightly; add about 1 inch of water and ¼ teaspoon salt to pan. Heat just to boiling. Break eggs, one at a time, into saucer or custard dish and carefully slip into simmering water. Cover and cook over low heat 3 to 5 minutes, or until of desired doneness. With slotted spatula or spoon, carefully remove eggs. Serve on buttered toast.

NUTRITION INFORMATION PER SERVING

Serving Size: 1 egg on 1 slice toast		Percent U.S. RDA Per Serving	
Calories	210	Protein	13%
Protein	8g	Vitamin A	17%
Carbohydrate	12g	Vitamin C	0%
Fat	14g	Thiamin	6%
Sodium	339mg	Riboflavin	10%
Potassium	92mg	Niacin	3%
		Calcium	5%
		Iron	9%

TIP: *Eggs may be poached in milk or in bouillon-flavored water.*

FRIED EGGS

In skillet, heat 1 to 2 tablespoons margarine, butter or bacon drippings until hot. Break egg, one at a time into custard cup or saucer; carefully slip each egg into skillet. Reduce heat to low and cook until of desired doneness. For SUNNY-SIDE-UP BASTED EGGS, spoon hot fat over eggs until whites are set and a white film forms over yolk. For SUNNY-SIDE-UP STEAMED EGGS, add 1 to 2 teaspoons water and cover skillet until whites are set and a white film forms over yolk, 3 to 5 minutes. For EGGS OVER EASY, cook eggs 2 to 3 minutes or until set on the bottom. Carefully turn eggs over to cook other side; cook until of desired doneness.

NUTRITION INFORMATION PER SERVING

Serving Size: 1 egg		Percent U.S. RDA Per Serving	
Calories	201	Protein	10%
Protein	6g	Vitamin A	22%
Carbohydrate	<1g	Vitamin C	0%
Fat	19g	Thiamin	3%
Sodium	296mg	Riboflavin	8%
Potassium	68mg	Niacin	*
		Calcium	3%
		Iron	6%

TIP: *To eliminate the need for margarine, butter or drippings, use a skillet coated with a non-stick surface. Add 1 tablespoon water with the eggs. Cook covered until of desired doneness.*

CREAMED EGGS

4 to 6 hard-cooked eggs
¼ cup finely chopped celery
1 small onion, finely chopped
2 tablespoons margarine or butter
2 tablespoons flour
1 teaspoon dry mustard
½ teaspoon salt
⅛ teaspoon pepper
1½ cups milk

In medium saucepan, cook celery and onion in margarine until tender. Blend in flour, salt and mustard; cook until mixture starts to bubble, stirring constantly. Add milk; cook over medium heat until mixture boils and thickens, stirring constantly. Shell eggs, cut into slices or wedges, add to cream sauce and heat through. Serve over toast or boiled potatoes. 3 to 4 servings

NUTRITION INFORMATION PER SERVING

Serving Size: 1/4 of recipe		Percent U.S. RDA Per Serving	
Calories	226	Protein	17%
Protein	11g	Vitamin A	21%
Carbohydrate	10g	Vitamin C	6%
Fat	15g	Thiamin	8%
Sodium	466mg	Riboflavin	20%
Potassium	270mg	Niacin	2%
		Calcium	15%
		Iron	9%

TIPS: *If desired, cook 2 to 4 slices bacon and use drippings for margarine. Use cooked crumbled bacon for garnish.*

If desired, add ½ to 1 cup dried beef or cooked cubed ham with eggs (omit salt), ¼ cup chopped green pepper with onions, ¼ cup sliced olives with eggs, 1 cup shredded cheese with eggs.

For MUSTARD EGGS, substitute 1 tablespoon prepared mustard for dry mustard, 1⅓ cups water for milk and add ½ tablespoon sugar. This is especially good with the bacon Tip.

For CURRIED EGGS, omit mustard and add 1 teaspoon curry powder. Garnish with peanuts, coconut, chutney or cooked crumbled bacon.

DEVILED EGGS

6 hard-cooked eggs, cooled
½ teaspoon dry or 1 teaspoon prepared mustard
⅛ teaspoon salt
Dash pepper
3 tablespoons mayonnaise, salad dressing or dairy sour cream
½ tablespoon vinegar
½ teaspoon Worcestershire sauce, if desired
Paprika

Remove shells from eggs and halve lengthwise. Carefully remove yolks and place in small bowl. Mash yolks with fork and add remaining ingredients except paprika; mix until fluffy. Fill egg white halves with yolk mixture. Sprinkle with paprika. 12 deviled eggs

NUTRITION INFORMATION PER SERVING

Serving Size: 1 deviled egg		Percent U.S. RDA Per Serving	
Calories	72	Protein	6%
Protein	4g	Vitamin A	7%
Carbohydrate	<1g	Vitamin C	*
Fat	6g	Thiamin	*
Sodium	81mg	Riboflavin	5%
Potassium	39mg	Niacin	*
		Calcium	*
		Iron	4%

TIP: *If desired, add one of the following: 2 tablespoons crumbled Roquefort or blue cheese, ¼ to ½ cup shredded cheese, ¼ cup chopped ripe olives, 1 teaspoon chopped chives, 2 chopped green onions, 1½ tablespoons anchovy paste (omit salt), ¼ cup drained flaked tuna, salmon, shrimp or crab meat, ¼ cup deviled ham (omit salt), ¼ teaspoon curry powder.*

BASIC OMELET

1½ tablespoons margarine or butter
4 eggs
¼ cup milk or water
¼ teaspoon salt
Dash pepper

In 9 or 10-inch skillet or omelet pan, melt margarine over medium-high heat, tilting pan to coat bottom. In small bowl, beat eggs, milk, salt and pepper until combined; pour into skillet. Reduce heat to low and cook without stirring. As edges set lift edges to allow the uncooked egg to flow to bottom of pan, tilting pan as necessary. Cook until mixture is set, but top still moist looking. Add any desired filling to omelet. With spatula, loosen edge of omelet and fold in half as omelet slides from pan to serving platter.

2 to 3 servings

NUTRITION INFORMATION PER SERVING

Serving Size: 1/2 of recipe		Percent U.S. RDA Per Serving	
Calories	282	Protein	24%
Protein	16g	Vitamin A	35%
Carbohydrate	3g	Vitamin C	*
Fat	23g	Thiamin	9%
Sodium	531mg	Riboflavin	23%
Potassium	193mg	Niacin	*
		Calcium	10%
		Iron	15%

TIPS: *For other size omelets, use 1 tablespoon milk or water for each egg and about 1 teaspoon margarine for each egg.*

For FILLED OMELETS, use sautéed mushrooms, cooked crumbled bacon, cooked chopped ham, shredded cheese, cottage cheese, diced tomato, jelly or marmalade (omit pepper), sweetened strawberries or raspberries. Add filling just before folding in half.

For SPANISH OMELET, cook 3 tablespoons chopped onion in 1½ tablespoons margarine or butter. Blend in 2 teaspoons flour; stir in 1 cup tomatoes, ⅓ cup sliced ripe olives, ¼ teaspoon salt and dash pepper. Simmer covered, about 15 minutes, stirring occasionally. Prepare omelet; spoon part of tomato mixture on omelet before folding and spoon remaining over omelet on serving platter.

For ORIENTAL OMELET, cook 2 tablespoons onion and 1 tablespoon green pepper in 1 tablespoon margarine or butter. Add ⅓ cup drained bean sprouts, ⅓ cup cooked chopped shrimp, ½ teaspoon soy sauce and dash ginger. Heat through. Spoon part of shrimp mixture on omelet before folding and spoon remaining over omelet on serving platter. If desired, serve with soy sauce or Creamy Mustard Sauce, page 551.

EGGS BENEDICT

Hollandaise sauce, page 543 or
1 pkg. hollandaise sauce mix
6 slices Canadian bacon or ham
6 eggs poached
3 English muffins
Margarine or butter

Prepare hollandaise sauce as directed. Keep warm over hot (not boiling) water. Broil or fry Canadian bacon. Split and toast English muffins while poaching eggs. Spread each muffin with margarine; place on serving plate and top with slice of hot Canadian bacon, poached egg and hollandaise sauce.

6 servings

NUTRITION INFORMATION PER SERVING

Serving Size: 1/6 of recipe		Percent U.S. RDA Per Serving	
Calories	475	Protein	28%
Protein	18g	Vitamin A	41%
Carbohydrate	17g	Vitamin C	6%
Fat	38g	Thiamin	26%
Sodium	1089mg	Riboflavin	18%
Potassium	188mg	Niacin	11%
		Calcium	11%
		Iron	20%

ORIENTAL OMELET

PUFFY OMELET

6 eggs, separated
1 teaspoon salt
6 tablespoons water
⅛ teaspoon pepper
2 tablespoons margarine or butter

Heat oven to 325°F. In large bowl, beat egg whites with salt and water until stiff peaks form. Using same beaters, in small bowl, beat egg yolks with pepper until thickened and light yellow in color. Fold into egg whites. Over medium heat, heat margarine in 10-inch ovenproof skillet until a drop of water sizzles in fat. Tilt pan to coat bottom and sides with margarine. Pour in omelet mixture. Reduce heat to low and cook uncovered until puffy and light brown on bottom, about 5 minutes. Place skillet in oven; bake at 325°F. for 15 to 18 minutes or until knife inserted in center comes out clean. To remove, tip skillet, loosening omelet with spatula. Fold in half and slip onto platter. Serve immediately with Cheese Sauce, page 540, or Mushroom Sauce, page 551, or with one of suggested fillings in Basic Omelet.
4 servings

NUTRITION INFORMATION PER SERVING

Serving Size: 1/4 of recipe		Percent U.S. RDA Per Serving	
Calories	190	Protein	17%
Protein	11g	Vitamin A	25%
Carbohydrate	<1g	Vitamin C	*
Fat	16g	Thiamin	6%
Sodium	707mg	Riboflavin	15%
Potassium	112mg	Niacin	*
		Calcium	5%
		Iron	11%

TIP: *To halve recipe, use half the ingredient amounts; cook in 6 or 8-inch skillet until puffy and light brown. Bake for 10 to 15 minutes. If desired, cut into wedges rather than folding in half.*

CHEESY SAUSAGE QUICHE

9-inch unbaked pastry shell, page 220
¾ lb. bulk pork sausage or links, sliced
½ cup chopped onion or 1 tablespoon instant minced onion
⅓ cup chopped green pepper or 4 teaspoons sweet pepper flakes
1½ cups (6 oz.) shredded Cheddar cheese
2 eggs
1 tablespoon flour
1 tablespoon chopped fresh parsley or 1 teaspoon parsley flakes
½ teaspoon seasoned salt
¼ teaspoon garlic salt
¼ teaspoon pepper
1 cup light cream or evaporated milk

Heat oven to 425°F. Prepare pastry shell. Bake 7 minutes. Remove from oven; reduce oven temperature to 350°F. In medium skillet, brown sausage; remove and drain on paper towel. Reserve 2 tablespoons fat; cook and stir onions and green pepper in reserved fat until crisp-tender, about 2 minutes. Stir in drained sausage. Spoon into partially baked shell. Sprinkle with cheese. In medium bowl, beat eggs until well blended. Add remaining ingredients; mix well. Pour over cheese. Bake at 350°F. for 30 to 35 minutes or until knife inserted in center comes out clean. Cool 5 to 10 minutes; cut into wedges to serve.
6 servings

NUTRITION INFORMATION PER SERVING

Serving Size: 1/6 of recipe		Percent U.S. RDA Per Serving	
Calories	555	Protein	27%
Protein	18g	Vitamin A	20%
Carbohydrate	19g	Vitamin C	22%
Fat	46g	Thiamin	22%
Sodium	860mg	Riboflavin	23%
Potassium	229mg	Niacin	9%
		Calcium	27%
		Iron	12%

EGGS FOO YONG

6 eggs
¼ cup instant minced onion or ½ cup finely chopped onion
2 tablespoons chopped green pepper
½ teaspoon salt
Dash pepper
16-oz. can (2 cups) bean sprouts, drained

SAUCE
1 tablespoon cornstarch
2 teaspoons sugar
1 cube or 1 teaspoon chicken bouillon
Dash ginger
1 cup water
2 tablespoons soy sauce

Heat oven to 300°F. In large bowl, beat eggs well. Add remaining ingredients, except Sauce ingredients; mix well. In large skillet, heat 2 tablespoons oil. Drop egg mixture by tablespoonfuls into skillet; fry until golden. Turn and brown other side. Drain on paper towel. Add additional oil to skillet if necessary and continue to cook the remaining egg mixture. Keep warm in 300°F. oven while preparing Sauce. In small saucepan, combine first 4 ingredients. Add water and soy sauce. Cook until mixture boils and thickens, stirring constantly. 4 servings

NUTRITION INFORMATION PER SERVING

Serving Size: 1/4 of recipe		Percent U.S. RDA Per Serving	
Calories	191	Protein	21%
Protein	14g	Vitamin A	20%
Carbohydrate	12g	Vitamin C	19%
Fat	10g	Thiamin	11%
Sodium	1274mg	Riboflavin	20%
Potassium	306mg	Niacin	3%
		Calcium	7%
		Iron	17%

TIP: *Sliced water chestnuts, cooked diced pork or shrimp may be added for variety.*

CHEESE 'N SAUSAGE QUICHE

CHEESE

SERVING

Cheese has the same high quality protein as meat, fish and eggs, so include it in your meals often. Cheese has fantastic flexibility–it can be cooked, uncooked, in a main dish, as a snack or a dessert. Here are some helpful hints:

As an appetizer, serve alone, with wine, fruit, crackers or bread. Except for unripened cheeses, cheese should always be served at room temperature for the best flavor.

In soups and sauces, add cubed or shredded cheese while heating to melt the cheese.

In salads, cheeses are cubed, shredded or cut into strips.

In *main dishes,* shred or cube cheese to be blended in, or added on top during the last few minutes.

As a dessert, serve with wine, sherry or fruit. Follow the hints for serving as an appetizer.

For specific serving suggestions see each type of cheese.

TYPES OF CHEESE

Today, there is an overwhelming assortment of cheeses available which may be confusing unless you know what you are looking for.

There are basically 9 groups of cheeses which are somewhat similar in their production, taste and use.

Cheddar Family

These are the most popular cheeses in the United States. The flavor ranges from mild, which is cured (aged) only a few weeks, to sharp which is aged several months. Cheddars are most often served on an appetizer tray, in sandwiches, grated in hot dishes and as a dessert with fruit.

Swiss Family

The Swiss cheeses are easily recognizable because of their large round holes or eyes which develop during aging. Swiss cheese in Switzerland is called Emmentaler. Gruyère is related to Swiss cheese but it has a stronger flavor. Most Gruyère cheese sold in the United States is a pasteurized process cheese. It is not the same as natural Gruyère. Swiss cheeses are served in sandwiches, salads and melted for cheese fondue.

Dutch Family

These cheeses in the United States often have a characteristic red wax coating, although in Holland, where they originated they are sold without. In manufacturing, the cheese is pressed into a mold which gives it its shape–Edam is round, Gouda is in wheels or rectangles. Baby Goudas are simply small Goudas. Both Gouda and Edam may have spices added, caraway being the most popular. Serve them on appetizer trays, in salads or with fruit for dessert.

Provolone Family

These cheeses originated in Italy. Alike because the cheese making process is the same, Provolone and Mozzarella differ greatly in flavor. Provolone is aged slightly and generally smoked. Mozzarella is actually a fresh, uncured cheese. Because they melt into a nice stringy mass, the Provolone cheeses are particularly suited for Italian dishes. Provolone is also served as an appetizer or dessert.

Blue Cheese Family

Easily recognizable because of the blue-green mold which grows throughout the cheese. Almost every cheese eating country has developed their own particular version. The blue cheese in the United States is made from cow's milk. Roquefort which is produced from sheep's milk is cured in caves in a region in southeast France. Blue cheeses are popularly served as appetizers, in salads and salad dressings and as a dessert with fruit.

Hard-grating Cheeses

These cheeses are so hard they are always grated or shredded. Because they have been aged for as long as 24 months, they have developed a strong pungent flavor that goes well in cooked dishes, particularly Italian. Romano is slightly stronger than Parmesan.

Uncured Cheeses

These are made in a slightly different method from the other cheeses. Coagulation of the curd is initiated by a lactic acid starter. This gives these cheeses their characteristic slightly acid taste. Cream cheese and Neufchatel (with a slightly lower fat content than cream cheese) have a mild flavor and smooth creamy texture which blend well with other ingredients. Thus, their uses are wide and varied. Cottage cheese is still in the curded form, although to improve its flavor and texture it is usually creamed by the addition of milk and cream. Cottage cheese may be purchased in either the large or small curd form. Although, not technically a member of the uncured family because lactic acid has not been added to initiate coagulation, we have inserted ricotta cheese in this group since Americans often substitute cottage cheese for ricotta and their uses are much the same. Ricotta is an uncured cheese that is a little drier than cottage cheese with a grainy texture rather than curds.

Surface Ripening Cheeses

In all cheeses of this type, a bacterial or mold culture is grown on the surface of the cheese. The enzymes produced penetrate the cheese and bring about the development of a particular flavor and texture. Camembert and Brie are mold ripened varieties; Limberger is a bacterial ripened cheese. Brick and Muenster no longer can be considered true members because due to consumer preference, they have little or no surface ripening. These cheeses are particularly popular served as desserts or appetizers.

Pasteurized Process Cheeses

These cheeses are a blend of fresh and aged natural cheeses that have been melted, pasteurized and mixed with an emulsifier. Other ingredients, such as fruits, vegetables, meats or spices may be added. Pasteurized process cheese food contains less cheese and fat than process cheese but has added milk or whey solids. Pasteurized process cheese spread has even more moisture and less milk fat than process cheese food. Usually a stabilizer is added to process cheese to prevent separation of the ingredients. Process cheeses are often used in cooked foods because they melt easily.

BUYING TIPS

- Cheeses should never be dry. Even hard cheeses should not be dried out with cracks on the surface. Softer cheeses should not be crumbly and dry.
- Cheeses which are packaged in paper, wax or foil should be fresh and clean. The outer wrapping should not be torn or broken.
- Check the Natural Cheese Identification Guide, page 250. The cheese should look as it has been described.

NATURAL CHEESE IDENTIFICATION GUIDE

NAME	SHAPE	TEXTURE	COLOR	FLAVOR
Cheddar Family				
Cheddar	varied, with or without rind	hard, firm	white to orange	mild to sharp depending on aging
Colby, Longhorn	cylindrical	hard but softer than Cheddar	light yellow to orange	mild
Monterey Jack	wheels	semi-soft, smooth	creamy white	mild
Swiss Family				
Swiss	blocks	hard, smooth	creamy white	sweet, mild
Emmentaler (em-en-tall-er)	wheels	with large holes	creamy white	nut-like
Gruyère (gree-air')	wheels	hard, tiny holes	light yellow	sweet, nut-like
Dutch Family				
Edam	ball shape, with or without red wax	hard type, crumbly texture	creamy yellow	mild, nut-like
Gouda	flattened, round	hard type, crumbly	creamy yellow	mild, nut-like
Provolone Family				
Provolone (pro-vo-lo'-nee)	round, pear or sausage bound with cord	semi-hard to hard, slices well	light creamy yellow to golden brown	mellow to sharp, usually smoked and salted
Mozzarella	rectangular	semi-soft	creamy white	mild
Seamorza	round	smooth, shiny, stretchy	light yellow	mild
Blue Cheese Family				
Blue Cheese - U.S. Roquefort - France (rōk-fert)	cylindrical	semi-soft moist and crumbly	white, marbled with blue-green mold	sharp, spicy salty taste
Hard-grating Cheese				
Parmesan	wheels, (wedges) grated	hard, brittle	creamy yellow	sharp, pungent
Romano	cylindrical, grated	hard, brittle	creamy white	sharp, very pungent
Uncured Cheeses				
Cream	foil wrapped rectangles	soft, smooth	white	slightly acidic
Neufchatel (new-sha-tel)	foil wrapped rectangles	creamy	white	buttery, mild
Cottage	curds in containers	large or small curds, moist, very soft	white	mild, slightly acidic
Ricotta (ri-kot'-ta)	in containers	moist, grainy, drier than cottage	white	bland, sweet

NATURAL CHEESE IDENTIFICATION GUIDE

NAME	SHAPE	TEXTURE	COLOR	FLAVOR
Surface Ripening Cheeses				
Camembert (cam'-em-bear)	wheels	soft, thin crust, creamy	light cream, white crust	mild to pungent
Brie (bree)	wheels	crust, creamy	white crust	mild to pungent
Brick	rectangles	semi-soft, smooth, elastic	creamy white	mild to moderately sharp
Muenster (mun'-ster)	wheels, rectangles	semi-soft, numerous openings, elastic	creamy white interior, tan surface	mild to mellow
Bel Paese (bel-pa-aye'-ze)	wheels	soft, smooth, waxy	gray surface, creamy yellow interior	mild to robust
Port du Salut (pord-a-sal-oo')	wheels, rectangles	semi-soft, buttery	creamy white interior, reddish brown surface	mellow to robust
Limburger	rectangles	soft, smooth	creamy white	robust, highly aromatic

STORAGE

Cheese is perishable and therefore should be stored in the refrigerator for longest storage.

- Cheese keeps best when unopened. After opening, wrap tightly in original wrapping or plastic wrap.
- Aromatic cheeses should be stored in tightly covered jars or containers.
- For longer storage, do not slice or shred the cheese in advance.
- Mold that develops on the surface of harder natural cheeses may be cut away without effect to the cheese.
- In general, the softer the cheese the more perishable it is. Use the following guide as an indication of refrigeration time for most cheeses:
  Cottage and riccota–5 days
  Cream and other soft cheeses–2 weeks
  Cheddar, Swiss and other harder cheeses–several months
  Cheese spreads–several weeks
- Long storage of harder cheeses will result in some additional aging which will sharpen the flavor.

FREEZING CHEESE

Cheese may be frozen without any effect on flavor. However, freezing does damage the texture of the cheese, usually causing it to crumble and become mealy. Therefore, cheese that has been frozen should be reserved for cooking purposes.

Store cheese in freezer wrap or store in airtight container. Cheese blocks should be no more than ½ pound or ½ inch thick.

COOKING WITH CHEESE

The secret to cooking with cheese is avoid overcooking. Cheese tends to get tough and stringy when cooked too long.

- When melting cheese, use low heat.
- Add cheese as a last ingredient to sauces or as toppings.
- Shred, grate or cube cheese so that it melts faster.
- Broil just until cheese is melted.
- When making cheese sauces or fondues, use a heavy pan or double boiler to prevent scorching.

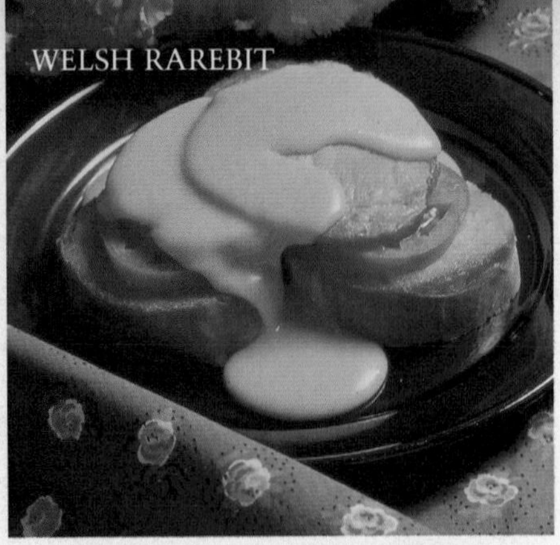

WELSH RAREBIT

3 tablespoons margarine or butter
3 cups (12 oz.) cubed American cheese
12-oz. can (1½ cups) beer
3 eggs, slightly beaten
1½ teaspoons dry mustard
1 teaspoon Worcestershire sauce
6 drops Tabasco sauce, if desired
6 slices toast

In medium saucepan, melt margarine over low heat. Add cheese and beer. Cook, stirring constantly, over very low heat until cheese melts. In small bowl, combine beaten egg, mustard, Worcestershire and Tabasco sauces. Add slowly to melted cheese, beating with a wire whisk or rotary beater. Continue cooking, about 10 minutes, stirring occasionally until thickened. Serve over toast points. 6 servings

NUTRITION INFORMATION PER SERVING

Serving Size: 1/6 of recipe		Percent U.S. RDA Per Serving	
Calories	410	Protein	30%
Protein	20g	Vitamin A	25%
Carbohydrate	18g	Vitamin C	*
Fat	27g	Thiamin	7%
Sodium	905mg	Riboflavin	23%
Potassium	131mg	Niacin	5%
		Calcium	44%
		Iron	11%

TIP: *For an interesting variation serve over toast points and thin tomato slices. Top with cooked crumbled bacon.*

MEXICAN FIESTA PIE

3 cups corn or tortilla chips
15-oz. can chili with beans
½ cup chopped onion
2 cups (8 oz.) shredded Cheddar, American or Monterey Jack cheese
Shredded or chopped lettuce, tomatoes and olives

Heat oven to 400°F. Lightly grease a 9-inch square pan or 1½-quart shallow casserole. Layer half the corn chips, chili, onion and cheese in pan; repeat. Bake uncovered at 400°F. for 15 minutes or until hot. Garnish with lettuce, tomatoes and olives. 4 servings

NUTRITION INFORMATION PER SERVING

Serving Size: 1/4 of recipe		Percent U.S. RDA Per Serving	
Calories	645	Protein	48%
Protein	31g	Vitamin A	17%
Carbohydrate	37g	Vitamin C	2%
Fat	41g	Thiamin	10%
Sodium	1317mg	Riboflavin	28%
Potassium	402mg	Niacin	17%
		Calcium	64%
		Iron	26%

CHEESE SOUFFLÉ

6 tablespoons margarine or butter
⅔ cup Pillsbury's Best® All Purpose or Unbleached Flour*
1 teaspoon salt
¼ teaspoon dry mustard
1½ cups milk
1½ cups (6 oz.) shredded Cheddar cheese
½ teaspoon Worcestershire sauce
6 eggs, separated

Heat oven to 350°F. Grease and lightly flour 1½-quart soufflé dish or casserole. Make a 4-inch band of double thickness aluminum foil 2 inches longer than the circumference of dish; grease one side. Extend depth of dish by wrapping foil, greased-side-in, around top of dish. Secure foil with clear tape.

In large saucepan, melt margarine. Blend in flour, salt and mustard. Heat until bubbly. Add milk; heat until mixture is very thick and smooth, stirring constantly. Add cheese and Worcestershire sauce; stir until cheese melts. Remove from heat; blend in egg yolks, one at a time, beating well after each. Beat egg whites until stiff peaks form (do not overbeat). Fold into cheese mixture. Carefully pour into soufflé dish. Bake at 350°F. for 55 to 60 minutes or until knife inserted near center comes out clean. Remove foil band. Serve immediately.

6 servings

NUTRITION INFORMATION PER SERVING

Serving Size: 1/6 of recipe		Percent U.S. RDA Per Serving	
Calories	395	Protein	27%
Protein	18g	Vitamin A	31%
Carbohydrate	15g	Vitamin C	*
Fat	29g	Thiamin	12%
Sodium	797mg	Riboflavin	27%
Potassium	199mg	Niacin	4%
		Calcium	32%
		Iron	11%

TIPS: *To halve recipe, use half the ingredient amounts and bake in 1-quart soufflé dish or casserole for 35 to 40 minutes.*

For TUNA or CHICKEN SOUFFLÉ, add 1 cup finely chopped tuna or chicken when adding cheese.

For BACON or HAM SOUFFLÉ, add 6 to 8 slices cooked crumbled bacon or 1 cup finely chopped ham when adding cheese.

**If using Pillsbury's Best® Self Rising Flour, omit salt.*

SWISS CHEESE FONDUE

1 garlic clove
¾ cup sauterne or Chablis white wine
3 cups (12 oz.) shredded natural Swiss cheese
2 tablespoons flour
¼ teaspoon salt
⅛ teaspoon nutmeg
Dash pepper
1 to 2 tablespoons kirsch, if desired
1 loaf French bread, cut into bite-size pieces

Rub inside of saucepan or fondue pot with cut garlic clove. Add wine and heat until bubbly. In medium bowl, combine cheese, flour, salt, nutmeg and pepper. Add about ¼ cup cheese mixture to wine; stir vigorously. Continue adding cheese in small amounts and stirring until all cheese is melted and mixture is thoroughly blended. Stir in kirsch. Keep hot while serving. Each guest uses fondue fork to dip bread into fondue.

4 to 5 servings

NUTRITION INFORMATION PER SERVING

Serving Size: 1/4 of recipe		Percent U.S. RDA Per Serving	
Calories	704	Protein	52%
Protein	34g	Vitamin A	19%
Carbohydrate	70g	Vitamin C	*
Fat	27g	Thiamin	24%
Sodium	1393mg	Riboflavin	36%
Potassium	238mg	Niacin	16%
		Calcium	83%
		Iron	20%

TIP: *If fondue becomes too thick during serving, stir in a little more warm wine.*

RICE

Rice is an economical, nutritional, easy to prepare addition to any meal. Because rice is bland, it is very compatible with many other foods. Served in main dishes, salads, desserts and vegetables, hot or cold, as a meal accompaniment or the main attraction – rice is certainly versatile.

TYPES OF RICE

There are many types of rice. Each has its own particular cooking features, taste and texture which make each type desirable in different ways for certain dishes.

REGULAR RICE: A white rice in which the hull and the entire outer coating of bran has been removed in processing. Almost all commercially available regular rice has been enriched (the nutrients lost in processing have been restored) and our nutritional information is based on enriched regular rice.

Regular rice is available in long, medium or short grains. Long grain rice cooks tender, with grains light, fluffy and separated. It is especially good in preparing curries, stews, chicken or meat dishes. Short and medium grain rices cook plump and moist so that the grains tend to cling together. They are especially good for croquettes, puddings and rice rings.

NUTRITION INFORMATION PER SERVING

Serving Size: 1/2 cup cooked (in salted water) white rice		Percent U.S. RDA Per Serving	
Calories	112	Protein	3%
Protein	2g	Vitamin A	0%
Carbohydrate	25g	Vitamin C	0%
Fat	<1g	Thiamin	8%
Sodium	385mg	Riboflavin	0%
Potassium	29mg	Niacin	5%
		Calcium	*
		Iron	5%

PARBOILED (CONVERTED RICE): A special steam treatment is used before milling to enable it to retain much of the natural vitamin and mineral content. It takes slightly longer to cook, but can be substituted for regular rice.

BROWN RICE: Only the outer husk has been removed, leaving the "brown" bran layer surrounding the rice. This layer of bran contains many vitamins and minerals. The nutty flavor and chewy texture go well with most dishes and can be subsituted for white rice. Because of the outer coating, the cooking time may be almost double.

NUTRITION INFORMATION PER SERVING

Serving Size: 1/2 cup cooked brown rice		Percent U.S. RDA Per Serving	
Calories	116	Protein	4%
Protein	2g	Vitamin A	0%
Carbohydrate	25g	Vitamin C	0%
Fat	<1g	Thiamin	6%
Sodium	275mg	Riboflavin	*
Potassium	68mg	Niacin	7%
		Calcium	*
		Iron	3%

WILD RICE: Although referred to as rice, this is actually the seed of a water grass. However, it is cooked and served in a manner similar to rice. Because it is relatively expensive and has a rather strong nutty flavor, it is often combined with white or brown rice.

NUTRITION INFORMATION PER SERVING

Serving Size: 1/2 cup cooked wild rice		Percent U.S. RDA Per Serving	
Calories	282	Protein	17%
Protein	11g	Vitamin A	0%
Carbohydrate	60g	Vitamin C	0%
Fat	<1g	Thiamin	24%
Sodium	6mg	Riboflavin	30%
Potassium	176mg	Niacin	25%
		Calcium	*
		Iron	19%

PRECOOKED OR QUICK-COOKING RICE: This is long-grain white rice which has been cooked, dehydrated and dried commercially. It is fast to cook and is good for main dish recipes.

NUTRITION INFORMATION PER SERVING

Serving Size: 1/2 cup cooked (in salted water) quick-cooking rice		Percent U.S. RDA Per Serving	
Calories	90	Protein	3%
Protein	2g	Vitamin A	0%
Carbohydrate	20g	Vitamin C	0%
Fat	0g	Thiamin	7%
Sodium	225mg	Riboflavin	0%
Potassium	0mg	Niacin	4%
		Calcium	*
		Iron	4%

BASIC PREPARATION

Rice is best when cooked in the amount of water that will be absorbed during cooking. This gives better flavor, texture and vitamin retention than cooking in a larger amount of water that must be drained off at the end of the cooking period. If too little water is used the cooked rice is likely to be hard, brittle and small in volume.

BROWN RICE: Add 1 teaspoon salt and 2½ cups water to 1 cup rice. Heat to boiling, stirring occasionally. Simmer tightly covered for 30 to 40 minutes. (Do not remove cover for 30 minutes.) Remove from heat and fluff with fork; cover and let steam for about 5 minutes.

WILD RICE: Add 1 teaspoon salt and 2½ cups water to 1 cup rice. Heat to boiling, stirring occasionally. Simmer tightly covered, 40 to 50 minutes or until tender. If necessary, add ¼ cup water.

REGULAR RICE: Add 1 teaspoon salt and 2 cups water to 1 cup rice. Heat to boiling, stirring occasionally. Simmer tightly covered for 14 minutes. (Do not remove cover.) Remove from heat and fluff with fork; cover and let steam about 5 minutes.

PARBOILED (CONVERTED) RICE and PRECOOKED OR QUICK-COOKING RICE: Follow package directions.

TIPS: *Cooked rice can be stored covered, in refrigerator for up to 1 week or in freezer 2 to 3 months. To reheat, thaw and place in saucepan with 2 to 3 tablespoons water. Simmer covered, until hot, 5 to 10 minutes. To reheat in oven, place rice in covered casserole with water in 350°F. oven for 20 to 25 minutes or until hot.*

When cooking add: chicken or beef bouillon to cooking water, chopped apple and raisins or orange peel and raisins (add with rice), chopped green pepper, onion or celery (add with rice), ½ teaspoon curry powder, celery or dill seed, marjoram or basil leaves (add with salt).

After cooking add: 2 tablespoons margarine or butter, 2 tablespoons poppy seed, ½ cup crushed pineapple, 2 cups cooked peas, ¼ to ½ cup toasted slivered almonds, chopped salted peanuts or cashews, 1 to 2 tablespoons minced parsley, 1 to 2 diced fresh tomatoes and ¼ cup grated Parmesan cheese, 2 to 3 tablespoons soy sauce (omit salt), ½ cup sliced water chestnuts or 1 cup sautéed mushrooms.

Note: *Do not rinse rice before or after cooking because of the possibility of losing some nutrients in the water.*

SERVING

Allow ½ cup cooked rice per serving.

Rice yields:

Regular—1 cup uncooked yields 3 cups cooked rice

Parboiled—1 cup uncooked yields 3 to 4 cups cooked rice

Brown—1 cup uncooked yields 3 cups cooked rice

Precooked or quick-cooking—1 cup uncooked yields 2 cups cooked rice

Wild rice—1 cup uncooked yields 3 cups cooked rice

RICE RING

Cook rice using basic directions, page 255. Stir in 2 tablespoons margarine or butter. Gently pack into greased 3 to 4-cup ring mold. Let stand 1 minute; invert on plate and remove mold. 4 to 5 servings

TIP: *If desired, add 2 to 3 tablespoons minced parsley, 1 cup hot cooked peas or ¼ cup chopped pimiento with margarine.*

RICE PILAF

2 cups water
1 tablespoon margarine or butter
1 cube or 1 teaspoon chicken bouillon
⅔ cup uncooked long grain rice
⅓ cup golden raisins
1 tablespoon minced onion
1 medium carrot, grated
1 celery stalk, finely chopped
¼ cup slivered almonds
1 teaspoon minced parsley

In medium saucepan, heat first 3 ingredients to boiling. Stir in rice, raisins, onion, carrot and celery; simmer covered 25 minutes. Add almonds and parsley; toss lightly.
4 servings

NUTRITION INFORMATION PER SERVING

Serving Size: 1/4 of recipe		Percent U.S. RDA Per Serving	
Calories	224	Protein	6%
Protein	4g	Vitamin A	37%
Carbohydrate	37g	Vitamin C	2%
Fat	7g	Thiamin	10%
Sodium	680mg	Riboflavin	5%
Potassium	253mg	Niacin	7%
		Calcium	5%
		Iron	10%

SPANISH RICE

6 slices bacon
1 cup uncooked regular or brown rice
¼ cup chopped green pepper
1 medium onion, sliced
1 teaspoon salt
⅛ teaspoon pepper
2 cups water
¼ cup catsup
16-oz. can (2 cups) tomatoes, undrained and cut up

In large skillet, fry bacon until crisp; drain on paper towel. Reserve 2 tablespoons drippings. Cook rice, onion and green pepper in drippings until onion is tender. Add crumbled bacon and remaining ingredients. Simmer covered, 30 to 45 minutes or until rice is tender and liquid is absorbed. 5 to 6 servings

NUTRITION INFORMATION PER SERVING

Serving Size: 1/6 of recipe		Percent U.S. RDA Per Serving	
Calories	208	Protein	9%
Protein	6g	Vitamin A	18%
Carbohydrate	36g	Vitamin C	42%
Fat	4g	Thiamin	15%
Sodium	1074mg	Riboflavin	4%
Potassium	308mg	Niacin	12%
		Calcium	3%
		Iron	11%

TIP: *For quick-cooking rice, cook onion and green pepper in drippings. Add remaining ingredients except rice. Simmer covered, 10 minutes. Add 2½ cups quick-cooking rice. Remove from heat. Let stand 5 minutes. Fluff with fork.*

WILD RICE CASSEROLE

1¼ cups uncooked wild rice
2 teaspoons salt
½ teaspoon thyme leaves
1 medium onion, sliced
3 cups water
2 tablespoons margarine or butter
4-oz. can (½ cup) sliced mushrooms, drained

Heat oven to 350°F. In 2-quart casserole, combine all ingredients. Bake covered at 350°F. for 1¼ to 1½ hours or until rice is tender, stirring occasionally during last half hour. 5 to 6 servings

NUTRITION INFORMATION PER SERVING

Serving Size: 1/6 of recipe		Percent U.S. RDA Per Serving	
Calories	164	Protein	8%
Protein	5g	Vitamin A	3%
Carbohydrate	28g	Vitamin C	4%
Fat	4g	Thiamin	11%
Sodium	762mg	Riboflavin	15%
Potassium	114mg	Niacin	12%
		Calcium	*
		Iron	9%

TIP: *For fluffier rice, soak rice in water several hours or overnight before cooking as directed.*

FRIED RICE

½ cup cooked finely chopped chicken, pork or ham
2 tablespoons chopped onion
4-oz. can (½ cup) mushroom stems and pieces, drained
2 tablespoons oil
3 cups cooked rice
¼ cup soy sauce
2 eggs, well-beaten
1 tablespoon chopped fresh parsley or 2 tablespoons dry parsley
⅛ teaspoon pepper

In medium skillet, cook chicken, onion and mushrooms in oil until tender. Add rice and soy sauce. Cook over low heat 5 minutes, stirring occasionally with a fork. Add egg, parsley and pepper. Cook over low heat 5 minutes, stirring constantly. If desired, serve with additional soy sauce. 5 to 6 servings

NUTRITION INFORMATION PER SERVING

Serving Size: 1/6 of recipe		Percent U.S. RDA Per Serving	
Calories	214	Protein	14%
Protein	9g	Vitamin A	6%
Carbohydrate	27g	Vitamin C	2%
Fat	8g	Thiamin	10%
Sodium	1300mg	Riboflavin	8%
Potassium	149mg	Niacin	12%
		Calcium	3%
		Iron	13%

CURRIED RICE

3 tablespoons margarine or butter
1 cup uncooked regular or brown rice
¼ cup chopped onion
¼ cup chopped green pepper
½ teaspoon salt
½ teaspoon curry powder
2 to 3 cubes or 2 or 3 teaspoons chicken bouillon
2½ cups water

In medium saucepan, melt margarine. Stir in rice, onion and green pepper; cook until rice is transparent and light golden brown in color, stirring occasionally. Stir in remaining ingredients; heat to boiling. Reduce heat, simmer covered until rice is tender and liquid is absorbed, 20 to 30 minutes (40 to 50 minutes for brown rice). 4 to 5 servings

NUTRITION INFORMATION PER SERVING

Serving Size: 1/4 of recipe		Percent U.S. RDA Per Serving	
Calories	270	Protein	6%
Protein	4g	Vitamin A	8%
Carbohydrate	43g	Vitamin C	22%
Fat	9g	Thiamin	13%
Sodium	1491mg	Riboflavin	*
Potassium	92mg	Niacin	9%
		Calcium	3%
		Iron	10%

TIPS: *One 10-oz. pkg. (1½ cups) frozen peas may be added with water.*

One-fourth cup chopped salted peanuts may be used as a garnish.

PASTA

Pasta is an Italian word for a variety of dried macaroni products which come in three basic forms: rod, tubular and flat. Macaroni is generally tubular, spaghetti and vermicelli are rod, and noodles are flat. Shells, rings, bows, alphabets are all variations of the basic three forms.

BUYING

The best pasta is made from durum wheat (or durum semolina) which gives the pasta its natural golden color. Pasta made from durum wheat retain their shape and firmness while cooking. When cooked properly they do not get mushy, sticky or leave a starchy residue.

Noodles are the only pasta products made with egg solids which gives noodles a more intense color than other pasta. Some pasta products contain spinach which gives the characteristic green color, however the flavor is similar to plain pasta products.

Most commercially distributed pasta has been enriched and is therefore a good source of the B vitamins. Our nutritional analysis for pasta products is determined on usage of enriched pasta.

NUTRITION INFORMATION PER SERVING

Serving Size: 1/2 cup cooked macaroni		Percent U.S. RDA Per Serving	
Calories	78	Protein	4%
Protein	2g	Vitamin A	0%
Carbohydrate	16g	Vitamin C	0%
Fat	<1g	Thiamin	7%
Sodium	<1mg	Riboflavin	3%
Potassium	43mg	Niacin	4%
		Calcium	*
		Iron	3%

SERVING

Although each of our recipes specify a certain pasta product, in most cases pastas may be interchanged.

Unless used in a cold salad, pasta should be served piping hot.

BASIC PREPARATION

The secret to making good pasta is lots of water. We recommend 2 quarts of water for 8 ounces of pasta. (Eight ounces pasta yields 3½ to 4 cups cooked pasta.)

In large deep saucepan, heat water to a rapid boil. Add 1 tablespoon oil to prevent boiling over and 2 teaspoons salt. Add pasta all at once. Stir to separate pasta. Start timing when water returns to a full boil. Stirring occasionally, cook uncovered for the amount of time listed in the chart below. Rinse cooked pasta with hot water if using in a hot dish or with cold water if using in a salad. The rinsing helps reduce the stickiness. Margarine or butter may be added to cooked noodles to further prevent them from sticking together.

Pasta	Cooking Time for 8 Ounces
long spaghetti	9-10 min. (al dente)* 11-12 min. (tender)
spaghetti	8-9 min. (al dente)* 10-11 min. (tender)
thin spaghetti	6 min. (al dente)* 7 min. (tender)
macaroni	8-9 min. (partially cooked)** 10-11 min. (fully cooked)
noodles	4-5 min. (partially cooked)** 6-7 min. (fully cooked)

*Al dente means firm to the tooth. This is the classic way to serve spaghetti.

**When using the pasta in a dish which will be cooked further, use this cooking time.

Other Pasta Tips

- If noodles or spaghetti are too long for container, let one end rest in water until soft; slowly force remaining portion into saucepan as it softens.
- Reheat cooked noodles by pouring hot water over them or place with a little water in a covered container in a heated oven.

MACARONI AND CHEESE

7-oz. pkg. (2 cups) uncooked macaroni
3 tablespoons margarine or butter
3 tablespoons flour
½ teaspoon salt
Dash pepper
2 cups milk
2 cups (8 oz.) shredded cheese

In medium saucepan, cook macaroni as directed on package; drain. In same saucepan, melt margarine; blend in flour, salt and pepper. Heat until bubbly. Add milk; heat until mixture boils and thickens, stirring constantly. Stir in cheese and macaroni. Heat through.

5 to 6 servings

NUTRITION INFORMATION PER SERVING

Serving Size: 1/6 of recipe		Percent U.S. RDA Per Serving	
Calories	388	Protein	25%
Protein	16g	Vitamin A	17%
Carbohydrate	33g	Vitamin C	*
Fat	21g	Thiamin	14%
Sodium	556mg	Riboflavin	24%
Potassium	219mg	Niacin	8%
		Calcium	39%
		Iron	8%

TIPS: *For oven casserole, pour macaroni-sauce mixture into 2-quart casserole. Top with crushed potato chips, shoestring potatoes or ¼ cup dry bread crumbs combined with 1 tablespoon melted margarine or butter. Bake uncovered at 350°F. for 30 to 35 minutes.*

Additions to macaroni and cheese: 2 tablespoons chopped pimiento or green pepper, ½ teaspoon dry or 1½ teaspoons prepared mustard, 1 to 2 chopped tomatoes, 4 to 5 sliced green onions, 1 can (6½ oz.) drained flaked tuna, 5 to 6 sliced wieners, 2 cups cooked cubed ham, chicken or turkey, ½ cup drained canned mushrooms.

SIMPLE MACARONI AND CHEESE

1 cup uncooked macaroni
2 tablespoons flour
¾ teaspoon salt
1 small onion, chopped
1 cup water
1 cup milk
2 tablespoons margarine or butter
Dash Tabasco sauce
1 cup (4 oz.) cubed or shredded cheese

Heat oven to 350°F. In 2-quart casserole, combine all ingredients except cheese; mix well. Bake covered at 350°F. for 45 to 50 minutes or until macaroni is tender, stirring occasionally. Stir in cheese; cover casserole until cheese melts.

3 to 4 servings

NUTRITION INFORMATION PER SERVING

Serving Size: 1/4 of recipe		Percent U.S. RDA Per Serving	
Calories	303	Protein	19%
Protein	12g	Vitamin A	14%
Carbohydrate	25g	Vitamin C	5%
Fat	17g	Thiamin	10%
Sodium	698mg	Riboflavin	18%
Potassium	192mg	Niacin	6%
		Calcium	30%
		Iron	6%

LASAGNA

1 lb. ground beef
½ cup chopped green pepper
2 medium onions, chopped
1 stalk celery, chopped
1 garlic clove, minced
1 teaspoon basil leaves
½ teaspoon salt
½ teaspoon oregano leaves
Dash pepper
1 teaspoon Worcestershire sauce
16-oz. can (2 cups) tomatoes, cut up or pureed in blender
15-oz. can (2 cups) tomato sauce
4-oz. can (½ cup) mushroom stems and pieces, drained
8-oz. pkg. lasagna noodles
12-oz. carton (1½ cups) creamed cottage cheese
2 cups (8 oz.) shredded Mozzarella cheese
½ cup grated Parmesan cheese

In large saucepan or Dutch oven, brown ground beef, green pepper, onions, celery and garlic; drain excess fat. Add basil, salt, oregano, pepper, Worcestershire sauce, tomatoes, tomato sauce and mushrooms. Simmer covered, 30 to 45 minutes.

In large deep saucepan cook noodles as directed on package. Heat oven to 350°F. In ungreased 13x9-inch pan or lasagna pan, layer ⅓ of noodles, ⅓ of the meat sauce, ½ of cottage cheese and ½ of Mozzarella cheese. Repeat with next layer of noodles, meat, cottage cheese and Mozzarella cheese. On last layer of noodles spread meat mixture and sprinkle with Parmesan cheese.* Bake at 350°F. for 40 to 45 minutes or until hot and bubbly. Let stand 10 minutes for ease in cutting.

8 servings

NUTRITION INFORMATION PER SERVING

Serving Size: 1/8 of recipe		Percent U.S. RDA Per Serving	
Calories	494	Protein	39%
Protein	25g	Vitamin A	32%
Carbohydrate	35g	Vitamin C	25%
Fat	28g	Thiamin	17%
Sodium	474mg	Riboflavin	34%
Potassium	517mg	Niacin	22%
		Calcium	34%
		Iron	19%

TIP: *To MAKE AHEAD prepare to *, cool, cover and refrigerate up to 2 days. To serve, bake at 350°F. for 50 to 55 minutes.*

NOODLES ALFREDO

8-oz. pkg. fine egg noodles
¼ cup margarine or butter
½ cup milk
½ cup grated Parmesan cheese

In large deep saucepan, cook egg noodles to desired doneness as directed on package. Combine margarine and milk with noodles. Heat until margarine melts, stirring gently until heated through. Remove from heat; toss with Parmesan cheese. Serve immediately.

4 servings

NUTRITION INFORMATION PER SERVING

Serving Size: 1/4 of recipe		Percent U.S. RDA Per Serving	
Calories	491	Protein	20%
Protein	13g	Vitamin A	24%
Carbohydrate	43g	Vitamin C	*
Fat	30g	Thiamin	17%
Sodium	387mg	Riboflavin	17%
Potassium	146mg	Niacin	11%
		Calcium	20%
		Iron	9%

SPAGHETTI WITH ITALIAN MEATBALLS

SAUCE

2 tablespoons olive oil or oil
½ cup finely chopped onion
1 garlic clove, minced
1 qt. (4 cups) water
28-oz. can (3½ cups) tomatoes, cut up
2 cans (6 oz. each) tomato paste
1 tablespoon sugar
2 teaspoons salt
1 teaspoon oregano leaves
½ teaspoon basil leaves
½ teaspoon pepper
1 large bay leaf

MEATBALLS

¾ lb. lean ground beef
½ lb. ground veal
⅔ cup fine dry bread crumbs
1 small onion, finely chopped
¼ cup grated Parmesan cheese
½ teaspoon salt
⅛ teaspoon pepper
1 egg
1 tablespoon oil

2 pkg. (8 oz. each) spaghetti

In Dutch oven, cook onion and garlic in oil until tender. Stir in remaining Sauce ingredients. Heat to boiling, stirring occasionally. Reduce heat; simmer uncovered 1 hour.

In medium bowl, combine all Meatball ingredients except oil; mix well. Shape into 1½-inch balls. In large skillet, add oil. Roll Meatballs in oil to coat all sides. Cook Meatballs over medium heat until brown on all sides. Drain excess fat; add Meatballs to Sauce; simmer additional 30 minutes or until Meatballs are done and Sauce is thickened.

In large deep saucepan, cook spaghetti to desired doneness as directed on package. Serve Sauce and Meatballs over hot spaghetti. If desired, sprinkle with Parmesan cheese.

6 to 8 servings

NUTRITION INFORMATION PER SERVING

Serving Size: 1/8 of recipe		Percent U.S. RDA Per Serving	
Calories	511	Protein	39%
Protein	26g	Vitamin A	50%
Carbohydrate	64g	Vitamin C	40%
Fat	17g	Thiamin	31%
Sodium	932mg	Riboflavin	25%
Potassium	900mg	Niacin	36%
		Calcium	10%
		Iron	32%

TIP: *If desired, ground beef may be substituted for ground veal.*

SPAGHETTI WITH BACON

8-oz. pkg. spaghetti
½ cup grated Parmesan cheese
3 eggs, beaten
½ cup milk
¼ teaspoon salt
Dash pepper
½ lb. bacon, fried, drained and crumbled

In large deep saucepan, cook spaghetti to desired doneness as directed on package. In small bowl, combine Parmesan cheese, eggs, milk, salt and pepper. Return spaghetti to saucepan. Pour cheese mixture over; sprinkle with bacon. Toss until well combined. Cook over medium heat, stirring constantly, until heated through.

4 servings

NUTRITION INFORMATION PER SERVING

Serving Size: 1/4 of recipe		Percent U.S. RDA Per Serving	
Calories	446	Protein	34%
Protein	22g	Vitamin A	13%
Carbohydrate	45g	Vitamin C	*
Fat	19g	Thiamin	27%
Sodium	468mg	Riboflavin	28%
Potassium	268mg	Niacin	15%
		Calcium	22%
		Iron	18%

EASY NOODLE PIZZA

8-oz. pkg. extra wide egg noodles
1 lb. ground beef
15-oz. can (2 cups) tomato sauce
½ teaspoon oregano leaves
½ teaspoon basil leaves
1 teaspoon garlic salt
2 cups (8 oz.) shredded Mozzarella cheese
4-oz. can (½ cup) mushroom stems and pieces, drained

Heat oven to 350°F. In large deep saucepan, cook egg noodles to partially cooked stage as directed on package.

In medium skillet, brown ground beef; drain excess fat. Stir in tomato sauce, oregano, basil and garlic salt.

Spread cooked noodles evenly in ungreased 12-inch pizza pan. Pour meat sauce over and spread evenly to sides of pan. Sprinkle with Mozzarella cheese. Top with mushrooms. Bake at 350°F. for 20 to 25 minutes. 12-inch pizza

NUTRITION INFORMATION PER SERVING

Serving Size: 1/4 of recipe		Percent U.S. RDA Per Serving	
Calories	855	Protein	52%
Protein	34g	Vitamin A	46%
Carbohydrate	56g	Vitamin C	0%
Fat	55g	Thiamin	27%
Sodium	688mg	Riboflavin	48%
Potassium	487mg	Niacin	40%
		Calcium	47%
		Iron	31%

MANICOTTI

7 to 8 manicotti macaroni
1 egg
2 cups (16 oz.) dry cottage, farmers or pot cheese*
⅓ cup grated Parmesan cheese
2 tablespoons chopped parsley
½ lb. ground beef**
2 teaspoons basil leaves, oregano leaves or Italian seasoning
1 small onion, chopped
2 medium garlic cloves, minced
½ cup water
2 cans (10¾ oz. each) condensed tomato soup
3 to 4 oz. Mozzarella cheese, shredded or sliced

Lightly grease (not oil) 12x8 or 13x9-inch baking dish. In large saucepan, cook manicotti as directed on package; drain. In medium bowl, beat egg slightly, add cottage cheese, Parmesan cheese and parsley; mix well. Fill each manicotti with cottage cheese mixture. Arrange manicotti in prepared dish. Heat oven to 350°F. In medium skillet, brown ground beef, onion and garlic. Stir in water and soup; pour over manicotti. Bake covered at 350°F. for 40 to 45 minutes. (Uncover for the last 15 minutes.) Top with Mozzarella cheese; return to oven until cheese melts and mixture is bubbly, about 5 minutes. 4 to 5 servings

NUTRITION INFORMATION PER SERVING

Serving Size: 1/4 of recipe		Percent U.S. RDA Per Serving	
Calories	556	Protein	54%
Protein	35g	Vitamin A	37%
Carbohydrate	47g	Vitamin C	22%
Fat	25g	Thiamin	20%
Sodium	1589mg	Riboflavin	40%
Potassium	718mg	Niacin	25%
		Calcium	38%
		Iron	25%

TIPS: **Creamed cottage cheese may be substituted for dry if rinsed under water and drained well.*

***If desired, substitute 2½ cups favorite prepared spaghetti sauce for ground beef, basil, onion, garlic, tomato soup and water.*

FISH & SEAFOOD

FISH & SEAFOOD

ABOUT FISH

BUYING

Not everyone is lucky enough to have an angler in the family and/or a well-stocked body of water nearby as an easily available source of fish. However, today's supermarkets are making many fish varieties easily available – fresh, frozen, canned, smoked or dried.

Since fish is quite perishable, make certain when purchasing that it is very fresh. Look for fish with a mild "fishy" odor – should not smell strong nor offensive. The flesh should be firm and elastic, leaving no imprint of the finger when pressed. If the heads remain, the eyes should be bright, clear and bulging, the gills reddish and the scales have a high sheen.

Fresh fish should be used as soon as possible since the flavors deteriorate rapidly. Prepare within 36 hours of purchase. If you are buying fresh fish for a later date, check with the grocer as to whether it had been frozen and thawed. Fish like any other meat, should never be refrozen.

Fresh and frozen fish are available in several forms:

Whole or round – correctly speaking, this refers to the fish simply as it comes from the water. However, most recipes which use whole fish actually mean whole dressed fish.

Dressed – fish which has been eviscerated and scaled if necessary. Often, the head, tail and fins are removed. The fish is ready for cooking. Allow ½ pound fish per serving.

Steaks – cross section slices of large dressed fish with a section of the backbone still remaining. Allow one steak, about ⅓ pound per serving.

Fillets – the sides of the fish removed from the backbone and cut lengthwise into serving size strips; they are boneless. Allow ⅓ pound per serving.

STORAGE

Fresh fish should be stored in the coldest part of your refrigerator and used within 36 hours of purchase. Place dry, dressed fish in container and cover with foil or plastic wrap.

If you do not plan to cook your fish immediately, the fish should be frozen. Fish under 2 pounds are usually dressed and frozen whole. Larger fish are easier to freeze and thaw if dressed and cut into steaks or fillets. Separate steaks and fillets between double layers of freezer wrap for ease in thawing.

PREPARATION

To thaw fish, place in refrigerator or under cold running water. Do not defrost at room temperature as fish will get mushy and lose flavor. Use immediately after thawing. Do not refreeze.

Cooking methods for fish depend on if it is considered a fat or lean species. In general, fat fish are preferred for baking, broiling and barbecuing as their natural oils help keep them moist as they cook. Fat fish include salmon, tuna (albacore), herring, whitefish, mackerel, shad, smelt, sardine and kipper. Lean fish is the larger category and includes haddock, sole, trout, red snapper, halibut, swordfish and cod. They are usually fried or poached, but can be baked or broiled successfully if melted fat or a sauce is used.

Fish is by nature a tender meat, high in protein. Like eggs, heat sets the protein, but will become tough and dry if overcooked. Cook fish just until done; *do not overcook.* Fish is done when a fork inserted in the thickest part easily flakes the fish. The fish should part easily in its natural divisions. Because fish needs only a short cooking time, it is perfect for a quick meal.

NUTRITION

Not only is lean fish relatively low in calories, but most of the fat they contain is polyunsaturated—needless to say an excellent source of food for dieters. All types of fish are excellent sources of protein. They are good sources of thiamine, riboflavin and niacin and those from the sea are rich in iodine. Fish canned with the bones such as sardines, are high in calcium if the bones, which become quite soft in canning, are eaten with the fish. Fat fish are comparatively high in vitamin A.

Note: Whitefish (which is a fat fish) was used in determining the nutritional information for recipes with fish fillets. If lean fish is used for the fillets, there will be slightly less vitamin A and calories. Below are the nutritional information for both a typical lean and fat fish for use as comparison.

NUTRITION INFORMATION PER SERVING

Serving Size: 1/3 lb. fat fish (Whitefish)		Percent U.S. RDA Per Serving	
Calories	234	Protein	64%
Protein	29g	Vitamin A	68%
Carbohydrate	0g	Vitamin C	*
Fat	12g	Thiamin	14%
Sodium	79mg	Riboflavin	11%
Potassium	452mg	Niacin	23%
		Calcium	†
		Iron	3%

NUTRITION INFORMATION PER SERVING

Serving Size: 1/3 lb. lean fish (Walleye)		Percent U.S. RDA Per Serving	
Calories	140	Protein	65%
Protein	29g	Vitamin A	*
Carbohydrate	0g	Vitamin C	*
Fat	2g	Thiamin	25%
Sodium	77mg	Riboflavin	14%
Potassium	483mg	Niacin	17%
		Calcium	†
		Iron	3%

Let fish marinate up to an hour in one of these tasty marinades before baking, broiling or grilling. Use remaining marinade to brush on fish during cooking.

MARINADES FOR FISH

LEMON MARINADE: Combine ¼ cup lemon juice, ¼ cup oil, 2 teaspoons anchovy paste, 2 teaspoons chopped onion or minced parsley, ½ teaspoon basil leaves and 1 teaspoon prepared horseradish.

WINE MARINADE: Combine ¼ cup dry white wine, ¼ cup oil, 1 lemon, thinly sliced and 1 tablespoon minced parsley.

ITALIAN MARINADE: Combine 1 cup Italian salad dressing, 1 tablespoon lemon juice and ½ teaspoon salt.

BROILED FISH

2 lb. fish fillets or steaks
¼ cup margarine or butter, melted
Salt and pepper

Cut fish into serving pieces; arrange on broiler pan (if fish has skin place skin-side-up) brushing both sides of fish with margarine. Season with salt and pepper. 6 servings

NUTRITION INFORMATION PER SERVING

Serving Size: 1/6 of recipe		Percent U.S. RDA Per Serving	
Calories	326	Protein	66%
Protein	43g	Vitamin A	12%
Carbohydrate	<1g	Vitamin C	*
Fat	16g	Thiamin	8%
Sodium	525mg	Riboflavin	10%
Potassium	618mg	Niacin	23%
		Calcium	5%
		Iron	9%

TIPS: *For FISH FILLETS (¼ to ½ inch thick) broil 2 inches from heat for 5 to 8 minutes or until fish flakes easily, turning once, basting with margarine.*

For FISH STEAKS (½ to 1 inch thick) broil 2 to 3 inches from heat for 10 to 12 minutes, turning once, basting with margarine.

OVEN-FRIED FISH

1 egg, slightly beaten
1 teaspoon salt
Dash pepper
1 tablespoon lemon juice
½ to ¾ cup crushed corn flakes or bread crumbs
2 tablespoons margarine or butter
1 lb. fish fillets*, cut into serving pieces

Heat oven to 350°F. In small bowl, combine first 4 ingredients; mix well. Dip fish in egg mixture, then coat with crumbs. Melt margarine in shallow baking pan. Arrange fish pieces in pan, turning to coat. Bake uncovered at 350°F. for 20 to 25 minutes or until fish flakes easily.

3 to 4 servings

NUTRITION INFORMATION PER SERVING

Serving Size: 1/4 of recipe		Percent U.S. RDA Per Serving	
Calories	310	Protein	54%
Protein	35g	Vitamin A	12%
Carbohydrate	10g	Vitamin C	3%
Fat	13g	Thiamin	10%
Sodium	853mg	Riboflavin	10%
Potassium	500mg	Niacin	18%
		Calcium	5%
		Iron	9%

TIP: **Perch, halibut, cod, flounder and haddock may be used.*

POOR MAN'S LOBSTER (TORSK)

3 qt. water
½ cup salt
½ cup sugar
4-lb. torsk, cut into 6 to 8 pieces (fresh or frozen, thawed)
Margarine or butter
Paprika, if desired

In Dutch oven or large saucepan, heat water, salt and sugar to boiling; remove from heat and add torsk. Cover and let stand 15 minutes. Drain carefully; pat dry with paper towels. Place torsk on foil-lined broiler pan or 15x10-inch jelly roll pan. Butter generously; broil 3 to 4 inches from heat until lightly browned. Serve immediately with melted margarine. 8 servings

NUTRITION INFORMATION PER SERVING

Serving Size: 1/8 of recipe		Percent U.S. RDA Per Serving	
Calories	534	Protein	100%
Protein	65g	Vitamin A	17%
Carbohydrate	12g	Vitamin C	0%
Fat	23g	Thiamin	12%
Sodium	388mg	Riboflavin	15%
Potassium	928mg	Niacin	34%
		Calcium	12%
		Iron	13%

POACHED FISH

2-lb. dressed whole fish or fish fillets
1 tablespoon salt
4 peppercorns
2 stalks celery, cut into pieces
2 carrots, cut into pieces
2 slices lemon
2 bay leaves
1 medium onion, sliced
1 quart (4 cups) water

Wrap fish in cheesecloth for ease in transferring fish after cooking. In large skillet, combine all ingredients except fish. Heat to boiling; simmer covered about 10 minutes. Carefully place fish in liquid; simmer covered about 20 minutes or until fish flakes easily. If liquid does not cover fish, turn fish over after 10 minutes for even cooking. Lift fish from liquid; carefully remove cheesecloth and place on platter.

4 to 6 servings

NUTRITION INFORMATION PER SERVING

Serving Size: 1/4 of recipe		Percent U.S. RDA Per Serving	
Calories	201	Protein	33%
Protein	21g	Vitamin A	12%
Carbohydrate	8g	Vitamin C	*
Fat	9g	Thiamin	13%
Sodium	26mg	Riboflavin	10%
Potassium	589mg	Niacin	18%
		Calcium	4%
		Iron	5%

TIP: *If desired, use ½ cup dry white wine for part of liquid.*

PAN-FRIED FISH

1 egg, slightly beaten
¼ cup milk
2-lb. dressed fish or 1 lb. fish fillets
½ cup Pillsbury's Best® All Purpose Flour, cornmeal or Hungry Jack® Buttermilk Pancake and Waffle Mix
Salt and pepper
¼ cup oil or shortening

In small bowl, combine egg and milk. Dip fish in egg mixture, then coat with flour. In large skillet, fry in hot oil over medium-high heat until golden brown, 5 to 7 minutes, turning fish only once. Season with salt and pepper.

3 to 4 servings

NUTRITION INFORMATION PER SERVING

Serving Size: 1/4 of recipe		Percent U.S. RDA Per Serving	
Calories	375	Protein	37%
Protein	24g	Vitamin A	12%
Carbohydrate	13g	Vitamin C	*
Fat	25g	Thiamin	18%
Sodium	216mg	Riboflavin	15%
Potassium	373mg	Niacin	20%
		Calcium	3%
		Iron	7%

TIP: *For PAN-FRIED SMELT, clean smelt, removing head. Prepare as for pan-fried fish, cooking 3 to 5 minutes or until fish flakes easily.*

FISH FILLETS WITH MUSHROOM-LEMON SAUCE

¼ cup margarine or butter
3 cups (8 oz.) sliced fresh mushrooms
4 to 6 green onions or 1 small onion, chopped
2 tablespoons flour
1 tablespoon chopped parsley
1 teaspoon salt
1 teaspoon grated lemon peel
⅛ teaspoon pepper
1 cup milk
2 lb. fish fillets*

In large skillet, sauté mushrooms and onions in margarine until tender. Blend in flour, parsley, salt, lemon peel, pepper and milk; heat to boiling. Add fish fillets, spooning sauce over fish. Simmer covered over low heat, about 15 minutes or until fish flakes easily. Remove fish to platter. Stir sauce until smooth and pour over fillets.

6 servings

NUTRITION INFORMATION PER SERVING

Serving Size: 1/6 of recipe		Percent U.S. RDA Per Serving	
Calories	229	Protein	25%
Protein	16g	Vitamin A	41%
Carbohydrate	7g	Vitamin C	9%
Fat	15g	Thiamin	11%
Sodium	512mg	Riboflavin	20%
Potassium	449mg	Niacin	19%
		Calcium	6%
		Iron	4%

TIPS: **Sole, haddock or pike are good with this recipe.*

To bake, prepare mushroom sauce as directed. Arrange fillets in lightly greased 11x7-inch pan. Pour sauce over fillets. Bake covered at 375°F. for 25 to 30 minutes or until fish flakes easily. Remove fish to platter. Stir sauce until smooth and pour over fillets.

CHEESE STUFFED TROUT

½ cup sliced fresh mushrooms
¼ cup chopped green onions or onion
2 tablespoons grated Parmesan cheese
2-lb. whole trout, cleaned
Salt and pepper

In small bowl, combine mushrooms, onion and cheese; spoon into cavity of each fish. Season with salt and pepper. Securely close cavities with toothpicks or skewers to keep stuffing inside. Place on lightly greased broiler pan. Broil 4 to 5 inches from heat about 5 to 10 minutes on each side or until fish flakes easily. 4 to 5 servings

NUTRITION INFORMATION PER SERVING

Serving Size: 1/4 of recipe		Percent U.S. RDA Per Serving	
Calories	180	Protein	33%
Protein	21g	Vitamin A	49%
Carbohydrate	1g	Vitamin C	3%
Fat	9g	Thiamin	11%
Sodium	75mg	Riboflavin	11%
Potassium	373mg	Niacin	18%
		Calcium	3%
		Iron	3%

TIP: *Fish fillets may be substituted for whole fish. Coat fillets with flour or dry pancake mix. In large skillet, sauté mushrooms and onion in small amount of oil until slightly tender; move to one side of skillet. Add fillets and fry until fish flakes. Serve fillets topped with mushrooms and onion; sprinkle with Parmesan cheese before serving.*

BAKED STUFFED FISH

2 to 3-lb. dressed whole fish
Salt
2 cups stuffing (see Bread Stuffing, this page)
2 tablespoons margarine or butter, melted

Heat oven to 400°F. Lightly sprinkle inside of fish with salt. Fill cavity with stuffing and secure edges of fish together with skewers or toothpicks. Place in greased shallow baking pan; brush with melted margarine. Bake uncovered at 400°F. for 45 minutes or until fish flakes easily, basting occasionally with margarine. Remove skewers before serving. To serve, cut sections by slicing through backbone and spoon out dressing.

4 to 6 servings

NUTRITION INFORMATION PER SERVING

Serving Size: 1/4 of recipe		Percent U.S. RDA Per Serving	
Calories	368	Protein	36%
Protein	23g	Vitamin A	67%
Carbohydrate	7g	Vitamin C	*
Fat	27g	Thiamin	13%
Sodium	1142mg	Riboflavin	10%
Potassium	399mg	Niacin	19%
		Calcium	3%
		Iron	5%

TIPS: *If desired, omit basting. Top fish with uncooked bacon slices; or pour 1 cup light cream or evaporated milk over fish before baking.*

Smaller fish may also be stuffed. Allow ½ cup stuffing per 12 to 16-oz. fish.

For BAKED FISH, bake as directed, omitting stuffing.

BREAD STUFFING

¼ cup margarine or butter
¼ cup chopped celery
2 tablespoons chopped onion
2 cups (2 slices) soft bread cubes
¼ teaspoon salt
¼ teaspoon thyme
⅛ teaspoon pepper

In medium skillet, cook celery and onion in margarine until tender. Stir in remaining ingredients.

2 cups stuffing

NUTRITION INFORMATION PER SERVING

Serving Size: 1/2 cup		Percent U.S. RDA Per Serving	
Calories	145	Protein	2%
Protein	2g	Vitamin A	10%
Carbohydrate	8g	Vitamin C	*
Fat	12g	Thiamin	3%
Sodium	360mg	Riboflavin	2%
Potassium	53mg	Niacin	*
		Calcium	2%
		Iron	3%

TIPS: *For LEMON STUFFING, add 2 teaspoons grated lemon peel and 2 tablespoons lemon juice with bread.*

For DILL STUFFING, add ¼ cup chopped dill pickle with bread or ¼ teaspoon dill weed.

For MUSHROOM STUFFING, cook ½ cup sliced fresh mushrooms with onion and celery.

For SHRIMP or CRAB STUFFING, add ½ cup cooked shrimp or crab meat with bread.

FISH CREOLE

1 lb. fish fillets
1 tablespoon margarine or butter
2 tablespoons finely chopped green pepper
1 small onion, chopped
½ stalk celery, chopped
2 tablespoons sugar
½ teaspoon salt
¼ teaspoon oregano leaves, if desired
⅛ teaspoon pepper
8-oz. can (1 cup) stewed tomatoes, cut into pieces

Heat oven to 350°F. Arrange fillets in 9-inch square or 11x7-inch pan. In medium skillet, cook green pepper, onion and celery in margarine until tender. Stir in remaining ingredients; mix well. Pour tomato mixture over fillets. Bake uncovered at 350°F. for 30 to 35 minutes or until fish flakes easily.

3 to 4 servings

NUTRITION INFORMATION PER SERVING

Serving Size: 1/4 of recipe		Percent U.S. RDA Per Serving	
Calories	265	Protein	51%
Protein	33g	Vitamin A	18%
Carbohydrate	11g	Vitamin C	31%
Fat	9g	Thiamin	9%
Sodium	519mg	Riboflavin	9%
Potassium	656mg	Niacin	20%
		Calcium	5%
		Iron	9%

FILLET AMANDINE

¼ cup margarine or butter
¼ cup slivered or sliced almonds
1 lb. fish fillets
½ teaspoon salt
Pepper
1 tablespoon lemon juice

In large skillet, sauté almonds in margarine until golden. Remove almonds; set aside. Add fish fillets and fry over medium heat until golden brown on both sides and fish flakes easily, turning only once. Season with salt and pepper. Remove fish to platter. Add lemon juice and almonds to pan drippings; heat and pour over fish.

4 servings

NUTRITION INFORMATION PER SERVING

Serving Size: 1/4 of recipe		Percent U.S. RDA Per Serving	
Calories	323	Protein	35%
Protein	23g	Vitamin A	61%
Carbohydrate	2g	Vitamin C	3%
Fat	25g	Thiamin	12%
Sodium	471mg	Riboflavin	12%
Potassium	404mg	Niacin	18%
		Calcium	2%
		Iron	5%

TIP: *For FILLETS IN WINE BUTTER, add 2 tablespoons white wine or sherry and ½ teaspoon dill weed when adding lemon juice.*

FISH FILLETS AU GRATIN

1 cup (4 oz.) shredded American cheese
¼ cup dry bread crumbs
1 teaspoon paprika
1 teaspoon minced parsley
½ teaspoon onion salt
¼ teaspoon salt
¼ teaspoon pepper
2 lb. fish fillets*

Heat oven to 400°F. In small bowl, combine all ingredients except fish. Place fish on individual squares of greased foil. Spoon crumb mixture over fish. Seal securely and bake at 400°F. for 30 to 35 minutes or until fish flakes easily.

6 servings

NUTRITION INFORMATION PER SERVING

Serving Size: 1/6 of recipe		Percent U.S. RDA Per Serving	
Calories	186	Protein	28%
Protein	18g	Vitamin A	37%
Carbohydrate	1g	Vitamin C	*
Fat	12g	Thiamin	7%
Sodium	483mg	Riboflavin	10%
Potassium	231mg	Niacin	11%
		Calcium	13%
		Iron	3%

TIPS: **Pike, trout, halibut, haddock, cod, red snapper, sole or flounder may be used.*

To halve recipe, use one half the ingredient amounts.

To grill, place packets 3 to 4 inches from hot coals; cook 20 to 25 minutes.

SAUCY FOILED FILLETS

- 2 lb. fish fillets or steaks
- Salt and pepper
- 1 small green pepper, cut into squares
- 1 small onion, sliced
- 1¼ cups barbecue sauce, catsup or tomato sauce
- 2 tablespoons margarine or butter
- 6 tablespoons grated Parmesan cheese

Heat oven to 350°F. Divide fish into 6 equal portions. Place each portion on a square piece of foil; season with salt and pepper. Top each with green pepper, onion and about 3 tablespoons of barbecue sauce. Dot each with margarine; sprinkle each portion with 1 tablespoon Parmesan cheese. Seal each packet securely. Place foil packet on cookie sheet. Bake at 350°F. for 20 minutes or until fish flakes easily. 6 servings

NUTRITION INFORMATION PER SERVING

Serving Size: 1/6 of recipe		Percent U.S. RDA Per Serving	
Calories	334	Protein	71%
Protein	46g	Vitamin A	12%
Carbohydrate	6g	Vitamin C	24%
Fat	13g	Thiamin	10%
Sodium	722mg	Riboflavin	13%
Potassium	770mg	Niacin	24%
		Calcium	12%
		Iron	12%

TIP: *Any lean fish may be used—red snapper, halibut, bass, walleyed pike or sole.*

SAUCY FOILED FISH FILLETS

SALMON STEAKS WITH MUSHROOM TOPPING

4 salmon steaks, cut ¾-inch thick
¼ teaspoon salt
¼ cup margarine or butter
1 small onion, chopped
1 stalk celery, chopped
3 cups (3 slices) bread, cubed
8-oz. (3 cups) sliced fresh mushrooms
2 tablespoons chopped parsley
¼ teaspoon salt
1 tablespoon lemon juice
¼ cup light cream

Heat oven to 350°F. In greased 9-inch square or other shallow baking pan, arrange salmon steaks in single layer; season with ¼ teaspoon salt. In large skillet, sauté onion and celery in margarine until tender. Add bread, mushrooms, parsley, salt and lemon juice; mix well. Spoon stuffing on top of salmon steaks. Drizzle cream over top. Bake uncovered at 350°F. for 25 to 30 minutes or until fish flakes easily.

4 servings

NUTRITION INFORMATION PER SERVING

Serving Size: 1/4 of recipe		Percent U.S. RDA Per Serving	
Calories	507	Protein	75%
Protein	48g	Vitamin A	16%
Carbohydrate	18g	Vitamin C	14%
Fat	26g	Thiamin	38%
Sodium	776mg	Riboflavin	28%
Potassium	359mg	Niacin	84%
		Calcium	8%
		Iron	19%

TIPS: *If desired, add 2 tablespoons sherry to stuffing.*

One cup (8 oz.) drained canned mushrooms may be substituted for fresh.

BROILED SALMON

Arrange 4 salmon steaks or fillets on lightly greased broiler pan. If desired, brush with glaze (below). Broil 5 to 6 inches from heat 8 to 10 minutes on each side or until fish flakes easily, brushing occasionally with remaining glaze. Spoon any leftover glaze over fish on serving plate. Season with salt and pepper.

4 servings

NUTRITION INFORMATION PER SERVING

Serving Size: 1/4 of recipe without glaze		Percent U.S. RDA Per Serving	
Calories	233	Protein	53%
Protein	34g	Vitamin A	4%
Carbohydrate	<1g	Vitamin C	*
Fat	9g	Thiamin	14%
Sodium	410mg	Riboflavin	5%
Potassium	565mg	Niacin	63%
		Calcium	*
		Iron	9%

TIPS: *If desired, marinate salmon in one of these glazes about 1 hour before broiling.*

TANGY GLAZE: In small saucepan, combine ¼ cup butter, ¼ cup firmly packed brown sugar and 2 tablespoons lemon juice. Heat to melt butter and combine ingredients.

NUTRITION INFORMATION PER SERVING

Serving Size: 1/4 of recipe		Percent U.S. RDA Per Serving	
Calories	387	Protein	53%
Protein	35g	Vitamin A	13%
Carbohydrate	14g	Vitamin C	5%
Fat	21g	Thiamin	14%
Sodium	554mg	Riboflavin	5%
Potassium	627mg	Niacin	63%
		Calcium	*
		Iron	11%

LEMON GLAZE: Omit brown sugar in Tangy Glaze. Proceed as directed.

DILL GLAZE: Omit brown sugar in Tangy Glaze, add ¾ teaspoon dill weed and proceed as directed.

BROILED SALMON

SALMON WITH DILL SAUCE

- 1 teaspoon salt
- 1 medium onion, sliced
- 1 cube or 1 teaspoon chicken bouillon
- 1½ cups water
- 1 tablespoon lemon juice
- 4 (2 to 3 lb.) salmon steaks or fillets

SAUCE

- 2 tablespoons margarine or butter
- 1 tablespoon finely chopped onion
- 2 tablespoons flour
- 1 teaspoon salt
- 1 teaspoon dill weed
- ⅛ teaspoon pepper
- 1½ cups milk

In large skillet, large enough to hold fish in single layer, combine first 5 ingredients. Heat to boiling. Add salmon steaks; simmer tightly covered about 10 minutes or until fish flakes easily. In small saucepan, cook onion in margarine until tender; stir in flour, salt, dill weed and pepper. Add milk, mixing well. Heat until mixture boils and thickens, stirring constantly. Remove salmon to platter; pour dill sauce over salmon and serve. 4 servings

NUTRITION INFORMATION PER SERVING

Serving Size: 1/4 of recipe		Percent U.S. RDA Per Serving	
Calories	426	Protein	75%
Protein	48g	Vitamin A	8%
Carbohydrate	12g	Vitamin C	*
Fat	20g	Thiamin	34%
Sodium	776mg	Riboflavin	19%
Potassium	210mg	Niacin	72%
		Calcium	16%
		Iron	14%

BAKED SALMON WITH CUCUMBER SAUCE

- 2 to 3-lb. section of salmon
- Butter, salt and pepper
- 1 cup dairy sour cream or yogurt
- 2 teaspoons chopped parsley
- ½ teaspoon chopped chives
- ½ medium cucumber, peeled and finely chopped or shredded
- 2 teaspoons lemon juice

Heat oven to 350°F. Place salmon in greased shallow baking pan; brush with butter and season with salt and pepper. Bake uncovered at 350°F. for 30 to 50 minutes or until fish flakes easily. Section salmon; remove large bones and place on heat-proof platter. In small bowl, combine remaining ingredients; spoon over salmon. Return to oven for 5 minutes to heat sauce. 4 to 6 servings

NUTRITION INFORMATION PER SERVING

Serving Size: 1/4 of recipe		Percent U.S. RDA Per Serving	
Calories	483	Protein	86%
Protein	56g	Vitamin A	17%
Carbohydrate	3g	Vitamin C	9%
Fat	26g	Thiamin	23%
Sodium	529mg	Riboflavin	12%
Potassium	940mg	Niacin	98%
		Calcium	7%
		Iron	14%

TIP: *Sauce is good served warm or cold with other fish. Try with salmon loaf, fried fish or serve cold with chilled canned salmon.*

SALMON LOAF

16- oz. can (2 cups) salmon, undrained
2 eggs
2 cups (2 slices) soft bread cubes or ⅓ cup dry bread crumbs
2 tablespoons minced parsley
¼ teaspoon salt
⅛ teaspoon pepper
1 small onion, chopped
2 tablespoons lemon juice

Heat oven to 350°F. In large bowl, flake salmon, removing bones and skin. With a fork, beat in eggs; mix in remaining ingredients. Place in well-greased 8x4-inch loaf pan or 8-inch square pan forming into loaf shape.* Bake uncovered at 375°F. for 50 to 60 minutes or until golden brown and knife inserted in center comes out clean. Loosen edges and lift out of pan; serve in slices. If desired, serve with Cheese-Dill Sauce, page 540 4 to 5 servings

NUTRITION INFORMATION PER SERVING

Serving Size: 1/4 of recipe		Percent U.S. RDA Per Serving	
Calories	259	Protein	44%
Protein	29g	Vitamin A	12%
Carbohydrate	11g	Vitamin C	15%
Fat	11g	Thiamin	8%
Sodium	689mg	Riboflavin	20%
Potassium	525mg	Niacin	48%
		Calcium	26%
		Iron	12%

TIPS: *For individual loaves, bake in 5 well-greased 5-oz. custard cups, filling ¾ full; bake 20 to 25 minutes.*

To MAKE AHEAD, prepare to, refrigerate up to 1 day. Bake as directed.*

TUNA-NOODLE BAKE

3 cups (6 oz.) uncooked noodles or macaroni
1½ cups (6 oz.) shredded American cheese
10- oz. pkg. (1¼ cups) chopped spinach or (1½ cups) cut asparagus
2 cans (6½ oz. each) tuna, drained and flaked
¼ teaspoon salt
2 eggs
13- oz. can (1⅔ cups) evaporated milk
Paprika

Heat oven to 350°F. In large saucepan, cook noodles as directed on package; drain. Stir in 1 cup cheese. Arrange in ungreased 12x8-inch (2 quart) baking dish. In medium saucepan, cook spinach as directed on package; drain and arrange on noodles. Sprinkle tuna over spinach. In small bowl, combine salt, eggs and milk; beat well. Pour over mixture; top with remaining cheese and sprinkle with paprika.* Bake uncovered at 350°F. for 25 to 30 minutes or until center is set.
5 to 6 servings

NUTRITION INFORMATION PER SERVING

Serving Size: 1/6 of recipe		Percent U.S. RDA Per Serving	
Calories	453	Protein	53%
Protein	35g	Vitamin A	74%
Carbohydrate	30g	Vitamin C	9%
Fat	21g	Thiamin	16%
Sodium	535mg	Riboflavin	35%
Potassium	432mg	Niacin	40%
		Calcium	43%
		Iron	19%

TIPS: *To MAKE AHEAD, prepare to *, cool and refrigerate up to 12 hours. Increase baking time to 30 to 35 minutes.*

Other canned or cooked seafoods such as shrimp, crab or lobster may be substituted for tuna.

TUNA BROCCOLI PIE

CRUST

⅓ cup margarine or butter, softened
¾ cup Hungry Jack® Mashed Potato Flakes
¾ cup Pillsbury's Best® All Purpose or Unbleached Flour*
¼ cup grated Parmesan cheese
¼ teaspoon salt
¼ cup water

FILLING

4 eggs
¼ cup finely chopped onion
½ teaspoon salt
10-oz. pkg. (2 cups) frozen chopped broccoli, cooked and drained
1 cup small curd creamed cottage cheese
6½-oz. can tuna, drained
1 small tomato, thinly sliced
1 cup (4 oz.) shredded Mozzarella cheese

Heat oven to 350°F. In medium bowl, cut margarine into potato flakes, flour, cheese and salt until crumbly. Add water; stir just until dough holds together. Press mixture into ungreased 9 or 10-inch pie pan; flute edge. Prick bottom and sides of pastry generously with fork. Bake at 350°F. for 5 minutes.

In large bowl, beat eggs until foamy. Stir in onion, salt, warm broccoli, cottage cheese and tuna. Bake at 350°F. for 40 minutes. Top with sliced tomatoes and sprinkle with Mozzarella cheese. Return to oven and bake for 10 minutes. Let stand 5 minutes before serving.

4 to 5 servings

NUTRITION INFORMATION PER SERVING

Serving Size: 1/5 of recipe		Percent U.S. RDA Per Serving	
Calories	501	Protein	44%
Protein	28g	Vitamin A	57%
Carbohydrate	22g	Vitamin C	40%
Fat	33g	Thiamin	17%
Sodium	768mg	Riboflavin	37%
Potassium	316mg	Niacin	27%
		Calcium	34%
		Iron	17%

TIP: **Self-rising flour is not recommended.*

CHEESY TUNA VEGETABLE BAKE

9¼-oz. can tuna, drained and flaked
1 cup (4 oz.) shredded Cheddar or American cheese
½ cup chopped celery
3 tablespoons chopped onion
½ cup milk
10¾-oz. can condensed cream of mushroom soup
10-oz. pkg. (1½ cups) frozen peas, thawed
8-oz. can Pillsbury Refrigerated Buttermilk or Country Style Biscuits
1 tablespoon margarine or butter, melted
½ cup crushed potato chips

Heat oven to 375°F. In ungreased shallow 2-quart casserole or 12x8-inch baking dish, spread tuna; sprinkle with cheese. In medium saucepan, combine celery, onion, milk, soup and peas; simmer while preparing biscuits. Separate biscuit dough into 10 biscuits; cut each biscuit into fourths. Pour hot soup mixture over tuna and cheese; arrange biscuit pieces over soup mixture. Drizzle with melted margarine; sprinkle with potato chips. Bake at 375°F. for 30 to 40 minutes or until golden brown. 4 to 5 servings

NUTRITION INFORMATION PER SERVING

Serving Size: 1/5 of recipe		Percent U.S. RDA Per Serving	
Calories	483	Protein	44%
Protein	29g	Vitamin A	17%
Carbohydrate	38g	Vitamin C	11%
Fat	24g	Thiamin	25%
Sodium	1235mg	Riboflavin	26%
Potassium	344mg	Niacin	47%
		Calcium	26%
		Iron	19%

SAUCY SEAFOOD SUPREME

1 cup chopped celery
2 tablespoons chopped chives or 1 tablespoon chopped green onion
2 cans (6½ oz. each) seafood, drained*
10¾-oz. can condensed cream of chicken soup**
2 tablespoons margarine or butter
½ cup slivered almonds
3-oz. can (2 cups) chow mein noodles

In medium saucepan, combine first 4 ingredients; mix well. Heat until hot and bubbly, stirring occasionally. In small skillet, brown almonds in melted margarine. Serve hot seafood mixture over chow mein noodles; sprinkle with toasted almonds. 4 to 5 servings

NUTRITION INFORMATION PER SERVING

Serving Size: 1/5 of recipe		Percent U.S. RDA Per Serving	
Calories	337	Protein	31%
Protein	20g	Vitamin A	11%
Carbohydrate	17g	Vitamin C	5%
Fat	21g	Thiamin	5%
Sodium	819mg	Riboflavin	12%
Potassium	243mg	Niacin	26%
		Calcium	6%
		Iron	10%

TIPS: **One variety of seafood or 2 different varieties may be used. A combination of tuna and crab is especially nice for this dish.*

***Cream of asparagus or other condensed cream soups may be substituted for the cream of chicken soup.*

The chow mein noodles may be placed in bottom of 2-quart casserole. Top with seafood mixture. Garnish with toasted almonds.

BOUILLABAISSE

1 medium onion, chopped
2 garlic cloves, minced
2 tablespoons olive or cooking oil
¼ cup chopped parsley
2½ teaspoons salt
¼ teaspoon saffron or curry powder
¼ teaspoon pepper
1 bay leaf
4 cups water
1 teaspoon lemon juice
1 lb. fish fillets, cut into 2-inch pieces
12-oz. pkg. (3 cups) frozen shrimp
6-oz. pkg. (¾ cup) frozen crab or lobster meat
1 pint oysters or clams, undrained
8-oz. can (1 cup) tomato sauce

In Dutch oven or large saucepan, sauté onion and garlic in oil until tender. Add remaining ingredients and stir to distribute evenly. Heat just to boiling. Simmer covered over low heat, 20 to 30 minutes or until seafood is done, stirring occasionally. Remove bay leaf. Serve in large soup bowls.

10 to 12 servings

NUTRITION INFORMATION PER SERVING

Serving Size: 1/12 of recipe		Percent U.S. RDA Per Serving	
Calories	161	Protein	25%
Protein	16g	Vitamin A	27%
Carbohydrate	5g	Vitamin C	5%
Fat	8g	Thiamin	8%
Sodium	649mg	Riboflavin	8%
Potassium	230mg	Niacin	15%
		Calcium	6%
		Iron	14%

TIPS: *Fish and seafood may be added either fresh or frozen although fresh fish give the most flavor. Fish may be added in the frozen state; use the maximum cooking time. Fresh and thawed fish require the minimum cooking time.*

Any combination of fish or seafood may be used depending on availability and taste. It is desirable to have some salt water fish varieties however. Cooking times may vary slightly, but should fall within range given.

LOBSTER

Lobster can be purchased whole or just the tail where most of the meat is concentrated. Whole lobster is available fresh or frozen. Because they spoil quickly, fresh lobster must be shipped and purchased live. If you are planning to serve fresh lobster, purchase that day and cook as soon as possible; live lobster will keep in the refrigerator a few hours if necessary. Frozen whole lobsters are usually cooked (characterized by the bright orange-red color) so you need only thaw the meat for cold dishes or heat it through for hot dishes. Lobster tails are most often frozen uncooked (characterized by the black-green color) and must be cooked before they are eaten.

Lobster is usually sold by the pound. A whole lobster for eating will weigh 1 to 2 pounds; allow one lobster per serving. Lobster tails vary in weight, however ½ pound per serving is sufficient.

BROILED LOBSTER TAILS

Allow ½ lb. per serving for lobster tails.* Prepare for broiling by cutting along underside of tail with shears; clip off fins along edges. Peel back soft undershell and discard. To prevent curling, bend tail back to crack shell or insert skewer between meat and shell. Lay cut-side-up on broiler pan. Brush with mixture of ¼ cup melted butter, ½ teaspoon salt and ¼ teaspoon paprika. Broil 4 inches from heat for 10 to 15 minutes or until lobster meat is firm. Serve with one of the butter sauces, pages 547 and 548.

NUTRITION INFORMATION PER SERVING

Serving Size: 1/4 of recipe		Percent U.S. RDA Per Serving	
Calories	285	Protein	25%
Protein	16g	Vitamin A	19%
Carbohydrate	<1g	Vitamin C	0%
Fat	24g	Thiamin	6%
Sodium	993mg	Riboflavin	3%
Potassium	160mg	Niacin	0%
		Calcium	6%
		Iron	4%

TIPS: **If desired, frozen lobster tail may be simmered covered, in salted boiling water for about 15 minutes. Prepare as directed for broiling. Cut broiling time to 2 to 3 minutes.*

For BUTTERFLIED LOBSTER TAILS, cut lengthwise through the center of the hard top shell with shears, then cut through the meat with a sharp knife without cutting through soft undershell. Spread open and cook as directed.

BOILED LIVE LOBSTER

In large saucepan, heat salted water to boiling. Plunge live lobster, head first, into boiling water. Return to boil; simmer covered about 15 minutes. Remove from water and turn on back. With sharp knife or shears, cut lobster in half lengthwise. Remove sac near head and dark vein which runs along underside of tail. Crack claws using claw or nut cracker. Serve with Drawn Butter Sauce, page 547. 1 serving

NUTRITION INFORMATION PER SERVING

Serving Size: 1 whole lobster		Percent U.S. RDA Per Serving	
Calories	80	Protein	24%
Protein	16g	Vitamin A	*
Carbohydrate	<1g	Vitamin C	*
Fat	1g	Thiamin	6%
Sodium	176mg	Riboflavin	3%
Potassium	151mg	Niacin	*
		Calcium	5%
		Iron	4%

LOBSTER THERMIDOR

10¾-oz. can condensed cream of shrimp or mushroom soup
8 oz. (1 cup) cooked lobster meat, cut into chunks
¼ teaspoon dry mustard
Dash cayenne pepper
¼ cup milk
4-oz. can (½ cup) sliced mushrooms, drained
Grated Parmesan cheese
Paprika

In medium saucepan, heat soup over low heat, stirring occasionally. Stir in lobster, mustard, pepper, milk and mushrooms. Heat through. Spoon into 4 lightly greased individual baking dishes or shells. Sprinkle with Parmesan cheese and paprika. Broil 3 to 4 inches from heat 2 to 3 minutes or until hot and bubbly. 4 servings

NUTRITION INFORMATION PER SERVING

Serving Size: 1/4 of recipe		Percent U.S. RDA Per Serving	
Calories	170	Protein	22%
Protein	15g	Vitamin A	2%
Carbohydrate	8g	Vitamin C	*
Fat	9g	Thiamin	5%
Sodium	754mg	Riboflavin	14%
Potassium	192mg	Niacin	5%
		Calcium	14%
		Iron	5%

TIPS: *Two 5-oz. cans lobster, drained may be substituted for the cooked lobster.*

With careful handling lobster shells may be used as individual baking dishes.

LOBSTER NEWBURG

¼ cup margarine or butter
1½ tablespoons flour
1 lb. (2 cups) cooked lobster meat, cut into chunks
½ teaspoon salt
Dash paprika
¼ cup dry sherry or dry white wine
2 egg yolks, slightly beaten
1½ cups light cream

In medium saucepan or top of double boiler, melt margarine. Stir in flour and let cook 1 minute. Add lobster, salt, paprika and sherry. In small bowl, combine beaten egg yolks and cream; gradually add to lobster mixture and blend well. Cook over very low heat or hot water until thickened, stirring frequently. Serve over toast points or patty shells. 4 servings

NUTRITION INFORMATION PER SERVING

Serving Size: 1/4 of recipe		Percent U.S. RDA Per Serving	
Calories	452	Protein	40%
Protein	26g	Vitamin A	30%
Carbohydrate	7g	Vitamin C	*
Fat	34g	Thiamin	12%
Sodium	684mg	Riboflavin	16%
Potassium	342mg	Niacin	*
		Calcium	18%
		Iron	8%

TIP: *For CRAB or SHRIMP NEWBURG, cooked crab meat, shrimp or a combination may be substituted for the lobster.*

SHRIMP

Since all of the meat is located in the tail, the shrimp that is usually bought in stores have the head sections removed. Shrimp are available cooked or raw, in the shell or shelled, and they can be purchased fresh, frozen or canned. In general they can be used interchangeably, however they do vary in size. Canned shrimp being the smallest are best suited for main dish recipes when pieces are desirable. Use fresh or frozen in appetizers where appearance is important.

Shrimp is usually sold according to count per pound. (The smaller the count per pound the larger the shrimp.) Two pounds of raw shrimp will yield about one pound cooked and shelled. Allow about ¼ pound cooked shelled shrimp per serving.

For a better appearance, remove the vein going down the back of the shrimp before cooking with a sharp knife or skewer. Simply pierce under the vein and pull out, either before or after shucking.

Calcium is unusually high in shrimp along with protein and iodine. Shrimp are also good sources of niacin, thiamine and riboflavin.

COOKING RAW SHRIMP

In saucepan, bring enough water to cover shrimp to a boil. Add shrimp and immediately reduce heat. Simmer, *do not boil* for 5 to 10 minutes. Shrimp will become tough if overcooked. Drain and serve warm or refrigerate for later use.

NUTRITION INFORMATION PER SERVING

Serving Size: 1/3 lb. shrimp		Percent U.S. RDA Per Serving	
Calories	89	Protein	30%
Protein	20g	Vitamin A	*
Carbohydrate	<1g	Vitamin C	12%
Fat	<1g	Thiamin	*
Sodium	119mg	Riboflavin	*
Potassium	191mg	Niacin	16%
		Calcium	7%
		Iron	9%

CHINESE SHRIMP

¼ cup margarine or butter
8-oz. can (⅔ cup) water chestnuts, drained and sliced
6-oz. can (¾ cup) bamboo shoots, drained
4-oz. (1½ cups) sliced fresh mushrooms
1 cube or 1 teaspoon chicken bouillon
1 tablespoon cornstarch
⅛ teaspoon ginger
4 green onions, sliced
12-oz. pkg. (3 cups) uncooked shrimp*
¾ cup water
2 tablespoons soy sauce
Green pepper rings, if desired

In large skillet, sauté water chestnuts, bamboo shoots and mushrooms in margarine 2 to 3 minutes. Blend in bouillon and cornstarch, mixing well. Stir in remaining ingredients except pepper rings. Heat to boiling; simmer covered 10 to 15 minutes or until shrimp are firm and pink. Serve over rice; garnish with green pepper rings.

4 to 5 servings

NUTRITION INFORMATION PER SERVING

Serving Size: 1/4 of recipe		Percent U.S. RDA Per Serving	
Calories	200	Protein	21%
Protein	14g	Vitamin A	16%
Carbohydrate	10g	Vitamin C	23%
Fat	12g	Thiamin	6%
Sodium	1116mg	Riboflavin	12%
Potassium	468mg	Niacin	16%
		Calcium	7%
		Iron	11%

TIP: **If using cooked shrimp, increase water to 1 cup and cook until mixture is thoroughly heated.*

SHRIMP CURRY

¼ cup margarine or butter
1 small onion, chopped
1 stalk celery, chopped
2 tablespoons chopped green pepper or drained pimiento
3 tablespoons flour
1½ to 2 teaspoons curry powder
⅛ teaspoon salt
1 cube or 1 teaspoon chicken bouillon
½ cup water
½ cup milk
12-oz. pkg. (3 cups) uncooked shrimp*

In large skillet, sauté onion and celery in margarine until tender. Stir in green pepper, flour, curry and bouillon. Add water and milk; heat to boiling. Add shrimp; simmer covered over low heat, 10 to 15 minutes or until shrimp are firm and pink. Serve over rice along with condiments (see Tips).

4 to 5 servings

NUTRITION INFORMATION PER SERVING

Serving Size: 1/4 of recipe		Percent U.S. RDA Per Serving	
Calories	203	Protein	21%
Protein	13g	Vitamin A	12%
Carbohydrate	8g	Vitamin C	17%
Fat	13g	Thiamin	5%
Sodium	545mg	Riboflavin	6%
Potassium	233mg	Niacin	11%
		Calcium	9%
		Iron	8%

TIPS: **Cooked shrimp may be substituted using minimum cooking time.*

Some condiments which could be served alongside of this dish are: toasted coconut, chopped peanuts, pickle relish, chutney, sliced green onions, raisins or crumbled bacon.

SHRIMP CREOLE

2 tablespoons margarine or butter
½ cup chopped green pepper
¼ cup chopped onion
3 tablespoons cornstarch
½ teaspoon salt
½ teaspoon paprika
½ teaspoon chili powder
½ teaspoon basil or marjoram leaves
⅛ teaspoon pepper
1 garlic clove, crushed
28-oz. can (3½ cups) tomatoes, undrained
16-oz. pkg. (4 cups) uncooked shrimp

In large skillet, sauté green pepper and onion in margarine until tender. Stir in remaining ingredients, mixing well. Heat to boiling. Simmer covered, 12 to 15 minutes or until shrimp are firm and pink, stirring occasionally. 5 servings

NUTRITION INFORMATION PER SERVING

Serving Size: 1/5 of recipe		Percent U.S. RDA Per Serving	
Calories	143	Protein	18%
Protein	12g	Vitamin A	37%
Carbohydrate	13g	Vitamin C	52%
Fat	5g	Thiamin	7%
Sodium	544mg	Riboflavin	5%
Potassium	493mg	Niacin	14%
		Calcium	5%
		Iron	10%

TIP: *If using cooked shrimp, reduce cooking time to 5 to 10 minutes and thin with additional water if necessary.*

SHRIMP JAMBALAYA

2 slices bacon, cut into pieces
¼ cup chopped green pepper
1 small onion, chopped
1 garlic clove, minced
¾ cup uncooked regular rice
1 teaspoon salt
½ teaspoon chili powder
¼ teaspoon basil leaves
2 cubes or 2 teaspoons chicken bouillon
½ bay leaf
1½ cups water
16-oz. can (2 cups) tomatoes, undrained
2 cups (8 oz.) uncooked shrimp
½ cup sliced ripe olives

In large skillet, fry bacon until crisp. Add green pepper, onion and garlic; sauté until tender. Stir in rice, salt, chili powder, basil, bouillon, bay leaf, water and tomatoes. Heat to boiling. Simmer covered over low heat 15 minutes or until rice is almost tender.* Add shrimp and olives. Cook covered, 10 to 15 minutes or until rice is tender and shrimp are firm and pink. Remove bay leaf and serve. 4 servings

NUTRITION INFORMATION PER SERVING

Serving Size: 1/4 of recipe		Percent U.S. RDA Per Serving	
Calories	272	Protein	27%
Protein	18g	Vitamin A	26%
Carbohydrate	37g	Vitamin C	40%
Fat	6g	Thiamin	17%
Sodium	1408mg	Riboflavin	5%
Potassium	473mg	Niacin	21%
		Calcium	9%
		Iron	18%

TIPS: *To MAKE AHEAD, prepare to*, cool and refrigerate up to 1 day. To serve, heat to boiling and continue from*. If necessary add more water.*

For quick-cooking rice, reduce water to 1 cup, increase rice to 1 cup. Combine all ingredients; cook covered 10 to 15 minutes or until rice is tender and shrimp are firm and pink.

If using cooked shrimp, cook rice mixture 20 minutes. Add shrimp and olives and cook about 5 minutes.

Shrimp may be added while frozen. Extend cooking time about 3 minutes after adding shrimp and olives. Uncover last 5 minutes of cooking time.

SAUTÉED SHRIMP AND MUSHROOMS

2 tablespoons margarine or butter
1 garlic clove, crushed
¼ cup dry sherry
12-oz. pkg. (3 cups) frozen uncooked shrimp*
4-oz. can (½ cup) button or sliced mushrooms, drained

In medium skillet, sauté garlic in margarine until light brown. Stir in remaining ingredients. Bring to boil; simmer uncovered over low heat, 10 to 15 minutes or until shrimp are firm and pink. Serve with rice. 3 to 4 servings

NUTRITION INFORMATION PER SERVING

Serving Size: 1/4 of recipe		Percent U.S. RDA Per Serving	
Calories	127	Protein	18%
Protein	12g	Vitamin A	5%
Carbohydrate	2g	Vitamin C	10%
Fat	6g	Thiamin	*
Sodium	138mg	Riboflavin	4%
Potassium	124mg	Niacin	11%
		Calcium	5%
		Iron	6%

TIP: **If using cooked shrimp, simmer covered over low heat, 5 to 10 minutes until flavors are blended.*

BATTER-FRIED SHRIMP OR SCALLOPS

1 lb. uncooked shrimp or scallops*
½ cup milk
1 egg
½ cup Pillsbury's Best® All Purpose Unbleached or Self Rising Flour
½ teaspoon salt
Dash Tabasco sauce

Rinse and drain shrimp well. Heat 1 to 1½ inches oil in skillet or saucepan to 375°F. In small bowl, beat together milk and egg; beat in flour, salt and Tabasco sauce until smooth. Dip shrimp in batter, draining off excess. Fry shrimp at 375°F. for 3 to 4 minutes or until golden brown. Drain slightly on paper towel and serve with Tartar Sauce page 544 or Sea Food Cocktail Sauce, page 552. 4 servings

NUTRITION INFORMATION PER SERVING

Serving Size: 1/4 of recipe		Percent U.S. RDA Per Serving	
Calories	153	Protein	25%
Protein	16g	Vitamin A	5%
Carbohydrate	14g	Vitamin C	11%
Fat	3g	Thiamin	9%
Sodium	375mg	Riboflavin	10%
Potassium	192mg	Niacin	14%
		Calcium	9%
		Iron	10%

TIPS: *Shrimp or scallops may be fresh or frozen. If frozen thaw and drain before cooking.*

**If shrimp are in shell, remove shell except for tail portion. Cut shrimp lengthwise to form butterfly shape, keeping tail intact. Dip in batter and fry as directed.*

SHRIMPLY GOOD CRÊPES

10 to 12 cooked Basic Crêpes, page 101
2 tablespoons margarine or butter
½ cup sliced water chestnuts
¼ cup chopped onion
2 cans (4½ oz. each) tiny or broken shrimp, drained or 10-oz. pkg. frozen shrimp, thawed and drained
¼ cup condensed cream of shrimp soup (reserve remainder for Sauce)

SHRIMP SAUCE
Remainder of 10¾-oz. can condensed cream of shrimp soup
¼ cup milk
1 tablespoon soy sauce, if desired
1 teaspoon lemon juice
¼ teaspoon Tabasco sauce

Prepare crêpes. Heat oven to 350°F. In medium skillet, sauté water chestnuts and onion in margarine until onion is tender. Add shrimp; cook and stir 2 minutes. Stir in ¼ cup soup; heat to bubbling. Spread about 2 tablespoons shrimp mixture over each crêpe. Roll up; arrange in 13x9 or 12x8-inch baking dish. Cover loosely with foil. Bake at 350°F. for 15 to 18 minutes or until heated through. While crêpes are baking, prepare Shrimp Sauce. In small saucepan, combine Sauce ingredients; heat until bubbly, stirring constantly. To serve, spoon Shrimp Sauce over hot crêpes.
10 to 12 crêpes

NUTRITION INFORMATION PER SERVING

Serving Size: 1/10 of recipe		Percent U.S. RDA Per Serving	
Calories	213	Protein	19%
Protein	13g	Vitamin A	9%
Carbohydrate	16g	Vitamin C	3%
Fat	11g	Thiamin	8%
Sodium	569mg	Riboflavin	12%
Potassium	154mg	Niacin	6%
		Calcium	9%
		Iron	10%

SWEET AND SOUR SHRIMP

3 medium green onions or 1 small onion, sliced
2 stalks celery, sliced
2 tablespoons margarine or butter
¼ cup sugar
3 tablespoons cornstarch
1 teaspoon paprika
½ teaspoon ginger
¼ cup soy sauce
¼ cup vinegar
15½-oz. can (2 cups) pineapple chunks, undrained
12-oz. pkg. (3 cups) uncooked or cooked shrimp
1 green pepper, cut into strips
1 large tomato, cut into small pieces

In large skillet, sauté onions and celery in margarine until tender. Stir in sugar, cornstarch, paprika and ginger. Add soy sauce, vinegar, pineapple and shrimp; mix well. Heat to boiling; simmer covered, 10 minutes or until shrimp are firm and pink, stirring occasionally. Add green pepper and continue cooking about 3 minutes. Stir in tomato and heat through. Serve with rice.

4 to 5 servings

NUTRITION INFORMATION PER SERVING

Serving Size: 1/4 of recipe		Percent U.S. RDA Per Serving	
Calories	293	Protein	21%
Protein	14g	Vitamin A	17%
Carbohydrate	48g	Vitamin C	92%
Fat	7g	Thiamin	11%
Sodium	1489mg	Riboflavin	8%
Potassium	572mg	Niacin	13%
		Calcium	9%
		Iron	16%

SCALLOPS, OYSTERS AND CLAMS

Scallops are most frequently sold shelled frozen or fresh but are also available in the shell. Clams are most often sold in the shell or canned. Oysters are sold in the shell, shucked or canned.

When purchased fresh in the shell, they should be alive and shells tightly closed. Although they can live a long time out of water, once they die, they spoil very quickly. Therefore, plan to use fresh shellfish the day of purchase.

To clean fresh shellfish, wash them several times in cold water. To open or shuck, place on table flat-side-up and force a sharp knife between the shells. To make it easier to insert the knife, you may wish to break off the thin end of the shell with a hammer. Force the shell all the way open until the muscle has been cut from one side. Cut the muscle from the other side and remove the shell. Wash the muscle again and proceed with the recipe.

COQUILLES ST. JACQUES

¼ cup margarine or butter
¼ cup chopped celery
4 oz. (1½ cups) sliced fresh mushrooms
2 medium green onions, sliced or 2 tablespoons chopped onion
2 tablespoons chopped green pepper
2 tablespoons flour
¼ teaspoon salt
⅛ teaspoon pepper
½ bay leaf
½ cup dry white wine
1 lb. fresh or frozen scallops
¼ cup whipping cream or evaporated milk
1 egg yolk
1 tablespoon chopped pimiento
2 tablespoons margarine or butter, melted
3 tablespoons dry bread crumbs
3 tablespoons grated Parmesan cheese

In large saucepan, sauté celery, mushrooms and onions in margarine until tender. Stir in green pepper, flour, salt, pepper, bay leaf and wine; mix well. Add scallops. Cook over medium heat until mixture boils and thickens, stirring occasionally. Cover and simmer 5 minutes (10 to 15 minutes if scallops are frozen) or until scallops are firm. Beat together cream and egg yolk until well mixed. Stir into scallops along with pimiento. Cook until mixture just begins to bubble. Remove bay leaf. Spoon mixture into 4 (8 small appetizer shells) lightly greased shells, individual baking dishes, or 1½-quart shallow casserole. Combine melted margarine, bread crumbs and cheese. Sprinkle over each serving. *Place under broiler a few minutes to brown crumbs and heat through.

4 main course or
8 appetizer servings

NUTRITION INFORMATION PER SERVING

Serving Size: 1/4 of recipe		Percent U.S. RDA Per Serving	
Calories	420	Protein	47%
Protein	30g	Vitamin A	23%
Carbohydrate	8g	Vitamin C	16%
Fat	27g	Thiamin	5%
Sodium	708mg	Riboflavin	13%
Potassium	762mg	Niacin	7%
		Calcium	21%
		Iron	24%

TIPS: *One-half cup (4-oz. can) drained sliced mushrooms may be substituted for fresh.*

*To MAKE AHEAD, prepare to * and refrigerate up to 12 hours. Place under broiler until hot and bubbly.*

SCALLOPS EN BROCHETTE

¼ teaspoon thyme leaves
2 garlic cloves, halved
¾ cup oil
¼ cup lemon juice
1½ lb. fresh or frozen scallops, thawed
12 slices (¾ lb.) bacon
18 cherry tomatoes
2 cups (4 oz.) fresh whole mushrooms*
1 green pepper, cut into 1-inch pieces

In deep bowl, combine first 5 ingredients. Marinate at least 1 hour. Starting with bacon and interlacing slices over and under other pieces, thread drained scallops, tomatoes, mushrooms and green pepper on skewers. Brush with oil marinade. Place on broiler pan and broil 3 inches from heat about 10 minutes or until scallops are firm and bacon crisp, turning occasionally.

6 servings

NUTRITION INFORMATION PER SERVING

Serving Size: 1/6 of recipe		Percent U.S. RDA Per Serving	
Calories	478	Protein	49%
Protein	32g	Vitamin A	6%
Carbohydrate	4g	Vitamin C	44%
Fat	37g	Thiamin	8%
Sodium	459mg	Riboflavin	9%
Potassium	761mg	Niacin	9%
		Calcium	14%
		Iron	24%

TIPS: **If desired, use only the mushroom caps. Cut stems off even with caps.*

Thin slices of bacon are necessary for cooking on skewers. If thick sliced bacon is substituted, partially cook until transparent, but still limp before threading on skewers.

Brochettes may be grilled over charcoal 4 inches from heat 10 to 15 minutes, turning occasionally.

FRIED OYSTERS

1 pint oysters
⅓ cup flour
1 teaspoon salt
⅛ teaspoon pepper
1 egg
1 tablespoon water
⅔ cup cracker or bread crumbs
¼ cup oil or butter

Drain oysters well; coat in mixture of flour, salt and pepper. In small bowl, beat together egg and water. Dip floured oysters in egg mixture; roll in crumbs to coat. In medium skillet, heat oil. Fry oysters until brown, about 5 minutes on each side, turning once. Serve with lemon wedges or Tartar Sauce, page 544.

4 servings

NUTRITION INFORMATION PER SERVING

Serving Size: 1/4 of recipe		Percent U.S. RDA Per Serving	
Calories	306	Protein	21%
Protein	13g	Vitamin A	10%
Carbohydrate	20g	Vitamin C	*
Fat	19g	Thiamin	16%
Sodium	761mg	Riboflavin	17%
Potassium	179mg	Niacin	18%
		Calcium	12%
		Iron	40%

TIPS: *If desired, fry in deep fat (375°F.) for about 2 to 3 minutes. For FRIED CLAMS, substitute shucked clams for oysters.*

NUTRITION INFORMATION PER SERVING

Serving Size: 1/4 of recipe		Percent U.S. RDA Per Serving	
Calories	292	Protein	20%
Protein	13g	Vitamin A	3%
Carbohydrate	20g	Vitamin C	*
Fat	17g	Thiamin	7%
Sodium	678mg	Riboflavin	13%
Potassium	197mg	Niacin	9%
		Calcium	8%
		Iron	30%

For FRIED FROG LEGS, substitute 3 lb. frog legs for oysters. Fry about 10 minutes on each side or until golden brown. If they are large, add a little water and simmer covered 10 minutes. Remove cover and continue frying until crisp.

NUTRITION INFORMATION PER SERVING

Serving Size: 1/4 of recipe		Percent U.S. RDA Per Serving	
Calories	384	Protein	58%
Protein	38g	Vitamin A	3%
Carbohydrate	17g	Vitamin C	*
Fat	17g	Thiamin	25%
Sodium	678mg	Riboflavin	35%
Potassium	43mg	Niacin	16%
		Calcium	5%
		Iron	21%

OYSTERS ROCKEFELLER

24 large oysters (about 2 pints), drained
2 pkg. (10 oz. each) frozen chopped spinach
2 cubes or 2 teaspoons chicken bouillon
1 tablespoon instant minced onion
2 tablespoons milk
Dash Tabasco sauce
8-oz. pkg. cream cheese, softened
½ cup buttered bread crumbs*

If oysters are not shelled, follow directions page 284 for shucking and cleaning. Place each oyster in lightly greased shell** or individual ramekins or baking dishes. Cook spinach as directed on package; omit salt but add 1 cube chicken bouillon for each package. Drain; press out liquid. Add onion, milk, Tabasco sauce and cream cheese; mix well. Heat through but do not boil. Broil oysters 3 inches from heat for 4 to 5 minutes or until thoroughly heated. Top each oyster with a spoonful of spinach mixture; sprinkle with buttered bread crumbs. Return to broiler for 3 to 5 minutes or until bubbly.

4 to 6 servings

NUTRITION INFORMATION PER SERVING

Serving Size: 1/4 of recipe		Percent U.S. RDA Per Serving	
Calories	385	Protein	25%
Protein	16g	Vitamin A	203%
Carbohydrate	13g	Vitamin C	36%
Fat	31g	Thiamin	15%
Sodium	928mg	Riboflavin	28%
Potassium	553mg	Niacin	14%
		Calcium	26%
		Iron	40%

TIPS: *To make in casserole, arrange oysters in lightly greased shallow casserole; top with cooked spinach mixture and sprinkle with bread crumbs. Bake uncovered at 375°F. for 25 to 30 minutes or until heated through.*

**For BUTTERED BREAD CRUMBS, melt 2½ tablespoons butter, add ½ cup dry bread crumbs and ⅛ teaspoon salt; mix well.*

***If preparing oysters in shells, place shells on a thin bed of rock salt in baking pan or jelly roll pan. The salt will keep the shells in place and hold the heat.*

SCALLOPED OYSTERS

¼ cup margarine or butter
2 cups (2 slices) soft bread crumbs
¼ cup grated Parmesan cheese
¼ teaspoon salt
Dash mace, if desired
1 pint oysters, drained
¼ cup dry sherry or dry white wine

Heat oven to 375°F. In 10x6 or 8-inch pan, melt margarine in oven. Stir in bread crumbs, cheese, salt and mace. Remove about half of crumbs; arrange remaining crumbs evenly in pan. Place oysters over crumbs; pour sherry over top. Sprinkle with remaining crumbs. Bake uncovered at 375°F. for 20 to 25 minutes or until lightly browned.
4 servings

NUTRITION INFORMATION PER SERVING

Serving Size: 1/4 of recipe		Percent U.S. RDA Per Serving	
Calories	275	Protein	22%
Protein	14g	Vitamin A	18%
Carbohydrate	16g	Vitamin C	0%
Fat	16g	Thiamin	15%
Sodium	512mg	Riboflavin	18%
Potassium	196mg	Niacin	18%
		Calcium	20%
		Iron	40%

TIPS: *Recipe may be halved and baked in small casserole.*

Two 8-oz. cans oysters, drained, may be substituted for fresh, but omit salt. Fresh shucked or canned clams may also be substituted for oysters.

The wine may be omitted; substitute liquor in which oysters or clams are packed or light cream.

STEAMED CLAMS

Select soft-shelled "steamer" clams, allowing about 1 lb. or ½ dozen clams per serving. Wash thoroughly and let stand in salt water 15 minutes; drain. In large saucepan, bring ½ inch water to boil. Add clams, cover tightly and steam over medium heat 5 to 10 minutes or until shells open. Remove any sand from cooking broth by straining through several layers of cheesecloth. Serve clams with cups of cooking broth and melted butter.

NUTRITION INFORMATION PER SERVING

Serving Size: 6 clams without butter		Percent U.S. RDA Per Serving	
Calories	45	Protein	12%
Protein	8g	Vitamin A	*
Carbohydrate	<1g	Vitamin C	*
Fat	1g	Thiamin	*
Sodium	20mg	Riboflavin	*
Potassium	128mg	Niacin	*
		Calcium	*
		Iron	10%

CLAMS IN SAUCE

10-oz. pkg. (1½ cups) frozen peas
9-oz. pkg. frozen onions in cream sauce
¼ cup milk
2 cans (6½ oz. each) minced clams (drain one can)

In medium saucepan, combine peas, onions, milk and liquor from 1 can of clams. Heat to boiling and simmer covered until peas are tender. Stir in clams and heat through. Serve over biscuits, toast points or rice.
4 servings

NUTRITION INFORMATION PER SERVING

Serving Size: 1/4 of recipe		Percent U.S. RDA Per Serving	
Calories	193	Protein	21%
Protein	14g	Vitamin A	10%
Carbohydrate	21g	Vitamin C	30%
Fat	7g	Thiamin	17%
Sodium	372mg	Riboflavin	13%
Potassium	195mg	Niacin	9%
		Calcium	10%
		Iron	19%

STEAMED CLAMS

CLAMS POULETTE

¼ cup margarine or butter
1 tablespoon finely chopped onion
4-oz. can (½ cup) mushroom stems and pieces, drained
¼ cup flour
½ teaspoon salt
⅛ teaspoon pepper
1 bay leaf
½ cup dry white wine
2 teaspoons lemon juice
2 cans (6½ oz. each) minced clams, undrained
½ cup light or whipping cream
1 egg yolk
1 tablespoon chopped parsley

In medium skillet, sauté onion and mushrooms in margarine until tender. Blend in flour. Stir in salt, pepper, bay leaf, wine, lemon juice and clams. Heat to boiling; simmer covered over low heat about 10 minutes. Remove bay leaf. Blend cream with egg yolk. Stir into clam mixture. Heat just until bubbles begin to form. Stir in parsley and serve over toast points or patty shells.

4 servings

NUTRITION INFORMATION PER SERVING

Serving Size: 1/4 of recipe		Percent U.S. RDA Per Serving	
Calories	291	Protein	16%
Protein	10g	Vitamin A	19%
Carbohydrate	12g	Vitamin C	5%
Fat	20g	Thiamin	6%
Sodium	429mg	Riboflavin	15%
Potassium	226mg	Niacin	9%
		Calcium	10%
		Iron	26%

CLAMS CASINO

24 hard-shell clams
¼ cup grated Parmesan cheese
¼ cup dry bread crumbs
2 tablespoons minced parsley
2 tablespoons minced green pepper
2 tablespoons minced onion
½ teaspoon oregano leaves
4 slices bacon, each cut into 6 pieces

Wash clams, discarding any open (dead) clams. Pry open shells (see page 284); discard top shell and loosen meat from bottom shell. Drain shells and meat on paper towel. Heat oven to 350°F. In small bowl, combine remaining ingredients except bacon. Return clams to bottom shell and arrange in shallow baking pan. Top each with heaping teaspoonful of crumb mixture and piece of bacon.* Bake at 350°F. for 20 to 25 minutes or until bacon is crisp and clams are set.

4 to 6 servings

NUTRITION INFORMATION PER SERVING

Serving Size: 1/4 of recipe		Percent U.S. RDA Per Serving	
Calories	155	Protein	23%
Protein	15g	Vitamin A	5%
Carbohydrate	8g	Vitamin C	16%
Fat	6g	Thiamin	4%
Sodium	323mg	Riboflavin	5%
Potassium	344mg	Niacin	3%
		Calcium	15%
		Iron	41%

TIPS: *To MAKE AHEAD, prepare to*, cover and refrigerate up to 6 hours. To serve, proceed from **

Two cans (6½ oz. each) drained clams may be substituted for the fresh. Mix clams with the crumb mixture. Fills 24 shells.

CRAB

Experts insist the only way to purchase crab is fresh live. Since crab can be easily overcooked, great care must be taken if preparing crab dishes from the cooked frozen variety as it is difficult to avoid overcooking when you reheat crab.

Hard shell crab is available in coastal areas almost all year and is frequently shipped in to specialty houses and supermarkets in the midwest. Soft shell crabs (a crab which has shed its hard shell) are in limited distribution during July and August.

The nutritive value of crab is similar to lobster.

BOILED CRAB

Select dressed Dungeness crab. Allow 1 crab for 2 servings. In large saucepan, heat salted water to boiling. Drop crabs into boiling water. Return to boil; simmer covered about 15 minutes. Remove from water, crack claws and legs and serve with one of seasoned butters, page 547 or serve with butter or tartar sauce.

NUTRITION INFORMATION PER SERVING

Serving Size: 1/2 whole crab		Percent U.S. RDA Per Serving	
Calories	79	Protein	23%
Protein	15g	Vitamin A	37%
Carbohydrate	<1g	Vitamin C	3%
Fat	2g	Thiamin	9%
Sodium	0mg	Riboflavin	4%
Potassium	0mg	Niacin	12%
		Calcium	4%
		Iron	4%

CRAB ROYALE

CRAB ROYALE

- **1 lb. (2 cups) cooked crab meat, drained and flaked**
- **1 cup (4 oz.) shredded Cheddar or Swiss cheese**
- **½ cup chopped celery**
- **⅓ cup dry bread crumbs**
- **3 tablespoons chopped green pepper, if desired**
- **3 tablespoons chopped pimiento, if desired**
- **1½ teaspoons instant minced onion**
- **¼ teaspoon salt**
- **Dash pepper**
- **½ cup salad dressing or mayonnaise**
- **⅓ cup milk or light cream**
- **1½ teaspoons lemon juice**

Heat oven to 375°F. In medium bowl, combine all ingredients; mix well. Spoon into 6 shells or individual baking dishes. Bake at 375°F. for 12 to 15 minutes or until lightly browned and heated through.

4 to 6 servings

NUTRITION INFORMATION PER SERVING

Serving Size: 1/6 of recipe		Percent U.S. RDA Per Serving	
Calories	234	Protein	21%
Protein	14g	Vitamin A	26%
Carbohydrate	7g	Vitamin C	14%
Fat	17g	Thiamin	6%
Sodium	393mg	Riboflavin	11%
Potassium	95mg	Niacin	7%
		Calcium	21%
		Iron	5%

TIP: *To MAKE AHEAD, prepare as directed; cover and refrigerate up to 8 hours. Bake at 375°F. for 20 minutes.*

DEVILED CRAB

3 tablespoons margarine or butter
2 tablespoons chopped onion
2 tablespoons chopped green pepper
2 tablespoons flour
¾ cup milk
1 lb. (2 cups) cooked crab meat, drained and flaked
1 tablespoon chopped parsley
½ teaspoon salt
½ teaspoon dry or 1 teaspoon prepared mustard
1 teaspoon Worcestershire sauce
⅛ teaspoon Tabasco sauce
1 egg, slightly beaten

Heat oven to 400°F. In medium saucepan, sauté onion and green pepper in margarine until tender. Blend in flour. Gradually stir in milk and heat until mixture boils and thickens, stirring constantly. Add remaining ingredients; mix well. Spoon into lightly greased 1-quart casserole or 4 individual baking dishes or shells. Bake uncovered at 400°F. for 20 to 25 minutes or until heated through.

4 servings

NUTRITION INFORMATION PER SERVING

Serving Size: 1/4 of recipe		Percent U.S. RDA Per Serving	
Calories	211	Protein	23%
Protein	15g	Vitamin A	14%
Carbohydrate	7g	Vitamin C	14%
Fat	13g	Thiamin	7%
Sodium	1059mg	Riboflavin	11%
Potassium	184mg	Niacin	8%
		Calcium	10%
		Iron	6%

DOWN EAST CRAB MEAT PIE

8-inch Single-Crust pastry, page 220

FILLING
5-oz. can crab meat, drained and flaked
⅔ cup chopped celery
⅓ cup chopped green pepper
2 tablespoons flour
1 tablespoon instant minced onion
½ teaspoon salt
⅓ cup chili sauce
2 teaspoons Worcestershire sauce

SAUCE
2 tablespoons margarine or butter
2 tablespoons flour
¼ teaspoon salt
¾ cup milk
1 cup shredded Swiss cheese
2 tablespoons cooking sherry, if desired
Paprika

Heat oven to 400°F. Prepare pastry. In large bowl, combine all Filling ingredients. Spoon into pastry-lined pie pan. In small saucepan, melt margarine. Blend in flour and salt; cook until bubbly. Gradually stir in milk. Cook over medium heat until mixture boils and thickens, stirring constantly. Remove from heat; stir in ¾ cup shredded cheese and sherry. Pour Sauce over Filling, spreading to cover. Sprinkle with remaining ¼ cup shredded cheese and paprika. Bake at 400°F. for 20 to 25 minutes or until bubbly and golden brown. Let cool 10 minutes. Cut in wedges to serve. 6 servings

NUTRITION INFORMATION PER SERVING

Serving Size: 1/6 of recipe		Percent U.S. RDA Per Serving	
Calories	460	Protein	19%
Protein	12g	Vitamin A	14%
Carbohydrate	28g	Vitamin C	15%
Fat	33g	Thiamin	15%
Sodium	1044mg	Riboflavin	16%
Potassium	241mg	Niacin	10%
		Calcium	24%
		Iron	7%

MEATS

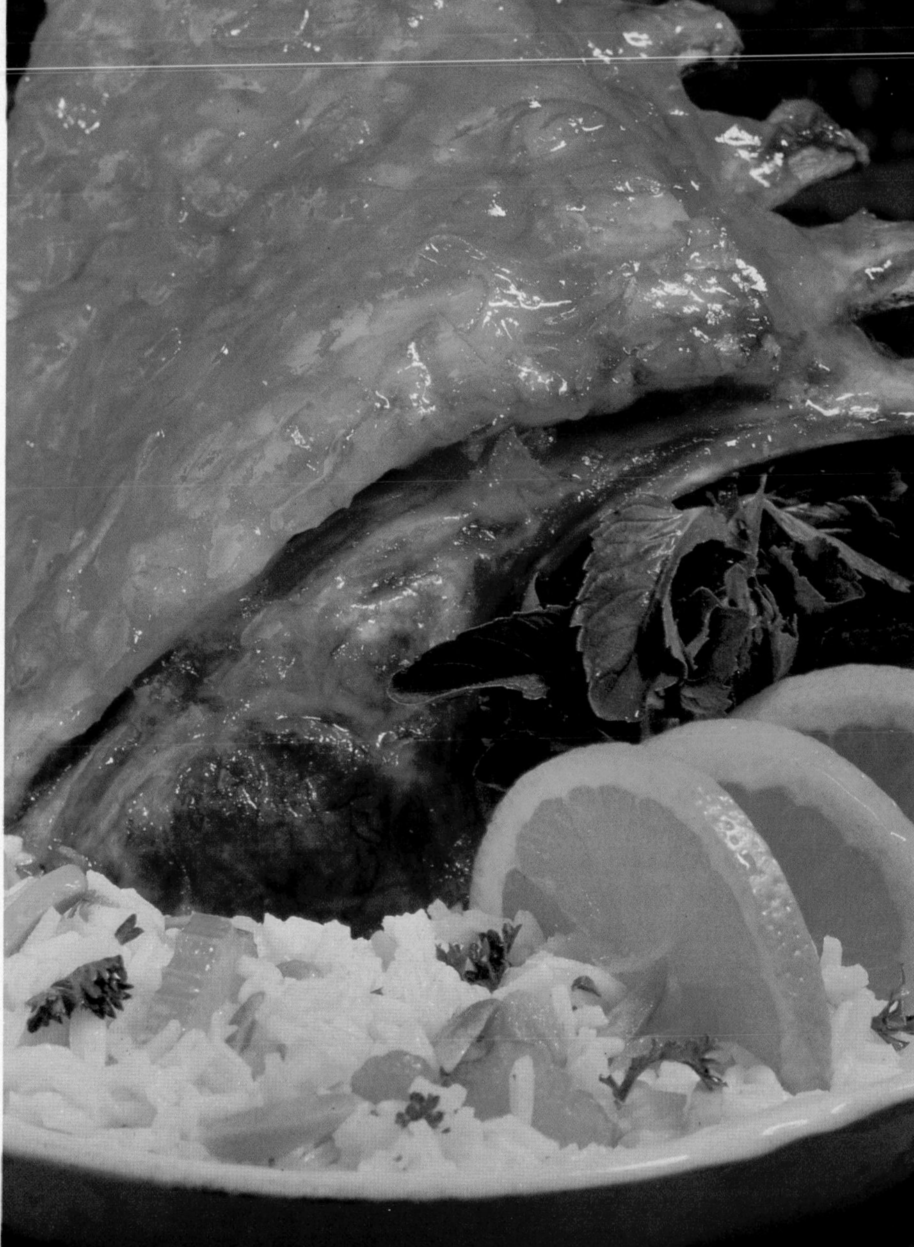

MEATS

BUYING

The greatest part of most food budgets usually is spent for meat, so naturally you want to get the best food value.

The price per lb. is not always the best clue to the bargain value of a meat cut. Since the number of servings that can be obtained from 1 lb. will depend upon the amount of bone and fat waste, the best way to figure the value of your meat is on the basis of the COST PER SERVING, not cost per lb.

Guide for Amount of Meat to Purchase:

You may use the following as a general guide. Take into consideration your family's eating habits and the other foods that will be served with the meal.

Fresh meat with no bone and very little fat – ¼ to ⅓ lb. per serving.

Fresh meat with small amount of bone and little fat – ⅓ to ½ lb. per serving.

Fresh meat with large amount of bone and little fat – ½ to ¾ lb. per serving.

STORAGE

- Store in the coldest part of refrigerator without actually freezing the meat.
- Prepackaged meats can be stored in the refrigerator in their original wrappings for 1 to 2 days. For longer storage, unwrap meat and cover loosely – some air helps retard bacteria growth. See Storage Chart.
- You can freeze meat in original packaging for short storage, 1 to 2 weeks. For longer storage, overwrap or rewrap the meat in moisture-vapor proof material and store in freezer at 0°F. or lower. See Storage Chart. Do not freeze canned meats in the can; seams may break.
- Meat which has not been tightly wrapped before freezing may appear whitish and dry with "freezer burn". It is not harmful, but the meat may be tough and tasteless after cooking.
- To judge when meat is spoiled, it changes from a bright red or pink to a dull gray color. The surface may become slippery, and it develops a pronounced off-odor. Spoiled meat should be discarded.

Storage Time Chart for Fresh and Processed Meats
(see page 455 for Freezing Cooked Meats)

Meat	Freezing at 0°F. or lower* (months)	Refrigerator at 35°F. to 40°F. (days)
Fresh Beef or Lamb	6 - 12	2 - 4
Fresh Veal	6 - 9	2 - 4
Fresh Pork	3 - 6	2 - 4
Ground Beef, Lamb or Veal	3 - 4	1 - 2
Ground Pork	1 - 3	1 - 2
Fresh Pork Sausage	2	7
Variety Meats	3 - 4	1 - 2
Bacon	1	5 - 7
Corned Beef	½	7
Ham, Whole	2	7
Ham Slices	2	3 - 4
Luncheon Meat	Not recommended	7
Wieners	1	4 - 5

*Some refrigerator freezers do not reach 0°F. Meat can still be frozen above 0°F., but should not be kept for the maximum time. Consult operator's manual for information on the freezing temperature of your freezer.

*We wish to express our appreciation to the National Livestock and Meat Board for the use of the LESSONS ON MEAT book as a reference and source book.

Thawing Time

Frozen meat should be left wrapped while defrosting in the refrigerator. Allow about 4 to 7 hours per lb. for a large roast, 3 to 5 hours per lb. for a small roast and 12 to 14 hours for a 1-inch steak. Also see Microwave Defrosting, page 386.

Cooking Frozen Meat

Recipes in this book assume that the meat is not frozen or has been defrosted. It is possible, however to cook meat from the frozen state. Frozen roasts must cook about ⅓ to ½ longer. A meat thermometer (inserted after thawing during cooking) is your best indicator for doneness.

Additional time required to cook frozen steaks, chops or patties depends on the thickness and surface area. To broil, place frozen meat directly on grill.

Meats to be breaded or floured must be partially thawed so breading mixture will adhere to the surface.

Meat Labels

The government requires that all meat and meat products transported across state lines sold commercially be inspected federally. Inspection is to guarantee consumers that the meat is wholesome and has been processed under sanitary conditions. A stamp appears on all wholesale cuts which pass federal inspection.

In addition to being inspected, meat and meat products may be graded for quality. The top grade of beef, USDA PRIME, is most frequently used by restaurants and hotels, although some supermarkets and specialty stores carry it. Most beef which is found in supermarkets is graded USDA CHOICE or USDA GOOD. The grading of meat is voluntary.

BEEF

When selecting cuts of beef, keep in mind the cooking method – tender cuts can be cooked to rare or well done; less tender cuts need to be tenderized by marinating or by long, slow cooking with liquid.

High quality beef should have abundant marbling of fat throughout the lean, be fine-textured and light to deep red in color, with smooth white fat.

ROASTS

Tender roasts are from the animal's back area where the meat muscles receive little exercise. The flavor of these cuts is best when the meat is cooked without added moisture. RIB ROASTS and TENDERLOIN ROASTS are two common types available.

STANDING RIB ROAST contains back and rib bones. For ease in carving, have your meat man loosen the backbone and tie the roast. In restaurants, this roast is usually referred to as "Prime Rib".

ROLLED RIB ROAST is a standing rib roast which has been boned, rolled and tied.

RIB EYE or DELMONICO ROAST is the large meaty rib muscle with outer fat layer and bones removed.

TENDERLOIN ROAST is usually the most tender muscle and one of the smallest parts of the dressed beef. It is generally quite expensive, but has no bone or waste. For a roast, the tenderloin is left whole, making a long, tapering roast.

Use this guide for Rib, Rolled Rib, Rib Eye or Whole Beef Tenderloin Roasts.

Set oven at 325°F., do not cover pan.

Weight	Doneness	Thermom-eter Reading	Approximate Cooking Time per lb.
4 to 6 lb.	rare	140°F.	26-32 min.
	medium	160°F.	34-38 min.
	well	170°F.	40-42 min.
6 to 8 lb.	rare	140°F.	23-25 min.
	medium	160°F.	27-30 min.
	well	170°F.	32-35 min.

RIB ROAST*

Heat oven to 325°F. Season meat with salt and pepper. Place roast, fat-side-up, on rack in shallow roasting pan. Insert meat thermometer so the bulb reaches the center of the largest muscle, being sure that the bulb does not rest in fat or on bone. Roast, uncovered, as directed in chart. For ease in carving, allow roast to stand 15 minutes to set juices.

NUTRITION INFORMATION PER SERVING

Serving Size: 1/2 lb. rib roast with bone, cooked		Percent U.S. RDA Per Serving	
Calories	673	Protein	47%
Protein	30g	Vitamin A	2%
Carbohydrate	0g	Vitamin C	0%
Fat	60g	Thiamin	5%
Sodium	74mg	Riboflavin	13%
Potassium	340mg	Niacin	28%
		Calcium	*
		Iron	22%

TIP: *Allow ½ to ¾ lb. per serving for Rib Roast and ⅓ to ½ lb. per serving for Rolled Rib Roast.*

CARVING STANDING RIB ROAST

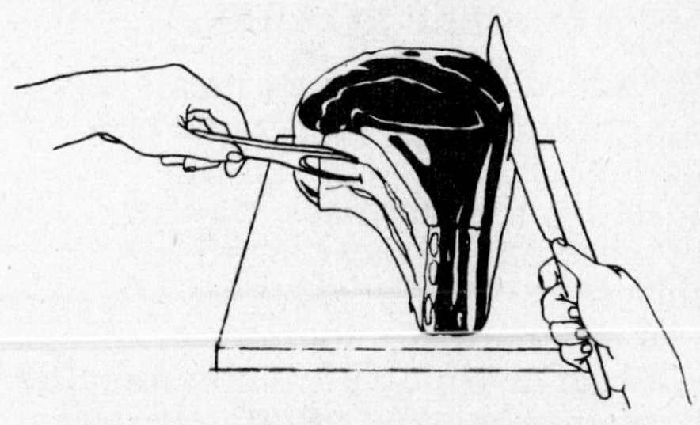

1. Slice from outside toward rib bone.

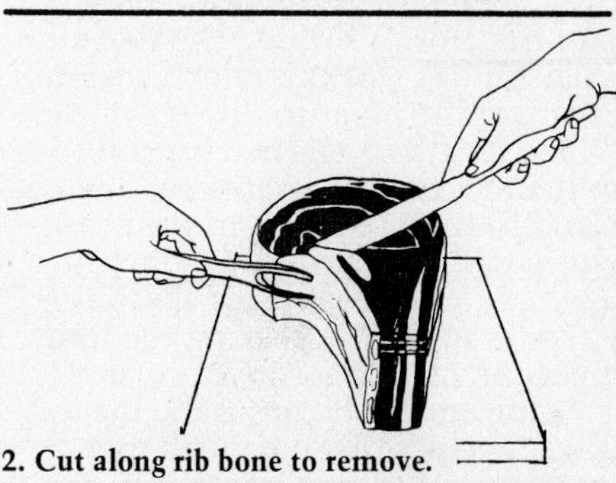

2. Cut along rib bone to remove.

ROAST WHOLE BEEF TENDERLOIN

Heat oven to 425°F. Remove excess surface fat and connective tissue from tenderloin; season with salt and pepper. Place roast on rack in shallow roasting pan. Turn thin ends under and brush roast with oil or margarine. Insert meat thermometer so the bulb reaches the thickest part. Roast uncovered 45 to 60 minutes or until meat thermometer registers 140°F. To serve, cut across grain into slices.

NUTRITION INFORMATION PER SERVING

Serving Size: 1/3 lb. raw beef tenderloin		Percent U.S. RDA Per Serving	
Calories	197	Protein	35%
Protein	23g	Vitamin A	0%
Carbohydrate	0g	Vitamin C	0%
Fat	11g	Thiamin	6%
Sodium	40mg	Riboflavin	24%
Potassium	384mg	Niacin	15%
		Calcium	*
		Iron	19%

TIP: *Allow approximately ⅓ to ½ lb. per serving.*

MARINADES FOR BEEF ROASTS

For added flavor, tender meats are marinated before roasting or preparing on a rotisserie. During roasting, the marinade may be brushed on the meat for added flavor.

If the marinade contains acid (vinegar or wine), use a non-metallic container to avoid reaction between the acid and metal. A deep bowl that fits closely around the roast or a plastic bag works well. Occasionally turn the meat to flavor evenly.

The length of marinating time will affect the penetration of flavors. Usually 12 to 18 hours in the refrigerator or 2 to 3 hours at room temperature are adequate for seasoning a tender roast. Marinating too long gives the meat a soft texture and overpowers the flavor of the meat. These recipes make enough marinade for a 4 to 5-lb. roast. After marinating meat, remove it from marinade and roast using Roasting Chart, page 297, until of desired degree of doneness.

PEPPER MARINADE

2 to 3 tablespoons coarse ground pepper
1 garlic clove, crushed
½ cup soy sauce
¼ cup dry white wine

Press pepper into roast with heel of hand. In small bowl, combine remaining ingredients; mix well.
¾ cup

BEER MARINADE

1½ tablespoons grated lemon peel
1 teaspoon sage leaves, if desired
½ teaspoon salt
¼ teaspoon pepper
1 medium onion, chopped
12-oz. can (1½ cups) beer

In small bowl, combine all ingredients; mix well. 2 cups

WINE MARINADE

1 tablespoon dry mustard
½ teaspoon marjoram, thyme or basil leaves
2 garlic cloves, minced
1 cup dry red wine
¼ cup oil
2 tablespoons soy sauce

In small bowl, combine all ingredients; mix well. 1⅓ cups

POT ROASTS

Pot roasts are from the meaty areas of a beef animal that receive more exercise which develops flavor and connective tissue. These areas are the shoulder (chuck) and hip (rump). Pot roasts are cooked with liquid to soften and tenderize the connective tissues.

CHUCK ROAST is the term used for a beef roast that comes from the shoulder. There are two shapes of bone. Blade bone connects to the shoulder and has the familiar blade shape. Arm bone comes from the front leg of the animal and is the round bone near the center of a roast. Chuck roasts have many small muscles running in various directions while rump roasts have much larger muscles.

NUTRITION INFORMATION PER SERVING

Serving Size: 3 oz. cooked lean chuck roast		Percent U.S. RDA Per Serving	
Calories	164	Protein	40%
Protein	26g	Vitamin A	*
Carbohydrate	0g	Vitamin C	†
Fat	6g	Thiamin	3%
Sodium	45mg	Riboflavin	12%
Potassium	207mg	Niacin	19%
		Calcium	*
		Iron	18%

NUTRITION INFORMATION PER SERVING

Serving Size: 3 oz. cooked lean rump roast		Percent U.S. RDA Per Serving	
Calories	177	Protein	38%
Protein	25g	Vitamin A	*
Carbohydrate	0g	Vitamin C	†
Fat	8g	Thiamin	4%
Sodium	61mg	Riboflavin	11%
Potassium	277mg	Niacin	22%
		Calcium	*
		Iron	17%

RUMP ROASTS make good pot roasts. They usually cost a little more per pound, but normally have less waste from fat and bone and are easier to carve for special occasions. Other cuts from this same area include SIRLOIN TIP, EYE OF ROUND and HEEL OF ROUND.

Most pot roasts are available with or without the bone. If the roast is boneless, you will get more servings from the same size roast.

BASIC POT ROAST

1 to 2 tablespoons oil
3 to 3½-lb. pot roast
2 teaspoons salt
¼ teaspoon pepper
4 medium onions, sliced
3 stalks celery, cut into pieces
1 bay leaf
1½ cups water
6 medium carrots, cut into pieces
4 medium potatoes, peeled and halved

In Dutch oven, brown meat in hot oil. Add salt, pepper, 1 onion, 1 stalk celery, bay leaf and water. Simmer covered, 2 to 2½ hours or until meat is tender. Add remaining vegetables; simmer 45 to 60 minutes or until tender. Remove meat and vegetables to platter. If desired, thicken juices with 3 tablespoons flour mixed with ¼ cup water. Stir into juices. Heat until mixture boils and thickens, stirring constantly. Serve with meat. 6 servings

NUTRITION INFORMATION PER SERVING

Serving Size: 1/6 of recipe		Percent U.S. RDA Per Serving	
Calories	499	Protein	43%
Protein	28g	Vitamin A	114%
Carbohydrate	29g	Vitamin C	54%
Fat	30g	Thiamin	14%
Sodium	832mg	Riboflavin	17%
Potassium	1119mg	Niacin	31%
		Calcium	7%
		Iron	25%

TIPS: *Dry red wine (about ½ cup) may be used for part of water.*

For BEER-FLAVORED POT ROAST, omit bay leaf and water and add 12-oz. can (1½ cups) beer.

POT ROAST IN FOIL

3 to 4-lb. pot roast
1 pkg. dry onion soup mix

Heat oven to 350°F. Place meat in center of a piece of double thick or heavy duty extra wide foil; sprinkle with dry soup mix. Bring edges of foil together and seal completely with double folds. Place seam-side-up in shallow baking pan. Bake at 350°F. for 2½ to 3 hours or until meat is tender.

6 to 8 servings

NUTRITION INFORMATION PER SERVING

Serving Size: 1/6 of recipe		Percent U.S. RDA Per Serving	
Calories	426	Protein	43%
Protein	28g	Vitamin A	*
Carbohydrate	4g	Vitamin C	*
Fat	32g	Thiamin	5%
Sodium	547mg	Riboflavin	13%
Potassium	467mg	Niacin	25%
		Calcium	*
		Iron	20%

TIPS: *For variety, add one of the following with the soup; sliced fresh or canned mushrooms, sliced celery, sliced carrots or green pepper rings.*

Roast may be baked in covered casserole rather than foil; potatoes, carrots or rutabagas may be added during last hour of cooking.

For an extra saucy roast baked in covered casserole without foil wrap, 1 can condensed cream of mushroom soup may be added.

For smaller roasts, add only half of the package of dry soup mix.

COMPANY POT ROAST

1 to 2 tablespoons oil
2½ to 3-lb. pot roast
1 medium onion, sliced
2 tablespoons sugar
1 cube or 1 teaspoon beef bouillon
1 stick cinnamon
1½ cups water
⅓ cup dry sherry
¼ cup soy sauce
8 carrots, halved lengthwise
4 potatoes, peeled and halved

In large skillet or Dutch oven, brown roast and onion in hot oil. Add remaining ingredients except carrots and potatoes. Simmer covered, 2 to 3 hours or until meat is tender. Add carrots and potatoes; simmer covered, 30 minutes or until vegetables are tender. Occasionally spoon juices over vegetables. If desired, thicken juices with 1½ tablespoons cornstarch mixed with ¼ cup cold water. Stir into juices. Heat mixture until it boils and thickens, stirring constantly. Serve with meat.

5 to 6 servings

NUTRITION INFORMATION PER SERVING

Serving Size: 1/5 of recipe

		Percent U.S. RDA Per Serving	
Calories	718	Protein	59%
Protein	38g	Vitamin A	287%
Carbohydrate	43g	Vitamin C	37%
Fat	42g	Thiamin	19%
Sodium	1406mg	Riboflavin	24%
Potassium	1556mg	Niacin	44%
		Calcium	9%
		Iron	38%

TIPS: *If meat becomes dry, add additional water.*

Skim off excess fat if necessary.

POT ROAST MILANO

2 tablespoons oil
3 to 4-lb. pot roast
1 teaspoon salt
½ teaspoon celery seed, if desired
½ teaspoon basil leaves or Italian seasoning
¼ teaspoon pepper
1 large onion, sliced
1 garlic clove, minced
1 cup Burgundy or dry red wine
8-oz. can (1 cup) tomato sauce
2 tablespoons flour
½ cup water

In large skillet or Dutch oven, brown meat in hot oil. Combine salt, celery seed, basil, pepper, onion, garlic, wine and tomato sauce; add to meat. Simmer covered 2½ to 3 hours or until tender. Remove meat to platter. Combine flour and water; stir into liquid in pan. Heat until mixture boils and thickens, stirring constantly. If necessary, thin with additional water. Spoon sauce over pot roast. Serve with spaghetti, buttered noodles or mashed potatoes.

6 to 8 servings

NUTRITION INFORMATION PER SERVING

Serving Size: 1/6 of recipe

		Percent U.S. RDA Per Serving	
Calories	542	Protein	59%
Protein	38g	Vitamin A	13%
Carbohydrate	11g	Vitamin C	6%
Fat	34g	Thiamin	8%
Sodium	442mg	Riboflavin	20%
Potassium	609mg	Niacin	31%
		Calcium	4%
		Iron	30%

TIP: *If desired, 2 cubes or 2 teaspoons beef bouillon and 1 cup water may be substituted for Burgundy.*

SAUERBRATEN

3 to 3½-lb. pot roast
1 cup red wine vinegar
1½ cups water
1 medium onion, sliced
1 stalk celery, sliced
5 whole cloves
2 bay leaves
3 teaspoons salt
4 peppercorns or ¼ teaspoon pepper
2 tablespoons oil
2 tablespoons firmly packed brown sugar
6 gingersnaps, crushed

Place meat in glass bowl. Add remaining ingredients except oil, brown sugar and gingersnaps. Cover and marinate in refrigerator 24 to 48 hours, turning meat several times to season evenly. Remove meat from marinade; drain well. In large skillet or Dutch oven, brown meat on all sides in hot oil. Add 1½ cups strained marinade. Simmer covered, 2½ to 3 hours or until tender. Place meat on warm platter. Spoon fat off juice; add brown sugar and gingersnaps. Cook until mixture comes to a boil, stirring constantly. If necessary, thin with water or remaining marinade. Pour over meat. Serve with potato dumplings, boiled potatoes or potato pancakes. 6 to 8 servings

NUTRITION INFORMATION PER SERVING

Serving Size: 1/8 of recipe		Percent U.S. RDA Per Serving	
Calories	224	Protein	37%
Protein	24g	Vitamin A	*
Carbohydrate	11g	Vitamin C	2%
Fat	9g	Thiamin	4%
Sodium	885mg	Riboflavin	11%
Potassium	393mg	Niacin	18%
		Calcium	3%
		Iron	19%

BRISKET

Brisket is available "fresh" or "corned". The meat is made up of long fibers similar to the flank, but thicker. Usually the bones have been removed and it is sold as BONELESS BRISKET. To tenderize the meat, long slow simmering is necessary and the meat should be carved into thin slices across the grain.

CORNED BEEF has been cured to give the distinct "corned beef" flavor. Unless already tenderized, it should be slowly simmered with liquid. Since salt is added during the curing process, additional salt is not needed during cooking.

To carve a brisket, cut across the grain in thin slices.

BRISKET

Brisket may be cooked covered with water. Add a bay leaf, 1½ teaspoons salt and 1 teaspoon peppercorns to the water; simmer 3 to 3½ hours. After cooking, serve plain or topped with a glaze. The brisket may be cooked one day, then glazed and heated the following day. These glazes may also be used on cooked whole corned beef.

NUTRITION INFORMATION PER SERVING

Serving Size: 1/4 lb. boneless beef brisket, cooked		Percent U.S. RDA Per Serving	
Calories	543	Protein	35%
Protein	23g	Vitamin A	0%
Carbohydrate	0g	Vitamin C	0%
Fat	49g	Thiamin	3%
Sodium	69mg	Riboflavin	17%
Potassium	376mg	Niacin	24%
		Calcium	*
		Iron	0%

TIP: *Allow approximately ⅓ to ½ lb. per serving.*

HONEY-SPICE GLAZE

¼ cup barbecue sauce
¼ cup soy sauce
2 tablespoons honey

Heat oven to 350°F. In small bowl, combine all ingredients; mix well. Spread on cooked brisket. Bake uncovered at 350°F. for 30 to 40 minutes, basting occasionally with pan juices.

½ cup

NUTRITION INFORMATION PER SERVING

Serving Size: 1/12 of recipe		Percent U.S. RDA Per Serving	
Calories	19	Protein	*
Protein	<1g	Vitamin A	*
Carbohydrate	4g	Vitamin C	*
Fat	<1g	Thiamin	*
Sodium	485mg	Riboflavin	*
Potassium	33mg	Niacin	*
		Calcium	*
		Iron	*

BARBECUED BRISKET OF BEEF

5 to 6-lb. beef brisket
3½-oz. bottle liquid smoke
Garlic salt
Onion salt
Celery salt
18-oz. bottle barbecue sauce
Salt
Pepper
Worcestershire sauce

Place brisket in 13x9-inch baking dish; pour liquid smoke on meat. Sprinkle all sides of brisket generously with garlic salt, onion salt and celery salt. Cover and refrigerate 6 to 8 hours. Drain liquid smoke. Heat oven to 250°F. Pour barbecue sauce over meat. Sprinkle with salt, pepper and Worcestershire sauce. Bake covered with foil at 250°F. for 4 to 5 hours or until tender. Sauce may be thickened and served with meat.

12 to 15 servings

NUTRITION INFORMATION PER SERVING

Serving Size: 1/15 of recipe		Percent U.S. RDA Per Serving	
Calories	470	Protein	29%
Protein	19g	Vitamin A	2%
Carbohydrate	3g	Vitamin C	3%
Fat	42g	Thiamin	2%
Sodium	457mg	Riboflavin	14%
Potassium	363mg	Niacin	20%
		Calcium	*
		Iron	*

TIP: *Cut meat in thin diagonal slices across grain at a slanting angle.*

NEW ENGLAND BOILED DINNER

- **3 lb. corned beef**
- **1 teaspoon peppercorns or ¼ teaspoon pepper**
- **6 whole cloves**
- **1 bay leaf**
- **6 potatoes, peeled and quartered**
- **6 carrots, halved lengthwise**
- **1 medium head cabbage, cut into 6 wedges**

In large saucepan, cover corned beef with water. Add peppercorns, cloves and bay leaf. Simmer covered, 3 to 3½ hours or until tender. Add potatoes and carrots. Simmer covered, 15 minutes longer. Add cabbage; cook 15 minutes or until vegetables are tender. Remove bay leaf. Cut meat into pieces. Serve with cooking liquid and vegetables.

6 to 8 servings

NUTRITION INFORMATION PER SERVING

Serving Size: 1/8 of recipe		Percent U.S. RDA Per Serving	
Calories	529	Protein	45%
Protein	30g	Vitamin A	121%
Carbohydrate	24g	Vitamin C	68%
Fat	35g	Thiamin	11%
Sodium	2022mg	Riboflavin	16%
Potassium	773mg	Niacin	17%
		Calcium	7%
		Iron	25%

TIP: *If corned beef is packaged with spice packet, omit peppercorns, cloves and bay leaf.*

LEFTOVER BEEF ROAST

Leftover beef? Turn it into a new dish with one of these ideas or serve it with a sauce from the Sauce Chapter. Beef is especially good with: Brown Sauce, Bordelaise Sauce, Mushroom Sauce, Creamy Mustard Sauce, Hot Catsup Sauce, Horseradish Sauce, Mustard Sauce or Buttery Steak Sauce.

QUICK BEEF AND VEGETABLE STEW

- **4 cups cooked cubed beef**
- **3 potatoes, cut into 1-inch cubes**
- **3 carrots, cut into 1-inch cubes**
- **1 onion, quartered**
- **¾ cup water**
- **10¾-oz. can condensed golden mushroom soup**
- **10-oz. pkg. (1½ cups) frozen peas, if desired**

In large saucepan, combine all ingredients except peas. Simmer covered, 20 minutes. Add peas and continue cooking 15 minutes or until vegetables are tender.

4 to 6 servings

NUTRITION INFORMATION PER SERVING

Serving Size: 1/6 of recipe		Percent U.S. RDA Per Serving	
Calories	456	Protein	45%
Protein	29g	Vitamin A	86%
Carbohydrate	24g	Vitamin C	21%
Fat	27g	Thiamin	17%
Sodium	520mg	Riboflavin	19%
Potassium	791mg	Niacin	29%
		Calcium	6%
		Iron	26%

TIPS: *If desired, substitute 1 pkg. dry onion soup mix for mushroom soup, adding 1¼ cups water.*

Try other vegetables, or use leftover vegetables. Add to stew during last 5 to 10 minutes of cooking time.

OLD-FASHIONED HASH

2 tablespoons shortening or oil
1 medium onion, chopped
3 cups cooked diced potatoes
3 cups cooked finely diced beef
1 teaspoon salt
⅛ teaspoon pepper
½ cup gravy
2 tablespoons catsup
½ teaspoon prepared mustard

In large skillet, melt shortening. Cook onion in hot shortening until tender. Stir in remaining ingredients. Cook until well browned, about 10 minutes. Turn and brown other side. 6 servings

NUTRITION INFORMATION PER SERVING

Serving Size: 1/6 of recipe		Percent U.S. RDA Per Serving	
Calories	385	Protein	32%
Protein	21g	Vitamin A	2%
Carbohydrate	17g	Vitamin C	15%
Fat	26g	Thiamin	9%
Sodium	698mg	Riboflavin	16%
Potassium	557mg	Niacin	19%
		Calcium	2%
		Iron	17

TENDER STEAKS

Like tender roasts, tender steaks are cut from the back section of the beef. The tender steaks include: RIB, CLUB, T-BONE, PORTERHOUSE, SIRLOIN and TENDERLOIN.

Starting nearest the shoulder, the first are the RIB STEAKS with the characteristic rib bone along one side. Near the rib section are the CLUB STEAKS which resemble the rib, but may begin to show a little tenderloin outside of the rib bone. The next steaks are T-BONE, where the rib bone resembles a T-shape. The small tenderloin is evident. PORTERHOUSE STEAKS are like T-bone, but larger in size. The tenderloin muscle is largest in this steak.

SIRLOIN STEAKS are next to the rump area, large in size and usually with a wedge-shaped bone (hip bone). The largest muscle in sirloin steak is sometimes separated and sold as TOP SIRLOIN or STRIP STEAK.

Tender steaks may be broiled, grilled or pan-fried to desired doneness or cut into cubes or strips and cooked quickly for sukiyaki or fondue.

TIMETABLE FOR BROILED STEAKS

		Approximate Total Cooking Time	
Steak	**Thickness**	**Rare (140°F.)**	**Medium (160°F.)**
Rib, rib eye or club	1 inch	15 min.	20 min.
	1½ inches	25 min.	30 min.
	2 inches	35 min.	45 min.
Sirloin, porterhouse or T-bone	1 inch	20 min.	25 min.
	1½ inches	30 min.	35 min.
	2 inches	40 min.	45 min.
Tenderloin (filet mignon)	1 inch	10 min.	15 min.
	2 inches	15 min.	20 min.

When buying steak, allow ½ to ¾ lb. per serving of meat with a bone; ⅓ to ½ lb. per serving of boneless steak.

BROILED STEAK

Place steak on broiler pan. Place or adjust broiler pan so the top of a 1-inch steak is 2 to 3 inches from the heat and a 2-inch steak, 3 to 5 inches from the heat. When one side is browned, season with salt and pepper, then turn and finish cooking (see timetable) on the second side. Season with salt and pepper.

NUTRITION INFORMATION PER SERVING

Serving Size: 1/2 lb. beef steak with bone, cooked

		Percent U.S. RDA Per Serving	
Calories	397	Protein	67%
Protein	43g	Vitamin A	*
Carbohydrate	0g	Vitamin C	0%
Fat	23g	Thiamin	8%
Sodium	51mg	Riboflavin	20%
Potassium	260mg	Niacin	43%
		Calcium	*
		Iron	30%

DRESS-UPS FOR TENDER STEAKS

TRAFALGAR STEAK

½ teaspoon garlic salt
2 to 3 teaspoons prepared horseradish
½ cup dairy sour cream

Broil or grill steak. In small saucepan, combine garlic salt, horseradish and sour cream. Heat, stirring constantly, but do not boil. Serve steak with warm dip. 4 servings

NUTRITION INFORMATION PER SERVING

Serving Size: 1/4 of recipe without steak

		Percent U.S. RDA Per Serving	
Calories	58	Protein	*
Protein	<1g	Vitamin A	5%
Carbohydrate	1g	Vitamin C	0%
Fat	5g	Thiamin	*
Sodium	250mg	Riboflavin	2%
Potassium	7mg	Niacin	0%
		Calcium	3%
		Iron	*

STEAK DIANE

1 tablespoon chopped chives
2 tablespoons Chablis or dry sherry
2 tablespoons steak sauce
2 tablespoons cognac or brandy

Broil or grill steak. In small bowl, combine chives, Chablis and steak sauce. When steak is done, place on platter and spoon sauce over top. In long handled saucepan, quickly warm cognac *just* until vapors rise from mixture. Ignite and spoon or pour flaming mixture over steak. 4 servings

NUTRITION INFORMATION PER SERVING

Serving Size: 1/4 of recipe without steak

		Percent U.S. RDA Per Serving	
Calories	31	Protein	*
Protein	<1g	Vitamin A	*
Carbohydrate	2g	Vitamin C	*
Fat	<1g	Thiamin	*
Sodium	142mg	Riboflavin	*
Potassium	51mg	Niacin	*
		Calcium	*
		Iron	*

STEAK CHAMPIGNON

1 to 2 tablespoons margarine or butter
½ cup dairy sour cream
¼ cup dry red wine or milk
4-oz. can (½ cup) mushrooms, drained and sliced

In large skillet, fry 1 to 1½-inch thick steak, in margarine until desired doneness. Remove steak to platter, season and keep warm. Add remaining ingredients to pan drippings. Heat, stirring constantly, but do not boil. Spoon over steak. 4 servings

NUTRITION INFORMATION PER SERVING

Serving Size: 1/4 of recipe without steak

		Percent U.S. RDA Per Serving	
Calories	99	Protein	*
Protein	1g	Vitamin A	7%
Carbohydrate	2g	Vitamin C	0%
Fat	8g	Thiamin	*
Sodium	48mg	Riboflavin	6%
Potassium	14mg	Niacin	2%
		Calcium	3%
		Iron	*

PROVINCIAL STEAK WITH TOMATOES

2 tablespoons margarine or butter
2 tablespoons green onions, chopped
2 tablespoons minced parsley
½ teaspoon garlic salt
2 tablespoons dry white wine or vermouth
2 tomatoes, thinly sliced

About 5 minutes before steak is done, melt margarine in saucepan. Add onions, parsley, garlic salt and wine. Heat to boiling; add tomatoes and cook just until heated. Serve with seasoned steak. 4 servings

NUTRITION INFORMATION PER SERVING

Serving Size: 1/4 of recipe without steak		Percent U.S. RDA Per Serving	
Calories	73	Protein	*
Protein	<1g	Vitamin A	19%
Carbohydrate	4g	Vitamin C	21%
Fat	6g	Thiamin	3%
Sodium	300mg	Riboflavin	*
Potassium	178mg	Niacin	2%
		Calcium	*
		Iron	3%

CAESAR'S STEAK: Brush 6-oz. steak with 2 tablespoons Caesar salad dressing before and during broiling or grilling. When done, sprinkle steak with 1 tablespoon grated Parmesan cheese and season to taste. Creamy onion salad dressing may be substituted for Caesar salad dressing.

NUTRITION INFORMATION PER SERVING

Serving Size: 6-oz. steak		Percent U.S. RDA Per Serving	
Calories	489	Protein	54%
Protein	35g	Vitamin A	*
Carbohydrate	2g	Vitamin C	0%
Fat	37g	Thiamin	6%
Sodium	774mg	Riboflavin	17%
Potassium	430mg	Niacin	33%
		Calcium	7%
		Iron	23%

STEAK AU POIVRE: Using heel of hand, press coarsely ground pepper (if you don't have a peppermill, crush peppercorns with rolling pin) into each side of 6-oz. steak (about 1 teaspoon per steak). Broil or pan fry steak. Season with ¼ teaspoon salt. If desired, add 2 tablespoons cognac or brandy to skillet; mix with juices and pour over steak (for broiled steak, warm cognac slightly and spoon over steak).

NUTRITION INFORMATION PER SERVING

Serving Size: 6-oz. steak		Percent U.S. RDA Per Serving	
Calories	376	Protein	51%
Protein	33g	Vitamin A	*
Carbohydrate	1g	Vitamin C	*
Fat	18g	Thiamin	6%
Sodium	613mg	Riboflavin	15%
Potassium	430mg	Niacin	33%
		Calcium	*
		Iron	25%

BEEF FONDUE

For each serving allow about ½ lb. boneless sirloin or tenderloin, cut into 1-inch cubes. Arrange cubes of meat in individual dishes lined with lettuce leaves; place at each setting. Prepare 3 or 4 sauces. (Make your own–see recipes in Sauce Chapter –or try prepared steak sauces, horseradish sauce, cocktail dips, mustard sauce, teriyaki sauce or blue cheese salad dressing.) Place fondue pot in center of table. Heat oil to about 375°F. or until it browns a cube of bread quickly. Place fondue pot over heating unit. (If using electric fondue pot, heat oil in fondue pot.)

Each guest uses fondue fork to spear meat and cook it in hot oil until of desired doneness. Remove to plate and eat with dinner fork (the fondue fork becomes very hot in the oil), dipping meat into desired sauces. For an added treat, pass a bowl of chopped salted peanuts along with sauces. 4 servings

NUTRITION INFORMATION PER SERVING

Serving Size: 1/4 of recipe without sauces or condiments

Percent U.S. RDA Per Serving

Calories	640	Protein	59%
Protein	38g	Vitamin A	*
Carbohydrate	0g	Vitamin C	0%
Fat	53g	Thiamin	7%
Sodium	99mg	Riboflavin	18%
Potassium	612mg	Niacin	39%
		Calcium	*
		Iron	27%

TIPS: *Try other types of fondue–cubes of lamb served with chutney, sweet-sour and curry sauces; thawed and well-drained fresh or frozen shrimp served with cocktail, sweet-sour and curry sauces; or cubes of boneless chicken breast served with sweet-sour, chive butter and curry sauces.*

For vegetables with fondue, add whole fresh mushrooms or sliced zucchini to dishes of meat. Each guest cooks vegetable along with meat.

If oil becomes too cool, place on burner for a few minutes to reheat.

Leftover oil may be strained and stored in refrigerator to be used the next time fondue is served or for other frying.

Suggested recipes from Sauce Chapter:
Brown Sauce
Bordelaise Sauce
Horseradish Sauce
Creamy Mustard Sauce
Mushroom Sauce

BEEF STROGANOFF

¼ cup flour
½ teaspoon salt
⅛ teaspoon pepper
1½ lb. beef sirloin, cut into thin strips
¼ cup shortening
10½-oz. can condensed beef bouillon or broth
3 tablespoons tomato juice
1 tablespoon prepared mustard
1 tablespoon Worcestershire sauce
4-oz. can (½ cup) sliced mushrooms, drained
1 cup dairy sour cream
¼ cup sherry, if desired

In large bowl or plastic bag, coat strips of sirloin with flour, salt and pepper mixture. In large skillet or Dutch oven, brown meat in hot shortening. Stir in bouillon, tomato juice, mustard, Worcestershire sauce and mushrooms. Heat to boiling; simmer covered, 20 to 30 minutes. Stir in sour cream and sherry; heat through but do not boil. Serve over rice or noodles. 4 to 6 servings

NUTRITION INFORMATION PER SERVING

Serving Size: 1/6 of recipe

Percent U.S. RDA Per Serving

Calories	308	Protein	31%
Protein	20g	Vitamin A	7%
Carbohydrate	8g	Vitamin C	2%
Fat	20g	Thiamin	7%
Sodium	631mg	Riboflavin	15%
Potassium	275mg	Niacin	22%
		Calcium	5%
		Iron	14%

SUKIYAKI

- **1 to 1½-lb. sirloin steak**
- **2 tablespoons oil**
- **3 tablespoons sugar**
- **½ teaspoon monosodium glutamate, if desired**
- **⅔ cup water**
- **½ cup soy sauce**
- **1 cup green onions, cut into 1-inch pieces**
- **2 medium onions, sliced**
- **6-oz. can (¾ cup) bamboo shoots, drained**
- **1½ cups (4 oz.) sliced fresh mushrooms or 8-oz. can (1 cup) mushrooms, drained**
- **16-oz. can (2 cups) bean sprouts, drained**
- **8-oz. can (⅔ cup) water chestnuts, sliced**

Cut meat into paper-thin slices across grain (freezing meat makes slicing easier), then into strips 1-inch wide. In large skillet or wok, brown meat in hot oil 2 to 3 minutes. Combine sugar, monosodium glutamate, water and soy sauce; pour over meat. Push meat to one side of skillet. Keeping ingredients separate, add green onions, onion slices and bamboo shoots; stir-fry 5 to 10 minutes or until vegetables are crisp-tender. Push vegetables to one side. Add mushrooms, bean sprouts and water chestnuts, still keeping ingredients separate. Cook 2 minutes or until heated through. Serve with rice.
4 servings

NUTRITION INFORMATION PER SERVING

Serving Size: 1/4 of recipe		Percent U.S. RDA Per Serving	
Calories	294	Protein	35%
Protein	23g	Vitamin A	*
Carbohydrate	27g	Vitamin C	10%
Fat	12g	Thiamin	13%
Sodium	2966mg	Riboflavin	24%
Potassium	659mg	Niacin	25%
		Calcium	8%
		Iron	28%

SKILLET BEEF BOURGUIGNONNE

1 tablespoon margarine or butter
1½-lb. sirloin steak*, cut into 1-inch cubes
4 oz. (1½ cups) sliced fresh mushrooms
1 small onion, sliced
1 garlic clove, minced
⅛ teaspoon pepper
½ to 1 green pepper, cut into 1-inch pieces
1¼-oz. pkg. dry beef-mushroom or onion soup mix
1 cup water
½ cup Burgundy or dry red wine
16-oz. can (2 cups) whole onions, drained

In large skillet, brown meat in margarine. Add mushrooms, onion and garlic; cook until tender. Add remaining ingredients; simmer covered, 15 to 20 minutes or until meat is tender, stirring occasionally. May be served with French bread, noodles or mashed potatoes.

4 to 5 servings

NUTRITION INFORMATION PER SERVING

Serving Size: 1/5 of recipe		Percent U.S. RDA Per Serving	
Calories	449	Protein	36%
Protein	23g	Vitamin A	5%
Carbohydrate	14g	Vitamin C	48%
Fat	31g	Thiamin	8%
Sodium	672mg	Riboflavin	16%
Potassium	607mg	Niacin	25%
		Calcium	5%
		Iron	19%

TIPS: **Stew meat may be substituted for sirloin. Increase water to 1½ cups and cook 1½ hours or until meat is tender, adding green pepper and wine during last 15 minutes of cooking time.*

To use cubed cooked beef, add 2 to 3 cups cubed beef with green pepper. Simmer 10 to 15 minutes or until heated through.

TERIYAKI BEEF

¼ cup sliced green onion
1 tablespoon brown sugar or honey
½ teaspoon ginger
1 garlic clove, minced
½ to ¾ cup soy sauce
¼ cup dry sherry
2 to 2½-lb. boneless sirloin steak*, cut into 1 to 1½-inch cubes

In medium bowl, combine all ingredients except steak; mix well. Add steak; stir to coat with marinade. Cover; let stand 2 hours at room temperature or several hours in refrigerator, turning meat occasionally. Thread meat on skewers. Broil 3 to 4 inches from heat or grill over hot coals until medium rare, turning occasionally. Serve with rice.

6 servings

Length of marinating time and surface area of meat present too many variables to accurately determine nutritional information.

TIPS: **Top or bottom round steak or flank steak, may be substituted for sirloin.*

Whole mushrooms may be marinated with steak and threaded with meat on skewers.

Steak may be left whole and marinated. Broil or grill as directed.

LESS TENDER STEAKS

Less tender steaks need to be marinated or simmered in liquid to soften the connective tissue. Like pot roast, these steaks come from areas of the animal that are well exercised. These areas include the chuck (shoulder) and rump (hip).

ROUND STEAK is from the rump section and has the characteristic round bone. It is composed of three distinct meat muscles. These muscles are often separated and sold as TOP ROUND STEAK, BOTTOM ROUND STEAK and EYE OF ROUND STEAK.

CHUCK STEAK is from the shoulder area and can contain either the blade or the arm bone. It can always be recognized by its many small muscles.

FLANK STEAK, a thin muscle with no bone and very little fat, can be marinated or simmered in liquid and cut across the long fibers into thin slices.

MARINADES FOR LESS TENDER STEAK

Less tender steak can be marinated in commercial tenderizers, in beer, or in a mixture containing lemon juice, vinegar or wine. The acid helps tenderize the tough connective tissues. Marinades are usually very flavorful and may also be used to add flavor to tender steak. No more than 2 hours is suggested for tender steaks; longer marinating can make the meat mushy.

Meats are marinated in a nonmetallic container to avoid a reaction between the metal and acid. It should be shallow enough for the steak to lie flat with as much area covered by the marinade as possible. If using a plastic bag, force out as much air as possible before closing and place it in a shallow dish to guard against leakage. Turn meat occasionally during marinating period to tenderize evenly.

These marinade recipes make enough for about 2 lb. of steak. To allow time to tenderize steak, marinate overnight (about 12 hours) in refrigerator or at room temperature 2 to 3 hours (the warmer room temperature speeds the tenderizing).

To serve, remove meat from marinade and broil or grill as directed in chart, page 304. Pan frying is not recommended because of excessive spattering from the liquid marinade in the hot fat. Marinated steak is most tender when cooked to medium rare doneness. Additional cooking toughens and dries the tender fibers, making the steak less tender.

BURGUNDY MARINADE

½ teaspoon salt
¼ teaspoon pepper
1 garlic clove, minced
½ cup oil
½ cup Burgundy or dry red wine
2 tablespoons catsup
2 tablespoons molasses

In small bowl, combine all ingredients; mix well. 1¼ cups

SOY MARINADE

½ teaspoon ginger
1 green onion, chopped, if desired
1 garlic clove, minced
¾ cup oil
¼ cup soy sauce
3 tablespoons honey or sugar
2 tablespoons vinegar or lemon juice

In small bowl, combine all ingredients; mix well. 1⅓ cups

LEMON-LIME MARINADE

2 limes
1 lemon
1 garlic clove, minced
½ cup oil

Cut limes and lemon into ½-inch slices. In medium saucepan, combine all ingredients. Heat over medium heat about 5 minutes or until hot, pressing fruit with back of spoon as it heats. Pour hot mixture over steak. 1 cup

SWISS STEAK

2 to 2½-lb. round steak, cut ½ to ¾-inch thick
¼ cup flour
1 teaspoon salt
¼ teaspoon pepper
1 to 2 tablespoons oil
1 large onion, sliced
7½-oz. can (1 cup) tomatoes, undrained, cut up
8-oz. can (1 cup) tomato sauce

Cut meat into serving pieces. In small bowl, combine flour, salt and pepper. Coat meat with seasoned flour (use all the flour). In large skillet, brown meat in hot oil. Add remaining ingredients; simmer covered, 1¼ to 1½ hours or until tender. Serve with potatoes or noodles. 6 servings

NUTRITION INFORMATION PER SERVING

Serving Size: 1/6 of recipe		Percent U.S. RDA Per Serving	
Calories	279	Protein	46%
Protein	30g	Vitamin A	19%
Carbohydrate	12g	Vitamin C	11%
Fat	12g	Thiamin	10%
Sodium	196mg	Riboflavin	16%
Potassium	462mg	Niacin	31%
		Calcium	3%
		Iron	22%

TIPS: *If desired, substitute one 10½-oz. can condensed tomato soup and ½ cup water for tomatoes and tomato sauce.*

Vegetables such as peas, beans or mushrooms may be added to Swiss Steak. Add peas and beans toward end of cooking; add mushrooms with onion.

BEEF IN OYSTER SAUCE

1½ to 2-lb. round steak
3 tablespoons flour
2 tablespoons oil
¼ cup sherry or water
10½-oz. can condensed oyster stew
4 green onions, sliced

Cut steak into serving pieces and coat with flour. In large skillet, brown meat in hot oil. Reduce heat. Sprinkle any remaining flour over meat. Add sherry and oyster stew. Simmer covered, 1 to 1¼ hours or until meat is tender. Add onions during last 10 minutes of cooking.

4 to 6 servings

NUTRITION INFORMATION PER SERVING

Serving Size: 1/4 of recipe		Percent U.S. RDA Per Serving	
Calories	450	Protein	53%
Protein	35g	Vitamin A	*
Carbohydrate	10g	Vitamin C	6%
Fat	27g	Thiamin	9%
Sodium	701mg	Riboflavin	17%
Potassium	474mg	Niacin	34%
		Calcium	2%
		Iron	24%

TIP: *For ORIENTAL BEEF IN OYSTER SAUCE, cut meat into small pieces. Prepare as directed, adding one 9-oz. pkg. frozen pea pods during last 10 minutes of cooking.*

BEEF BIRDS

2 to 2½-lb. (1 large or 2 small) flank or round steak, cut ½-inch thick
½ teaspoon salt
⅓ cup margarine or butter
1 medium onion, chopped
2 tablespoons chopped parsley
½ teaspoon poultry seasoning or sage
4 to 6 slices bread, cubed
2 tablespoons oil
½ cup water
10½-oz. can condensed beef consommé
2 tablespoons cornstarch or ¼ cup flour
¼ cup water

Cut steak into 6 equal portions. Season with salt. In large skillet, cook onion in margarine until tender. Remove from heat. Add parsley, poultry seasoning and bread cubes; mix well. Divide stuffing mixture among pieces of steak. Roll up steaks with stuffing inside and fasten with skewers, toothpicks or tie with a string. In same skillet, brown rolled steaks in hot oil. Add ½ cup water and consommé. Reduce heat; simmer covered, 1½ to 2 hours or until tender. Combine cornstarch with ¼ cup water; add to broth. Heat until gravy boils and thickens, stirring constantly.

6 servings

NUTRITION INFORMATION PER SERVING

Serving Size: 1/6 of recipe		Percent U.S. RDA Per Serving	
Calories	413	Protein	54%
Protein	35g	Vitamin A	11%
Carbohydrate	15g	Vitamin C	5%
Fat	23g	Thiamin	8%
Sodium	787mg	Riboflavin	17%
Potassium	495mg	Niacin	28%
		Calcium	4%
		Iron	26%

CITRUS SIMMERED STEAK

2 tablespoons oil
1¾ to 2-lb. top or bottom round steak, cut 1¾-inches thick
½ teaspoon salt
⅛ teaspoon thyme, if desired
1 medium onion, sliced
2 tablespoons barbecue sauce or catsup
1 tablespoon lemon juice
1 tablespoon soy sauce
4-oz. can (½ cup) mushroom stems and pieces, drained
1 tablespoon sugar
1 tablespoon cornstarch
¼ cup water
1 lemon, sliced

In large skillet, brown meat in hot oil. Add salt, thyme, onion, barbecue sauce, lemon juice, soy sauce and mushrooms. Simmer covered, 1½ to 2 hours or until meat is tender. In small bowl, combine sugar, cornstarch and water; mix well. Add cornstarch mixture and lemon slices to meat; stir to blend. Continue simmering until sauce thickens, stirring occasionally.

5 to 6 servings

NUTRITION INFORMATION PER SERVING

Serving Size: 1/6 of recipe		Percent U.S. RDA Per Serving	
Calories	297	Protein	39%
Protein	26g	Vitamin A	*
Carbohydrate	8g	Vitamin C	17%
Fat	18g	Thiamin	6%
Sodium	498mg	Riboflavin	14%
Potassium	425mg	Niacin	26%
		Calcium	3%
		Iron	20%

TIPS: *If desired, orange juice and orange slices may be used for the lemon.*

A chuck (arm or blade) pot roast may be substituted for the round steak. Cook 2 to 2½ hours. Skim excess fat before thickening sauce.

ROUND STEAK BARBECUE

1½ to 2-lb. round steak, cut ½ to ¾-inch thick
2 tablespoons oil
3 tablespoons sugar
2 teaspoons salt or seasoned salt
1 medium onion, chopped
½ cup water
3 tablespoons Worcestershire sauce
2 tablespoons prepared mustard
8-oz. can (1 cup) tomato sauce

Cut meat into serving pieces. In large skillet, brown meat in hot oil. Stir in remaining ingredients. Simmer covered, 1 to 1¼ hours or until meat is tender. 5 to 6 servings

NUTRITION INFORMATION PER SERVING

Serving Size: 1/5 of recipe		Percent U.S. RDA Per Serving	
Calories	386	Protein	41%
Protein	26g	Vitamin A	15%
Carbohydrate	16g	Vitamin C	4%
Fat	24g	Thiamin	7%
Sodium	1103mg	Riboflavin	13%
Potassium	371mg	Niacin	27%
		Calcium	3%
		Iron	20%

TOURNEDOS

1 to 1½-lb. top round steak, cut 1-inch thick
Meat tenderizer
½ teaspoon pepper
¼ to ½ teaspoon garlic salt
½ lb. (8 slices) bacon
2 tablespoons chopped parsley
¾ cup hollandaise sauce, page 543
¼ teaspoon tarragon leaves

Cut steak into 8 lengthwise strips. Pound each strip with a meat hammer until ¼-inch thick. Sprinkle with meat tenderizer, pepper and garlic salt. Partially cook bacon and place on top steak; sprinkle with parsley. Roll up with bacon inside and secure with toothpicks. Broil or grill 6 to 8 inches from heat about 15 minutes for medium doneness. Serve with hollandaise sauce and tarragon. 4 to 6 servings

NUTRITION INFORMATION PER SERVING

Serving Size: 1/6 of recipe		Percent U.S. RDA Per Serving	
Calories	332	Protein	30%
Protein	20g	Vitamin A	17%
Carbohydrate	<1g	Vitamin C	6%
Fat	27g	Thiamin	8%
Sodium	865mg	Riboflavin	11%
Potassium	241mg	Niacin	17%
		Calcium	3%
		Iron	15%

PAPRIKASH BEEF

2 tablespoons oil
5 to 6 cube steaks
2 tablespoons chopped onion
1 tablespoon paprika
1 teaspoon chopped parsley
½ teaspoon salt
½ teaspoon garlic salt
¼ cup water
8-oz. can (1 cup) tomato sauce
½ cup dairy sour cream

In large skillet, brown steaks in hot oil; drain excess fat. Add remaining ingredients except sour cream. Reduce heat and simmer covered, 15 to 20 minutes, stirring occasionally. Blend in sour cream. Heat, but do not boil. Serve over noodles. 5 to 6 servings

NUTRITION INFORMATION PER SERVING

Serving Size: 1/5 of recipe		Percent U.S. RDA Per Serving	
Calories	337	Protein	45%
Protein	29g	Vitamin A	18%
Carbohydrate	6g	Vitamin C	*
Fat	21g	Thiamin	6%
Sodium	470mg	Riboflavin	16%
Potassium	345mg	Niacin	23%
		Calcium	5%
		Iron	21%

TIP: *Ground beef patties (about 1½ lb. ground beef) may be substituted for cube steak. Omit oil for browning.*

MINUTE STEAK LORRAINE

2 tablespoons flour
½ teaspoon salt
¼ teaspoon oregano leaves
⅛ teaspoon minced garlic
6 cube steaks
2 tablespoons oil
½ green pepper, cut into 1-inch pieces
1 pkg. Pillsbury Brown Gravy Mix
¾ cup water
⅓ cup dry red wine
4-oz. can (½ cup) mushroom stems and pieces, drained

In small bowl, combine flour, salt, oregano and garlic. Lightly coat steaks with flour mixture. In large skillet, brown steaks in hot oil. Reduce heat; add remaining ingredients. Simmer covered, 20 to 25 minutes or until steaks are tender. 6 servings

NUTRITION INFORMATION PER SERVING

Serving Size: 1/6 of recipe		Percent U.S. RDA Per Serving	
Calories	243	Protein	41%
Protein	27g	Vitamin A	*
Carbohydrate	5g	Vitamin C	20%
Fat	11g	Thiamin	6%
Sodium	361mg	Riboflavin	15%
Potassium	363mg	Niacin	22%
		Calcium	*
		Iron	20%

STEW MEAT

STEW MEAT is cut in cubes from the less tender sections of beef. This meat is very flavorful but requires long, slow simmering for tenderness.

BEEF STEW

1½ to 2 lb. beef stew meat
¼ cup flour
1 teaspoon salt
¼ teaspoon pepper
3 tablespoons oil
2 cubes or 2 teaspoons beef bouillon
2 medium onions, quartered
1 stalk celery, cut into pieces
1 bay leaf
3 cups water
2 cups (4 oz.) whole fresh mushrooms
4 potatoes, peeled and quartered
4 carrots, cut into pieces
2 tablespoons flour
¼ cup water

In large bowl or plastic bag, coat beef cubes with flour, salt and pepper mixture. In Dutch oven or large skillet, brown meat in hot oil. Add bouillon, onions, celery, bay leaf and 3 cups water. Simmer covered, 1½ hours or until tender. Remove bay leaf. Add mushrooms, potatoes and carrots. Cover; continue cooking until vegetables are tender, 30 to 45 minutes. Combine 2 tablespoons flour with ¼ cup water; stir into stew juices. Heat mixture until it thickens and boils, stirring constantly. 5 to 6 servings

NUTRITION INFORMATION PER SERVING

Serving Size: 1/6 of recipe		Percent U.S. RDA Per Serving	
Calories	405	Protein	42%
Protein	27g	Vitamin A	107%
Carbohydrate	31g	Vitamin C	14%
Fat	19g	Thiamin	17%
Sodium	730mg	Riboflavin	20%
Potassium	968mg	Niacin	35%
		Calcium	6%
		Iron	23%

TIPS: *If desired, ½ cup dry red wine or one 8-oz. can (1 cup) tomato sauce may be substituted for part of the water.*

For OXTAIL STEW, substitute oxtails for part or all of the stew meat. You may wish to use more oxtails or more vegetables since there is bone with oxtails. Two pounds would serve only 3 to 4 people.

OVEN BAKED STEW

2 lb. stew meat
1 tablespoon sugar
1 teaspoon salt
⅛ teaspoon pepper
⅛ teaspoon thyme leaves
⅛ teaspoon marjoram leaves
⅛ teaspoon rosemary leaves
6 whole carrots, cut into chunks
3 celery stalks, thickly sliced
1 large onion, chopped
¼ to ½ cup red wine
16-oz. can (2 cups) tomatoes, undrained

Heat oven to 250°F. In 3-quart casserole, combine raw meat and remaining ingredients; mix well. Bake covered at 250°F. for 5 to 6 hours, stirring occasionally.
6 to 8 servings

NUTRITION INFORMATION PER SERVING

Serving Size: 1/8 of recipe		Percent U.S. RDA Per Serving	
Calories	299	Protein	33%
Protein	21g	Vitamin A	95%
Carbohydrate	10g	Vitamin C	19%
Fat	18g	Thiamin	7%
Sodium	425mg	Riboflavin	12%
Potassium	625mg	Niacin	19%
		Calcium	4%
		Iron	18%

HUNGARIAN GOULASH

2 lb. beef stew meat
¼ cup flour
2 to 3 medium onions, sliced
2 tablespoons oil
2 tablespoons paprika
2 teaspoon salt
1 teaspoon marjoram leaves
¼ teaspoon pepper
1 medium green pepper, chopped
1 garlic clove, minced
½ cup water
16-oz. can (2 cups) tomatoes, undrained
3 tablespoons flour
½ cup water

In large bowl or plastic bag, coat beef cubes with ¼ cup flour. In large skillet or Dutch oven, brown meat and onions in hot oil.Stir in paprika, salt, marjoram, pepper, green pepper, garlic, ½ cup water and tomatoes; heat to boiling. Reduce heat; simmer covered, 2 hours or until meat is tender. Combine 3 tablespoons flour with ½ cup water; stir into hot liquid. Heat mixture until it boils and thickens, stirring constantly. Serve over noodles or potatoes. 6 to 8 servings

NUTRITION INFORMATION PER SERVING

Serving Size: 1/8 of recipe		Percent U.S. RDA Per Serving	
Calories	333	Protein	34%
Protein	22g	Vitamin A	13%
Carbohydrate	12g	Vitamin C	46%
Fat	22g	Thiamin	9%
Sodium	658mg	Riboflavin	13%
Potassium	507mg	Niacin	20%
		Calcium	3%
		Iron	18%

BEEF RAGOUT WITH DUMPLINGS

2 lb. beef stew meat
¼ cup flour
2 teaspoons salt
¼ teaspoon pepper
2 medium onions, sliced
2 tablespoons oil
1 cube or 1 teaspoon beef bouillon
1 stick cinnamon, if desired
1 bay leaf
1 cup Burgundy dry red wine or water
½ cup water
4-oz. can (½ cup) mushroom stems and pieces, undrained
4 medium carrots, sliced
2 stalks celery, chopped
Fluffy Dumplings, page 88

In large bowl or plastic bag, coat beef cubes with flour, salt and pepper mixture. In large skillet or Dutch oven, brown meat and onion in hot oil. Add bouillon, cinnamon, bay leaf, wine, water and mushrooms. Heat to boiling; simmer covered, 1½ hours. Add celery and carrots; continue simmering covered, 20 to 25 minutes until vegetables are just about tender. Prepare Fluffy Dumplings. Drop by rounded tablespoonfuls onto top of hot stew. Simmer covered, 12 to 15 minutes or until dumplings are no longer doughy. Remove cinnamon stick and bay leaf. 6 to 8 servings

NUTRITION INFORMATION PER SERVING

Serving Size: 1/8 of recipe		Percent U.S. RDA Per Serving	
Calories	486	Protein	39%
Protein	25g	Vitamin A	60%
Carbohydrate	29g	Vitamin C	7%
Fat	27g	Thiamin	17%
Sodium	965mg	Riboflavin	23%
Potassium	547mg	Niacin	25%
		Calcium	9%
		Iron	23%

SHORT RIBS

SHORT RIBS are cut from the bony tip of the ribs. They contain a cross section of rib bone and alternate layers of meat and fat. Usually cooked with liquid for tenderness.

BARBECUED SHORT RIBS

3 to 3½ lb. beef short ribs, cut into serving pieces
¼ cup firmly packed brown sugar
2 teaspoons garlic salt
¼ teaspoon thyme
1 medium onion, chopped
1 lemon, sliced
1 cup catsup
½ cup water
2 tablespoons Worcestershire sauce
2 teaspoons prepared mustard

Heat oven to 450°F. In shallow baking pan, bake ribs uncovered at 450°F. for 20 minutes; drain excess fat. Reduce oven temperature to 350°F. In small bowl, combine remaining ingredients and pour over ribs. Bake covered at 350°F. for 1¼ to 1½ hours or until tender. Brush sauce on ribs occasionally. Serve sauce with ribs. 4 servings

NUTRITION INFORMATION PER SERVING

Serving Size: 1/4 of recipe		Percent U.S. RDA Per Serving	
Calories	300	Protein	37%
Protein	24g	Vitamin A	20%
Carbohydrate	38g	Vitamin C	28%
Fat	29g	Thiamin	13%
Sodium	1842mg	Riboflavin	16%
Potassium	751mg	Niacin	35%
		Calcium	7%
		Iron	27%

TIP: *For a quick barbecue sauce, combine 1 cup of prepared barbecue sauce with the water, onion and lemon. Pour over meat and continue as directed.*

GROUND BEEF

GROUND BEEF is composed of meat and trimmings from less tender sections that are ground. The lean content should not be less than 70%. In addition to being labeled GROUND BEEF, it may also be labeled according to the type of beef used:

CHUCK from the shoulder (chuck) area.

ROUND from the round steak area usually contains less fat than ground chuck.

SIRLOIN from the sirloin steak area and is usually the highest in price.

Ground beef is sometimes categorized as LEAN, and EXTRA LEAN depending on the fat content of the meat.

Occasionally ground meat is sold in meatloaf mixtures or other precombined foods. If these mixtures include ingredients other than meat, the ingredients should be listed on the label.

HAMBURGERS

1 lb. ground beef
½ teaspoon salt
⅛ teaspoon pepper

In small bowl, mix all ingredients. Shape into 3 or 4 patties. In medium skillet, fry patties over medium heat 5 to 10 minutes on each side or until browned and cooked to desired doneness. 3 to 4 servings

NUTRITION INFORMATION PER SERVING

Serving Size: 1/3 of recipe		Percent U.S. RDA Per Serving	
Calories	311	Protein	40%
Protein	26g	Vitamin A	*
Carbohydrate	<1g	Vitamin C	*
Fat	22g	Thiamin	7%
Sodium	413mg	Riboflavin	13%
Potassium	489mg	Niacin	29%
		Calcium	*
		Iron	19%

See TIPS, page 318.

TIPS: *To broil or barbecue, place patties 2 to 3 inches from heat, allowing about 5 minutes on each side for rare and about 7 minutes for medium.*

For HAMBURGER VARIATIONS, add 1 small chopped onion, 1 to 2 teaspoons lemon pepper marinade (omit pepper), ½ teaspoon garlic salt (omit salt), 1 tablespoon barbecue sauce or catsup, 1 teaspoon prepared mustard, 2 to 4 tablespoons pickle relish, ¼ cup chopped mushrooms or 1 tablespoon Worcestershire sauce.

For HAMBURGER TOPPINGS, add cheese slices, cheese sauce, sour cream, onion dip or cream soups.

For FILLED HAMBURGERS, form each patty into 2 thin patties; place one of the following fillings between patties and seal edges well:
thinly sliced tomato and cheese
cheese and chopped green chilies
crumbled blue cheese
cheese and sautéed onions

SALISBURY STEAK

10¾-oz. can condensed golden mushroom soup
1½ lb. ground beef
½ cup dry bread or cracker crumbs
½ teaspoon salt
⅛ teaspoon pepper
1 onion, finely chopped
1 egg, slightly beaten
⅓ cup water

Heat oven to 350°F. In medium bowl, combine ¼ of the soup with remaining ingredients except water; mix well. Shape into 6 patties; arrange in single layer in 13x9 or 12x8-inch baking dish. Bake uncovered at 350°F. for 30 minutes. Skim off fat. In small bowl, combine remaining soup and water; spoon over patties. Return to oven and bake for 10 minutes. If desired, garnish with mushroom slices.

6 servings

NUTRITION INFORMATION PER SERVING

Serving Size: 1/6 of recipe		Percent U.S. RDA Per Serving	
Calories	322	Protein	35%
Protein	23g	Vitamin A	4%
Carbohydrate	8g	Vitamin C	4%
Fat	22g	Thiamin	7%
Sodium	646mg	Riboflavin	16%
Potassium	457mg	Niacin	24%
		Calcium	4%
		Iron	18%

TIP: *To prepare in skillet, brown meat patties in 1 tablespoon hot oil; drain excess fat. Add soup and water; simmer covered, 10 to 15 minutes.*

BASIC MEATBALLS

1 lb. ground beef
¼ cup dry bread or cracker crumbs
½ teaspoon salt
⅛ teaspoon pepper
1 small onion, chopped
1 egg
1 tablespoon oil

In medium bowl, combine all ingredients except oil; mix well. Shape into 1½ to 2-inch balls. In large skillet, brown meatballs in hot oil; drain excess fat. Add desired sauce to meatballs; cook as directed in recipe.

4 servings

NUTRITION INFORMATION PER SERVING

Serving Size: 1/4 of recipe		Percent U.S. RDA Per Serving	
Calories	318	Protein	35%
Protein	23g	Vitamin A	4%
Carbohydrate	7g	Vitamin C	2%
Fat	22g	Thiamin	7%
Sodium	375mg	Riboflavin	14%
Potassium	427mg	Niacin	23%
		Calcium	3%
		Iron	18%

TIPS: *To brown in oven, arrange on ungreased shallow baking pan and bake at 400°F. for 15 minutes or until browned.*

For cocktail-size meatballs, shape into 1-inch balls; continue as directed.

24 meatballs

MEATBALL STEW

One recipe Basic Meatballs, page 318
1 cube or 1 teaspoon beef bouillon
½ teaspoon marjoram leaves
3 carrots, cut into ½-inch pieces
2 potatoes, cut into 1-inch pieces
1 medium onion, sliced
1¼ cups water
10¾-oz. can tomato soup

Heat oven to 375°F. In 3-quart casserole, combine browned meatballs with remaining ingredients. Bake at 375°F. for 1 hour or until vegetables are tender.

4 to 5 servings

NUTRITION INFORMATION PER SERVING

Serving Size: 1/4 of recipe		Percent U.S. RDA Per Serving	
Calories	453	Protein	41%
Protein	27g	Vitamin A	135%
Carbohydrate	35g	Vitamin C	45%
Fat	24g	Thiamin	16%
Sodium	1249mg	Riboflavin	19%
Potassium	998mg	Niacin	32%
		Calcium	7%
		Iron	25%

TIP: *Stew may be simmered covered in Dutch oven or large skillet, 30 to 45 minutes or until vegetables are tender.*

MEATBALLS IN GINGER SAUCE

One recipe Basic Meatballs, page 318
½ cup gingersnap crumbs
⅓ cup firmly packed brown sugar
¼ cup raisins, if desired
2 cubes or 2 teaspoons beef bouillon
1½ cups water
2½ tablespoons lemon juice

In large skillet, combine browned meatballs with remaining ingredients. Simmer covered, 20 to 25 minutes, stirring occasionally.

4 to 5 servings

NUTRITION INFORMATION PER SERVING

Serving Size: 1/4 of recipe		Percent U.S. RDA Per Serving	
Calories	461	Protein	35%
Protein	24g	Vitamin A	4%
Carbohydrate	41g	Vitamin C	9%
Fat	23g	Thiamin	7%
Sodium	923mg	Riboflavin	14%
Potassium	623mg	Niacin	23%
		Calcium	6%
		Iron	25%

SPEEDY SWEDISH MEATBALLS

One recipe Basic Meatballs, page 318
¼ teaspoon celery seed, if desired
⅛ teaspoon nutmeg
⅝-oz. pkg. Pillsbury Brown Gravy Mix
1 cup water

In large skillet, combine browned meatballs with remaining ingredients. Simmer covered, 15 minutes, stirring occasionally.

4 servings

NUTRITION INFORMATION PER SERVING

Serving Size: 1/4 of recipe		Percent U.S. RDA Per Serving	
Calories	333	Protein	35%
Protein	23g	Vitamin A	4%
Carbohydrate	9g	Vitamin C	4%
Fat	22g	Thiamin	7%
Sodium	564mg	Riboflavin	14%
Potassium	434mg	Niacin	23%
		Calcium	4%
		Iron	19%

TIP: *Cream of chicken or mushroom soup may be substituted for gravy mix. Decrease water to ¼ cup. If desired, substitute ¼ cup milk or white wine for water.*

SWEET-SOUR MEATBALLS

One recipe Basic Meatballs, page 318
2 tablespoons sugar
1½ tablespoons cornstarch
½ cup water
20-oz. can (2½ cups) pineapple chunks, drained (reserve ½ cup syrup)
½ cup reserved syrup
3 tablespoons vinegar
2 tablespoons soy sauce
1½ to 2 green peppers, cut into 1-inch pieces

In large skillet, add sugar and cornstarch to browned meatballs. Stir in water, syrup, vinegar and soy sauce. Heat mixture until it boils and thickens, stirring constantly. Add pineapple and green pepper. Simmer covered, 15 to 20 minutes. Serve over rice.

4 to 5 servings

NUTRITION INFORMATION PER SERVING

Serving Size: 1/4 of recipe		Percent U.S. RDA Per Serving	
Calories	478	Protein	38%
Protein	25g	Vitamin A	11%
Carbohydrate	48g	Vitamin C	104%
Fat	22g	Thiamin	18%
Sodium	1044mg	Riboflavin	20%
Potassium	738mg	Niacin	26%
		Calcium	6%
		Iron	26%

BASIC MEAT LOAF

1½ lb. ground beef
⅓ cup dry bread or cracker crumbs
1 teaspoon salt
¼ teaspoon pepper
1 small onion, chopped
⅓ cup catsup, chili sauce or barbecue sauce
1 teaspoon Worcestershire sauce
1 egg

Heat oven to 350°F. In large bowl, combine all ingredients; mix well. Press into greased 8x4-inch loaf pan or 6-cup ring mold. Bake at 350°F. for 1 hour. Let stand 5 minutes, lift onto serving platter.

5 to 6 servings

NUTRITION INFORMATION PER SERVING

Serving Size: 1/6 of recipe		Percent U.S. RDA Per Serving	
Calories	279	Protein	34%
Protein	22g	Vitamin A	29%
Carbohydrate	6g	Vitamin C	6%
Fat	18g	Thiamin	7%
Sodium	458mg	Riboflavin	14%
Potassium	409mg	Niacin	24%
		Calcium	3%
		Iron	18%

TIPS: *For individual meat loaves, make in 12 individual muffin cups. Bake at 350°F. for 25 to 30 minutes.*

For variety, add one of the following to meat mixture:

1 cup cubed cheese (enclose in hamburger mixture)
¼ cup chopped sweet or dill pickle
2 tablespoons pickle relish
½ cup crushed pineapple, drained
½ cup mushroom pieces, drained
¼ cup chopped green pepper

For STUFFED MEAT LOAF, prepare ¼ of recipe for Bread Stuffing, page 416. Press half of meat mixture into 9x5-inch loaf pan. Top with stuffing, then remaining meat mixture; press to form loaf.

MEXICALI MEAT LOAF

1 egg
1 lb. ground beef
½ cup dry bread or cracker crumbs
½ teaspoon oregano leaves
1 small onion, chopped
½ cup chili sauce or catsup
7-oz. can (1 cup) Mexicorn Brand Golden Whole Kernel Corn With Sweet Peppers, drained

TOPPING
1 egg, slightly beaten
1 cup (4 oz.) shredded Cheddar cheese
½ teaspoon salt
½ teaspoon dry mustard
2 tablespoons milk
½ teaspoon Worcestershire sauce
4 slices bacon, fried, drained and crumbled, if desired
4 stuffed green olives, sliced

Heat oven to 375°F. In large bowl, beat egg slightly. Add remaining ingredients; mix well. Press meat mixture into 8x4-inch loaf pan. Bake at 375°F. for 45 minutes. In small bowl, combine first 6 Topping ingredients; spread on meat loaf. top with bacon and olives. Return to oven and bake for 3 to 5 minutes or until cheese melts. Let stand 10 minutes before lifting from pan.

4 servings

NUTRITION INFORMATION PER SERVING

Serving Size: 1/4 of recipe		Percent U.S. RDA Per Serving	
Calories	531	Protein	55%
Protein	35g	Vitamin A	16%
Carbohydrate	21g	Vitamin C	15%
Fat	34g	Thiamin	14%
Sodium	1256mg	Riboflavin	28%
Potassium	654mg	Niacin	29%
		Calcium	27%
		Iron	26%

FLAVORFUL MEAT LOAF

1 lb. ground beef
2 tablespoons dry onion soup mix
5-oz. can (⅔ cup) evaporated milk
2 tablespoons firmly packed brown sugar
½ teaspoon dry or prepared mustard
2 tablespoons catsup

Heat oven to 350°F. In 8x4-inch loaf pan, combine first 3 ingredients; mix well (mixture will be very moist). Press evenly in pan. Combine brown sugar, mustard and catsup; spoon over meat mixture. Bake at 350°F. for 45 minutes. Using spatulas, lift meat loaf from pan to serving plate.

3 to 4 servings

NUTRITION INFORMATION PER SERVING

Serving Size: 1/4 of recipe		Percent U.S. RDA Per Serving	
Calories	336	Protein	36%
Protein	23g	Vitamin A	5%
Carbohydrate	15g	Vitamin C	4%
Fat	20g	Thiamin	7%
Sodium	432mg	Riboflavin	19%
Potassium	561mg	Niacin	23%
		Calcium	12%
		Iron	17%

TIP: *To double recipe, use double the ingredient amounts; bake in 9x5-inch loaf pan for 1¼ hours.*

GROUND BEEF STROGANOFF

1 lb. ground beef
1 small onion, chopped
½ teaspoon garlic salt
¼ teaspoon pepper
10¾-oz. can condensed cream of mushroom or celery soup
4-oz. can (½ cup) mushroom stems and pieces, drained
¾ cup dairy sour cream or yogurt

In medium skillet, brown ground beef and onion; drain excess fat. Stir in garlic salt, pepper, soup and mushrooms. Simmer covered, 15 to 20 minutes. Stir in sour cream; heat through, but do not boil. Serve over rice, noodles or chow mein noodles.

4 to 5 servings

NUTRITION INFORMATION PER SERVING

Serving Size: 1/4 of recipe		Percent U.S. RDA Per Serving	
Calories	415	Protein	35%
Protein	23g	Vitamin A	9%
Carbohydrate	10g	Vitamin C	4%
Fat	31g	Thiamin	7%
Sodium	878mg	Riboflavin	22%
Potassium	461mg	Niacin	27%
		Calcium	9%
		Iron	17%

TIP: *For an oven casserole, spoon cooked mixture into 1½ or 2-quart casserole. Top with French-fried onions. Bake uncovered at 350°F. for 20 to 25 minutes or until heated through.*

STUFFED GREEN PEPPERS

4 large green peppers
1 lb. ground beef
¼ cup chopped celery
2 tablespoons chopped onion
1 cup cooked rice
½ teaspoon salt
1 medium tomato, chopped
Dash pepper
¼ cup catsup
8-oz. can (1 cup) tomato sauce
1 teaspoon sugar
¼ teaspoon basil leaves
¼ cup grated Cheddar cheese

Heat oven to 350°F. Cut tops from peppers; remove membrane and seeds. In large saucepan, cook peppers 5 minutes in boiling water to cover. Drain; set aside. In large skillet, brown ground beef, celery and onion; drain excess fat. Add rice, salt, tomato, pepper and catsup; mix well.

Spoon mixture into peppers. Place peppers in shallow baking pan. Combine tomato sauce, sugar and basil; mix well. Spoon half of sauce over peppers. Bake uncovered at 350°F. for 30 to 40 minutes or until peppers are tender. Spoon on remaining sauce and sprinkle with cheese during last 5 minutes of baking.

4 servings

NUTRITION INFORMATION PER SERVING

Serving Size: 1/4 of recipe		Percent U.S. RDA Per Serving	
Calories	447	Protein	40%
Protein	26g	Vitamin A	44%
Carbohydrate	30g	Vitamin C	221%
Fat	25g	Thiamin	21%
Sodium	704mg	Riboflavin	23%
Potassium	905mg	Niacin	33%
		Calcium	10%
		Iron	27%

STROGANOFF CRÊPES

12 to 14 cooked Basic Crêpes, page 101
1 lb. ground beef
½ cup chopped onion
1 garlic clove, minced
4-oz. can (½ cup) mushroom stems and pieces, drained
2 tablespoons flour
½ to 1 teaspoon salt
¼ teaspoon pepper
¼ teaspoon paprika
10¾-oz. can condensed cream of mushroom soup
2 cups dairy sour cream

Prepare crêpes. In large skillet, brown ground beef, onion, garlic and mushrooms; drain. Stir in flour until smooth. Stir in salt, pepper, paprika and soup; simmer 10 minutes. Remove from heat; stir in 1 cup sour cream. Heat oven to 350°F. Spoon about ¼ cup meat mixture along center of each crêpe. Fold opposite edges over filling. Arrange in ungreased 13x9-inch baking dish. Brush crêpes with melted margarine, if desired. Cover loosely with foil. Bake at 350°F. for 15 to 20 minutes or until heated through. Serve immediately topped with remaining sour cream.

12 to 14 crêpes

NUTRITION INFORMATION PER SERVING

Serving Size: 1 crêpe		Percent U.S. RDA Per Serving	
Calories	296	Protein	20%
Protein	13g	Vitamin A	12%
Carbohydrate	15g	Vitamin C	*
Fat	20g	Thiamin	10%
Sodium	444mg	Riboflavin	18%
Potassium	229mg	Niacin	12%
		Calcium	10%
		Iron	10%

TIP: *For crispier crêpes, bake uncovered.*

STROGANOFF CRÊPES

CHILI

1 lb. ground beef
1 medium onion, chopped
1 stalk celery, chopped
2 teaspoons chili powder
1 teaspoon salt
Dash pepper
16-oz. can (2 cups) stewed tomatoes
8-oz. can (1 cup) tomato sauce
15-oz. can (2 cups) kidney beans, undrained

In large skillet, brown ground beef, onion and celery; drain excess fat. Stir in remaining ingredients except beans. Simmer covered, 30 to 45 minutes until flavors are blended. Stir in beans; heat through.

6 servings

NUTRITION INFORMATION PER SERVING

Serving Size: 1/6 of recipe		Percent U.S. RDA Per Serving	
Calories	292	Protein	29%
Protein	19g	Vitamin A	36%
Carbohydrate	21g	Vitamin C	26%
Fat	15g	Thiamin	10%
Sodium	505mg	Riboflavin	12%
Potassium	658mg	Niacin	21%
		Calcium	5%
		Iron	21%

STUFFED CABBAGE LEAVES

12 large cabbage leaves
1 lb. ground beef
¼ cup chopped celery
2 tablespoons chopped onion
1 cup cooked rice
½ teaspoon salt
1 medium tomato, chopped
Dash pepper
¼ cup catsup
1 egg
8-oz. can (1 cup) tomato sauce
1 teaspoon sugar
¼ teaspoon basil leaves
1 cup (4 oz.) grated Cheddar or American cheese

Heat oven to 350°F. In large sauce-pan, cook cabbage leaves 5 minutes in boiling water. Drain; set aside. In large skillet, brown ground beef, celery and onion; drain excess fat. Add rice, salt, tomato, pepper, catsup and egg. Mix well; heat through. Divide meat mixture equally on each cabbage leaf. Fold edges in; roll filling inside each leaf. Secure with toothpicks. Place cabbage rolls in 12x8-inch or 13x9-inch baking dish. In small bowl, combine tomato sauce, sugar and basil; spoon over cabbage rolls. Cover with foil. Bake at 350°F. for 45 minutes. Remove foil, sprinkle with cheese during last 5 minutes of baking.

5 to 6 servings

NUTRITION INFORMATION PER SERVING

Serving Size: 1/6 of recipe		Percent U.S. RDA Per Serving	
Calories	362	Protein	33%
Protein	21g	Vitamin A	27%
Carbohydrate	19g	Vitamin C	14%
Fat	22g	Thiamin	10%
Sodium	606mg	Riboflavin	16%
Potassium	441mg	Niacin	20%
		Calcium	18%
		Iron	17%

BEEF ENCHILADAS

- 4 to 5 teaspoons chili powder
- 2 teaspoons salt
- ½ teaspoon cumin, if desired
- 2 garlic cloves, minced
- 3½ cups water
- 2 cans (6 oz. each) tomato paste
- Dash Tabasco sauce or red pepper
- Oil
- 12 corn tortillas
- 1 to 1½ lb. ground beef
- 1 medium onion, chopped
- 2 cups (8 oz.) shredded Cheddar, Monterey Jack or American cheese
- ½ cup sliced or chopped ripe olives

Heat oven to 350°F. In medium saucepan, combine first 7 ingredients; simmer 20 minutes. In medium skillet, fry tortillas in about ¼-inch hot oil just until softened, a few seconds on each side. Drain on paper towel. In large skillet, brown ground beef and onion; drain excess fat. Remove from heat; add 1 cup shredded cheese, 1 cup tomato paste mixture and olives. Pour remaining tomato paste mixture in greased 13x9-inch baking dish. Spoon about 2 heaping tablespoonfuls of beef mixture down center of each tortilla; fold or roll tortilla around filling. Place seam-side-down in dish. Pour any remaining beef and tomato mixture over tortillas; sprinkle with remaining cheese. Bake uncovered at 350°F. for 20 to 25 minutes or until hot and bubbly. 6 servings

NUTRITION INFORMATION PER SERVING

Serving Size: 1/6 of recipe		Percent U.S. RDA Per Serving	
Calories	588	Protein	43%
Protein	28g	Vitamin A	71%
Carbohydrate	42g	Vitamin C	30%
Fat	35g	Thiamin	18%
Sodium	1148mg	Riboflavin	24%
Potassium	840mg	Niacin	28%
		Calcium	45%
		Iron	36%

TIP: *To halve recipe, use half the ingredient amounts; bake in 10x6 or 9-inch square pan.*

MEXICAN BEEF AND DUMPLINGS

- 2 lb. ground beef
- 3 teaspoons chili powder
- 1½ teaspoons salt
- 1 small onion, chopped
- 16-oz. can (2 cups) whole kernel corn, undrained
- 16-oz. can (2 cups) tomatoes, undrained
- 15-oz. can (2 cups) tomato sauce with onion, celery and green pepper

DUMPLINGS

- 1 cup Hungry Jack® Buttermilk Pancake and Waffle Mix
- ½ cup cornmeal
- ½ cup water
- 2 tablespoons oil
- 1 egg

In large Dutch oven, brown ground beef; drain excess fat. Stir in remaining ingredients except Dumpling ingredients. Simmer covered, 15 minutes. In medium bowl, combine all Dumpling ingredients; mix until well blended. Spoon Dumplings on top of boiling mixture. Cook covered, 12 to 15 minutes or until Dumplings are no longer doughy. 8 servings

NUTRITION INFORMATION PER SERVING

Serving Size: 1/8 of recipe		Percent U.S. RDA Per Serving	
Calories	485	Protein	39%
Protein	26g	Vitamin A	43%
Carbohydrate	38g	Vitamin C	34%
Fat	26g	Thiamin	18%
Sodium	925mg	Riboflavin	21%
Potassium	654mg	Niacin	33%
		Calcium	11%
		Iron	25%

TIPS: *To halve recipe, use half the ingredient amounts. In large skillet, cook as directed. For Dumplings, use half the ingredient amounts except for water (use 2 tablespoons) and egg (use 1 egg).*

Regular tomato sauce may be used, adding ½ cup chopped celery and ¼ cup chopped green pepper.

BEAN AND MEAT HOT DISH

1 lb. ground beef
4 cups cooked dry beans*
3 tablespoons firmly packed brown sugar
1 pkg. dry onion soup mix
1½ cups water
1 cup catsup
1 teaspoon prepared mustard

In large skillet, brown ground beef; drain excess fat. Stir in remaining ingredients. Simmer covered about 30 minutes. 6 to 8 servings

NUTRITION INFORMATION PER SERVING

Serving Size: 1/6 of recipe		Percent U.S. RDA Per Serving	
Calories	396	Protein	38%
Protein	24g	Vitamin A	13%
Carbohydrate	48g	Vitamin C	8%
Fat	13g	Thiamin	18%
Sodium	999mg	Riboflavin	14%
Potassium	973mg	Niacin	23%
		Calcium	9%
		Iron	32%

TIPS: **Great northern or navy beans may be used.*

Mixture may be baked in covered casserole at 350°F. for about 45 minutes or until hot and bubbly.

BEEFY BEAN 'N BISCUIT CASSEROLE

1½ lb. ground beef
½ cup chopped onion or 2 tablespoons instant minced onion
½ cup chopped green pepper or 2 tablespoons sweet pepper flakes
½ to 1 cup chopped celery
1 tablespoon firmly packed brown sugar
1 teaspoon garlic salt
1 teaspoon paprika or ½ teaspoon pepper
¾ cup water
1 tablespoon vinegar
¼ teaspoon Tabasco sauce
½ teaspoon Worcestershire sauce
16-oz. can (2 cups) pork and beans
10-oz. pkg. (1½ cups) frozen peas or lima beans, thawed
6-oz. can tomato paste

BISCUIT TOPPING
1½ cups Pillsbury's Best® All Purpose or Unbleached Flour*
2 teaspoons baking powder
½ teaspoon salt
¼ cup margarine or butter
½ cup milk
10 to 12 (½-inch) cubes Cheddar or American cheese, if desired

Heat oven to 400°F. In 10-inch ovenproof skillet, brown ground beef, onion and green pepper; drain excess fat. Add remaining ingredients except Biscuit Topping; simmer while preparing biscuits.

In medium bowl, combine flour, baking powder and salt; stir to blend. Using pastry blender or fork, cut in margarine until consistency of coarse meal. Add milk; stir with fork just until a soft dough forms. Turn dough onto floured surface; sprinkle lightly with flour. Knead gently 10 to 12 times until no longer sticky. Roll or press to ½-inch thickness; cut with 2-inch floured cutter. Place cheese cube in center of each biscuit. Fold dough over cheese; seal well. Arrange biscuits over hot meat mixture. Bake at 400°F. for 20 to 25 minutes or until deep golden brown. Serve immediately. 6 servings

NUTRITION INFORMATION PER SERVING

Serving Size: 1/6 of recipe		Percent U.S. RDA Per Serving	
Calories	601	Protein	50%
Protein	33g	Vitamin A	36%
Carbohydrate	54g	Vitamin C	65%
Fat	28g	Thiamin	35%
Sodium	1175mg	Riboflavin	27%
Potassium	984mg	Niacin	41%
		Calcium	15%
		Iron	38%

TIP: *If using Pillsbury's Best® Self Rising Flour, omit baking powder and salt.*

BEEFY BEAN 'N BISCUIT CASSEROLE

SOUTH-OF-THE-BORDER SPECIAL

1 lb. ground beef
1 medium onion, sliced
½ cup ripe olives
16-oz. can (2 cups) tomatoes, undrained
¾ teaspoon chili powder
1 pkg. Pillsbury Brown Gravy Mix
6-oz. pkg. corn chips

In large skillet, brown ground beef and onion; drain excess fat. Add olives, tomatoes, chili powder and gravy mix. Simmer covered, 5 to 10 minutes. Serve over corn chips.

4 servings

NUTRITION INFORMATION PER SERVING

Serving Size: 1/4 of recipe		Percent U.S. RDA Per Serving	
Calories	544	Protein	38%
Protein	24g	Vitamin A	28%
Carbohydrate	35g	Vitamin C	23%
Fat	34g	Thiamin	15%
Sodium	832mg	Riboflavin	17%
Potassium	741mg	Niacin	29%
		Calcium	24%
		Iron	28%

TIP: *If desired, part of corn chips may be stirred into ground beef mixture and remaining used as a topping.*

TAMALE BEEF CASSEROLE

1½ lb. ground beef
½ cup chopped onion or 2 tablespoons instant minced onion
½ cup chopped ripe olives
2 tablespoons chili powder
1 teaspoon salt
½ teaspoon pepper
16-oz. can (2 cups) whole kernel corn, drained
10¾-oz. can condensed tomato soup

CORN BREAD TOPPING

¾ cup cornmeal
½ cup Pillsbury's Best® All Purpose or Unbleached Flour*
1 teaspoon baking powder
1 teaspoon salt
½ teaspoon soda
1 cup buttermilk
2 tablespoons oil
1 egg, slightly beaten

Heat oven to 425°F. In 10 or 12-inch ovenproof skillet, brown ground beef and onion; drain excess fat. Add remaining ingredients except Topping ingredients; simmer while preparing Topping. In medium bowl, combine cornmeal, flour, baking powder, salt and soda; stir to blend. Combine buttermilk, oil and egg. Add to flour mixture. Stir *just* until dry ingredients are moistened. Spoon Topping over hot ground beef mixture. Bake at 425°F. for 20 to 25 minutes or until deep golden brown. Serve immediately.

6 to 8 servings

NUTRITION INFORMATION PER SERVING

Serving Size: 1/8 of recipe		Percent U.S. RDA Per Serving	
Calories	387	Protein	32%
Protein	21g	Vitamin A	32%
Carbohydrate	32g	Vitamin C	11%
Fat	20g	Thiamin	15%
Sodium	1198mg	Riboflavin	19%
Potassium	492mg	Niacin	25%
		Calcium	8%
		Iron	20%

TIP: **Self-rising flour is not recommended.*

PORK

Pork is a tender meat. Although it does not require long, slow cooking for tenderizing, it does require thorough cooking. Cuts of pork can be barbecued or broiled if they are cooked at a moderate temperature that allows the meat to cook thoroughly without drying the surface. Some cuts – bacon, ham and chops – are sold cured and smoked to give them a special flavor.

High quality pork should have a grayish-pink color and a firm, fine grain. The lean should be moderately marbled with a layer of firm, white fat.

PORK ROASTS

Pork roasts are cut from the shoulder and loin areas. The rump area is usually cured and made into ham, occasionally it is sold as FRESH HAM and roasted like roast pork.

PORK LOIN ROAST consists of the large loin muscle and sometimes the tenderloin muscle, also available as BONELESS LOIN ROAST. Rib sections are sometimes tied together to form a CROWN ROAST.

PORK SHOULDER ROASTS include ARM ROASTS or PICNICS and BOSTON SHOULDER ROASTS, sometimes called BOSTON BUTT. These roasts are tender, but contain more bone and fat than a loin roast. Also available boneless.

NUTRITION INFORMATION PER SERVING

Serving Size: 3 oz. cooked lean pork Boston butt		Percent U.S. RDA Per Serving	
Calories	207	Protein	35%
Protein	23g	Vitamin A	0%
Carbohydrate	0g	Vitamin C	†
Fat	12g	Thiamin	33%
Sodium	56mg	Riboflavin	14%
Potassium	258mg	Niacin	22%
		Calcium	*
		Iron	16%

PORK TENDERLOIN comes from the lean tenderloin muscle along the back; there is very little fat and no bone. It can be roasted whole or cut into slices and cooked like a boneless pork chop.

TIMETABLE FOR ROASTING PORK

Set oven at 325°F., do not cover pan.

Pork Roasts (fresh)	Weight	Thermometer Temperature	Approximate Cooking Time per lb.
Loin			
center	3-5 lb.	170°F.	30-35 min.
half	5-7 lb.	170°F.	35-40 min.
end	3-4 lb.	170°F.	40-45 min.
top (double)	3-5 lb.	170°F.	35-45 min.
top (boneless)	2-4 lb.	170°F.	30-35 min.
Crown	4-6 lb.	170°F.	35-40 min.
Arm Picnic Shoulder (fresh)			
bone-in	5-8 lb.	170°F.	30-35 min.
boneless	3-5 lb.	170°F.	30-35 min.
Blade Boston Shoulder	4-6 lb.	170°F.	40-45 min.
Leg (fresh ham)			
whole, bone-in	12-16 lb.	170°F.	22-26 min.
whole, boneless	10-14 lb.	170°F.	24-28 min.
half, bone-in	5-8 lb.	170°F.	35-40 min.
Tenderloin	½-1 lb.	170°F.	45-60 min.

HOW TO CARVE LOIN ROAST

For easier carving, have butcher saw backbone free of ribs but do not cut into meaty center.

Before roast is served, remove backbone. Do this by cutting close along the bone, leaving as much meat on roast as possible. Place roast with bone side facing carver.

Insert a fork in the top of the roast and make slices by cutting close along each side of the rib bone. One slice will contain the rib, the next will be boneless.

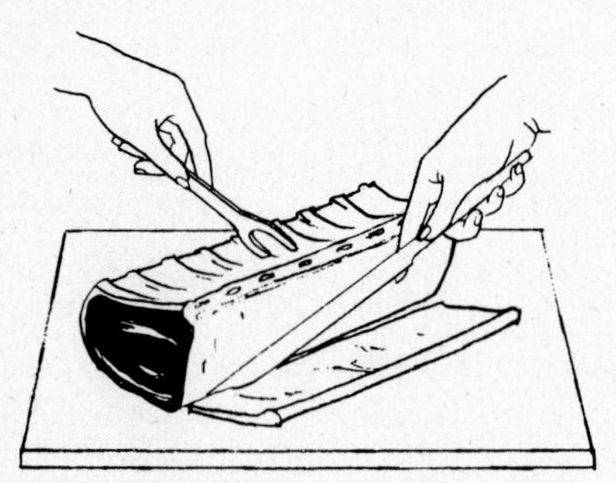

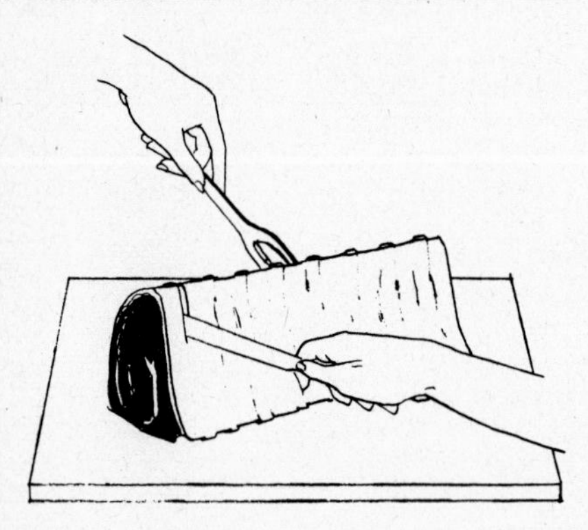

MARINADES FOR PORK ROASTS

(See Marinades for Beef Roasts, page 298, for information on marinating.)

WINE MARINADE

2 tablespoons chopped parsley
2 teaspoons salt
¼ teaspoon pepper
2 garlic cloves, sliced
1 cup dry wine

1 cup

SHERRY-SOY MARINADE

1 tablespoon dry mustard
1 teaspoon ginger
1 teaspoon sage or thyme leaves
1 garlic clove, minced
½ cup dry sherry
⅓ cup soy sauce

¾ cup

For each marinade, combine all ingredients; mix well. Use to marinate 4 to 6-lb. pork roast 2 to 4 hours at room temperature or several hours in refrigerator.

PORK LOIN ROAST

Heat oven to 325°F. Have butcher remove backbone from center-cut pork loin roast. Place roast, fat-side-up, on a rack in open shallow roasting pan. Season meat with salt and pepper. Insert meat thermometer so the bulb reaches the center of the thickest part, being sure that the bulb does not rest in fat or on bone. Roast 30 to 35 minutes per lb. or until thermometer registers 170°F.

NUTRITION INFORMATION PER SERVING

Serving Size: 1/2 lb. raw pork loin with bone		Percent U.S. RDA Per Serving	
Calories	442	Protein	46%
Protein	30g	Vitamin A	0%
Carbohydrate	0g	Vitamin C	0%
Fat	35g	Thiamin	75%
Sodium	0mg	Riboflavin	19%
Potassium	0mg	Niacin	34%
		Calcium	*
		Iron	22%

TIP: *Allow approximately ⅓ to ½ lb. per serving.*

STUFFED CROWN ROAST OF PORK

7-lb. pork crown roast
1½ teaspoons salt
¼ teaspoon pepper

For easy carving, have butcher cut off backbone. Heat oven to 325°F. Season meat with salt and pepper. Place in roasting pan, rib bones up. Wrap tips of bones in foil to prevent excess browning. Insert meat thermometer so ball reaches center of thickest part but does not rest in fat or on bone. (Do not add water; do not cover.) Roast on lowest oven rack at 325°F. for 2 hours. Meanwhile, prepare 1 quart of favorite stuffing. Cranberry, Sesame or Apple-Raisin Stuffing, page 416 and 417, or Rice Stuffing with orange peel and raisins added, page 417, are some suggestions. Fill center of roast with stuffing and roast 1½ to 2 hours longer, until meat thermometer registers 170°F. Cover stuffing with foil if top becomes too brown. To serve, remove foil and cover bone ends with paper frills or spiced crab apples.

6 to 8 servings

NUTRITION INFORMATION PER SERVING

Serving Size: 1/8 of recipe without stuffing		Percent U.S. RDA Per Serving	
Calories	693	Protein	50%
Protein	33g	Vitamin A	0%
Carbohydrate	<1g	Vitamin C	*
Fat	61g	Thiamin	45%
Sodium	1576mg	Riboflavin	19%
Potassium	369mg	Niacin	27%
		Calcium	*
		Iron	23%

PROVENCE-STYLE PORK ROAST

4 to 6-lb. pork loin roast
2 garlic cloves, slivered
2 teaspoons salt
¼ teaspoon pepper
1 cup dry white wine
2 tablespoons parsley flakes or chopped parsley

Heat oven to 325°F. Make small cuts between ribs and insert garlic slivers. Rub roast with salt and pepper. In large plastic bag or shallow dish, pour wine over roast; rub on parsley. Marinate covered, 2 to 4 hours at room temperature. Drain wine; sprinkle with salt and pepper again. Place roast, fat-side-up, on a rack in shallow roasting pan. Roast at 325°F. for 2 to 3 hours or until thermometer registers 170°F.

8 to 10 servings

NUTRITION INFORMATION PER SERVING

Serving Size: 1/10 of recipe		Percent U.S. RDA Per Serving	
Calories	375	Protein	37%
Protein	24g	Vitamin A	*
Carbohydrate	1g	Vitamin C	*
Fat	28g	Thiamin	60%
Sodium	495mg	Riboflavin	15%
Potassium	299mg	Niacin	28%
		Calcium	*
		Iron	18%

LEFTOVER PORK ROAST

Substitute pork for beef in Barbecued Sliced Beef, page 536, Cornish Pasties, page 536, Quick Beef and Vegetable Stew, page 303.

PORK CHOPS AND STEAKS

Pork chops and steaks include rib chops, loin chops, shoulder chops or steaks, either blade or arm. All the chops should be tender but usually the shoulder steaks have more waste and are made up of several smaller muscles.

RIB CHOPS have one large muscle and the rib bone. Sometimes they are cut extra thick and slit to make a pocket for stuffing. BUTTERFLY CHOPS are extra-thick with the bone removed, cut almost in half and opened to make butterfly shape.

LOIN CHOPS are similar to rib chops, but in addition have the small tenderloin on one side of the T-shaped bone.

Loin and rib chops are sometimes cured and available as SMOKED PORK CHOPS.

NUTRITION INFORMATION PER SERVING

Serving Size: 1 pork loin chop with bone, broiled

Nutrient	Amount	Percent U.S. RDA Per Serving	
Calories	454	Protein	44%
Protein	29g	Vitamin A	0%
Carbohydrate	0g	Vitamin C	0%
Fat	37g	Thiamin	74%
Sodium	71mg	Riboflavin	19%
Potassium	323mg	Niacin	34%
		Calcium	*
		Iron	22%

BREADED PORK CUTLETS

Purchase boneless pork chops or pork tenderloin, allowing about ¼ lb. per serving. Cut tenderloin into ½-inch slices. Flatten and prepare as for Breaded Veal Cutlets, page 349.

NUTRITION INFORMATION PER SERVING

Serving Size: 1/4 of recipe

Nutrient	Amount	Percent U.S. RDA Per Serving	
Calories	337	Protein	39%
Protein	25g	Vitamin A	3%
Carbohydrate	13g	Vitamin C	*
Fat	20g	Thiamin	8%
Sodium	80mg	Riboflavin	17%
Potassium	324mg	Niacin	25%
		Calcium	3%
		Iron	20%

PORK CHOPS WITH PEARS

4 to 6 pork chops or steaks
Salt and pepper
3 to 4 fresh pears, peeled, halved and cored*
2 tablespoons orange juice
¼ cup firmly packed brown sugar
¼ teaspoon cinnamon
¼ cup dry sherry or orange juice
1 tablespoon margarine or butter
1 tablespoon cornstarch
1 tablespoon water

Heat oven to 350°F. Grease bottom of large skillet with small piece of pork fat. Brown chops; place in shallow pan and season with salt and pepper. Arrange pears hollow-side-up around chops; drizzle orange juice over all. Sprinkle with brown sugar and cinnamon; pour sherry over pears and chops. Divide margarine and place in hollow of pears. Bake covered at 350°F. for 50 minutes. Uncover during last 20 minutes. Place pears and chops on platter. Dissolve cornstarch in water. Add to juices in pan and heat until mixture boils and thickens, stirring constantly. Pour over chops and pears.

4 to 6 servings

NUTRITION INFORMATION PER SERVING

Serving Size: 1/4 of recipe

Nutrient	Amount	Percent U.S. RDA Per Serving	
Calories	374	Protein	35%
Protein	23g	Vitamin A	3%
Carbohydrate	36g	Vitamin C	8%
Fat	14g	Thiamin	56%
Sodium	357mg	Riboflavin	17%
Potassium	408mg	Niacin	25%
		Calcium	4%
		Iron	21%

TIPS: **Canned pear or peach halves may be substituted for fresh pears; add to pork chops during last 15 minutes of cooking.*

To prepare in skillet, brown chops; add remaining ingredients. Simmer covered, 35 minutes, occasionally spooning sauce over chops and pears. Remove chops and pears; thicken sauce as directed.

BAKED PORK CHOPS AND STUFFING

4 pork chops or steaks
2 cups (2 slices) soft bread cubes
2 tablespoons chopped onion
¼ teaspoon poultry seasoning or ⅛ teaspoon sage and ⅛ teaspoon celery salt
2 tablespoons water
2 tablespoons margarine or butter, melted
⅓ cup water or dry sherry
10¾-oz. can condensed cream of mushroom soup

Heat oven to 350°F. Grease bottom of medium skillet with small piece of pork fat. Brown chops; place in single layer in shallow 2 to 2½-quart casserole. In small bowl, combine bread cubes, onion, poultry seasoning, 2 tablespoons water and margarine. Top each chop with ¼ of mixture. Combine ⅓ cup water and soup in skillet used for browning chops; pour over stuffing and chops. Bake uncovered at 350°F. for 1 hour or until chops are tender.

4 servings

NUTRITION INFORMATION PER SERVING

Serving Size: 1/4 of recipe		Percent U.S. RDA Per Serving	
Calories	372	Protein	40%
Protein	26g	Vitamin A	6%
Carbohydrate	14g	Vitamin C	*
Fat	23g	Thiamin	59%
Sodium	734mg	Riboflavin	20%
Potassium	86mg	Niacin	29%
		Calcium	5%
		Iron	20%

TIPS: *Condensed cream of celery or golden mushroom soup may be substituted for mushroom soup.*

For 6 servings, use 6 pork chops and 3 cups bread cubes. Increase poultry seasoning to ½ teaspoon.

RICE AND HONEY CHOPS

4 to 6 pork chops
¾ cup uncooked white or brown rice
½ cup raisins
1 teaspoon salt
1½ cups orange juice
½ cup water
2 tablespoons dry sherry, if desired
2 tablespoons honey

Grease bottom of large skillet with small piece of pork fat. Brown chops and remove. Add remaining ingredients; arrange chops over top. Simmer covered over low heat, 30 to 40 minutes or until tender. If rice mixture becomes dry, add additional liquid; if too moist, remove cover during last 5 minutes of cooking.

4 to 5 servings

NUTRITION INFORMATION PER SERVING

Serving Size: 1/4 of recipe		Percent U.S. RDA Per Serving	
Calories	441	Protein	39%
Protein	25g	Vitamin A	4%
Carbohydrate	58g	Vitamin C	42%
Fat	11g	Thiamin	69%
Sodium	972mg	Riboflavin	15%
Potassium	524mg	Niacin	32%
		Calcium	4%
		Iron	25%

TIP: *For quick-cooking rice, cook chops with remaining ingredients except rice for 35 minutes. Remove chops; stir in 1 cup quick-cooking rice. Arrange chops over rice. Simmer covered, 10 minutes. Fluff rice with fork and serve.*

CREOLE PORK STEAKS

4 to 6 pork steaks or chops
1 stalk celery, sliced
1 cup uncooked long grain or brown rice
2 tablespoons brown sugar
1 teaspoon salt
¼ to ½ teaspoon basil leaves
1½ cups water
15-oz. can (2 cups) tomato sauce

Grease bottom of large skillet with small piece of pork fat. Brown steaks over medium heat, turning once. Add celery and brown slightly; drain excess fat. Stir in remaining ingredients. Simmer covered, 30 minutes (40 minutes for brown rice) or until rice and steaks are tender.

4 to 6 servings

NUTRITION INFORMATION PER SERVING

Serving Size: 1/4 of recipe		Percent U.S. RDA Per Serving	
Calories	490	Protein	41%
Protein	27g	Vitamin A	16%
Carbohydrate	50g	Vitamin C	8%
Fat	20g	Thiamin	67%
Sodium	1110mg	Riboflavin	16%
Potassium	274mg	Niacin	35%
		Calcium	5%
		Iron	27%

SAVORY PORK AND RICE BAKE

2 to 3 cups cooked cubed pork
1 cup uncooked white or brown rice
1 teaspoon salt
½ to 1 teaspoon poultry seasoning or sage
1 small onion, chopped
1 stalk celery, sliced
2 cups water
10¾-oz. can condensed cream of chicken, celery or mushroom soup

Heat oven to 375°F. In 2½-quart casserole, combine all ingredients; mix well. Bake covered at 375°F. for 45 to 60 minutes or until rice is tender, stirring occasionally.

4 to 5 servings

NUTRITION INFORMATION PER SERVING

Serving Size: 1/4 of recipe		Percent U.S. RDA Per Serving	
Calories	484	Protein	32%
Protein	21g	Vitamin A	6%
Carbohydrate	45g	Vitamin C	3%
Fat	24g	Thiamin	36%
Sodium	1774mg	Riboflavin	12%
Potassium	361mg	Niacin	25%
		Calcium	5%
		Iron	22%

SWEET-SOUR PORK

1 lb. lean boneless pork, cut into 1-inch cubes
1 tablespoon oil
½ teaspoon salt
½ cup water
¼ cup sugar
2 green peppers, cut into 1-inch pieces
¼ cup vinegar
15½-oz. can (2 cups) pineapple chunks, undrained
2½ tablespoons cornstarch
2 tablespoons soy sauce
1 medium or 2 small tomatoes, cut into 8 pieces

In large skillet, brown meat in hot oil. Add salt and water; simmer covered, 30 minutes. Add sugar, green pepper, vinegar and pineapple. Combine cornstarch and soy sauce; stir into meat mixture. Heat mixture until it boils and thickens, stirring constantly. Simmer covered, 10 minutes. Add tomatoes; simmer 5 minutes, stirring occasionally. Serve over rice or chow mein noodles.

4 servings

NUTRITION INFORMATION PER SERVING

Serving Size: 1/4 of recipe		Percent U.S. RDA Per Serving	
Calories	377	Protein	31%
Protein	20g	Vitamin A	15%
Carbohydrate	49g	Vitamin C	121%
Fat	13g	Thiamin	56%
Sodium	988mg	Riboflavin	19%
Potassium	657mg	Niacin	25%
		Calcium	5%
		Iron	24%

CHOW MEIN

1 lb. chow mein meat
1 tablespoon oil
4 oz. (1½ cups) sliced fresh mushrooms or 4-oz. can mushrooms, drained
1 medium onion, sliced
2 medium stalks celery, sliced
1 cube or 1 teaspoon beef bouillon
½ teaspoon ginger
1 cup water
2 tablespoons soy sauce
16-oz. can (2 cups) bean sprouts, drained
8-oz. can (⅔ cup) water chestnuts, drained and sliced
8½-oz. can (1 cup) bamboo shoots, drained
1 tablespoon cornstarch
2 tablespoons water

In large skillet, brown meat in hot oil. Add mushrooms and onions; brown slightly. Add celery, bouillon, ginger, water and soy sauce; simmer covered, 20 minutes. Add bean sprouts, water chestnuts and bamboo shoots. Combine cornstarch and water; stir into meat mixture. Heat to boiling, stirring constantly. Simmer covered, 10 to 15 minutes. Serve over rice or chow mein noodles. 4 servings

NUTRITION INFORMATION PER SERVING

Serving Size: 1/4 of recipe		Percent U.S. RDA Per Serving	
Calories	324	Protein	36%
Protein	24g	Vitamin A	*
Carbohydrate	15g	Vitamin C	11%
Fat	20g	Thiamin	23%
Sodium	998mg	Riboflavin	24%
Potassium	597mg	Niacin	28%
		Calcium	5%
		Iron	22%

TIPS: *For GROUND BEEF CHOW MEIN, one pound ground beef may be substituted for chow mein meat. Brown ground beef; drain excess fat; omit oil.*

A 16-oz. can (2 cups) drained chow mein vegetables may be substituted for bean sprouts, water chestnuts and bamboo shoots.

For crisper vegetables, add onion and celery when bean sprouts are added.

CHINESE PORK STRIPS

1 lb. lean boneless pork, cut into thin strips, 2½ to 3-inches long
¼ teaspoon salt
Dash pepper
½ cup water
½ cup pineapple or orange juice
2 to 3 tablespoons soy sauce
2 cups thinly sliced Chinese cabbage
8-oz. can (⅔ cup) water chestnuts, drained and sliced
7-oz. pkg. (1½ cups) frozen Chinese pea pods
1½ tablespoons cornstarch
1 tablespoon water

Grease bottom of large skillet with small piece of pork fat. Brown pork over medium-high heat. Add salt, pepper, water, pineapple juice and soy sauce. Simmer covered, 30 minutes. Add cabbage, water chestnuts and pea pods. Simmer covered, 10 minutes or until vegetables are desired doneness. Mix cornstarch with 1 tablespoon water; stir into pork mixture. Heat until mixture boils and thickens, stirring constantly. Serve over rice. 4 servings

NUTRITION INFORMATION PER SERVING

Serving Size: 1/4 of recipe without pea pods		Percent U.S. RDA Per Serving	
Calories	219	Protein	30%
Protein	20g	Vitamin A	*
Carbohydrate	15g	Vitamin C	26%
Fat	9g	Thiamin	47%
Sodium	853mg	Riboflavin	15%
Potassium	416mg	Niacin	22%
		Calcium	5%
		Iron	18%

TIP: *Shredded cabbage may be substituted for Chinese cabbage.*

PORK RIBS

Spareribs come from the breast and rib areas. A thin covering of meat surrounds these bones.

COUNTRY-STYLE RIBS have more meat than spareribs and come from the rib section of the loin area.

Both types of ribs can be used interchangeably in our recipes, but the same weight of spareribs will serve fewer people. The fat may need to be skimmed from sauces on spareribs.

NUTRITION INFORMATION PER SERVING

Serving Size: 1 lb. spareribs, cooked

Nutrient	Amount	Percent U.S. RDA Per Serving	
Calories	792	Protein	58%
Protein	37g	Vitamin A	0%
Carbohydrate	0g	Vitamin C	0%
Fat	70g	Thiamin	52%
Sodium	75mg	Riboflavin	22%
Potassium	307mg	Niacin	31%
		Calcium	*
		Iron	26%

SHERRY-GLAZED RIBS

3 to 4-lb. spareribs or country-style ribs
¼ cup firmly packed brown sugar
1 tablespoon cornstarch
¼ cup orange juice
¼ cup sherry
3 tablespoons soy sauce

Heat oven to 325°F. Cut ribs into serving pieces and arrange in shallow baking pan. In small bowl, combine remaining ingredients; pour over ribs. Bake covered at 325°F. for 1½ hours or until tender, turning occasionally. Skim off excess fat before serving. If desired, garnish with orange slices cut in half. 4 to 5 servings

NUTRITION INFORMATION PER SERVING

Serving Size: 1/4 of recipe

Nutrient	Amount	Percent U.S. RDA Per Serving	
Calories	681	Protein	45%
Protein	29g	Vitamin A	*
Carbohydrate	19g	Vitamin C	7%
Fat	53g	Thiamin	40%
Sodium	1051mg	Riboflavin	19%
Potassium	369mg	Niacin	24%
		Calcium	4%
		Iron	26%

KENTUCKY-STYLE RIBS

3 to 4-lb. spareribs or country-style ribs
1 medium onion, sliced, if desired
¼ cup firmly packed brown sugar
1 tablespoon cornstarch
¼ cup bourbon
3 tablespoons soy sauce

Heat oven to 350°F. Cut ribs into serving pieces and arrange in shallow baking pan. Top with onion slices. In small bowl, combine remaining ingredients; pour over ribs. Bake covered at 350°F. for 1 hour, turning occasionally. Bake uncovered ½ to 1 hour or until ribs are tender, turning occasionally. 4 to 5 servings

NUTRITION INFORMATION PER SERVING

Serving Size: 1/4 of recipe

Nutrient	Amount	Percent U.S. RDA Per Serving	
Calories	715	Protein	45%
Protein	29g	Vitamin A	*
Carbohydrate	19g	Vitamin C	5%
Fat	53g	Thiamin	40%
Sodium	1052mg	Riboflavin	20%
Potassium	376mg	Niacin	24%
		Calcium	4%
		Iron	27%

TIP: *Ribs may be grilled or broiled about 5 to 6 inches from heat for 45 to 60 minutes; brush frequently with sauce ingredients. Before grilling, ribs should be either marinated in sauce mixture 2 hours at room temperature or overnight in refrigerator.*

BAKED RIBS AND SAUERKRAUT

3-lb. spareribs or country-style ribs
1½ teaspoons salt
¼ teaspoon pepper
32-oz. jar (4 cups) sauerkraut, undrained
2 tablespoons firmly packed brown sugar
2 tart apples, peeled and chopped
1 small onion, chopped
¼ cup water

Heat oven to 450°F. Cut ribs into serving pieces. Place in 13x9-inch pan; season with salt and pepper. Bake uncovered at 450°F. for 20 minutes. Reduce oven temperature to 350°F. Remove ribs; drain fat from pan. In same pan, combine sauerkraut, brown sugar, apples, onion and water; spread evenly. Arrange ribs on top; bake uncovered at 350°F. for 1½ to 2 hours or until ribs are tender, stirring occasionally.
5 to 6 servings

NUTRITION INFORMATION PER SERVING

Serving Size: 1/6 of recipe		Percent U.S. RDA Per Serving	
Calories	470	Protein	32%
Protein	21g	Vitamin A	*
Carbohydrate	18g	Vitamin C	39%
Fat	35g	Thiamin	30%
Sodium	1701mg	Riboflavin	16%
Potassium	452mg	Niacin	17%
		Calcium	8%
		Iron	19%

HAMS AND PICNICS

SMOKED HAMS and PICNICS are available fully cooked (need no further cooking) and cook-before-eating (partially cooked in processing, but need further cooking before eating).

SMOKED PICNIC is from the shoulder area. It tastes like ham, but is less expensive because of more bone and waste.

SMOKED HAMS have the characteristic round leg bone and have been cured and smoked. They are available as bone-in, semi-boneless, boneless or rolled. They can be sold whole, halved or as pieces.

ROLLED or SHAPED HAM cuts have been boned and are sometimes in a casing. They are fully cooked; however, heating enhances the flavor. Slices can be baked, broiled or fried.

SEMI-BONELESS HAMS are trimmed hams with all bones removed except the leg bone. Usually in a casing or wrapped in paper; most are fully cooked.

CANNED HAMS are cured (some are smoked, too) and have been fully cooked. They have almost no waste from fat or bone.

CENTER HAM SLICES are cut crosswise through the center section of ham.

BAKED SMOKED HAM

Heat oven to 325°F. Place ham, fat-side-up, on rack in shallow roasting pan. Insert meat thermometer so the bulb reaches the center of the thickest part, but does not rest in fat or on bone. Bake as directed in timetable, page 339.

To glaze baked ham, pour drippings from pan. If necessary, trim fat, leaving only a thin layer on ham. Score ham by cutting diamond shapes about ¼-inch deep through the fat. If desired, insert a whole clove in each diamond. Spoon one of the suggested glazes, page 339, over ham; return to oven and bake 15 to 20 minutes more.

NUTRITION INFORMATION PER SERVING

Serving Size: 1/3 lb. boneless smoked ham, cooked		Percent U.S. RDA Per Serving	
Calories	358	Protein	40%
Protein	26g	Vitamin A	0%
Carbohydrate	0g	Vitamin C	0%
Fat	27g	Thiamin	39%
Sodium	928mg	Riboflavin	13%
Potassium	212mg	Niacin	22%
		Calcium	*
		Iron	18%

GLAZED HAM SLICE

TIMETABLE FOR BAKED HAM

Set oven at 325°F., do not cover pan.

Ham	Weight	Thermometer Temperature	Approximate Cooking Time per lb.
Cook-before-eating			
whole ham	10-14 lb.	160°F.	18-20 min.
half ham	5-7 lb.	160°F.	22-25 min.
shank or rump portion	3-4 lb.	160°F.	35-40 min.
arm picnic shoulder	5-8 lb.	170°F.	30-35 min.
Fully Cooked			
whole ham	10-14 lb.	140°F.	10-15 min.
half ham	5-7 lb.	140°F.	18-24 min.
shank or rump portion	3-4 lb.	140°F.	18-24 min.
arm picnic shoulder	5-8 lb.	140°F.	25-30 min.

Choose a cook-before-eating, fully cooked or a canned ham, then bake it to perfection topped with a shiny glaze. Allow ⅓ to ½ lb. of ham per serving.

GLAZES FOR BAKED HAM

BROWN SUGAR: Combine 1 cup firmly packed brown sugar, 2 tablespoons flour, ½ teaspoon dry or prepared mustard, ⅛ teaspoon cinnamon and 3 tablespoons dry sherry, vinegar or water; mix well. Spread on ham.

JELLY: Heat 1 cup currant or apple jelly until melted. Spread on ham.

ORANGE MARMALADE: Use 1 cup orange marmalade to spread on ham.

PINEAPPLE: Combine 1 cup firmly packed brown sugar with ¾ cup drained crushed pineapple; spread on ham.

TIP: *Score ham well before spreading on glaze. Glaze will not run off as easily and flavor will penetrate more.*

SPICY AUTUMN HAM

1 tablespoon whole cloves
4 to 5-lb. picnic ham or ham
2 to 3 qts. apple cider
1 teaspoon whole or ½ teaspoon ground allspice
2 sticks cinnamon or ¼ teaspoon ground cinnamon

Insert cloves into fat layer around edge of ham rind. In Dutch oven, add ham, cider to cover, allspice and cinnamon sticks. Cover; heat to boiling. Reduce heat; simmer 1½ to 2 hours or until tender. Remove ham to platter. If desired, thicken 2½ cups of juice with 2 tablespoons cornstarch dissolved in 2 tablespoons water. Heat until mixture boils and thickens, stirring constantly. Serve over sliced ham.

8 to 10 servings

NUTRITION INFORMATION PER SERVING

Serving Size: 1/8 of recipe		Percent U.S. RDA Per Serving	
Calories	320	Protein	42%
Protein	28g	Vitamin A	*
Carbohydrate	30g	Vitamin C	3%
Fat	10g	Thiamin	43%
Sodium	895mg	Riboflavin	18%
Potassium	565mg	Niacin	25%
		Calcium	3%
		Iron	28%

TIP: *If desired, add vegetables such as sweet potatoes, rutabagas or turnips during last 30 minutes of cooking.*

BAKED HAM SLICE IN ORANGE SAUCE

½ cup firmly packed brown sugar
1 tablespoon cornstarch
⅛ teaspoon ginger
1 cup orange juice
1 ham slice, cut 1-inch thick
10 to 12 whole cloves

Heat oven to 325°F. In shallow baking dish, combine first 3 ingredients. Stir in orange juice. Add ham slice, turning to coat both sides. Sprinkle with cloves. Bake uncovered at 325°F. for 45 to 60 minutes, basting ham occasionally with sauce. 4 to 5 servings

NUTRITION INFORMATION PER SERVING

Serving Size: 1/4 of recipe		Percent U.S. RDA Per Serving	
Calories	325	Protein	40%
Protein	26g	Vitamin A	2%
Carobohydrate	35g	Vitamin C	28%
Fat	9g	Thiamin	42%
Sodium	937mg	Riboflavin	14%
Potassium	536mg	Niacin	24%
		Calcium	4%
		Iron	23%

TIPS: *If desired, cut 1-inch slices or several thinner slices from ready-to-eat ham.*

To halve recipe, use ½ to 1 lb. ham; use half the remaining ingredients. Bake about 30 minutes.

HAM LOAF

2 eggs
1½ lb. (5 cups) cooked ground ham
2 cups soft bread crumbs
¼ cup firmly packed brown sugar
2 tablespoons chopped green pepper
2 tablespoons chopped onion
1 tablespoon prepared mustard
¼ cup milk or pineapple syrup

Heat oven to 350°F. In large bowl, slightly beat eggs; stir in remaining ingredients; mix well. Press into 8x4-inch loaf pan. Bake at 350°F. for 60 to 70 minutes or until set in center. Let stand 5 minutes before removing from pan.

5 to 6 servings

NUTRITION INFORMATION PER SERVING

Serving Size: 1/6 of recipe		Percent U.S. RDA Per Serving	
Calories	381	Protein	36%
Protein	23g	Vitamin A	5%
Carbohydrate	18g	Vitamin C	5%
Fat	23g	Thiamin	33%
Sodium	822mg	Riboflavin	16%
Potassium	319mg	Niacin	19%
		Calcium	6%
		Iron	20%

TIPS: *For PINEAPPLE-GLAZED HAM LOAF, top unbaked ham loaf with 8-oz. can (1 cup) drained crushed pineapple mixed with 2 tablespoons brown sugar.*

For HONEY-GLAZED HAM LOAF, top unbaked ham loaf with 2 tablespoons honey.

For HAM LOAF SQUARES, press ham mixture into 8 or 9-inch square pan. Arrange 8-oz. can drained pineapple slices on top of meat. Halve 3 to 4 maraschino cherries and arrange with pineapple. Bake at 350°F. for 50 to 60 minutes. Cut into squares.

HAM ASPARAGUS HOLLANDAISE

10- oz. pkg. frozen asparagus spears
3 tablespoons (1½ oz.) cream cheese, softened
¼ cup mayonnaise or salad dressing
½ lb. cooked, thinly sliced ham
Hollandaise Sauce, page 543
1 hard-cooked egg, sliced or chopped

Heat oven to 350°F. In medium saucepan, cook asparagus as directed on package; drain. In small bowl, blend cream cheese and mayonnaise until smooth. Spread cream cheese mixture on ham slices. Roll 2 or 3 asparagus spears inside each ham slice. Secure with toothpicks if necessary. Arrange seam-side-down in 12x8-inch baking dish or shallow pan. Prepare Hollandaise Sauce as directed. Pour cooked Sauce over center of ham rolls. Garnish with egg. Bake uncovered at 350°F. for 10 to 15 minutes or until heated through.

4 to 5 servings

NUTRITION INFORMATION PER SERVING

Serving Size: 1/4 of recipe		Percent U.S. RDA Per Serving	
Calories	567	Protein	27%
Protein	18g	Vitamin A	44%
Carbohydrate	3g	Vitamin C	25%
Fat	54g	Thiamin	25%
Sodium	701mg	Riboflavin	17%
Potassium	170mg	Niacin	10%
		Calcium	6%
		Iron	19%

TIPS: *Canned asparagus spears may be substituted for frozen; omit cooking asparagus. Assemble as directed.*

One pkg. hollandaise sauce mix may be substituted for Hollandaise Sauce. Prepare as directed on package.

BROILED HAM AND FRUIT KABOBS

½ cup orange marmalade or apricot preserves
½ teaspoon ginger, if desired
¼ cup orange juice
1 tablespoon lemon juice
1½ cups (8 oz.) cooked ham, cut into 1-inch cubes
2 medium bananas, cut into 1-inch slices
8-oz. can (1 cup) pineapple chunks, drained

In small bowl, combine first 4 ingredients; mix well. Thread ham, bananas and pineapple on 4 large or 8 small skewers, beginning and ending with ham. Grill or broil kabobs, 6 to 8 inches from heat for 15 to 20 minutes, turning occasionally. Brush frequently with basting sauce until ham and fruit are heated.

4 servings

NUTRITION INFORMATION PER SERVING

Serving Size: 1/4 of recipe		Percent U.S. RDA Per Serving	
Calories	308	Protein	22%
Protein	14g	Vitamin A	4%
Carbohydrate	56g	Vitamin C	15%
Fat	5g	Thiamin	27%
Sodium	495mg	Riboflavin	11%
Potassium	506mg	Niacin	15%
		Calcium	3%
		Iron	14%

TIP: *If desired, marinate ham, bananas and pineapple, 1 to 2 hours in basting sauce before cooking.*

HAM AND CHEESE CRÊPES

12 cooked Basic Crêpes, page 101
1½ cups (6 oz.) shredded Cheddar or American cheese
12 slices (12 oz.) cooked, thinly sliced ham
1 tablespoon chopped green onion
½ teaspoon salt
⅛ teaspoon pepper
½ cup dairy sour cream
½ teaspoon prepared mustard
⅓ cup bread crumbs
3 tablespoons margarine or butter, melted

Prepare crêpes. Heat oven to 350°F. Sprinkle each crêpe with about 2 tablespoons cheese; top each with ham slice. In small bowl, combine onion, salt, pepper, sour cream and mustard; mix well. Spread about 1 tablespoon sour cream mixture over ham. Roll up; arrange in 13x9-inch pan. Combine margarine and bread crumbs; sprinkle over crêpes. Cover loosely with foil; bake at 350°F. for 15 to 20 minutes or until cheese is melted. Serve immediately.

12 crêpes

NUTRITION INFORMATION PER SERVING

Serving Size: 1 crêpe		Percent U.S. RDA Per Serving	
Calories	263	Protein	24%
Protein	16g	Vitamin A	13%
Carbohydrate	11g	Vitamin C	*
Fat	17g	Thiamin	18%
Sodium	628mg	Riboflavin	17%
Potassium	180mg	Niacin	10%
		Calcium	17%
		Iron	10%

TIPS: *For crispier crêpes, bake on ungreased cookie sheet 12 to 15 minutes.*

For variety, serve with cheese or cream soup sauce.

WIENERS, BACON AND SAUSAGES

There are a great number of sausages and luncheon meats, so read the label in determining your preferences. All should be stored in the refrigerator and can be left in their original wrappings.

BOLOGNA

Available in rings, rolls or slices, this fully cooked sausage is generally made of beef and pork with mild seasonings similar to wieners.

WIENERS

Also called frankfurters, franks and Vienna-style sausage.

Several types of wieners are available. Read the label to check on the ingredients: all beef or a combination of beef and pork, also note different sizes, weight, type of grind. Wieners are fully cooked and may be eaten hot or cold.

How to Cook:

Simmer (do not boil), covered with water, 5 to 10 minutes or until heated through.

Fry in partially covered skillet over medium heat 5 to 10 minutes or until browned on all sides. If desired, fry in a little margarine, butter or oil.

Broil or grill 3 to 4 inches from heat 10 to 12 minutes, turning occasionally to brown evenly. If desired, brush with barbecue sauce during cooking.

SAUSAGE

FRESH PORK SAUSAGE is made of selected fresh pork with spices added. It is available in links, patties, rolls and bulk. It must be cooked thoroughly before serving.

FRESH COUNTRY-STYLE SAUSAGE is ground more coarsely than fresh pork sausage. It is generally linked in casings, but is sometimes sold in bulk. It also must be cooked before serving.

Some other sausages which will add variety to your menu are: SMOKED SAUSAGE, BRATWURST, KNACKWURST and POLISH SAUSAGE. All must be cooked.

How to Cook Fresh Sausage:
Place sausages in cold skillet, fry partially covered over medium heat 5 to 10 minutes on each side until browned and well done. Thick patties may be covered for a few minutes to cook center.

Oven-cook by placing on rack in shallow baking pan. Bake uncovered, at 400°F. for 15 to 20 minutes or until well done, turning once.

BACON

Available in slabs (unsliced) or already sliced in varying thicknesses, bacon is cut from the side of pork, cured and smoked.

How to Cook:
Fry in skillet (place bacon in cold pan), heating slowly and separating slices so they lie flat in pan. Fry slowly 2 to 3 minutes on each side or until crisp. Drain on paper towel.

Oven-cook by placing separated bacon slices on rack in shallow baking pan. Bake at 400°F. for 10 to 12 minutes or until crisp.

Broil by placing separated bacon slices on cold broiler rack. Broil 3 inches from heat 3 to 4 minutes on each side or until crisp, watching carefully.

NUTRITION INFORMATION PER SERVING

Serving Size: 2 slices cooked bacon		Percent U.S. RDA Per Serving	
Calories	86	Protein	6%
Protein	4g	Vitamin A	0%
Carbohydrate	<1g	Vitamin C	†
Fat	8g	Thiamin	5%
Sodium	153mg	Riboflavin	3%
Potassium	35mg	Niacin	4%
		Calcium	*
		Iron	3%

CANADIAN BACON

This cut is the boneless loin that has been cured and smoked. It is available whole, cut into sections or sliced. It should be labeled "fully cooked" or "cook-before-eating" to indicate the need for cooking.

How to Cook:
Fry by placing ¼-inch slices in cold skillet. Cook over medium heat about 10 minutes, turning once to brown evenly.

Oven-cook by placing a 1 to 1½-lb. piece of unsliced Canadian bacon in shallow baking pan. Bake uncovered, at 325°F. for about 1 hour (35 to 40 minutes per pound). If desired, brush with a glaze suggested for ham.

NUTRITION INFORMATION PER SERVING

Serving Size: 1 slice cooked Canadian Bacon		Percent U.S. RDA Per Serving	
Calories	58	Protein	9%
Protein	6g	Vitamin A	0%
Carbohydrate	<1g	Vitamin C	†
Fat	4g	Thiamin	13%
Sodium	537mg	Riboflavin	2%
Potassium	91mg	Niacin	5%
		Calcium	*
		Iron	5%

POLISH SAUSAGE AND SAUERKRAUT

28 or 32-oz. can or jar (4 cups) sauerkraut, undrained
2 tablespoons firmly packed brown sugar
½ teaspoon caraway seed
1 medium apple, chopped
¼ cup water
1 to 1½ lb. Polish sausage or ring bologna

In large saucepan, combine all ingredients except sausage; mix well. Place sausage on top. Simmer covered, 20 to 30 minutes.

4 to 6 servings

NUTRITION INFORMATION PER SERVING

Serving Size: 1/4 of recipe		Percent U.S. RDA Per Serving	
Calories	427	Protein	31%
Protein	20g	Vitamin A	3%
Carbohydrate	21g	Vitamin C	29%
Fat	30g	Thiamin	30%
Sodium	2736mg	Riboflavin	18%
Potassium	340mg	Niacin	20%
		Calcium	9%
		Iron	23%

TIP: *One pound whole or sliced wieners may be substituted for Polish sausage.*

SAUERKRAUT AND WIENERS

¼ cup margarine or butter
1 small onion, sliced
1 stalk celery, sliced
¼ cup sugar
1½ tablespoons cornstarch
1 tablespoon chopped pimiento, drained
1 cube or 1 teaspoon beef bouillon
¼ teaspoon ginger
1½ cups water
2 tablespoons vinegar
16-oz. can (2 cups) sauerkraut, drained
8 wieners

In large saucepan, cook onion and celery in margarine until tender. Stir in remaining ingredients except wieners; mix well. Arrange wieners on top. Simmer covered, about 10 minutes or until heated through, stirring occasionally. Serve with boiled or baked potatoes.

4 to 5 servings

NUTRITION INFORMATION PER SERVING

Serving Size: 1/5 of recipe		Percent U.S. RDA Per Serving	
Calories	365	Protein	15%
Protein	10g	Vitamin A	9%
Carbohydrate	18g	Vitamin C	17%
Fat	29g	Thiamin	9%
Sodium	1515mg	Riboflavin	10%
Potassium	303mg	Niacin	10%
		Calcium	3%
		Iron	9%

TIP: *Ring bologna or Polish sausage may be substituted for wieners.*

BEER AND BRATWURST

1 lb. (6 to 8) bratwurst or other smoked sausage
1 teaspoon celery seed
1 bay leaf
1 medium onion, sliced
12-oz. can beer

In large saucepan, combine all ingredients. Heat until almost boiling. Simmer covered about 5 minutes. Remove bratwurst and continue simmering onions until tender. Broil or grill bratwursts 3 to 4 inches from heat about 3 to 5 minutes on each side. Before serving, drain onions and serve with bratwurst.

4 to 5 servings

NUTRITION INFORMATION PER SERVING

Serving Size: 1/5 of recipe		Percent U.S. RDA Per Serving	
Calories	318	Protein	23%
Protein	15g	Vitamin A	*
Carbohydrate	6g	Vitamin C	3%
Fat	24g	Thiamin	21%
Sodium	1008mg	Riboflavin	12%
Potassium	262mg	Niacin	16%
		Calcium	3%
		Iron	14%

SNAPPY WIENERS

1 lb. (10) wieners
1 small onion, chopped
2 tablespoons catsup
1 tablespoon vinegar
1 tablespoon prepared mustard
2 teaspoons Worcestershire sauce
¾ teaspoon prepared horseradish

Heat oven to 350°F. Score wieners diagonally. In 1½-quart casserole, combine remaining ingredients; mix well. Arrange wieners in sauce, turning to coat well. Bake covered at 350°F. for 30 minutes or until heated through.

5 to 6 servings

NUTRITION INFORMATION PER SERVING

Serving Size: 1/6 of recipe		Percent U.S. RDA Per Serving	
Calories	237	Protein	15%
Protein	10g	Vitamin A	*
Carbohydrate	4g	Vitamin C	3%
Fat	20g	Thiamin	8%
Sodium	910mg	Riboflavin	9%
Potassium	209mg	Niacin	10%
		Calcium	*
		Iron	7%

TIP: *To prepare in skillet, heat 10 to 15 minutes or until heated through.*

BEER AND BRATWURST

CREAMED CHIPPED BEEF

- **¼ cup margarine or butter**
- **¼ cup flour**
- **Dash pepper**
- **2 cups milk**
- **1 or 2 pkg. (3 oz. each) sliced dried beef**

In medium saucepan, melt margarine. Blend in flour and pepper. Stir in milk. Cook over medium heat until mixture boils and thickens, stirring constantly. Reduce heat. Cut beef into shreds; add to cream sauce and heat through. Serve over toast points or mashed potatoes. 3 to 4 servings

NUTRITION INFORMATION PER SERVING

Serving Size: 1/4 of recipe		Percent U.S. RDA Per Serving	
Calories	295	Protein	30%
Protein	20g	Vitamin A	13%
Carbohydrate	12g	Vitamin C	*
Fat	18g	Thiamin	8%
Sodium	2007mg	Riboflavin	22%
Potassium	270mg	Niacin	11%
		Calcium	16%
		Iron	13%

TIPS: *One 2½-oz. jar sliced dried beef may be substituted for the package. To eliminate salty flavor, separate slices, cover with boiling water; drain immediately. Continue as directed.*

Other seasonings could include: ½ teaspoon dry mustard (add with flour), 2 tablespoons chopped onion (cook in margarine until tender), 1 cup shredded Cheddar cheese (add with beef), 1 tablespoon parsley (add with beef).

ORANGE-GLAZED LUNCHEON LOAF

- **12-oz. can luncheon meat**
- **4 thin orange slices, cut in half**
- **8 whole cloves**
- **¼ cup orange marmalade**
- **1 teaspoon flour**
- **⅛ teaspoon dry mustard or ¼ teaspoon prepared mustard**

Heat oven to 350°F. Place luncheon meat in 8-inch square pan. Cut meat halfway through into 8 slices. Insert orange slices in slashes and 1 whole clove in each section of meat. Combine marmalade, flour and mustard; spread over loaf.* Bake uncovered at 350°F. for 20 to 30 minutes or until heated through. 4 servings

NUTRITION INFORMATION PER SERVING

Serving Size: 1/4 of recipe		Percent U.S. RDA Per Serving	
Calories	312	Protein	20%
Protein	13g	Vitamin A	*
Carbohydrate	19g	Vitamin C	18%
Fat	21g	Thiamin	19%
Sodium	1052mg	Riboflavin	11%
Potassium	236mg	Niacin	14%
		Calcium	3%
		Iron	12%

TIP: *To MAKE AHEAD, prepare to * and refrigerate up to 1 day. Bake just before serving.*

ZESTY LUNCHEON SLICES

- **¼ cup firmly packed brown sugar**
- **¼ cup currant or apple jelly**
- **1 tablespoon prepared horseradish**
- **12-oz. can luncheon meat**
- **16-oz. can (2 cups) pear halves, peach halves or pineapple slices, drained**

Heat oven to 350°F. In shallow pan, combine brown sugar, jelly and horseradish. Slice meat into 6 slices. Dip in glaze mixture, turning to coat both sides; arrange in pan. Place fruit along side or on top of meat slices. Spoon glaze over each. Bake uncovered at 350°F. for 20 to 30 minutes or until heated through, occasionally spooning glaze over meat. If desired, garnish fruit with maraschino cherry half. 4 to 5 servings

NUTRITION INFORMATION PER SERVING

Serving Size: 1/5 of recipe		Percent U.S. RDA Per Serving	
Calories	329	Protein	16%
Protein	10g	Vitamin A	*
Carbohydrate	34g	Vitamin C	2%
Fat	17g	Thiamin	15%
Sodium	848mg	Riboflavin	10%
Potassium	260mg	Niacin	11%
		Calcium	2%
		Iron	12%

VEAL

Veal is from a young beef animal but it is not thought of as a form of beef. It has a very mild flavor. Recipes which include a sauce, stuffing or coating help retain the natural juices and enhance the flavor.

When purchasing veal, look for light grayish-pink lean, very fine grain, fairly firm and velvety texture with very little fat.

VEAL ROASTS

SHOULDER ROASTS include several muscles and occasionally contain some rib bones. Arm roasts contain the round bone. Roast or cook with liquid. Blade roasts contain the blade bone and are cut from the shoulder area near the ribs. Cook with liquid for tenderness. Boneless cuts are available.

RUMP ROASTS contain the round muscles and usually part of the round bone. A rolled rump roast is boneless. Roast or cook with liquid.

VEAL CHOPS AND STEAKS

These are commonly available: LOIN CHOPS, RIB CHOPS, SHOULDER or ROUND STEAKS, SHOULDER CHOPS, BLADE STEAKS and CUTLETS. Veal chops and steaks are usually cooked with liquid or pan-fried.

VEAL ROAST

Heat oven to 325°F. Place roast, fat-side-up, on rack in shallow roasting pan. Season with salt and pepper. Brush with margarine, butter or oil or lay several slices of bacon over roast. Insert meat thermometer so the bulb reaches the center of the thickest part of meat, being sure the bulb does not rest in fat or on bone. Roast to 170°F. (well done), see Timetable for Roasting Veal. Occasionally baste with additional margarine or pan drippings. Let roast stand, covered with foil, about 20 minutes before slicing.

TIMETABLE FOR ROASTING VEAL

Set oven at 325°F., do not cover pan.

Cut	Weight	Thermometer Reading	Approximate Cooking Time Per lb.
Rump	5-8 lb.	170°F.	25-35 min.
Loin	4-6 lb.	170°F.	30-35 min.
Rib (rack)	3-5 lb.	170°F.	35-40 min.
Shoulder	4-6 lb.	170°F.	40-45 min.

VEAL ROAST AND MUSHROOM SAUCE

3 to 4-lb. veal rump, blade or shoulder roast
1 medium onion, sliced
½ cup dry white wine or sherry
10 ¾-oz. can condensed golden mushroom soup
¼ teaspoon salt
Dash pepper

Heat oven to 325°F. Place roast fat-side-up, in 2½ to 3-quart covered casserole. Sprinkle with onion; pour wine and soup over roast. Add salt and pepper. Bake covered at 325°F. for 2 to 2½ hours or until tender. Serve sauce over roast.

5 to 6 servings

NUTRITION INFORMATION PER SERVING

Serving Size: 1/6 of recipe		Percent U.S. RDA Per Serving	
Calories	347	Protein	53%
Protein	35g	Vitamin A	*
Carbohydrate	7g	Vitamin C	4%
Fat	18g	Thiamin	7%
Sodium	587mg	Riboflavin	22%
Potassium	710mg	Niacin	35%
		Calcium	4%
		Iron	24%

TIPS: *To cook on top of range, place roast in Dutch oven and simmer covered, 2 to 2½ hours or until tender. Add water if necessary.*

For additional seasoning, add ½ teaspoon crushed thyme or marjoram leaves or ¼ teaspoon garlic powder.

GLAZED VEAL ROLL

3-lb. boneless rolled veal shoulder or rump roast
½ teaspoon salt
⅛ teaspoon pepper
½ cup firmly packed brown sugar
1 tablespoon grated lemon peel
⅛ teaspoon cloves
1 tablespoon lemon juice
12-oz. can (1½ cups) apricot nectar

Heat oven to 325°F. Season meat with salt and pepper. Place on rack in shallow roasting pan. Insert meat thermometer so bulb reaches center of the thickest part. (Do not add water; do not cover.) Roast at 325°F. for 1½ hours. In small saucepan, combine remaining ingredients; mix well. Simmer 10 minutes. Cool. After meat has roasted 1½ hours, spoon ⅓ apricot glaze over meat every 20 minutes. Roast until well done, about 2½ hours total roasting time until meat thermometer registers 170°F. If desired, serve drippings as sauce with meat.

8 to 10 servings

NUTRITION INFORMATION PER SERVING

Serving Size: 1/10 of recipe		Percent U.S. RDA Per Serving	
Calories	274	Protein	39%
Protein	25g	Vitamin A	7%
Carbohydrate	16g	Vitamin C	4%
Fat	12g	Thiamin	6%
Sodium	184mg	Riboflavin	16%
Potassium	547mg	Niacin	29%
		Calcium	3%
		Iron	20%

VEAL CUTLETS CORDON BLEU

6 boneless veal cutlets (about 4 oz. each) or 1½ lb. veal round steak
6 thin slices Swiss cheese
6 thin slices cooked ham
¼ cup flour
¼ teaspoon salt
¼ teaspoon pepper
⅛ teaspoon nutmeg
⅛ teaspoon cloves
2 eggs, slightly beaten
½ cup dry bread or cornflake crumbs
½ cup margarine or butter

Cut veal cutlets in half. Place veal between sheets of plastic wrap; pound with flat side of meat hammer or rolling pin until ¼-inch thick. Place 1 slice cheese and 1 slice ham (cut slightly smaller than veal) on 6 veal slices. Top with remaining veal. Pound edges together to seal. In small bowl, combine flour, salt, pepper, nutmeg and cloves. Coat cutlets with seasoned flour; dip in eggs and coat with crumbs. In large skillet, brown in hot margarine 4 to 5 minutes on each side or until tender.

5 to 6 servings

NUTRITION INFORMATION PER SERVING

Serving Size: 1/6 of recipe		Percent U.S. RDA Per Serving	
Calories	526	Protein	55%
Protein	36g	Vitamin A	21%
Carbohydrate	7g	Vitamin C	*
Fat	39g	Thiamin	16%
Sodium	910mg	Riboflavin	24%
Potassium	464mg	Niacin	28%
		Calcium	22%
		Iron	24%

BREADED VEAL CUTLETS

2 tablespoons flour
½ teaspoon salt
½ teaspoon paprika
⅛ teaspoon pepper
1 egg, slightly beaten
1 to 2 teaspoons Worcestershire sauce
½ cup dry bread crumbs
4 to 6 veal cutlets*
2 to 3 tablespoons oil

In small bowl, combine first 4 ingredients. In another small bowl, combine egg and Worcestershire sauce. Coat cutlets with seasoned flour; dip in egg mixture, and coat with crumbs. In large skillet, brown cutlets in hot oil until golden brown. Continue cooking over medium heat 5 to 7 minutes or until veal is done. 4 servings

NUTRITION INFORMATION PER SERVING

Serving Size: 1/4 of recipe		Percent U.S. RDA Per Serving	
Calories	313	Protein	39%
Protein	25g	Vitamin A	3%
Carbohydrate	6g	Vitamin C	*
Fat	20g	Thiamin	8%
Sodium	401mg	Riboflavin	17%
Potassium	454mg	Niacin	25%
		Calcium	2%
		Iron	18%

TIPS: **If desired, use 1 to 1½ lb. veal round steak. Cut into serving pieces and flatten to ¼-inch thickness by placing between sheets of plastic wrap and pounding with flat side of meat hammer or rolling pin.*

For CHEESE-TOPPED VEAL, decrease bread crumbs to ¼ cup. Mix crumbs with ¼ cup grated Parmesan cheese. After turning browned cutlets, top each with slice of Mozzarella cheese and tomato slice. Cover and heat until tomato is hot and cheese begins to melt.

VEAL PARMIGIANA

⅓ cup grated Parmesan cheese
2 tablespoons cornflake or dry bread crumbs
1 egg, slightly beaten
1 to 1½-lb. veal cutlets or veal round steak, cut into 4 serving pieces
2 tablespoons oil
1 medium onion, chopped
¼ teaspoon salt
⅛ teaspoon pepper
⅛ teaspoon oregano leaves or Italian seasoning
8-oz. can (1 cup) tomato sauce
1 cup (4 oz.) shredded Mozzarella cheese

Heat oven to 375°F. In small bowl, combine Parmesan cheese and crumbs. Dip veal in egg, then coat with cheese and crumb mixture. In large skillet, brown veal in hot oil. Remove veal to shallow 8-inch square or round pan. Add onion to skillet and cook until tender. Stir in salt, pepper, oregano and tomato sauce. Top pieces of veal with cheese; pour tomato mixture over cheese, spreading to cover. Sprinkle with additional Parmesan cheese. Bake uncovered at 375°F. for 30 minutes or until bubbly. 4 servings

NUTRITION INFORMATION PER SERVING

Serving Size: 1/4 of recipe		Percent U.S. RDA Per Serving	
Calories	525	Protein	46%
Protein	30g	Vitamin A	27%
Carbohydrate	12g	Vitamin C	5%
Fat	39g	Thiamin	9%
Sodium	400mg	Riboflavin	32%
Potassium	510mg	Niacin	25%
		Calcium	34%
		Iron	21%

VEAL CHOPS PERU

⅓ cup flour
1 teaspoon salt
1 teaspoon oregano leaves
2 tablespoons margarine or butter
5 to 6 veal chops
1 medium onion, sliced
¼ cup water
6 thin slices (3x3-inch) Swiss cheese
⅛ teaspoon instant coffee
½ cup dairy sour cream

Combine flour, salt and oregano; coat chops with mixture. In large skillet, brown chops and onion in hot margarine. Add water; simmer covered, 20 minutes or until chops are tender. Remove chops to platter. Top each chop with slice of cheese. (Heat from chops will melt cheese.) Add instant coffee and sour cream to pan drippings; stir to combine. Heat through, but do not boil. Pour sauce over chops. If desired, garnish with parsley. 5 to 6 servings

NUTRITION INFORMATION PER SERVING

Serving Size: 1/6 of recipe		Percent U.S. RDA Per Serving	
Calories	378	Protein	46%
Protein	30g	Vitamin A	11%
Carbohydrate	8g	Vitamin C	4%
Fat	25g	Thiamin	8%
Sodium	725mg	Riboflavin	21%
Potassium	488mg	Niacin	25%
		Calcium	23%
		Iron	18%

TIPS: *If desired, substitute ¼ cup prepared coffee for water and omit instant coffee.*

For LAMB CHOPS PERU, substitute lamb chops for veal chops, prepare as directed.

VEAL STROGANOFF

1½ lb. boneless veal, cubed
1 small onion, chopped
2 tablespoons oil
1½ teaspoons chopped parsley
½ teaspoon oregano or basil leaves
¼ cup dry white wine or sherry
10¾-oz. can condensed cream of mushroom soup
4-oz. can (½ cup) mushroom stems and pieces, undrained
½ cup dairy sour cream

In large skillet, brown veal and onion in hot oil. Add parsley, oregano, wine, soup and mushrooms. Heat to boiling. Simmer covered, about 1¼ hours or until veal is tender, stirring occasionally.* Before serving, stir in sour cream; heat, but do not boil. Serve over noodles or rice. 4 to 5 servings

NUTRITION INFORMATION PER SERVING

Serving Size: 1/4 of recipe		Percent U.S. RDA Per Serving	
Calories	500	Protein	53%
Protein	34g	Vitamin A	6%
Carbohydrate	11g	Vitamin C	6%
Fat	32g	Thiamin	9%
Sodium	797mg	Riboflavin	30%
Potassium	734mg	Niacin	41%
		Calcium	8%
		Iron	25%

TIPS: *To double recipe, double the ingredient amounts.*

A 1½-oz. pkg. sour cream sauce mix may be substituted for sour cream.

*To MAKE AHEAD, prepare to *, cool and refrigerate up to 2 days; continue as directed.*

VEAL SCALLOPINI

¼ cup flour
1 teaspoon salt
⅛ teaspoon pepper
6 veal cutlets*
2 tablespoons oil
3 tomatoes, coarsely chopped
1 cube or 1 teaspoon beef bouillon
½ cup dry white wine
⅓ cup margarine or butter
12 oz. (4 cups) sliced fresh mushrooms
1 small onion, chopped
1 green pepper, sliced
1 garlic clove
8 oz. noodles
Grated Parmesan cheese

In small bowl, combine flour, salt and pepper. Coat meat with flour mixture. In large skillet, brown meat in hot oil for 5 to 7 minutes. Stir in wine, tomatoes and bouillon; simmer covered, 15 minutes. In another large skillet, melt margarine. Cook mushrooms, onion, green pepper and garlic in margarine until tender. Cook noodles as directed on package. Add vegetables to meat and simmer uncovered, about 10 minutes to blend flavors; remove garlic. Serve over noodles; sprinkle with Parmesan cheese.

4 to 6 servings

NUTRITION INFORMATION PER SERVING

Serving Size: 1/6 of recipe		Percent U.S. RDA Per Serving	
Calories	630	Protein	54%
Protein	35g	Vitamin A	27%
Carbohydrate	46g	Vitamin C	68%
Fat	32g	Thiamin	29%
Sodium	1131mg	Riboflavin	44%
Potassium	1429mg	Niacin	51%
		Calcium	11%
		Iron	31%

TIP: **If desired, 1½-lb. veal round steak cut into 6 pieces may be substituted for the veal cutlets. Pound round steak with meat hammer until about ¼-inch thick. Continue as directed.*

LAMB

Lamb is a tender, flavorful meat that is best served very hot or chilled rather than lukewarm. Lamb is frequently served with stuffings and sauces, of which mint is one of the most well known.

The color of lean lamb is light pink. The texture should be fine and velvety; fat should be white.

LAMB ROASTS

LEG OF LAMB is the back leg section of the lamb. It is available whole cut into sections or boned.

RIB ROASTS contain the rib and back bones. They are cut from the rib area. Also called LAMB RACK.

SHOULDER ROASTS can be identified by their square shape. They contain the rib bones, blade bone and part of the arm bone and are covered with a layer of fat. They are sometimes boned and sold as ROLLED SHOULDER ROASTS. CUSHION SHOULDER ROASTS have the bones removed and are then tied without rolling, making a flatter roast.

LAMB ROASTS

Heat oven to 325°F. Place roast, fat-side-up, on rack in shallow roasting pan. Season with salt and pepper unless using glaze with salt or soy sauce added. Insert meat thermometer so the bulb reaches the center of the thickest part of meat, being sure the bulb does not rest in fat or on bone. Roast to desired degree of doneness using Timetable for Roasting Lamb, page 352.

NUTRITION INFORMATION PER SERVING

Serving Size: 1/2 lb. lamb roast with bone, cooked		Percent U.S. RDA Per Serving	
Calories	374	Protein	52%
Protein	34g	Vitamin A	0%
Carbohydrate	0g	Vitamin C	0%
Fat	25g	Thiamin	13%
Sodium	94mg	Riboflavin	21%
Potassium	389mg	Niacin	37%
		Calcium	*
		Iron	13%

TIMETABLE FOR ROASTING LAMB

Set oven at 325°F., do not cover pan.

Lamb Roasts	Weight	Thermometer Reading	Approximate Cooking Time per lb.
Leg, bone-in	5-8 lb.	175°F.-180°F.	30-35 min.
Shoulder, bone-in	4-6 lb.	175°F.-180°F.	30-35 min.
Shoulder, cushion	3-5 lb.	175°F.-180°F.	30-35 min.
Shoulder, boneless	3-5 lb.	175°F.-180°F.	40-45 min.

HOW TO CARVE LEG OF LAMB

Place leg of lamb on platter with the shank to the carver's right. Remove several slices from the thin side to form a solid base on which to set roast.

Turn roast on its base. Starting at the shank end, remove a small wedge cut; then carve perpendicular to the leg bone.

Release slices by cutting under them and along the leg bone, starting at shank end. For additional servings, turn over to original position and make slices to the bone. Release and serve.

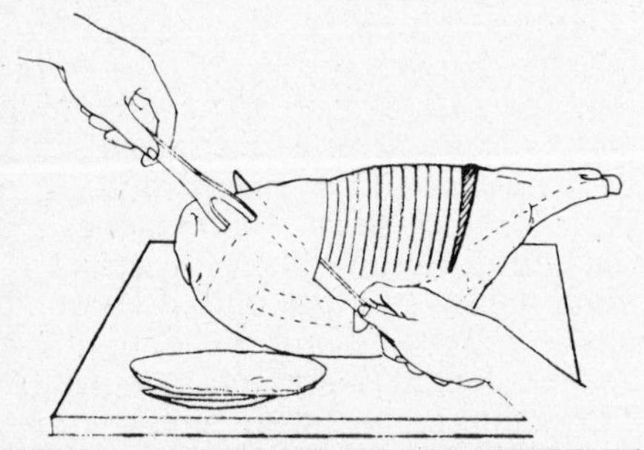

GLAZES FOR LAMB ROASTS

GARLIC GLAZE: Combine 1 tablespoon paprika, 3 cloves minced garlic, ½ teaspoon basil leaves, ⅓ cup water, ⅓ cup sherry, 2 tablespoons oil and 2 tablespoons soy sauce. Brush lamb with Glaze every 30 minutes during roasting.

JELLY GLAZE: Melt ¾ cup mint, currant or apricot jelly over low heat. Brush on lamb during last hour of roasting.

SPICY GLAZE: Combine ¼ cup firmly packed brown sugar, 1½ teaspoons salt, ½ teaspoon dry mustard, ½ teaspoon chili powder, 1 clove minced garlic, ¼ teaspoon ginger, ¼ teaspoon cloves and 1 tablespoon lemon juice. Brush on lamb during last hour of roasting.

PLUM GLAZE: In blender, combine 1 teaspoon basil leaves, 17-oz. can (2 cups) pitted and drained blue plums (reserve ¼ cup syrup), reserved syrup, 2 tablespoons lemon juice, 1 tablespoon soy sauce and 1 teaspoon Worcestershire sauce. Blend at medium speed until smooth. Brush lamb with Glaze every 30 minutes during roasting.

LAMB CHOPS

LOIN CHOPS are cut from the loin area. The T-shaped bone in these chops divides the tenderloin and rib muscles.

RIB CHOPS are cut from the rib area and have only one muscle and usually one or two rib bones, depending on the thickness of the chops.

SHOULDER CHOPS or STEAKS are tender chops containing several small muscles and the arm or blade bone.

NUTRITION INFORMATION PER SERVING

Serving Size: 1 lamb chop, cooked		Percent U.S. RDA Per Serving	
Calories	513	Protein	48%
Protein	31g	Vitamin A	0%
Carbohydrate	0g	Vitamin C	0%
Fat	42g	Thiamin	11%
Sodium	100mg	Riboflavin	19%
Potassium	415mg	Niacin	36%
		Calcium	*
		Iron	10%

GROUND LAMB
GROUND LAMB and LAMB PATTIES are made by grinding lean meat and trimmings. Patties may be seasoned or unseasoned.

LAMB RIBLETS
RIBLETS contain part of the rib bones and are from the breast section. Cuts are made between the ribs. They are sometimes sold boneless for stew.

STEW MEAT
STEW MEAT contains less tender sections of lamb cut into meaty pieces. They are tenderized by slow simmering in liquid.

LAMB SHANKS
LAMB SHANKS contain the leg and several muscles. They are usually cut from the front legs and require long simmering in liquid for tenderness.

ORANGE BLOSSOM LAMB CHOPS

2 tablespoons margarine or butter
6 lamb chops
1 teaspoon salt
1 medium onion, sliced
Dash pepper
1 to 2 teaspoons soy sauce, if desired
6-oz. can (¾ cup) frozen concentrated orange juice

In large skillet, brown chops in margarine. Reduce heat; add remaining ingredients. Stir until orange juice has blended with pan juices. Simmer covered, 15 to 20 minutes or until meat is tender. If desired, garnish with orange slices. Serve with rice. 4 to 6 servings

NUTRITION INFORMATION PER SERVING

Serving Size: 1/6 of recipe		Percent U.S. RDA Per Serving	
Calories	204	Protein	26%
Protein	17g	Vitamin A	8%
Carbohydrate	15g	Vitamin C	49%
Fat	8g	Thiamin	13%
Sodium	517mg	Riboflavin	11%
Potassium	433mg	Niacin	19%
		Calcium	3%
		Iron	8%

GLAZES AND MARINADES FOR LAMB CHOPS (for 4 to 6 chops)

GARLIC MARINADE: In small bowl, combine 1 teaspoon salt, 2 cloves minced garlic, 1 crushed bay leaf, ⅓ cup oil and 1 tablespoon vinegar. Pour over chops and marinate 2 hours. Drain well and broil as directed.

ORANGE GLAZE: In small bowl, combine ¼ cup orange marmalade and 2 tablespoons dry sherry or orange juice. Brush on chops during broiling or grilling.

APRICOT GLAZE: In small bowl, combine 1 teaspoon salt, ½ teaspoon nutmeg, ¼ teaspoon ginger, ⅓ cup apricot preserves and 2 tablespoons lemon juice. Brush on chops during broiling or grilling.

MINT GLAZE: In small saucepan, melt ¼ cup mint jelly with 1 tablespoon lemon juice over low heat. Stir to blend. Brush on chops during broiling or grilling. If desired, place canned pear halves on broiler during last half of cooking; brush pears with mint glaze also.

BROILED LAMB CHOPS

Place lamb rib, loin or shoulder chops on broiler pan. Place or adjust broiler pan so tops of 1-inch chops are 2 inches from heat and 2-inch chops are 3 inches from heat. When one side is browned, season with salt and pepper, turn and finish cooking on second side. (One-inch thick chops require 10 to 12 minutes; 2-inch thick chops require 20 to 22 minutes total cooking time.) Season with salt and pepper unless using glaze or marinade containing salt or soy sauce.

TIP: *Other seasonings for lamb chops include a dash of garlic salt, paprika or curry powder added with salt and pepper.*

LAMB CHOPS DELUXE

LAMB CHOPS DELUXE

1 tablespoon oil
6 to 8 lamb chops
1 teaspoon salt
1 teaspoon caraway seed or dill weed
1 medium onion, sliced
Dash pepper
¼ cup water
¾ cup dairy sour cream

In large skillet, brown chops in hot oil; drain excess fat. Add salt, caraway seed, onion, pepper and water. Simmer covered, 20 to 25 minutes or until chops are done. Remove chops to platter. Skim excess fat from pan drippings; stir in sour cream. Heat through, but do not boil. Pour sauce over chops. If desired, garnish with parsley.

6 to 8 servings

NUTRITION INFORMATION PER SERVING

Serving Size: 1/6 of recipe		Percent U.S. RDA Per Serving	
Calories	127	Protein	11%
Protein	7g	Vitamin A	5%
Carbohydrate	3g	Vitamin C	3%
Fat	9g	Thiamin	3%
Sodium	384mg	Riboflavin	6%
Potassium	96mg	Niacin	7%
		Calcium	4%
		Iron	3%

LAMB PATTIES

1 lb. ground lamb
2 tablespoons chopped onion
½ teaspoon salt
⅛ teaspoon pepper

In medium bowl, combine all ingredients; shape into 4 patties. Broil or grill 3 to 4 inches from heat 6 to 8 minutes on each side. If desired, brush with one of Glazes for Lamb Chops, page 353.

4 patties

NUTRITION INFORMATION PER SERVING

Serving Size: 1 patty		Percent U.S. RDA Per Serving	
Calories	125	Protein	29%
Protein	19g	Vitamin A	*
Carbohydrate	<1g	Vitamin C	*
Fat	5g	Thiamin	7%
Sodium	318mg	Riboflavin	12%
Potassium	199mg	Niacin	21%
		Calcium	*
		Iron	8%

LAMB AND RICE CURRY

5 to 6 lamb shoulder chops or steaks
1 teaspoon salt
1 medium onion, sliced
½ cup water
1 cup uncooked rice
¼ cup slivered almonds
2 tablespoons firmly packed brown sugar
1 cube or 1 teaspoon beef bouillon
½ teaspoon curry powder
1½ cups water
2 tablespoons chopped pimiento, drained
½ cup dairy sour cream

In large skillet, brown lamb chops. Add salt, onion and ½ cup water. Reduce heat; simmer covered, 15 minutes. Remove chops. Add remaining ingredients except sour cream; mix well. Arrange chops on top. Simmer 20 to 25 minutes longer or until most of water is absorbed. Stir in sour cream. If desired, garnish with parsley.

5 to 6 servings

NUTRITION INFORMATION PER SERVING

Serving Size: 1/6 of recipe		Percent U.S. RDA Per Serving	
Calories	380	Protein	41%
Protein	27g	Vitamin A	3%
Carbohydrate	33g	Vitamin C	4%
Fat	15g	Thiamin	19%
Sodium	589mg	Riboflavin	19%
Potassium	348mg	Niacin	31%
		Calcium	6%
		Iron	17%

TIP: *For PORK AND RICE CURRY, substitute pork steak for lamb chops.*

LAMB STEW

2 lb. boneless lamb, cut into 1-inch cubes
½ teaspoon sugar
1 tablespoon oil
⅓ cup flour
1½ teaspoons salt
¼ teaspoon pepper
1 garlic clove, minced
1½ cups water
¾ cup dry red wine
1 teaspoon Worcestershire sauce
6 to 8 carrots, peeled and cut into pieces
4 small onions, quartered
4 stalks celery, cut into 1-inch slices
2 to 3 potatoes, peeled and cubed

Sprinkle meat with sugar. In large skillet or Dutch oven, brown meat in hot oil. Stir in flour, salt and pepper. Add garlic, water, wine and Worcestershire sauce. Simmer covered, 45 minutes or until meat is tender, stirring occasionally. Add vegetables; cover and cook 30 to 45 minutes or until vegetables are tender. 5 to 6 servings

NUTRITION INFORMATION PER SERVING

Serving Size: 1/6 of recipe		Percent U.S. RDA Per Serving	
Calories	331	Protein	38%
Protein	25g	Vitamin A	160%
Carbohydrate	29g	Vitamin C	29%
Fat	10g	Thiamin	19%
Sodium	693mg	Riboflavin	20%
Potassium	900mg	Niacin	31%
		Calcium	8%
		Iron	17%

TIPS: *If desired, omit wine and increase water to 2¼ cups.*

To use cooked lamb, use 3 cups cooked cubed lamb, omit browning, and add 1 cube or 1 teaspoon beef bouillon. Omit first 45 minute cooking period.

APPLE LAMB CASSEROLE

⅓ cup flour
1 teaspoon salt
1-lb. lamb shoulder, cubed
2 tablespoons oil or shortening
1 teaspoon parsley flakes
½ teaspoon thyme
¼ to ½ teaspoon curry powder
⅛ teaspoon pepper
1 small whole onion
1 bay leaf
2 cups water
3 cups sliced apples, peeled
2 tablespoons sugar
10-oz. can Hungry Jack® Refrigerated Big Flaky Biscuits

In paper or plastic bag, combine flour and salt. Shake lamb cubes in flour mixture. In large skillet, brown lamb in hot oil. Stir in parsley flakes, thyme, curry powder, pepper, onion, bay leaf and water. Simmer covered, 1 hour or until meat is tender, stirring occasionally. Heat oven to 425°F. Remove onion and bay leaf from meat mixture. Stir in apples and sugar. Heat to boiling. Remove to 8 or 9-inch (2 to 2½ qt.) square baking dish.* Separate biscuit dough into 10 biscuits. Arrange around edge of baking dish. Bake at 425°F. for 15 to 18 minutes or until biscuits are done. 5 to 6 servings

NUTRITION INFORMATION PER SERVING

Serving Size: 1/6 of recipe		Percent U.S. RDA Per Serving	
Calories	423	Protein	24%
Protein	16g	Vitamin A	*
Carbohydrate	40g	Vitamin C	5%
Fat	22g	Thiamin	20%
Sodium	874mg	Riboflavin	16%
Potassium	282mg	Niacin	22%
		Calcium	3%
		Iron	12%

TIPS: **If skillet is ovenproof, there is no need to remove to baking dish.*

Cooked cubed lamb may be substituted for lamb shoulder; omit browning.

One 20-oz. can (2 cups) sliced pie apples may be substituted for fresh apples.

SHEPHERD'S PIE

2 to 3 cups cooked cubed lamb
10-oz. pkg. (1½ cups) frozen peas
10¾-can condensed golden mushroom, cream of celery or mushroom soup
½ teaspoon salt
⅛ teaspoon pepper
1 small onion, chopped
1 teaspoon Worcestershire sauce
2 cups prepared mashed potatoes*
Paprika

Heat oven to 375°F. In 2-quart casserole, combine first 7 ingredients; arrange evenly in casserole. Spread mashed potatoes over top to cover meat mixture (or mound dollops of potatoes over top of meat mixture). Sprinkle with paprika. Bake at 375°F. for 45 to 50 minutes or until light golden brown and bubbly.

NUTRITION INFORMATION PER SERVING

Serving Size: 1/4 of recipe using Hungry Jack® mashed potatoes

		Percent U.S. RDA Per Serving	
Calories	485	Protein	34%
Protein	22g	Vitamin A	14%
Carbohydrate	28g	Vitamin C	27%
Fat	32g	Thiamin	26%
Sodium	1289mg	Riboflavin	20%
Potassium	561mg	Niacin	38%
		Calcium	8%
		Iron	16%

TIPS: *Cooked cubed beef or veal may be substituted for cooked lamb.*

**For mashed potatoes, prepare 4-serving recipe of Hungry Jack® Mashed Potato Flakes or cook 2 medium potatoes and mash with ¼ cup milk and 2 tablespoons margarine or butter.*

Fresh ground lamb may be substituted. Cook 1-lb. ground lamb with onion until brown; combine in casserole with other ingredients as directed.

LAMB LOAF

1½ lb. ground lamb
1 cup (1 slice) soft bread cubes
½ cup pickle relish
1½ teaspoons salt
1 small onion, chopped
Dash pepper
½ cup milk
2 eggs

Heat oven to 350°F. In medium bowl, combine all ingredients; mix well. Press into greased 8x4-inch loaf pan or 8-inch round or square pan, shaping into a loaf. Bake uncovered at 350°F. for 50 to 60 minutes. If desired, spoon catsup, barbecue sauce, mint sauce or jelly over top during last 5 to 10 minutes of baking. 4 to 6 servings

NUTRITION INFORMATION PER SERVING

Serving Size: 1/6 of recipe

		Percent U.S. RDA Per Serving	
Calories	213	Protein	35%
Protein	23g	Vitamin A	5%
Carbohydrate	12g	Vitamin C	3%
Fat	8g	Thiamin	10%
Sodium	778mg	Riboflavin	18%
Potassium	272mg	Niacin	21%
		Calcium	6%
		Iron	12%

TIPS: *For variety, add one of the following to meat mixture in place of pickle relish: 1 cup cubed cheese, ½ cup mushroom pieces or ½ cup drained crushed pineapple.*

To make LAMB RING, press meat mixture into 4-cup ring mold. Bake 30 minutes. Unmold on heat-proof platter. Spoon mint jelly or cranberry sauce over ring and bake 5 minutes longer.

MOUSSAKA

MOUSSAKA

1 lb. ground lamb
1 tablespoon chopped parsley
1 teaspoon salt
⅛ teaspoon pepper
⅛ teaspoon nutmeg
1 medium onion, chopped
¼ cup dry red wine or water
16-oz. can (2 cups) tomatoes, drained
1 medium eggplant
2 eggs
¼ cup milk
¼ cup grated Parmesan cheese

Heat oven to 375°F. In large skillet, brown lamb; drain excess fat. Add parsley, salt, pepper, nutmeg, onion, wine and tomatoes. Peel eggplant and slice crosswise into ¼-inch thick slices. Arrange half of eggplant slices in bottom of 8-inch square pan or 1½ quart shallow casserole. Top with half of meat mixture, remaining eggplant slices and remaining meat.* Bake at 375°F. for 40 minutes or until eggplant is tender. Beat eggs and milk together; pour over partially baked casserole. Sprinkle with cheese. Return to oven and bake uncovered for 10 to 15 minutes or until egg mixture is set. Let stand about 10 minutes before serving; cut into squares.
4 servings

NUTRITION INFORMATION PER SERVING

Serving Size: 1/4 of recipe		Percent U.S. RDA Per Serving	
Calories	429	Protein	40%
Protein	26g	Vitamin A	29%
Carbohydrate	14g	Vitamin C	26%
Fat	27g	Thiamin	17%
Sodium	818mg	Riboflavin	25%
Potassium	778mg	Niacin	26%
		Calcium	15%
		Iron	18%

TIP: *To MAKE AHEAD, prepare to * and refrigerate up to 2 days. To serve, increase first baking time to 45 minutes.*

LAMB SHISH KABOBS

8-oz. (4 cups) fresh mushrooms
12 medium green onions
3 firm tomatoes
1 large cucumber
1½ lb. boneless lamb shoulder, cut into 1½-inch cubes
¾ lb. (12 slices) bacon

MARINADE
¼ teaspoon thyme leaves
2 garlic cloves, minced
1 cup oil
¼ cup lemon juice

Wash mushrooms, onions, tomatoes and cucumber. Remove tops from onions; cut tomatoes into quarters; slice cucumber in half lengthwise and cut into ½-inch pieces. In large bowl, combine all Marinade ingredients. Add vegetables and lamb. Marinate at room temperature for 1 hour.

Starting with bacon, thread meat and vegetables on skewers, interlacing bacon over and under pieces. Broil 5 inches from heat for 30 minutes, basting with Marinade and turning occasionally until brown. Season with salt. 6 servings

NUTRITION INFORMATION PER SERVING

Serving Size: 1/6 of recipe		Percent U.S. RDA Per Serving	
Calories	468	Protein	37%
Protein	24g	Vitamin A	15%
Carbohydrate	10g	Vitamin C	31%
Fat	37g	Thiamin	18%
Sodium	219mg	Riboflavin	24%
Potassium	685mg	Niacin	31%
		Calcium	5%
		Iron	15%

TIPS: *For a quick marinade, substitute prepared Italian or French dressing.*

One 10-oz. pkg. (1½ cups) frozen brussels sprouts may be substituted for onions. Cook brussels sprouts as directed on pkg. until almost tender; drain.

VARIETY MEATS

Variety meats are often priced economically. Because no bone or fat is usually included in these meats, there is very little waste.

Available from beef, veal, pork and lamb, variety meats include liver, heart, kidneys, brain, tongue and sweetbreads. Each varies somewhat in flavor and tenderness; the price normally fluctuates with availability and demand.

LIVER

Beef and pork liver are frequently fried or cooked in liquid, while the liver from younger animals – veal, lamb and baby beef or calf – is usually broiled or pan fried.

BROILED LIVER

Arrange slices of baby beef, veal or lamb liver on broiler pan. Broil 4 to 5 inches from heat for 3 minutes. Season with salt and pepper. Turn and broil second side 2 to 3 minutes or until it just loses red color (overcooking will toughen liver cooked this way).

NUTRITION INFORMATION PER SERVING

Serving Size: 1/4 lb. beef liver, cooked		Percent U.S. RDA Per Serving	
Calories	259	Protein	46%
Protein	30g	Vitamin A	1207%
Carbohydrate	6g	Vitamin C	31%
Fat	12g	Thiamin	20%
Sodium	208mg	Riboflavin	279%
Potassium	429mg	Niacin	93%
		Calcium	*
		Iron	55%

LIVER, BACON AND ONIONS

- 1 lb. beef, veal, lamb or pork liver
- ¼ cup flour
- ½ teaspoon salt
- ⅛ teaspoon pepper
- 4 slices bacon
- 2 medium onions, sliced

Cut liver into serving pieces. Combine flour, salt and pepper. Coat liver with seasoned flour. In large fry pan, fry bacon until crisp; remove bacon from pan. Brown liver and onions in bacon drippings, 2 to 3 minutes on each side. Serve topped with crisp bacon. 4 servings

NUTRITION INFORMATION PER SERVING

Serving Size: 1/4 of recipe		Percent U.S. RDA Per Serving	
Calories	444	Protein	59%
Protein	38g	Vitamin A	1202%
Carbohydrate	15g	Vitamin C	33%
Fat	25g	Thiamin	32%
Sodium	726mg	Riboflavin	285%
Potassium	533mg	Niacin	101%
		Calcium	3%
		Iron	62%

CALORIE WATCHERS CREOLE LIVER

- ½ teaspoon margarine or butter
- 1½ lb. baby beef or beef liver, cut into 1½-inch strips
- ¼ cup chopped green pepper
- ½ teaspoon salt
- ⅛ teaspoon marjoram or rosemary leaves
- ⅛ teaspoon thyme or poultry seasoning
- 1 medium onion, chopped
- ½ cup condensed beef consommé*
- ¼ cup water
- 6-oz. can tomato paste

In large skillet, brown liver in hot margarine. Add remaining ingredients. Simmer covered, 10 to 15 minutes for baby beef liver or 15 to 20 minutes for beef liver, adding small amount of water if liquid becomes too thick. 6 servings

NUTRITION INFORMATION PER SERVING

Serving Size: 1/6 of recipe		Percent U.S. RDA Per Serving	
Calories	302	Protein	50%
Protein	32g	Vitamin A	1232%
Carbohydrate	14g	Vitamin C	55%
Fat	13g	Thiamin	24%
Sodium	541mg	Riboflavin	283%
Potassium	754mg	Niacin	99%
		Calcium	3%
		Iron	64%

TIP: **If desired, ½ cup water, 1 cube or 1 teaspoon beef bouillon and 1 teaspoon Worcestershire sauce may be substituted for beef consommé.*

MICROWAVE

MICROWAVE COOKING

About Microwave Cooking

Microwave ovens have been "growing up" over the years and in many homes they have become standard kitchen equipment. Getting to know your own oven is important and learning what you can do best to satisfy you and your family's food needs will help you use your microwave to its greatest capacity. The manual that comes with your oven is your best source of information specifically for your model, from there you can go on toward developing confidence in your own ability to be creative with cooking.

Speed was the original advantage of microwave cooking and remains one of the main reasons for their popularity in today's fast paced lifestyle. In addition, microwave ovens are energy efficient, safe and easy to use. All microwave ovens comply with stringent requirements of the Federal Government.

How do microwave ovens work? When microwaves enter food, they simply cause the liquid or moisture molecules in the food to vibrate at a fantastic rate; friction created by this vibration produces heat throughout the food. Microwaves are attracted to items containing moisture and produce heat *within* the food. This is opposite of the cooking process that occurs by conventional ranges where the heat is outside the food as in a hot oven or on a surface unit. Since microwaves work on moisture, the foods will not have the browning or crispness they normally get from ovens, broilers or skillets. Moistness is highly desirable for certain foods, other foods need recipe additions to offset browning or crispness needs.

A number of cooking speeds are available in the various microwave oven models. All microwave ovens have HIGH; in addition many have variable cooking speeds which make them more adaptable to a wide range of cooking needs. Just as you use a variety of heat settings when cooking on a surface unit, you can select a variety of settings for using your microwave oven. Watch so that you can see how your food is cooking. You may stop and start the cooking process as often as necessary.

The cooking utensils that should be used in a microwave oven include the following items: most glass ovenware, ceramics, ovenproof dinnerware, heavy plastics and paper products. All of these are suitable because they allow the passage of the microwaves into the food. Clear plastic wrap can be used to cover the food. This retains steam helping the food cook more evenly and prevents drying out of the food.

You may want to consider selecting a dish that can be used for both cooking and serving because the food can go directly from the microwave oven to the table.

Although metal which reflects microwaves away from the food should generally not be used, it can be used under the following conditions:

- Aluminum foil, metal skewers or clamps – if the amount of food is much greater than the amount of foil or metal. Be certain the foil or metal is not touching the walls of the oven because this could cause "arcing" or sparking.
- TV breakfast and dinner trays – if the containers are less than ¾ inch deep. Although cooking in TV trays occurs from the top surfaces only, the food will heat.
- NOTE: Remove paper wrapped metal twist closures from packages before inserting in microwave.

Many of the techniques of cooking with microwaves are similar to conventional cooking. However, because of the increased speed when cooking with microwave energy, they become especially important to remember. Microwaves first contact the outer section of food, creating heat that is then conducted toward the center of the food. This fact of cooking from outside toward the center is the reason behind several of the techniques of cooking with microwaves. Most food should be turned during microwave cooking to allow for even cooking; this means turning over, stirring or rotating because the outside edges of the food tend to cook first. Many foods should also be allowed to stand after cooking to provide for more even doneness by equalizing the heat throughout the food.

Many variables affect the timing of recipes – the microwave oven itself, the size and shape of the food and doneness required for the food as you desire it. Foods should be placed in a ring at the outer edge of the cooking dish, leaving the center empty; the larger portion of the foods should be pointing to the outer edge of the dish. Experience with your own microwave oven will teach you how to select settings and timing for cooking and reheating foods.

Home canning is not recommended for microwave ovens; pressure cooking requires temperatures above boiling and microwave cooking can go to boiling (212°F.) but no higher.

Microwave cooking can be fun and gives you a new flexibility in your life that you are sure to enjoy.

Microwave Oven Power Settings

The manufacturers of microwave ovens use a wide variety of terms to describe the power settings for their ovens; the following chart indicates some of the terms. Each microwave oven has a specific wattage output for its full power or HIGH setting; it may be stamped on the nameplate of your microwave oven or stated in the instruction book that came with your oven. If not, your dealer should have the information. Wattage output for the lower settings also varies; the chart below and on page 364 gives you an indication of the variable power provided by some of the manufacturers of microwave ovens. Note the blue bands on the chart which divide the variable power settings into 5 levels.

	power	watts
MEDIUM-HIGH	⅔ power	425 to 475 watts
MEDIUM	½ power	300 to 350 watts
LOW	⅓ power	175 to 225 watts
WARM		75 to 125 watts

The microwave oven power setting information is provided to assist you in determining which setting to use for cooking with your own microwave oven. For example, if your oven has the same settings as Oven B on the chart and you are preparing a recipe that calls for MEDIUM, then you would set your microwave oven at simmer to achieve the same results.

MANUFACTURER'S MICROWAVE POWER SETTINGS

	Watts	Oven A	Oven B	Oven C	Oven D	Oven E	Oven F	Oven G	Oven H	Oven I
							High			
	700									
		High			High					
High	650		High	High		High		Normal Cook	High	High
	600				Defrost		Med-High	High		
		Roast	Reheat		Reheat			Reheat		
	550									
	500				Warm	Reheat	Flash Defrost		Warm	Med-Hig
								Warm		
Medium-High	450		Warm			Bake	Medium			
	400				Medium	Warm				
				Medium Defrost						
	350						Med-Low			
Medium		Medium				Simmer		Defrost	Simmer	Mediun
	300		Simmer					Simmer-High		
	250				Simmer	Defrost				
		Defrost	Defrost				Defrost			
Low	200	Low				Sauté				Med-Lo Defrost
	150	Simmer					Low	Simmer-Low	Defrost	
					Warm					
				Warm		Warm				
Warm	100		Warm							Simme Low
	50	Warm			Defrost Low	Low	Warm	Warm		

Microwave Cooking Time Conversion Chart

Pillsbury recipes were developed in counter top microwave ovens with 600 to 650 watts.

If your microwave oven has a lower wattage, use the following conversion chart to determine cooking times.

Recipe Times for 600 to 700 Watts Oven	Convert to Times Below for 500 to 600 Watts Oven	Convert to Times Below for 400 to 500 Watts Oven
15 Sec.	18 Sec.	20 Sec.
30 Sec.	35 Sec.	45 Sec.
45 Sec.	55 Sec.	1 Min.
1 Min.	1 Min. 15 Sec.	1 Min. 30 Sec.
2 Min.	2 Min. 30 Sec.	2 Min. 50 Sec.
3 Min.	3 Min. 30 Sec.	4 Min. 15 Sec.
4 Min.	4 Min. 50 Sec.	5 Min. 45 Sec.
5 Min.	6 Min.	7 Min.
6 Min.	7 Min. 15 Sec.	8 Min. 30 Sec.
7 Min.	8 Min. 30 Sec.	9 Min. 50 Sec.
8 Min.	9 Min. 30 Sec.	11 Min. 15 Sec.
9 Min.	10 Min. 50 Sec.	12 Min. 30 Sec.
10 Min.	12 Min.	14 Min.

APPETIZERS & SANDWICHES

Thin strips of sirloin steak marinate in a teriyaki mixture and are then wrapped around water chestnuts.

TERIYAKI WRAP UPS

1 tablespoon sugar
1 tablespoon chopped onion or 1 teaspoon instant minced onion
¼ teaspoon ginger
1 garlic clove, minced, or ⅛ teaspoon instant minced garlic
¼ cup soy sauce
½ lb. sirloin steak, cut into thin strips
8-oz. can (⅔ cup) water chestnuts, drained

In small bowl, combine first 5 ingredients; mix well. Add steak strips, tossing to coat with soy mixture. Let stand 15 to 30 minutes, stirring occasionally. Drain steak strips and wrap each around water chestnut (cut larger water chestnuts in half), fastening with toothpicks. Place on plate or shallow GLASS baking dish. MICROWAVE uncovered on HIGH 3 MINUTES or until steak is desired doneness
About 16 snacks

Length of marinating time and surface area of meat present too many variables to accurately determine nutritional information.

TIPS: *To MAKE AHEAD, marinate the steak strips and wrap around water chestnuts. Refrigerate until ready to cook. Increase microwaving time to 3 MINUTES, 30 SECONDS.*

If desired, ⅓ cup bottled prepared teriyaki sauce may be substituted for the first 5 ingredients.

NACHOS

Place a single layer of taco or corn chips on a paper plate or plastic tray. Cut ¼-inch thick slices of cheese into 1-inch squares. Place a square of cheese on each corn chip. MICROWAVE uncovered on HIGH 45 SECONDS to 1 MINUTE or until cheese is melted. Serve. Prepare additional nachos as needed.

NUTRITION INFORMATION PER SERVING

Serving Size: 1/8 of recipe*		Percent U.S. RDA Per Serving	
Calories	113	Protein	6%
Protein	4g	Vitamin A	3%
Carbohydrate	7g	Vitamin C	0%
Fat	8g	Thiamin	*
Sodium	176mg	Riboflavin	4%
Potassium	28mg	Niacin	*
		Calcium	15%
		Iron	3%

*This recipe was analyzed with 2 cups of corn chips and 3½ oz. of cheese.

HOT CLAM DIP

8-oz. pkg. cream cheese
2 tablespoons chopped almonds
1 tablespoon instant minced onion
1 tablespoon prepared horseradish
¼ teaspoon garlic salt
¼ teaspoon salt
Dash pepper
3 tablespoons milk
8-oz. can minced clams, drained

In 1½-quart GLASS bowl or serving dish, soften cream cheese (MICROWAVE 30 SECONDS). Stir in remaining ingredients. MICROWAVE uncovered on HIGH 2 MINUTES or until hot, stirring occasionally. If desired, garnish with paprika or parsley. About 2½ cups

NUTRITION INFORMATION PER SERVING

Serving Size: 1 tablespoon		Percent U.S. RDA Per Serving	
Calories	31	Protein	2%
Protein	1g	Vitamin A	*
Carbohydrate	<1g	Vitamin C	*
Fat	3g	Thiamin	*
Sodium	40mg	Riboflavin	*
Potassium	12mg	Niacin	*
		Calcium	*
		Iron	*

QUESADILLAS

4 flour tortillas
¼ cup chopped onion
¼ cup chopped tomato
¼ cup chopped green chilies or green pepper
1 cup (4 oz.) shredded Cheddar or American cheese

Layer tortillas between paper towels or napkins. MICROWAVE on HIGH about 45 SECONDS to soften. Place tortillas in 12x8-inch GLASS baking dish. Sprinkle each tortilla with 1 tablespoon onion, tomato, green chilies and ¼ cup cheese. MICROWAVE on HIGH 2 to 3 MINUTES or until cheese melts. Fold in half or serve open, cut into wedges. If desired, serve with taco or green chili sauce. 4 servings

NUTRITION INFORMATION PER SERVING

Serving Size: 1/4 of recipe		Percent U.S. RDA Per Serving	
Calories	187	Protein	14%
Protein	9g	Vitamin A	12%
Carbohydrate	17g	Vitamin C	25%
Fat	10g	Thiamin	5%
Sodium	199mg	Riboflavin	10%
Potassium	83mg	Niacin	3%
		Calcium	28%
		Iron	8%

Wiener slices in a peppy sauce make tasty hot snacks served on toothpicks.

TANGY WIENER PICK UPS

1 pkg. Pillsbury Homestyle or Brown Gravy Mix
½ cup cold water
½ cup apple or currant jelly
2 tablespoons catsup
1 lb. wieners or smokie links, cut into ½-inch slices

In 1½-quart GLASS casserole, combine gravy mix and water; blend well. Stir in remaining ingredients. MICROWAVE uncovered on HIGH 7 MINUTES or until sauce thickens and wieners are heated through, stirring occasionally. Serve with toothpicks. 8 to 10 servings

NUTRITION INFORMATION PER SERVING

Serving Size: 4 appetizers		Percent U.S. RDA Per Serving	
Calories	183	Protein	9%
Protein	6g	Vitamin A	*
Carbohydrate	12g	Vitamin C	*
Fat	12g	Thiamin	5%
Sodium	541mg	Riboflavin	6%
Potassium	122mg	Niacin	6%
		Calcium	*
		Iron	5%

CRAB ON THE HALF-SHELL

¼ cup margarine or butter
3 tablespoons flour
7¾-oz. can crab meat, drained and flaked (reserve liquor)
Milk
1 tablespoon minced pimiento
2 tablespoons minced green pepper
½ teaspoon salt
Grated Parmesan cheese
Paprika

In 2-cup GLASS measuring cup or bowl, melt margarine (MICROWAVE 30 SECONDS). Blend in flour. Reserve crab liquor and add milk to make 1 cup. Add liquid to margarine and flour and MICROWAVE uncovered on HIGH 2 MINUTES, 30 SECONDS or until thickened, stirring occasionally. Add crab meat, pimiento, green pepper and salt; mix well. Spoon mixture into about 12 small or 6 medium shells, top with Parmesan cheese and sprinkle with paprika. Place filled shells on hard plastic tray or platter. Loosely cover with waxed paper and MICROWAVE on HIGH 2 MINUTES or until bubbly. 6 medium or 12 small shells

NUTRITION INFORMATION PER SERVING

Serving Size: 1 appetizer		Percent U.S. RDA Per Serving	
Calories	143	Protein	12%
Protein	8g	Vitamin A	8%
Carbohydrate	5g	Vitamin C	7%
Fat	10g	Thiamin	4%
Sodium	604mg	Riboflavin	7%
Potassium	98mg	Niacin	4%
		Calcium	8%
		Iron	2%

Shrimp are tucked between toast squares and a buttery cheese topping. Very tasty hot or cold.

CHEESE SHRIMP PUFFS

8 slices bread or 32 crackers
¼ cup margarine or butter
2 cups (8 oz.) shredded Cheddar cheese
1 egg, separated
4½-oz. can small cooked shrimp

Toast bread and cut each slice into 4 squares. Arrange on 2 napkin-lined plates. In medium bowl, soften margarine (MICROWAVE 10 SECONDS). Cream together margarine and cheese. Mix in egg yolk, (reserve white in small bowl). Beat egg white until soft peaks form. Fold into cheese mixture. Drain shrimp well and divide among toast squares. Top each with spoonful of cheese mixture so there is space for spreading during heating. Cook 1 plate at a time. MICROWAVE uncovered on HIGH about 1 MINUTE or until hot.

32 snacks

NUTRITION INFORMATION PER SERVING

Serving Size: 2 appetizers		Percent U.S. RDA Per Serving	
Calories	128	Protein	11%
Protein	7g	Vitamin A	7%
Carbohydrate	6g	Vitamin C	0%
Fat	8g	Thiamin	3%
Sodium	195mg	Riboflavin	6%
Potassium	41mg	Niacin	2%
		Calcium	13%
		Iron	4%

TIPS: *Large shrimp may be used, but they are usually more expensive. If using large shrimp, cut into pieces to divide among the pieces of bread.*

These may be assembled up to 2 hours ahead and left at room temperature until ready to heat.

DENVER SANDWICH

2 tablespoons margarine or butter
1 cup cooked chopped ham or luncheon meat
¼ cup chopped green pepper
1 small onion, chopped
4 eggs, slightly beaten
Salt and pepper to taste
Hot buttered toast
Catsup or chili sauce

Place 2 tablespoons margarine in 8 or 9-inch GLASS pie pan. MICROWAVE on HIGH about 1 MINUTE or until margarine is melted. Add ham, green pepper and onion. MICROWAVE covered on HIGH 2 MINUTES. Stir in eggs. MICROWAVE covered on HIGH 1½ MINUTES or until almost set in center. LET STAND covered 3 MINUTES before serving. Season. Cut into wedges; serve on toast with catsup or chili sauce.

4 servings

NUTRITION INFORMATION PER SERVING

Serving Size: 1 sandwich		Percent U.S. RDA Per Serving	
Calories	212	Protein	25%
Protein	16g	Vitamin A	19%
Carbohydrate	2g	Vitamin C	13%
Fat	15g	Thiamin	18%
Sodium	465mg	Riboflavin	15%
Potassium	224mg	Niacin	8%
		Calcium	4%
		Iron	14%

DILLY BUNS

¼ cup margarine or butter, softened
¼ teaspoon dill weed
½ teaspoon prepared mustard
4 hamburger or hot dog buns, sliced

In small GLASS bowl, blend margarine, dill and mustard; spread on sliced surface of buns. Place on paper plate or towel. MICROWAVE on LOW 1 to 2 MINUTES or until hot. Serve warm. 4 servings

NUTRITION INFORMATION PER SERVING

Serving Size: 1/4 of recipe		Percent U.S. RDA Per Serving	
Calories	222	Protein	5%
Protein	3g	Vitamin A	9%
Carbohydrate	21g	Vitamin C	*
Fat	14g	Thiamin	7%
Sodium	351mg	Riboflavin	4%
Potassium	43mg	Niacin	4%
		Calcium	3%
		Iron	4%

TOASTY CHEESE LOAF

⅓ cup margarine or butter, softened
5-oz. jar process cheese spread
1 loaf French bread (about 12-inches long)
Paprika or minced parsley

In small bowl, blend margarine and cheese. Cut bread in half lengthwise. Cut each half almost through to bottom crust every 2 inches. Spread cheese mixture between and on top of slices. Sprinkle with paprika or minced parsley. Place on paper towel or napkin. MICROWAVE on HIGH 1 to 1½ MINUTES or until cheese is melted. 4 servings

NUTRITION INFORMATION PER SERVING

Serving Size: 1/4 of recipe		Percent U.S. RDA Per Serving	
Calories	337	Protein	14%
Protein	9g	Vitamin A	19%
Carbohydrate	22g	Vitamin C	0%
Fat	24g	Thiamin	7%
Sodium	960mg	Riboflavin	16%
Potassium	120mg	Niacin	4%
		Calcium	22%
		Iron	5%

TACO CHIP FRANKS

½ cup crushed corn tortilla chips
½ cup (2 oz.) shredded cheese
1 tablespoon barbecue sauce
5 to 6 frankfurters, split almost through lengthwise

In small bowl, combine first 3 ingredients. Spoon onto frankfurters. Place on paper plate or in 8-inch square GLASS baking dish. MICROWAVE on HIGH 2 to 2½ MINUTES or until hot. 4 servings

NUTRITION INFORMATION PER SERVING

Serving Size: 1/4 of recipe		Percent U.S. RDA Per Serving	
Calories	333	Protein	20%
Protein	13g	Vitamin A	4%
Carbohydrate	8g	Vitamin C	*
Fat	28g	Thiamin	9%
Sodium	989mg	Riboflavin	13%
Potassium	190mg	Niacin	10%
		Calcium	16%
		Iron	10%

CHILI CON QUESO BURGER SPREAD

5-oz. jar process cheese spread
1 to 2 tablespoons minced mild chilies, drained
1 teaspoon instant minced onion or 1 tablespoon chopped onion
1 tablespoon milk

In small GLASS bowl, combine all ingredients. MICROWAVE on HIGH 1 to 2 MINUTES or until warm. Spoon onto cooked hamburgers. ⅔ cup

NUTRITION INFORMATION PER SERVING

Serving Size: 1 tablespoon		Percent U.S. RDA Per Serving	
Calories	43	Protein	4%
Protein	2g	Vitamin A	3%
Carbohydrate	2g	Vitamin C	6%
Fat	3g	Thiamin	*
Sodium	232mg	Riboflavin	5%
Potassium	39mg	Niacin	*
		Calcium	8%
		Iron	*

VEGETABLES

MICROWAVE BLANCHING OF FRESH VEGETABLES FOR FREEZING

STEP-BY-STEP BLANCHING IN YOUR MICROWAVE OVEN:

1. PREPARE VEGETABLE by washing, peeling, slicing or dicing as you normally would.
2. MEASURE only 1 pound or about 1 quart of vegetables per batch into recommended casserole. This amount is also recommended for best results conventionally.
3. ADD WATER as given in chart. DO NOT ADD SALT.
4. Cover casserole. SET POWER AT HIGH OR COOK SETTING.
5. STIR vegetables after half of time and after blanching. When blanched, vegetable will have a bright color evenly throughout. Check vegetable at minimum time on chart; if color is not evenly bright throughout all of vegetables, stir well and continue cooking to maximum time.
6. PLUNGE INTO ICE WATER IMMEDIATELY to prevent further cooking. Spread on paper towels, blotting with additional towels to remove excess moisture.
7. PACKAGE in freezing containers, labeling amounts and date. Note: Pint-size freezer containers most closely resemble the size boxes used for packaging commercially frozen vegetables. If this size container is used for freezing, reconstituting is easy by following cooking instructions in "Cooking Blanched Vegetables From Your Freezer," page 370.

VEGETABLE BLANCHING CHART

Vegetable	Amount	Casserole Size	Amount of Water	Time in Minutes
Asparagus	1-lb. cut into 1 to 2-in pieces	2-qt.	¼ cup	2½ to 3½ min.
Beans, Green or Wax	1-lb.	1½-qt.	½ cup	3½ to 5½ min.
Broccoli (1-inch cuts)	1 bunch 1¼-1½-lb.	2-qt.	½ cup	3 to 5 min.
Carrots	1-lb., sliced	1½-qt.	¼ cup	3½ to 5½ min.
Cauliflower	1 head, cut into flowerets	2-qt.	½ cup	3 to 5 min.
Onions	4 medium, quartered	1-qt.	½ cup	2½ to 4 min.
Parsnips	1-lb., cubed	1½-qt.	¼ cup	2 to 3½ min.
Peas	2-lb., shelled	1-qt.	¼ cup	3 to 4½ min.
Spinach	1-lb., washed	2-qt.	none	2 to 3 min.
Squash, Summer Yellow, Zucchini	1-lb., sliced or cubed	1½-qt.	¼ cup	2½ to 4 min.
Turnips	1-lb., cubed	1½-qt.	¼ cup	2½ to 4 min.

Microwave blanching information courtesy of General Electric Company.

COOKING BLANCHED VEGETABLES FROM YOUR FREEZER

As stated in "Step-By-Step Blanching" information, pint size containers most closely resemble the boxes of commercially frozen vegetables from the supermarket. Those packages hold about 2 cups of blanched vegetables.

Frozen vegetables from 1-pint containers may be cooked in the microwave oven the same as 10 oz. pkg. of commercially frozen vegetables.

If you package blanched vegetables in amounts different than 1 pint, change instructions accordingly. For larger amounts, allow a proportionately larger casserole, more water and a longer cooking time.

A LONGER STANDING TIME IS MORE DESIRABLE THAN OVERCOOKING. We have found that home blanched vegetables are best when cooked to a "crisp-tender" state, then allowed to stand (covered) an additional 5 to 10 minutes to finish softening and to develop flavor. Done this way they are delicious!!

This is a good combination for late fall when corn, tomatoes and green pepper are plentiful. Hollowed-out tomatoes make good "servers" for many cooked vegetables.

CORN-FILLED TOMATOES

6 large or 8 medium tomatoes
Salt
2 tablespoons margarine or butter
1 tablespoon chopped onion or 1 teaspoon instant minced onion
2 tablespoons chopped green pepper
16-oz. can (2 cups) whole kernel corn, drained
¼ cup crushed potato chips, crackers or bread crumbs
Grated Parmesan cheese

Cut off tops of tomatoes and hollow out inside (grapefruit knife or spoon works well). (Save inside of tomatoes and add to salad, casserole or other vegetable dishes.) Place hollowed-out tomatoes on serving plate; sprinkle with salt. In medium GLASS bowl, combine margarine, onion and green pepper. MICROWAVE on HIGH 2 MINUTES, stirring once after margarine melts. Stir in corn and crushed chips. Spoon into tomatoes, sprinkle with Parmesan cheese. MICROWAVE on HIGH 5 MINUTES or until heated through. 6 to 8 servings.

NUTRITION INFORMATION PER SERVING

Serving Size: 1/6 of recipe		Percent U.S. RDA Per Serving	
Calories	142	Protein	7%
Protein	5g	Vitamin A	29%
Carbohydrate	17g	Vitamin C	33%
Fat	7g	Thiamin	6%
Sodium	385mg	Riboflavin	7%
Potassium	391mg	Niacin	7%
		Calcium	8%
		Iron	5%

CREAMY CAULIFLOWER

10- oz. pkg. (1½ cups) frozen cauliflower
½ cup mayonnaise or salad dressing
1 teaspoon instant minced onion or 1 tablespoon chopped onion
1 teaspoon prepared mustard
½ cup (2 oz.) shredded Cheddar or American cheese

Place cauliflower in 1½-quart GLASS casserole. MICROWAVE covered on HIGH 4 MINUTES. Stir. MICROWAVE covered on HIGH 4 to 5 MINUTES or until tender. Drain well. In small bowl, combine remaining ingredients; add to cauliflower and toss lightly. MICROWAVE covered on HIGH 1½ to 2 MINUTES or until heated through. LET STAND 3 minutes before serving. 4 servings

NUTRITION INFORMATION PER SERVING

Serving Size: 1/4 of recipe		Percent U.S. RDA Per Serving	
Calories	271	Protein	8%
Protein	5g	Vitamin A	6%
Carbohydrate	4g	Vitamin C	38%
Fat	27g	Thiamin	3%
Sodium	287mg	Riboflavin	7%
Potassium	182mg	Niacin	*
		Calcium	13%
		Iron	4%

The microwave oven helps make this attractive casserole easy by cooking the broccoli and the cheese sauce.

CHEESY BROCCOLI

2 pkg. (10 oz. each) frozen broccoli spears
2 tablespoons margarine or butter
2 tablespoons flour
½ teaspoon salt
1 cup milk
½ to 1 cup (2 to 4 oz.) shredded Cheddar cheese
1 fresh tomato, sliced

Remove waxed or foil overwrap, place packages of frozen broccoli in oven and MICROWAVE on HIGH 6 MINUTES. Open packages and rearrange broccoli. Close packages and MICROWAVE on HIGH 2 MINUTES or until broccoli is just about tender. After broccoli cooks, prepare cheese sauce by melting margarine in 2-cup GLASS measuring cup (MICROWAVE 30 SECONDS). Blend in flour and salt. Stir in milk. MICROWAVE uncovered on HIGH 2 MINUTES or until mixture boils and thickens, stirring occasionally during last half of cooking time. Stir in cheese until melted. Arrange broccoli on serving plate. Sprinkle with salt to taste. Top with cheese sauce; arrange sliced tomatoes on cheese sauce. MICROWAVE uncovered on HIGH 2 MINUTES to heat tomatoes.
6 to 8 servings

NUTRITION INFORMATION PER SERVING

Serving Size: 1/6 of recipe		Percent U.S. RDA Per Serving	
Calories	133	Protein	10%
Protein	7g	Vitamin A	54%
Carbohydrate	9g	Vitamin C	65%
Fat	9g	Thiamin	6%
Sodium	327mg	Riboflavin	14%
Potassium	295mg	Niacin	4%
		Calcium	17%
		Iron	5%

TIP: *Fresh broccoli may be used; MICROWAVE covered in casserole.*

HONEY-GLAZED CARROTS

4 medium carrots, sliced or cut into strips
2 tablespoons margarine or butter
2 tablespoons honey
2 tablespoons water
¼ teaspoon salt

In 1-quart GLASS casserole, combine first 4 ingredients. MICROWAVE covered on HIGH 7 to 8 MINUTES or until carrots are just about tender, stirring occasionally. Stir in salt. 4 servings

NUTRITION INFORMATION PER SERVING

Serving Size: 1/4 of recipe		Percent U.S. RDA Per Serving	
Calories	105	Protein	*
Protein	<1g	Vitamin A	156%
Carbohydrate	14g	Vitamin C	4%
Fat	6g	Thiamin	2%
Sodium	230mg	Riboflavin	2%
Potassium	167mg	Niacin	*
		Calcium	3%
		Iron	3%

TIP: *If desired, add ¼ teaspoon ginger or 1 teaspoon chopped candied ginger with honey.*

GREEN BEANS CAESAR

2 cups frozen green beans
1 tablespoon instant minced onion or ¼ cup chopped onion
2 tablespoons cider or red wine vinegar
2 tablespoons oil
Dash salt
Dash pepper
¾ cup herb-seasoned croutons
Grated Parmesan cheese

Place beans in 1-quart GLASS casserole. MICROWAVE covered on HIGH 5 MINUTES. Drain and break apart. Add onion, vinegar, oil, salt and pepper; toss lightly. MICROWAVE covered on HIGH 4 to 6 MINUTES or until tender. Gently stir in croutons and sprinkle with Parmesan cheese. 4 servings

NUTRITION INFORMATION PER SERVING

Serving Size: 1/4 of recipe		Percent U.S. RDA Per Serving	
Calories	139	Protein	6%
Protein	4g	Vitamin A	8%
Carbohydrate	10g	Vitamin C	6%
Fat	9g	Thiamin	3%
Sodium	148mg	Riboflavin	6%
Potassium	126mg	Niacin	*
		Calcium	10%
		Iron	3%

This very colorful dish uses frozen peas that taste like they are garden fresh.

PEAS WITH ONIONS AND MUSHROOMS

2 tablespoons margarine or butter
¼ cup chopped onion or 1 tablespoon instant minced onion
4-oz. can (½ cup) mushroom stems and pieces, drained
10-oz. pkg. (1½ cups) frozen peas
Dash pepper
Dash allspice
¼ teaspoon salt

In 1-quart GLASS casserole, combine margarine and onion. MICROWAVE covered on HIGH 2 MINUTES or until onion is tender. Add mushrooms, peas, pepper and allspice. MICROWAVE covered on HIGH 5 MINUTES, 30 SECONDS or until peas are just about tender, stirring once. Stir in salt. 4 servings

NUTRITION INFORMATION PER SERVING

Serving Size: 1/4 of recipe		Percent U.S. RDA Per Serving	
Calories	103	Protein	6%
Protein	4g	Vitamin A	12%
Carbohydrate	9g	Vitamin C	10%
Fat	6g	Thiamin	12%
Sodium	280mg	Riboflavin	7%
Potassium	104mg	Niacin	8%
		Calcium	*
		Iron	8%

Brown sugar and nuts make a caramel topping on these sweet potatoes.

SWEET POTATOES BRULÉE

23-oz. can (2 cups) cooked mashed sweet potatoes or yams
2 tablespoons margarine or butter
3 tablespoons orange juice
Dash salt
⅛ teaspoon cinnamon, if desired
3 tablespoons chopped pecans or walnuts
¼ cup firmly packed brown sugar

In 1-quart GLASS casserole, combine first 5 ingredients; mix well. Arrange evenly in casserole. Sprinkle with pecans and brown sugar. MICROWAVE covered on HIGH 4 MINUTES or until hot.

4 to 5 servings

NUTRITION INFORMATION PER SERVING

Serving Size: 1/4 of recipe		Percent U.S. RDA Per Serving	
Calories	280	Protein	5%
Protein	3g	Vitamin A	199%
Carbohydrate	46g	Vitamin C	23%
Fat	10g	Thiamin	8%
Sodium	202mg	Riboflavin	4%
Potassium	353mg	Niacin	4%
		Calcium	5%
		Iron	9%

TIPS: *The amount of orange juice needed may vary with potatoes. We used a vacuum pack which does not contain liquid. If using potatoes with liquid, drain and add only enough orange juice to moisten.*

Try this topping with cooked squash, too.

Sour cream and cheese turn mashed potatoes into something special.

SAVORY POTATOES

1½ cups water
½ teaspoon salt
2 tablespoons margarine or butter
½ cup milk
1½ cups Hungry Jack® Mashed Potato Flakes
½ cup dairy sour cream
½ teaspoon onion salt
1 egg
Shredded cheese

In 1½ or 2-quart GLASS casserole, combine water, salt and margarine. MICROWAVE covered on HIGH 2 MINUTES, 30 SECONDS or until mixture boils. Add milk. With fork, stir in potato flakes. Stir in sour cream, onion salt and egg; mix well. Sprinkle with cheese.* MICROWAVE covered on HIGH 4 MINUTES or until hot. 4 to 5 servings

NUTRITION INFORMATION PER SERVING

Serving Size: 1/4 of recipe		Percent U.S. RDA Per Serving	
Calories	298	Protein	11%
Protein	7g	Vitamin A	20%
Carbohydrate	18g	Vitamin C	12%
Fat	22g	Thiamin	6%
Sodium	660mg	Riboflavin	13%
Potassium	339mg	Niacin	5%
		Calcium	17%
		Iron	4%

TIPS: *To MAKE AHEAD, prepare to *, and refrigerate. When ready to serve, complete final cooking, adding 1 minute.*

If desired, 3 cups mashed potatoes may be used, adding sour cream, onion salt, egg and cheese as directed.

To halve recipe, use half the ingredient amounts, except use 1 egg. Prepare in 1-quart GLASS casserole. MICROWAVE on HIGH 1 MINUTE, 30 SECONDS to heat water and 2 MINUTES, 30 SECONDS to heat finished potatoes.

STUFFED CORNISH HENS
ORANGE BURGUNDY CHICKEN
SPEEDY CHICKEN STEW

POULTRY

A fryer makes a quick and often economical chicken stew. We found the flavor as good as with stewing chicken cooked conventionally.

SPEEDY CHICKEN STEW

2½ to 3-lb. frying chicken, cut up
1 tablespoon salt
2 stalks celery, cut into 1-inch pieces
1 medium onion, sliced
1 bay leaf
4 peppercorns
3 cubes or 3 teaspoons chicken bouillon
3 cups water
4 carrots, cut into thin slices
¼ cup flour
½ cup water

DUMPLINGS

1½ cups Pillsbury's Best® All Purpose or Unbleached Flour
2 teaspoons baking powder
½ teaspoon salt
1 teaspoon parsley flakes
⅔ cup milk
1 egg, slightly beaten
2 tablespoons oil

In 4-quart GLASS casserole, combine first 8 ingredients. MICROWAVE covered on HIGH 24 MINUTES, stirring once. Add carrots. Combine ¼ cup flour with ½ cup water. Stir into chicken mixture. MICROWAVE covered on HIGH 8 MINUTES. In medium bowl, combine first 4 Dumpling ingredients. Stir in remaining ingredients *just* until dry ingredients are moistened. (Mixture will be soft.)

Remove bay leaf and peppercorns; if desired, remove meat from bone at this point. Spoon Dumplings by rounded tablespoonfuls onto hot chicken mixture. MICROWAVE covered on HIGH 6 MINUTES or until Dumplings are no longer doughy on underside.

4 to 6 servings

NUTRITION INFORMATION PER SERVING

Serving Size: 1/6 of recipe		Percent U.S. RDA Per Serving	
Calories	373	Protein	57%
Protein	37g	Vitamin A	109%
Carbohydrate	37g	Vitamin C	13%
Fat	8g	Thiamin	25%
Sodium	2019mg	Riboflavin	22%
Potassium	808mg	Niacin	79%
		Calcium	12%
		Iron	18%

TIPS: *For stewed chicken without vegetables and dumplings, cover chicken and MICROWAVE on HIGH 28 MINUTES or until tender.*

For variety, add ½ cup raisins and ⅛ teaspoon nutmeg to flour mixture for Dumplings.

A mild, tomato-flavored chicken dish. Canned soups make this traditional dish very easy.

CHICKEN MARENGO

2½ to 3-lb. frying chicken, cut up
1 garlic clove, minced, or ⅛ teaspoon garlic powder or instant minced garlic
1 lb. (about 16) small whole onions or 16-oz. can (1⅔ cups) drained pearl onions
10¾-oz. can condensed golden mushroom soup
10¾-oz. can condensed tomato soup

Place chicken in 2 or 3-quart GLASS casserole. In medium bowl, combine remaining ingredients; pour over chicken. MICROWAVE covered on HIGH 28 MINUTES, stirring once. If desired, thicken sauce with 1 to 2 teaspoons cornstarch dissolved in 2 tablespoons water.

4 to 6 servings

NUTRITION INFORMATION PER SERVING

Serving Size: 1/6 of recipe		Percent U.S. RDA Per Serving	
Calories	243	Protein	49%
Protein	32g	Vitamin A	9%
Carbohydrate	15g	Vitamin C	19%
Fat	6g	Thiamin	9%
Sodium	906mg	Riboflavin	12%
Potassium	704mg	Niacin	72%
		Calcium	6%
		Iron	12%

CHICKEN SUBGUM

1½ cups sliced celery
2 tablespoons cornstarch
3 tablespoons soy sauce
1½ to 2 cups cooked cut-up chicken
16-oz. can (2 cups) chow mein vegetables or bean sprouts, drained
4-oz. can (½ cup) mushrooms, drained or 8-oz. can (⅔ cup) water chestnuts, drained and sliced
1 cup water
2 teaspoons granulated chicken bouillon
1½ teaspoons instant minced onion or 1 tablespoon chopped onion

Place celery in 2-quart GLASS shallow casserole. MICROWAVE on HIGH 2 MINUTES or until crisp-tender. Blend cornstarch and soy sauce; stir into celery. Add chicken, chow mein vegetables, mushrooms, water, bouillon and onion. MICROWAVE uncovered on HIGH 6 MINUTES. Stir. MICROWAVE uncovered on HIGH 5 to 7 MINUTES or until sauce is thickened. Serve over chow mein noodles or rice. 4 servings

NUTRITION INFORMATION PER SERVING

Serving Size: 1/4 of recipe		Percent U.S. RDA Per Serving	
Calories	252	Protein	35%
Protein	23g	Vitamin A	3%
Carbohydrate	24g	Vitamin C	9%
Fat	7g	Thiamin	6%
Sodium	1322mg	Riboflavin	12%
Potassium	516mg	Niacin	36%
		Calcium	5%
		Iron	12%

Chicken goes well with this soy-flavored sauce. Bamboo shoots and water chestnuts add a crunchy texture.

ORIENTAL CHICKEN

2½ to 3-lb. frying chicken, cut up
¼ teaspoon salt
⅛ teaspoon pepper
1 medium onion, cut into wedges
½ cup chicken broth or bouillon*
¼ cup soy sauce
1 tablespoon cornstarch
1 tablespoon sugar
2 tablespoons water
6-oz. can (½ cup) bamboo shoots, drained
8-oz. can (⅔ cup) water chestnuts, drained and sliced

Cut larger pieces of chicken in half for uniform size. In 2-quart or 12x8-inch GLASS baking dish, combine salt, pepper, onion, chicken broth and soy sauce. Add chicken, skin-side-down. MICROWAVE covered on HIGH 30 MINUTES, turning chicken over once. Remove chicken to serving platter. Combine cornstarch, sugar and water. Add to pan drippings. MICROWAVE covered on HIGH 1 MINUTE, 30 SECONDS, stirring once. Add bamboo shoots and water chestnuts. MICROWAVE on HIGH 2 MINUTES or until hot, stirring once. Serve over rice along with chicken. 4 to 6 servings

NUTRITION INFORMATION PER SERVING

Serving Size: 1/6 of recipe served over ½ cup rice		Percent U.S. RDA Per Serving	
Calories	298	Protein	53%
Protein	34g	Vitamin A	*
Carbohydrate	35g	Vitamin C	7%
Fat	1g	Thiamin	16%
Sodium	1601mg	Riboflavin	11%
Potassium	618mg	Niacin	76%
		Calcium	5%
		Iron	18%

TIP: **For bouillon you may add 1 chicken bouillon cube or ½ teaspoon instant chicken bouillon to ½ cup water.*

STUFFED CORNISH HENS

4 Cornish game hens (1 lb. each)
1 teaspoon salt
Nut Stuffing, page 416 (use almonds)
¼ cup margarine or butter, melted
1 teaspoon paprika

Wash hens and set aside giblets (use however you prefer, but they are best cooked conventionally). Sprinkle the inside of cavities with salt; fill body and neck cavity with stuffing. Secure openings with toothpicks or wooden skewers. On each, tie legs together and wings to body with string. Cover the end of legs with small pieces of foil. Place inverted saucers or small casserole lids in 2-quart or 12x8-inch GLASS baking dish to hold hens out of juices. Place hens, breast-side-down, on saucers. Brush with mixture of margarine and paprika. MICROWAVE covered on HIGH 12 MINUTES. Turn breast-side-up and reverse outside edges to inside. Brush with remainder of margarine mixture. MICROWAVE covered on HIGH 12 MINUTES or until MICROWAVE meat thermometer* registers 185°F. (will increase to 190°F during standing). LET STAND covered 5 to 10 MINUTES to finish cooking. 4 servings

Insufficient data with regard to Cornish Game Hens to provide nutritional information.

TIPS: *For variety, use water chestnuts for almonds in stuffing and brush with a glaze of 2 tablespoons margarine, 2 tablespoons soy sauce and 2 tablespoons dark corn syrup.*

**Do not use conventional meat thermometer in oven when cooking.*

ORANGE BURGUNDY CHICKEN

2½ to 3-lb. frying chicken, cut up
2 tablespoons firmly packed brown sugar
2 tablespoons cornstarch
1 teaspoon salt
½ cup orange marmalade
½ cup orange juice
½ cup burgundy or red wine
1 tablespoon lemon juice

Cut larger pieces of chicken in half for uniform size. Arrange skin-side-up in 2-quart or 12x8-inch GLASS baking dish. Combine remaining ingredients. Pour over chicken. MICROWAVE covered on HIGH 28 MINUTES or until chicken is done, spooning sauce over chicken during last half of cooking time. If desired, place under broiler for additional browning. Serve over rice.

4 to 6 servings

NUTRITION INFORMATION PER SERVING

Serving Size: 1/6 of recipe with 1/2 cup rice		Percent U.S. RDA Per Serving	
Calories	378	Protein	50%
Protein	32g	Vitamin A	*
Carbohydrate	54g	Vitamin C	15%
Fat	<1g	Thiamin	15%
Sodium	860mg	Riboflavin	8%
Potassium	585mg	Niacin	73%
		Calcium	5%
		Iron	15%

TIPS: *To halve recipe, use half the ingredient amounts; MICROWAVE covered in 1-quart or 8-inch square GLASS baking dish on HIGH 20 MINUTES.*

A 1¼ to 1½-lb. turkey thigh may be used with half this sauce. MICROWAVE covered on HIGH in 1½-quart GLASS casserole 15 MINUTES or until done, occasionally spooning sauce over turkey.

STUFFED WALLEYED PIKE, TURBAN OF SOLE, SALMON RING AND HALIBUT DIVAN

FISH & SEAFOOD

This salmon loaf gets its ring shape from a casserole dish with a glass in the center. Canned tuna may be substituted.

SALMON RING

3 eggs, beaten
16-oz. can (2 cups) red salmon, drained and flaked
1 cup fine dry bread crumbs
½ cup (1 stalk) chopped celery
¼ cup chopped green pepper
2 tablespons minced onion or 2 teaspoons instant minced onion
¾ cup milk
1 tablespoon lemon juice

In 1½-quart GLASS casserole, combine all ingredients; mix well. Move mixture away from center and place glass in center to make the ring shape. MICROWAVE uncovered on HIGH 8 MINUTES or until mixture is set around glass. Remove glass and invert onto serving plate.

6 servings

NUTRITION INFORMATION PER SERVING

Serving Size: 1/6 of recipe		Percent U.S. RDA Per Serving	
Calories	195	Protein	28%
Protein	18g	Vitamin A	11%
Carbohydrate	7g	Vitamin C	13%
Fat	10g	Thiamin	6%
Sodium	421mg	Riboflavin	15%
Potassium	356mg	Niacin	24%
		Calcium	22%
		Iron	9%

TIPS: *You may substitute 2 cans (6½ oz. each) tuna for salmon.*

The center of the ring may be filled with creamed peas or other vegetables before serving.

FISH FILLETS AMANDINE

¼ cup margarine or butter
1 lb. fish fillets
Dash salt
Dash pepper
¼ cup slivered or sliced almonds
2 teaspoons lemon juice
2 tablespoons dry white wine or sherry, if desired

Place margarine in 1½-quart shallow GLASS casserole. MICROWAVE on HIGH 1 MINUTE or until melted. Arrange fish in casserole with thickest parts to outside. MICROWAVE covered on HIGH 4 MINUTES. Rotate ½ turn. MICROWAVE on HIGH 2 to 4 MINUTES or until fish flakes easily. Season with salt and pepper. Remove fish to serving platter. Add almonds, lemon juice and wine to pan drippings. MICROWAVE on HIGH 1 MINUTE or until hot; pour over fish.

4 servings

NUTRITION INFORMATION PER SERVING

Serving Size: 1/4 of recipe		Percent U.S. RDA Per Serving	
Calories	393	Protein	28%
Protein	18g	Vitamin A	54%
Carbohydrate	9g	Vitamin C	*
Fat	31g	Thiamin	9%
Sodium	427mg	Riboflavin	11%
Potassium	395mg	Niacin	14%
		Calcium	2%
		Iron	5%

TURBAN OF SOLE

2 tablespoons margarine or butter
½ cup (1 stalk) finely chopped celery
¼ cup finely chopped onion or 1 tablespoon instant minced onion
1½ teaspoons parsley flakes or 3 tablespoons minced parsley
¼ teaspoon chervil, if desired
1 teaspoon lemon juice
Dash white or black pepper
Dash thyme
1½ cups (1½ slices) soft bread cubes
16-oz. pkg. fresh or frozen sole fillets, thawed

SAUCE
Half of 10¾-oz. can condensed cream of mushroom soup
1 tablespoon chopped pimiento or ripe olives
1 tablespoon milk or cream

Butter four 6-oz. custard cups. In 1-quart GLASS bowl or casserole, combine first 8 ingredients. MICROWAVE covered on HIGH 3 MINUTES, stirring once. Stir bread cubes into mixture. Line sides and bottoms of prepared custard cups with thin pieces of fish, reserving small scraps for top. (You may have to cut thick pieces in half.) Evenly divide stuffing between the 4 custard cups (about ½ cup each). Top with any leftover pieces of fish. Place custard cups on a dinner plate. Cover with a dinner plate and MICROWAVE on HIGH 4 MINUTES or until fish flakes easily. With both hands, invert dinner plates with custard cups between them. Let stand covered while making Sauce.

In small GLASS bowl, combine all ingredients for Sauce. MICROWAVE uncovered on HIGH 1 MINUTE, 30 SECONDS or until mixture bubbles. Remove top plate and custard cups. Spoon Sauce over turbans and serve. 4 servings

NUTRITION INFORMATION PER SERVING

Serving Size: 1/4 of recipe		Percent U.S. RDA Per Serving	
Calories	390	Protein	30%
Protein	20g	Vitamin A	51%
Carbohydrate	20g	Vitamin C	6%
Fat	25g	Thiamin	12%
Sodium	691mg	Riboflavin	13%
Potassium	458mg	Niacin	16%
		Calcium	5%
		Iron	7%

TIPS: *The stuffing may also be used to stuff four 8 to 10 oz. whole fish.*

You may substitute seasoned bread cubes and eliminate seasonings in recipe.

BUTTER SCALLOPS

3 tablespoons margarine or butter
2 teaspoons granulated chicken bouillon
½ teaspoon dill weed
1 lb. uncooked scallops
1 tablespoon dry sherry

Place margarine in 1-quart GLASS casserole. MICROWAVE on HIGH 1 MINUTE or until margarine melts. Stir in bouillon and dill. Add scallops. MICROWAVE covered on HIGH 6 to 7 MINUTES. Stir in sherry. 4 servings

NUTRITION INFORMATION PER SERVING

Serving Size: 1/4 of recipe		Percent U.S. RDA Per Serving	
Calories	211	Protein	41%
Protein	27g	Vitamin A	7%
Carbohydrate	<1g	Vitamin C	*
Fat	10g	Thiamin	*
Sodium	646mg	Riboflavin	*
Potassium	548mg	Niacin	*
		Calcium	13%
		Iron	19%

TIP: *One pound uncooked shrimp may be substituted for scallops.*

Frozen broccoli and fish are thawed in packages, then cooked together and topped with an easy and colorful sauce made from shrimp soup. Ready to serve in about 20 minutes.

HALIBUT DIVAN

16-oz. pkg. frozen halibut fillets
10-oz. pkg. frozen broccoli spears
½ teaspoon tarragon leaves, if desired
7-oz. container frozen semi-condensed cream of shrimp soup

Place packages of frozen fillets and broccoli in microwave oven. MICROWAVE on HIGH 3 MINUTES. Remove from packages and separate. Place fillets in 2-quart GLASS baking dish. Top with broccoli, placing stems toward outside of dish, but not extending beyond edge of fish (if they extend beyond, they may overcook). Sprinkle with tarragon. MICROWAVE covered on HIGH 11 MINUTES or until fish flakes easily. LET STAND covered. Remove frozen soup from container and place in 2-cup GLASS measuring cup and MICROWAVE on HIGH 4 to 5 MINUTES or until thawed and heated, stirring occasionally. Pour sauce over fillets and broccoli. 4 servings

NUTRITION INFORMATION PER SERVING

Serving Size: 1/4 of recipe		Percent U.S. RDA Per Serving	
Calories	214	Protein	40%
Protein	26g	Vitamin A	45%
Carbohydrate	6g	Vitamin C	59%
Fat	9g	Thiamin	6%
Sodium	538mg	Riboflavin	8%
Potassium	612mg	Niacin	39%
		Calcium	5%
		Iron	6%

TIPS: *If fish is fresh, omit first cooking time that is primarily for thawing. MICROWAVE frozen broccoli uncovered on HIGH 2 MINUTES to thaw and separate.*

If broccoli is fresh, place in covered 2-qt. GLASS casserole with 1 tablespoon water and MICROWAVE on HIGH 3 MINUTES to start cooking.

This recipe may be used for many types of pike, such as Northern, Channel, Pickerel, as well as perch or trout. The stuffing enhances the mild flavor of the fish.

STUFFED WALLEYED PIKE

1½-lb. whole walleyed pike
Salt
2 tablespoons margarine or butter
2 tablespoons chopped green onion
⅛ teaspoon fennel, if desired
⅓ cup white wine
1 cup crumbled herb-seasoned stuffing

Cut off large fin on back (dorsal) since it's very sharp. Salt inside of fish. In medium GLASS bowl, melt margarine (MICROWAVE 20 SECONDS). Add onion and fennel. MICROWAVE covered on HIGH 1 MINUTE, 30 SECONDS. Add wine and crumbled stuffing; toss to combine. Stuff fish and secure with string, toothpicks or small wooden skewers. Place fish diagonally on waxed or parchment paper. Wrap fish in paper and secure ends if necessary with rubber bands. MICROWAVE on HIGH 8 MINUTES or until fish flakes easily, turning once. LET STAND wrapped 2 MINUTES to finish cooking.
4 servings

NUTRITION INFORMATION PER SERVING

Serving Size: 1/4 of recipe		Percent U.S. RDA Per Serving	
Calories	254	Protein	28%
Protein	18g	Vitamin A	47%
Carbohydrate	7g	Vitamin C	*
Fat	14g	Thiamin	9%
Sodium	524mg	Riboflavin	7%
Potassium	296mg	Niacin	14%
		Calcium	*
		Iron	3%

TIP: *Place several towels in bottom of oven for absorption of moisture and easy removal of fish after cooking.*

LASAGNA, MEATY MEAT LOAF, GROUND BEEF PATTIES AND STUFFED GREEN PEPPERS

BEEF

Gravy mix coating combines with meat juices during cooking to give meat patties a brown color and flavor. For quick meals, shape patties ahead of time and refrigerate or freeze.

GROUND BEEF PATTIES

1 to 1½ lb. ground beef
Salt and pepper
1 pkg. Pillsbury Brown Gravy Mix

Season ground beef with salt and pepper. Shape into ¼-lb. patties. Coat patties with gravy mix. Arrange in shallow GLASS baking dish. MICROWAVE covered on HIGH:

1 patty –2 MINUTES, 30 SECONDS
2 patties–3 MINUTES
3 patties–3 MINUTES, 30 SECONDS
4 patties–4 MINUTES
5 patties–4 MINUTES, 30 SECONDS
6 patties–5 MINUTES

4 to 6 patties

NUTRITION INFORMATION PER SERVING

Serving Size: 1/4 of recipe		Percent U.S. RDA Per Serving	
Calories	243	Protein	30%
Protein	20g	Vitamin A	*
Carbohydrate	<1g	Vitamin C	0%
Fat	17g	Thiamin	5%
Sodium	82mg	Riboflavin	11%
Potassium	371mg	Niacin	22%
		Calcium	*
		Iron	15%

TIPS: *Patties may be topped with one of the following during last minute of cooking: Cheese, sour cream, onion dip, cream of mushroom soup or cheese sauce.*

Patties may be seasoned, shaped, coated with gravy mix and frozen. To cook frozen patties, MICROWAVE covered on HIGH:

1 patty –2 MINUTES; let stand 1 MINUTE; MICROWAVE 1 MINUTE
2 patties–2 MINUTES, 30 SECONDS; let stand 1 MINUTE; MICROWAVE 2 MINUTES
3 patties–3 MINUTES; let stand 1 MINUTE; MICROWAVE 3 MINUTES
4 patties–4 MINUTES; let stand 1 MINUTE; MICROWAVE 3 MINUTES, 30 SECONDS

MEATY MEAT LOAF

1 lb. ground beef
2 tablespoons dry onion soup mix
¼ teaspoon salt
5-oz. can (⅔ cup) evaporated milk
2 tablespoons firmly packed brown sugar
½ teaspoon dry mustard
2 tablespoons catsup

In 1 or 1½-quart (8x4-inch) GLASS loaf dish, combine first 4 ingredients; mix well. (Mixture will be very moist.) Press evenly in dish. Combine remaining ingredients; spoon and spread over top of meat. MICROWAVE covered on HIGH 7 MINUTES or until done. LET STAND 5 MINUTES before removing to serving platter and slicing.

3 to 4 servings

NUTRITION INFORMATION PER SERVING

Serving Size: 1/4 of recipe		Percent U.S. RDA Per Serving	
Calories	350	Protein	37%
Protein	24g	Vitamin A	6%
Carbohydrate	17g	Vitamin C	4%
Fat	21g	Thiamin	7%
Sodium	781mg	Riboflavin	19%
Potassium	586mg	Niacin	23%
		Calcium	13%
		Iron	17%

TIPS: *To MAKE AHEAD, prepare as directed, refrigerate 1 day or freeze up to 1 month. After refrigerating, MICROWAVE, as directed; after freezing, MICROWAVE on HIGH 8 MINUTES, LET STAND 5 MINUTES and MICROWAVE on HIGH 5 MORE MINUTES.*

Meat loaf may be microwaved covered in 1-quart GLASS casserole, by pushing meat away from center and inserting a small glass to form a tube. MICROWAVE 6 MINUTES. Remove glass and drain juices before inverting meat loaf onto serving plate.

SWEET-SOUR MEATBALLS

¼ cup milk
1 egg
1 lb. ground beef
½ cup chopped onion or 2 tablespoons instant minced onion
2 tablespoons fine dry bread or cracker crumbs
1 teaspoon salt
⅛ teaspoon pepper
½ teaspoon Worcestershire sauce
20-oz. can pineapple chunks, drained (reserve ½ cup syrup)
½ cup reserved pineapple syrup
½ cup water
2 tablespoons vinegar
1 large green pepper, cut into cubes or thin strips
2 tablespoons cornstarch
1 tablespoon sugar
2 tablespoons soy sauce

In large bowl, blend milk and egg. Stir in ground beef, onion, crumbs, salt, pepper and Worcestershire sauce. Shape into one dozen 1½-inch balls. Place in 2-quart GLASS baking dish. MICROWAVE covered on HIGH 5 MINUTES. Rotate dish ½ turn after 3 minutes. Drain excess fat. Add ½ cup pineapple syrup, water, vinegar and green pepper. Stir gently. MICROWAVE covered on HIGH 4 MINUTES. Blend cornstarch, sugar and soy sauce; stir into meatball mixture. MICROWAVE covered on HIGH 2 to 4 MINUTES or until sauce is clear and thickened. Stir in pineapple. Serve over rice. 4 servings

NUTRITION INFORMATION PER SERVING

Serving Size: 1/4 of recipe with 1/2 cup rice

Calories	537
Protein	26g
Carbohydrate	66g
Fat	19g
Sodium	1663mg
Potassium	734mg

Percent U.S. RDA Per Serving	
Protein	40%
Vitamin A	9%
Vitamin C	80%
Thiamin	24%
Riboflavin	20%
Niacin	30%
Calcium	8%
Iron	29%

We found we could cook stuffed peppers without first precooking peppers and rice. Easy to prepare and cook in 20 minutes.

STUFFED GREEN PEPPERS

1 lb. ground beef
½ cup chopped onion or 2 tablespoons instant minced onion
½ cup (1 stalk) chopped celery
¼ cup chopped green pepper
½ cup quick-cooking rice
½ teaspoon salt
⅛ teaspoon pepper
½ cup water
½ cup catsup
4 large green peppers
8-oz. can (1 cup) tomato sauce
1 teaspoon basil leaves
Grated Parmesan cheese, if desired

Crumble ground beef into 1-quart GLASS casserole. Stir in onion, celery and green pepper. MICROWAVE uncovered on HIGH 5 MINUTES, stirring once. Drain. Stir in rice, salt, pepper, water and ¼ cup catsup. MICROWAVE covered on HIGH 5 MINUTES.

Cut tops from peppers; remove membrane and seeds. Place in 2-quart GLASS casserole. Spoon hamburger mixture into peppers. Combine ¼ cup catsup, tomato sauce and basil. Spoon over peppers. MICROWAVE uncovered on HIGH 10 to 12 MINUTES or until peppers are tender. Sprinkle with cheese.

4 servings

NUTRITION INFORMATION PER SERVING

Serving Size: 1/4 of recipe

Calories	461
Protein	27g
Carbohydrate	36g
Fat	24g
Sodium	858mg
Potassium	952mg

Percent U.S. RDA Per Serving	
Protein	41%
Vitamin A	44%
Vitamin C	230%
Thiamin	22%
Riboflavin	24%
Niacin	34%
Calcium	11%
Iron	28%

Because of their shape, lasagna noodles cook well in the baking dish which you will later use for assembling the complete lasagna. Start about 45 minutes before serving time.

LASAGNA

8-oz. pkg. lasagna noodles
1 teaspoon salt
1 lb. ground beef
1 pkg. spaghetti sauce mix
15-oz. can (2 cups) tomato sauce
4-oz. can (½ cup) mushroom stems and pieces, drained
12-oz. carton (1½ cups) creamed cottage cheese
6 to 8-oz. pkg. sliced Mozzarella cheese
½ cup grated Parmesan cheese

Place noodles in 2-quart or 12x8-inch GLASS baking dish. Cover with water and sprinkle with salt. MICROWAVE uncovered on HIGH 15 MINUTES. Remove from oven and LET STAND in cooking water while preparing meat sauce.

In medium GLASS bowl, crumble ground beef. MICROWAVE uncovered on HIGH 5 MINUTES, stirring occasionally to break beef into small pieces. Drain off juices. Stir in spaghetti sauce mix, tomato sauce and mushrooms. Drain noodles and rinse well to remove excess starch. Assemble in 2-quart or 12x8-inch GLASS baking dish by layering ⅓ of noodles, ⅓ of meat mixture, ½ of cottage cheese and ½ of Mozzarella cheese. Repeat with next layer of noodles. On last layer of noodles, spread last ⅓ of meat mixture and sprinkle with Parmesan cheese. Cover loosely with waxed paper.* MICROWAVE on HIGH 10 MINUTES or until heated through. LET STAND covered about 5 minutes for ease in cutting and serving. 6 to 8 servings

NUTRITION INFORMATION PER SERVING

Serving Size: 1/6 of recipe		Percent U.S. RDA Per Serving	
Calories	621	Protein	49%
Protein	32g	Vitamin A	31%
Carbohydrate	42g	Vitamin C	44%
Fat	36g	Thiamin	19%
Sodium	1088mg	Riboflavin	40%
Potassium	418mg	Niacin	27%
		Calcium	39%
		Iron	22%

TIPS: *To MAKE AHEAD, prepare to *and refrigerate. If it has chilled completely, MICROWAVE on HIGH 12 MINUTES or until hot.*

Recipe may be assembled in two 8-inch square or two 10x6-inch GLASS baking dishes. For these sizes it is easier to assemble in 2 layers and sprinkle Parmesan cheese on top of Mozzarella. You may freeze one dish for use at a later time. When ready to serve, cover loosely with waxed paper. MICROWAVE on HIGH 8 MINUTES, LET STAND 5 MINUTES and MICROWAVE on HIGH 6 MORE MINUTES or until hot.

GUIDE FOR DEFROSTING MEAT, POULTRY AND FISH

Use the following times as a guide when defrosting these or similar cuts of frozen meat, poultry or fish. Since shape of cut and package, starting temperature and total weight will vary, it may be necessary to make slight adjustments in the times.

With items as dense as meats, a rest period (standing time) after each cooking period is necessary to allow the heat to penetrate the center of the meat without cooking the outside edges. REST PERIODS SHOULD BE AT LEAST 2 MINUTES FOR LARGER, MORE DENSE CUTS AND 1 MINUTE FOR SMALLER, LESS DENSE CUTS. With smaller cuts, you can separate or rearrange the pieces to speed the defrosting of the center.

Large items such as roasts can begin with cooking periods of 2 to 3 minutes. As the roast thaws on the outside, the cooking times must be decreased to avoid cooking these thawed areas. Once the outside of the meat feels warm and is thawed, the cooking periods should be reduced to 30 seconds to 1 minute, depending on the size of the cut. It is more difficult to know when the center of a large cut is thawed but a meat thermometer (do not use conventional meat thermometer in microwave oven when cooking) will quickly tell you if the temperature has climbed above 32°F.

With these times, there may be some cooking that begins on the outside edge. This is acceptable if the meat will be cooked immediately. If not planning to cook the meat immediately, it is better to use shorter cooking periods while defrosting to eliminate the chance of spoilage during additional storage.

The times given in chart under Microwave Defrost Times are alternately **MICROWAVE; LET STAND; MICROWAVE.**

This chart *does not* pertain to automatic defrost features.

MEAT	WEIGHT	MICROWAVE DEFROST TIMES*
Chops	2 lb.	2 min; 1 min; 1 min.
Ground	2 lb. 1 lb.	2 min; 1 min; 1 min; 30 sec. 2 min; 1 min; 30 sec; 30 sec.
Ribs	2 lb. 1 lb.	2 min; 1 min; 1 min; 1 min. 2 min; 1 min; 30 sec.
Roast	4 lb. 3 lb.	3 min; 3 min; 2 min; 2 min; 1 min; 1 min; 1 min. 3 min; 3 min; 2 min; 1 min; 1 min; 30 sec.
Steak (¾ inch thick)	1½ - 2 lb.	2 min; 1 min; 1 min.
Steak (1½ inch thick)	1½ - 2 lb.	2 min; 2 min; 2 min; 1 min.
POULTRY		
Chicken, Breasts (4)	1 lb.	2 min; 1 min; 1 min.
Chicken, Fryer	2½ to 3lb.	3 min; 2 min; 2 min; 1 min; 1 min.
Cornish Hens (2) (4)	1 lb. each 1 lb. each	2 min; 2 min; 2 min; 1 min; 1 min. 3 min; 2 min; 2 min; 2 min; 1 min; 1 min.
Goose	10 lb.	3 min; 3 min; 3 min; 3 min; 3 min; 2 min; 2 min; 2 min; 2 min; 2 min; 2 min.
Turkey, Boneless Rolled Roast	4 lb.	3 min; 2 min; 2 min; 2 min; 2 min; 2 min.
Turkey, Breast (1)	2 lb. 2 oz.	3 min; 2 min; 2 min; 1 min; 1 min; 1 min.
Turkey, Thighs (1)	1 lb. 7 oz.	3 min; 2 min; 1 min; 1 min.
Turkey, Wings (2)	2 lb. 7 oz.	3 min; 2 min; 2 min; 1 min; 1 min.
FISH AND SEAFOOD		
Fillets	1 lb.	2 min; 1 min; 1 min; 30 sec.
Whole Fish	12 oz.	30 sec; 30 sec; 30 sec.
Lobster Tail	8 - 10 oz.	30 sec; 30 sec; 30 sec.
Shrimp	8 - 10 oz.	1 min; 30 sec.

*Allow a rest period of at least 2 minutes for larger cuts and 1 minute for smaller cuts after each microwave time.

CAKES

BASIC INSTRUCTIONS FOR MAKING PILLSBURY PLUS CAKE MIXES IN THE MICROWAVE OVEN

This collection of delicious new microwave cakes using Pillsbury Plus cake mixes was developed by the home economists of the Pillsbury Consumer Service Kitchens. It includes both long-time family favorites updated for microwave and new recipe ideas that will soon become favorites. You'll also find other hints to improve your microwave baking plus basic instructions for microwaving all flavors of Pillsbury Plus mixes in a variety of pan sizes.

Tips for success in microwave baking

- Our tests show that a LOW/HIGH power combination produces the best baking results. But since ovens vary, directions for LOW/HIGH combination and HIGH only power ovens are included in recipe directions.

  *If your microwave oven has a multi-power setting, LOW in our directions refers to power ratings of 30 to 50%.
- Since foods cook so quickly in the microwave, baked products will be somewhat different than those baked in conventional ovens: texture will have a finer grain and crusts will not brown. Microwaving does not affect flavor. We suggest that you choose products that have darker colored crusts or add frostings or toppings to light colored baked goods.
- It is easy to overbake in microwave ovens, and baking times vary with oven models, so Pillsbury recipes give a range in time. Start with the minimum time and add more cook-time as needed. Remember products will continue to bake after they are removed from the oven.
- To ensure even baking, turn pans frequently. (Recipes indicate optimum number of turns.)
- Since not all pans are suitable for microwave baking, use the kind indicated in the recipe.
- Cool baked products on a flat, heat resistant surface (not a wire rack) to insure that the bottom will be completely baked.

Pan preparation

8-inch round GLASS pans: line with waxed paper.
13x9 and 12x8-inch GLASS pans: no pan preparation necessary.
Cupcakes: for best results use cupcake liners in GLASS custard cups.

Amount of batter per pan

8-inch round GLASS pans: divide batter evenly between two pans. (Bake each layer separately)
13x9-inch GLASS pan: use all batter.
12x8-inch GLASS pan: use 3¼ cups batter; use remaining batter to make cupcakes.
Cupcakes: use 2 tablespoons of batter per cupcake.

Number of turns

8-inch round GLASS pans: rotate ½ turn halfway through baking cycle.
13x9-inch GLASS pan: rotate ½ turn every 3 to 4 minutes during baking.
12x8-inch GLASS pan: rotate ½ turn every 3 to 4 minutes during baking.
Cupcakes: no turning necessary.

To defrost and bake frozen batter:

Cover with plastic wrap; MICROWAVE on LOW 5 minutes, rotating ¼ turn every minute. Remove plastic wrap and MICROWAVE on HIGH 5½ to 6½ MINUTES. (LOW refers to 30% to 50% power.)

MICROWAVING TIMES FOR PILLSBURY PLUS CAKE MIX

Prepare cake according to package directions
and MICROWAVE as directed below:

	8-Inch Round Pans		13x9-Inch Pan		12x8-Inch Pan		Cupcakes:* All Flavors
	LOW/HIGH combination**	**HIGH only**	**LOW**/HIGH combination**	**HIGH only**	**LOW**/HIGH combination**	**HIGH only**	**HIGH only**
Butter	LOW: 5 min. HIGH: 2½ to 3½ min.	4½ to 5½ min.	LOW: 7 min. HIGH: 7½ to 8½ min.	11 to 12 min.	LOW: 6 min. HIGH: 4 to 5 min.	8 to 9 min.	1 cupcake: 30 sec.
Dark Chocolate	LOW: 5 min. HIGH: 2½ to 3½ min.	4½ to 6 min.	LOW: 7 min. HIGH: 7½ to 8½ min.	12 to 14 min.	LOW: 6 min. HIGH: 4 to 5 min.	7 to 8 min.	2 cupcakes: 1 min.
Devil's Food	LOW: 4 min. HIGH: 3 to 3½ min.	4½ to 5 min.	LOW: 7 min. HIGH: 7½ to 8½ min.	13 to 14 min.	LOW: 6 min. HIGH: 3½ to 4½ min.	7 to 8 min.	3 cupcakes: 1½ min.
Fudge Marble	LOW: 5 min. HIGH: 2½ to 3½ min.	4½ to 5½ min.	LOW: 7 min. HIGH: 7½ to 8½ min.	12 to 14 min.	not recommended		4 cupcakes: 2 min.
German Chocolate	LOW: 5 min. HIGH: 2½ to 3½ min.	4½ to 5½ min.	LOW: 10 min. HIGH: 7 to 8 min.	12 to 13 min.	LOW: 6 min. HIGH: 4½ to 5½ min.	8 to 9 min.	5 cupcakes: 2½ min.
Lemon	LOW: 5 min. HIGH: 2½ to 3½ min.	4½ to 5½ min.	LOW: 7 min. HIGH: 7½ to 8½ min.	11 to 12 min.	LOW: 6 min. HIGH: 4 to 4½ min.	8 to 9 min.	6 cupcakes: 3 min.
White	LOW: 5 min. HIGH: 2 to 3 min.	4 to 5 min.	LOW: 7 min. HIGH: 7 to 8 min.	11 to 12 min.	LOW: 6 min. HIGH: 4 to 5 min.	8 to 9 min.	
Yellow, Strawberry or Banana	LOW: 5 min. HIGH: 2½ to 3 min.	4½ to 5 min.	LOW: 7 min. HIGH: 7½ to 8½ min.	10½ to 11½ min.	LOW: 6 min. HIGH: 4 to 4½ min.	8 to 9 min.	

Cool all pans on flat surface, not a wire rack. Remove round cakes from pans after 10 minutes. Remove cupcakes from pan immediately; cool on flat surface.

*Microwaving more than 6 cupcakes at one time is not recommended. Determine number of cupcakes desired; MICROWAVE the time indicated on cupcake column above.

**LOW: Refers to 30% to 50% power.

DESSERTS

CRUMB PIE SHELL

1¼ cups fine crumbs (vanilla wafer, graham cracker, chocolate wafer or gingersnaps)
2 tablespoons sugar
¼ cup melted margarine or butter

In small bowl, blend crumbs with sugar and margarine. Press firmly and evenly into 9-inch GLASS pie pan. MICROWAVE on HIGH 2 to 2½ MINUTES, rotating plate ¼ turn after 1 minute. 9-inch pie shell

NUTRITION INFORMATION PER SERVING

Serving Size: 1/6 of recipe		Percent U.S. RDA Per Serving	
Calories	168	Protein	3%
Protein	2g	Vitamin A	6%
Carbohydrate	20g	Vitamin C	0%
Fat	10g	Thiamin	*
Sodium	240mg	Riboflavin	3%
Potassium	86mg	Niacin	*
		Calcium	*
		Iron	*

TIP: *Melt margarine in microwave.*

PILLSBURY PIE CRUST MIX SHELL

Prepare 1 pkg. Pillsbury Pie Crust Mix according to package directions. Roll dough and place in 9-inch GLASS pie pan. Flute edge and prick generously. Place directly on floor of oven. MICROWAVE on HIGH 4 to 5 MINUTES, rotating ½ turn after 2 minutes.

9-inch pastry shell

NUTRITION INFORMATION PER SERVING

Serving Size: 1/6 of recipe		Percent U.S. RDA Per Serving	
Calories	140	Protein	2%
Protein	2g	Vitamin A	*
Carbohydrate	13g	Vitamin C	*
Fat	9g	Thiamin	7%
Sodium	205mg	Riboflavin	4%
Potassium	0mg	Niacin	4%
		Calcium	*
		Iron	2%

TIP: *Freeze unbaked pastry shell for thawing and baking later.*

CHOCOLATE PASTRY SHELL

1¼ cups Pillsbury's Best® All Purpose or Unbleached Flour*
¼ teaspoon salt
2 tablespoons unsweetened cocoa
½ cup shortening
2½ tablespoons water

In small bowl, combine flour, salt and cocoa. Using pastry blender cut in shortening until particles are size of small peas. Sprinkle flour mixture with water, tossing and mixing lightly with a fork until mixture forms a ball. Flatten ball slightly; smooth edges.

With stockinette-covered rolling pin, roll dough on floured pastry cloth or surface to ⅛-inch thickness. Line 9-inch GLASS pie pan; trim edge of pastry 1 inch from rim of pan; flute. Prick pastry generously. MICROWAVE on HIGH 2 to 3 MINUTES, rotating ½ turn after 1 minute, then ¼ turn after 2 minutes. Pastry is done when it looks set and loses its shiny appearance.

9-inch pie shell

NUTRITION INFORMATION PER SERVING

Serving Size: 1/6 of recipe		Percent U.S. RDA Per Serving	
Calories	247	Protein	5%
Protein	3g	Vitamin A	*
Carbohydrate	21g	Vitamin C	0%
Fat	17g	Thiamin	11%
Sodium	91mg	Riboflavin	7%
Potassium	52mg	Niacin	7%
		Calcium	*
		Iron	5%

TIP: **If using Pillsbury's Best® Self Rising Flour, omit salt.*

BRANDY ALEXANDER PIE

1 Crumb Pie Shell made with chocolate wafers, page 390
24 large marshmallows
½ cup milk
¼ cup dark creme de cacao
3 tablespoons brandy
1½ cups whipping cream, whipped

Make crumb mixture as recipe directs. Reserve 2 tablespoons crumbs to decorate top of pie. Press remainder into 9-inch GLASS pie pan and MICROWAVE as recipe directs. Cool.

Place marshmallows and milk in 3-quart GLASS casserole. MICROWAVE on HIGH about 3 MINUTES or until melted marshmallows can be blended with milk. Chill 30 to 40 minutes or until cool.

Stir creme de cacao and brandy into cooled marshmallow mixture then fold in whipped cream. Pour into crust and decorate with reserved chocolate cookie crumbs. Freeze or refrigerate until serving.

9-inch pie

NUTRITION INFORMATION PER SERVING

Serving Size: 1/6 of recipe		Percent U.S. RDA Per Serving	
Calories	493	Protein	6%
Protein	4g	Vitamin A	16%
Carbohydrate	53g	Vitamin C	*
Fat	27g	Thiamin	*
Sodium	286mg	Riboflavin	5%
Potassium	80mg	Niacin	*
		Calcium	6%
		Iron	4%

TIP: *This pie is soft and creamy when served from refrigerator; for firm pieces which hold sharp cut, serve frozen. Frozen pie releases easily from bottom of pie pan if set on towel dampened with hot water a few minutes.*

Fresh apple pie hot from the oven in 20 minutes! Use this combination microwave and conventional oven method, the microwave speeds up cooking and the regular oven browns the crust.

MICROWAVE APPLE PIE

Prepare 1 pkg. Pillsbury Pie Crust Mix according to package directions for two-crust pie. Use an 8 or 9-inch GLASS pie pan. Fill with your favorite apple filling. Place pie directly on floor of microwave oven. MICROWAVE on HIGH 6½ to 7½ MINUTES, rotating ½ turn after 4 minutes. While microwaving, heat conventional oven to 450°F. Bake for 10 minutes or until crust is golden brown.

8 or 9-inch pie

CHOCOLATE COVERED CHERRY PIE

1 Crumb Pie Shell*, page 390
6-oz. pkg. (1 cup) semi-sweet chocolate chips
14-oz. can sweetened condensed milk (not evaporated)
½ teaspoon salt
21-oz. can (2 cups) cherry fruit filling
½ teaspoon almond extract
8 stemmed maraschino cherries, for garnish

Cook and cool pie shell. Put chocolate, milk and salt in 1½-quart GLASS casserole. MICROWAVE on HIGH 2 MINUTES or until boiling. Stir vigorously until well blended. Mix in fruit filling and almond extract. Pour into shell. Chill at least 2 hours or overnight. Garnish with cherries. 9-inch pie

NUTRITION INFORMATION PER SERVING

Serving Size: 1/6 of recipe		Percent U.S. RDA Per Serving	
Calories	695	Protein	14%
Protein	9g	Vitamin A	18%
Carbohydrate	115g	Vitamin C	23%
Fat	26g	Thiamin	6%
Sodium	606mg	Riboflavin	21%
Potassium	482mg	Niacin	4%
		Calcium	20%
		Iron	8%

TIP: **Graham cracker or vanilla wafer crumb crusts are best with this pie.*

FRUIT PARFAIT PIE

1 Crumb Pie Shell, page 390
2 pkg. (10 oz. each) frozen berries, thawed
3-oz. pkg. fruit-flavored gelatin
1 pint vanilla ice cream

Cook and cool pie shell. Drain syrup from fruit into measuring cup. Reserve fruit. Add enough water to syrup to make 1½ cups. Pour into 1½-quart GLASS casserole. MICROWAVE on HIGH 2½ to 3 MINUTES or until liquid is boiling. Add gelatin and stir until dissolved. To hot gelatin mixture, add ice cream by spoonfuls until all is added. Stir well. Chill 20 to 30 minutes or until thickened but not set. Fold in the reserved fruit and pour into crust. Chill until set, about 1 hour. 9-inch pie

NUTRITION INFORMATION PER SERVING

Serving Size: 1/6 of recipe		Percent U.S. RDA Per Serving	
Calories	409	Protein	9%
Protein	6g	Vitamin A	11%
Carbohydrate	68g	Vitamin C	84%
Fat	15g	Thiamin	3%
Sodium	314mg	Riboflavin	12%
Potassium	273mg	Niacin	4%
		Calcium	9%
		Iron	6%

NO BAKE PEANUT BUTTER COOKIES

½ cup sugar
½ cup light corn syrup
2 cups corn flakes, toasted oat or crisp rice cereal
1 cup peanut butter

In medium GLASS bowl, blend sugar and syrup. MICROWAVE on HIGH 2½ to 3 MINUTES or until mixture comes to a full boil. Stir in cereal and peanut butter. Drop by teaspoonfuls onto waxed paper or shape into balls. 36 cookies

NUTRITION INFORMATION PER SERVING

Serving Size: 2 cookies		Percent U.S. RDA Per Serving	
Calories	143	Protein	6%
Protein	4g	Vitamin A	0%
Carbohydrate	17g	Vitamin C	0%
Fat	7g	Thiamin	*
Sodium	121mg	Riboflavin	*
Potassium	94mg	Niacin	11%
		Calcium	*
		Iron	4%

OUTDOOR COOKING

OUTDOOR COOKING

Outdoor cooking conjures up images of fresh air, hearty appetites and casual mealtimes. Maybe most of your outdoor cooking has been in your backyard but it is also just as easy to have a tailgate party, using one or two hibachis. Or perhaps breakfast in the park with foods that need only to be heated. A patio brunch, a boating excursion or a camping trip are all good times made even better by cooking outdoors.

However, the good flavor of barbecuing is going indoors more frequently too. Fireplaces, indoor grills, or outdoor grills placed in a well-ventilated garage make barbecuing a year-round pleasure.

Whether you are cooking on a charcoal grill, a gas grill, a camp stove, a hibachi, an open fire or a kettle cooker, we suggest you consider expanding your menu planning to include vegetables, breads, desserts and appetizers prepared on a barbecue, as well as the meat dish. Use special caution to prevent spoilage if marinating meat at room temperature during hot weather.

BASIC WAYS TO BARBECUE

HOT OFF THE GRILL: Familiar method of cooking over direct heat used for most barbecue cooking. For the beginner, the first rule to know is that a good, even bed of coals is the key to success.

- Light the charcoal about ½ hour before you wish to cook food.
- Judge the readiness of the briquets for cooking by their appearance after lighting. They should look gray in the daytime; glow red at night. There should be no flame showing at all. After coals are burning evenly, spread briquets one layer deep with about 1-inch between. Space between the briquets helps prevent flare-ups from dripping fat. If cooker has a hood, the grill may be covered to give more flavor to food and speed cooking time.
- To reduce heat when cooking, raise the height of the grill. To increase heat near the end of cooking time, tap the ashes off the coals because they tend to blanket the fire.
- If more coals are needed, add charcoal around the edge of the fire. Unlit coals placed on top of burning coals produce cool spots. As the charcoal catches fire, it can be added to replace burned-down coals.
- For controlling flare-ups and smoke, trim as much fat from meat as possible before placing on grill. Have water available to extinguish any flames.

ROTISSERIE ROASTING: When using a rotisserie; coals are arranged along the back of the grill. Place a drip pan (you can make one from several thicknesses of foil) under the meat. The juices from the meat may be used as a sauce to serve along with meat or for basting. Follow use and care instructions for using your specific rotisserie; however, here are some extra tips:

- Center meat on rotisserie so that weight is balanced equally.
- Thread ribs on spit in accordion fashion.
- When threading a cut of meat containing bone that runs the length of the meat, follow the bone, if possible.
- Meats over 12 lb. generally do not cook well by rotisserie.

COVERED GRILL ROASTING: In covered kettle or wagon cookers, large cuts of meat may be roasted without a rotisserie. For the kettle cooker, coals are arranged around the sides of the meat and a drip pan is placed underneath. For the wagon cooker, charcoal is placed at one end, with the meat and drip pan at the other end.

- You can improvise a cover by making a hood with heavy duty foil.

FOIL COOKING: The "no clean-up" convenience of wrapping foods in foil before grilling gives barbecue cooking another dimension. One-dish meals make their appearance as vegetables, fruits, and sauces are added to these handy packets. Other foil baking or roasting pans may be used. When testing recipes for this book, we used a single thickness of heavy duty foil. For steaks and chops with small bones that might tear the foil when handled, two thicknesses can be used.

ADDING SMOKED FLAVOR: Smoke cooking is used by the barbecue chef to give food a distinctive flavor. Foods cook over slow coals in a covered grill. (This popular cooking method should not be confused with smoking as a curing process for such meats as ham. While these meats have smokehouse flavor, cooking is still required.)

Coals for smoke cooking are arranged depending on the food you are cooking. Once the coals are going, dampened wood chips are tossed on the fire. While hickory chips are most popular, wood from other fruit and nut trees have distinctive flavors, too. Avoid using resinous woods such as pine, as foods acquire a taste somewhat like turpentine!

Soak wood chips in water about 30 minutes before using. If they should catch fire, simply remove them with tongs and soak again. Sometimes, it is helpful to wrap the dampened chips in several foil packets. Punch holes in one side of the packet; place them on the coals with punched side up.

Fresh herbs, too, can give their subtle flavor to barbecued foods—and a delightful aroma to the whole patio area as well. Mint, bay, thyme, rosemary and marjoram can be added periodically as roasts are cooking or during the last 10 minutes when cooking smaller cuts and fish.

SAFETY AND TASTE TIPS

- Use tongs to handle meat and vegetables whenever possible. A fork pierces the food, allowing juices to escape.
- Season meats *after* cooking (unless recipe instructions specify otherwise) to keep juices from running too early in the cooking process.
- It is usually advisable to baste extremely lean meat. (A small paint brush works well.) Use either drippings or a prepared marinade or sauce.
- Utilize foil or a metal drip pan to catch delicious juices and to help avoid fires caused from drippings.
- Keep meat from sticking by rubbing grill with some fat trimmings, a piece of bacon or a special spray-on product.
- To keep meat lying flat on the grill, score edges or use a special wire holder.
- Avoid burning your hands by using asbestos gloves to handle hot cooking equipment and briquets which may need rearranging.
- A water-filled sprinkler bottle is handy to keep sudden flare-ups from getting out of control.
- Heat can be reduced by moving grill, adjustable firebox and/or coals away from food.

Add fruit to your next barbecued burgers for a Polynesian touch.

BEEF BURGERS POLYNESIAN

1½ lb. ground beef
1½ teaspoons salt
½ teaspoon pepper
¼ cup margarine or butter, melted
½ cup prepared sweet and sour sauce
2 bananas
4 pineapple slices

BEFORE GRILLING: Combine beef, salt and pepper; mix well. Shape into 4 oval patties. Combine margarine and sauce.

ON THE GRILL: Brush patties with sauce. Place on grill 3 to 4 inches from hot coals. Cook until browned on one side; turn. Meanwhile, cut banana lengthwise and crosswise in quarters. Lay a pineapple slice and 2 banana quarters on each burger. Spoon on remaining sauce. Continue cooking until of desired doneness. These burgers are best served open-face on toasted English muffins or bread. 4 servings

NUTRITION INFORMATION PER SERVING

Serving Size: 1 patty		Percent U.S. RDA Per Serving	
Calories	574	Protein	47%
Protein	31g	Vitamin A	14%
Carbohydrate	30g	Vitamin C	13%
Fat	37g	Thiamin	14%
Sodium	695mg	Riboflavin	19%
Potassium	897mg	Niacin	36%
		Calcium	3%
		Iron	26%

CHEESEBURGERS CANTONESE

1 lb. ground beef
½ teaspoon onion salt
2 tablespoons soy sauce
16-oz. can (2 cups) bean sprouts, drained
6 slices American cheese
6 hamburger buns, sliced
Salad dressing or mayonnaise

BEFORE GRILLING: Combine first 4 ingredients; mix well. Form mixture into 6 patties.

ON THE GRILL: Place patties on grill 3 to 4 inches from hot coals. Cook until browned on both sides and of desired doneness. For each sandwich, place bun tops on grill to toast. When toasted, place a piece of cheese on each patty and top with toasted bun. While cheese melts, toast bottom half of buns. If desired, spread with salad dressing before topping with meat patty.

6 sandwiches

NUTRITION INFORMATION PER SERVING

Serving Size: 1 sandwich		Percent U.S. RDA Per Serving	
Calories	360	Protein	34%
Protein	22g	Vitamin A	5%
Carbohydrate	24g	Vitamin C	2%
Fat	19g	Thiamin	13%
Sodium	1155mg	Riboflavin	19%
Potassium	377mg	Niacin	20%
		Calcium	18%
		Iron	18%

When grilling steaks, trim excess fat so drippings will not catch fire. Slash the fat edge at 1 to 2-inch intervals to prevent steak from curling during cooking.

GRILLING TIME FOR TENDER STEAKS*

THICKNESS	RARE	MEDIUM	WELL
1 inch	8 to 12 min.	14 to 20 min.	20 to 30 min.
1½ inches	14 to 18 min.	16 to 25 min.	25 to 35 min.
2 inches	16 to 20 min.	30 to 35 min.	40 or more min.

*Timetable may also be used for pre-tenderized meat cuts or for less tender cuts that have been seasoned with meat tenderizer, as directed on label.

SIRLOIN STEAK WITH ROQUEFORT

¼ cup margarine or butter
¼ cup (2 oz.) Roquefort or blue cheese
Salt and pepper
2-lb. sirloin steak, cut 1½ inches thick

BEFORE GRILLING: In small bowl, cream margarine, cheese, salt and pepper. Trim excess fat from steak; slash fat edges to prevent curling.

ON THE GRILL: Place steak on grill 6 inches from hot coals. Cook 10 minutes; turn. Spread with cheese mixture and cook 10 to 15 minutes longer for medium steak or until of desired doneness.

6 to 8 servings

NUTRITION INFORMATION PER SERVING

Serving Size: 1/6 of recipe		Percent U.S. RDA Per Serving	
Calories	507	Protein	40%
Protein	26g	Vitamin A	10%
Carbohydrate	<1g	Vitamin C	*
Fat	44g	Thiamin	4%
Sodium	201mg	Riboflavin	15%
Potassium	382mg	Niacin	25%
		Calcium	5%
		Iron	17%

TEXAS CHILI BEEF SLICES

2-lb. round or family steak, cut 2 inches thick
Instant meat tenderizer
1 small onion, chopped
2 garlic cloves, minced
2 tablespoons vinegar
2 tablespoons oil
2 tablespoons Worcestershire sauce
2 to 3 teaspoons chili powder or cayenne pepper
8-oz. can (1 cup) tomato sauce
1 lemon, sliced
2 tablespoons firmly packed brown sugar
½ teaspoon dry mustard or 1½ teaspoons prepared mustard
¼ teaspoon Tabasco sauce

BEFORE GRILLING: Sprinkle meat with tenderizer as directed on label. Combine onion, garlic, vinegar, oil, Worcestershire sauce and chili powder to make marinade. Pour marinade over steak in shallow non-metallic container or plastic bag. Marinate 15 to 20 minutes at room temperature or 2 hours in refrigerator. Remove steak from marinade. Combine marinade with remaining ingredients in saucepan; simmer 10 minutes. Keep warm until serving time.

ON THE GRILL: Center steak on grill 4 to 6 inches from hot coals. Cook 30 to 40 minutes for medium rare or until of desired doneness, turning once. To serve, cut across grain into slices. Spoon sauce over steak.

5 to 6 servings

NUTRITION INFORMATION PER SERVING

Serving Size: 1/5 of recipe		Percent U.S. RDA Per Serving	
Calories	464	Protein	55%
Protein	36g	Vitamin A	28%
Carbohydrate	13g	Vitamin C	*
Fat	29g	Thiamin	9%
Sodium	451mg	Riboflavin	18%
Potassium	57mg	Niacin	37%
		Calcium	3%
		Iron	28%

Use this recipe as a timing guide when grilling boneless beef roasts.

WINE AND GARLIC ROLLED ROAST

½ cup red wine vinegar or red wine
¼ cup oil
1 garlic clove, minced
1 teaspoon dry mustard or 1 tablespoon prepared mustard
3 to 4-lb. rolled rump, sirloin tip or top round roast, 4 inches in diameter
3 to 4 tablespoons coarsely ground black pepper

BEFORE GRILLING: Combine all ingredients except roast and pepper to make marinade. Pour marinade over roast in non-metallic bowl or plastic bag. Marinate 12 to 14 hours or overnight in refrigerator, turning several times to season. Remove roast; reserve marinade for basting sauce. Dry roast with paper towel; press pepper into all sides of roast. Insert meat thermometer.

ON THE GRILL: Arrange coals for covered grill roasting, page 395. Center meat on grill 6 to 8 inches from coals; cover with hood or foil tent. Roast over slow fire to 160°F. for medium rare (about 1¾ hours) or until of desired doneness, basting with marinade and turning a quarter turn every 30 minutes. For ease in carving, let stand 15 minutes.

8 to 12 servings

Length of marinating time and surface area of meat present too many variables to accurately determine nutritional information.

TIP: *Roast may be cooked on rotisserie also; omit turning step.*

LAMB SHISH KABOBS

SHASLIK

1-lb. round steak, ¼ inch thick, cut into strips
Russian dressing
1½ cups cherry tomatoes
4-oz. can (½ cup) canned or fresh mushroom caps
16-oz. can (2 cups) whole potatoes, drained
1 zucchini, cubed

BEFORE GRILLING: In shallow non-metallic bowl or plastic bag, marinate meat overnight in enough dressing to cover. Thread alternately meat and vegetables on skewers, interlacing meat over and under vegetables.

ON THE GRILL: Place skewers on grill 3 to 4 inches from coals. Cook 10 minutes or until of desired doneness, brushing frequently with marinade. 4 to 6 servings

Length of marinating time and surface area of meat present too many variables to accurately determine nutritional information.

TIP: *If round steak ¼-inch thick is unavailable, just cut a thicker steak into ¼-inch strips.*

Cubes of lamb and vegetables alternated on skewers. Serve with rice or crusty rolls.

LAMB SHISH KABOBS

1 cup oil or olive oil
¼ cup lemon juice
2 garlic cloves, minced
¼ teaspoon crushed thyme leaves
8 oz. (4 cups) fresh mushrooms
4 to 5 tomatoes, quartered
1 green pepper, cut into 1-inch pieces
1½ lb. boneless lamb, cut into 1½-inch cubes
¾ lb. (12 slices) bacon

BEFORE GRILLING: Combine oil, lemon juice, garlic and thyme. Pour oil mixture over vegetables and lamb in large non-metallic bowl. Marinate at room temperature 1 hour or in refrigerator overnight.

ON THE GRILL: Starting with bacon, thread lamb and vegetables on skewers, interlacing bacon over and under pieces. Grill over hot coals 30 minutes or broil 5 inches from heat until brown, basting with marinade and turning occasionally. Season with salt. 5 to 6 servings

Length of marinating time and surface area of meat present too many variables to accurately determine nutritional information.

TIPS: *For a quick marinade, use bottled Italian or French dressing.*

Bacon may be omitted; cook kabobs 20 to 25 minutes.

GINGER-SHERRY LAMB CHOPS

¼ cup soy sauce
¼ cup dry sherry
1 garlic clove, minced
1 teaspoon dry or prepared mustard
¼ teaspoon ginger
¼ teaspoon thyme, if desired
4 lamb chops or steaks

BEFORE GRILLING: In non-metallic bowl or plastic bag, combine all ingredients except chops. Add chops, coating with marinade. Marinate 2 to 4 hours at room temperature or overnight in refrigerator.

ON THE GRILL: Place chops on grill 4 to 6 inches from hot coals. Cook about 10 minutes on each side or until of desired doneness, brushing occasionally with marinade. 4 servings

Length of marinating time and surface area of meat present too many variables to accurately determine nutritional information.

GRILLED TURKEY

BEFORE GRILLING: Rinse turkey; pat dry. Rub inside with salt. If desired, stuff cavity. Skewer neck skin to back. Wrap string around wings and breast to fasten securely. Insert spit from tail end of bird toward front part of breast. Insert skewers or spit forks firmly in place in bird and secure, making sure turkey is evenly balanced on spit. Tie drumsticks to spit. For moisture, place a small pan of water behind bed of coals.

ON THE GRILL: Arrange coals for rotisserie roasting, page 394. Brush turkey with oil. Insert rotisserie 4 to 6 inches from coals. Cover; roast according to timetable, adding 4 to 6 pieces of charcoal and brushing with oil every 30 minutes. For easier slicing, allow roast to stand 15 to 20 minutes.

TIPS: *To check temperature, insert meat thermometer in thickest part of breast, or test doneness by raising drumstick up and down–leg should move easily. Thermometer should register 180° to 185°F.*

Use hot pads or paper towels to protect your fingers when checking doneness.

TIMETABLE FOR GRILLING TURKEY

WHOLE TURKEY (180° to 185°F.)
(Medium coals)

Ready-to-Cook Weight (lb.)	Approximate Time (hours)	Approximate Servings
4 to 6	2 to 3	6 to 8
6 to 8	3 to 3½	8 to 10
8 to 10	3½ to 4	10 to 14
10 to 12	4 to 5	14 to 18

BONELESS TURKEY ROAST
(170° to 175°F.)
(Medium coals)

Ready-to-Cook Weight (lb.)	Approximate Time (hours)	Approximate Servings
2 to 5	1½ to 2	6 to 12
5 to 7	2 to 3	12 to 16
7 to 9	3 to 3½	16 to 24

Precooking the chicken in foil allows a shorter grilling time and less chance of burning.

EASY BUTTER-BASTED CHICKEN

2½ to 3 lb. frying chicken, cut up
½ cup margarine or butter
½ teaspoon salt
½ teaspoon lemon pepper seasoning
¼ teaspoon basil leaves, crushed, if desired

BEFORE GRILLING: Heat oven to 350°F. Place chicken on large square of heavy duty foil; wrap tightly. Roast in foil for 30 minutes. Melt margarine in small saucepan; add lemon pepper seasoning and basil to make basting sauce.

ON THE GRILL: Place chicken, skin-side-up on grill 4 to 6 inches from hot coals. Cook about 20 minutes or until done, turning and brushing often with basting sauce.

4 servings

NUTRITION INFORMATION PER SERVING

Serving Size: 1/4 of recipe		Percent U.S. RDA Per Serving	
Calories	445	Protein	55%
Protein	36g	Vitamin A	47%
Carbohydrate	<1g	Vitamin C	*
Fat	33g	Thiamin	8%
Sodium	553mg	Riboflavin	42%
Potassium	9mg	Niacin	53%
		Calcium	3%
		Iron	21%

CHICKEN WITH PINEAPPLE GLAZE

2 (2½ to 3 lb. each) frying chickens, quartered or halved
2 tablespoons margarine or butter
Salt
Pepper
Paprika
1 cup firmly packed brown sugar
2 tablespoons lemon juice
2 tablespoons prepared mustard or 1 teaspoon dry mustard
Dash salt
8-oz. can (1 cup) crushed pineapple, undrained

BEFORE GRILLING: Rub chicken with margarine; sprinkle with salt, pepper and paprika. Combine remaining ingredients for basting sauce; mix well.

ON THE GRILL: Place chicken on grill, skin-side-up, 6 to 8 inches from hot coals. Cook 30 to 45 minutes, turning once to brown both sides. Brush with basting sauce during last 10 to 15 minutes. If desired, heat any remaining sauce and serve with chicken. 8 servings

NUTRITION INFORMATION PER SERVING

Serving Size: 1/8 of recipe		Percent U.S. RDA Per Serving	
Calories	391	Protein	55%
Protein	36g	Vitamin A	31%
Carbohydrate	33g	Vitamin C	4%
Fat	12g	Thiamin	10%
Sodium	101mg	Riboflavin	43%
Potassium	131mg	Niacin	54%
		Calcium	5%
		Iron	26%

CHILI BARBECUED CHICKEN

2½ to 3 lb. frying chicken, cut up
1 cup catsup or chili sauce
¼ cup chopped onion or 2 tablespoons instant minced onion
¼ cup firmly packed brown sugar
1 garlic clove, crushed
1 tablespoon grated lemon peel, if desired
2 tablespoons lemon juice
1 tablespoon Worcestershire sauce
1 teaspoon chili powder
1 teaspoon paprika

BEFORE GRILLING: Heat oven to 350°F. Place chicken on large square of heavy duty foil; wrap tightly. Roast in foil for 30 minutes. In small bowl, combine all remaining ingredients.

ON THE GRILL: Place chicken skin-side-up on grill 4 to 6 inches from hot coals. Cook about 20 minutes or until done, turning and brushing often with basting sauce. 4 servings

NUTRITION INFORMATION PER SERVING

Serving Size: 1/4 of recipe		Percent U.S. RDA Per Serving	
Calories	374	Protein	58%
Protein	38g	Vitamin A	56%
Carbohydrate	33g	Vitamin C	28%
Fat	10g	Thiamin	13%
Sodium	777mg	Riboflavin	46%
Potassium	335mg	Niacin	59%
		Calcium	6%
		Iron	27%

TACO INSIDE-OUTS

1 cup (4 oz.) shredded Cheddar or American cheese
½ cup crushed corn chips
¼ cup taco or barbecue sauce
1 lb. wieners

BEFORE GRILLING: In small bowl, combine cheese, corn chips and taco sauce. Cut a narrow slit, lengthwise in wieners, to make a pocket. Insert about 2 tablespoons cheese mixture in each wiener. Place wieners on skewers, long-handled forks or green sticks.

ON THE GRILL: Hold wieners 2 to 3 inches from hot coals. Cook for 3 to 5 minutes, until heated and cheese melts. 4 to 5 servings

NUTRITION INFORMATION PER SERVING

Serving Size: 1/4 of recipe		Percent U.S. RDA Per Serving	
Calories	525	Protein	34%
Protein	22g	Vitamin A	9%
Carbohydrate	9g	Vitamin C	*
Fat	44g	Thiamin	14%
Sodium	1640mg	Riboflavin	22%
Potassium	313mg	Niacin	16%
		Calcium	26%
		Iron	16%

SWEET 'N SOUR RIBS POLYNESIA

GUIDE FOR COOKING RIBS

There is more than one accepted way to cook spareribs or country-style ribs. Like other pork cuts, they should be cooked until well done. One of these methods will become a favorite of yours; adapt it to other recipes you have for ribs. Length of cooking time will vary with the meatiness of the ribs. Meat will shrink from the ends of bones when done. For each serving, allow about 1 pound of spareribs or ½ pound country-style ribs.

PRECOOKING IN WATER METHOD: Cut ribs into 2 to 3-rib sections. In large saucepan, cover ribs with water; add 1 teaspoon salt. Simmer over medium-low heat about 1 hour or until tender. Drain ribs; brush both sides with basting sauce. Place on grill. Cook 10 minutes on each side or until ribs are crisp and nicely browned, basting often.

PRECOOKING IN FOIL METHOD: Wrap uncooked ribs securely in heavy duty foil. Grill 30 minutes, turning once, or heat in 350°F. oven. Unwrap; place ribs on grill. Cook 30 minutes or until browned on all sides. Brush with basting sauce during last 15 minutes.

COOKING ON THE ROTISSERIE METHOD: Weave spit rod in and out of the uncooked rack of spareribs, forming accordion-like folds. Keep ribs in balance so they turn evenly while cooking. Cook 45 minutes to 1 hour, basting with barbecue sauce during last 5 minutes.

SWEET 'N SOUR RIBS POLYNESIA

4 lb. country-style or spareribs, cut into serving pieces
¼ cup firmly packed brown sugar
1 teaspoon dry mustard
1 teaspoon paprika
2 cubes or 2 teaspoons beef bouillon
1 cup pineapple juice
¼ cup vinegar
2 tablespoons cornstarch
½ cup water

BEFORE GRILLING: Precook ribs using method in Guide for Cooking Ribs. In small saucepan, combine remaining ingredients except cornstarch and water. Cook over low heat, stirring until bouillon is dissolved. Combine cornstarch and water; stir into cooked mixture. Cook until mixture is thickened and clear, stirring constantly.

ON THE GRILL: Place ribs on grill 6 to 8 inches from hot coals. Brush with sauce and grill; see cooking times in Guide for Cooking Ribs.

4 to 6 servings

NUTRITION INFORMATION PER SERVING

Serving Size: 1/4 of recipe		Percent U.S. RDA Per Serving	
Calories	899	Protein	59%
Protein	38g	Vitamin A	*
Carbohydrate	26g	Vitamin C	5%
Fat	70g	Thiamin	54%
Sodium	485mg	Riboflavin	23%
Potassium	161mg	Niacin	32%
		Calcium	4%
		Iron	30%

GLAZED HAM

1 boneless fully-cooked ham (about 4 lb.)
1 cup port or red wine
½ teaspoon cinnamon
12-oz. can (1½ cups) apricot nectar

BEFORE GRILLING: Pierce ham deeply with meat fork or ice pick. Combine remaining ingredients. Pour over ham in non-metallic bowl or plastic bag; cover. Marinate several hours at room temperature or overnight in refrigerator, turning several times to season. Remove ham from marinade; reserve marinade for basting sauce. Insert meat thermometer.

ON THE GRILL: Arrange coals for rotisserie or covered grill roasting. Center meat on grill or on rotisserie 6 to 8 inches from coals; cover unless using rotisserie. Roast over slow fire to 130°F. (about 2 hours) turning and basting with marinade every 30 minutes. 12 to 16 servings

Length of marinating time and surface area of meat present too many variables to accurately determine nutritional information.

GRILLING GUIDE FOR SHELLFISH

LOBSTER

Either frozen lobster, thawed, fresh split whole lobster or lobster tails may be used. To prepare lobster tails, cut along the underside of the tail with scissors; clip off fins along edges. Peel back soft undershell; discard. To prevent curling, bend tail back to crack shell or insert skewers between meat and shell.

HOW TO BARBECUE: Place on grill 6 to 8 inches from hot coals. Cooked lobster need only reheat about 5 minutes. Do not overcook. For uncooked lobster, begin with meat-side-down; turn and continue cooking shell-side-down for about 10 minutes or until meat is opaque. Brush with melted margarine, butter or lemon butter (1 teaspoon lemon juice for ¼ cup butter) while cooking. Allow about 1 pound whole lobster or ½ pound lobster tail per serving.

SHRIMP OR SCALLOPS

Thawed frozen or fresh shrimp or scallops may be used. Fresh shrimp may be cooked in the shell or shelled before cooking. Thaw frozen scallops; remove any shell particles and wash before using.

HOW TO BARBECUE: Place on grill 4 to 6 inches from hot coals. Cook about 15 to 20 minutes, turning and brushing occasionally with melted margarine or butter until shell is reddish and meat is opaque. (If too small to rest on grill, thread on skewers or place on foil.) Allow about ¼ pound shelled shrimp or ⅓ pound scallops per serving.

OYSTERS OR CLAMS

Live in-the-shell oysters may be placed directly on the grill for cooking. Wash first to remove any dirt or sand, then rinse. When using clams that are to be eaten from the shell, first cover with clean salt water (⅓ cup salt to 1 gallon tap water) and allow to stand 15 to 20 minutes; change the water 2 or 3 times. Clams will open and cleanse themselves of sand.

HOW TO BARBECUE: Place whole oysters on the grill 4 to 6 inches from hot coals. Cook 10 to 15 minutes. When shells pop open, oysters are done. Drain any juice. Shells will be hot; use hot pads when removing top shell. Allow about 6 oysters per serving.

DILL MARINATED SALMON STEAKS

4 fresh or frozen salmon steaks, cut 1 inch thick
2 tablespoons lemon juice
1 tablespoon oil
¾ teaspoon dill weed
Salt and pepper

BEFORE GRILLING: Thaw frozen steaks. Combine remaining ingredients to make marinade. Pour over salmon in shallow non-metallic container or pastic bag, turning to coat both sides of fish. Cover and marinate 1 hour at room temperature or several hours in refrigerator. Remove salmon; reserve marinade for basting sauce.

ON THE GRILL: Place salmon on greased grill 4 to 6 inches from hot coals. Cook 10 to 15 minutes or until fish flakes easily, turning once and brushing occasionally with marinade. 4 servings

Length of marinating time and surface area of meat present too many variables to accurately determine nutritional information.

BARBECUED WHOLE FISH

BEFORE GRILLING: Fill the cavity of a whole dressed fish with about 2 cups favorite stuffing. Fasten edges together with metal skewers or sew opening closed with heavy thread.

ON THE GRILL: Brush both sides of fish with melted margarine or butter; place on piece of heavy duty foil. Grill 6 to 8 inches from hot coals; cover. Cook, allowing 15 to 20 minutes per pound of fish, turning several times. Brush occasionally with melted margarine. Allow about ½ lb. of whole fish per serving.

TIP: *If grill does not have cover, wrap fish in foil before grilling.*

SHRIMP IN GARLIC BUTTER

½ cup margarine or butter
3 garlic cloves, minced
1 tablespoon minced parsley
2 tablespoons lemon juice
¼ teaspoon salt
1½ to 2 lb. cleaned and shelled fresh shrimp

BEFORE GRILLING: Melt margarine; add garlic, parsley, lemon juice and salt. Set aside. Thread shrimp on 4 to 6 skewers.

ON THE GRILL: Place shrimp on greased grill, 4 to 6 inches from hot coals. Cook 15 to 20 minutes or until done, turning and brushing occasionally with garlic butter.

4 to 6 servings

NUTRITION INFORMATION PER SERVING

Serving Size: 1/4 of recipe		Percent U.S. RDA Per Serving	
Calories	277	Protein	23%
Protein	15g	Vitamin A	21%
Carbohydrate	2g	Vitamin C	13%
Fat	24g	Thiamin	*
Sodium	507mg	Riboflavin	*
Potassium	179mg	Niacin	12%
		Calcium	6%
		Iron	7%

TIP: *Two pkg. (12 oz. each) frozen large shrimp, thawed may be substituted for fresh.*

CLAM BAKE IN FOIL

6 clams
1 lb. lobster
½ to ¾ lb. frying chicken pieces
2 medium potatoes, unpeeled
2 small onions
2 unhusked ears of corn, silks removed
½ cup water

BEFORE GRILLING: Clams should be scrubbed and lobster freshly killed. Place all ingredients on large square of double thickness heavy duty foil. Seal packet carefully but securely (wrap loosely as lobster may puncture foil).

ON THE GRILL: Place about 4 inches from hot coals. Cook about 1 hour, turning packet frequently while cooking. Serve with melted margarine and fresh lemon wedges.

2 servings

NUTRITION INFORMATION PER SERVING

Serving Size: 1/2 of recipe		Percent U.S. RDA Per Serving	
Calories	505	Protein	74%
Protein	48g	Vitamin A	16%
Carbohydrate	58g	Vitamin C	41%
Fat	10g	Thiamin	25%
Sodium	336mg	Riboflavin	32%
Potassium	1354mg	Niacin	44%
		Calcium	14%
		Iron	52%

VEGETABLES TO COOK OVER COALS

CORN-ON-THE-COB: Husk corn; wrap in heavy duty foil. Place directly on the coals. Cook about 20 minutes, turning frequently until tender. Check doneness by pressing a kernel with your thumbnail. It should be tender, but juicy.

CORN-IN-THE-HUSK: Pull husks back on ears of corn and remove silks. Replace husks; soak in cold water about 30 minutes. Remove from water; cook about 4 inches from hot coals for about 20 minutes or until tender. Turn frequently to roast evenly.

MUSHROOMS: Large mushroom caps can be placed on skewers either alone or combined with meat. To prevent splitting, mushrooms can be cooked in a small amount of boiling water for about 5 minutes before placing on skewers. Brush with seasoned butters, meat marinades or basting sauces before grilling. Cook over coals about 10 minutes, brushing occasionally with margarine or butter. Allow about 5 mushrooms per serving.

POTATOES: Scrub potatoes; oil skin lightly and pierce with fork. Wrap each potato securely in squares of heavy duty foil. Place potatoes on grill 4 to 6 inches from hot coals. Roast about 1 hour or until tender, turning several times. Unwrap potatoes; slit top of each lengthwise; serve with margarine, butter or sour cream.

SUMMER SQUASH: Small whole yellow, zucchini or patty pan squash may be placed on skewers before grilling or put directly on the grill. One to 2-inch slices or quartered patty pan squash can be placed on skewers. Brush with seasoned butter or prepared French or Italian dressing before grilling. Cook over coals 20 to 30 minutes or until tender, brushing occasionally with margarine or butter. Allow about 1 small squash per serving.

TOMATOES: Tomatoes cook more quickly than firmer vegetables. Both cherry and larger tomatoes may be used. No need to baste; place small tomatoes on skewers or halves on the grill or on a sheet of foil to prevent skin from breaking. Small tomatoes cook in about 5 minutes; larger ones take about 10 minutes. Allow about 5 cherry tomatoes or 1 large tomato per serving.

VEGETABLE KABOBS

1 zucchini squash
1 small yellow summer squash
¼ cup Italian dressing
20 cherry tomatoes
20 fresh mushroom caps

BEFORE GRILLING: Cut zucchini and yellow squash into 1 or 2-inch slices. Because squash needs longer cooking, the squash pieces should be placed on separate skewers from the tomatoes and mushrooms. Place squash alternately on 2 skewers, then place tomatoes and mushroom caps alternately on 2 other skewers. Brush dressing over squash and mushrooms, tomatoes need no basting.

ON THE GRILL: Place vegetable kabobs on grill 4 to 6 inches from heat. Cook squash 20 to 30 minutes or until tender, basting occasionally. Cook tomatoes and mushrooms 5 minutes. 4 servings

NUTRITION INFORMATION PER SERVING

Serving Size: 1/4 of recipe		Percent U.S. RDA Per Serving	
Calories	186	Protein	3%
Protein	2g	Vitamin A	10%
Carbohydrate	6g	Vitamin C	23%
Fat	18g	Thiamin	5%
Sodium	623mg	Riboflavin	12%
Potassium	287mg	Niacin	10%
		Calcium	3%
		Iron	4%

INDIVIDUAL BEAN AND APPLE POTS

¼ lb. (4 to 8 slices) bacon, diced
½ cup (1 medium) chopped onion
2 cans (16 oz. each) pork and beans with tomato sauce
2 tablespoons firmly packed brown sugar
1 teaspoon dry or prepared mustard
1 apple, cut into 16 thin wedges

BEFORE GRILLING: Partially cook bacon; pour off all but 2 tablespoons drippings. Add onion; cook until tender. Stir in remaining ingredients except apple. Spoon individual servings on squares of heavy duty foil. Top with apple wedges. Seal securely. Wrap again in another square of foil.

ON THE GRILL: Place 4 to 6 inches from hot coals. Heat 30 to 45 minutes, turning every 15 minutes. 6 servings

NUTRITION INFORMATION PER SERVING

Serving Size: 1/6 of recipe		Percent U.S. RDA Per Serving	
Calories	269	Protein	18%
Protein	12g	Vitamin A	4%
Carbohydrate	36g	Vitamin C	4%
Fat	9g	Thiamin	12%
Sodium	761mg	Riboflavin	5%
Potassium	379mg	Niacin	8%
		Calcium	9%
		Iron	17%

TIP: *To heat in pan, add all ingredients to skillet; simmer covered, on stove or grill until heated through.*

SPUDS 'N ONIONS

4 medium baking potatoes
½ cup margarine or butter, softened
2 medium mild onions, sliced
Salt
Pepper
Paprika, if desired

BEFORE GRILLING: Peel potatoes; cut into 4 or 5 crosswise slices. Spread margarine generously between slices. Place 1 onion slice between each potato slice; reassemble. Secure slices with toothpick or skewer. Spread tops with margarine; sprinkle with salt, pepper and paprika. Place each potato on large square of heavy duty foil; seal securely.

ON THE GRILL: Place over medium coals; cook 45 to 50 minutes or until soft. Serve in opened packages.

4 servings

NUTRITION INFORMATION PER SERVING

Serving Size: 1/4 of recipe		Percent U.S. RDA Per Serving	
Calories	346	Protein	7%
Protein	4g	Vitamin A	19%
Carbohydrate	32g	Vitamin C	51%
Fat	23g	Thiamin	10%
Sodium	358mg	Riboflavin	4%
Potassium	743mg	Niacin	12%
		Calcium	3%
		Iron	6%

CHEDDAR APPLE DANDY

6 medium cooking apples, peeled and sliced
1 cup (4 oz.) shredded Cheddar cheese
¾ cup Pillsbury's Best® All Purpose or Unbleached Flour*
½ cup firmly packed brown sugar
½ teaspoon cinnamon
¼ teaspoon salt
½ cup margarine or butter

BEFORE GRILLING: Slice each apple onto a 12-inch square of foil. Top with cheese. Combine flour, brown sugar, cinnamon and salt; cut in margarine until crumbly. Spoon equally over tops of apples. Bring foil up and seal well. Wrap in another square of foil.

ON THE GRILL: Place packets 4 to 6 inches from coals. Cook 45 to 55 minutes or until apples are tender, turning packets every 15 minutes. Serve warm.

6 servings

NUTRITION INFORMATION PER SERVING

Serving Size: 1/6 of recipe		Percent U.S. RDA Per Serving	
Calories	405	Protein	10%
Protein	7g	Vitamin A	18%
Carbohydrate	48g	Vitamin C	5%
Fat	22g	Thiamin	10%
Sodium	415mg	Riboflavin	11%
Potassium	240mg	Niacin	5%
		Calcium	17%
		Iron	9%

TIP: **If using Pillsbury's Best® Self Rising Flour, omit salt.*

LAST OF THE COALS FRUIT JUBILEE

- **2 teaspoons grated orange peel**
- **3 to 4 oranges**
- **16-oz. can (1½ cups) pear halves, drained (reserve ½ cup syrup)**
- **21-oz. can (2 cups) cherry fruit filling**
- **⅓ cup sugar**
- **2 tablespoons margarine or butter**
- **2 to 3 tablespoons brandy, if desired**
- **Angel food or pound cake**

BEFORE GRILLING: Cut oranges into bite-size pieces; cut pears into slices. In large skillet, combine orange peel, oranges, pears and fruit filling. Carefully stir in ½ cup reserved pear syrup and sugar. Top with margarine.

ON THE GRILL: Place on grill 8 to 10 inches from coals. Warm, stirring occasionally. If desired, just before serving, add brandy and flame. Serve spooned over cake slices or ice cream. 8 to 10 servings

NUTRITION INFORMATION PER SERVING

Serving Size: 1/8 of recipe with Fruit and Cake		Percent U.S. RDA Per Serving	
Calories	413	Protein	8%
Protein	5g	Vitamin A	7%
Carbohydrate	91g	Vitamin C	12%
Fat	3g	Thiamin	3%
Sodium	207mg	Riboflavin	8%
Potassium	195mg	Niacin	*
		Calcium	2%
		Iron	3%

DESSERT APPLES IN FOIL

- **6 apples**
- **⅓ cup raisins**
- **⅓ cup chopped nuts**
- **3 tablespoons firmly packed brown sugar**
- **2 tablespoons margarine or butter**

BEFORE GRILLING: Wash and core apples; remove 1 inch of peel around top. In small bowl, combine remaining ingredients. Stuff center of each apple with 2 tablespoons mixture. Wrap each apple in heavy duty foil.

ON THE GRILL: Place apple packets on grill 4 to 6 inches from hot coals and cook about 10 minutes or until tender. 6 servings

NUTRITION INFORMATION PER SERVING

Serving Size: 1/6 of recipe		Percent U.S. RDA Per Serving	
Calories	206	Protein	2%
Protein	1g	Vitamin A	6%
Carbohydrate	34g	Vitamin C	6%
Fat	9g	Thiamin	5%
Sodium	52mg	Riboflavin	3%
Potassium	267mg	Niacin	*
		Calcium	3%
		Iron	6%

GRILLED BANANAS

- **4 bananas, unpeeled**
- **¼ cup miniature marshmallows**
- **¼ cup semi-sweet chocolate chips**

BEFORE GRILLING: Peel back one section of banana skin. Lengthwise, scoop out about ¼ of the banana. Stuff with miniature marshmallows and chocolate chips. Replace peel on banana; wrap tightly in foil.

ON THE GRILL: Place 2 to 3 inches from hot coals. Cook about 5 minutes, turning occasionally.

4 servings

NUTRITION INFORMATION PER SERVING

Serving Size: 1/4 of recipe		Percent U.S. RDA Per Serving	
Calories	88	Protein	*
Protein	<1g	Vitamin A	*
Carbohydrate	15g	Vitamin C	3%
Fat	4g	Thiamin	*
Sodium	2mg	Riboflavin	*
Potassium	142mg	Niacin	*
		Calcium	*
		Iron	3%

POULTRY

POULTRY

BUYING

- Ready-to-cook poultry may be bought whole, quartered, cut up or in a selection of serving pieces. It is sold chilled or frozen.
- Poultry includes chickens that are either broilers or fryers, roasters, stewing hens, Rock Cornish game hens, turkey, ducks and geese.

STORAGE

- Fresh poultry can be kept in the refrigerator (38°F.) about 2 days; loosely cover to allow air to circulate. Store giblets separately.
- To freeze fresh poultry, wrap in moisture-vapor proof material and store in freezer at 0°F. Use chicken and turkey within 1 year, duck and goose within 6 months, giblets within 3 months.
- To refrigerate leftover stuffed poultry, remove stuffing, cool quickly and store in separate container. Wrap cooked poultry loosely and store in coldest part of refrigerator, use within 2 days.

BASIC PREPARATION

- Roasting chickens, whole fryers, Rock Cornish game hens, turkeys, ducks and geese can all be roasted.
- Broilers, fryers, smaller turkeys and turkey parts can be broiled, fried, barbecued, baked or cooked on a rotisserie.
- Stewing chickens need a moist cooking method to make them more tender. Braising, simmering and pressure cooking are 3 good methods.

PREPARING WHOLE BIRDS

Buying

Allow ¾ to 1 lb. per serving for birds under 12 lb. and ½ to ¾ lb. for those over 12 lb.

Thawing

To thaw in refrigerator, leave in original wrap and allow 12 hours thawing time for 3 to 5-lb. birds and 3 days for a 12-lb. turkey. To thaw in water, leave in original water-tight wrap and place under cold running water or immerse in cold water, changing water every 30 to 60 minutes. This method takes about 8 hours to thaw a 12-lb. turkey. Room temperature thawing is not recommended because parts of the bird could become warm enough for spoilage to start. Also see Microwave Defrosting, page **386**.

Do not thaw commercially frozen stuffed poultry; cook from the frozen state according to package directions.

Cleaning

After bird is thawed, remove giblets from body cavity. Rinse bird inside and out with cold water. Drain and pat dry. Sprinkle cavity with salt (lightly, if planning to stuff).

Stuffing

Allow about ½ cup stuffing per pound of ready-to-cook poultry. Stuff poultry lightly, just before roasting. If stuffing and bird are prepared the day before, refrigerate separately. Never stuff poultry with dressing before freezing or refrigerating.

ROAST DUCK

Trussing
Close neck cavity by bringing loose skin over opening and holding in place with a metal skewer or "sew" in place with heavy thread. Close body cavity by inserting metal skewers across opening and then lacing together with heavy thread or string or "sew" opening closed using heavy thread. Tuck wing tips between the wing and body to prevent overcooking. Tie wings and legs to body with string to hold in place during cooking.

Roasting
Roast stuffed poultry in uncovered shallow pan, without water at 325°F. See Roasting Timetable, this page.

To test doneness, move poultry leg. Bird is done if leg joint moves easily. The softness of the flesh on drumstick and thigh are further signs or doneness.

To Roast in Paper Bag
Rub turkey generously with ¼ cup margarine or butter. Place stuffed or unstuffed bird (12 lb. maximum) on baking pan to catch drippings. Slide into large paper bag, folding ends up and securing with paper clips or small skewers. Bake at 325°F. See minimum times in Roasting Timetable, this page. No basting or turning necessary.

To Roast in Cooking Bag or Clear Cooking Film
Place stuffed or unstuffed bird in cooking bag or wrap in cooking film. Puncture several small holes in top of bag. Place in baking pan. Bake at 325°F. for larger birds, 350°F. for smaller birds. Reduce cooking time ½ to ⅔ of that suggested in Roasting Timetable, this page. A meat thermometer may be used by inserting through the bag into the inside thigh muscle of the bird.

Ducks and Geese
Stuff with bread-type stuffing or with fruits such as oranges, prunes, apples, raisins or dried apricots. Begin roasting at 400°F. for 15 minutes, then reduce temperature to 325°F. Baste occasionally with drippings, remove excess drippings as they accumulate. A cooking bag or paper bag also will prevent spattering. For paper bag, puncture a few holes in top of paper bag during last hour of cooking to help crisp skin. Carve as for turkey. If desired, use kitchen shears to cut duck into quarters for serving.

TIMETABLE FOR ROASTING POULTRY

Set oven at 325°F., do not cover pan.

Poultry	Weight	Thermometer Temp.	Total Roasting Time
Turkey—Whole, Stuffed	4-6 lb.	180°F.-185°F.	2-3 hrs.
	6-8 lb.	180°F.-185°F.	3-3½ hrs.
	8-12 lb.	180°F.-185°F.	3½-4½ hrs.
	12-16 lb.	180°F.-185°F.	4½-5½ hrs.
	16-20 lb.	180°F.-185°F.	5½-6½ hrs.
	20-24 lb.	180°F.-185°F.	6½-7 hrs.
Turkey—Boneless Rolled Roasts	3-5 lb.	170°F.-175°F.	2½-3 hrs.
	5-7 lb.	170°F.-175°F.	3-3½ hrs.
	7-9 lb.	170°F.-175°F.	3½-4 hrs.
Chicken	2½-4½ lb.	180°F.-185°F.	2-3⅓ hrs.
Capon	4-8 lb.	180°F.-185°F.	3-5 hrs.
Duck	3-5 lb.	180°F.-185°F.	2½-3 hrs.*
Goose	4-8 lb.	180°F.-185°F.	2¾-3½ hrs.*
	8-14 lb.	180°F.-185°F.	3½-5 hrs.*
Cornish Game Hen	1-1½ lb.	180°F.-185°F.	¾-1 hr.**

*Roast at 400°F. for 15 minutes, then at 325°F.
**Roast at 350°F.

NUTRITION INFORMATION PER SERVING

Serving Size: 3 oz. cooked turkey

Calories	162
Protein	27g
Carbohydrate	0g
Fat	5g
Sodium	111mg
Potassium	312mg

Percent U.S. RDA Per Serving

Protein	41%
Vitamin A	0%
Vitamin C	0%
Thiamin	3%
Riboflavin	9%
Niacin	33%
Calcium	*
Iron	9%

Carving

Allow birds to stand covered loosely with foil 15 to 30 minutes before carving. This allows the juices to "set" giving juicier meat and making carving easier. Carve with sharp knife or with electric knife, always cutting across grain of meat.

Cut leg from body, cutting through joint that joins thigh to backbone. Remove leg and cut joint to separate drumstick and thigh. On large birds, carve in slices, cutting parallel to bone.

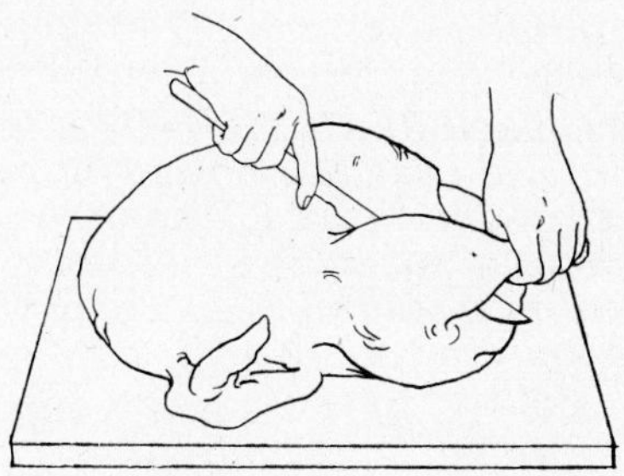

Make a deep horizontal cut into breast meat, parallel to and close to wing.

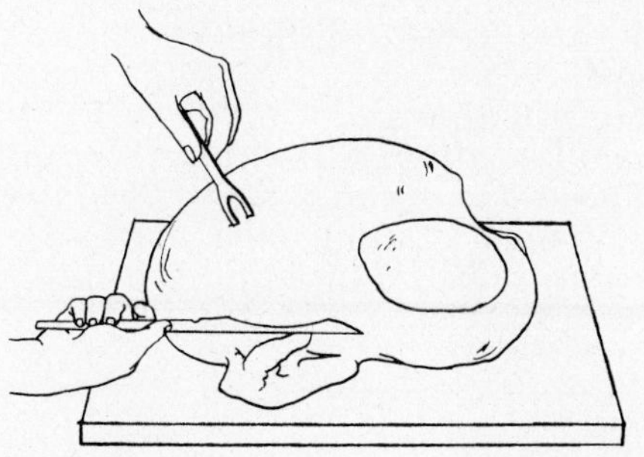

Beginning near front of breast, cut thin slices of white meat, slicing parallel to the wing.

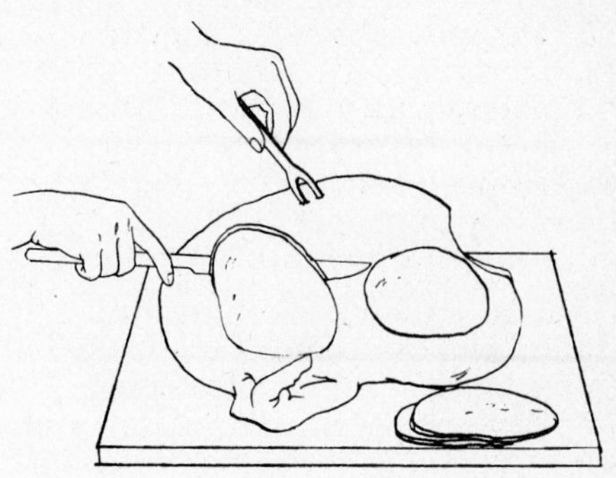

BREAD STUFFING

½ cup margarine or butter
1 medium onion, chopped
2 stalks celery, chopped
8 cups dry bread cubes
2 tablespoons minced parsley, if desired
2 tablespoons poultry seasoning, sage or savory
1 teaspoon salt
¼ teaspoon pepper
About ½ cup broth* or water

In large skillet, cook margarine, onion and celery until tender. In large bowl, combine bread cubes, parsley, poultry seasoning, salt and pepper; mix well. Add broth and margarine-onion mixture, stirring until of desired moistness (stuffing will become a little more moist during cooking because it absorbs juices from bird). 2 quarts

NUTRITION INFORMATION PER SERVING

Serving Size: 1/2 cup		Percent U.S. RDA Per Serving	
Calories	65	Protein	*
Protein	<1g	Vitamin A	6%
Carbohydrate	3g	Vitamin C	3%
Fat	6g	Thiamin	*
Sodium	293mg	Riboflavin	*
Potassium	38mg	Niacin	*
		Calcium	*
		Iron	*

TIPS: **Broth can be chicken bouillon dissolved in water or cooking liquid from giblets.*

Day-old soft bread cubes may be substituted for dry bread cubes. Decrease broth to about ¼ cup. If desired, add 1 beaten egg before adding broth.

For CHESTNUT STUFFING, roast chestnuts by cutting x-shaped slit on one side of shell. Place on cookie sheet and bake at 400°F. for 15 to 20 minutes, stirring occasionally. Cool enough to handle and remove shell. Chop finely and add desired amount to stuffing (1 cup added to this amount of stuffing will give a mild flavor).

For MUSHROOM STUFFING, cook 1 cup sliced or chopped fresh or drained canned mushrooms with onion and celery.

For OYSTER STUFFING, simmer ½ pint (1 cup) oysters with liquor for about 5 minutes or until oysters are set. Drain. Chop oysters and add to stuffing. If desired, double the amount oysters may be added.

For SAUSAGE STUFFING, in small skillet, brown ½ lb. pork sausage; add to bread cube mixture. Decrease poultry seasoning to 1 teaspoon and salt to ¼ teaspoon (sausage is highly seasoned). Use drippings for part of margarine and cook onion and celery in drippings and margarine, continuing as directed.

For CORNBREAD STUFFING, use crumbled baked cornbread for part or all of bread cubes. Decrease poultry seasoning to 1 teaspoon. Cornbread stuffing is also good with the sausage variation.

For NUT STUFFING, add ¼ cup chopped nuts–almonds, filberts, pecans, walnuts or peanuts. For a toasted flavor, cook nuts with onion mixture.

For SESAME STUFFING, cook ¼ cup sesame seed with onion mixture.

For WATER CHESTNUT STUFFING, add ½ to 1 cup chopped water chestnuts to stuffing and glaze bird with Soy-Butter Glaze, page 418.

For APPLE-RAISIN STUFFING, add 2 medium peeled and chopped apples and ⅔ cup raisins. (Apples will make stuffing more moist, so decrease liquid by 2 tablespoons.)

CRANBERRY STUFFING

4 cups dry bread cubes
1½ cups chopped cranberries
¼ cup sugar
2 tablespoons finely chopped onion or 2 teaspoons instant minced onion
2 tablespoons grated orange peel
1 teaspoon salt
½ teaspoon marjoram leaves
¼ teaspoon thyme leaves
½ cup margarine or butter, melted
½ cup orange juice

In large bowl, combine all stuffing ingredients; toss lightly. Use to stuff 4 to 5-lb. bird or 7-lb. pork crown roast. For crown roast, cover stuffing with foil if top becomes too brown.
1 quart

NUTRITION INFORMATION PER SERVING

Serving Size: 1/2 cup		Percent U.S. RDA Per Serving	
Calories	100	Protein	*
Protein	2g	Vitamin A	6%
Carbohydrate	12g	Vitamin C	11%
Fat	6g	Thiamin	*
Sodium	360mg	Riboflavin	*
Potassium	57mg	Niacin	*
		Calcium	*
		Iron	*

TIP: *If desired, use seasoned bread cubes for stuffing, omitting salt, marjoram and thyme.*

SAUERKRAUT STUFFING

27-oz. can (4 cups) sauerkraut, drained
1 medium apple, peeled and chopped
1 medium onion, chopped
½ to 1 teaspoon caraway seed or marjoram leaves

In large bowl, combine all ingredients and use to stuff one 4 to 5-lb. duck or 5 to 6-lb. goose. 1 quart

NUTRITION INFORMATION PER SERVING

Serving Size: 1/2 cup		Percent U.S. RDA Per Serving	
Calories	29	Protein	*
Protein	1g	Vitamin A	*
Carbohydrate	7g	Vitamin C	20%
Fat	<1g	Thiamin	2%
Sodium	528mg	Riboflavin	2%
Potassium	143mg	Niacin	*
		Calcium	3%
		Iron	3%

RICE STUFFING

¼ cup margarine or butter
2 tablespoons chopped onion
2 cups cooked rice (white, brown, wild or combination)
½ teaspoon salt
½ teaspoon poultry seasoning

In medium skillet, cook margarine and onion until tender. Mix in cooked rice, salt and poultry seasoning. ½ quart

NUTRITION INFORMATION PER SERVING

Serving Size: 1/2 cup		Percent U.S. RDA Per Serving	
Calories	216	Protein	3%
Protein	2g	Vitamin A	9%
Carbohydrate	25g	Vitamin C	*
Fat	12g	Thiamin	8%
Sodium	795mg	Riboflavin	*
Potassium	41mg	Niacin	5%
		Calcium	*
		Iron	6%

TIPS: *Cooked seasoned rice mixes may be substituted for rice; omit salt and poultry seasoning.*

For variety, add any of the following to Rice Stuffing: ¼ cup chopped or slivered almonds or chopped pecans, ½ cup drained canned mushrooms, ¼ cup raisins or currants, 1 tablespoon grated orange peel, ½ to ¾ cup drained crushed pineapple or 1 stalk chopped celery (cook with onion).

COOKING GIBLETS

Cover giblets with water. Add 1 teaspoon salt, ¼ teaspoon pepper, 2 sliced stalks of celery and 1 medium sliced onion. Simmer 1 to 2 hours or until tender. Giblets may be chopped and added to stuffing, gravy or eaten plain. Broth may be used in dressing, gravy or added to sauces for leftovers.

GLAZES FOR POULTRY*

HONEY-PINEAPPLE GLAZE: Melt ¼ cup margarine or butter. Stir in ¼ cup pineapple syrup or juice, ¼ cup honey and ½ teaspoon mace or nutmeg.

HONEY-LEMON GLAZE: Melt ¼ cup margarine or butter. Stir in ¼ cup honey and 1 tablespoon lemon juice.

ORANGE GLAZE: Melt 2 tablespoons margarine or butter. Stir in ⅓ cup frozen concentrated orange juice or orange marmalade and ½ teaspoon ginger.

CURRY-PEACH GLAZE: Melt ¼ cup margarine or butter. Stir in ½ cup peach preserves and 1 teaspoon curry powder.

SOY-BUTTER GLAZE: Melt 2 tablespoons margarine or butter. Stir in ⅓ cup soy sauce, ¼ cup light or dark corn syrup and ¼ teaspoon garlic salt.

TIPS: **Enough for 1 turkey, 4 Cornish hens. Halve recipe for 1 chicken.*

If poultry becomes too brown, place piece of foil lightly over breast.

DUCKLING Á LA ORANGE

4½ to 5-lb. duckling
1 teaspoon salt
2 oranges, unpeeled and quartered
3 peppercorns or ⅛ teaspoon pepper
1 garlic clove, minced
3 to 4 tablespoons orange marmalade

ORANGE SAUCE

2 tablespoons sugar
1 tablespoon cornstarch
1 tablespoon grated orange peel
⅔ cup orange juice
3 tablespoons pan drippings
2 tablespoons curacao, Cointreau or Grand Marnier

Heat oven to 400°F. Prepare duckling for roasting as directed on page 414, using salt, oranges, peppercorns and garlic as stuffing. Roast as directed on Poultry Roasting Timetable, page 414 (2½ to 3 hours) spreading with orange marmalade during last 15 minutes of cooking time.

In small saucepan, combine sugar, cornstarch and orange peel. Stir in orange juice and drippings (from roasting pan). Heat to boiling, stirring occasionally. Keep hot or reheat to serve. Stir in curacao before serving. Discard stuffing from duckling. Serve duckling over rice with Orange Sauce.

4 servings

NUTRITION INFORMATION PER SERVING

Serving Size: 1/4 of recipe		Percent U.S. RDA Per Serving	
Calories	855	Protein	98%
Protein	64g	Vitamin A	6%
Carbohydrate	36g	Vitamin C	24%
Fat	50g	Thiamin	8%
Sodium	537mg	Riboflavin	3%
Potassium	252mg	Niacin	3%
		Calcium	11%
		Iron	54%

TURKEY PARTS

Turkey parts – breasts, thighs, legs and wings – can be used in most of the fryer recipes. However, cooking time should be doubled to tenderize the turkey and cook the thicker parts.

Recipes for fryers that would also be good with turkey parts include: Orange Burgundy Chicken, Chicken Magnifico, Chicken Cacciatore and Oriental Chicken.

We've included a recipe for turkey drumsticks, but any turkey parts may be used interchangeably in these recipes – just use about the same total weight of turkey.

DRUMSTICKS FRICASSEE

½ cup Pillsbury's Best® All Purpose or Unbleached Flour
4 turkey drumsticks or thighs (about 5 lb. total)
2 to 3 tablespoons oil or shortening
1½ teaspoons salt
¼ teaspoon pepper
1 cube or 1 teaspoon chicken bouillon
Water
10-oz. pkg. (1½ cups) frozen peas and carrots
2 tablespoons flour
½ cup water

Flour drumsticks. In large skillet or Dutch oven, brown drumsticks in hot oil; drain excess oil. Add salt, pepper, bouillon and just enough water to cover bottom of skillet. Simmer covered, about 1½ hours or until turkey is tender, adding water as necessary.* Add peas and carrots and cook about 10 minutes. Remove drumsticks to platter. Combine 2 tablespoons flour with water; stir into broth and vegetables. Heat mixture until it boils and thickens, stirring constantly. Serve over drumsticks. 4 servings

NUTRITION INFORMATION PER SERVING

Serving Size: 1/4 of recipe		Percent U.S. RDA Per Serving	
Calories	748	Protein	138%
Protein	90g	Vitamin A	132%
Carbohydrate	22g	Vitamin C	12%
Fat	31g	Thiamin	25%
Sodium	1401mg	Riboflavin	46%
Potassium	1270mg	Niacin	69%
		Calcium	3%
		Iron	44%

TIPS: *Frozen vegetables such as carrots or beans may be substituted for peas and carrots.*

*To MAKE AHEAD, prepare to *, cool and refrigerate up to 1 day. Add vegetables and allow to simmer 15 minutes to heat through and cook vegetables.*

TURKEY DIVAN

2 pkg. (10 oz. each) frozen broccoli spears
6 thick slices cooked turkey or 10 slices cooked chicken
¼ cup mayonnaise or salad dressing
1 teaspoon lemon juice
10¾-oz. can condensed cream of chicken soup
½ cup dry bread crumbs
1 tablespoon margarine or butter, melted

Heat oven to 350°F. Grease 12x8-inch (2 qt.) baking dish. Cook broccoli as directed on package until almost done (crisp-tender); drain. Arrange broccoli in prepared baking dish. Lay turkey slices on top. In small bowl, combine mayonnaise, lemon juice and soup; pour over turkey. Combine bread crumbs and margarine; sprinkle on top. Bake uncovered at 350°F. for 25 to 35 minutes or until heated through.
4 to 6 servings

NUTRITION INFORMATION PER SERVING

Serving Size: 1/6 of recipe		Percent U.S. RDA Per Serving	
Calories	338	Protein	49%
Protein	32g	Vitamin A	37%
Carbohydrate	14g	Vitamin C	71%
Fat	17g	Thiamin	8%
Sodium	662mg	Riboflavin	17%
Potassium	546mg	Niacin	38%
		Calcium	6%
		Iron	15%

PIONEER TURKEY CASSEROLE

6-oz. pkg. white and wild rice mix
2 to 3 cups cooked cubed turkey or chicken
2 tablespoons chopped onion
1 stalk celery, chopped
1 cup water
1 teaspoon Worcestershire sauce
10¾-oz. can condensed cream of chicken, celery, mushroom or golden mushroom soup
8-oz. can (⅔ cup) water chestnuts, drained and sliced
4-oz. can (½ cup) mushroom stems and pieces, undrained
¼ cup chopped roasted almonds

Heat oven to 375°F. Grease 2-quart casserole. In casserole, combine uncooked rice and packet of seasonings with remaining ingredients, except nuts; mix well. Bake covered at 375°F. for 45 minutes. Uncover; sprinkle with nuts and continue baking for 15 minutes or until rice is done. 5 to 6 servings

NUTRITION INFORMATION PER SERVING

Serving Size: 1/6 of recipe		Percent U.S. RDA Per Serving	
Calories	275	Protein	31%
Protein	20g	Vitamin A	4%
Carbohydrate	27g	Vitamin C	2%
Fat	9g	Thiamin	8%
Sodium	498mg	Riboflavin	13%
Potassium	335mg	Niacin	26%
		Calcium	4%
		Iron	12%

CRUNCHY TURKEY HOT DISH

10¾-oz. can condensed cream of chicken soup
¼ cup water
2 cups cooked cubed turkey or chicken
½ cup coarsely chopped cashews, if desired
1 tablespoon chopped pimiento, drained or 1 tablespoon chopped green pepper
2 stalks celery, chopped
1 small onion, chopped
3-oz. can (2 cups) chow mein noodles

Heat oven to 350°F. In 1½-quart casserole, combine soup and water. Add turkey, cashews, pimiento, celery, onion and 1 cup chow mein noodles; mix well.* Top with remaining 1 cup noodles. Bake uncovered at 350°F. for 30 to 40 minutes or until bubbly.

4 servings

NUTRITION INFORMATION PER SERVING

Serving Size: 1/4 of recipe		Percent U.S. RDA Per Serving	
Calories	406	Protein	46%
Protein	30g	Vitamin A	7%
Carbohydrate	25g	Vitamin C	7%
Fat	21g	Thiamin	9%
Sodium	724mg	Riboflavin	13%
Potassium	489mg	Niacin	31%
		Calcium	4%
		Iron	14%

TIP: *To MAKE AHEAD, prepare to *. Refrigerate up to 1 day. Top with remaining 1 cup noodles; bake as directed.*

NUT STUFFING

TURKEY AND DRESSING BAKE

2 stalks celery, sliced or chopped
8-oz. pkg. (5 cups) herb-seasoned stuffing
4-oz. can (½ cup) mushroom stems and pieces, drained
4 cups cooked cubed turkey or chicken
1½ cups milk
5 eggs
2 cans (10¾ oz. each) condensed cream of chicken soup
½ cup slivered almonds
¼ cup grated Parmesan cheese
¼ cup margarine or butter, melted

Heat oven to 375°F. In greased 13x9-inch (3 qt.) baking dish or pan, combine celery, croutons and mushrooms; mix well. Arrange turkey evenly over crouton mixture. Combine milk, eggs and soup; mix well and pour over turkey. Sprinkle with almonds and Parmesan cheese; drizzle with margarine. Bake uncovered at 375°F. for 35 to 40 minutes or until knife inserted in center comes out clean.

8 to 10 servings

NUTRITION INFORMATION PER SERVING

Serving Size: 1/10 of recipe		Percent U.S. RDA Per Serving	
Calories	415	Protein	44%
Protein	28g	Vitamin A	16%
Carbohydrate	22g	Vitamin C	*
Fat	21g	Thiamin	6%
Sodium	1006mg	Riboflavin	21%
Potassium	410mg	Niacin	25%
		Calcium	12%
		Iron	13%

TIPS: *To halve recipe, use half the ingredient amounts, using 2 large or 3 small eggs; bake in 8 or 9-inch square pan for 30 to 35 minutes.*

Unseasoned dry bread cubes may be substituted for seasoned stuffing; add 2 teaspoons poultry seasoning and ½ teaspoon salt.

How to Cut Up a Chicken

With a sharp knife, cut leg and thigh from body by cutting through joint that connects thigh to backbone. To help find joint, pull leg away from body of chicken.

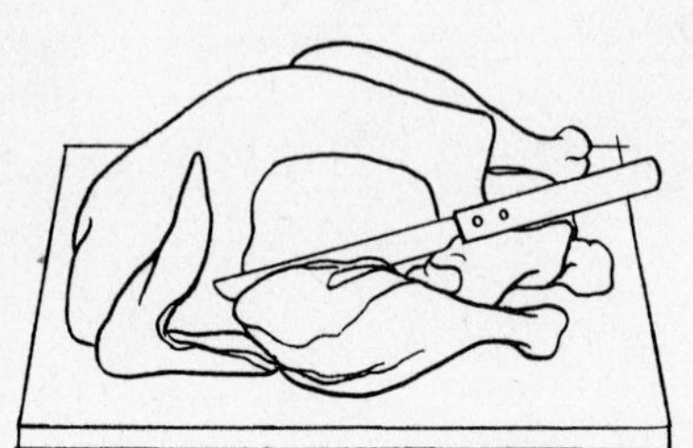

Bend thigh and leg together to find joint (small indentation where skin is held tight). Cut through joint to separate. Remove leg from other side of bird.

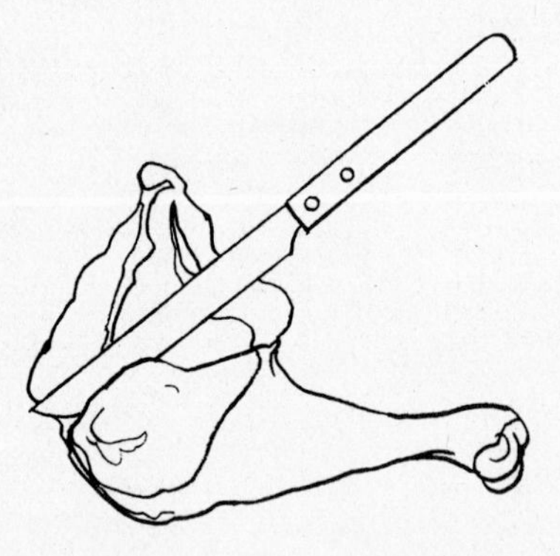

Remove wings by pulling the wing away from body and cutting through joint where it is attached to the body.

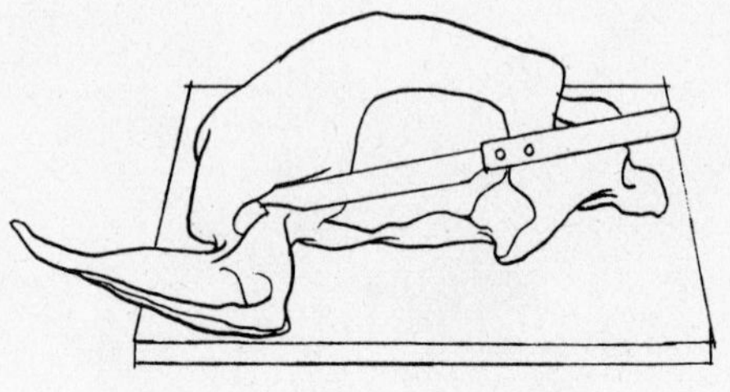

Stand bird upright on neck end. With knife or sharp scissors, cut along breast to neck, through joints, to separate breast and back. Bend back portion in half crosswise to break at joint; cut through broken joint. Divide breast portion lengthwise by cutting just to one side of the breast bone.

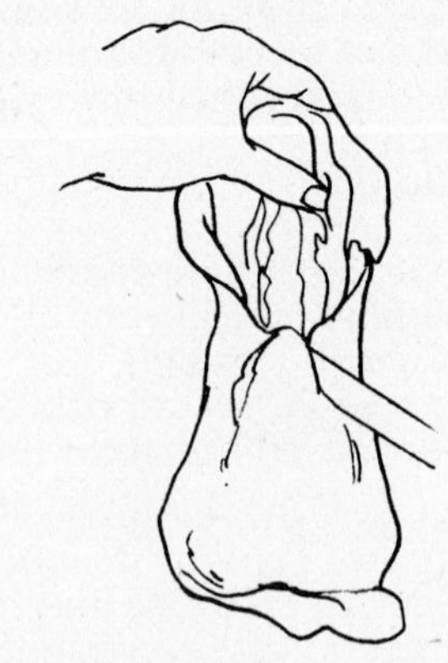

FRIED CHICKEN

⅓ cup flour
1½ teaspoons salt
1 teaspoon paprika
½ teaspoon pepper
2½ to 3-lb. frying chicken, cut up
1 cup oil or shortening

In paper or plastic bag, combine first 4 ingredients. Shake chicken, a few pieces at a time, in flour mixture. Heat oil in large skillet; add chicken and brown over medium heat. Reduce heat; simmer covered about 30 minutes or until tender. Remove cover last 10 minutes to crisp chicken. If gravy is desired, drain oil except for about 3 tablespoons. See page 541, for making Pan Gravy.

4 to 6 servings

NUTRITION INFORMATION PER SERVING

Serving Size: 1/6 of recipe		Percent U.S. RDA Per Serving	
Calories	584	Protein	46%
Protein	30g	Vitamin A	16%
Carbohydrate	8g	Vitamin C	*
Fat	48g	Thiamin	7%
Sodium	536mg	Riboflavin	34%
Potassium	7mg	Niacin	45%
		Calcium	*
		Iron	13%

TIPS: *For crustier chicken, dip chicken first in mixture of 1 egg beaten with 2 tablespoons water and then in flour mixture, increasing flour to ½ cup.*

Additional seasonings may be added to flour mixture: ½ teaspoon poultry seasoning, ⅛ teaspoon garlic or onion powder, or ½ teaspoon lemon pepper marinade.

For an onion flavor, shake chicken pieces in mixture of ½ cup dry bread crumbs, 2 tablespoons dry onion soup mix, ½ teaspoon salt and ⅛ teaspoon pepper. Fry as directed.

After browning, chicken may be placed in shallow baking pan and baked uncovered, at 350°F. for about 45 minutes.

Leftover oil or shortening may be drained from pan into covered storage container and refrigerated for use again when frying chicken.

GOLDEN OVEN-FRIED CHICKEN

½ cup margarine or butter
1 garlic clove, crushed or minced
1 cup dry bread crumbs
¼ cup grated Parmesan cheese
¼ cup finely chopped almonds
2 tablespoons chopped parsley
1 teaspoon salt
¼ teaspoon thyme or poultry seasoning
⅛ teaspoon pepper
2½ to 3-lb. frying chicken, cut up or quartered

Heat oven to 400°F. In 13x9-inch pan, melt margarine with garlic. In medium bowl or shallow pan, combine bread crumbs, cheese, almonds, parsley, salt, thyme and pepper; mix well. Dip chicken pieces in garlic butter; coat with crumb mixture. Place skin-side-up in pan containing garlic butter. Bake uncovered at 400°F. about 1 hour or until tender, basting occasionally with pan drippings.

4 to 6 servings

NUTRITION INFORMATION PER SERVING

Serving Size: 1/6 of recipe		Percent U.S. RDA Per Serving	
Calories	385	Protein	53%
Protein	35g	Vitamin A	15%
Carbohydrate	14g	Vitamin C	3%
Fat	21g	Thiamin	10%
Sodium	811mg	Riboflavin	15%
Potassium	564mg	Niacin	71%
		Calcium	11%
		Iron	14%

OTHER VARIATIONS FOR OVEN-FRIED CHICKEN

Dip chicken in mixture of ⅓ cup honey, 1 tablespoon lemon juice, 1 tablespoon soy sauce and ¼ cup melted margarine. Roll (lightly) in ⅔ cup sesame seed. Place skin-side-up in 13x9-inch pan; sprinkle with salt. Bake as directed.

In 13x9-inch pan, melt ¼ cup margarine. Dip chicken in 1 can (10¾ oz.) condensed cream of mushroom soup, then roll in 3 cups croutons crushed to 1½ cups or crumb mixture for Golden Oven-Fried Chicken. Place skin-side-up in baking pan containing margarine. Bake as directed.

LEMON BROILED CHICKEN

2½ to 3-lb. frying chicken, cut up
1 lemon, halved or 3 tablespoons lemon juice
1 teaspoon salt
½ teaspoon paprika
⅛ teaspoon pepper
2 tablespoons margarine or butter, melted
1 teaspoon sugar, if desired

Rub chicken pieces on all sides with cut surface of lemon, squeezing lemon halves to release juice. Place chicken pieces skin-side-down on broiler pan. Combine salt with paprika and pepper. Brush chicken with half of melted margarine; sprinkle with half of seasoning mixture. Broil about 6 inches from heat 15 to 20 minutes or until deep golden brown. Turn chicken; brush with remaining margarine and sprinkle with remaining seasoning mixture. Continue broiling 10 to 15 minutes or until chicken is tender and deep golden brown. For a special flavor, sprinkle chicken pieces with sugar about 3 minutes before end of broiling time.

4 to 6 servings

NUTRITION INFORMATION PER SERVING

Serving Size: 1/6 of recipe		Percent U.S. RDA Per Serving	
Calories	198	Protein	37%
Protein	24g	Vitamin A	22%
Carbohydrate	1g	Vitamin C	4%
Fat	10g	Thiamin	5%
Sodium	415mg	Riboflavin	28%
Potassium	12mg	Niacin	35%
		Calcium	*
		Iron	14%

TIPS: *For SWEET-SOUR BROILED CHICKEN, season chicken with salt and pepper. Broil as directed, brushing with prepared sweet 'n sour sauce during last 5 minutes of broiling on each side.*

For BARBECUE-BROILED CHICKEN, use barbecue sauce for sweet 'n sour sauce in above Tip.

For TARRAGON-BROILED CHICKEN, omit lemon and add ½ teaspoon tarragon leaves to margarine.

TATER-CRISP CHICKEN

¼ cup margarine or butter
1 cup Hungry Jack® Mashed Potato Flakes
1 teaspoon salt
2 to 3-lb. frying chicken, cut up

Heat oven to 400°F. Place margarine in 13x9-inch baking dish; melt in oven. In plastic bag, combine potato flakes and salt. Rinse chicken pieces in cold water; shake in plastic bag. Place chicken skin-side-down in melted margarine. Bake uncovered at 400°F. for 30 minutes; turn chicken. Bake 30 minutes longer.

4 to 6 servings

NUTRITION INFORMATION PER SERVING

Serving Size: 1/6 of recipe		Percent U.S. RDA Per Serving	
Calories	229	Protein	47%
Protein	30g	Vitamin A	6%
Carbohydrate	6g	Vitamin C	4%
Fat	8g	Thiamin	7%
Sodium	571mg	Riboflavin	7%
Potassium	597mg	Niacin	69%
		Calcium	2%
		Iron	9%

TIP: *Paprika, tarragon, basil, marjoram or thyme may be added to the potato mixture. Onion, garlic or seasoned salt may be substituted for regular salt.*

CHICKEN CACCIATORE

2½ to 3-lb. frying chicken, cut up
3 tablespoons oil or olive oil
1 teaspoon salt
1 teaspoon Italian seasoning or oregano leaves
⅛ teaspoon pepper
1 medium onion, sliced or chopped
2 garlic cloves, minced
15-oz. can (2 cups) tomato sauce
6-oz. can tomato paste

In large skillet or Dutch oven, brown chicken in hot oil; drain excess oil. Stir in remaining ingredients. Simmer covered, 45 to 50 minutes or until tender. If desired, serve chicken and sauce over spaghetti. 4 to 6 servings

NUTRITION INFORMATION PER SERVING

Serving Size: 1/6 of recipe		Percent U.S. RDA Per Serving	
Calories	331	Protein	50%
Protein	33g	Vitamin A	42%
Carbohydrate	15g	Vitamin C	19%
Fat	15g	Thiamin	13%
Sodium	484mg	Riboflavin	11%
Potassium	765mg	Niacin	75%
		Calcium	4%
		Iron	17%

TIP: *If desired, add 1 pkg. spaghetti sauce mix and 1¼ cups water. Omit salt, Italian seasoning, pepper, garlic and tomato sauce.*

ORANGE AND CHICKEN BURGUNDY

2½ to 3-lb. frying chicken, cut up
2 tablespoons margarine or butter
½ teaspoon seasoned salt or salt
⅛ teaspoon pepper, if desired
3 tablespoons firmly packed brown sugar
1 tablespoon cornstarch
¼ teaspoon salt
⅛ teaspoon ginger, if desired
⅓ cup orange marmalade
⅓ cup orange juice
1 teaspoon lemon juice
⅓ cup Burgundy or dry red wine*
1 orange thinly sliced, if desired

In large skillet, brown chicken in margarine. Season with salt and pepper. Add remaining ingredients, except Burgundy and orange slices; reduce heat. Simmer covered about 25 to 35 minutes or until tender, stirring occasionally. Add Burgundy and orange slices. Continue simmering 10 minutes.

4 to 6 servings

NUTRITION INFORMATION PER SERVING

Serving Size: 1/6 of recipe		Percent U.S. RDA Per Serving	
Calories	386	Protein	46%
Protein	30g	Vitamin A	21%
Carbohydrate	30g	Vitamin C	31%
Fat	15g	Thiamin	7%
Sodium	249mg	Riboflavin	33%
Potassium	134mg	Niacin	44%
		Calcium	5%
		Iron	16%

TIPS: **One-third cup additional orange juice may be used for wine. Increase lemon juice to 1 tablespoon; prepare as directed.*

To bake in oven, brown chicken and arrange in 13x9-inch pan. Combine remaining ingredients except Burgundy and orange slices. Pour over chicken. Cover with foil and bake at 350°F. for 1 hour, adding Burgundy and orange slices during last 15 minutes of baking time.

Peach or apricot preserves may be substituted for orange marmalade.

CHICKEN MAGNIFICO

¼ cup flour
1 teaspoon paprika
½ teaspoon salt
⅛ teaspoon pepper
2½ to 3-lb. frying chicken, cut up
2 tablespoons oil or shortening
¾ cup cooked cubed ham (½-inch cubes)
1 teaspoon basil leaves
1 large onion, chopped
11-oz. can condensed Cheddar cheese soup
8-oz. can (1 cup) stewed tomatoes, undrained

In paper or plastic bag, combine first 4 ingredients. Shake chicken, a few pieces at a time, in flour mixture. In large skillet, brown chicken in hot oil. In medium bowl, combine remaining ingredients; spoon over chicken. Simmer covered over low heat, 30 to 35 minutes or until chicken is tender. Remove cover; continue cooking until sauce thickens (about 5 minutes). If desired, serve over rice or noodles.

4 to 6 servings

NUTRITION INFORMATION PER SERVING

Serving Size: 1/6 of recipe		Percent U.S. RDA Per Serving	
Calories	426	Protein	56%
Protein	36g	Vitamin A	26%
Carbohydrate	16g	Vitamin C	11%
Fat	23g	Thiamin	15%
Sodium	623mg	Riboflavin	40%
Potassium	138mg	Niacin	56%
		Calcium	11%
		Iron	18%

TIPS: *To bake in oven, brown chicken in Dutch oven. Combine remaining ingredients; spoon over chicken. Bake covered at 350°F. for 1 hour.*

Two chopped fresh tomatoes may be substituted for stewed tomatoes.

CHICKEN ATOP RICE

1¼ cups rice, uncooked
2 tablespoons chopped onion
½ teaspoon salt
1 stalk celery, chopped
2 cups water
10¾-oz. can condensed cream of chicken soup
4-oz. can (½ cup) mushroom stems and pieces, drained
2½ to 3-lb. frying chicken, cut up
2 tablespoons margarine or butter, melted
½ teaspoon salt
½ teaspoon paprika
¼ to ½ teaspoon poultry seasoning

Heat oven to 375°F. In 13x9-inch pan, combine first 7 ingredients; mix well. Arrange chicken on rice mixture skin-side-up; drizzle with margarine. Sprinkle with ½ teaspoon salt, paprika and poultry seasoning. Bake uncovered at 375°F. for 1 hour or until chicken is tender.

5 to 6 servings

NUTRITION INFORMATION PER SERVING

Serving Size: 1/6 of recipe		Percent U.S. RDA Per Serving	
Calories	366	Protein	53%
Protein	34g	Vitamin A	7%
Carbohydrate	38g	Vitamin C	*
Fat	7g	Thiamin	17%
Sodium	1461mg	Riboflavin	10%
Potassium	577mg	Niacin	77%
		Calcium	5%
		Iron	17%

TIPS: *For CHICKEN ATOP DRESSING, substitute 8-oz. pkg. herb-seasoned stuffing mix for rice. Omit first ½ teaspoon salt. Bake covered with foil at 375°F. for 1 hour; remove foil and bake 30 minutes longer. (This makes a moist dressing; if you prefer a drier dressing, decrease water to 1½ cups.)*

Wild rice may be substituted for half of rice.

For PORK CHOPS ATOP RICE, in large skillet, brown 6 pork chops. Arrange pork chops on rice mixture; omit margarine.

OVEN BARBECUED CHICKEN AND BISCUITS

2½ to 3-lb. frying chicken, cut up
¼ teaspoon salt
2 tablespoons firmly packed brown sugar
2 tablespoons instant minced onion or ½ cup chopped onion
½ teaspoon salt
⅛ teaspoon pepper
1 garlic clove, minced
½ cup catsup
¼ cup vinegar
¼ cup water
1 teaspoon Worcestershire sauce
8-oz. can Pillsbury Refrigerated Buttermilk or Country Style Biscuits
2 tablespoons grated Parmesan cheese
½ teaspoon Italian seasoning or oregano

Heat oven to 375°F. In ungreased 13x9-inch pan, arrange chicken pieces skin-side-down; sprinkle with ¼ teaspoon salt. In small saucepan, combine brown sugar, onion, ½ teaspoon salt, pepper, garlic, catsup, vinegar, water and Worcestershire sauce; heat to boiling. Pour over chicken. Bake uncovered at 375°F. for 30 minutes. Turn chicken pieces and spoon sauce over. Bake 10 to 15 minutes longer or until tender. If necessary, add 2 to 3 tablespoons water to sauce to prevent sticking. Move chicken to one end of pan; spoon sauce over chicken. Separate biscuit dough into 10 biscuits. Dip each in sauce; place sauce-side-up in opposite end of pan. Combine Parmesan cheese with Italian seasoning; sprinkle over biscuits. Return to oven and continue baking 15 to 20 minutes or until biscuits are brown. 4 to 6 servings

NUTRITION INFORMATION PER SERVING

Serving Size: 1/6 of recipe		Percent U.S. RDA Per Serving	
Calories	277	Protein	52%
Protein	34g	Vitamin A	7%
Carbohydrate	30g	Vitamin C	7%
Fat	2g	Thiamin	17%
Sodium	1062mg	Riboflavin	14%
Potassium	635mg	Niacin	75%
		Calcium	6%
		Iron	15%

TIP: *If desired, biscuits may be omitted. After turning chicken pieces and spooning on sauce, sprinkle the Parmesan cheese mixture on each piece. Bake 20 to 30 minutes longer or until tender.*

CHICKEN BASQUE

2½ to 3-lb. frying chicken, cut up
2 tablespoons oil or olive oil
1½ teaspoons salt
½ teaspoon ground basil
½ teaspoon thyme
¼ teaspoon pepper
1 medium onion, chopped
1 garlic clove, minced
1 bay leaf
1 cup vermouth or dry white wine
16-oz. can (2 cups) tomatoes, undrained and cut up
6-oz. can tomato paste
1 tablespoon cornstarch

In Dutch oven or large skillet, brown chicken in hot oil. Add remaining ingredients except cornstarch. Heat to boiling; reduce heat. Simmer covered until tender, about 30 minutes. Place chicken on heated platter. Combine cornstarch with 2 tablespoons water; stir into tomato mixture. Heat until it boils and thickens, stirring constantly. Remove bay leaf and serve sauce over chicken. 4 to 6 servings

NUTRITION INFORMATION PER SERVING

Serving Size: 1/6 of recipe		Percent U.S. RDA Per Serving	
Calories	363	Protein	48%
Protein	31g	Vitamin A	48%
Carbohydrate	16g	Vitamin C	33%
Fat	16g	Thiamin	11%
Sodium	650mg	Riboflavin	36%
Potassium	492mg	Niacin	51%
		Calcium	4%
		Iron	23%

ORIENTAL CHICKEN

2½ to 3-lb. frying chicken, cut up
¼ to ½ teaspoon salt
⅛ teaspoon pepper
1 tablespoon oil or shortening
1 medium onion, cut into wedges
½ cup chicken broth or bouillon*
¼ cup soy sauce
1 tablespoon cornstarch
1 tablespoon sugar
2 tablespoons water
11-oz. can (1 cup) mandarin oranges, drained, if desired
6-oz. can (½ cup) bamboo shoots, drained
8-oz. can (⅔ cup) water chestnuts, drained and sliced

Season chicken pieces with salt and pepper. In large skillet, brown chicken in hot oil. Add onion, broth and soy sauce. Simmer covered, 35 to 40 minutes or until chicken is tender. Remove chicken while preparing sauce. Combine cornstarch with sugar; stir in water. Add cornstarch mixture to skillet; heat until mixture boils and thickens, stirring constantly. Add mandarin oranges, bamboo shoots and water chestnuts; heat through. Pour over chicken and serve with rice.

4 to 6 servings

NUTRITION INFORMATION PER SERVING

Serving Size: 1/6 of recipe		Percent U.S. RDA Per Serving	
Calories	322	Protein	49%
Protein	32g	Vitamin A	16%
Carbohydrate	16g	Vitamin C	13%
Fat	14g	Thiamin	8%
Sodium	1101mg	Riboflavin	36%
Potassium	156mg	Niacin	48%
		Calcium	4%
		Iron	18%

TIP: **If desired, 1 chicken bouillon cube or ½ teaspoon instant bouillon and ½ cup water may be substituted for chicken broth.*

FRUITY BAKED CHICKEN

2 tablespoons margarine or butter
⅓ cup flour
1½ teaspoons salt
½ teaspoon paprika
⅛ teaspoon pepper
2½ to 3-lb. frying chicken, cut up or quartered
16-oz. can (2 cups) fruit cocktail, drained (reserve ½ cup syrup)
1 tablespoon firmly packed brown sugar or honey
¼ teaspoon cinnamon
¼ teaspoon nutmeg
1 teaspoon lemon juice
½ cup reserved syrup

Heat oven to 375°F. In 13x9-inch pan, melt margarine. In paper or plastic bag, combine flour, salt, paprika and pepper. Shake chicken, a few pieces at a time, in flour mixture. Arrange chicken in pan, skin-side-up. Combine remaining ingredients except fruit cocktail; pour over chicken pieces. Bake at 375°F. for 50 minutes, basting occasionally with sauce. Spoon fruit cocktail over chicken; sprinkle with additional cinnamon, if desired. Return to oven and bake for 15 to 20 minutes or until chicken is tender.

4 to 6 servings

NUTRITION INFORMATION PER SERVING

Serving Size: 1/6 of recipe		Percent U.S. RDA Per Serving	
Calories	260	Protein	48%
Protein	31g	Vitamin A	5%
Carbohydrate	23g	Vitamin C	2%
Fat	5g	Thiamin	10%
Sodium	703mg	Riboflavin	9%
Potassium	614mg	Niacin	71%
		Calcium	3%
		Iron	11%

TIPS: *Other fruits may be substituted for fruit cocktail; such as peaches or pineapple.*

To cook in skillet, coat chicken in flour mixture as suggested above; brown in margarine. Add seasoning mixture with reserved fruit syrup; simmer covered 20 minutes; add fruit cocktail and cook 10 minutes or until chicken is tender.

SPEEDY CHICKEN AND DUMPLINGS

2½ to 3-lb. frying chicken, cut up
2 tablespoons margarine or butter
1 tablespoon salt
2 stalks celery, cut into 1-inch pieces
1 medium onion, sliced
3 cubes or 3 teaspoons chicken bouillon
4 peppercorns or ¼ teaspoon pepper
1 bay leaf
3 cups water
4 carrots, cut into 1-inch pieces
3 tablespoons flour
½ cup cold water
Fluffy Dumplings, page 88

In Dutch oven or large skillet, brown chicken in hot margarine. Add salt, celery, onion, bouillon, peppercorns, bay leaf and water. Heat to boiling; reduce heat. Simmer covered, 20 minutes. Add carrots, simmer covered 15 minutes or until just about tender. Combine flour with ½ cup water, stir into chicken mixture. Heat until it boils and thickens, stirring constantly. Prepare Dumplings and drop by rounded tablespoonfuls on top of hot mixture. Cover tightly; boil gently 12 to 15 minutes or until Dumplings are fluffy and dry.

4 to 6 servings

NUTRITION INFORMATION PER SERVING

Serving Size: 1/6 of recipe		Percent U.S. RDA Per Serving	
Calories	493	Protein	55%
Protein	36g	Vitamin A	129%
Carbohydrate	36g	Vitamin C	14%
Fat	22g	Thiamin	22%
Sodium	1982mg	Riboflavin	46%
Potassium	333mg	Niacin	54%
		Calcium	11%
		Iron	21%

TIP: *Dumplings may be omitted and additional vegetables such as potatoes, frozen peas or corn may be added with carrots. Cook vegetables 20 to 30 minutes or until tender.*

CHICKEN AND DUMPLINGS

4 to 5-lb. stewing chicken*, cut up
3 cups water
1 tablespoon salt
1 large onion, sliced
1 or 2 stalks celery, cut into 1-inch pieces
1 bay leaf
4 peppercorns or ¼ teaspoon pepper
¼ cup flour
½ cup cold water
1½ to 3 cups (10 or 20-oz. pkg.) frozen mixed vegetables
Fluffy Dumplings, page 88

In large saucepan, combine first 7 ingredients. Heat to boiling; reduce heat. Simmer covered, 2 to 3 hours or until chicken is tender. Remove chicken from bones; cut into desired pieces. Skim fat from broth. Combine flour with ½ cup water; stir into broth. Heat mixture until it boils and thickens, stirring constantly. Add vegetables and chicken pieces. Prepare Dumplings and drop by rounded tablespoonfuls on top of hot mixture. Cover tightly; boil gently 12 to 15 minutes or until Dumplings are fluffy and dry.

4 to 6 servings

NUTRITION INFORMATION PER SERVING

Serving Size: 1/6 of recipe		Percent U.S. RDA Per Serving	
Calories	721	Protein	73%
Protein	48g	Vitamin A	79%
Carbohydrate	38g	Vitamin C	9%
Fat	41g	Thiamin	25%
Sodium	1450mg	Riboflavin	36%
Potassium	247mg	Niacin	78%
		Calcium	11%
		Iron	27%

TIP: **A 3 to 4-lb. cut-up frying chicken may be substituted. Simmer covered about 1 hour or until chicken is tender.*

Refrigerated biscuits make easy dumplings. Arrange on hot stew; simmer covered as directed.

HOW TO BONE CHICKEN

To bone chicken breasts, start on thickest side and cut along bone to release meat.

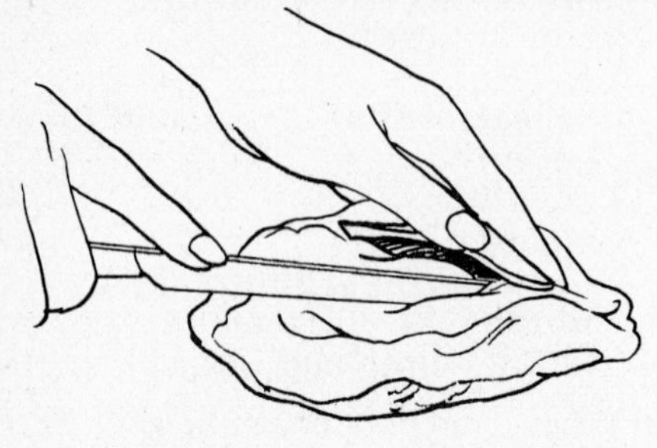

CHICKEN BREASTS IN WINE SAUCE

3 whole chicken breasts, halved
2 tablespoons margarine or butter
½ teaspoon salt
3 medium carrots, thinly sliced
Pepper
¼ cup white wine or milk
4-oz. can (½ cup) mushroom stems and pieces, drained
10¾-oz. can condensed cream of chicken soup

If desired, bone chicken breasts and remove skin. In large skillet, brown chicken breasts in hot margarine. Add remaining ingredients. Simmer covered, 25 to 35 minutes or until chicken and carrots are tender. Serve with rice or noodles. 4 to 6 servings

NUTRITION INFORMATION PER SERVING

Serving Size: 1/6 of recipe		Percent U.S. RDA Per Serving	
Calories	260	Protein	42%
Protein	27g	Vitamin A	87%
Carbohydrate	9g	Vitamin C	3%
Fat	11g	Thiamin	5%
Sodium	647mg	Riboflavin	15%
Potassium	166mg	Niacin	62%
		Calcium	4%
		Iron	11%

TIP: *To MAKE AHEAD, cook as directed. Cool and refrigerate or freeze. To serve, thaw and reheat.*

GOURMET CHICKEN IN FOIL

4 whole chicken breasts, halved
¼ cup margarine or butter
½ teaspoon salt
Pepper
2 to 4 tablespoons chopped chives
1½-oz. pkg. sour cream sauce mix
4-oz. can (½ cup) mushroom stems and pieces, drained
4 tablespoons sherry or white wine, if desired

Heat oven to 375°F. If desired, bone and skin chicken breasts. In medium skillet, brown chicken breasts in hot margarine. Place 2 pieces of chicken on double thick or heavy duty 12-inch square of foil; spoon remaining margarine in pan over chicken. Season each with ⅛ teaspoon salt, dash pepper and sprinkle with ½ to 1 tablespoon chopped chives. Divide dry sour cream sauce mix among foil packets (about 2 tablespoons each). Divide mushrooms and place on top. Spoon on wine. Seal packets using tight double folds.* Place packets on cookie sheet; bake 35 to 40 minutes or until chicken is tender. Serve with rice or noodles. 6 to 8 servings

NUTRITION INFORMATION PER SERVING

Serving Size: 1/8 of recipe		Percent U.S. RDA Per Serving	
Calories	167	Protein	30%
Protein	20g	Vitamin A	6%
Carbohydrate	2g	Vitamin C	*
Fat	7g	Thiamin	4%
Sodium	397mg	Riboflavin	6%
Potassium	335mg	Niacin	43%
		Calcium	*
		Iron	6%

TIPS: *To MAKE AHEAD, prepare to *, refrigerate up to 6 hours.*

Chicken may be placed in covered 13x9-inch pan instead of wrapping in foil.

Packets may be grilled over medium coals about 30 minutes, turning once.

CHICKEN ELEGANTÉ

8 slices dried beef
4 whole chicken breasts, boned and halved
10¾-oz. can condensed cream of mushroom soup
1 cup dairy sour cream
½ cup slivered almonds
⅓ cup imitation bacon bits

Heat oven to 325°F. Roll slice of dried beef around each half of chicken breast; arrange in 13x9-inch baking dish or 3-quart casserole. In small bowl, combine soup and sour cream; pour over chicken.* Sprinkle with almonds and imitation bacon bits. Bake covered at 325°F. for 1¼ to 1½ hours or until chicken is tender. 6 to 8 servings

NUTRITION INFORMATION PER SERVING

Serving Size: 1/8 of recipe		Percent U.S. RDA Per Serving	
Calories	310	Protein	41%
Protein	27g	Vitamin A	19%
Carbohydrate	7g	Vitamin C	0%
Fat	19g	Thiamin	6%
Sodium	1244mg	Riboflavin	31%
Potassium	114mg	Niacin	31%
		Calcium	7%
		Iron	16%

TIP: *To MAKE AHEAD, prepare to *, cover and refrigerate up to 1 day; prepare as directed.*

CHICKEN ELEGANTE

CHICKEN KIEV

4 whole chicken breasts, halved
Salt and pepper
1½ teaspoons chopped chives or ½ teaspoon tarragon leaves
1 tablespoon minced parsley
1 stick (¼ lb.) cold margarine or butter
¼ cup flour
1 egg, slightly beaten
½ cup dry bread crumbs

Bone chicken breasts and remove skin. Place one breast at a time, boned-side-up, between pieces of plastic wrap. Using the flat side of a meat mallet or a rolling pin, flatten each until about ⅛ inch thick; peel off wrap. Flatten remaining breasts in same way. Sprinkle with salt and pepper. Divide chives and parsley among the chicken breasts. Cut margarine in quarters lengthwise and then in half crosswise to make 8 pieces. Place a piece of margarine on each chicken breast. Roll up chicken with margarine inside, tucking in ends and sealing well. Roll in flour, then dip in egg and coat with bread crumbs. Cover loosely and refrigerate until ready to cook.

About 15 minutes before serving, in medium skillet, heat 1½ to 2-inches oil to 340°F. Cook chicken in hot oil about 10 minutes or until golden brown, turning once if necessary to brown all sides.

4 to 8 servings*

NUTRITION INFORMATION PER SERVING

Serving Size: 1/8 of recipe		Percent U.S. RDA Per Serving	
Calories	312	Protein	43%
Protein	28g	Vitamin A	13%
Carbohydrate	9g	Vitamin C	*
Fat	18g	Thiamin	6%
Sodium	461mg	Riboflavin	14%
Potassium	29mg	Niacin	60%
		Calcium	3%
		Iron	10%

TIPS: **For hearty appetites or when light side dishes are planned, allow 2 per serving. When several side dishes are planned, allow 1 per serving.*

If desired, freeze 4 for later use. To cook 4 frozen Chicken Kiev, decrease temperature of oil to 320°F. and increase time to 15 minutes. The oil will be below 300°F. for the cooking of the frozen chicken pieces. Cooking more than 4 at a time is not suggested because the oil would cool too much.

For CHICKEN CORDON BLEU, omit margarine in chicken breasts and fill each with ½ thin slice cooked ham and ½ slice Swiss cheese. Continue as directed.

TANGY CORNISH HENS

TANGY CORNISH HENS

2 Cornish game hens, halved
2 tablespoons margarine or butter, melted
Salt and pepper
½ cup maple-flavored syrup
¼ cup lemon juice
2 tablespoons prepared mustard
2 teaspoons soy sauce
8-oz. can (1 cup) crushed pineapple, drained

Heat oven to 350°F. In 13x9-inch pan, arrange hens, skin-side-up. Brush with melted margarine; season with salt and pepper. Bake uncovered at 350°F. for 30 minutes. In small bowl, combine syrup, lemon juice, mustard, soy sauce and pineapple; spoon over hens. Return to oven for 30 minutes or until well browned and tender, basting occasionally. 4 servings

Insufficient data with regard to Cornish Game Hens to provide nutritional information.

TIP: *Other types of poultry such as quartered or cut-up chicken or turkey parts may be substituted for Cornish hens. Allow 2½ to 3½ lb. poultry for amount of sauce.*

CORNISH HEN AND RICE BAKE

3 (12 to 16 oz. each) Cornish game hens
6-oz. pkg. white and wild rice mix
2 tablespoons chopped onion
1 stalk celery, chopped
4-oz. can (½ cup) mushroom stems and pieces, drained
2 cups water
3 cubes or 3 teaspoons chicken bouillon
2 tablespoons margarine or butter
2 tablespoons honey

Heat oven to 375°F. Using kitchen shears or sharp knife, cut game hens in half lengthwise through breastbone. In 13x9-inch (3 qt.) glass baking dish, combine rice mix, onion, celery and mushrooms. Heat water and dissolve bouillon; stir into rice mixture. Dot with margarine. Place game hens cut-side-down over rice. Brush with 1 tablespoon honey; lightly sprinkle with salt. Cover with foil and bake at 375°F. for 45 minutes. Uncover; brush game hens with remaining honey. Bake uncovered 30 minutes longer or until tender and brown. 4 to 5 servings

Insufficient data with regard to Cornish Game Hens to provide nutritional information.

TIPS: *One 10¾-oz. can condensed chicken broth plus enough water to equal 2 cups may be substituted for the 2 cups water and 3 cubes or 3 teaspoons chicken bouillon.*

For CHICKEN AND RICE BAKE, substitute 2½ lb. to 3½ lb. quartered or cut-up frying chicken.

CHICKEN AND NOODLE CASSEROLE

- **10-oz. pkg. (5 cups) egg noodles, uncooked**
- **¼ cup margarine or butter**
- **¼ cup flour**
- **1 cup light cream or milk**
- **½ teaspoon salt**
- **10¾-oz. can condensed chicken broth**
- **4 cups cooked cubed chicken or turkey**
- **4-oz. can (½ cup) mushroom stems and pieces, undrained**
- **½ to 1 cup buttered bread cubes**
- **¼ cup grated Parmesan cheese**

Heat oven to 350°F. Grease 2½-quart casserole. Cook noodles as directed on package; drain. In medium saucepan, melt margarine; blend in flour. Stir in cream, salt and chicken broth. Cook until thickened, stirring constantly. In prepared casserole, combine chicken, mushrooms and noodles. Pour sauce over mixture.* Sprinkle with buttered bread cubes and Parmesan cheese. Bake uncovered at 350°F. for 1 hour or until center is bubbly and top is lightly browned.

6 to 8 servings

NUTRITION INFORMATION PER SERVING

Serving Size: 1/8 of recipe		Percent U.S. RDA Per Serving	
Calories	432	Protein	46%
Protein	30g	Vitamin A	15%
Carbohydrate	32g	Vitamin C	*
Fat	20g	Thiamin	16%
Sodium	613mg	Riboflavin	19%
Potassium	379mg	Niacin	43%
		Calcium	9%
		Iron	13%

TIPS: *To MAKE AHEAD, prepare to *, cool and refrigerate up to 2 days. Top with bread cubes and cheese just before baking; increase baking time to 1 hour, 15 minutes.*

Casserole may be prepared, cooled and frozen up to 3 months. Thaw partially or completely before baking as directed.

CHICKEN RICE HOT DISH

- **4-oz. can (½ cup) mushroom stems and pieces**
- **1 cube or 1 teaspoon chicken bouillon**
- **1 small onion, chopped**
- **¼ cup margarine or butter**
- **2 tablespoons flour**
- **1½ cups light cream or milk**
- **1½ cups uncooked quick-cooking rice**
- **3 cups cooked cubed chicken or turkey**
- **¼ cup chopped pimiento, drained**
- **2 tablespoons chopped parsley**
- **¾ teaspoon salt**
- **¼ teaspoon pepper**

Drain mushrooms; reserve liquid. Add enough hot water to reserved mushroom liquid to measure 1½ cups; add bouillon cube. In large skillet, cook onion and drained mushrooms in margarine until tender. Stir in flour; add bouillon and cream. Heat mixture until it boils and slightly thickens, stirring constantly. Add rice, chicken, pimiento, parsley, salt and pepper. Simmer covered, 15 minutes or until rice is tender.

6 servings

NUTRITION INFORMATION PER SERVING

Serving Size: 1/6 of recipe		Percent U.S. RDA Per Serving	
Calories	504	Protein	41%
Protein	27g	Vitamin A	20%
Carbohydrate	44g	Vitamin C	7%
Fat	24g	Thiamin	17%
Sodium	1174mg	Riboflavin	16%
Potassium	409mg	Niacin	41%
		Calcium	10%
		Iron	16%

CHICKEN ALMOND PARTY BAKE

- **3 cups cooked cubed chicken**
- **¼ cup slivered almonds**
- **¼ cup chopped pimiento, drained**
- **2 tablespoons chopped onion**
- **½ teaspoon salt**
- **½ cup white wine or chicken broth**
- **10¾-oz. can condensed cream of chicken soup**
- **4-oz. can (½ cup) mushroom stems and pieces, drained**

POTATO TOPPING

- **2 tablespoons margarine or butter**
- **½ teaspoon salt**
- **1 cup water**
- **¼ cup milk**
- **1½ cups Hungry Jack® Mashed Potato Flakes**
- **½ cup dairy sour cream or yogurt**
- **1 egg**
- **¼ cup slivered almonds**

Heat oven to 375°F. In 8-inch square pan, combine all ingredients except Potato Topping; mix well. In medium saucepan, heat margarine, salt and water to boiling. Remove from heat. Add milk; stir in potato flakes with fork just until moistened. Let stand until liquid is absorbed (about ½ minute). Blend in sour cream; add egg and beat well. Drop Potato Topping by tablespoonfuls onto filling. Sprinkle with remaining ¼ cup almonds. Bake uncovered at 375°F. for 40 to 45 minutes or until topping is golden brown. 4 to 6 servings

NUTRITION INFORMATION PER SERVING

Serving Size: 1/6 of recipe		Percent U.S. RDA Per Serving	
Calories	370	Protein	44%
Protein	28g	Vitamin A	13%
Carbohydrate	17g	Vitamin C	7%
Fat	19g	Thiamin	7%
Sodium	891mg	Riboflavin	18%
Potassium	625mg	Niacin	48%
		Calcium	9%
		Iron	13%

CHICKEN ENCHILADAS

- **1 large or 2 medium onions, chopped**
- **2 tablespoons oil**
- **1 teaspoon chili powder**
- **½ teaspoon salt**
- **½ teaspoon garlic salt**
- **¼ teaspoon Tabasco sauce**
- **15-oz. can (2 cups) tomato sauce**
- **3 cups cooked diced chicken or turkey**
- **½ cup sliced ripe or stuffed green olives**
- **12 frozen or canned tortillas**
- **2 cups (8 oz.) shredded Cheddar cheese**

Heat oven to 350°F. In small skillet, cook onion in oil until tender. Stir in chili powder, salt, garlic salt, Tabasco sauce and tomato sauce. In medium bowl, combine chicken with olives and ½ cup sauce mixture. Over medium heat, fry tortillas in about ¼-inch hot oil just until softened, a few seconds on each side. Drain on paper towels. Divide chicken mixture among the 12 tortillas. Roll up each tortilla and place seam-side-down in lightly greased 13x9-inch (3 qt.) baking dish. Pour remaining sauce over tortillas; sprinkle with cheese.* Bake uncovered at 350°F. for 30 to 35 minutes or until heated through. 4 to 5 servings

NUTRITION INFORMATION PER SERVING

Serving Size: 1/5 of recipe		Percent U.S. RDA Per Serving	
Calories	668	Protein	67%
Protein	44g	Vitamin A	45%
Carbohydrate	45g	Vitamin C	4%
Fat	35g	Thiamin	13%
Sodium	890mg	Riboflavin	23%
Potassium	445mg	Niacin	56%
		Calcium	53%
		Iron	26%

TIPS: *To MAKE AHEAD, prepare to * Refrigerate up to 1 day. Bake uncovered at 350°F. for 40 to 45 minutes.*

To halve recipe, use half the ingredient amounts; bake in 11x7 or 8-inch square pan for 25 to 30 minutes.

CHICKEN TETRAZZINI

7 to 8-oz. pkg. spaghetti
8 oz. (3 cups) sliced fresh mushrooms or 8-oz. can (1 cup) mushrooms, drained
4 tablespoons margarine or butter
2 tablespoons flour
2 cups chicken broth
1 cup light cream or evaporated milk
3 tablespoons sherry, if desired
1 teaspoon salt
⅛ teaspoon nutmeg
Dash pepper
3 cups cooked cubed chicken or turkey
¼ cup grated Parmesan cheese

Cook spaghetti as directed on package; drain. In large skillet, cook mushrooms in 2 tablespoons margarine until tender. Add to spaghetti. Heat oven to 375°F. In same skillet, melt remaining 2 tablespoons margarine; blend in flour. Stir in chicken broth. Heat, stirring constantly until sauce thickens; boil 1 minute. Remove from heat; stir in cream, sherry and seasonings. Pour half of sauce into spaghetti and mushrooms. Stir chicken into remaining sauce. Turn spaghetti mixture into greased 12x8-inch baking dish or shallow 2-quart casserole. Make a well in the center. Pour chicken mixture into well. Sprinkle with cheese.* Bake covered at 375°F. for 30 minutes or until heated through.

6 to 8 servings

NUTRITION INFORMATION PER SERVING

Serving Size: 1/8 of recipe		Percent U.S. RDA Per Serving	
Calories	359	Protein	39%
Protein	25g	Vitamin A	11%
Carbohydrate	27g	Vitamin C	*
Fat	16g	Thiamin	13%
Sodium	775mg	Riboflavin	20%
Potassium	430mg	Niacin	48%
		Calcium	8%
		Iron	10%

TIP: *To MAKE AHEAD, prepare to *, cool and refrigerate up to 1 day. Bake covered, 40 minutes.*

CHICKEN OLÉ CRÊPES

12 cooked Basic Crêpes, page 101
½ cup chopped green pepper
¼ cup chopped onion
1 garlic clove, finely minced
3 tablespoons margarine or butter
½ teaspoon salt
¼ teaspoon chili powder
⅛ teaspoon pepper
16-oz. can (2 cups) tomatoes, drained and chopped
3 cups cooked cubed chicken or turkey
10¾-oz. can condensed cream of chicken soup
1 cup milk
½ cup shredded Monterey Jack or Cheddar cheese

Prepare Crêpes. In large skillet, sauté green pepper, onion and garlic in margarine until onion is tender. Add seasonings and tomatoes; simmer 15 minutes. Stir in chicken; cook 5 minutes longer. Heat oven to 350°F. In medium saucepan, combine soup, milk and cheese; heat until cheese melts, stirring constantly. Spoon about ¼ cup chicken mixture along center of each crêpe. Fold one edge over filling; fold opposite edge over this. Arrange in ungreased 13x9-inch baking dish. Pour hot cheese sauce over crêpes. Bake at 350°F. for 15 to 20 minutes or until heated through. Serve immediately.

12 crêpes

NUTRITION INFORMATION PER SERVING

Serving Size: 1 crêpe		Percent U.S. RDA Per Serving	
Calories	250	Protein	28%
Protein	18g	Vitamin A	19%
Carbohydrate	15g	Vitamin C	15%
Fat	13g	Thiamin	10%
Sodium	566mg	Riboflavin	15%
Potassium	363mg	Niacin	25%
		Calcium	8%
		Iron	8%

TIP: *Sauce may be served over crêpes at serving time. Arrange filled crêpes in baking dish; cover loosely with foil; bake as directed.*

CHICKEN LIVERS STROGANOFF

1 lb. chicken livers
2 tablespoons margarine or butter
½ teaspoon oregano leaves
½ teaspoon Worcestershire sauce
1 small onion, chopped
2 tablespoons flour
½ teaspoon salt
⅛ teaspoon pepper
4-oz. can (½ cup) mushroom stems and pieces, undrained
¼ cup dry white wine
¼ cup dairy sour cream
Hot cooked rice

Cut chicken livers in half. In large skillet, heat margarine with oregano and Worcestershire sauce. Add livers and onion; brown slowly over medium heat for 5 to 7 minutes. Remove livers from pan; set aside. Blend in flour, salt, pepper and mushrooms. Heat until boiling, stirring constantly; boil 1 minute. Return livers to pan; add wine. Simmer covered, 3 to 5 minutes or until hot. Stir in sour cream. Heat through; but do not boil. Serve over hot rice. 4 to 6 servings

NUTRITION INFORMATION PER SERVING

Serving Size: 1/6 of recipe		Percent U.S. RDA Per Serving	
Calories	316	Protein	36%
Protein	23g	Vitamin A	191%
Carbohydrate	32g	Vitamin C	14%
Fat	9g	Thiamin	18%
Sodium	729mg	Riboflavin	124%
Potassium	213mg	Niacin	52%
		Calcium	4%
		Iron	43%

ITALIAN-STYLE CHICKEN LIVERS

1 lb. chicken livers, chopped
2 tablespoons oil or shortening
½ teaspoon Italian seasoning
½ teaspoon garlic salt
2 medium zucchini, unpeeled and sliced
1 small onion, chopped
Dash pepper
16-oz. can (2 cups) stewed tomatoes
6-oz. can tomato paste
4-oz. can (½ cup) mushroom stems and pieces, drained

In large skillet, brown chicken livers in hot oil; drain excess oil. Add remaining ingredients. Simmer covered, 10 minutes or until zucchini is tender. If desired, serve over spaghetti with grated Parmesan cheese. 4 to 5 servings

NUTRITION INFORMATION PER SERVING

Serving Size: 1/4 of recipe		Percent U.S. RDA Per Serving	
Calories	332	Protein	53%
Protein	34g	Vitamin A	333%
Carbohydrate	22g	Vitamin C	74%
Fat	12g	Thiamin	26%
Sodium	463mg	Riboflavin	192%
Potassium	981mg	Niacin	83%
		Calcium	6%
		Iron	68%

TIP: *To MAKE AHEAD, prepare, cook and cool. Refrigerate up to 2 days. Heat to serve.*

PICKLES, CANNING & FREEZING

PICKLES CANNING & FREEZING

PICKLES

Pickles and relishes are welcome additions to a meal; they can be served as an accent to a sandwich or as a meat accompaniment. Often a relish can be served as a salad.

A small amount of relish can be stored in the refrigerator. For longer storage of pickles and relishes, sealing is necessary to keep out oxygen.

When preparing pickles and relishes, choose fruits and vegetables at their peak of perfection. Discard food that shows any trace of mold because it may acquire an off-flavor during the pickling process. Wash produce carefully under cold running water or through several changes of water.

Vinegar provides the acid solution in which pickles and relishes are preserved. Some of our recipes call for cider vinegar which has a more mellow flavor than white distilled vinegar. When a sharper flavor or a light color of vegetable or fruit is desirable, the white distilled vinegar is used.

Pickling salt is called for in the recipes rather than iodized or non-iodized table salt. Iodized salt may cause pickles to darken and non-iodized table salt may make the brine cloudy.

For more information about preparing pickles and relishes, contact your local Agricultural Extension Service County Extension Office or the manufacturers of canning jars.

Nutritional Information: Because of inconsistent variables in making pickles we are unable to give specific nutritional information for each recipe. However, below is nutritional information for typical dill and sweet pickles.

NUTRITION INFORMATION PER SERVING

Serving Size: 1 medium dill pickle		Percent U.S. RDA Per Serving	
Calories	7	Protein	*
Protein	<1g	Vitamin A	*
Carbohydrate	1g	Vitamin C	6%
Fat	<1g	Thiamin	0%
Sodium	928mg	Riboflavin	*
Potassium	130mg	Niacin	0%
		Calcium	*
		Iron	4%

NUTRITION INFORMATION PER SERVING

Serving Size: 2 sweet pickles–gherkins		Percent U.S. RDA Per Serving	
Calories	44	Protein	*
Protein	0g	Vitamin A	*
Carbohydrate	11g	Vitamin C	3%
Fat	<1g	Thiamin	0%
Sodium	0mg	Riboflavin	*
Potassium	0mg	Niacin	0%
		Calcium	*
		Iron	2%

For heating pickling liquids, use unchipped enamalware, stainless steel, aluminum or heat-proof glass pots.

DILL PICKLES

24 to 30 (3-inch long) cucumbers
12 to 16 sprigs fresh dill
4 teaspoons mustard seed
1 quart (4 cups) water
2 cups cider vinegar
2 tablespoons pickling salt

Wash cucumbers and pack in hot sterilized quart jars. To each jar, add 3 or 4 sprigs fresh dill and 1 teaspoon mustard seed. In large saucepan, combine water, vinegar and salt. Heat to boiling. Fill jars leaving ½ inch at top. Seal according to canning directions. Process in simmering water bath at 200° to 205°F. for 10 minutes. Store without removing screw bands. 4 quarts

TIP: *A garlic clove may be added to each jar along with dill.*

SWEET PICKLE CHUNKS

5 quarts medium cucumbers
8 cups sugar
4 cups cider vinegar
2 tablespoons mixed pickling spice
5 teaspoons pickling salt

Place cucumbers in large container; cover with boiling water. Drain and repeat process each day for 4 days.

On 5th day, cut cucumbers into 1 or 2-inch chunks and return to container. In large saucepan, combine sugar, vinegar, spice and salt. Heat to boiling. Pour over cucumber chunks to cover. (If additional syrup is needed, use 2 parts sugar to 1 part vinegar.)

On 6th day, drain syrup and heat to boiling; pour over pickles.

On 7th day, drain syrup and heat to boiling; pack cucumbers in jars and fill with syrup leaving ½ inch at top of jar. Seal according to canning directions; process in boiling water bath at 212°F. for 5 minutes.

7 pints

MIXED PICKLE SLICES

5 quarts (20 cups) thinly sliced unpeeled cucumbers
6 medium onions, thinly sliced
3 medium green peppers, thinly sliced
3 garlic cloves or ¼ teaspoon instant minced garlic
⅓ cup pickling salt
Ice cubes
5 cups sugar
2 cups cider vinegar
2 tablespoons mustard seed
1½ teaspoons celery seed
1½ teaspoons turmeric

In large container, combine cucumber, onion, green pepper and garlic. Sprinkle with salt and cover with layer of ice cubes; mix lightly. Let stand 3 hours. Drain well; remove garlic. In large saucepan, combine sugar, vinegar, seeds and turmeric. Heat to boiling. Fill jars with pickle slices and syrup leaving ½ inch at top. Clean top of jar; seal with vacuum-seal lids. Process in simmering water bath at 200° to 205°F. for 5 minutes.

10 pints

TIP: *For ZUCCHINI PICKLES, use sliced unpeeled zucchini for part or all of cucumbers.*

PICKLED BEETS

16-oz. can (2 cups) sliced or whole beets, drained (reserve ⅓ cup liquid)
⅓ cup sugar
⅓ cup reserved beet liquid or water
⅓ cup vinegar
1 teaspoon pickling spice, if desired

In medium saucepan, combine drained beets, sugar, liquid and vinegar. Tie pickling spice in piece of cheesecloth or paper towel; add to beets. Cook until mixture comes to boil, stirring occasionally. Cool and remove pickling spices before serving. Leftovers will keep several weeks in refrigerator.

2 cups

TIPS: *If desired, use 3 whole cloves, 2 whole allspice and ½ stick cinnamon for pickling spice.*

For longer storage, fill jars to within ½ inch of top with hot pickles and liquid; seal with vacuum-seal lids and process in boiling water bath at 212°F. for 30 minutes.

For pickles using fresh beets, cook beets as directed in Vegetables Chapter 18. *Slice or leave whole. Continue as directed above.*

REFRIGERATOR CUCUMBER PICKLES

7 medium unpeeled cucumbers, thinly sliced
1 tablespoon pickling salt
2 medium (2 cups) onions, thinly sliced or chopped
1 green pepper (1 cup), chopped
2 cups sugar
1 tablespoon celery seed
1 tablespoon mustard seed
1 cup vinegar

In large bowl, mix cucumbers and salt; let stand ½ hour. Drain well. Stir in onions and green pepper. In small bowl, combine remaining ingredients. Pour syrup over cucumber mixture; mix well. Store in covered container or pack in quart jars; refrigerate several hours or up to 3 months. About 3 quarts

PUMPKIN PICKLES

1 pumpkin (about 5 lb.)
4½ cups vinegar
4½ cups water
1½ cups wine vinegar
7½ cups sugar
1 lemon, sliced and quartered
1 piece whole ginger or 1 teaspoon ginger

Cut pumpkin into pieces and remove seeds; peel and cut into ½ or 1-inch cubes (about 4 quarts cubes). Place in large glass bowl; add vinegar and water to cover. Let stand overnight. Drain vinegar liquid, reserving 2 cups. Place pumpkin cubes in large saucepan. Add the 2 cups reserved liquid, wine vinegar, sugar, lemon and ginger. Heat to boiling and cook until pumpkin is clear and transparent, about 30 minutes, stirring occasionally. Fill jars with pumpkin leaving ½ inch at top. Cover with liquid leaving ½ inch at top and seal with vacuum-seal lids. Process in simmering water bath at 200° to 205°F. for 5 minutes. 7 pints

TIP: *Cooking pumpkin is recommended because the Jack-o-lantern variety may be tough and stringy.*

FRESH VEGETABLE RELISH

2 medium tomatoes, chopped
2 medium cucumbers, chopped
1 stalk celery, sliced or chopped
1 small onion, chopped
¼ cup firmly packed brown sugar
2 teaspoons salt
¼ cup vinegar
½ teaspoon mustard seed or dill weed

In 1-quart container, combine all ingredients; mix well. Cover and refrigerate several hours or up to 3 months. 3 cups

NUTRITION INFORMATION PER SERVING

Serving Size: 1 tablespoon		Percent U.S. RDA Per Serving	
Calories	8	Protein	*
Protein	<1g	Vitamin A	*
Carbohydrate	2g	Vitamin C	4%
Fat	<1g	Thiamin	*
Sodium	91mg	Riboflavin	*
Potassium	36mg	Niacin	*
		Calcium	*
		Iron	*

TIP: *For a flavor variation, add any of the following: green pepper, red pepper, onion or cabbage.*

CRANBERRY-ORANGE RELISH

1 orange
1 lb. (4 cups) cranberries
1¾ cups sugar

Juice orange. Grind cranberries and peel of orange. Add sugar and orange juice; mix well. Refrigerate several hours or up to 2 weeks. 3 cups

NUTRITION INFORMATION PER SERVING

Serving Size: 1/4 cup		Percent U.S. RDA Per Serving	
Calories	136	Protein	*
Protein	<1g	Vitamin A	*
Carbohydrate	35g	Vitamin C	19%
Fat	<1g	Thiamin	*
Sodium	1mg	Riboflavin	*
Potassium	61mg	Niacin	*
		Calcium	*
		Iron	*

CORN RELISH

16-oz. can (2 cups) whole kernel corn, drained
⅓ cup pickle relish
⅓ cup chopped pimiento
⅓ cup chopped green pepper
¼ cup sugar
1 small onion, chopped
¼ cup vinegar
1 teaspoon cornstarch
½ teaspoon celery seed
1 tablespoon prepared mustard

In medium saucepan, combine all ingredients; mix well. Cook, stirring occasionally, until mixture comes to a boil and thickens slightly. Cool before serving. Store covered, in refrigerator for 2 to 3 weeks. 2½ cups

NUTRITION INFORMATION PER SERVING

Serving Size: 1 tablespoon		Percent U.S. RDA Per Serving	
Calories	16	Protein	*
Protein	<1g	Vitamin A	*
Carbohydrate	4g	Vitamin C	3%
Fat	<1g	Thiamin	*
Sodium	37mg	Riboflavin	*
Potassium	15mg	Niacin	*
		Calcium	*
		Iron	*

TIP: *Fresh corn may be substituted for canned; cover, heat to boiling and simmer about 5 minutes.*

CANNING

Canning preserves the flavor of produce and allows you to store it for use at a much later date. Fruits and vegetables picked in the summer at their peak of ripeness can be preserved for serving in the middle of winter.

In the canning process, heat destroys food spoiling agents such as yeasts, mold and bacteria. Some bacteria is killed by temperatures of 212°F. in the boiling water bath; other bacteria which causes botulism food poisoning is only destroyed by temperatures of 240°F. in the pressure cooker. Home canning is safe when canning procedures are carefully followed.

Acid Foods

Fruits and tomatoes need to reach boiling temperature (212°F.) to kill any organisms which could cause spoilage. The boiling water bath is one method used for canning these acid foods. A container is needed large enough to hold the canning jars on a rack, allowing them to be covered with water that will boil. The pressure cooker may also be used for canning acid foods – 5 pounds of pressure is recommended and the time needed is shorter than in a boiling water bath. During the hot summer this advantage may be important to you. The open kettle method is no longer recommended for any fruits or tomatoes because it is impossible to prevent contamination at the time the jar is filled.

Low Acid Foods

Vegetables need to reach a temperature higher than boiling water so they are pressure cooked to assure safe canning without danger of botulism. Follow manufacturer's directions carefully when using a pressure canner. Vegetables should not be canned by the boiling water bath method.

Syrup Pack

Our recipes for canning fruit call for a medium syrup, but a water pack can be used. Follow the same directions, using hot water instead of syrup. We suggest that you add ascorbic acid to fruits that darken easily. Artificial sweeteners can also be added to the water pack.

Jars

Use standard canning jars because they are specifically designed for canning. Do not use other types such as empty salad dressing jars. Such jars are not designed to withstand sudden changes in temperature or the high temperatures of pressure cooking.

Sealing of Jars

We recommend vacuum-seal lids because they are the easiest and most convenient to use. The seal can be checked at a glance by noting a depressed center of the lid when the content of the jar is cooled.

Do Not Can Food in the Oven

Conventional and microwave ovens are not satisfactory for canning because the jars may explode or the temperature of the food will not get high enough to kill botulism producing bacteria.

Canning Fruits and Tomatoes Using Boiling Water Bath Method

1. Select jars without nicks, cracks or rough spots on top where lid will provide seal. A crack or rough spot can prevent the lid from sealing to the jar.
2. Wash jars in hot soapy water, rinse well and let stand with hot water in them to warm the jar and prevent breakage when hot syrup is added. (Dishwasher may be used.)
3. Prepare syrup, see Syrup for Canning Fruits, page 446.
4. Place metal sealing lids in pan with water to cover; heat to boiling and keep hot.
5. Prepare fruit and pack into jars to within ½ inch of top of jar. See Timetable for Canning Fruits and Tomatoes, page 448. If fruits tend to darken, use ascorbic acid according to manufacturer's directions.
6. Add hot syrup (or water), filling to within ½ inch of top of jar. Run knife between fruit and jar to remove any air bubbles. Add additional syrup if necessary.
7. Wipe rim of jar with clean cloth, being certain there are no food particles remaining that would prevent sealing.
8. Place scalded lid on jar with sealing compound next to jar. Screw metal bands down tightly by hand. Do not tighten with a wrench because this would not allow air to escape during processing.
9. Place filled jars on rack in canner filled ⅓ full with hot water. Add additional hot water to cover jars; cover canner.
10. Heat water to boiling; start counting the processing time when water begins to boil. Reduce heat to hold water at a steady, but gentle boil.
11. Remove jars from canner and set upright, 2 to 3 inches apart, on wooden board, newspapers or several layers of cloth. Cool away from any draft which could cause hot jars to break.
12. About 12 hours after processing, remove bands and check to be sure the top of lid is depressed which means the jar is sealed. Do not retighten bands. (Lids are used only once; bands can be used many times.)
13. If for any reason jars are not sealed, store in refrigerator and use contents within a few days. Or, check jar rim again for nicks or food particles; top with a new lid and process again for 15 minutes.
14. Store canned fruits in a dark cool area to prevent fading of the fruit color.

Canning Fruits and Tomatoes Using Pressure Cooker Method

Follow directions for Canning Vegetables but use 5 pounds of pressure instead of 10 pounds. See Timetable for Canning Fruits and Tomatoes, page 448.

Syrup for Canning Fruits

Allow 1 to 1½ cups syrup for each quart.

Medium Syrup: 1 cup sugar and 2 cups water or fruit juice makes 2½ cups syrup (for most fruits).

Heavy Syrup: 1 cup sugar and 1 cup water or fruit juice makes 1½ cups syrup (for sour fruits).

Thin Syrup: 1 cup sugar and 3 cups water or fruit juice makes 3½ cups syrup (for a less sweet product).

In large saucepan, combine sugar and water; heat to boiling to dissolve sugar. Keep syrup hot until used.

TIP: *Most fruits have better texture, color and flavor when canned with sugar syrup, but sugar is not necessary to prevent spoilage. Lower calorie fruit may be canned by omitting sugar and canning in water.*

Special Flavors for Canned Fruit

Make canned fruits special by adding liqueurs, spices, wines or fruit peel before canning.

- For LIQUEURS, such as creme de menthe, Grand Marnier, Galiano and others, add 2 to 3 tablespoons per pint, before adding hot syrup.
- For BRANDY, add 2 to 3 tablespoons per pint, before adding hot syrup. Fruit-flavored brandies can be added to fruits with compatible flavors.
- For SPICES, add 3 to 4 whole spices or 1 stick cinnamon or ginger per pint when packing fruit in jar.
- For WINES, make a heavy syrup, but before adding syrup to jar, fill jar half full with wine and finish filling with the heavy syrup.
- For FRUIT PEEL, use a vegetable peeler to remove a 2-inch outer strip from orange or grapefruit peel. Add to each pint jar.

Some fruits and flavors especially enhance each other. We have found these to be some of the combinations we like:

- Applesauce–add brandy or fruit-flavored brandy, orange-flavored liqueurs, sherry, muscatel wine or sweet vermouth.
- Apricots–add brandy, Galiano, orange-flavored liqueurs, cloves, allspice or cinnamon.
- Berries–add brandy, port or rosé wine.
- Cherries–add brandy, Galiano, sherry, port or creme de cacao.
- Peaches–add brandy, muscatel wine, Galiano, sherry, port, allspice, cloves, cinnamon, ginger or orange peel.
- Pears–add brandy, creme de cacao, creme de menthe, muscatel wine, sherry, port, Galiano, allspice, cloves, cinnamon, ginger or orange peel.
- Plums–add brandy, sherry, port, Burgundy, allspice, cloves, cinnamon or orange peel.

Canning Vegetables Using Pressure Cooker Method

1. Select jars without nicks, cracks or rough spots on rim where lid will provide seal. A crack or rough spot can prevent the lid from sealing to the jar.
2. Wash jars in hot soapy water, rinse well and let stand with hot water in them to warm the jar and prevent breakage when hot syrup is added. (Dishwasher may be used.)
3. Place metal sealing lids in pan with water to cover, heat to boiling and keep hot.
4. Prepare vegetables and pack into jars. See Timetable for Canning Vegetables, page 449.
5. Add boiling water or the boiling water in which vegetables were heated for packing, filling to within ½ inch of top of jar.
6. Wipe rim of jar with clean cloth, being certain there are no food particles that would prevent sealing.
7. Place scalded lid on jar with sealing compound next to jar. Screw metal bands down tightly by hand. Do not tighten with a wrench because this would not allow air to escape during processing.
8. Place filled jars on rack in pressure canner containing 2 or 3 inches of hot water or the amount recommended by canner manufacturer.
9. Place canner over high heat. Lock cover according to manufacturer's directions. Leave petcock or vent open for steam to escape.
10. After steam has escaped for 10 minutes, close petcock or vent and let pressure rise to 10 pounds. Start counting processing time after it has reached 10 pounds. Watch heat to keep pressure at 10 pounds during processing time. (Fluctuating pressure causes the liquid to cook out of the jars.)
11. When time is up, remove from heat and allow pressure to slowly fall to zero before trying to open canner.
12. Slowly open petcock; if steam escapes the pressure is not down yet. After petcock is open, remove cover and take jars from canner. Place upright 2 to 3 inches apart on wooden board, newspapers or several layers of cloth. Cool away from any draft which could cause hot jars to break.
13. About 12 hours after processing, remove bands and check to be sure that top of lid is depressed which means the jar is sealed. (Lids are used only once; bands can be used many times.)
14. If for any reason jars are not sealed, store in refrigerator and use contents within a few days. Or, check jar top again for nicks and food particles; top with a new lid and process for original time.

Safety Note: For home canned vegetables, it is recommended that the vegetables come to a full, hard boil, then cover and boil for 10 minutes before eating. Boil corn 20 minutes. This is a safety precaution in case any phase of the canning process was not correct. The boiling destroys botulism toxins which can cause death. If using home canned vegetables for a salad, boil and cool before using.

TIMETABLE FOR CANNING FRUIT AND TOMATOES

FRUIT	AMOUNT TO BUY FOR 1 QUART	BASIC PREPARATION	BOILING WATER BATH		TIME IN PRESSURE COOKER *WITH 5 POUNDS PRESSURE*	
			PINTS	QUARTS	PINTS	QUARTS
Apples	2½ lb. or 8 medium	Wash, peel, core and slice. Boil 5 minutes in syrup. Pack in jars leaving ½ inch at top.	15 min.	20 min.	8 min.	8 min.
Applesauce	3 lb. or 10 medium	Prepare applesauce. Pack hot into jars leaving ½ inch at top.	25 min.	25 min.	8 min.	8 min.
Apricots	2½ lb. or 24 medium	Wash, halve and pit. Pack into jars; add hot syrup leaving ½ inch at top.	25 min.	30 min.	8 min.	8 min.
Berries (except) strawberries and cranberries)	1½ quarts	Wash, stem and pack into jars; add hot syrup leaving ½ inch at top.	10 min.	15 min.	8 min.	8 min.
Cherries	2½ lb. unpitted	Wash, stem and pit if desired. Pack into jars; add hot syrup leaving ½ inch at top.	20 min.	25 min.	8 min.	8 min.
Cranberries	2 lb. or 1½ quarts	Wash, stem and heat to boiling in heavy syrup. Pack into jars leaving ½ inch at top.	10 min.	15 min.	8 min.	8 min.
Fruit Juices	3 to 4 lb. fruit	Crush fruit, heat slowly to simmering point; strain. Add sugar if desired. Heat and simmer 10 minutes (do not boil); pour into jars leaving ½ inch at top.	10 min.	10 min.	5 min.	5 min.
Peaches	2 lb. or 8 medium	Peel by dipping fruit into boiling water a few seconds to loosen peel. Halve or slice and pit. Pack into jars; add hot syrup leaving ½ inch at top.	25 min.	30 min.	8 min.	8 min.
Pears	2 lb. or 8 medium	Peel, halve or slice and core. Pack into jars; add hot syrup leaving ½ inch at top.	25 min.	30 min.	8 min.	8 min.
Plums	2 lb. or 20 medium	Wash, prick skins if canning whole or cut in half and pit. Pack into jars; add hot syrup leaving ½ inch at top.	20 min.	25 min.	8 min.	8 min.
Rhubarb	1½ lb. or 10 stalks	Wash, cut into pieces. Cook in heavy syrup until tender. Pack into jars leaving ½ inch at top.	10 min.	10 min.	5 min.	5 min.

TIMETABLE FOR CANNING FRUIT AND TOMATOES

FRUIT	AMOUNT TO BUY FOR 1 QUART	BASIC PREPARATION	BOILING WATER BATH		TIME IN PRESSURE COOKER *WITH 5 POUNDS PRESSURE*	
			PINTS	QUARTS	PINTS	QUARTS
Strawberries	2½ quarts	Wash, stem and heat to boiling in syrup. Pack into jars leaving ½ inch at top.	15 min.	15 min.	8 min.	8 min.
Tomatoes*	3 lb. or 12 small	Peel by dipping tomatoes into boiling water a few seconds to loosen skin. Core and quarter. Pack into jars, pressing in to form juice; add 1 teaspoon salt per quart. Leave ½ inch at top. DO NOT add water.	40 min.	50 min.	10 min.	10 min.
Tomato Juice*	4 lb. or 16 small	Wash, remove core, cut into pieces and simmer to soften. Put through strainer or food mill. Add 1 teaspoon salt per quart. Heat to boiling; pour into jars leaving ½ inch at top. DO NOT add water.	35 min.	35 min.	5 min.	5 min.

***** *"Low acid" tomatoes taste less tart but are not low acid and may be canned satisfactorily.*

HIGH ALTITUDE: If processing time is less than 20 minutes, add 1 minute additional time for each 1000 feet above sea level. If processing time is more than 20 minutes, add 2 minutes for each 1000 feet.

TIMETABLE FOR CANNING VEGETABLES

VEGETABLE	AMOUNT TO BUY FOR 1 QUART	BASIC PREPARATION (If desired, add ½ teaspoon salt per pint.)	TIME IN PRESSURE COOKER *WITH 10 POUNDS PRESSURE*	
			PINTS	QUARTS
Asparagus	About 48 spears or 3 lb.	Wash and trim; break or cut into 1-inch pieces. Pack tightly into jars leaving ½ inch at top. Cover with boiling water leaving ½ inch at top.	25 min.	30 min.
Beans, green or wax	2 lb.	Wash and trim; break or cut into 1-inch pieces. Pack tightly into jars leaving ½ inch at top. Cover with boiling water leaving ½ inch at top.	20 min.	25 min.
Beans, lima or butter	4 lb. (in pod)	Shell and wash. Pack into jars. For small type, leave 1 inch at top for pints and 1½ inches at top for quarts. For large beans, leave ¾ inch at top for pints and 1¼ inches for quarts. Cover with boiling water leaving ½ inch at top.	40 min.	50 min.
Beets	2 lb.	Wash, cut off tops, leaving 1-inch stem. Boil, covered with water, until skins can be slipped. Remove skins, leave whole, slice or dice. Pack into jars leaving ½ inch at top. Cover with boiling water leaving ½ inch at top.	30 min.	35 min.

TIMETABLE FOR CANNING VEGETABLES

VEGETABLE	AMOUNT TO BUY FOR 1 QUART	BASIC PREPARATION (If desired, add ½ teaspoon salt per pint.)	TIME IN PRESSURE COOKER *WITH 10 POUNDS PRESSURE*	
			PINTS	QUARTS
Carrots	2½ lb.	Remove tops, wash and peel. Slice, dice or leave whole. Pack into jars leaving 1 inch at top. Cover with boiling water leaving ½ inch at top.	25 min.	30 min.
Corn, whole kernel	12 to 14 ears	Husk, remove silk and trim. Cut corn from cob. Pack loosely into jars leaving 1 inch at top. Cover with boiling water leaving ½ inch at top.	55 min.	85 min.*
Okra	1½ lb.	Wash and trim; leave whole or slice. Cover with hot water and boil 2 minutes. Pack into jars leaving 1 inch at top. Cover with cooking liquid leaving ½ inch at top.	25 min.	40 min.
Peas, green	4 lb. (in pod)	Shell and wash. Pack peas lightly in jars leaving 1 inch at top. Cover with boiling water leaving 1 inch at top.	40 min.	40 min.
Pumpkin, see Winter Squash				
Squash, summer or zucchini	2 or 3 lb.	Wash squash and cut into slices. Cover with water and boil 2 minutes. Pack into jars leaving ½ inch at top. Cover with cooking liquid leaving ½ inch at top.	25 min.	30 min.
Squash, winter	2 lb.	Wash, remove seeds, peel and cut into cubes.** Cover with water and heat to boiling. Pack in jars leaving ½ inch at top. Cover with cooking liquid leaving ½ inch at top.	55 min.	90 min.
Tomatoes, see Timetable for Canning Fruits and Tomatoes, pages 448 and 449.				

*The State Department of Agriculture recommends all corn be canned in pints because the long processing time for quarts tends to darken it.

**Straining or mashing of squash or pumpkin should be done at time of use, not before processing.

HIGH ALTITUDE: Increase pressure 1 pound for each 2000 feet above sea level.

FREEZING

Materials and Containers for Freezing

When freezing foods, it is necessary to wrap or cover well to seal in moisture and flavor. This also prevents development of off flavors by sealing out air and the flavor of other foods. A variety of materials are available for freezing, each giving an airtight seal.

ALUMINUM FOIL is an excellent moisture vapor-proof material. Freezer foil is recommended for freezing because its thickness makes it resistant to tearing or piercing. A double thickness of regular weight foil can be used when freezer foil is not available. Foil is especially good for wrapping poultry and other unevenly shaped foods because it easily molds to the food, eliminating air pockets.

PLASTIC WRAPS AND BAGS are usually moisture vapor-proof and are suitable for freezing. Plastic bags are especially convenient for individual foods like rolls or cookies because you may wish to remove only a portion, leaving the remainder in the freezer. With plastic wrap, the ends of the wrap should be taped in place as the wrap often does not cling to itself at freezing temperatures.

FREEZER PAPER is specially coated with an airtight film to give an airtight package. This is often used for home freezing of meats, but should not be confused with regular waxed butcher's paper which does not give an airtight package.

PLASTIC FREEZER CONTAINERS AND FREEZER JARS should have large openings for ease in removing frozen foods. They usually come with tight fitting lids that give an airtight seal. Jars and containers with straight sides and a narrow opening can be used when the contents will be thawed before removing from the container.

FREEZER-TO-OVEN CASSEROLES and dishes are convenient for mixtures you plan to bake from the frozen state. Seal cover on casserole with freezer tape; slip those without lids into plastic bags or wrap in foil. If the number of your casserole dishes is limited, you can freeze the food in a foil-lined casserole until the contents are solid; then lift from casserole and finish wrapping in foil or slip into a plastic bag. When ready to use, remove foil and return to casserole dish.

How to Wrap: To preserve the quality of food, the wrap should eliminate air pockets and provide a tight seal that prevents air from reaching the food during freezer storage.

The "freezer wrap" is one of the easiest methods of insuring an airtight seal. To make the freezer wrap, place the food in center of foil or freezer paper. Bring the two longest sides of the wrap together over the food and fold the edges over, as many times as necessary to bring the wrap flat against the top of the food. (To avoid waste, the wrap should only be long enough to make two folds.) Fold end corners toward each other and then fold the ends over, stretching tightly. If necessary, fastening in place with freezer tape or string.

Freezing Tips:

- To separate layers of frozen chops, fish, steaks, meat patties, cut poultry, etc., place freezer or waxed paper between the pieces before freezing. Keep the shape of the package as flat as possible for speed in thawing.
- Some foods are more convenient to use if frozen loosely rather than in a solid block. Freeze vegetables and berries in shallow pans until firm, then package and store. It is easy to remove the amount needed and return the rest to the freezer.
- Liquids such as soup stocks, pureed foods or beverages can be frozen in ice cube trays until firm, then removed and stored in plastic bags. Individual cubes can be removed and used as desired.
- To make your own "TV dinners", arrange slightly undercooked foods on divided foil trays. Use gravies and sauces on meats and vegetables to fill air spaces. Seal trays by pressing foil tightly over the tops and freeze immediately. To serve, place tray of frozen dinner in 425°F. oven and heat 30 to 40 minutes or until hot.

Freezing Temperatures: Rapid freezing helps retain the original texture of foods so freeze in coldest part of freezer (10° to 20°F. below zero). Once frozen, the food should be stored at 0°F. or below for maximum keeping quality.

Check manufacturer's information if storing food in freezer compartment of refrigerator. If refrigerator-freezer does not go below 0°F., use the minimum time when given for freezer storage period for optimum quality of food item.

How to Freeze Fruits

Fruits may be frozen dry without sugar, combined with sugar or covered with a syrup mixture.

DRY PACK: Wash and drain fruits well. Fill freezer containers to within ½ inch of top. Cover tightly, label and freeze.

SUGAR PACK: Wash and drain fruits well. Sugar only enough fruit for 2 to 3 pints at a time. Add sugar to fruit and fold carefully to distribute. Fill freezer containers to within ½ inch of top. Cover tightly, label and freeze.

SYRUP PACK: Prepare medium syrup on page 446. Cool and chill. Wash and drain fruit. Fill freezer container ⅓ full with syrup. Add fruit leaving 1 inch at top. (More head space is needed with syrup because it expands when frozen.) If necessary, add more syrup to cover fruit. Place a small piece of crumpled plastic wrap or waxed paper on top of fruit, pressing down to hold fruit under syrup. Cover tightly, label and freeze.

FRUIT	AMOUNT TO BUY FOR ONE QUART	PREPARATION	SYRUP PACK	SUGAR PACK	DRY PACK
Apples	2½ lb. or 8 medium	Wash, peel and core. Slice.	Medium with ½ tsp. ascorbic acid	½ cup sugar and ½ tsp. ascorbic acid	Yes with ½ tsp. ascorbic acid
Applesauce	3 lb. or 10 medium	Prepare Applesauce, page 198. Cool and pack into containers.			
Apricots	2 lb. or 24 medium	Wash, halve and pit. If not peeled, place in boiling water ½ minute to prevent peel from toughening.	Medium with 1½ tsp. ascorbic acid	½ cup sugar and ½ tsp. ascorbic acid	No
Berries, except Blueberries, Cranberries or Gooseberries	1½ qt.	Stem, wash and drain. With strawberries, slice or leave whole.	Medium	¾ cup sugar	Yes
Blueberries, Cranberries or Gooseberries	1 qt.	Stem, sort, wash and drain.	Medium	No	Yes
Cherries	2½ lb. unpitted	Stem, sort, wash and drain. Pit or leave whole.	Medium or Heavy ½ tsp. ascorbic acid	½ to ¾ cup sugar and ½ tsp. ascorbic acid	Yes
Grapefruit or Oranges	4 to 5 medium	Wash, peel, section fruit removing membrane and seeds.	Medium syrup ½ tsp. ascorbic acid	No	No
Grapes	1 qt.	Wash and stem. Leave seedless grapes whole. Halve and remove seeds from others.	Medium	No	Yes
Melons	1 medium cantaloupe	Cut in half, remove seeds and peel. Cut into slices, cubes or balls.	Light	No	No
Peaches or Nectarines	2 lb. or 8 medium	Peel by dipping into boiling water a few seconds to loosen peel. Halve and pit; slice if desired.	Medium ½ tsp. ascorbic acid	¾ cup sugar and ½ tsp. ascorbic acid	No
Pears	2 lb. or 8 medium	Peel, halve or quarter and core. Heat in boiling syrup 1 to 2 minutes. Cool, then pack into containers.	Medium ½ tsp. ascorbic acid	No	No
Pineapple	1 large	Peel, remove core and eyes.	Medium	No	Yes
Plums or Prunes	2 lb. or 20 medium	Wash, leave whole, halve or quarter.	Medium ½ tsp. ascorbic acid	No	Yes with ½ tsp. ascorbic acid
Rhubarb	1½ lb. or 10 stalks	Wash and cut into ½-inch pieces.	Medium	No	Yes

TIP: *Serve fruit as soon as defrosted, preferably with a few ice crystals. Thaw at room temperature, submerge package in cool water or use a microwave oven for quick defrosting.*

When using frozen fruit in cooked mixtures, you may need to decrease liquid or add a small amount of tapioca or cornstarch.

HOW TO FREEZE VEGETABLES

1. Prepare vegetables.
2. Blanch according to timetable using minimum time for small pieces, maximum time for larger pieces. (This heating is necessary to stop enzyme action that would cause loss of color,. flavor and freshness.) To blanch, heat a large deep saucepan ⅔ filled with water to a full boil. Place vegetable in wire strainer, basket or cheesecloth, and lower into water to cover vegetable. Cover container and start counting time immediately. (See blanching directions also in Microwave section, page 369.)
3. When time is complete, lift vegetable from boiling water and immerse in ice cold water, changing water until vegetable is cold.
4. Drain thoroughly and fill freezer containers leaving ½ inch at top.
5. Cover tightly and freeze.

VEGETABLE	AMOUNT TO BUY FOR ONE QUART	PREPARATION	BLANCHING TIME
Asparagus	about 32 spears (2 lb.)	Wash and trim. Break or cut into desirable length.	3 to 4 min.
Beans, Green or Wax	1½ lb.	Wash and trim. Cut or break into pieces or leave whole.	3½ min.
Beans, Lima	4 lb. (in pod)	Shell and wash.	3 to 4 min.
Broccoli	2 lb.	Wash, remove large leaves and tough stalks; split lengthwise so stalks are no more than 1 inch thick.*	4 min.
Brussels Sprouts	2 lb.	Remove outer leaves; wash.*	4 to 5 min.
Carrots	2½ lb.	Remove tops, wash and peel. Slice, dice or cut into strips.	3½ min.
Corn-on-the-Cob	—	Husk, remove silk and trim.	medium ears-8 min. large ears-11 min.
Corn, Whole Kernel	12 ears	Husk, remove silk and trim. Blanch, then cool and cut kernels from cob.	4½ min.
Okra	1½ lb.	Wash and trim. Slice or leave whole.	3 to 4 min.
Peas, Green	4 lb. (in pod)	Shell and wash.	1½ min.
Peppers, Green		Wash, remove stem and seeds; cut into strips or chop. Package and freeze.	2 min. May freeze chopped without blanching
Pumpkin, see Winter Squash			
Spinach and Other Greens	2-3 lb.	Sort, wash and trim.	leafy greens-2 min. stem portions of Swiss Chard-3 to 4 min.
Squash, Summer and Zucchini	2 lb.	Wash, cut into ½ inch slices.	3 min.
Squash, Winter or Pumpkin	3 lb.	Wash, remove seeds and cut into larger pieces. Steam or bake until tender. Scoop out pulp; put through sieve or blender. Cool. Package and freeze.	0

TIP: **To remove small insects, soak ½ hour in salt brine, ¼ cup salt to 1 quart water.*

HIGH ALTITUDE–Above 2,000 Feet: Add ½ minute to blanching time.
–Above 4,000 Feet: Add 1 minute to blanching time.
–Above 6,000 Feet: Add 2½ minutes to blanching time.

HOW TO FREEZE PREPARED FOODS

FOOD	BEFORE FREEZING	BEFORE USING*	STORAGE TIME AT 0°F. OR BELOW
Main Dishes			
Cooked Meats or Poultry	Cook as for serving. Cool; wrap tightly. Gravies, broths or sauces added to meat before freezing help prevent drying. Not recommended: fried meats and poultry because they may develop a rancid flavor.	Leave wrapped and thaw in refrigerator about 8 hours. Meats with sauces can be thawed over low heat in a saucepan or in 350°F. oven in a covered casserole, about 45 minutes.	Without broth – 1 month With broth – 6 months
Casseroles	Most casserole mixtures freeze well. Select ones with a condensed soup base or use minimal fat in a sauce to prevent it separating when reheated. Cook meats until just tender. Cook vegetables, pasta or rice until just about tender. Cool mixture quickly. Package in meal-size amounts or in "freezer-to-oven dishes". Wrap tightly. If sour cream is to be added, add after thawing and heating mixture.	Mixture can be thawed in refrigerator before heating or heated and thawed at the same time. To thaw and heat in oven, cover and heat at 375°F. for 1 to 1½ hours, stirring occasionally. If mixture cannot be stirred, bake 1½ to 2 hours. For a crisp top, remove cover last 15 minutes.	3 months In sauce or gravy – 6 months
Chili and Spaghetti	Cook as for serving (time can be reduced to half since flavors blend during storage). Beans may become mushy so it is advisable to add them after freezing and thawing.	Thaw in saucepan over low heat about 20 minutes, in double boiler over boiling water about 45 minutes or in covered casserole at 350°F. about 45 minutes.	3 months
Soups and Stews	Prepare as for serving; undercook vegetables or wait and add vegetables when thawing. Soups with large amount of milk may curdle or separate during thawing but will recombine when heated.	Thaw and heat in saucepan over low heat about 20 minutes, in double boiler over boiling water about 45 minutes or in covered casserole at 350°F. about 45 minutes.	3 months
Sandwiches	Use cooked meats, poultry, tuna, salmon, peanut butter or cheese. Use cream cheese, margarine or butter for spread and add pickle, nuts or hard-cooked egg yolk. Not recommended: vegetables such as lettuce, tomato, celery or cucumber (they lose their crunchy texture); mayonnaise and salad dressing (they separate); cooked egg white (it becomes tough and rubbery).	Thaw wrapped sandwich at room temperature about 3 hours.	Less than 1 month

**See also microwave thawing directions accompanying your microwave oven.*

HOW TO FREEZE PREPARED FOODS (continued)

FOOD	BEFORE FREEZING	BEFORE USING*	STORAGE TIME AT 0°F. OR BELOW
Meal Accompaniments			
Vegetables	For freezing fresh vegetables, see page 454. Other vegetables that freeze well include: stuffed baked potatoes, baked potatoes to freeze and use later in potato salad or au gratin potatoes, mashed potatoes, cooked sweet potatoes and squash, chopped chives, parsley, onion and green pepper freeze well for use in cooking. Not recommended: uncooked potatoes (they turn mushy), lettuce, tomato, celery, radishes, cucumber or other fresh vegetables that will be eaten raw.	*Stuffed baked potato:* leave wrapped and heat at 350°F. for 1 hour, unwrapping during last half hour. *Baked potato:* thaw at room temperature or slice or chop frozen potato and use. *Mashed potato, sweet potatoes, or cooked squash:* cover and heat in shallow container at 350°F. for about 45 minutes.	Cooked vegetables 3 months Fresh vegetables 12 to 18 months except onions 3 to 6 months
Baked Beans	Cool and package.	Heat in covered casserole at 350°F. about 45 to 60 minutes.	6 months
Salads	Most salads are not recommended because mayonnaise and salad dressing separate and crisp vegetables become soft during freezing.		
Stuffings	Cool, package and freeze.	Thaw and heat in foil or covered casserole at 350°F. about 30 to 45 minutes.	2 months
Biscuits, Muffins and Popovers	Bake as usual, remove from pan and cool completely. Package.	To thaw and heat, place on cookie sheet and heat at 400°F. about 10 minutes.	2-3 months
Nut Breads	Bake as usual, remove from pan and cool completely. Package.	Thaw in original wrappings in refrigerator about 12 hours or at room temperature about 4 hours.	2-3 months
Doughnuts, Cinnamon Rolls and Coffeecake	Fry or bake as usual, remove from pan; cool completely. Frost or glaze after thawing since frosting may crack and fall off during freezing.	Thaw and heat uncovered, on cookie sheet at 350°F. about 15 minutes.	2 months

**See also microwave thawing directions accompanying your microwave oven.*

HOW TO FREEZE PREPARED FOODS (continued)

FOOD	BEFORE FREEZING	BEFORE USING*	STORAGE TIME AT 0°F. OR BELOW
Yeast Breads	Bake as usual, remove from pan and cool completely. (For bakery bread, place in airtight wrap).	Thaw in original wrapping at room temperature 2 to 3 hours.	9 to 12 months
Yeast Rolls	Bake as usual, remove from pan and cool completely. For Brown 'N Serve Rolls, see page 70.	Thaw wrapped in foil, at 375°F. about 20 minutes. For crisp crust, open foil during last 5 minutes.	9 to 12 months
Pancakes, Waffles, Crêpes and French Toast	Prepare as usual, cool on rack and package.	Thaw and heat waffles and French Toast in toaster. Thaw and heat pancakes and French Toast uncovered, at 350°F. about 15 minutes. Thaw and heat crêpes covered, at 350°F. about 20 minutes.	2 months
Desserts			
Cakes and Cupcakes, Gingerbread and Shortcakes	Most cakes freeze well—unfrosted cakes freeze a little better than frosted cakes. *Unfrosted:* Bake as usual. Cool, remove from pan if desired. Wrap and freeze.	*Unfrosted:* thaw wrapped, at room temperature, 1-2 hours or in 350°F. oven 10 to 15 minutes.	Unfrosted—4 to 6 months
	Frosted: Frost and freeze unwrapped until frosting is firm so it won't stick to wrapping. Wrap and freeze. Not recommended: 7-minute type frostings or cream fillings because they separate and will make cake soggy.	*Frosted:* thaw by removing wrapping and covering with cake cover.	Frosted—2 to 3 months Gingerbread—1 month Shortcakes—2 to 3 months
Angel and Sponge Cakes	Bake as usual, cool. Best left in pan or place in rigid container to avoid crushing. Wrap and freeze. If frosted, freeze before wrapping. Cakes can be filled or frosted with whipped cream or whipped topping before freezing.	*Unfrosted:* thaw wrapped, at room temperature 2 to 3 hours. *Frosted:* thaw by removing wrapping and covering with cake cover.	2 months With whipped cream or topping—1 month
Cookies	Most cookies freeze well. Bake as usual and cool. Package, using rigid containers if cookies tend to crumble. *Unbaked:* some doughs can be formed into rolls and frozen for slicing and baking later. See cookie chapter for recipes.	Thaw wrapped, at room temperature 1 to 2 hours.	9 to 12 months
Candy	Most candies freeze well. Prepare and allow to set. Package and freeze.	Thaw wrapped, at room temperature 1 to 2 hours.	12 months

**See also microwave thawing directions accompanying your microwave oven.*

HOW TO FREEZE PREPARED FOODS (continued)

FOOD	BEFORE FREEZING	BEFORE USING*	STORAGE TIME AT 0°F. OR BELOW
Pies	*Baked:* bake as usual, cool and package. Recommended: fruit, pumpkin, pecan and cheesecake pies.	*Baked:* Thaw wrapped, at room temperature. Open and heat at 350°F. for 20 minutes. Or, thaw and heat unwrapped, at 325°F. about 45 minutes.	Baked – 4 to 6 months
	Unbaked: prepare as usual, except wait to slit top crust until just before baking to avoid drying filling during freezing. Using tapioca as thickener allows less crust soakage than cornstarch. Recommended: fruit and pumpkin pies.	*Unbaked:* unwrap, slit crust and bake at 425°F. for 15 minutes, then at 375°F. for 30 to 40 minutes or until bubbly in center.	Unbaked – 2 to 3 months
	Chiffon Pies: Prepare as usual and refrigerate to set. Freeze, then wrap. Not recommended: cream-type fillings because they separate; meringue topped pies because they get watery.	Unwrap and thaw in refrigerator 2 to 3 hours.	1 month
Pies Shells	*Baked:* Leave in pan or remove, cool and wrap carefully. Cookie crumb crusts also freeze well but must be left in pan.	*Bakes:* fill without thawing.	2 months
	Unbaked: Fit crust into pan, wrap and freeze.	*Unbaked:* If baking with filling, fill without thawing and bake. For a baked pastry shell, prick frozen unbaked pie shell and bake as for normal pastry shell.	2 months
Cheesecake	Bake as usual and cool. Wrap.	Thaw wrapped, in refrigerator 6 to 8 hours.	4 to 5 months
Cream Puffs	Bake, cool and package or freeze mounds of dough and package.	Crisp and thaw by unwrapping and placing on cookie sheet. Heat at 400°F. 15 minutes.	Baked – 3 months
		For unbaked batter, thaw on cookie sheet; bake as usual.	Unbaked – 1 month
Crisps and Cobblers	Most fruit crisps and cobblers freeze well after baking and cooling.	Thaw and heat uncovered at 350°F. about 45 minutes.	2 to 3 months

**See also microwave thawing directions accompanying your microwave oven.*

FREEZER STRAWBERRY JAM

2 cups (1 quart) strawberries
4 cups sugar
1 cup water
1 pkg. (1¾ oz.) powdered fruit pectin

Crush strawberries or process in blender until in small pieces. Measure into large bowl. Stir in sugar; let stand 10 minutes. In small saucepan, combine water and pectin. Heat to boiling and boil 1 minute, stirring constantly. Stir into fruit mixture and continue stirring 3 minutes to dissolve most of sugar. Ladle into freezer glasses or containers leaving ½-inch at top; cover with lids. Let stand until set, about 24 hours. Store in freezer up to 1 year or in refrigerator 2 to 3 weeks.

5 (1 cup) glasses

NUTRITION INFORMATION PER SERVING

Serving Size: 1 tablespoon		Percent U.S. RDA Per Serving	
Calories	44	Protein	*
Protein	<1g	Vitamin A	*
Carbohydrate	11g	Vitamin C	5%
Fat	<1g	Thiamin	*
Sodium	<1mg	Riboflavin	*
Potassium	14mg	Niacin	*
		Calcium	*
		Iron	*

FREEZER GRAPE JELLY

6½ cups sugar
2½ cups water
6-oz. bottle liquid fruit pectin
3 cans (6 oz. each) frozen grape juice concentrate, thawed

In large saucepan, combine sugar and water. Heat to boiling and boil 1 minute, stirring occasionally. Remove from heat; stir in pectin and grape juice. Ladle into glasses leaving ½-inch at top. Cover and let stand until set, about 12 hours. Cover tightly and store in freezer up to 1 year or in refrigerator 2 to 3 weeks.

9 (1 cup) glasses

NUTRITION INFORMATION PER SERVING

Serving Size: 1 tablespoon		Percent U.S. RDA Per Serving	
Calories	43	Protein	*
Protein	<1g	Vitamin A	*
Carbohydrate	11g	Vitamin C	*
Fat	0g	Thiamin	*
Sodium	<1mg	Riboflavin	*
Potassium	6mg	Niacin	*
		Calcium	*
		Iron	*

COOKING FROZEN VEGETABLES

Because most vegetables have been partially cooked in the blanching process prior to freezing, the cooking time will be less than required for fresh vegetables. Cook frozen vegetables in a small amount of salted water. Defrosting is unnecessary before cooking except for corn on the cob which should be partially defrosted before cooking.

The following guide is to help you determine cooking times for frozen vegetables. Water should be boiling when vegetables are added, then water needs to return to a boil before you start timing.

Frozen Vegetable	Approximate Cooking Time
Asparagus	6 to 10 min.
Beans, Green or Wax	8 to 12 min.
Beans, Lima (small)	8 to 10 min.
(large)	12 to 15 min.
Broccoli	5 to 8 min.
Brussels Sprouts	4 to 8 min.
Carrots	7 to 10 min.
Corn on the Cob (partially thawed)	5 to 8 min.
Corn, Whole Kernel	4 to 6 min.
Peas, Green	5 to 8 min.
Spinach	4 to 6 min.
Swiss Chard	7 to 10 min.
Squash and Pumpkin	Were cooked before freezing so need only to be heated to serving temperature.

TIPS: *Frozen vegetables may also be cooked in a microwave, see directions accompanying your microwave oven.*

A pressure saucepan may be used for cooking frozen vegetables, see directions from manufacturer. Watch timing to prevent overcooking of vegetables.

SALADS & DRESSINGS

SALADS & DRESSINGS

ABOUT TOSSED SALADS

SERVING

Crisp, chilled greens are the first commandment in the art of salad making. They add variety in color and flavor, as well as texture. If using a combination of vegetables with the greens, you may wish to choose one kind of lettuce to complement your other ingredients. If using only greens in the salad, you may wish to use a combination of greens for contrasting flavor, texture and color.

PREPARATION

The easiest way to loosen lettuce leaves on a head of lettuce is to cut out the core and place head, cut-side up, under a stream of cold water, removing lettuce leaves.

Wash the greens carefully in cold water, discarding wilted outer leaves. Dry thoroughly (placing on paper towels will help) and store in refrigerator. Salad greens may be stored unwrapped in the crisper for a few days or in a tightly sealed plastic container or bag on the lower shelves of the refrigerator for longer periods of time.

To avoid discoloration of lettuce, tear rather than cut the leaves into bite-size pieces.

Be sure to keep greens well chilled right up to serving time, however, do not freeze or they will become soggy and translucent.

To give your salad a subtle garlic flavor simply rub the inside of your salad bowl with a cut clove of garlic.

Add nuts, croutons or other foods which become soggy just before serving to keep them crisp.

The reason for "tossing" a salad is to coat the greens and vegetables with the salad dressing. Tossing means to lightly stir so that the greens are not bruised.

An easy way to toss a large salad is to put all ingredients into a large plastic bag, add the dressing and tightly close the bag. Shake to mix thoroughly. Pour mixture into the desired serving dish.

Crispness and color may be added to vegetable salads with celery, green onions, fresh spinach leaves, parsley, fresh chives, mustard greens or shredded red cabbage.

VARIETIES OF LETTUCE

Iceberg or Head: The most commonly used variety; available almost anywhere year round. It has a rather watery taste and very crisp leaves.

Bibb: Has a rather sweet flavor, velvety texture and very small, pliable dark leaves.

Boston or Butter: Resembles Bibb lettuce in flavor and texture but usually larger leaves.

Romaine: Has a strong green flavor, fiberous texture and deep green straight leaves.

Leaf (green or red)**:** Delicate in flavor with crisp, ruffly leaf edges. There is no flavor difference between the red and green varieties.

Escarole: Has a bitter flavor, rough in texture with broad curling leaves.

Curly Endive or Chicory: A bitter flavor with wiry, feathered leaves.

Watercress: Slightly bitter flavor with extremely fragile small leaves. Makes a nice garnish.

TOSSED SALAD

4 cups assorted salad greens, torn into bite-size pieces*
3 medium tomatoes, cut into wedges
1 medium cucumber, sliced
½ teaspoon salt
Dash pepper
½ cup prepared French or other favorite dressing

Chill salad greens. In salad bowl, combine all ingredients; toss lightly. Serve immediately.

5 to 6 servings

NUTRITION INFORMATION PER SERVING

Serving Size: 1/5 of recipe		Percent U.S. RDA Per Serving	
Calories	135	Protein	3%
Protein	2g	Vitamin A	22%
Carbohydrate	11g	Vitamin C	48%
Fat	10g	Thiamin	6%
Sodium	569mg	Riboflavin	5%
Potassium	408mg	Niacin	4%
		Calcium	4%
		Iron	7%

TIPS: **Any type of salad greens may be used such as:*

Boston lettuce
Bibb lettuce
Iceberg lettuce
Bronze lettuce
Curly endive
Romaine
Escarole
Spinach
Watercress

Vegetable additions to tossed salad:

Fresh Vegetables
Sliced zucchini squash
Cauliflowerets
Bean sprouts
Mushrooms
Shredded or thinly sliced carrots
Sliced green peppers
Sliced radishes
Thinly sliced onions
Sliced celery

Cooked Vegetables
French fried onion rings
Bamboo shoots
Water chestnuts
Julienne beets
Artichoke hearts
Green beans
Garbanzo beans
Pimiento or sliced olives

Fruit additions to tossed salad:

Thinly sliced avocado
Mandarin oranges
Grapefruit segments
Green grapes
Pomegranate seeds
Sliced unpeeled apples

Protein additions to tossed salad:

Cubed or shredded cheese
Anchovy fillets
Slices or wedges of hard-cooked eggs
Drained seafood
Salami
Summer sausage
Pickled herring

CAESAR SALAD

1 garlic clove, cut into quarters
⅓ cup oil
½ teaspoon salt
⅛ teaspoon pepper
2 qt. romaine lettuce, torn into bite-sized pieces
1 egg
2 tablespoons lemon juice
1 cup seasoned croutons
¼ cup Parmesan cheese
6 anchovy fillets, if desired

In small bowl, marinate garlic in oil 30 minutes; stir in salt and pepper. Place romaine in salad bowl. Remove garlic pieces from oil; discard garlic. Pour oil over romaine; toss lightly. Break egg over salad; add lemon juice and toss again. Add croutons and cheese. Garnish with anchovies. Serve immediately.

4 to 6 servings

NUTRITION INFORMATION PER SERVING

Serving Size: 1/6 of recipe		Percent U.S. RDA Per Serving	
Calories	191	Protein	8%
Protein	5g	Vitamin A	31%
Carbohydrate	7g	Vitamin C	26%
Fat	16g	Thiamin	3%
Sodium	320mg	Riboflavin	7%
Potassium	222mg	Niacin	*
		Calcium	11%
		Iron	7%

SPINACH AND MUSHROOM SALAD

¾ teaspoon salt
¼ teaspoon sugar
⅛ teaspoon dry mustard
⅛ teaspoon freshly ground pepper
½ to 1 garlic clove, finely minced
4 to 5 tablespoons olive oil
2 tablespoons lemon juice
1 egg yolk
10 to 12-oz. pkg. fresh spinach, torn into bite-size pieces
6 strips bacon, diced, fried and drained
¾ cup sliced mushrooms
2 green onions, sliced

In small bowl, combine the first 8 ingredients. Mix well and chill about 3 hours. In large bowl, toss spinach, bacon, mushrooms and onions. Pour dressing over salad; toss. 8 servings

NUTRITION INFORMATION PER SERVING

Serving Size: 1/8 of recipe		Percent U.S. RDA Per Serving	
Calories	116	Protein	5%
Protein	3g	Vitamin A	59%
Carbohydrate	3g	Vitamin C	35%
Fat	10g	Thiamin	5%
Sodium	284mg	Riboflavin	8%
Potassium	225mg	Niacin	4%
		Calcium	4%
		Iron	8%

Garnish your tossed salad with garlic or onion croutons.

CROUTONS

Heat oven to 350°F. Remove crusts from slices of day-old bread; cut into cubes. Place in single layer in shallow baking pan. Bake at 350°F. for 10 to 15 minutes or until brown and crisp. Croutons may be prepared in skillet; toss bread cubes in melted margarine or butter over low heat until lightly browned and crisp. Add dash of garlic or onion powder to melted margarine for garlic or onion croutons.

WILTED LETTUCE SALAD

5 slices bacon
1 head lettuce, torn into bite-size pieces
2 green onions, sliced
1 tablespoon sugar
½ teaspoon salt
¼ teaspoon dry mustard, if desired
¼ teaspoon pepper
¼ cup cider vinegar
2 tablespoons water

Fry bacon until crisp; drain on paper towel and crumble. Reserve 2 tablespoons drippings. In large salad bowl, combine lettuce and onions. Combine reserved bacon drippings with remaining ingredients; heat just to boiling. Pour over lettuce; toss lightly. Garnish with crumbled bacon; serve immediately. 8 servings

NUTRITION INFORMATION PER SERVING

Serving Size: 1/8 of recipe		Percent U.S. RDA Per Serving	
Calories	47	Protein	3%
Protein	2g	Vitamin A	5%
Carbohydrate	5g	Vitamin C	9%
Fat	3g	Thiamin	5%
Sodium	190mg	Riboflavin	4%
Potassium	152mg	Niacin	2%
		Calcium	*
		Iron	3%

TIPS: *For WILTED SPINACH SALAD, substitute spinach for part or all of lettuce.*

Crumbled blue cheese, sliced hard-cooked egg, chopped tomato, sliced radishes or sliced fresh mushrooms may be sprinkled over salad before serving.

LAYERED MIXED VEGETABLE SALAD

1 head lettuce, torn into bite-size pieces
½ cup chopped green or red onion
½ cup (1 stalk) chopped celery
½ cup (1 small) chopped green pepper
10-oz. pkg. (1½ cups) frozen peas, thawed and drained
1 cup mayonnaise or salad dressing
2 tablespoons sugar
2 cups (8 oz.) shredded Cheddar cheese
10 slices bacon, fried, drained and crumbled or ½ cup imitation bacon bits
8-oz. can (⅔ cup) water chestnuts, drained and sliced

In large bowl or 13x9-inch pan, layer lettuce and onion. Spoon ½ cup mayonnaise evenly over top. Layer celery, green pepper and peas; spread remaining mayonnaise over top. Sprinkle sugar, cheese and bacon over top. Cover and refrigerate at least 8 hours. Add water chestnuts. Toss before serving.

10 to 12 servings

NUTRITION INFORMATION PER SERVING

Serving Size: 1/12 of recipe		Percent U.S. RDA Per Serving	
Calories	276	Protein	12%
Protein	8g	Vitamin A	11%
Carbohydrate	8g	Vitamin C	25%
Fat	24g	Thiamin	8%
Sodium	333mg	Riboflavin	10%
Potassium	187mg	Niacin	4%
		Calcium	16%
		Iron	6%

TIP: *Grated Romano or Parmesan cheese may be substituted for Cheddar cheese.*

LAYERED MIXED VEGETABLE SALAD

VEGETABLE SALAD TIPS

Celery, carrots and radishes can be sliced or chopped ahead of time. Place in ice water and store in the refrigerator until ready to use.

Parsley makes a lovely addition or nice garnish on almost any salad. To get parsley to look its freshest wash and shake off excess water. Place in tightly covered jar (without additional water) and store in refrigerator overnight.

To prepare potatoes for potato salad, boil potatoes in their jackets in salted water until tender. Drain and let dry slightly. Peel potatoes while still very warm by holding on fork or in paper toweling.

If at all possible use hot potatoes when preparing potato salad. During chilling, hot potatoes will absorb the flavors better than cold potatoes.

MARINATED ARTICHOKE HEARTS

9-oz. pkg. (1 cup) frozen artichoke hearts
1 small onion, sliced
1 cup prepared Italian dressing
2 tablespoons water
Salad greens

In medium saucepan, combine all ingredients except greens. Cook as directed on package; cool. Cover and chill. Before serving, add to greens for tossed salad. 4 servings

NUTRITION INFORMATION PER SERVING

Serving Size: 1/4 of recipe		Percent U.S. RDA Per Serving	
Calories	354	Protein	4%
Protein	2g	Vitamin A	6%
Carbohydrate	11g	Vitamin C	12%
Fat	35g	Thiamin	6%
Sodium	1266mg	Riboflavin	8%
Potassium	138mg	Niacin	4%
		Calcium	2%
		Iron	3%

TIP: *Marinated artichoke hearts may be kept in refrigerator several weeks.*

For maximum flavor blend–allow to refrigerate overnight.

TRIPLE BEAN SALAD

½ cup sugar
1 medium onion, thinly sliced
¼ cup chopped green pepper
1 teaspoon celery seed or celery salt
½ teaspoon salt
¼ teaspoon pepper
½ cup vinegar
¼ cup oil
1 tablespoon soy sauce, if desired
3 cans (16 oz. each) beans*, drained

In large bowl, combine all ingredients; mix well. Cover and refrigerate several hours.

8 to 10 servings

NUTRITION INFORMATION PER SERVING

Serving Size: 1/10 of recipe		Percent U.S. RDA Per Serving	
Calories	133	Protein	4%
Protein	3g	Vitamin A	3%
Carbohydrate	19g	Vitamin C	15%
Fat	6g	Thiamin	2%
Sodium	367mg	Riboflavin	3%
Potassium	172mg	Niacin	*
		Calcium	4%
		Iron	9%

TIP: **Cooked green, yellow, red kidney, garbanzo, lima or soy beans may be used.*

CARROT-RAISIN SALAD

½ cup raisins
2 cups (4 medium) shredded carrots
⅓ cup mayonnaise or salad dressing

In serving bowl, combine all ingredients; mix well. Cover and chill.
4 to 6 servings

NUTRITION INFORMATION PER SERVING

Serving Size: 1/4 of recipe		Percent U.S. RDA Per Serving	
Calories	203	Protein	*
Protein	1g	Vitamin A	122%
Carbohydrate	20g	Vitamin C	8%
Fat	14g	Thiamin	4%
Sodium	137mg	Riboflavin	3%
Potassium	332mg	Niacin	2%
		Calcium	3%
		Iron	6%

TIP: *Dairy sour cream or yogurt may be substituted for mayonnaise; add 1 tablespoon honey or sugar.*

An easy salad to bring to the Fourth of July wiener roast—nicely complements sausage of any kind.

KRAUT SALAD

8-oz. can (1 cup) sauerkraut, drained
⅓ cup sugar
½ cup finely chopped green pepper
1 small onion, finely chopped, or 6 green onions, sliced
1 tablespoon chopped pimiento, drained
Radishes, if desired

In medium bowl, combine all ingredients except radishes; mix well. Cover and chill. Garnish with radishes. 4 servings

NUTRITION INFORMATION PER SERVING

Serving Size: 1/4 of recipe		Percent U.S. RDA Per Serving	
Calories	84	Protein	*
Protein	<1g	Vitamin A	2%
Carbohydrate	21g	Vitamin C	52%
Fat	<1g	Thiamin	2%
Sodium	268mg	Riboflavin	2%
Potassium	123mg	Niacin	*
		Calcium	2%
		Iron	3%

MUSHROOM SALAD

2 cups water
2 tablespoons lemon juice
16-oz. (6 cups) sliced mushrooms
2 tablespoons sliced green onions or finely chopped onion
½ teaspoon salt
½ teaspoon grated lemon peel
¼ teaspoon sugar
⅛ teaspoon pepper
½ cup cream or evaporated milk
Lettuce leaves

In large saucepan, heat water and lemon juice to boiling; add mushrooms. Reduce heat; simmer covered, 2 to 3 minutes; drain. In medium bowl, combine remaining ingredients except lettuce leaves. Add mushrooms; toss lightly. Cover and refrigerate at least 3 hours. Serve on lettuce leaves.
4 to 5 servings

NUTRITION INFORMATION PER SERVING

Serving Size: 1/4 of recipe		Percent U.S. RDA Per Serving	
Calories	90	Protein	5%
Protein	3g	Vitamin A	6%
Carbohydrate	6g	Vitamin C	14%
Fat	6g	Thiamin	6%
Sodium	297mg	Riboflavin	22%
Potassium	379mg	Niacin	15%
		Calcium	4%
		Iron	4%

TIPS: *Mushrooms may be refrigerated in dressing several days. Leftover dressing may be used on salad greens.*

Two cans (8 oz. each) mushrooms, drained, may be substituted for fresh mushrooms. Omit mushroom cooking step.

TARRAGON-MARINATED VEGETABLES

- **2 cups vegetables, cooked and drained**
- **¼ teaspoon tarragon leaves**
- **¼ cup oil**
- **¼ cup vinegar**
- **Salad greens**

Combine vegetables, tarragon, oil and vinegar. Chill several hours. Add to salad greens or serve on lettuce leaves. 4 servings

NUTRITION INFORMATION PER SERVING

Serving Size: 1/4 of recipe		Percent U.S. RDA Per Serving	
Calories	148	Protein	3%
Protein	2g	Vitamin A	31%
Carbohydrate	6g	Vitamin C	55%
Fat	14g	Thiamin	6%
Sodium	9mg	Riboflavin	5%
Potassium	215mg	Niacin	4%
		Calcium	3%
		Iron	4%

TIP: *Vegetables that may be used for salad: beans, carrots, peas, brussels sprouts, celery root, kohlrabi or artichoke hearts.*

PENNSYLVANIA HOT SLAW

- **2 slices bacon**
- **1 tablespoon firmly packed brown sugar**
- **1 tablespoon chopped green onion or chopped chives**
- **1½ teaspoons salt**
- **¼ cup vinegar**
- **3 cups (½ medium head) shredded cabbage**
- **5 to 6 radishes, thinly sliced**
- **1 small stalk celery, thinly sliced**

Fry bacon until crisp; drain on paper towel and crumble. Reserve 1 tablespoon drippings. To reserved drippings, add brown sugar, green onion, salt and vinegar; stir until smooth. Add crumbled bacon and remaining ingredients; toss lightly. Heat through. 4 servings

NUTRITION INFORMATION PER SERVING

Serving Size: 1/4 of recipe		Percent U.S. RDA Per Serving	
Calories	53	Protein	3%
Protein	2g	Vitamin A	2%
Carbohydrate	8g	Vitamin C	45%
Fat	2g	Thiamin	3%
Sodium	859mg	Riboflavin	3%
Potassium	192mg	Niacin	*
		Calcium	4%
		Iron	3%

POTATO SALAD

- **3 to 4 medium potatoes, cooked, peeled and cubed**
- **3 hard-cooked eggs, chopped**
- **1 small onion, chopped or 6 green onions, chopped**
- **2 stalks celery, chopped**
- **¼ cup chopped pickle or pickle relish**
- **1 teaspoon salt**
- **⅛ teaspoon pepper**
- **¾ cup mayonnaise or salad dressing**
- **1 tablespoon prepared mustard**

In large bowl, combine all ingredients; mix well. Cover and chill. 4 to 6 servings

NUTRITION INFORMATION PER SERVING

Serving Size: 1/4 of recipe		Percent U.S. RDA Per Serving	
Calories	482	Protein	14%
Protein	9g	Vitamin A	13%
Carbohydrate	28g	Vitamin C	39%
Fat	38g	Thiamin	11%
Sodium	908mg	Riboflavin	12%
Potassium	647mg	Niacin	9%
		Calcium	6%
		Iron	12%

TIPS: *For MARINATED POTATO SALAD, toss warm potato slices, onion, pickle, salt and pepper with ¼ cup French dressing. Cover and refrigerate several hours. Before serving, mix in eggs, celery and ½ cup mayonnaise; omit mustard.*

Other additions to potato salad: cooked cubed beef; 1 to 2 tablespoons chopped green pepper or chives; 4 to 5 sliced radishes; 1 tomato, cut into wedges; chopped cucumber or zucchini squash; ½ cup cottage cheese; ¼ cup sliced olives; ¼ teaspoon curry powder or dill weed.

GERMAN POTATO SALAD

4 medium potatoes, cooked and peeled warm
4 slices bacon
6 green onions, sliced or 1 small onion, chopped
2 tablespoons sugar
1 tablespoon flour
1 teaspoon salt
1 teaspoon or 1 cube beef bouillon
¼ teaspoon celery seed
¼ teaspoon allspice, if desired
Dash pepper
½ cup water
¼ cup vinegar

Fry bacon until crisp; drain on paper towel and crumble. Reserve 3 tablespoons drippings. Cook onion in reserved bacon drippings until tender. Add sugar, flour, salt, bouillon, celery seed, allspice and pepper; stir until smooth. Stir in water and vinegar; heat until bubbly. Slice warm potatoes and add to sauce mixture with crumbled bacon. Stir gently; heat through.

4 to 5 servings

NUTRITION INFORMATION PER SERVING

Serving Size: 1/4 of recipe		Percent U.S. RDA Per Serving	
Calories	205	Protein	9%
Protein	6g	Vitamin A	*
Carbohydrate	37g	Vitamin C	49%
Fat	4g	Thiamin	13%
Sodium	736mg	Riboflavin	6%
Potassium	701mg	Niacin	14%
		Calcium	3%
		Iron	8%

STUFFED TOMATOES

Remove stem and core of tomato. Hollow out inside (save pulp to add to other salads or cut up and add to mixture that will be used to stuff tomato). Fill with: corn relish, seafood or chicken salad, marinated cooked vegetables, coleslaw, cottage cheese, cucumbers in sour cream or rice salad. Garnish with chives, crumbled bacon, shredded or crumbled cheese or chopped parsley.

CRUNCHY CABBAGE SALAD

4 cups shredded Chinese cabbage
8-oz. can (⅔ cup) water chestnuts, drained and sliced
½ cup fresh sliced mushrooms or 4-oz can (½ cup) mushrooms, drained
1 tablespoon chopped onion
½ cup mayonnaise or salad dressing
1 to 2 tablespoons soy sauce
¾ cup chow mein noodles

In large bowl, combine first 4 ingredients. Combine mayonnaise and soy sauce; pour over cabbage mixture. Toss lightly. Before serving, add chow mein noodles; toss lightly. If desired, garnish with toasted almonds.

6 servings

NUTRITION INFORMATION PER SERVING

Serving Size: 1/6 of recipe		Percent U.S. RDA Per Serving	
Calories	180	Protein	3%
Protein	2g	Vitamin A	3%
Carbohydrate	8g	Vitamin C	27%
Fat	16g	Thiamin	3%
Sodium	346mg	Riboflavin	4%
Potassium	219mg	Niacin	3%
		Calcium	3%
		Iron	4%

TIP: *Leftover cooked cubed pork or chicken makes a tasty addition to this salad.*

CRISP OVERNIGHT SLAW

⅓ cup sugar
½ teaspoon garlic salt
¼ teaspoon celery seed
3 tablespoons vinegar
3 tablespoons lemon juice
3 cups (½ medium head) shredded cabbage
¼ cup chopped green pepper
1 stalk celery, chopped
3 to 4 green onions, sliced
5 to 6 radishes, sliced

In large bowl, combine first 5 ingredients. Add remaining ingredients except radishes; toss lightly. Cover and refrigerate at least 4 hours. Before serving, add radishes.

5 to 6 servings

NUTRITION INFORMATION PER SERVING

Serving Size: 1/5 of recipe		Percent U.S. RDA Per Serving	
Calories	74	Protein	*
Protein	<1g	Vitamin A	2%
Carbohydrate	19g	Vitamin C	63%
Fat	<1g	Thiamin	3%
Sodium	206mg	Riboflavin	2%
Potassium	202mg	Niacin	*
		Calcium	3%
		Iron	3%

TIP: *If desired, chopped cucumber, zucchini, or halved cherry tomatoes may be added with cabbage.*

SOUR CREAM COLESLAW

1 small head cabbage, shredded or thinly sliced
2 tablespoons sugar
2 tablespoons chopped onion
½ teaspoon salt
½ cup dairy sour cream
1 teaspoon lemon juice

In large bowl, combine all ingredients; toss lightly. 6 servings

NUTRITION INFORMATION PER SERVING

Serving Size: 1/6 of recipe		Percent U.S. RDA Per Serving	
Calories	73	Protein	2%
Protein	2g	Vitamin A	5%
Carbohydrate	9g	Vitamin C	60%
Fat	4g	Thiamin	3%
Sodium	204mg	Riboflavin	4%
Potassium	183mg	Niacin	*
		Calcium	6%
		Iron	*

TIPS: *For extra crispy coleslaw, chill shredded cabbage in ice water for 1 hour. Drain and combine with remaining ingredients.*

For COCONUTTY SLAW, add ¼ cup chopped cucumber and ¼ cup flaked coconut to cabbage mixture; omit onion.

For FRUIT SLAW, add 2 cups miniature marshmallows, 1 small stalk celery, chopped and a 15¼-oz. can (2 cups) drained crushed pineapple to cabbage mixture; omit onion. Drained maraschino cherries may be used as a garnish. 8 servings

For APPLE SLAW, add 1 large cubed apple, 1 teaspoon grated orange peel, ⅛ teaspoon cinnamon and ⅛ teaspoon cloves to cabbage mixture; omit onion.

For SEAFOOD SLAW, add ½ cup cooked crab meat, shrimp or lobster.

SWEET AND SOUR COLESLAW

6 cups (1 medium head) shredded cabbage
1 teaspoon salt
1½ cups (3 medium stalks) chopped celery
½ cup (1 small) chopped green pepper
1¼ cups sugar
1 teaspoon celery seed
1 teaspoon mustard seed
1 cup white vinegar
½ cup water

In large bowl, sprinkle salt over cabbage; let stand 1 hour. Squeeze out liquid. Add celery and green pepper. In medium saucepan, combine remaining ingredients, boil 1 minute. Cool and pour over cabbage. Cover and refrigerate several hours. May be refrigerated up to 2 weeks. 12 servings

NUTRITION INFORMATION PER SERVING

Serving Size: 1/12 of recipe		Percent U.S. RDA Per Serving	
Calories	97	Protein	*
Protein	<1g	Vitamin A	2%
Carbohydrate	25g	Vitamin C	42%
Fat	<1g	Thiamin	*
Sodium	205mg	Riboflavin	*
Potassium	151mg	Niacin	*
		Calcium	3%
		Iron	*

TIP: *May be frozen in 9-inch square pan or in individual serving portions. Thaw at room temperature about 2 hours before serving, cutting through occasionally with a knife. Serve slightly frosty.*

CUCUMBERS IN VINEGAR AND OIL

1 cucumber, thinly sliced
1 small onion, thinly sliced
1 to 2 tablespoons sugar
½ teaspoon salt
Dash pepper
½ cup vinegar
¼ cup oil
Salad greens

In small bowl, combine all ingredients. Cover and refrigerate several hours. Drain and serve on lettuce leaves or toss with green salad, using oil and vinegar mixture as dressing. 3 to 4 servings

NUTRITION INFORMATION PER SERVING

Serving Size: 1/4 of recipe		Percent U.S. RDA Per Serving	
Calories	156	Protein	*
Protein	1g	Vitamin A	4%
Carbohydrate	9g	Vitamin C	17%
Fat	14g	Thiamin	*
Sodium	278mg	Riboflavin	2%
Potassium	184mg	Niacin	*
		Calcium	3%
		Iron	6%

CUCUMBERS IN SOUR CREAM

2 medium cucumbers, thinly sliced
½ teaspoon salt
1 tablespoon sugar
¼ teaspoon dill weed, if desired
Dash pepper
½ cup dairy sour cream
1 tablespoon vinegar

In medium bowl, sprinkle salt over cucumbers. Let stand 20 minutes; drain. Add remaining ingredients; toss lightly. Cover and chill. 3 to 4 servings

NUTRITION INFORMATION PER SERVING

Serving Size: 1/4 of recipe		Percent U.S. RDA Per Serving	
Calories	84	Protein	3%
Protein	2g	Vitamin A	9%
Carbohydrate	8g	Vitamin C	18%
Fat	6g	Thiamin	3%
Sodium	289mg	Riboflavin	5%
Potassium	161mg	Niacin	*
		Calcium	6%
		Iron	6%

FRUIT SALADS

Often fruit salads can double as light refreshing desserts. To keep fruit salads cool and refreshing serve on greens on chilled salad plates. Stack the plates and chill in refrigerator before assembling salad and serving.

Vary the fruit shapes with balls, spears, cubes and triangles.

An easy salad variation is to serve a platter of fruits using one of the fruit dressings as a dip.

To keep fruits from turning dark, dip fruit pieces in lemon or other citrus juice, or use a commercial fruit freshener; follow directions on package.

For more specific information about individual fruits see Chapter 8 FRUITS, DESSERTS, SAUCES AND PIES.

FRUIT SALAD-DRESSING COMBINATIONS

HONEY CELERY SEED DRESSING, page 498: Melon, pineapple and blueberries; pears, blueberries and apples; grapefruit, oranges, bananas and coconut; bananas, oranges and dates; peaches, bananas and cantaloupe; honeydew melon, blueberries and bananas.

WHIPPED CREAM DRESSING, page 503: Tangerines, apricots and cashews; bananas, pineapple and dates; plums, green grapes and apples; oranges, grapefruit and avocados; apples, celery and walnuts.

SOUR CREAM DRESSING, page 502: Apricots, oranges and dates; pineapple, bananas, coconut and raspberries; peaches, dark sweet cherries and pecans; watermelon, avocados, green grapes and peaches.

Bright red apples offer a colorful contrast to the cream cheese topping.

CINNAMON APPLE SALAD

4 apples, peeled and sliced
1 cup water
½ cup red cinnamon candies
Lettuce leaves
1 tablespoon lemon juice
3-oz. pkg. cream cheese, softened
2 tablespoons chopped walnuts

In saucepan, combine apples, water and cinnamon candies. Heat to boiling and cook uncovered, about 10 minutes or until apples are tender, stirring occasionally. Cool and chill. To serve, drain apple slices and arrange on lettuce. Combine lemon juice and cream cheese; beat until smooth. Spoon over apples; garnish with walnuts. 6 to 8 servings

NUTRITION INFORMATION PER SERVING

Serving Size: 1/6 of recipe		Percent U.S. RDA Per Serving	
Calories	157	Protein	3%
Protein	2g	Vitamin A	7%
Carbohydrate	22g	Vitamin C	7%
Fat	8g	Thiamin	4%
Sodium	48mg	Riboflavin	4%
Potassium	171mg	Niacin	*
		Calcium	2%
		Iron	3%

TIPS: *Leftover liquid may be reused with other apples or added to fruit punches or apple cider.*

TIPS: *Apples may also be halved with core and peel removed. Cook with ¾ cup cinnamon candies and 2 cups water. Add ½ stalk chopped celery and ¼ cup chopped dates to cream cheese.*

Pretty glazed melon balls with pears and pineapple are a refreshing treat.

MINTY MELON BOWL

2 cups honeydew melon balls
1 cup green grapes
8-oz. can (1 cup) pineapple chunks, drained
1 cup cubed fresh or canned pears
¼ cup apple-mint or mint jelly

In salad bowl, combine all ingredients except jelly. Melt jelly or stir with fork until soft; pour over fruit. Toss lightly. Cover and chill. If desired, garnish with fresh mint leaves. 6 servings

NUTRITION INFORMATION PER SERVING

Serving Size: 1/6 of recipe		Percent U.S. RDA Per Serving	
Calories	108	Protein	*
Protein	<1g	Vitamin A	*
Carbohydrate	28g	Vitamin C	29%
Fat	<1g	Thiamin	4%
Sodium	11mg	Riboflavin	3%
Potassium	261mg	Niacin	3%
		Calcium	*
		Iron	4%

CITRUS-AVOCADO SALAD

1 ripe avocado, peeled and sliced lengthwise
Lemon juice
Dash salt
1 orange or grapefruit, peeled and sectioned
Lettuce leaves

Sprinkle avocado slices with lemon juice and salt. On salad plates lined with lettuce leaves, alternate avocado slices and fruit sections. Serve with Sour Cream Dressing, page 502 or Honey Celery Seed Dressing, page 498. 2 servings

NUTRITION INFORMATION PER SERVING

Serving Size: 1/2 of recipe		Percent U.S. RDA Per Serving	
Calories	301	Protein	7%
Protein	4g	Vitamin A	14%
Carbohydrate	22g	Vitamin C	118%
Fat	25g	Thiamin	18%
Sodium	144mg	Riboflavin	21%
Potassium	1138mg	Niacin	14%
		Calcium	6%
		Iron	8%

CURRIED FRUIT COCKTAIL

1 medium avocado, peeled and sliced
1 medium apple, cubed
1 cup orange sections, halved
1 cup grapefruit sections, cut into thirds
15½-oz. can (2 cups) pineapple chunks, drained
½ cup dairy sour cream or yogurt*
½ teaspoon curry powder
¼ teaspoon salt

In bowl, combine fruit. In small bowl, blend remaining ingredients; serve over fruit. 4 to 6 servings

NUTRITION INFORMATION PER SERVING

Serving Size: 1/6 of recipe		Percent U.S. RDA Per Serving	
Calories	228	Protein	4%
Protein	2g	Vitamin A	9%
Carbohydrate	31g	Vitamin C	65%
Fat	12g	Thiamin	12%
Sodium	102mg	Riboflavin	10%
Potassium	516mg	Niacin	6%
		Calcium	5%
		Iron	5%

TIP: **When using yogurt, add ½ tablespoon honey or sugar.*

PINEAPPLE-PIMIENTO SALAD

8-oz. can (1 cup) crushed pineapple, drained
5-oz. jar Neufchatel cheese spread with pimiento
½ cup whipping cream, whipped
¼ cup mayonnaise or salad dressing
3 cups miniature marshmallows

In medium bowl, combine all ingredients; mix well. Pour into 8-inch square pan or serving bowl. Cover and refrigerate at least 3 hours. If desired, garnish with maraschino cherries. 6 to 9 servings

NUTRITION INFORMATION PER SERVING

Serving Size: 1/6 of recipe		Percent U.S. RDA Per Serving	
Calories	306	Protein	8%
Protein	5g	Vitamin A	11%
Carbohydrate	29g	Vitamin C	5%
Fat	20g	Thiamin	3%
Sodium	455mg	Riboflavin	9%
Potassium	116mg	Niacin	*
		Calcium	16%
		Iron	4%

WALDORF SALAD

¼ cup chopped nuts
¼ cup chopped dates
2 tablespoons sugar
4 medium apples, cored and cubed
1 stalk celery, chopped
⅔ cup mayonnaise or salad dressing
1 teaspoon lemon juice

In large bowl, combine all ingredients; mix well. Cover and chill. 6 servings

NUTRITION INFORMATION PER SERVING

Serving Size: 1/6 of recipe		Percent U.S. RDA Per Serving	
Calories	299	Protein	2%
Protein	1g	Vitamin A	3%
Carbohydrate	24g	Vitamin C	8%
Fat	23g	Thiamin	4%
Sodium	156mg	Riboflavin	3%
Potassium	204mg	Niacin	*
		Calcium	2%
		Iron	4%

TIPS: *Dairy sour cream or yogurt may be substituted for part of mayonnaise.*

Raisins may be substituted for dates.

This is the original "overnight fruit salad".

CUSTARD FRUIT SALAD

20-oz. can (2½ cups) pineapple chunks, well-drained (reserve syrup)
16-oz. can (2 cups) fruit cocktail, well-drained (reserve syrup)
1 cup reserved syrup
1 cup sugar
1 tablespoon margarine or butter
4 eggs
¼ cup cornstarch
10-oz. pkg. (6 cups) miniature marshmallows
1 cup (½ pint) whipping cream, whipped
11-oz. can (1 cup) mandarin oranges, well-drained
2 large bananas, sliced
½ cup whole or halved green grapes

In medium saucepan, heat reserved syrup, sugar and margarine to boiling. Beat eggs until foamy. Add cornstarch; mix well. Pour egg mixture into boiling juice, stirring constantly. Cook over medium heat until very thick; cool to lukewarm. Pour into large bowl; add marshmallows, pineapple and fruit cocktail. Mix well. Cover and refrigerate about 4 hours. Before serving, fold in whipped cream; stir in oranges, bananas and grapes.

10 to 12 servings

NUTRITION INFORMATION PER SERVING

Serving Size: 1/12 of recipe		Percent U.S. RDA Per Serving	
Calories	362	Protein	6%
Protein	4g	Vitamin A	14%
Carbohydrate	66g	Vitamin C	23%
Fat	11g	Thiamin	7%
Sodium	54mg	Riboflavin	7%
Potassium	310mg	Niacin	3%
		Calcium	5%
		Iron	8%

TIPS: *Half the recipe may be reserved for later use. Divide custard fruit mixture in half after chilling. Add half the whipped cream and fruit before serving. The remaining portion may be kept in refrigerator up to 2 days.*

Prepared, canned or frozen lemon pudding make an easy dressing for fruit. Omit cooked dressing; fold 1 cup pudding into fruit; chill. If desired, whipping cream, whipped may be added to fruit with pudding.

This is an easy version of the classic overnight salad—but without having to cook a custard base.

OVERNIGHT FRUIT SALAD

15½-oz. can (2 cups) pineapple chunks, drained (reserve syrup)
1¾ cups liquid (reserved syrup plus water)
3-oz. pkg. lemon-flavored gelatin
1 cup (½ pint) whipping cream, whipped or 1 pkg. dessert topping mix
4 cups miniature marshmallows
1¼ cups halved grapes
2 oranges, cut up or one 11-oz. can (1 cup) mandarin oranges, drained

In small saucepan, heat 1 cup of liquid to boiling. In large bowl, add boiling liquid to gelatin; stir to dissolve. Add remaining liquid; chill until thickened but not set. Fold in whipped cream. Add remaining ingredients; blend well. Cover and refrigerate several hours or overnight. Will keep for 2 days when dessert topping mix is used.

8 servings

NUTRITION INFORMATION PER SERVING

Serving Size: 1/8 of recipe		Percent U.S. RDA Per Serving	
Calories	292	Protein	4%
Protein	3g	Vitamin A	12%
Carbohydrate	48g	Vitamin C	36%
Fat	11g	Thiamin	6%
Sodium	54mg	Riboflavin	4%
Potassium	193mg	Niacin	*
		Calcium	5%
		Iron	4%

A fall favorite, sharp cheddar cheese and fresh oranges make a perfect flavor combination.

MOHAVE FRUIT SALAD

- 2 cups chopped apples
- 1½ cups (6-oz.) cubed sharp natural Cheddar cheese
- ½ teaspoon grated orange rind
- 1 cup fresh orange sections
- ½ cup chopped walnuts
- ½ cup salad dressing or mayonnaise
- 1 teaspoon lemon juice

In medium bowl, combine all ingredients; mix lightly. Chill.

4 to 6 servings

NUTRITION INFORMATION PER SERVING

Serving Size: 1/4 of recipe		Percent U.S. RDA Per Serving	
Calories	454	Protein	21%
Protein	14g	Vitamin A	15%
Carbohydrate	22g	Vitamin C	27%
Fat	36g	Thiamin	9%
Sodium	472mg	Riboflavin	15%
Potassium	266mg	Niacin	2%
		Calcium	36%
		Iron	7%

MOHAVE FRUIT SALAD

An old-fashioned favorite, this can double as a light refreshing dessert topped with whipped cream.

GLORIFIED RICE

- ¼ cup cold water
- 1 pkg. unflavored gelatin
- 3 cups cold cooked rice
- 2 medium bananas, sliced and halved
- ⅓ cup sugar
- ½ teaspoon salt
- 2 cups (1 pint) whipping cream, whipped, or 4 cups frozen whipped topping, thawed
- 1 teaspoon vanilla
- ½ teaspoon almond extract
- 20-oz. can (2½ cups) crushed pineapple, drained
- 10-oz. jar (1¼ cups) maraschino cherries, drained and chopped

In small saucepan, sprinkle gelatin over water. Stir over low heat until gelatin is dissolved; cool. In very large bowl, combine remaining ingredients. Add gelatin; blend well. Spoon into oiled 12-cup fluted tube pan; pack lightly. Chill until firm.

10 to 12 servings

NUTRITION INFORMATION PER SERVING

Serving Size: 1/12 of recipe		Percent U.S. RDA Per Serving	
Calories	274	Protein	4%
Protein	3g	Vitamin A	14%
Carbohydrate	34g	Vitamin C	10%
Fat	15g	Thiamin	6%
Sodium	239mg	Riboflavin	4%
Potassium	194mg	Niacin	3%
		Calcium	4%
		Iron	4%

TIP: *To halve recipe, use half the ingredient amounts; spoon into oiled 5½-cup mold.*

MOLDED SALADS

GELATIN

These are one of the loveliest salads for hot summer luncheons and dinners however, the problem is to keep their shape. Serve molds on a well-chilled plate. If they are to be on display for any length of time, such as a buffet, it would be wise to set the platter on a bed of ice.

To unmold a gelatin salad, place hot wet towels around the bottom of the mold, or dip bottom of mold in warm water for a *few seconds* (don't overdo or you can melt your salad). Place inverted plate on top of mold. Grasping plate and mold together, quickly invert to release salad on plate. Remove mold. If gelatin doesn't release shake slightly or tap mold lightly with a knife handle.

Many molds have the size marked on the bottom. If unmarked, measure the amount of water required to fill it. Another mold size may be substituted. However, slightly larger molds or two smaller molds may alter the chilling time. A gelatin salad may also be chilled in a square or loaf pan if a mold is not available.

Except for pineapple, frozen fruits may be substituted for fresh in any salad. Fresh or frozen pineapple cannot be used in gelatin salads unless it is boiled, as it contains a substance which prevents the gelatin from thickening and becoming firm. If the frozen fruit is packed in syrup, unless otherwise specified in the recipe, drain the syrup before using the fruit in gelatin salads.

Easy ideas for gelatin salads:

- For part of liquid use fruit or vegetable juice, carbonated beverages, or a few tablespoons of wine, champagne or sherry.
- When dissolving gelatin with boiling water add one stick cinnamon, 5 whole cloves or one piece of ginger. Remove spice after 10 minutes.
- Layer gelatins by combining colors and flavors that accentuate each other. Pour first layer into dish or mold and allow it to set until firm before adding next layer. Each layer must be firmly set before the next layer is added.
- Chill gelatin in shallow pan until set. Cut into cubes and fold into whipped cream, pudding or another flavor of partially set gelatin.

FROZEN

These are terrific for make-ahead salads since they can be prepared and frozen weeks ahead of the scheduled event – be sure to cover properly before freezing.

Before serving, allow a frozen salad to stand at room temperature a few moments to ease in slicing. Be careful not to let the salad thaw.

Lining your pan with foil will aid in the removal of the salad from the pan. Simply peel off the foil after the salad is unmolded. However, if you do not wish to remove the salad before slicing, the foil is not necessary.

To keep fruits from turning dark, dip pieces into lemon or other citrus juice before adding to salad.

Tabasco sauce gives the snap to a tomato-vegetable mold.

GAZPACHO SALAD

1 pkg. unflavored gelatin
½ cup cold water
¼ teaspoon salt
10¾-oz. can condensed tomato soup
1 tablespoon vinegar or lemon juice
Dash Tabasco sauce
1 medium cucumber, chopped
1 green pepper, chopped
1 small onion, chopped

In medium saucepan, sprinkle gelatin over cold water. Stir over low heat until gelatin is dissolved. Remove from heat. Add salt, tomato soup, vinegar and Tabasco sauce; blend well. Chill until slightly thickened but not set, about 45 minutes. Stir in remaining ingredients. Pour into oiled 3-cup mold or individual molds. Chill until firm. Unmold to serve. 4 to 5 servings

NUTRITION INFORMATION PER SERVING

Serving Size: 1/5 of recipe		Percent U.S. RDA Per Serving	
Calories	69	Protein	5%
Protein	3g	Vitamin A	14%
Carbohydrate	12g	Vitamin C	61%
Fat	1g	Thiamin	4%
Sodium	599mg	Riboflavin	4%
Potassium	269mg	Niacin	4%
		Calcium	3%
		Iron	6%

Aspic is a perfect beginning to a rich main dish.

VEGETABLE COCKTAIL ASPIC

2 cups cocktail vegetable juice
3-oz. pkg. lemon-flavored gelatin
Dash salt
1½ teaspoons lemon juice

In small saucepan, heat cocktail vegetable juice to boiling; remove from heat. Add remaining ingredients; stir until gelatin dissolves. Pour into oiled 3-cup mold or 8-inch square pan. Chill until firm, about 2 hours. To serve, unmold or cut into squares. 4 to 6 servings

NUTRITION INFORMATION PER SERVING

Serving Size: 1/6 of recipe		Percent U.S. RDA Per Serving	
Calories	67	Protein	3%
Protein	2g	Vitamin A	11%
Carbohydrate	15g	Vitamin C	13%
Fat	<1g	Thiamin	3%
Sodium	252mg	Riboflavin	*
Potassium	180mg	Niacin	3%
		Calcium	*
		Iron	2%

TIP: *One sliced celery stalk and 1 shredded carrot may be added before pouring into mold.*

An easy recipe with dramatic results—many guests are puzzled as to how this creation was assembled.

FILLED MELON WEDGES

3-oz. pkg. raspberry or strawberry-flavored gelatin
2 cups pineapple juice
1 ripe cantaloupe

In medium bowl, dissolve gelatin in 1 cup boiling pineapple juice; add remaining juice. Cut cantaloupe in half; remove seeds. Remove fruit, leaving ½-inch shell. Chop fruit; stir into gelatin. Fill shells with gelatin mixture. Chill until firm. Cut into slices or wedges to serve.
4 to 6 servings

NUTRITION INFORMATION PER SERVING

Serving Size: 1/6 of recipe		Percent U.S. RDA Per Serving	
Calories	151	Protein	4%
Protein	3g	Vitamin A	121%
Carbohydrate	37g	Vitamin C	110%
Fat	<1g	Thiamin	7%
Sodium	67mg	Riboflavin	4%
Potassium	568mg	Niacin	6%
		Calcium	4%
		Iron	5%

MOLDED CRANAPPLE SALAD

6-oz. pkg. cherry or raspberry-flavored gelatin
1 cup boiling water
1 cup cranberry juice
½ teaspoon salt
2 cups (2 medium) chopped apple
10-oz. pkg. (1¼ cups) frozen cranberry-orange relish, partially thawed

In large bowl, dissolve gelatin in boiling water. Stir in remaining ingredients. Chill until thickened but not set. Stir and pour into oiled 4-cup mold. Chill until firm, about 4 hours. Unmold to serve.
6 to 8 servings

NUTRITION INFORMATION PER SERVING

Serving Size: 1/6 of recipe		Percent U.S. RDA Per Serving	
Calories	241	Protein	5%
Protein	3g	Vitamin A	*
Carbohydrate	59g	Vitamin C	17%
Fat	<1g	Thiamin	2%
Sodium	272mg	Riboflavin	*
Potassium	84mg	Niacin	*
		Calcium	*
		Iron	2%

CREAMY MOLDED VEGETABLE SALAD

2 cups cold water
2 pkg. unflavored gelatin
½ cup sugar
½ teaspoon salt
⅓ cup vinegar
2 tablespoons lemon juice
1½ cups salad dressing or mayonnaise
Yellow or green food coloring, if desired
1 cup shredded cabbage
2 medium carrots, shredded
1 stalk celery, sliced
1 green pepper
Lettuce leaves

In medium saucepan, sprinkle gelatin over ½ cup of the cold water. Stir over low heat until gelatin is dissolved. Add sugar, salt, remaining 1½ cups water and lemon juice; stir until sugar is dissolved. Remove from heat, add salad dressing and food coloring, stir until well blended. Stir in cabbage, carrots and celery. Cut green pepper into rings; reserve for later use. Chop remaining green pepper and stir into salad. Pour into oiled 6-cup mold. Refrigerate until firm, about 4 hours.

To serve, unmold and garnish with green pepper rings. 6 to 8 servings

NUTRITION INFORMATION PER SERVING

Serving Size: 1/8 of recipe		Percent U.S. RDA Per Serving	
Calories	266	Protein	4%
Protein	3g	Vitamin A	37%
Carbohydrate	24g	Vitamin C	70%
Fat	19g	Thiamin	4%
Sodium	414mg	Riboflavin	4%
Potassium	200mg	Niacin	*
		Calcium	3%
		Iron	3%

CHERRY YOGURT SHIMMER

3-oz. pkg. cherry-flavored gelatin
1 cup boiling water
½ cup cold water
8-oz. carton (1 cup) cherry yogurt

In small bowl, dissolve gelatin in boiling water. Stir in cold water. Chill until thickened but not set, about 45 minutes. Beat until frothy; fold in yogurt. Pour into oiled 3-cup mold or serving dish. Chill until firm, about 2 hours. To serve, unmold or serve from dish.

4 to 5 servings

NUTRITION INFORMATION PER SERVING

Serving Size: 1/4 of recipe		Percent U.S. RDA Per Serving	
Calories	141	Protein	7%
Protein	5g	Vitamin A	*
Carbohydrate	31g	Vitamin C	0%
Fat	<1g	Thiamin	2%
Sodium	96mg	Riboflavin	8%
Potassium	81mg	Niacin	0%
		Calcium	7%
		Iron	0%

TIPS: *Any flavor combination of gelatin and yogurt may be substituted.*

If desired, 3 drops peppermint or almond extract may be added with cold water. Try lime and pineapple with peppermint or orange and peach with almond.

MOLDED WALDORF SALAD WITH ORANGE CREAM DRESSING

SALAD

3-oz. pkg. cherry, raspberry or strawberry-flavored gelatin
1 cup boiling water
1 cup cranberry juice or cold water
1 cup halved green grapes
1 medium apple, chopped
1 stalk celery, chopped
¼ cup chopped walnuts or pecans

DRESSING

¼ cup whipping cream, whipped or ½ cup frozen whipped topping, thawed
½ cup mayonnaise or salad dressing
⅓ cup orange marmalade or 2 tablespoons frozen orange juice concentrate, thawed

In medium bowl, dissolve gelatin in boiling water. Add cranberry juice; mix well. Stir in remaining Salad ingredients. Pour into oiled 5½-cup mold or 8-inch square pan. Chill until firm, about 2 hours.

In small bowl, fold together Dressing ingredients; blend well. Cover and chill. To serve, unmold or cut into squares. Top with Dressing.

6 to 8 servings

NUTRITION INFORMATION PER SERVING

Serving Size: 1/6 of recipe		Percent U.S. RDA Per Serving	
Calories	359	Protein	4%
Protein	3g	Vitamin A	5%
Carbohydrate	42g	Vitamin C	7%
Fat	22g	Thiamin	4%
Sodium	170mg	Riboflavin	3%
Potassium	146mg	Niacin	*
		Calcium	3%
		Iron	4%

TIP: *An 8-oz. can drained white seedless grapes may be substituted for the halved green grapes.*

COTTAGE CHEESE LIME SALAD

2 pkg. (3 oz. each) lemon-flavored gelatin
2 pkg. (3 oz. each) lime-flavored gelatin
2 cups boiling water
2 cups cold water
1 cup mayonnaise or salad dressing
24-oz. carton (3 cups) creamed small-curd cottage cheese
1 cup chopped nuts
8-oz. can (1 cup) crushed pineapple, undrained
5⅓-oz. can (⅔ cup) evaporated milk or whole milk

In very large bowl, dissolve gelatin in boiling water. Stir in cold water. Chill until thickened, but not set, about 45 minutes. Add mayonnaise; blend well. Stir in remaining ingredients. Spoon into oiled 12-cup fluted tube pan. Chill until firm. Unmold to serve. 12 to 14 servings

NUTRITION INFORMATION PER SERVING

Serving Size: 1/12 of recipe		Percent U.S. RDA Per Serving	
Calories	391	Protein	19%
Protein	13g	Vitamin A	4%
Carbohydrate	34g	Vitamin C	3%
Fat	24g	Thiamin	5%
Sodium	337mg	Riboflavin	12%
Potassium	157mg	Niacin	*
		Calcium	10%
		Iron	4%

TIP: *To halve recipe, use half the ingredient amounts; spoon into oiled 5½-cup mold.*

CHRISTMAS SALAD

29-oz. can (3½ cups) sliced pears, drained (reserve syrup)
2 cups liquid (reserved syrup plus water)
6-oz. pkg. lime-flavored gelatin
4 pkg. (3 oz. each) cream cheese, softened
2 cups (1 pint) whipping cream, whipped
1 cup maraschino cherries, drained and chopped
½ cup chopped walnuts

In small saucepan, heat liquid to boiling; add gelatin and stir to dissolve. Chill until slightly thickened, but not set. Beat until frothy. Add pears and cream cheese; beat until smooth. Fold in whipped cream, cherries and nuts. Pour into oiled 12-cup mold or 13x9-inch pan. Chill until firm, about 2 hours. To serve, unmold or cut into squares.
12 to 15 servings

NUTRITION INFORMATION PER SERVING

Serving Size: 1/12 of recipe		Percent U.S. RDA Per Serving	
Calories	413	Protein	8%
Protein	5g	Vitamin A	21%
Carbohydrate	36g	Vitamin C	*
Fat	29g	Thiamin	2%
Sodium	129mg	Riboflavin	8%
Potassium	136mg	Niacin	*
		Calcium	6%
		Iron	*

ORANGE SHERBET SALAD

Very tangy but a favorite of our tasters.

ORANGE SHERBET SALAD

6-oz. pkg. orange-flavored gelatin
1 cup boiling water
1 cup orange juice
1 pint (2 cups) lemon, orange or pineapple sherbet
11- oz. can (1 cup) mandarin oranges, drained

In small bowl, dissolve gelatin in boiling water. Add orange juice and sherbet; blend until sherbet is melted and mixture is smooth. Chill until thickened but not set, about 30 minutes. Fold in oranges. Pour into oiled 4-cup mold or 8-inch square pan. Chill until firm, about 2 hours. To serve, unmold or cut into squares. 6 to 9 servings

NUTRITION INFORMATION PER SERVING

Serving Size: 1/6 of recipe		Percent U.S. RDA Per Serving	
Calories	222	Protein	6%
Protein	4g	Vitamin A	2%
Carbohydrate	52g	Vitamin C	56%
Fat	<1g	Thiamin	5%
Sodium	97mg	Riboflavin	3%
Potassium	139mg	Niacin	*
		Calcium	2%
		Iron	*

A creamy whipped topping highlights this pretty gelatin mold.

APRICOT SALAD

6-oz. pkg. orange-flavored gelatin
2 cups boiling water
1½ cups cold water
29-oz. can (3½ cups) apricots, drained and cut up (reserve syrup)
8-oz. can (1 cup) crushed pineapple, undrained
1 to 2 cups miniature marshmallows
½ cup sugar
2 tablespoons flour
1 cup liquid (reserved syrup plus water)
1 egg
2 tablespoons margarine or butter
1 pkg. dessert topping mix

In medium bowl, dissolve gelatin in boiling water; add cold water, apricots and pineapple. Pour into 13x9-inch pan. Sprinkle with miniature marshmallows and chill until firm. In small saucepan, combine sugar, flour, liquid and egg. Heat to boiling; boil 1 minute. Add margarine and stir until melted; cool. Prepare dessert topping as directed on package. Fold cooked mixture into topping and spread on salad. Chill. Cut into squares.

15 servings

NUTRITION INFORMATION PER SERVING

Serving Size: 1/15 of recipe		Percent U.S. RDA Per Serving	
Calories	175	Protein	3%
Protein	2g	Vitamin A	16%
Carbohydrate	36g	Vitamin C	5%
Fat	3g	Thiamin	2%
Sodium	67mg	Riboflavin	*
Potassium	117mg	Niacin	*
		Calcium	*
		Iron	2%

TIP: *1 cup (½ pint) whipping cream, whipped and sweetened may be used instead of dessert topping mix.*

CREAMY RHUBARB RING

¼ cup water
8 cups sliced fresh or frozen rhubarb
1⅓ cups sugar
6-oz. pkg. raspberry or strawberry-flavored gelatin
2 pkg. (10 oz. each) frozen raspberries or strawberries, thawed and drained (reserve syrup)
1½ pints (3 cups) vanilla ice cream

TOPPING

1 cup reserved syrup
2 tablespoons cornstarch
1 cup (½ pint) whipping cream, whipped and sweetened or 2 cups frozen whipped topping, thawed

In large saucepan, combine water and rhubarb; heat to boiling. Cover; simmer until rhubarb is tender, about 15 minutes. Remove from heat; stir in sugar and gelatin until dissolved. Blend in raspberries and ice cream until ice cream is melted and mixture is slightly thickened. Spoon into oiled 12-cup fluted tube pan. Chill until firm. Unmold to serve.

In small saucepan, combine reserved syrup and cornstarch; blend well. Cook over low heat until mixture is clear and thickened, stirring constantly. Cover and chill. Fold into whipped cream. Serve as a topping on individual slices.

10 to 12 servings

NUTRITION INFORMATION PER SERVING

Serving Size: 1/12 of recipe		Percent U.S. RDA Per Serving	
Calories	336	Protein	6%
Protein	4g	Vitamin A	11%
Carbohydrate	58g	Vitamin C	30%
Fat	11g	Thiamin	3%
Sodium	75mg	Riboflavin	10%
Potassium	330mg	Niacin	3%
		Calcium	15%
		Iron	5%

A double-layered delight with tangy strawberries on top and a cool creamy lemon base.

STRAWBERRIES 'N CREAM MOLD

3 pkg. (3 oz. each) strawberry-flavored gelatin
2⅓ cups boiling water
2 pkg. (10 oz. each) frozen strawberries
3 pkg. (3 oz. each) lemon-flavored gelatin
3 cups boiling water
2 pkg. (8 oz. each) cream cheese, softened
⅔ cup mayonnaise or salad dressing
Yellow food coloring, if desired
Whipped cream or frozen whipped topping, thawed

In large bowl, dissolve strawberry-flavored gelatin in 2⅓ cups boiling water. Stir in frozen strawberries until gelatin is thickened and strawberries are thawed. Spoon into oiled 12-cup fluted tube pan. Chill until firm. In large bowl, dissolve lemon-flavored gelatin in 3 cups boiling water. Chill until thickened, but not set.

In medium bowl, beat cream cheese until light and fluffy. Add mayonnaise; blend well. Beat thickened lemon-flavored gelatin until light-colored and foamy. Blend in cream cheese mixture and food coloring. Spoon over firm strawberry mixture in pan. Chill until firm. Serve with whipped cream.

12 to 14 servings

NUTRITION INFORMATION PER SERVING

Serving Size: 1/12 of recipe		Percent U.S. RDA Per Serving	
Calories	491	Protein	12%
Protein	8g	Vitamin A	17%
Carbohydrate	52g	Vitamin C	42%
Fat	30g	Thiamin	*
Sodium	308mg	Riboflavin	8%
Potassium	98mg	Niacin	*
		Calcium	4%
		Iron	3%

CUCUMBER SALAD

6-oz. pkg. lime-flavored gelatin
2 cups boiling water
1 cup cold water
⅛ teaspoon salt
2 small cucumbers, grated
1 small onion, grated
1 cup mayonnaise or salad dressing

In medium bowl, dissolve gelatin in boiling water; add cold water. Chill until slightly thickened, but not set, about 45 minutes. Add remaining ingredients; stir until well blended. Pour into oiled 5½-cup mold. Refrigerate until firm, about 3 hours. Unmold to serve. 6 to 8 servings

NUTRITION INFORMATION PER SERVING

Serving Size: 1/8 of recipe		Percent U.S. RDA Per Serving	
Calories	287	Protein	4%
Protein	3g	Vitamin A	4%
Carbohydrate	22g	Vitamin C	10%
Fat	22g	Thiamin	*
Sodium	269mg	Riboflavin	*
Potassium	94mg	Niacin	*
		Calcium	*
		Iron	4%

CRANBERRY FREEZE

16-oz. can (2 cups) whole cranberry sauce
8-oz. can (1 cup) crushed pineapple, drained
1 cup dairy sour cream or yogurt
⅓ cup chopped pecans

In medium bowl, combine all ingredients; mix well. Pour into 8-inch square pan or ice cube tray. Freeze 2 hours until firm. To serve, cut into squares. If desired garnish with pecan halves. 6 servings

NUTRITION INFORMATION PER SERVING

Serving Size: 1/6 of recipe		Percent U.S. RDA Per Serving	
Calories	260	Protein	3%
Protein	2g	Vitamin A	7%
Carbohydrate	38g	Vitamin C	7%
Fat	12g	Thiamin	7%
Sodium	17mg	Riboflavin	4%
Potassium	100mg	Niacin	*
		Calcium	5%
		Iron	2%

A tablespoon of rum added with the lime concentrate will give an authentic flavor addition.

DAIQUIRI FRUIT SALAD

15¼-oz. can (2 cups) crushed pineapple, drained (reserve syrup)
1 cup liquid (reserved syrup plus water)
3-oz. pkg. lime or lemon-flavored gelatin
½ cup frozen limeade concentrate thawed
⅓ cup salad dressing or mayonnaise
1 cup (½ pint) whipping cream, whipped or 2 cups frozen whipped topping, thawed
2 medium bananas, sliced
½ cup chopped nuts, if desired

In small saucepan, heat 1 cup of liquid to boiling. In large bowl, dissolve gelatin in hot liquid. Add frozen limeade concentrate and salad dressing; stir until well blended. Chill until thickened, but not set, about 45 minutes. Fold in pineapple and remaining ingredients. Pour into oiled 6-cup ring mold or 8-inch square pan. Freeze until firm, about 3 hours. To serve, unmold or cut into squares. 5 to 6 servings

NUTRITION INFORMATION PER SERVING

Serving Size: 1/6 of recipe		Percent U.S. RDA Per Serving	
Calories	485	Protein	7%
Protein	5g	Vitamin A	16%
Carbohydrate	62g	Vitamin C	26%
Fat	27g	Thiamin	9%
Sodium	135mg	Riboflavin	7%
Potassium	388mg	Niacin	3%
		Calcium	6%
		Iron	6%

TIP: *Salad may be refrigerated as well as frozen.*

May be served as a light refreshing summer dessert, too.

FROZEN SHERBET SALAD

1 pint (2 cups) orange, lemon or lime sherbet
¾ cup halved green grapes
½ cup chopped maraschino cherries
8¾-oz. can (1 cup) peaches, drained and cubed
8-oz. can (1 cup) crushed pineapple, drained
¼ cup whipping cream, whipped or ½ cup frozen whipped topping, thawed

In small bowl, blend sherbet until softened. Fold in remaining ingredients. Pour into 8-inch square pan. Freeze 2 hours or until firm. To serve, cut into squares.

9 servings

NUTRITION INFORMATION PER SERVING

Serving Size: 1/9 of recipe		Percent U.S. RDA Per Serving	
Calories	140	Protein	*
Protein	<1g	Vitamin A	5%
Carbohydrate	29g	Vitamin C	6%
Fat	3g	Thiamin	2%
Sodium	7mg	Riboflavin	*
Potassium	83mg	Niacin	*
		Calcium	*
		Iron	*

TIP: *An 8-oz. can white seedless grapes, drained may be substituted for the halved green grapes.*

If properly wrapped in foil, this salad can be made several weeks ahead.

FROZEN FRUIT SALAD

15¼-oz. can (2 cups) crushed pineapple, drained (reserve syrup)
1 cup liquid (reserved syrup plus water)
⅓ cup sugar
1 tablespoon flour
1 egg, beaten
8-oz. pkg. cream cheese, softened
2½ cups miniature marshmallows
½ cup chopped red maraschino cherries, drained
½ cup chopped green maraschino cherries, drained
29-oz. can (3½ cups) fruit cocktail, drained
1 cup (½ pint) whipping cream, whipped

In medium saucepan, heat liquid to boiling. Combine sugar and flour; stir into egg. Remove liquid from heat. Add sugar mixture to hot liquid, stirring constantly. Return to heat and boil 1 minute until thickened; cool. In large bowl, blend cooled egg mixture and cream cheese. Stir in marshmallows, cherries, pineapple and fruit cocktail. Fold in whipped cream. Spoon into two 8x4-inch loaf pans or 24 muffin cups lined with paper baking cups. If desired, garnish with cherry halves. Freeze until firm, about 2 hours. Slice ½ to 1 inch thick.

18 to 24 servings

NUTRITION INFORMATION PER SERVING

Serving Size: 1/18 of recipe		Percent U.S. RDA Per Serving	
Calories	194	Protein	3%
Protein	2g	Vitamin A	10%
Carbohydrate	25g	Vitamin C	4%
Fat	10g	Thiamin	3%
Sodium	44mg	Riboflavin	4%
Potassium	112mg	Niacin	*
		Calcium	3%
		Iron	2%

MAIN DISH SALAD TIPS

SERVING

Main dish salads can be served in large individual bowls or on dinner plates. If serving a vegetable along with the salad, the plate would be best. If only a roll and relish accompany the salad, individual bowls may be used along with bread and butter plates. Or, the entire salad may be placed in a large bowl and served individually at the table.

PREPARATION

Leftover chicken, canned chicken or cooked fresh chicken may be used for cooked cubed chicken. One 3-lb. 4-oz. can whole chicken yields about 2½ cups cubed chicken. A 5-lb. stewing chicken yields 5 cups cooked cubed chicken.

In all our recipes turkey and chicken may be used interchangeably. A 3-lb. turkey roast yields about 5 cups cooked cubed turkey.

Canned ham, fully cooked ham, or leftover baked ham may be used for cooked cubed ham. In most recipes, cubed luncheon meat may be substituted for the ham.

To prevent hard-cooked eggs from getting dark around the yolk, bring to a boil, then reduce heat and simmer for 15 minutes. Immediately immerse in cold water.

Almost any leftover cooked or raw vegetable may be added to a main dish salad. Be careful to stir very lightly when adding cooked vegetables so they do not become mushy. Green beans add color and flavor to a beef salad; asparagus to seafood salads; and carrots to chicken or turkey salads.

To store cheese, wrap tightly and refrigerate.

Salads may be garnished with carrot curls, radish slices or flowers, hard-cooked egg slices, pimiento strips, tomato wedges, shredded cheese or cucumber slices. Parsley and watercress are also colorful garnishes.

MACARONI SALAD

1 cup uncooked macaroni
1 stalk celery, chopped
¼ cup pickle relish or chopped sweet pickle
¼ teaspoon salt
1 tablespoon chopped onion
¾ cup mayonnaise or salad dressing

Prepare macaroni as directed on package. In large bowl, combine macaroni with remaining ingredients; toss lightly. Cover and chill.

5 to 6 servings

NUTRITION INFORMATION PER SERVING

Serving Size: 1/5 of recipe		Percent U.S. RDA Per Serving	
Calories	345	Protein	5%
Protein	4g	Vitamin A	2%
Carbohydrate	24g	Vitamin C	*
Fat	27g	Thiamin	15%
Sodium	403mg	Riboflavin	6%
Potassium	89mg	Niacin	7%
		Calcium	*
		Iron	6%

TIPS: *For RICE SALAD, use 1 cup uncooked rice. Cook as directed on package, cool and substitute for macaroni.*

NUTRITION INFORMATION PER SERVING

Serving Size: 1/5 of recipe		Percent U.S. RDA Per Serving	
Calories	398	Protein	5%
Protein	3g	Vitamin A	2%
Carbohydrate	37g	Vitamin C	*
Fat	27g	Thiamin	12%
Sodium	405mg	Riboflavin	*
Potassium	78mg	Niacin	7%
		Calcium	2%
		Iron	8%

For TUNA SALAD, use 6½-oz. can tuna, drained. Stir into macaroni salad.

Additions to Macaroni Salad: Protein—2 to 3 chopped hard-cooked eggs; ½ to 1 cup canned seafood; 1 to 2 cups cooked cubed meat; sausage or cubed cheese; ½ cup chopped nuts; 1 to 2 cups canned kidney or garbanzo beans; cooked crumbled bacon.

Vegetable—1 cup cooked peas or carrots, 1 tablespoon green pepper or pimiento, 1 shredded carrot, ¼ cup stuffed olives or chopped cucumber.

HEARTY MEAT SALAD

2 cups (2 medium) cooked cubed potatoes
2 cups cooked cubed beef, pork or lamb
2 hard-cooked eggs, cut into wedges
1 medium carrot, shredded
½ cup prepared French or Russian dressing
⅓ cup mayonnaise or salad dressing
8-oz. can (1 cup) peas, drained

In large bowl, combine all ingredients except peas; mix well. Add peas and toss lightly. Cover and chill. If desired, garnish with parsley. 3 to 4 servings

NUTRITION INFORMATION PER SERVING

Serving Size: 1/4 of recipe		Percent U.S. RDA Per Serving	
Calories	640	Protein	37%
Protein	24g	Vitamin A	58%
Carbohydrate	26g	Vitamin C	29%
Fat	49g	Thiamin	13%
Sodium	674mg	Riboflavin	16%
Potassium	394mg	Niacin	22%
		Calcium	5%
		Iron	24%

An easy to eat version of the famous sandwich.

TACO SALAD

1 lb. ground beef
1 medium onion, chopped
1¼-oz. pkg. taco seasoning mix*
½ cup hot water
½ head lettuce, torn into pieces
6-oz. pkg. corn chips
¾ cup (3-oz.) shredded Cheddar or American cheese
2 medium tomatoes, cut into wedges
⅓ cup chili sauce
¼ teaspoon Tabasco sauce

In large skillet, brown ground beef and onion; drain. Stir in dry taco seasoning mix and water; simmer 10 minutes over low heat. Line separate salad bowls or plates with lettuce; sprinkle with corn chips. Spoon about ½ cup beef mixture in center; sprinkle with cheese. Garnish with tomatoes. Serve immediately with combination of chili sauce and Tabasco sauce or with prepared French or Russian dressing. 4 to 6 servings

NUTRITION INFORMATION PER SERVING

Serving Size: 1/4 of recipe		Percent U.S. RDA Per Serving	
Calories	614	Protein	47%
Protein	30g	Vitamin A	36%
Carbohydrate	40g	Vitamin C	57%
Fat	37g	Thiamin	20%
Sodium	925mg	Riboflavin	26%
Potassium	951mg	Niacin	31%
		Calcium	40%
		Iron	30%

TIP: **To substitute for taco seasoning mix: add ½ cup chili sauce, 1 teaspoon salt, 1 teaspoon chili powder and ¼ teaspoon Tabasco sauce when adding water.*

TACO SALAD

CHICKEN SALAD

3 cups cooked cubed chicken
2 stalks celery, chopped
¼ teaspoon salt
½ cup mayonnaise or salad dressing
2 tablespoons lemon juice

In medium bowl, combine all ingredients; mix well. Cover and chill. Serve plain or use to fill green pepper, avocado or pineapple halves, hollowed out tomatoes or lettuce cups. 4 servings

NUTRITION INFORMATION PER SERVING

Serving Size: 1/4 of recipe		Percent U.S. RDA Per Serving	
Calories	377	Protein	52%
Protein	34g	Vitamin A	4%
Carbohydrate	2g	Vitamin C	9%
Fat	26g	Thiamin	4%
Sodium	392mg	Riboflavin	7%
Potassium	520mg	Niacin	61%
		Calcium	3%
		Iron	9%

TIP: *For variety, add 3 slices bacon, fried, drained and crumbled; 1 cup cooked cubed ham or ½ cup cubed jellied cranberry sauce.*

Water chestnuts, celery and bamboo shoots give the crunch, soy sauce adds the flavor.

CHINESE CHICKEN SALAD

2 cups cooked cubed chicken or turkey
1 cup (2 medium stalks) chopped celery
2 green onions, thinly sliced
2 tablespoons pimiento, drained, chopped or sliced
8-oz. can (⅔ cup) water chestnuts, drained and sliced
8½-oz. can (1 cup) bamboo shoots, drained
¾ cup mayonnaise or salad dressing
2 tablespoons soy sauce
1 tablespoon lemon juice

In medium bowl, toss chicken and vegetables together. Stir mayonnaise, soy sauce and lemon juice together. Chill both mixtures. Before serving, toss chicken mixture and dressing. 4 to 6 servings

NUTRITION INFORMATION PER SERVING

Serving Size: 1/4 of recipe		Percent U.S. RDA Per Serving	
Calories	451	Protein	38%
Protein	25g	Vitamin A	5%
Carbohydrate	9g	Vitamin C	15%
Fat	36g	Thiamin	7%
Sodium	993mg	Riboflavin	9%
Potassium	500mg	Niacin	43%
		Calcium	5%
		Iron	12%

Very popular for the afternoon tea such as showers and receptions, this recipe may be doubled to serve 16 to 20 guests.

COMPANY TURKEY SALAD

7-oz. pkg. macaroni rings
3 cups cooked cubed turkey
6 hard-cooked eggs, chopped
½ cup sliced stuffed green olives
1½ cups halved green grapes or 16-oz. can white seedless grapes, drained and halved
¼ cup (1 small) chopped onion
1½ cups (3 medium stalks) chopped celery
½ to 1 cup slivered almonds
½ cup whipping cream, whipped
2 tablespoons sugar
½ teaspoon salt
⅛ teaspoon pepper
1¼ cups salad dressing or mayonnaise

Prepare macaroni rings as directed on package. In large bowl, combine macaroni, turkey, eggs, olives, grapes, onion, celery and almonds. In small bowl, fold remaining ingredients together for dressing. Combine turkey mixture and dressing; mix well. Cover and chill.

8 to 10 servings

NUTRITION INFORMATION PER SERVING

Serving Size: 1/8 of recipe		Percent U.S. RDA Per Serving	
Calories	556	Protein	44%
Protein	28g	Vitamin A	18%
Carbohydrate	36g	Vitamin C	7%
Fat	33g	Thiamin	15%
Sodium	679mg	Riboflavin	21%
Potassium	537mg	Niacin	36%
		Calcium	8%
		Iron	17%

HAM SALAD

2 hard-cooked eggs, chopped
3 cups cooked cubed ham
1 stalk celery, chopped
½ cup pickle relish or chopped sweet pickle
½ cup mayonnaise or salad dressing
2 teaspoons prepared or ½ teaspoon dry mustard
Dash pepper

In large bowl, combine all ingredients; mix well. Cover and chill. Serve in lettuce cups. If desired, garnish with tomato wedges.

4 servings

NUTRITION INFORMATION PER SERVING

Serving Size: 1/4 of recipe		Percent U.S. RDA Per Serving	
Calories	447	Protein	39%
Protein	26g	Vitamin A	9%
Carbohydrate	12g	Vitamin C	*
Fat	33g	Thiamin	35%
Sodium	1242mg	Riboflavin	17%
Potassium	357mg	Niacin	19%
		Calcium	4%
		Iron	21%

TIPS: *A 12-oz. can luncheon meat, cubed, or 3 cups sliced wieners, salami, bologna or Vienna sausage may be substituted for ham.*

One cup cubed or shredded cheese may be added or substituted for eggs.

SWEET-SOUR WIENER SALAD

1 lb. wieners, cut into 1-inch slices
2 cups cooked macaroni
1 to 2 tablespoons firmly packed brown sugar
2 tablespoons chopped green pepper
1 tablespoon chopped pimiento, drained
½ cup mayonnaise or salad dressing
8-oz. can (1 cup) sauerkraut, well-drained
Cabbage leaves

In large bowl, combine all ingredients; mix well. Cover and chill. Serve on cabbage leaves. If desired, garnish with green pepper rings or cucumber slices. 4 to 5 servings

NUTRITION INFORMATION PER SERVING

Serving Size: 1/4 of recipe		Percent U.S. RDA Per Serving	
Calories	676	Protein	29%
Protein	19g	Vitamin A	3%
Carbohydrate	30g	Vitamin C	53%
Fat	54g	Thiamin	23%
Sodium	1687mg	Riboflavin	20%
Potassium	486mg	Niacin	21%
		Calcium	6%
		Iron	20%

CHEF'S SALAD

1 garlic clove, if desired
2 heads lettuce, torn into bite-size pieces
6 radishes, sliced
½ teaspoon salt
Dash pepper
1 cup julienne strips cooked chicken or turkey
1 cup julienne strips cooked ham
1 cup (4 oz.) julienne strips Swiss or Cheddar cheese
3 hard-cooked eggs, sliced
2 tomatoes, cut into wedges
½ cup mayonnaise or salad dressing

Rub large salad bowl with cut garlic clove; discard garlic. Add lettuce, radishes, salt and pepper; toss lightly. Arrange chicken, ham and cheese over lettuce. Top with eggs and tomatoes. Serve with mayonnaise or favorite dressing. 6 servings

NUTRITION INFORMATION PER SERVING

Serving Size: 1/6 of recipe		Percent U.S. RDA Per Serving	
Calories	364	Protein	35%
Protein	23g	Vitamin A	30%
Carbohydrate	8g	Vitamin C	33%
Fat	27g	Thiamin	20%
Sodium	749mg	Riboflavin	21%
Potassium	652mg	Niacin	22%
		Calcium	24%
		Iron	16%

TIP: *Any combination of salad greens may be substituted for some of the lettuce; such as fresh spinach leaves, watercress, romaine and endive.*

TURKEY SALAD POLYNESIAN

TURKEY SALAD POLYNESIAN

3 cups cooked cubed turkey
2 stalks celery, thinly sliced
1 teaspoon curry powder
¼ teaspoon salt
¾ cup mayonnaise or salad dressing
2 tablespoons chopped chutney
15½-oz. can (2 cups) pineapple chunks, drained
1 banana, sliced
½ cup salted peanuts or cashews
½ cup flaked coconut, if desired
11-oz. can (1 cup) mandarin oranges, drained
Lettuce leaves

In large bowl, combine first 7 ingredients; toss lightly. Cover and chill, at least 2 hours. Before serving, slice banana; add to turkey mixture with peanuts. Serve in lettuce cups; garnish with coconut and oranges.
4 to 6 servings

NUTRITION INFORMATION PER SERVING

Serving Size: 1/4 of recipe		Percent U.S. RDA Per Serving	
Calories	774	Protein	64%
Protein	42g	Vitamin A	7%
Carbohydrate	45g	Vitamin C	54%
Fat	50g	Thiamin	19%
Sodium	592mg	Riboflavin	16%
Potassium	1042mg	Niacin	78%
		Calcium	6%
		Iron	17%

SHRIMP AND RICE SALAD

1½ cups cooked rice
1½ cups cooked shrimp*, cut into pieces
1 stalk celery, chopped
1 carrot, shredded
3 to 4 tablespoons mayonnaise or salad dressing
1 tablespoon lemon juice
10-oz. pkg. (1¼ cups) frozen cut asparagus, cooked and drained or 10-oz. can asparagus, drained

In large bowl, combine all ingredients except asparagus; mix well. Add asparagus and toss lightly. Cover and chill. If desired, garnish with pimiento strips, tomato wedges or hard-cooked egg slices. 4 servings

NUTRITION INFORMATION PER SERVING

Serving Size: 1/4 of recipe		Percent U.S. RDA Per Serving	
Calories	238	Protein	33%
Protein	22g	Vitamin A	56%
Carbohydrate	18g	Vitamin C	26%
Fat	9g	Thiamin	12%
Sodium	396mg	Riboflavin	7%
Potassium	424mg	Niacin	20%
		Calcium	10%
		Iron	16%

TIPS: **A 12-oz. pkg. frozen shrimp or 2 cans (4½ oz. each) shrimp, drained, may be substituted.*

For additional color and flavor, ¼ cup sliced ripe olives, 1 tablespoon drained chopped pimiento, and 2 tablespoons chili sauce may be added.

Tuna and chicken noodle soup team together with crunchy vegetables for a surprisingly good main dish molded salad.

MYSTERY SALAD

3 pkg. (3 oz. each) lemon-flavored gelatin
1½ cups boiling water
1½ cups chopped celery
⅓ cup chopped onion
⅓ cup chopped green pepper
3 cans (6½ oz. each) tuna, drained
3 cans (10¾ oz. each) condensed chicken noodle soup
8-oz. can (⅔ cup) water chestnuts, drained and sliced
1½ cups salad dressing or mayonnaise
1½ cups whipping cream (not whipped)

In large bowl, dissolve gelatin in boiling water; cool to lukewarm. Add remaining ingredients; blend well. Pour into 13x9-inch pan. Chill until firm. 15 servings

NUTRITION INFORMATION PER SERVING

Serving Size: 1/15 of recipe		Percent U.S. RDA Per Serving	
Calories	355	Protein	22%
Protein	14g	Vitamin A	10%
Carbohydrate	25g	Vitamin C	10%
Fat	23g	Thiamin	3%
Sodium	703mg	Riboflavin	6%
Potassium	115mg	Niacin	23%
		Calcium	4%
		Iron	6%

A very basic salad that lets you use your creativity.

SEAFOOD SALAD

1½ to 2 cups cooked or canned seafood*
¼ teaspoon salt
1 stalk celery, finely chopped
½ cup mayonnaise or salad dressing
1 tablespoon lemon juice

In medium bowl, combine all ingredients; mix well. Cover and chill. Serve plain or use to fill green pepper, avocado or pineapple halves, hollowed out tomatoes or lettuce cups. 3 to 4 servings

NUTRITION INFORMATION PER SERVING

Serving Size: 1/4 of recipe made with tuna

		Percent U.S. RDA Per Serving	
Calories	355	Protein	35%
Protein	23g	Vitamin A	3%
Carbohydrate	1g	Vitamin C	4%
Fat	28g	Thiamin	3%
Sodium	312mg	Riboflavin	6%
Potassium	49mg	Niacin	47%
		Calcium	*
		Iron	9%

TIPS: **Two cans (6½ oz. each) tuna, drained and flaked; 2 cans (7½ oz. each) crab or lobster meat, drained and flaked; 12-oz. package frozen shrimp, cooked; 2 cans (4½ oz. each) shrimp, drained and chopped into pieces or 16-oz. can salmon, drained, may be used.*

- *Additions to basic recipe: Vegetable–½ to 1 cup cooked vegetable such as mushrooms, peas, asparagus or beans; 1 small peeled and cubed cucumber, 2 tablespoons chopped green pepper, ¼ cup sliced olives or pimiento, 1 tablespoon minced parsley, 1 tablespoon chopped chives. Protein–2 chopped hard-cooked eggs, ⅓ to ½ cup cubed or shredded cheese or chopped nuts. Fruit–½ to 1 cup chopped fresh or drained canned fruit; such as pineapple, mandarin oranges or avocado. Seasonings–¼ to ½ teaspoon curry powder, ¼ cup pickle relish, 2 tablespoons chopped chutney. Heartiness–1 cup cooked rice or macaroni, shoestring potatoes or chow mein noodles, adding more dressing if necessary.*

Serve this as a rich first course or as an elegant main dish.

CRAB LOUIS

1 cup mayonnaise or salad dressing
¼ cup chili sauce
2 pkg. (6 oz. each) frozen crab meat, thawed, drained and flaked
2 tablespoons finely chopped green pepper
1 stalk celery, chopped
1 tablespoon finely chopped onion
½ teaspoon salt
⅛ teaspoon pepper
½ cup whipping cream, whipped
Lettuce leaves

In large bowl, combine mayonnaise and chili sauce; blend until smooth. Add crab meat, green pepper, celery, onion, salt and pepper. Fold in whipped cream. Chill. Serve in lettuce cups. 4 to 6 servings

NUTRITION INFORMATION PER SERVING

Serving Size: 1/4 of recipe

		Percent U.S. RDA Per Serving	
Calories	573	Protein	19%
Protein	13g	Vitamin A	44%
Carbohydrate	5g	Vitamin C	22%
Fat	57g	Thiamin	6%
Sodium	1249mg	Riboflavin	8%
Potassium	197mg	Niacin	7%
		Calcium	7%
		Iron	6%

TIP: *Two 7½-oz. cans crabmeat, drained and flaked maybe substituted for the frozen crab meat. Shrimp or lobster may also be substituted for the crab meat.*

DRESSINGS

A good salad dressing should complement the salad—never overpower. The salad dressing is the final important touch in salad making.

With most salads, especially tossed, the dressing should be added just before serving. For variety, serve the salad without and offer two or three complementary dressings from which to choose.

ABOUT OILS AND VINEGARS

There are a wide variety of oils and vinegars from which to choose and experiment. Each will lend a subtle difference to your dressing.

Distilled (white) vinegar is the clear colorless variety made from grain alcohol. Considered to be rather sharp and strong it is not preferred for most salad dressing. Its primary use in food preparation is for pickling when the food must remain light in color.

Cider vinegar is made from the hard cider of apples, (you will note an apple juice odor). It has a golden, cider color and a sharp vinegar taste. Like distilled vinegar, it is best used in pickling. Although often used in dressings, its overpowering taste is considered by many to be undesirable.

Malt vinegar has a light beer aroma and flavor. Very commonly used in England with Fish and Chips, it varies in color from pale to clear dark brown.

Wine vinegar is the preferred vinegar for use in most salad dressings. They are made from wines, most often of the grape variety, and have a full-bodied, wine-like aroma. Red or white wine vinegars can generally be used interchangeably unless specified in the recipe. Not as sharp in flavor as distilled or cider vinegar, wine vinegar complements rather than dominates the salad.

Herb or Seasoned vinegars start with a wine vinegar base to which herbs and spices may be added. The most popular vinegar herbs include basil, burnet, chervil, marjoram, mint, oregano, rosemary, savory, tarragon and thyme. You may purchase commercially made herb vinegars or make your own.

To make an herb vinegar choose an individual herb or a combination of herbs. Use 3 tablespoons of fresh herbs (3 teaspoons dry herbs) per quart of wine vinegar. Allow to set for 4 weeks. Strain through a cheesecloth and store in glass corked bottles.

NOTE: All vinegars are corrosive so mix and store in glass, enamel or stainless vessels.

Olive oil is the preferred dressing oil by many salad connoisseurs. It has a distinct heavy flavor which may be too much for some. Therefore, it can be found blended with other oils to give a little more subtle flavor to the salad. Olive oil comes in a wide variety of colors and flavor strengths depending on the origin. French olive oil is the most delicate, Italian is the most commonly used. Other varieties include Greek and Spanish.

Vegetable oil because of its mildness and versatility is a favorite. Pressed from a variety of seeds and fruits the color will vary depending on the prominent ingredient used. Read the label ingredients for the exact blend.

Corn oil can be bought pure or blended and is a common ingredient in salads and cooking.

Safflower oil has a subtle flavor which makes it a good choice for making mayonnaise or cooked dressings. High in polyunsaturates it is favored among the diet conscious.

Sesame oil has a strong, nutty flavor so use sparingly. It is best to use sesame oil only when specified in the recipe. This is a very common oil in oriental cooking.

Peanut oil is perfect when you don't want to alter the taste or color of the food. It is also a good oil to use in fondue cooking and deep fat frying.

NOTES: If a particular oil is desired to create a desired taste the recipe will state the oil by name. If no particular oil is stated use the one which you prefer.

Oils should be stored at temperatures less than 70°F. in dark, tightly closed bottles as they will have a tendency to become rancid.

OTHER SALAD DRESSING INGREDIENTS

When available **fresh herbs** are preferred over dried. Snip with a kitchen shears. See GUIDE TO USING HERBS AND SPICES, page 15, for more detailed information on each particular herb.

Garlic is a popular ingredient. If you enjoy making your own dressing, garlic press is a handy gadget to have since fresh garlic gives the better flavor.

Onions come in many varieties. Green onions (scallions), chives and the milder shallots are the most common additions to salad dressings. The Italian onion (purple in color) is a mild onion used for slicing in a salad.

VINEGAR AND OIL DRESSING

¼ to ½ cup oil
½ cup vinegar
½ teaspoon salt
Dash pepper
½ teaspoon Worcestershire sauce

In pint jar or blender, combine all ingredients. Shake covered or blend until well mixed. Cover and chill. Mix well before using.

NUTRITION INFORMATION PER SERVING

Serving Size: 1 tablespoon		Percent U.S. RDA Per Serving	
Calories	31	Protein	0%
Protein	0g	Vitamin A	0%
Carbohydrate	<1g	Vitamin C	0%
Fat	3g	Thiamin	0%
Sodium	70mg	Riboflavin	0%
Potassium	4mg	Niacin	0%
		Calcium	*
		Iron	*

ITALIAN DRESSING

¼ to ½ cup olive oil
1 tablespoon chopped onion
1 tablespoon chopped pimiento, drained
1 tablespoon chopped parsley
1 garlic clove, cut in half
½ teaspoon oregano leaves or Italian seasoning

In pint jar, combine all ingredients. Shake covered until well mixed. Cover and refrigerate several hours. Remove garlic; shake well before serving. 1 cup

NUTRITION INFORMATION PER SERVING

Serving Size: 1 tablespoon		Percent U.S. RDA Per Serving	
Calories	31	Protein	*
Protein	<1g	Vitamin A	*
Carbohydrate	<1g	Vitamin C	*
Fat	3g	Thiamin	*
Sodium	<1mg	Riboflavin	*
Potassium	3mg	Niacin	*
		Calcium	*
		Iron	*

EASY THOUSAND ISLAND DRESSING

½ cup mayonnaise
2 tablespoons pickle relish
2 tablespoons chili sauce
1 hard-cooked egg, chopped
½ teaspoon Worcestershire sauce

In small bowl, combine all ingredients; blend well. Cover and chill.

¾ cup

NUTRITION INFORMATION PER SERVING

Serving Size: 1 tablespoon		Percent U.S. RDA Per Serving	
Calories	80	Protein	*
Protein	<1g	Vitamin A	2%
Carbohydrate	2g	Vitamin C	*
Fat	8g	Thiamin	*
Sodium	115mg	Riboflavin	*
Potassium	18mg	Niacin	*
		Calcium	*
		Iron	*

THOUSAND ISLAND DRESSING

½ cup whipping cream, whipped
1 hard-cooked egg, chopped
¼ cup chopped stuffed olives
¼ cup chopped dill pickle
1 tablespoon finely chopped green onion
Dash paprika
1 cup mayonnaise or salad dressing
¼ cup chili sauce
1 teaspoon Worcestershire sauce
Dash Tabasco sauce

In small bowl, beat cream until thick. Add remaining ingredients; blend well. Cover and chill.

2¾ cups

NUTRITION INFORMATION PER SERVING

Serving Size: 1 tablespoon		Percent U.S. RDA Per Serving	
Calories	50	Protein	*
Protein	<1g	Vitamin A	*
Carbohydrate	<1g	Vitamin C	*
Fat	5g	Thiamin	*
Sodium	83mg	Riboflavin	*
Potassium	13mg	Niacin	*
		Calcium	*
		Iron	*

HONEY CELERY SEED DRESSING

½ teaspoon dry mustard
½ teaspoon paprika
⅛ teaspoon salt
½ cup oil
½ cup honey
2 tablespoons vinegar
½ teaspoon celery seed

In small bowl or blender, combine all ingredients except celery seed; blend well. Stir in celery seed. Cover and chill.

1 cup

NUTRITION INFORMATION PER SERVING

Serving Size: 1 tablespoon		Percent U.S. RDA Per Serving	
Calories	93	Protein	*
Protein	<1g	Vitamin A	*
Carbohydrate	9g	Vitamin C	*
Fat	7g	Thiamin	*
Sodium	18mg	Riboflavin	*
Potassium	9mg	Niacin	*
		Calcium	*
		Iron	*

LOW-CALORIE THOUSAND ISLAND DRESSING

8-oz. carton (1 cup) plain yogurt
¼ cup finely chopped celery
1 tablespoon finely chopped onion
1 tablespoon sugar or honey
½ teaspoon chopped chives
½ teaspoon salt
½ teaspoon garlic salt
⅛ teaspoon pepper
¼ cup catsup

In small bowl or blender, combine all ingredients. Blend until smooth. Cover and chill. Mix well before using.

1½ cups

NUTRITION INFORMATION PER SERVING

Serving Size: 1 tablespoon		Percent U.S. RDA Per Serving	
Calories	10	Protein	*
Protein	<1g	Vitamin A	*
Carbohydrate	2g	Vitamin C	*
Fat	<1g	Thiamin	*
Sodium	120mg	Riboflavin	*
Potassium	29mg	Niacin	*
		Calcium	*
		Iron	*

FRENCH-RUSSIAN DRESSING

¼ cup sugar
½ teaspoon salt
2 tablespoons finely chopped onion
1 garlic clove, crushed
1 cup oil
⅓ cup chili sauce
¼ cup vinegar
½ teaspoon Worcestershire sauce

In small bowl or blender, combine all ingredients. Blend until smooth. Cover and chill. Mix well before using. 1¾ cups

NUTRITION INFORMATION PER SERVING

Serving Size: 1 tablespoon		Percent U.S. RDA Per Serving	
Calories	80	Protein	*
Protein	<1g	Vitamin A	*
Carbohydrate	3g	Vitamin C	*
Fat	8g	Thiamin	*
Sodium	84mg	Riboflavin	*
Potassium	16mg	Niacin	*
		Calcium	*
		Iron	*

TANGY FRENCH DRESSING

½ cup firmly packed brown sugar
½ teaspoon salt
1 garlic clove, minced
½ cup vinegar
½ cup catsup
½ cup chili sauce
¼ to ½ cup oil
¼ teaspoon Worcestershire sauce
Dash Tabasco sauce

In pint jar or blender, combine all ingredients. Shake well or blend at medium speed until smooth. Cover and chill. Mix well before using. 2½ cups

NUTRITION INFORMATION PER SERVING

Serving Size: 1 tablespoon		Percent U.S. RDA Per Serving	
Calories	30	Protein	*
Protein	<1g	Vitamin A	*
Carbohydrate	5g	Vitamin C	*
Fat	1g	Thiamin	*
Sodium	110mg	Riboflavin	*
Potassium	38mg	Niacin	*
		Calcium	*
		Iron	*

This traditional dressing is the final touch for any green salad– simple but elegant.

BASIC FRENCH DRESSING

¾ cup oil
¼ cup vinegar or lemon juice
1 teaspoon paprika
½ teaspoon salt
½ teaspoon dry mustard
Dash pepper

In pint jar or blender, combine all ingredients. Shake well or blend at medium speed until smooth. Cover and chill. Mix well before using. 1 cup

NUTRITION INFORMATION PER SERVING

Serving Size: 1 tablespoon		Percent U.S. RDA Per Serving	
Calories	91	Protein	*
Protein	<1g	Vitamin A	0%
Carbohydrate	<1g	Vitamin C	0%
Fat	10g	Thiamin	*
Sodium	68mg	Riboflavin	*
Potassium	4mg	Niacin	*
		Calcium	*
		Iron	*

TIPS: *For use with fruit, add ¼ cup sugar or 2 tablespoons honey.*

For GARLIC FRENCH DRESSING, add 1 crushed garlic clove and let stand several hours.

For BLUE CHEESE FRENCH DRESSING, add 2 oz. crumbled blue or Roquefort cheese and 2 tablespoons sugar, if desired.

For MINT FRENCH DRESSING, add 1 to 2 tablespoons crushed mint leaves and 2 tablespoons sugar. Serve over fruit.

LOW-CALORIE FRENCH DRESSING

2 teaspoons cornstarch
¾ cup cold water
1 tablespoon sugar
½ teaspoon salt
½ teaspoon onion powder
½ teaspoon dry mustard
½ teaspoon celery seed
½ teaspoon paprika
¼ cup lemon juice
¼ cup catsup
1 tablespoon oil
1 teaspoon Worcestershire sauce

In medium saucepan, combine cornstarch and water; blend well. Cook until thickened, stirring constantly; cool. Stir in remaining ingredients; beat well. Chill. Mix well before using.

1¼ cups

NUTRITION INFORMATION PER SERVING

Serving Size: 1 tablespoon		Percent U.S. RDA Per Serving	
Calories	14	Protein	*
Protein	<1g	Vitamin A	*
Carbohydrate	2g	Vitamin C	3%
Fat	<1g	Thiamin	*
Sodium	93mg	Riboflavin	*
Potassium	18mg	Niacin	*
		Calcium	*
		Iron	*

BERRY FRUIT DRESSING

½ teaspoon dry or prepared mustard
¼ teaspoon salt
2 tablespoons lemon juice or vinegar
10-oz. pkg. (1¼ cups) frozen sweetened raspberries or strawberries, partially thawed

In small bowl or blender, combine all ingredients. Blend until well combined. Cover and chill.

1¼ cups

NUTRITION INFORMATION PER SERVING

Serving Size: 1 tablespoon		Percent U.S. RDA Per Serving	
Calories	14	Protein	*
Protein	<1g	Vitamin A	*
Carbohydrate	4g	Vitamin C	6%
Fat	<1g	Thiamin	*
Sodium	27mg	Riboflavin	*
Potassium	17mg	Niacin	*
		Calcium	*
		Iron	*

GREEN GODDESS SALAD DRESSING

¼ cup snipped parsley
3 tablespoons chopped green onion
1 garlic clove, crushed
½ teaspoon salt
⅛ teaspoon freshly ground pepper
2-oz. can anchovy fillets, drained and chopped
1 cup mayonnaise
½ cup dairy sour cream
2 tablespoons tarragon vinegar
1 tablespoon lemon juice
2 drops green food coloring

In small bowl, combine all ingredients; mix well. Cover and chill.

2 cups

NUTRITION INFORMATION PER SERVING

Serving Size: 1 tablespoon (without anchovies)*		Percent U.S. RDA Per Serving	
Calories	60	Protein	*
Protein	<1g	Vitamin A	*
Carbohydrate	<1g	Vitamin C	2%
Fat	6g	Thiamin	*
Sodium	77mg	Riboflavin	*
Potassium	9mg	Niacin	*
		Calcium	*
		Iron	*

*Insufficient data to give nutritional information with regard to anchovies.

EASY GREEN GODDESS DRESSING

½ cup mayonnaise
½ cup dairy sour cream
3 tablespoons chopped green onion
2 tablespoons finely chopped parsley
½ teaspoon salt
⅛ teaspoon garlic powder
⅛ teaspoon pepper
1 tablespoon vinegar or lemon juice
Half 2-oz. can anchovy fillets, chopped or 1 tablespoon anchovy paste, if desired
3 drops green food coloring

In small bowl, combine all ingredients; blend well. Cover and chill.
1½ cups

NUTRITION INFORMATION PER SERVING

Serving Size: 1 tablespoon (without anchovies)* — Percent U.S. RDA Per Serving

Calories	45	Protein	*
Protein	<1g	Vitamin A	*
Carbohydrate	<1g	Vitamin C	*
Fat	5g	Thiamin	*
Sodium	75mg	Riboflavin	*
Potassium	6mg	Niacin	*
		Calcium	*
		Iron	*

*Insufficient data to give nutritional information with regard to anchovies.

COOKED SALAD DRESSING

2 tablespoons flour
2 tablespoons sugar
1 teaspoon salt
1 teaspoon dry or prepared mustard
¾ cup milk
1 egg, slightly beaten
3 tablespoons vinegar
1 tablespoon margarine or butter

In small saucepan, combine first 4 ingredients; mix well. Stir in milk and egg; mix until smooth. Cook over medium heat until mixture boils and thickens, stirring constantly. Blend in vinegar and margarine. Cool. (For potato salad, warm dressing penetrates the potatoes quicker.)
1 cup

NUTRITION INFORMATION PER SERVING

Serving Size: 1 tablespoon — Percent U.S. RDA Per Serving

Calories	29	Protein	*
Protein	1g	Vitamin A	*
Carbohydrate	3g	Vitamin C	*
Fat	2g	Thiamin	*
Sodium	152mg	Riboflavin	*
Potassium	25mg	Niacin	*
		Calcium	*
		Iron	*

TIPS: *For FRUIT DRESSING, cool cooked dressing. Before adding to fruit, fold in 1 cup thawed whipped topping or ½ cup whipping cream, whipped and sweetened.*

For SOUR CREAM COOKED DRESSING, cool cooked dressing. Fold in ½ cup dairy sour cream. Try on meat, seafood, coleslaw, potato and other vegetable salads.

SOUR CREAM DRESSING

1 cup dairy sour cream or plain yogurt
2 tablespoons honey
2 teaspoons lemon juice
¼ teaspoon salt

In small bowl, combine all ingredients; blend well. Cover and chill.

1 cup

NUTRITION INFORMATION PER SERVING

Serving Size: 1 tablespoon		Percent U.S. RDA Per Serving	
Calories	37	Protein	*
Protein	<1g	Vitamin A	2%
Carbohydrate	3g	Vitamin C	*
Fat	3g	Thiamin	*
Sodium	40mg	Riboflavin	*
Potassium	2mg	Niacin	*
		Calcium	*
		Iron	*

TIP: *OTHER FLAVOR VARIATIONS: Omit lemon juice and add 2 tablespoons creme de menthe, Galiano, Grand Marnier or fruit-flavored brandy; add fruit-flavored yogurt and decrease honey to 1 tablespoon; add a dash of cinnamon, nutmeg or ginger; add ¼ teaspoon celery or poppy seed; add grated orange or lemon peel; fold in ½ cup shredded Cheddar or Swiss cheese or chopped nuts.*

SOUR CREAM-BLUE CHEESE DRESSING

2 to 4-oz. blue cheese, softened
¾ cup salad oil
1 teaspoon salt
½ teaspoon sugar
⅛ teaspoon pepper
1 garlic clove, crushed
1 cup dairy sour cream
¼ cup cider vinegar

In small bowl, mash blue cheese with fork. Beat at low speed, gradually add ¼ cup salad oil; beat until smooth. Add remaining salad oil; continue beating. Add remaining ingredients and beat until well blended.

2⅓ cups

NUTRITION INFORMATION PER SERVING

Serving Size: 1 tablespoon		Percent U.S. RDA Per Serving	
Calories	58	Protein	*
Protein	<1g	Vitamin A	*
Carbohydrate	<1g	Vitamin C	*
Fat	6g	Thiamin	*
Sodium	60mg	Riboflavin	*
Potassium	2mg	Niacin	*
		Calcium	*
		Iron	*

HORSERADISH DRESSING

2 teaspoons sugar
½ teaspoon salt
¼ teaspoon paprika
Dash pepper
½ to 1 cup mayonnaise or salad dressing
½ cup dairy sour cream or plain yogurt
3 to 4 tablespoons prepared horseradish
½ teaspoon prepared or ¼ teaspoon dry mustard
½ teaspoon Worcestershire sauce
Dash Tabasco sauce

In pint jar or blender, combine all ingredients. Shake covered or blend at medium speed until smooth. Cover and chill.

1⅔ cups

NUTRITION INFORMATION PER SERVING

Serving Size: 1 tablespoon		Percent U.S. RDA Per Serving	
Calories	41	Protein	*
Protein	<1g	Vitamin A	*
Carbohydrate	<1g	Vitamin C	*
Fat	4g	Thiamin	*
Sodium	73mg	Riboflavin	*
Potassium	7mg	Niacin	*
		Calcium	*
		Iron	*

CREAMY SWEET-SOUR DRESSING

¼ cup sugar
¼ cup cream or dairy sour cream
¼ cup vinegar or lemon juice

In small bowl, combine all ingredients; mix well. Pour over salad greens or shredded cabbage; toss lightly. ⅔ cup

NUTRITION INFORMATION PER SERVING

Serving Size: 1 tablespoon		Percent U.S. RDA Per Serving	
Calories	33	Protein	*
Protein	<1g	Vitamin A	*
Carbohydrate	6g	Vitamin C	*
Fat	1g	Thiamin	*
Sodium	3mg	Riboflavin	*
Potassium	13mg	Niacin	*
		Calcium	*
		Iron	*

Perfect atop a gelatin mold. Use complementary flavors such as raspberry jam with a peach gelatin, orange marmalade on a cranberry mold or strawberries on lemon molds.

WHIPPED CREAM DRESSING

¼ cup whipping cream, whipped or ½ cup frozen whipped topping, thawed
½ cup mayonnaise or salad dressing
⅓ cup fruit jam or preserves

In small bowl, fold together all ingredients. Cover and chill. 1⅓ cups

NUTRITION INFORMATION PER SERVING

Serving Size: 1 tablespoon		Percent U.S. RDA Per Serving	
Calories	62	Protein	*
Protein	<1g	Vitamin A	*
Carbohydrate	4g	Vitamin C	*
Fat	5g	Thiamin	*
Sodium	33mg	Riboflavin	*
Potassium	9mg	Niacin	*
		Calcium	*
		Iron	*

YOGURT DRESSING

8-oz. carton (1 cup) plain yogurt or dairy sour cream
1 tablespoon sugar or honey
¼ teaspoon onion salt
1½ teaspoons prepared mustard
1 teaspoon lemon juice

In small bowl,combine all ingredients; blend well. Cover and chill. 1 cup

NUTRITION INFORMATION PER SERVING

Serving Size: 1 tablespoon		Percent U.S. RDA Per Serving	
Calories	10	Protein	*
Protein	<1g	Vitamin A	*
Carbohydrate	2g	Vitamin C	*
Fat	<1g	Thiamin	*
Sodium	38mg	Riboflavin	*
Potassium	21mg	Niacin	*
		Calcium	*
		Iron	*

TIPS: *For CHIVE YOGURT DRESSING, add 2 tablespoons chopped chives. If desired, add 2 slices cooked crumbled bacon or 1 tablespoon bacon-flavored bits. Try on salads, vegetables or baked potatoes.*

For HORSERADISH YOGURT DRESSING, decrease sugar to 1 teaspoon and add 1 teaspoon prepared horseradish and ½ teaspoon Worcestershire sauce. Try on meat or vegetable salads.

For BLUE CHEESE YOGURT DRESSING, omit sugar and mustard and add 2 oz. crumbled blue cheese. Try on fruit or vegetable salads.

For CURRY YOGURT DRESSING, add 1 teaspoon curry powder. Try on meat, coleslaw, macaroni or potato salads. Add ¼ cup chopped chutney to salads. Garnish with peanuts or coconut.

Homemade mayonnaise has a snappier flavor than the commercial version but many experts feel it is the only way to make a salad.

MAYONNAISE

1 egg yolk
½ teaspoon salt
½ teaspoon sugar
¼ teaspoon prepared or dry mustard
Dash pepper or cayenne
2 tablespoons lemon juice or vinegar
1 cup oil

In small bowl, combine egg yolk, salt, sugar, mustard, pepper and 1 tablespoon lemon juice; blend well. Add oil by teaspoonfuls, beat at medium speed until half the oil has been added. Add the remaining 1 tablespoon of lemon juice; blend well. Add the remaining oil by tablespoonfuls; continue beating until all the oil has been added and the mayonnaise is thick and smooth. Cover and chill. 1 cup

NUTRITION INFORMATION PER SERVING

Serving Size: 1 tablespoon		Percent U.S. RDA Per Serving	
Calories	125	Protein	*
Protein	<1g	Vitamin A	*
Carbohydrate	<1g	Vitamin C	*
Fat	14g	Thiamin	*
Sodium	69mg	Riboflavin	*
Potassium	4mg	Niacin	*
		Calcium	*
		Iron	*

TIPS: *To make in blender, use a whole egg instead of just the yolk. Combine all ingredients with ¼ cup oil. Blend at high speed until smooth. Remove cover, gradually add remaining ¾ cup oil; blending until smooth.*

If mayonnaise separates, in small bowl, slowly add curdled mixture to 1 egg yolk, beating constantly until it thickens again.

ADDITIONS TO MAYONNAISE
(Using ½ cup mayonnaise)

SOUR CREAM-MAYONNAISE DRESSING: Fold in ½ cup dairy sour cream. Makes a tart creamy dressing for meat, seafood, coleslaw, potato and macaroni salads.

1 cup

NUTRITION INFORMATION PER SERVING

Serving Size: 1 tablespoon		Percent U.S. RDA Per Serving	
Calories	64	Protein	*
Protein	<1g	Vitamin A	*
Carbohydrate	<1g	Vitamin C	0%
Fat	7g	Thiamin	*
Sodium	44mg	Riboflavin	*
Potassium	2mg	Niacin	0%
		Calcium	*
		Iron	*

CREAMY RUSSIAN DRESSING: Fold in 2 tablespoons chili sauce, ⅛ teaspoon garlic powder and ⅛ teaspoon onion powder.

½ cup

NUTRITION INFORMATION PER SERVING

Serving Size: 1 tablespoon		Percent U.S. RDA Per Serving	
Calories	103	Protein	*
Protein	<1g	Vitamin A	*
Carbohydrate	1g	Vitamin C	*
Fat	11g	Thiamin	*
Sodium	132mg	Riboflavin	*
Potassium	20mg	Niacin	*
		Calcium	*
		Iron	*

CREAMY CUCUMBER DRESSING: Fold in ½ cup dairy sour cream, ½ cup chopped cucumber, 2 sliced green onions, and ¼ teaspoon onion salt. Try on lettuce salad or sliced tomatoes.

1½ cups

NUTRITION INFORMATION PER SERVING

Serving Size: 1 tablespoon		Percent U.S. RDA Per Serving	
Calories	43	Protein	*
Protein	<1g	Vitamin A	*
Carbohydrate	<1g	Vitamin C	*
Fat	5g	Thiamin	*
Sodium	46mg	Riboflavin	*
Potassium	8mg	Niacin	*
		Calcium	*
		Iron	*

SOUPS, SAUCES,
&
SANDWICHES

SOUPS

SERVING

The versatility of soup can never be overestimated from the hot and hearty meal-in-one soup bowl to the cool and light first course sipper; almost any meal can accommodate a soup.

Soup can be elegant. Served as a first course, it can be an impressive beginning to a formal dinner party. Serve warm soups from a decorative soup tureen or serve cold soups on ice.

Soup can be homey. Serve a hearty meat and vegetable soup along with bread and fresh fruit for a complete meal – wonderful for a family supper or just casual entertaining.

PREPARATION

Making soup can be a very individual affair. Ingredients may be substituted to suit personal tastes and product availability, especially with vegetable soups.

Soups make great use of the unwanted meat trimmings – chicken backs aren't a barbecuing favorite but they are perfect for soup.

Have some of your vegetables been in the refrigerator too long? Are they wilted or shriveled? Add them to your next soup pot. The slow cooking draws out the flavors and nutrients into the stock.

Here are a few additional tips:

- Do not boil soups thickened with egg; this will cause curdling.
- If using canned vegetables, do not drain but instead use the liquid as part of the water needed as it contains many valuable nutrients.
- Frozen vegetables offer as much food value as fresh vegetables.
- Freeze any meat pieces you wish to use later for soups; they may be added frozen to the pot.
- Instant bouillon, canned meat stock and fresh stock may be used interchangeably. One cube or teaspoon instant bouillon plus 1 cup water equals 1 cup canned or fresh meat stock.

GARNISHES FOR SOUP

Top off bowls of soup with one or several of these ideas; select flavors to complement the flavors of the soup.

Croutons, cheese crackers, crushed potato chips, shoestring potatoes, chow mein noodles, popcorn, pretzels.

Shredded cheese, grated Parmesan cheese, crumbled blue cheese, toasted almonds, cooked crumbled bacon, sieved egg yolk, sliced wieners, chopped peanuts, dairy sour cream, yogurt.

Chopped chives, sliced green onions, sliced radishes, chopped dill pickle, sliced cucumber, green pepper strips, chopped celery tops, shredded carrots, sliced water chestnuts, sliced lemon, sliced avocado.

Caraway seed, rosemary, marjoram, parsley, watercress, dill weed, basil leaves, curry powder, nutmeg, mint leaves.

OLD-FASHIONED VEGETABLE SOUP

2 to 3 lb. beef shank or meaty soup bones
3 teaspoons salt
¼ teaspoon thyme leaves or marjoram leaves
6 peppercorns or ¼ teaspoon pepper
2 whole allspice
2 cubes or 2 teaspoons beef bouillon
1 bay leaf
2 quarts (8 cups) water
2 medium potatoes, peeled and cubed
2 stalks celery, sliced
2 medium carrots, sliced
1 small onion, chopped
16-oz. can (2 cups) tomatoes, undrained
12-oz. can (1½ cups) whole kernel corn, drained, if desired

In large saucepan or Dutch oven, combine first 8 ingredients. Simmer covered, 2½ to 3 hours or until meat is tender. Remove beef shank, peppercorns, allspice and bay leaf. Cut meat from bones and return to soup. Add remaining ingredients; simmer covered, 30 minutes or until vegetables are tender.

6 to 8 servings

NUTRITION INFORMATION PER SERVING

Serving Size: 1/6 of recipe		Percent U.S. RDA Per Serving	
Calories	194	Protein	16%
Protein	10g	Vitamin A	71%
Carbohydrate	26g	Vitamin C	28%
Fat	7g	Thiamin	9%
Sodium	1488mg	Riboflavin	8%
Potassium	498mg	Niacin	15%
		Calcium	4%
		Iron	11%

MINESTRONE SOUP

- 2 tablespoons salt
- ¼ teaspoon pepper
- 2 to 3 lb. beef shank or soup bones
- 1 bay leaf
- 1 garlic clove, minced
- 3 quarts (12 cups) water
- 2 cups chopped cabbage
- 1 cup (4 oz.) vermicelli or spaghetti, broken into 2 to 3-inch pieces
- 4 medium carrots, sliced
- 2 stalks celery, sliced
- ⅛ teaspoon Kitchen Bouquet, if desired
- 16-oz. can (2 cups) chick peas or kidney beans, undrained
- 16-oz. can (2 cups) tomatoes, undrained
- 8-oz. can (1 cup) tomato sauce

In Dutch oven, combine first 6 ingredients. Heat to boiling; reduce heat and simmer covered, 2½ to 3 hours or until meat is tender. Remove beef shank from soup and cut meat from bone; cut into bite-size pieces. Add meat* and remaining ingredients to soup. Cover and continue simmering 30 to 45 minutes or until vegetables are tender. Remove bay leaf. If desired, sprinkle each serving with grated Parmesan cheese. 10 to 12 servings

NUTRITION INFORMATION PER SERVING

Serving Size: 1/10 of recipe		Percent U.S. RDA Per Serving	
Calories	186	Protein	14%
Protein	9g	Vitamin A	76%
Carbohydrate	23g	Vitamin C	15%
Fat	6g	Thiamin	9%
Sodium	1361mg	Riboflavin	7%
Potassium	358mg	Niacin	10%
		Calcium	5%
		Iron	13%

TIP: *To MAKE AHEAD, prepare to*. Refrigerate up to 2 days or freeze up to 3 months. To serve, proceed as directed. Completed soup may be frozen up to 3 months.*

GROUND BEEF-VEGETABLE SOUP

- 1 lb. ground beef
- 2 teaspoons salt
- ⅛ teaspoon pepper
- 2 medium carrots, chopped
- 1 medium potato or rutabaga, cubed
- 1 medium onion, sliced
- 1 stalk celery, chopped
- 1 bay leaf
- 3 cups water
- 1 tablespoon Worcestershire sauce
- 16-oz. can tomatoes, undrained

In Dutch oven or deep skillet, brown ground beef; drain excess fat. Stir in remaining ingredients. Simmer covered, 20 to 25 minutes or until vegetables are tender, stirring occasionally. 5 to 6 servings

NUTRITION INFORMATION PER SERVING

Serving Size: 1/6 of recipe		Percent U.S. RDA Per Serving	
Calories	210	Protein	23%
Protein	15g	Vitamin A	67%
Carbohydrate	12g	Vitamin C	37%
Fat	11g	Thiamin	9%
Sodium	890mg	Riboflavin	10%
Potassium	638mg	Niacin	20%
		Calcium	3%
		Iron	14%

CHICKEN NOODLE SOUP

3 to 4-lb. stewing chicken, cut into pieces
1 tablespoon salt
¼ teaspoon poultry seasoning, if desired
6 peppercorns
3 quarts (12 cups) water
3 carrots, sliced
2 medium stalks celery, chopped
1 small onion, chopped
1 to 2 cups noodles, uncooked

In large saucepan or Dutch oven, combine first 5 ingredients. Heat to boiling; reduce heat. Simmer covered, 2 to 2½ hours or until chicken is tender. Remove chicken and peppercorns. Skim off fat. Cut meat from bone and return to soup. Add remaining ingredients except noodles. Continue simmering covered, until vegetables are almost tender. Add noodles; cook about 10 minutes longer until noodles are tender. 6 to 8 servings

NUTRITION INFORMATION PER SERVING

Serving Size: 1/6 of recipe		Percent U.S. RDA Per Serving	
Calories	384	Protein	56%
Protein	36g	Vitamin A	97%
Carbohydrate	33g	Vitamin C	6%
Fat	11g	Thiamin	27%
Sodium	1161mg	Riboflavin	19%
Potassium	535mg	Niacin	62%
		Calcium	5%
		Iron	17%

TIP: *For CHICKEN RICE SOUP, omit noodles and add ⅓ cup uncooked brown or white rice when vegetables are added. Simmer 30 to 40 minutes or until rice is tender.*

HAM AND SPLIT PEA SOUP

16-oz. pkg. (2 cups) dried split peas
2-lb. smoked ham shank
1 teaspoon salt
½ teaspoon basil leaves
1 small onion, chopped
6 peppercorns
2 quarts (8 cups) water
2 medium stalks celery, sliced
1 medium carrot, chopped, if desired

In large saucepan, combine first 7 ingredients. Simmer covered, 1 hour. Stir in celery and carrots. Continue simmering covered, for ½ to 1 hour or until peas are tender and soup thickens. Remove peppercorns and ham shank; cut meat from bone and return to soup. Heat through.
6 to 8 servings

NUTRITION INFORMATION PER SERVING

Serving Size: 1/6 of recipe		Percent U.S. RDA Per Serving	
Calories	402	Protein	41%
Protein	26g	Vitamin A	29%
Carbohydrate	38g	Vitamin C	4%
Fat	17g	Thiamin	36%
Sodium	401mg	Riboflavin	17%
Potassium	602mg	Niacin	21%
		Calcium	4%
		Iron	26%

TIPS: *Whole peas may be substituted for split peas, but soak overnight in the 2 quarts water before cooking as directed.*

Smoked pork hocks may be substituted for ham shank.

For HAM AND BEAN SOUP, substitute dried navy beans for split peas. Soak beans overnight in the 2 quarts water. Increase first cooking time to 2 hours. Stir in celery and carrots. Continue cooking as directed.

Perfect for the day after Thanksgiving—nourishing but not heavy. Cut up the turkey carcass enough to fit the soup pot if necessary.

"LEFTOVER TURKEY" SOUP

1½ teaspoons salt
¼ teaspoon poultry seasoning or sage
Bones and trimmings from 1 turkey or 2 chickens
3 cubes or 3 teaspoons chicken bouillon
1 bay leaf
1½ quarts (6 cups) water
½ cup barley or rice or 1 cup noodles
3 medium carrots, sliced
2 stalks celery, sliced
2 medium onions, sliced or chopped
2 tablespoons chopped parsley

In large saucepan, combine first 6 ingredients. Simmer covered, 1½ hours. Remove bones; cut off meat and return meat to broth. Add remaining ingredients except parsley to broth. Simmer covered, 30 minutes or until vegetables and barley are tender. Garnish with parsley.
6 to 8 servings

NUTRITION INFORMATION PER SERVING

Serving Size: 1/6 of recipe		Percent U.S. RDA Per Serving	
Calories	144	Protein	12%
Protein	8g	Vitamin A	82%
Carbohydrate	21g	Vitamin C	17%
Fat	3g	Thiamin	4%
Sodium	1053mg	Riboflavin	3%
Potassium	268mg	Niacin	4%
		Calcium	4%
		Iron	5%

TIP: *Other vegetables may be added or substituted such as: corn, zucchini, tomatoes, potatoes, peas and mushrooms.*

Feel free to experiment with other cream soup variations such as asparagus, broccoli or cauliflower.

BASIC CREAM SOUP

¼ cup margarine or butter
1 small onion, chopped
1 stalk celery, chopped
3 tablespoons flour
3 cups milk
1 teaspoon salt
⅛ teaspoon pepper

In medium saucepan, cook onion and celery in margarine until tender. Stir in flour. Add milk; heat mixture until it thickens and boils, stirring constantly. Season with salt and pepper. (Any desired cooked vegetables or meat may be added with milk.) 3 to 4 servings

NUTRITION INFORMATION PER SERVING

Serving Size: 1/3 of recipe		Percent U.S. RDA Per Serving	
Calories	332	Protein	15%
Protein	10g	Vitamin A	20%
Carbohydrate	20g	Vitamin C	5%
Fat	24g	Thiamin	9%
Sodium	1038mg	Riboflavin	27%
Potassium	431mg	Niacin	4%
		Calcium	31%
		Iron	*

TIPS: *For CREAM OF CORN SOUP, add ¼ teaspoon dry mustard with flour and 16-oz. can (2 cups) drained corn with milk; use vegetable liquid for part of milk. Garnish with nutmeg or cooked crumbled bacon.*

For CREAM OF MUSHROOM SOUP, cook 8-oz. (3 cups) sliced fresh or 8-oz. can (1 cup) drained canned mushrooms along with onion. Continue as directed, adding 2 cubes or 2 teaspoons chicken bouillon along with milk. If desired, substitute ¼ cup dry white wine or sherry for part of milk.

Some old-fashioned tomato base soups include a small amount of soda to help eliminate curdling when the milk is added. This has been found to destroy some of the nutrients. To prevent curdling, use very fresh whole milk. Milk refrigerated for several days tends to curdle easily.

CREAM OF TOMATO SOUP

¼ cup margarine or butter
1 small onion, chopped
1 stalk celery, chopped
3 tablespoons flour
3 cups milk
1 tablespoon sugar
1 teaspoon salt
⅛ teaspoon pepper
28-oz. can (3½ cups) tomatoes, undrained

In large saucepan, cook onion and celery in margarine until tender. Stir in flour. Add milk and sugar. Heat mixture until it boils and thickens, stirring constantly. In medium saucepan, heat tomatoes. (If desired, process tomatoes in blender until smooth.) Before serving, slowly add tomatoes to milk mixture, stirring constantly. Serve immediately. Soup may be reheated, but do not boil. Avoid storing soup in metal, as it may pick up a metallic taste. 6 servings

NUTRITION INFORMATION PER SERVING

Serving Size: 1/6 of recipe		Percent U.S. RDA Per Serving	
Calories	203	Protein	10%
Protein	6g	Vitamin A	34%
Carbohydrate	18g	Vitamin C	25%
Fat	12g	Thiamin	9%
Sodium	691mg	Riboflavin	16%
Potassium	514mg	Niacin	7%
		Calcium	16%
		Iron	5%

POTATO SOUP

2 to 3 slices bacon, cut in half
3 medium potatoes, peeled and cubed
2 stalks celery, chopped
2 medium carrots, diced
1 small onion, chopped
1 teaspoon salt
⅛ teaspoon pepper
1 cup water
2 tablespoons flour
2 cups milk

In large saucepan, fry bacon until crisp; drain on paper towel. To drippings, add potatoes, celery, carrots, onion, salt, pepper and water. Cook covered about 15 minutes or until tender. Combine flour with small amount of milk until smooth. Add to potato mixture along with remaining milk. Cook over medium heat until mixture boils. Garnish with crumbled bacon.

4 to 5 servings

NUTRITION INFORMATION PER SERVING

Serving Size: 1/4 of recipe		Percent U.S. RDA Per Serving	
Calories	193	Protein	13%
Protein	8g	Vitamin A	60%
Carbohydrate	26g	Vitamin C	24%
Fat	6g	Thiamin	12%
Sodium	673mg	Riboflavin	17%
Potassium	615mg	Niacin	9%
		Calcium	18%
		Iron	6%

TIPS: *Bacon may be omitted. Cook vegetables in water as directed.*

Add 2 tablespoons margarine when adding milk.

CHEESE SOUP DELIGHT

2 tablespoons margarine or butter
3 tablespoons flour
1 cup milk
10¾-oz. can (1¼ cups) condensed chicken broth
⅛ teaspoon salt
Dash pepper
2 to 4 tablespoons white wine or beer
¼ teaspoon Worcestershire sauce
Dash Tabasco sauce
1 cup (4 oz.) grated sharp Cheddar cheese

In medium saucepan, melt margarine; add flour and blend. Heat until bubbly, stirring constantly. Add milk and chicken broth; stir until smooth. Add salt, pepper, wine, Worcestershire and Tabasco; heat to boiling, stirring occasionally. Remove from heat; add cheese and stir until cheese is melted and smooth. Garnish with broken pretzels or popcorn. 4 servings

NUTRITION INFORMATION PER SERVING

Serving Size: 1/4 of recipe		Percent U.S. RDA Per Serving	
Calories	245	Protein	18%
Protein	12g	Vitamin A	14%
Carbohydrate	10g	Vitamin C	*
Fat	17g	Thiamin	4%
Sodium	819mg	Riboflavin	15%
Potassium	125mg	Niacin	2%
		Calcium	29%
		Iron	7%

CORNY WIENER CHOWDER

1 tablespoon margarine or butter
2 stalks celery, sliced
1 lb. wieners, sliced
¼ teaspoon salt
1 cup milk
2 teaspoons Worcestershire sauce
16-oz. can (2 cups) cream-style corn
10¾-oz. can condensed cream of celery or potato soup

In large saucepan, cook celery in margarine until tender. Add remaining ingredients. Simmer covered, 15 to 20 minutes or until heated through and flavors are well blended. If desired, garnish with paprika or pimiento. 5 to 6 servings

NUTRITION INFORMATION PER SERVING

Serving Size: 1/6 of recipe		Percent U.S. RDA Per Serving	
Calories	370	Protein	20%
Protein	13g	Vitamin A	10%
Carbohydrate	23g	Vitamin C	10%
Fat	26g	Thiamin	10%
Sodium	747mg	Riboflavin	16%
Potassium	223mg	Niacin	14%
		Calcium	8%
		Iron	10%

TIP: *Cooked cubed ham, bologna or canned luncheon meat may be substituted for wieners.*

Leeks are a member of the onion family. They look like very large green onion plants. Delicately flavored leeks make a very pleasant and not overpowering soup.

CREAM OF LEEK SOUP

4 to 6 medium leeks
6 tablespoons margarine or butter
3 tablespoons flour
2 teaspoons chopped chives
½ teaspoon salt
6 cups milk or light cream
6 cubes or 6 teaspoons chicken bouillon

Thinly slice leeks, discarding top green portion. In medium saucepan, cook leeks in margarine 8 to 10 minutes or until tender, stirring occasionally. Stir in flour, chives, and salt; add milk and bouillon. Cook over medium heat, until boiling, stirring occasionally. Boil 1 to 2 minutes. If desired, garnish with nutmeg. 6 servings

NUTRITION INFORMATION PER SERVING

Serving Size: 1/6 of recipe		Percent U.S. RDA Per Serving	
Calories	290	Protein	16%
Protein	10g	Vitamin A	17%
Carbohydrate	18g	Vitamin C	6%
Fat	20g	Thiamin	8%
Sodium	1404mg	Riboflavin	26%
Potassium	435mg	Niacin	3%
		Calcium	30%
		Iron	*

Lobster or crab are perfect shellfish for this rich first course soup.

SEAFOOD BISQUE

1 tablespoon margarine or butter
2 tablespoons chopped onion
1 teaspoon chopped chives
1 cube or 1 teaspoon chicken bouillon
1 cup milk
Dash Tabasco sauce
½ cup condensed tomato soup
1 tablespoon lemon juice
1 cup cooked seafood
1 cup light cream

In medium saucepan, cook onion in margarine until tender. Stir in chives, bouillon, milk and Tabasco. Cook until steaming hot. Stir in tomato soup and lemon juice; heat through, stirring constantly. Stir in seafood and cream; heat but do not boil. 3 to 4 servings

NUTRITION INFORMATION PER SERVING

Serving Size: 1/4 of recipe		Percent U.S. RDA Per Serving	
Calories	253	Protein	16%
Protein	11g	Vitamin A	20%
Carbohydrate	11g	Vitamin C	11%
Fat	19g	Thiamin	5%
Sodium	917mg	Riboflavin	14%
Potassium	273mg	Niacin	5%
		Calcium	15%
		Iron	3%

TIP: *Soup may appear curdled after lemon juice is added to milk. Further cooking and addition of cream results in a smooth soup.*

OYSTER STEW

1 pint (2 cups) fresh oysters, drained (reserve liquor)
1 small onion, chopped
¼ to ½ cup margarine or butter
1 teaspoon salt
½ teaspoon celery salt, if desired
⅛ teaspoon white pepper
4 cups milk
½ teaspoon Worcestershire sauce
Reserved liquor

In medium saucepan, slowly cook oysters and onion in margarine until edges of oysters begin to curl. Add remaining ingredients. Heat through, but do not boil. If desired, garnish with chopped parsley. 4 to 5 servings

NUTRITION INFORMATION PER SERVING

Serving Size: 1/4 of recipe		Percent U.S. RDA Per Serving	
Calories	348	Protein	29%
Protein	19g	Vitamin A	24%
Carbohydrate	18g	Vitamin C	5%
Fat	22g	Thiamin	17%
Sodium	1108mg	Riboflavin	38%
Potassium	533mg	Niacin	16%
		Calcium	41%
		Iron	37%

TIP: *One 16-oz. can oysters may be substituted for fresh oysters.*

NEW ENGLAND CLAM CHOWDER

3 slices bacon
1 large potato, peeled and cubed
1 medium stalk celery, chopped
1 small onion, chopped
¾ teaspoon salt
⅛ teaspoon pepper
⅛ teaspoon thyme
2 cans (6½ oz. each) minced clams, drained (reserve liquor)
Reserved liquor
¼ cup flour
3 cups milk

In large saucepan, fry bacon until crisp; drain on paper towel. To drippings add potato, celery, onion, salt, pepper, thyme and liquor from clams. Heat to boiling and cook covered, about 10 minutes or until vegetables are tender. Combine flour and milk, add to vegetable mixture. Heat over medium heat until mixture thickens, stirring occasionally. Stir in clams. Heat through, but do not boil. Garnish with crumbled bacon.

5 to 6 servings

NUTRITION INFORMATION PER SERVING

Serving Size: 1/6 of recipe		Percent U.S. RDA Per Serving	
Calories	186	Protein	19%
Protein	13g	Vitamin A	4%
Carbohydrate	18g	Vitamin C	10%
Fat	7g	Thiamin	9%
Sodium	381mg	Riboflavin	20%
Potassium	427mg	Niacin	9%
		Calcium	20%
		Iron	20%

TIP: *To omit bacon, cook vegetables in clam liquor. Add 2 tablespoons margarine or butter when adding milk.*

EASY MANHATTAN CLAM CHOWDER

1 tablespoon margarine or butter
¼ cup finely chopped celery
2 tablespoons finely chopped onion
10¾-oz. can condensed cream of potato soup
6½-oz. can (¾ cup) minced clams, undrained
8-oz. can (1 cup) stewed tomatoes, cut up
½ cup milk

In medium saucepan, cook celery and onion in margarine until tender. Add remaining ingredients except milk. Heat just to boiling; simmer covered, 5 to 10 minutes to blend flavors. Add milk, heat but do not boil.

4 to 6 servings

NUTRITION INFORMATION PER SERVING

Serving Size: 1/4 of recipe		Percent U.S. RDA Per Serving	
Calories	168	Protein	11%
Protein	7g	Vitamin A	15%
Carbohydrate	12g	Vitamin C	12%
Fat	10g	Thiamin	4%
Sodium	731mg	Riboflavin	12%
Potassium	335mg	Niacin	7%
		Calcium	10%
		Iron	14%

TIP: *For EASY NEW ENGLAND CLAM CHOWDER, omit tomatoes; increase milk to 1 cup and add 2 teaspoons minced parsley.*

CREOLE GUMBO

½ cup chopped green pepper
2 medium stalks celery, chopped
1 small onion, chopped
2 tablespoons olive oil or oil
1½ teaspoons salt
1 garlic clove, minced
1 tablespoon Worcestershire sauce
16-oz. can (2 cups) tomatoes, undrained
8-oz. can (1 cup) tomato sauce
1 tablespoon chopped parsley
¼ cup dry sherry, if desired
10-oz. pkg. (1¼ cups) frozen okra, partially thawed and cut into ½-inch pieces
7½-oz. can (1 cup) crab meat, drained and flaked
4¼-oz. can (1 cup) shrimp, drained and cut into pieces

In large saucepan, cook green pepper, celery and onion in oil until tender. Stir in salt, garlic, Worcestershire sauce, tomatoes and tomato sauce. Simmer covered, 45 to 60 minutes. Add remaining ingredients. Continue simmering covered, 15 to 20 minutes or until okra is tender. If desired, top with garlic-flavored croutons. 6 to 8 servings

NUTRITION INFORMATION PER SERVING

Serving Size: 1/6 of recipe		Percent U.S. RDA Per Serving	
Calories	200	Protein	20%
Protein	13g	Vitamin A	32%
Carbohydrate	15g	Vitamin C	44%
Fat	10g	Thiamin	11%
Sodium	988mg	Riboflavin	10%
Potassium	398mg	Niacin	12%
		Calcium	10%
		Iron	11%

CREOLE GUMBO

SPINACH SOUP

10-oz. pkg. (1¼ cups) frozen chopped spinach
¼ cup chopped onion
¼ cup water
13¾-oz. can (2 cups) chicken stock
2 tablespoons margarine or butter
1 tablespoon flour
½ teaspoon salt
Dash pepper
½ cup light cream or milk
1 lemon, sliced, if desired

In medium saucepan, cook spinach with onion and water until thawed and tender. Pour mixture into blender with 1 cup of chicken stock. Process on medium speed until pureed. In same saucepan, melt margarine; stir in flour, salt and pepper. Add remaining chicken stock and cook until mixture boils, stirring constantly. Stir in spinach mixture, simmer covered, 10 minutes. Add cream; heat through. Serve garnished with lemon slices or a dollop of sour cream.

4 servings

NUTRITION INFORMATION PER SERVING

Serving Size: 1/4 of recipe		Percent U.S. RDA Per Serving	
Calories	154	Protein	11%
Protein	7g	Vitamin A	95%
Carbohydrate	7g	Vitamin C	20%
Fat	11g	Thiamin	4%
Sodium	973mg	Riboflavin	10%
Potassium	240mg	Niacin	12%
		Calcium	10%
		Iron	7%

TIP: *One 10¾-oz. can condensed chicken broth plus water to equal 2 cups, may be substituted for the chicken stock.*

A Greek specialty served as a first course. Delicately seasoned to stimulate the appetite.

EGG AND LEMON SOUP

⅓ cup white or brown rice
4 cubes or 4 teaspoons chicken bouillon
4 cups chicken broth
3 eggs
2 tablespoons lemon juice

In large saucepan, combine rice, bouillon and chicken broth. Simmer covered until rice is tender, about 20 minutes (40 minutes for brown rice). In small bowl, beat eggs well; beat in lemon juice. Slowly blend in half of hot chicken broth; return mixture to saucepan. Heat over low heat until mixture becomes creamy and hot, stirring occasionally; do not boil. (Boiling will cause the mixture to curdle.) If desired, garnish with fresh lemon slices or parsley sprigs.

4 servings

NUTRITION INFORMATION PER SERVING

Serving Size: 1/4 of recipe		Percent U.S. RDA Per Serving	
Calories	114	Protein	15%
Protein	10g	Vitamin A	10%
Carbohydrate	7g	Vitamin C	4%
Fat	5g	Thiamin	4%
Sodium	1797mg	Riboflavin	7%
Potassium	73mg	Niacin	*
		Calcium	4%
		Iron	13%

Often served as a first course soup. Mildly sweet onions flavor the beef broth; French bread and Parmesan cheese float on the soup.

FRENCH ONION SOUP

2 large or 3 medium onions, sliced
¼ cup margarine or butter
6 cubes or 6 teaspoons beef bouillon
Dash pepper
1 quart (4 cups) water
1 teaspoon Worcestershire sauce
4 to 6 slices French bread, toasted
Grated Parmesan cheese

In large saucepan, cook onions in margarine until tender. Add bouillon, pepper, water and Worcestershire sauce. Simmer covered, 20 to 25 minutes to blend flavors. To serve, top each serving with a slice of toasted French bread and sprinkle with Parmesan cheese. If desired, place under broiler until cheese is bubbly. 4 to 6 servings

NUTRITION INFORMATION PER SERVING

Serving Size: 1/4 of recipe		Percent U.S. RDA Per Serving	
Calories	206	Protein	9%
Protein	6g	Vitamin A	11%
Carbohydrate	16g	Vitamin C	7%
Fat	14g	Thiamin	5%
Sodium	1729mg	Riboflavin	6%
Potassium	164mg	Niacin	3%
		Calcium	9%
		Iron	4%

TIP: *For a rich wine flavor, use ½ cup dry white wine or sherry for part of water.*

PUMPKIN SOUP

A fall favorite that has a flavor similar to squash. For an interesting soup tureen serve from a hollowed out pumpkin.

PUMPKIN SOUP

4 cups cubed raw pumpkin*, peeled
¼ cup margarine or butter
2 carrots, cut into pieces
¼ cup water
1 teaspoon salt
¼ teaspoon thyme
½ bay leaf
3 sprigs parsley or 1 tablespoon parsley flakes
2 stalks celery, cut into pieces
1 medium onion, quartered
Pepper
4 cups chicken stock
½ cup dry white wine or sherry

In large saucepan, cook pumpkin in margarine 3 minutes. Add carrots and water; simmer covered, 30 minutes or until pumpkin is tender. Simmer remaining ingredients in another covered saucepan, 30 minutes. Strain to remove celery and onion. Process pumpkin and carrots in blender until smooth. Stir in broth. Heat through.
6 to 8 servings

NUTRITION INFORMATION PER SERVING

Serving Size: 1/6 of recipe		Percent U.S. RDA Per Serving	
Calories	187	Protein	13%
Protein	8g	Vitamin A	158%
Carbohydrate	14g	Vitamin C	14%
Fat	10g	Thiamin	3%
Sodium	1491mg	Riboflavin	6%
Potassium	367mg	Niacin	20%
		Calcium	5%
		Iron	5%

TIP: **If desired, one 16-oz. can (2 cups) cooked pumpkin may be substituted for raw pumpkin. Omit first cooking of pumpkin and add canned pumpkin to strained broth. If desired, ½ cup cooked carrots, processed in blender may be added. Stir until smooth. Heat through.*

This is a very versatile soup—serve it warm or cold, as a first course or a dessert. For a fast simple version see Mock Fruit Soup, page 204.

SWEDISH FRUIT SOUP

2 quarts (8 cups) boiling water
½ cup large pearl tapioca
⅛ teaspoon salt
1 cup pitted prunes
1 cup dried apricots
1 cup raisins
3 cinnamon sticks
1 cup sugar
3 medium apples, peeled and sliced
1 lemon, sliced
1 cup grape juice

In large saucepan, pour boiling water over tapioca and salt; mix well. Add prunes, apricots, raisins and cinnamon sticks. Simmer covered, 1 hour. Add remaining ingredients, continue simmering covered for 30 to 35 minutes or until tapioca is clear and apples are tender. Remove cinnamon sticks. Serve hot or chilled. 8 to 10 servings

NUTRITION INFORMATION PER SERVING

Serving Size: 1/8 of recipe		Percent U.S. RDA Per Serving	
Calories	341	Protein	3%
Protein	2g	Vitamin A	43%
Carbohydrate	89g	Vitamin C	17%
Fat	<1g	Thiamin	5%
Sodium	47mg	Riboflavin	6%
Potassium	566mg	Niacin	6%
		Calcium	5%
		Iron	16%

VICHYSSOISE

3 medium potatoes, peeled and sliced
3 medium leeks, peeled and sliced
46-oz. can (5¾ cups) chicken broth
1 teaspoon salt
1 cup light cream or evaporated milk
Chopped chives

In large saucepan, combine potatoes, leeks and chicken broth. Simmer covered, about 15 minutes or until tender. Process in blender until creamy. Cool. Add salt and cream. Serve garnished with chopped chives. 6 to 8 servings

NUTRITION INFORMATION PER SERVING

Serving Size: 1/6 of recipe		Percent U.S. RDA Per Serving	
Calories	214	Protein	19%
Protein	12g	Vitamin A	7%
Carbohydrate	16g	Vitamin C	14%
Fat	11g	Thiamin	6%
Sodium	1748mg	Riboflavin	8%
Potassium	299mg	Niacin	28%
		Calcium	6%
		Iron	3%

TIP: *If desired, 6 cubes or 6 teaspoons chicken bouillon and 5¾ cups water may be substituted for chicken broth.*

CUCUMBER-TOMATO SOUP

3 green onions or 1 teaspoon chopped chives
1 medium cucumber, peeled and cut into pieces
¼ teaspoon salt
⅛ teaspoon pepper
2½ cups milk
1 teaspoon Worcestershire sauce
10¾-oz. can condensed tomato soup

In blender, combine all ingredients. Blend at medium speed until smooth. Refrigerate several hours. Process again to mix just before serving. Garnish with sliced green onion tops or chives. 6 servings

NUTRITION INFORMATION PER SERVING

Serving Size: 1/6 of recipe		Percent U.S. RDA Per Serving	
Calories	111	Protein	7%
Protein	5g	Vitamin A	11%
Carbohydrate	13g	Vitamin C	19%
Fat	5g	Thiamin	5%
Sodium	557mg	Riboflavin	12%
Potassium	312mg	Niacin	3%
		Calcium	13%
		Iron	3%

TIP: *If the cucumber has large seeds, remove them before blending for a smoother consistency.*

Of Spanish origin, this makes a nutritious meal on a hot summer day.

COLD GAZPACHO

2 medium tomatoes, chopped
1 cucumber, thinly sliced
1 small onion, chopped
½ green pepper, chopped
1 garlic clove, minced
1 tablespoon oil or olive oil
1 tablespoon wine vinegar or lemon juice
Dash Tabasco sauce
24-oz. can (3 cups) cocktail vegetable juice

In large bowl, combine all ingredients; cover and refrigerate at least 6 hours. Serve chilled.
5 to 6 servings

NUTRITION INFORMATION PER SERVING

Serving Size: 1/5 of recipe		Percent U.S. RDA Per Serving	
Calories	78	Protein	4%
Protein	3g	Vitamin A	33%
Carbohydrate	12g	Vitamin C	89%
Fat	3g	Thiamin	9%
Sodium	281mg	Riboflavin	6%
Potassium	583mg	Niacin	9%
		Calcium	4%
		Iron	9%

SANDWICHES

Credited to the Earl of Sandwich who wanted a meal to eat in hand. Actually the sandwich is known in many countries and has probably existed for many centuries in some form.

Today's sandwich can take many shapes and sizes from the dainty tea sandwich to the hearty hero. Sandwiches are served hot or cold, open-faced or many layers, plain or fancy. Some sandwiches are not so neat to eat with the hand but their popularity remains undiminished.

Most experienced cooks can make these sandwiches blindfolded. But if you are new to cooking here are a few basic instructions.

ALL-TIME FAVORITES

B.L.T. (BACON, LETTUCE AND TOMATO)

Lightly toast 2 slices of bread; spread with mayonnaise. Layer toasted bread with lettuce leaf, slices of tomato and 3 slices crisp fried bacon. Top with second slice of toast. Cut into thirds or fourths.

1 sandwich

NUTRITION INFORMATION PER SERVING

Serving Size: 1 sandwich		Percent U.S. RDA Per Serving	
Calories	497	Protein	19%
Protein	12g	Vitamin A	7%
Carbohydrate	31g	Vitamin C	12%
Fat	36g	Thiamin	17%
Sodium	683mg	Riboflavin	13%
Potassium	217mg	Niacin	14%
		Calcium	6%
		Iron	14%

CLUB SANDWICH

Lightly toast 3 slices of bread; spread with mayonnaise. Layer toasted bread with sliced cold chicken or turkey, second slice of bread, lettuce leaf, sliced tomato and 3 slices of crisp fried bacon. Top with third slice of toast. Secure with toothpicks. Cut into thirds or fourths.

1 sandwich

NUTRITION INFORMATION PER SERVING

Serving Size: 1 sandwich		Percent U.S. RDA Per Serving	
Calories	756	Protein	47%
Protein	31g	Vitamin A	9%
Carbohydrate	46g	Vitamin C	12%
Fat	50g	Thiamin	22%
Sodium	940mg	Riboflavin	20%
Potassium	457mg	Niacin	46%
		Calcium	9%
		Iron	22%

GRILLED CHEESE SANDWICH

Make cheese sandwiches. Spread soft margarine or butter on outsides of sandwich and grill on heated skillet or electric grill until golden brown.

NUTRITION INFORMATION PER SERVING

Serving Size: 1 sandwich		Percent U.S. RDA Per Serving	
Calories	493	Protein	28%
Protein	18g	Vitamin A	26%
Carbohydrate	29g	Vitamin C	0%
Fat	34g	Thiamin	8%
Sodium	1105mg	Riboflavin	20%
Potassium	108mg	Niacin	7%
		Calcium	44%
		Iron	11%

Secure with large toothpicks for ease in cutting and serving.

HERO SANDWICH

14- inch loaf French or Italian bread
8-oz. pkg. braunschweiger
4 to 6 slices (4 to 6 oz.) Swiss cheese
4 to 6 thin slices cooked ham
1 large (2 small) tomatoes, thinly sliced
1 large Bermuda onion, thinly sliced
4 to 6 lettuce leaves
¼ cup chopped celery
¼ cup chopped sweet pickle
½ teaspoon salt
Dash pepper
4 hard-cooked eggs, chopped
¼ cup mayonnaise or salad dressing

Cut bread in half lengthwise. Spread braunschweiger evenly over bottom half of loaf. Arrange slices of cheese, ham, tomatoes, onion and lettuce over braunschweiger. In small bowl, combine celery, pickle, salt, pepper, eggs and mayonnaise; mix well. Spread over lettuce. Replace top half of loaf. Cut diagonally into 6 to 8 servings. 6 to 8 servings

NUTRITION INFORMATION PER SERVING

Serving Size: 1/6 of recipe		Percent U.S. RDA Per Serving	
Calories	667	Protein	47%
Protein	30g	Vitamin A	72%
Carbohydrate	55g	Vitamin C	22%
Fat	36g	Thiamin	31%
Sodium	1586mg	Riboflavin	60%
Potassium	333mg	Niacin	31%
		Calcium	33%
		Iron	35%

TIP: *Vary filling by substituting sliced salami, bologna, meat loaf, turkey or other cold cuts or sliced green pepper rings.*

CHICKEN OR TURKEY SANDWICH FILLING

2 cups cooked finely chopped chicken or turkey
¼ cup pickle relish, drained
2 tablespoons chopped pimiento, drained
¼ teaspoon salt
Dash pepper
1 stalk celery, finely chopped
¼ cup mayonnaise or salad dressing

In medium bowl, combine all ingredients; mix well. Chill.

2½ cups

NUTRITION INFORMATION PER SERVING

Serving Size: 1/4 cup		Percent U.S. RDA Per Serving	
Calories	97	Protein	13%
Protein	8g	Vitamin A	*
Carbohydrate	2g	Vitamin C	*
Fat	6g	Thiamin	*
Sodium	153mg	Riboflavin	3%
Potassium	118mg	Niacin	12%
		Calcium	*
		Iron	3%

SEAFOOD FILLING

6½-oz. can crab meat, tuna or shrimp, drained and flaked
2 tablespoons chopped dill pickle
2 tablespoons mayonnaise or salad dressing
½ teaspoon lemon juice

In medium bowl, combine all ingredients; mix well. Chill. 1 cup

NUTRITION INFORMATION PER SERVING

Serving Size: 1/4 cup (using crab meat)		Percent U.S. RDA Per Serving	
Calories	83	Protein	9%
Protein	6g	Vitamin A	*
Carbohydrate	<1g	Vitamin C	*
Fat	6g	Thiamin	*
Sodium	461mg	Riboflavin	*
Potassium	53mg	Niacin	3%
		Calcium	*
		Iron	2%

EGG SALAD SANDWICH FILLING

2 hard-cooked eggs, chopped
1 teaspoon chopped pimiento, drained
½ teaspoon chopped chives
⅛ teaspoon salt
Dash pepper
2 tablespoons mayonnaise or salad dressing

In small bowl, combine all ingredients; mix well. Chill. ¾ cup

NUTRITION INFORMATION PER SERVING

Serving Size: 1/4 cup		Percent U.S. RDA Per Serving	
Calories	128	Protein	7%
Protein	5g	Vitamin A	9%
Carbohydrate	<1g	Vitamin C	*
Fat	12g	Thiamin	2%
Sodium	191mg	Riboflavin	6%
Potassium	51mg	Niacin	*
		Calcium	2%
		Iron	5%

PINEAPPLE-CHEESE FILLING

5-oz. jar pasteurized process cheese spread
¼ cup drained crushed pineapple

In small bowl, combine cheese and pineapple; mix well. ¾ cup

NUTRITION INFORMATION PER SERVING

Serving Size: 1 tablespoon		Percent U.S. RDA Per Serving	
Calories	38	Protein	3%
Protein	2g	Vitamin A	2%
Carbohydrate	2g	Vitamin C	*
Fat	3g	Thiamin	*
Sodium	192mg	Riboflavin	4%
Potassium	34mg	Niacin	*
		Calcium	7%
		Iron	*

DEVILED HAM SANDWICH FILLING

2 cans (3 oz. each) deviled ham
2 tablespoons chopped stuffed green olives
2 tablespoons mayonnaise or salad dressing

In medium bowl, combine all ingredients; mix well. Chill. ¾ cup

NUTRITION INFORMATION PER SERVING

Serving Size: 1/4 cup		Percent U.S. RDA Per Serving	
Calories	272	Protein	12%
Protein	8g	Vitamin A	*
Carbohydrate	<1g	Vitamin C	0%
Fat	26g	Thiamin	5%
Sodium	189mg	Riboflavin	4%
Potassium	6mg	Niacin	5%
		Calcium	*
		Iron	7%

TIP: *Two cups cooked finely chopped ham may be substituted for deviled ham. Increase mayonnaise to ¼ cup.* 2 cups

CREAMY PIMIENTO SPREAD

8-oz. pkg. cream cheese, softened
Dash salt
2 tablespoons milk or cream
¼ teaspoon Worcestershire sauce
½ cup (2 oz.) shredded Cheddar cheese
2 tablespoons chopped pimiento

In small bowl, combine first 4 ingredients; beat until light and fluffy. Fold in cheese and pimiento. 1½ cups

NUTRITION INFORMATION PER SERVING

Serving Size: 1 tablespoon		Percent U.S. RDA Per Serving	
Calories	46	Protein	2%
Protein	1g	Vitamin A	4%
Carbohydrate	<1g	Vitamin C	*
Fat	4g	Thiamin	*
Sodium	53mg	Riboflavin	2%
Potassium	11mg	Niacin	*
		Calcium	3%
		Iron	*

HAM SALAD FILLING

1 cup (8 oz.) cooked ground ham
2 tablespoons mayonnaise or salad dressing
1 to 2 tablespoons pickle relish
1 tablespoon minced onion

In small bowl, combine all ingredients; mix well. 1 cup

TIP: *Ground canned luncheon meat may be substituted for ham.*

NUTRITION INFORMATION PER SERVING

Serving Size: 1/4 cup		Percent U.S. RDA Per Serving	
Calories	140	Protein	11%
Protein	7g	Vitamin A	*
Carbohydrate	3g	Vitamin C	*
Fat	11g	Thiamin	11%
Sodium	333mg	Riboflavin	4%
Potassium	5mg	Niacin	6%
		Calcium	*
		Iron	5%

Need a change of pace from the ordinary? Below are several new and different ways to spark up a sandwich.

SANDWICH FILLING COMBINATIONS

MEAT AND POULTRY

Cooked sliced beef, radish slices and lettuce leaf.
Cooked sliced pork, onion slices and mustard.
Cooked sliced turkey, turkey stuffing and cranberry sauce.
Cooked sliced chicken, sliced avocado and cream cheese.
Cooked sliced lamb, green pepper rings and cream cheese.
Cooked sliced ham, sliced Swiss cheese and lettuce leaf.

COLD CUTS AND FISH

Sliced salami, sliced tomato and sliced American cheese.
Sliced corned beef, sliced Swiss cheese and mustard.
Sliced bologna, baked beans and green pepper rings.
Sliced pastrami, coleslaw and sliced tomato.
Flaked tuna, tartar sauce and lettuce leaf.
Flaked crab meat, chili sauce and mayonnaise.
Sliced smoked salmon, cream cheese.

PEANUT BUTTER

Peanut butter, sliced apple and shredded carrot.
Peanut butter, jelly or jam.
Peanut butter, honey and sunflower nuts.
Peanut butter, sliced banana and raisins.
Peanut butter, cooked crumbled bacon and sliced dill pickle.

CHEESE

Cream cheese, jelly and chopped nuts.
Cream cheese, sliced banana, coconut and chopped peanuts.
Pimiento cheese spread, sliced olives and mayonnaise.
Cottage cheese, chopped green pepper and onion salt.

AVOCADO-BACON SANDWICHES

1 medium avocado, mashed
1 tablespoon chopped onion
¼ cup mayonnaise or salad dressing
1 tablespoon lemon juice
4 slices bacon, fried, drained and crumbled
4 to 8 slices bread

In small bowl, blend first 4 ingredients. Stir in bacon. Spread on bread to make open-face or regular sandwiches. 4 sandwiches

NUTRITION INFORMATION PER SERVING

Serving Size: 1 sandwich		Percent U.S. RDA Per Serving	
Calories	319	Protein	9%
Protein	6g	Vitamin A	4%
Carbohydrate	19g	Vitamin C	17%
Fat	25g	Thiamin	12%
Sodium	305mg	Riboflavin	12%
Potassium	404mg	Niacin	10%
		Calcium	3%
		Iron	8%

TIP: *Two tablespoons imitation bacon bits may be substituted for crumbled bacon.*

An open-face sandwich, delicious with a cream soup.

BROILED CRAB-TOMATO SANDWICHES

3 English muffins, split and toasted
6-oz. pkg. (1 cup) frozen cooked crab meat, thawed and drained
1 cup (4 oz.) shredded American or natural Swiss cheese
¼ cup dairy sour cream or mayonnaise
1 teaspoon lemon juice
½ teaspoon Worcestershire sauce
Dash Tabasco sauce
6 thin slices fresh tomato
Paprika

Split and toast muffins; arrange on broiler pan or cookie sheet. In medium bowl, combine remaining ingredients except tomato slices and paprika; mix well. Top each muffin half with slice of tomato and some of crab meat mixture. Sprinkle with paprika. Broil about 5 inches from heat for 3 to 5 minutes or until cheese is melted.

6 sandwiches

NUTRITION INFORMATION PER SERVING

Serving Size: 1 sandwich		Percent U.S. RDA Per Serving	
Calories	196	Protein	20%
Protein	13g	Vitamin A	9%
Carbohydrate	17g	Vitamin C	6%
Fat	9g	Thiamin	10%
Sodium	507mg	Riboflavin	11%
Potassium	85mg	Niacin	8%
		Calcium	21%
		Iron	7%

TIP: *Canned crab meat may be substituted for frozen.*

OPEN-FACE BROILED SANDWICH IDEAS

Toasted bread, sliced buns or English muffins all perform well for broiled sandwiches. Assemble your choice and broil 5 to 6 inches from heat for 3 to 5 minutes or until hot and bubbly. Choose one of the following:

Sliced turkey, cooked vegetable, gravy and sliced cheese.
Flaked tuna, mushroom soup and sliced or cubed cheese.
Sliced Mozzarella cheese, sliced tomato and Italian seasoning.
Sliced American or Cheddar cheese, sliced onion and green pepper rings.
Baked beans, cottage cheese and sliced American cheese.
Sliced mushrooms, sliced onion and cubed cheese.

TIP: *For broiled hamburger or hot dog combinations, see HAMBURGER IDEAS and HOTDOG IDEAS.*

The king of sandwiches! Serve the sauce as a dipper for the sandwich.

MONTE CRISTO

Oil
15 slices bread
5 slices (8 oz.) cooked ham
5 slices (8 oz.) Swiss cheese
5 slices (8 oz.) cooked turkey

BATTER
1 cup light cream
5 eggs
1½ cups Pillsbury's Best® All Purpose or Unbleached Flour*
1¼ cups sugar

SAUCE
½ cup dairy sour cream
¼ cup strawberry preserves

In large saucepan or deep skillet, heat 1 to 1½ inches oil to 375°F. Layer each sandwich with 1 slice bread, ham, cheese, second slice of bread, turkey and third slice of bread. Secure with toothpicks. In medium bowl, beat light cream and eggs together. Add flour and sugar; beat well. Dip entire sandwich in batter; allow excess batter to drip into bowl. Fry in hot oil (375°F.) until deep golden brown, turning once, about 5 minutes. Drain on paper towels. Lightly sprinkle sandwich with powdered sugar.

In small bowl, combine sour cream and preserves for Sauce. Serve with hot sandwich. 5 sandwiches

NUTRITION INFORMATION PER SERVING

Serving Size: 1 sandwich		Percent U.S. RDA Per Serving	
Calories	1330	Protein	82%
Protein	53g	Vitamin A	35%
Carbohydrate	138g	Vitamin C	*
Fat	62g	Thiamin	52%
Sodium	1556mg	Riboflavin	51%
Potassium	469mg	Niacin	30%
		Calcium	59%
		Iron	35%

TIP: **Self-rising flour is not recommended.*

HOT DOG IDEAS

Prepare hot dogs as desired. Place in bun or on bread and add one of the following accompaniments:

- Chili
- Sloppy Joe filling
- Barbecue sauce and chopped green pepper
- Chili sauce, chopped lettuce and shredded cheese
- Catsup and pineapple
- Sauerkraut
- Sauerkraut and baked beans
- Sauerkraut and shredded Swiss cheese; broil
- Shredded cheese and cooked crumbled bacon
- Cottage cheese and sliced green onions; broil

See page 317 for directions on how to make ground beef patties.

HAMBURGER IDEAS

Prepare your favorite ground beef patties. Serve on buns, toasted English muffins or slices of bread. Top with one of these:

- Guacamole dip
- Prepared onion dip
- Sour cream and sliced cucumber
- Garlic butter
- Sautéed mushrooms
- Mushroom or cheese soup
- Crumbled blue cheese; broil
- Sliced cheese; broil
- Cheddar cheese and chopped green chilies; broil
- Sauerkraut and Swiss cheese; broil
- Onion and tomato slices
- Grilled eggplant slices and Italian salad dressing
- Sliced pineapple and sweet-sour sauce
- Warm bean sprouts and soy sauce

PIZZA BURGERS

1 lb. ground beef
½ teaspoon garlic salt
½ teaspoon oregano leaves
4 tablespoons tomato paste or pizza sauce
4 slices (4 oz.) Mozzarella cheese
4 hamburger buns, sliced

In medium bowl, combine ground beef, garlic salt and oregano; mix well. Shape into 4 patties. Fry or broil until of desired doneness, turning once. Top each with 1 tablespoon of tomato paste and slice of cheese; continue cooking until cheese melts. Serve in hamburger buns. 4 sandwiches

NUTRITION INFORMATION PER SERVING

Serving Size: 1 sandwich		Percent U.S. RDA Per Serving	
Calories	456	Protein	39%
Protein	25g	Vitamin A	16%
Carbohydrate	20g	Vitamin C	9%
Fat	30g	Thiamin	13%
Sodium	523mg	Riboflavin	26%
Potassium	566mg	Niacin	25%
		Calcium	25%
		Iron	23%

BARBECUED LUNCHEON SANDWICHES

1 tablespoon margarine or butter
½ cup chopped green pepper
12-oz. can luncheon meat
½ to ¾ cup barbecue sauce
3 to 4 hamburger buns, sliced or 6 slices bread
6 to 8 slices (6 to 8 oz.) American cheese

In medium skillet, cook green pepper in hot margarine until tender. Cut luncheon meat into strips or cubes. Add meat and barbecue sauce to green pepper; mix well. Simmer covered, until mixture is hot. Spoon mixture onto buns or toast; top each with cheese slice. Broil until cheese melts.

6 to 8 sandwiches

NUTRITION INFORMATION PER SERVING

Serving Size: 1 sandwich		Percent U.S. RDA Per Serving	
Calories	349	Protein	25%
Protein	16g	Vitamin A	10%
Carbohydrate	11g	Vitamin C	11%
Fat	26g	Thiamin	15%
Sodium	1276mg	Riboflavin	15%
Potassium	213mg	Niacin	9%
		Calcium	21%
		Iron	11%

REUBEN SANDWICHES

8 slices pumpernickel or other dark bread
½ lb. thinly sliced corned beef
8-oz. can (1 cup) sauerkraut, well-drained
2 to 3 tablespoons thousand island dressing
4 slices Swiss cheese
2 tablespoons margarine or butter, softened

Top 4 slices of bread with corned beef, then sauerkraut, salad dressing and cheese. Top with other bread slices. Spread margarine on outsides of each sandwich. Grill on hot (375°F.) griddle, skillet or under broiler until bread is browned and cheese melts.

4 sandwiches

NUTRITION INFORMATION PER SERVING

Serving Size: 1 sandwich		Percent U.S. RDA Per Serving	
Calories	551	Protein	38%
Protein	25g	Vitamin A	13%
Carbohydrate	37g	Vitamin C	9%
Fat	35g	Thiamin	12%
Sodium	1742mg	Riboflavin	19%
Potassium	421mg	Niacin	9%
		Calcium	40%
		Iron	19%

TIPS: *For thoroughly drained sauerkraut, drain liquid and place sauerkraut in 2 or 3 layers of paper towel; squeeze out excess liquid.*

If desired, ½ teaspoon prepared mustard and ¼ teaspoon caraway seed may be added with dressing.

For open-face sandwiches, toast bread and arrange filling on bread, ending with cheese. Broil until cheese melts. Garnish each with cherry tomato. Party rye bread may be used and served as hearty hors d'oeuvres.

REUBEN SALAD BUNS

12-oz. can corned beef or 8 oz. thinly sliced corned beef
1 cup (4 oz.) shredded Swiss cheese
1 teaspoon dill weed
1 small apple, peeled, cored and shredded
2 tablespoons thousand island dressing
2 teaspoons prepared mustard
8-oz. can (1 cup) sauerkraut, drained
10 pumpernickel rolls or hamburger buns

Heat oven to 350°F. In medium bowl, break up canned corned beef with fork or cut sliced corned beef into shreds. Add remaining ingredients except buns; mix well. Spoon corned beef onto bottom half of rolls; top with other half of roll. Wrap each in foil. Bake at 350°F. for 15 to 20 minutes or until cheese melts. 10 sandwiches

NUTRITION INFORMATION PER SERVING

Serving Size: 1 sandwich		Percent U.S. RDA Per Serving	
Calories	228	Protein	22%
Protein	14g	Vitamin A	3%
Carbohydrate	19g	Vitamin C	5%
Fat	11g	Thiamin	6%
Sodium	747mg	Riboflavin	11%
Potassium	76mg	Niacin	6%
		Calcium	14%
		Iron	13%

Try serving for breakfast!

HEARTY BUNWICHES

8 slices (12 oz.) Canadian bacon or ham
8 hamburger buns
8 slices (8 oz.) American cheese
8 tomato slices

Broil Canadian bacon 5 inches from heat 3 to 4 minutes on each side. If desired, toast hamburger buns. Layer bottom half of hamburger bun with Canadian bacon, tomato and cheese slice. Return to broiler; broil 3 to 5 minutes or until cheese melts. Top with other half bun. Serve hot. 8 sandwiches

NUTRITION INFORMATION PER SERVING

Serving Size: 1 sandwich		Percent U.S. RDA Per Serving	
Calories	286	Protein	28%
Protein	18g	Vitamin A	11%
Carbohydrate	18g	Vitamin C	9%
Fat	16g	Thiamin	26%
Sodium	1280mg	Riboflavin	13%
Potassium	243mg	Niacin	9%
		Calcium	23%
		Iron	13%

HEARTHSIDE SANDWICHES

2 cups cooked chopped ham
1 cup (4 oz.) shredded American or Cheddar cheese
2 to 3 tablespoons pickle relish, drained
1 tablespoon finely chopped onion
2 tablespoons mayonnaise or salad dressing
1 teaspoon prepared mustard
8 hamburger or rye buns, sliced

Heat oven to 350°F. In medium bowl, combine all ingredients except buns; mix well. Fill buns with mixture. Wrap each sandwich in foil. Bake at 350°F. for about 20 minutes or until hot.

8 sandwiches

NUTRITION INFORMATION PER SERVING

Serving Size: 1 sandwich		Percent U.S. RDA Per Serving	
Calories	240	Protein	19%
Protein	12g	Vitamin A	4%
Carbohydrate	18g	Vitamin C	*
Fat	13g	Thiamin	18%
Sodium	753mg	Riboflavin	10%
Potassium	162mg	Niacin	7%
		Calcium	13%
		Iron	10%

Leftover turkey gravy may be used in place of the mix.

TURKEY BUNS AND GRAVY

1½ cups cooked cubed turkey
¼ cup chopped celery
2 tablespoons chopped onion
¾ teaspoon poultry seasoning or sage
¼ teaspoon salt
3 tablespoons margarine or butter, melted
4 hamburger or other buns, unsliced
1 pkg. Pillsbury Brown Gravy Mix

Heat oven to 350°F. In medium bowl, combine first 6 ingredients. Leaving buns whole, hollow out top of buns leaving ½-inch thick ring around edge. Crumble this extra bread into turkey mixture; mix well. Fill hollowed-out buns with turkey mixture. Wrap each in foil. Bake at 350°F. for 15 minutes or until hot. Prepare gravy mix as directed on package. Serve gravy over warm buns.

4 sandwiches

NUTRITION INFORMATION PER SERVING

Serving Size: 1 sandwich		Percent U.S. RDA Per Serving	
Calories	257	Protein	30%
Protein	20g	Vitamin A	5%
Carbohydrate	19g	Vitamin C	2%
Fat	11g	Thiamin	7%
Sodium	626mg	Riboflavin	9%
Potassium	261mg	Niacin	20%
		Calcium	3%
		Iron	9%

TUNA SALAD BUNS

1 cup (4 oz.) cubed or shredded American or Cheddar cheese
¼ cup sliced stuffed green olives
2 tablespoons chopped onion
2 tablespoons chopped green pepper
2 tablespoons pickle relish, drained
⅓ cup mayonnaise or salad dressing
6½-oz. can tuna, drained
6 hamburger or hot dog buns, sliced

Heat oven to 350°F. In medium bowl, combine all ingredients except buns; mix well. Fill buns with mixture. Wrap each in foil. Bake at 350°F. for 15 minutes or until cheese melts. 6 sandwiches

NUTRITION INFORMATION PER SERVING

Serving Size: 1 sandwich		Percent U.S. RDA Per Serving	
Calories	344	Protein	24%
Protein	16g	Vitamin A	6%
Carbohydrate	24g	Vitamin C	7%
Fat	21g	Thiamin	9%
Sodium	660mg	Riboflavin	11%
Potassium	72mg	Niacin	20%
		Calcium	17%
		Iron	9%

TIP: *For open-face sandwiches, spread filling on bun halves or toasted bread. Broil 3 to 5 minutes or until cheese melts.*

HOT TURKEY SALAD BUNS

2 cups cooked cubed turkey
1 cup (4 oz.) shredded Cheddar cheese
¼ cup chopped celery
¼ cup chopped roasted almonds, if desired
¼ teaspoon salt
1 sweet pickle, chopped
½ cup mayonnaise or salad dressing
4 to 6 hamburger buns

Heat oven to 350°F. In medium bowl, combine all ingredients except buns; mix well. Fill buns with mixture. Wrap each in foil. Bake at 350°F. for 15 minutes or until cheese is melted. 4 to 6 sandwiches

NUTRITION INFORMATION PER SERVING

Serving Size: 1 sandwich		Percent U.S. RDA Per Serving	
Calories	464	Protein	37%
Protein	24g	Vitamin A	6%
Carbohydrate	25g	Vitamin C	*
Fat	30g	Thiamin	10%
Sodium	617mg	Riboflavin	18%
Potassium	299mg	Niacin	24%
		Calcium	20%
		Iron	13%

TIP: *Sandwiches may be served cold or made into open-face sandwiches and broiled.*

Tangy and mildly spiced, this is a kid favorite!

SLOPPY JOES

1 lb. ground beef
½ cup chopped green pepper or celery
1 small onion, chopped
8-oz. can (1 cup) tomato sauce
½ cup catsup
1 tablespoon firmly packed brown sugar
1 teaspoon dry mustard
¼ teaspoon salt
⅛ teaspoon pepper
1 tablespoon Worcestershire sauce
1 tablespoon vinegar

In large skillet, brown ground beef, green pepper and onion; drain excess fat. Stir in remaining ingredients. Simmer covered, 15 to 20 minutes, stirring occasionally. Serve over toasted buns.

4 to 5 servings

NUTRITION INFORMATION PER SERVING

Serving Size: 1/5 of recipe without bun		Percent U.S. RDA Per Serving	
Calories	292	Protein	27%
Protein	18g	Vitamin A	21%
Carbohydrate	16g	Vitamin C	29%
Fat	17g	Thiamin	8%
Sodium	468mg	Riboflavin	11%
Potassium	466mg	Niacin	22%
		Calcium	3%
		Iron	16%

Leftover roast beef simmers in a barbecue sauce for a hot hearty sandwich.

BARBECUED SLICED BEEF

1½ cups chopped onion
2 tablespoons margarine or butter
1½ cups catsup
¼ cup firmly packed brown sugar
1 tablespoon dry or 2 tablespoons prepared mustard
1½ teaspoons salt
¼ teaspoon pepper
⅛ teaspoon cloves
2 tablespoons lemon juice or vinegar
1 tablespoon Worcestershire sauce
12 cooked thin slices beef
6 hamburger buns

In large skillet, cook onion in margarine until tender. Stir in remaining ingredients except beef and buns. Heat to boiling; simmer covered, 30 minutes. Add beef; simmer 10 to 15 minutes or until beef is heated through. Serve on warm buns.

6 servings

NUTRITION INFORMATION PER SERVING

Serving Size: 1 sandwich		Percent U.S. RDA Per Serving	
Calories	430	Protein	45%
Protein	29g	Vitamin A	23%
Carbohydrate	47g	Vitamin C	17%
Fat	14g	Thiamin	15%
Sodium	1481mg	Riboflavin	18%
Potassium	388mg	Niacin	28%
		Calcium	8%
		Iron	27%

If desired, one recipe for Two-Crust Pastry, page 220 may be used.

CORNISH PASTIES

1 lb. ground beef
1 cup uncooked finely cubed potato
½ cup thinly sliced carrots
¼ cup chopped celery
½ teaspoon salt
¼ teaspoon poultry seasoning
1 small onion, chopped
Dash pepper
10¾-oz. can condensed cream of mushroom soup
1 pkg. Pillsbury Pie Crust Mix

Heat oven to 375°F. In medium skillet, brown ground beef; drain excess fat. Add potatoes, carrots, celery, salt, poultry seasoning, onion, pepper and soup; mix well. Prepare double pie crust recipe using mix. Divide dough into 6 equal portions. Roll each portion on floured surface to 7-inch circle. Place generous ½ cup meat mixture on each pastry circle. Moisten edges with water; fold in half. Seal edges and prick top with fork. Place on ungreased cookie sheet. Bake at 375°F. for 25 to 30 minutes or until light golden brown. Eat from hand like a sandwich or serve with mushroom sauce or beef gravy.

6 pasties

NUTRITION INFORMATION PER SERVING

Serving Size: 1 pastie		Percent U.S. RDA Per Serving	
Calories	477	Protein	32%
Protein	21g	Vitamin A	23%
Carbohydrate	36g	Vitamin C	8%
Fat	27g	Thiamin	7%
Sodium	1090mg	Riboflavin	13%
Potassium	555mg	Niacin	22%
		Calcium	6%
		Iron	15%

TIPS: *Pasties may be assembled several hours ahead and refrigerated until ready to bake.*

Two cups finely cubed leftover roast beef may be substituted for ground beef.

FRENCH DIP

In medium saucepan, add 1½ lb. cooked sliced beef with 1½ cups of water and pan drippings or 2 beef bouillon cubes. Heat through. Add ½ teaspoon soy sauce and 1 teaspoon instant minced onion. Simmer 2 to 3 minutes. Remove beef slices. Serve between slices of crusty French bread. Individual portions of meat juices may be served for dipping sandwiches. 6 servings

NUTRITION INFORMATION PER SERVING

Serving Size: 1/6 of recipe		Percent U.S. RDA Per Serving	
Calories	605	Protein	52%
Protein	34g	Vitamin A	*
Carbohydrate	40g	Vitamin C	*
Fat	33g	Thiamin	18%
Sodium	755mg	Riboflavin	21%
Potassium	84mg	Niacin	33%
		Calcium	4%
		Iron	29%

DENVER SANDWICH

1 cup cooked chopped ham
3 tablespoons chopped green pepper
½ teaspoon salt
¼ teaspoon pepper
1 small onion, chopped
4 eggs, slightly beaten
2 tablespoons margarine or butter
4 slices bread, toasted

In medium bowl, combine first 5 ingredients with eggs. On griddle or in large skillet, melt margarine. Pour about ½ cup of egg mixture onto griddle for each sandwich. Allow eggs to begin to set and brown on bottom; turn and brown on other side, 1 to 2 minutes. Serve on toast with chili sauce or catsup. 4 sandwiches

NUTRITION INFORMATION PER SERVING

Serving Size: 1 sandwich		Percent U.S. RDA Per Serving	
Calories	294	Protein	25%
Protein	16g	Vitamin A	18%
Carbohydrate	17g	Vitamin C	19%
Fat	17g	Thiamin	21%
Sodium	938mg	Riboflavin	18%
Potassium	269mg	Niacin	11%
		Calcium	7%
		Iron	17%

TACOS

1 lb. ground beef
1 small onion, chopped
1 teaspoon chili powder
½ teaspoon salt
½ teaspoon garlic powder
8-oz. can (1 cup) tomato sauce
4-oz. pkg. taco shells or 12 tortillas*
1 cup (4 oz.) shredded American or Cheddar cheese
2 cups shredded lettuce
2 tomatoes, chopped
Taco sauce
½ cup dairy sour cream, if desired

Heat oven to 250°F. In medium skillet, brown ground beef and onion; drain excess fat. Stir in chili powder, salt, garlic powder and tomato sauce. Simmer covered, 10 minutes. Heat taco shells in oven at 250°F. for 5 minutes. Assemble tacos by layering meat, cheese, lettuce and tomatoes in each shell. Serve with taco sauce; top with sour cream. 10 tacos

NUTRITION INFORMATION PER SERVING

Serving Size: 1 taco		Percent U.S. RDA Per Serving	
Calories	289	Protein	22%
Protein	14g	Vitamin A	25%
Carbohydrate	24g	Vitamin C	16%
Fat	15g	Thiamin	9%
Sodium	469mg	Riboflavin	11%
Potassium	308mg	Niacin	14%
		Calcium	18%
		Iron	15%

TIPS: **If tortillas are used, fry in ¼-inch hot oil to soften. Remove from oil; drain on paper towel and fold in half.*

Heated refried beans may be added to meat mixture before assembling.

THICK CRUST PIZZA

SAUCE
- **2 tablespoons oil**
- **1 medium onion, chopped**
- **1 garlic clove, minced**
- **2 teaspoons firmly packed brown sugar**
- **1 teaspoon basil leaves**
- **1 teaspoon oregano leaves**
- **½ teaspoon salt**
- **¼ teaspoon pepper**
- **2 to 4 tablespoons water**
- **6-oz. can tomato paste**
- **4-oz. can (½ cup) mushroom stems and pieces, undrained**

CRUST
- **1 pkg. Pillsbury Hot Roll Mix**
- **1 cup warm water (105 to 115°F.)**
- **½ cup grated Parmesan cheese**
- **2 cups (8 oz.) shredded Mozzarella or other cheese**

Heat oven to 425°F. Grease (not oil) 14-inch pizza pan or 15x10-inch jelly roll pan. In medium saucepan, cook onion and garlic in oil until tender. Stir in remaining ingredients exept Crust ingredients. Simmer covered, 15 to 20 minutes, stirring occasionally. In large bowl, dissolve yeast from hot roll mix in water. Stir in flour mixture. Press dough into prepared pan forming a high rim around edge. Sprinkle Parmesan cheese over crust, spoon on Sauce and toppings,* if desired. Sprinkle with Mozzarella cheese. Bake at 425°F. for 20 to 25 minutes or until crust is golden brown.

14-inch pizza

NUTRITION INFORMATION PER SERVING

Serving Size: 1/4 of recipe		Percent U.S. RDA Per Serving	
Calories	795	Protein	34%
Protein	22g	Vitamin A	39%
Carbohydrate	82g	Vitamin C	25%
Fat	42g	Thiamin	47%
Sodium	1025mg	Riboflavin	61%
Potassium	664mg	Niacin	34%
		Calcium	63%
		Iron	30%

TIPS: **For variety, arrange one or more of the following toppings on pizza before sprinkling with Mozzarella cheese:*

Drained browned ground beef
Sliced pepperoni or wieners
Cooked drained and sliced brown and serve sausage
Cooked shrimp
Cooked crab meat or lobster
Drained anchovies
Sliced mushrooms
Chopped or sliced green pepper
Sliced olives
Sliced zucchini or eggplant

For a thin crust, divide dough in half and make 2 pizzas; double Sauce and topping amounts. If necessary to hold dough to bake later, cover and refrigerate dough until ready to press into pan.

SAUCES

ABOUT WHITE SAUCES

SERVING

There are two basic white sauces. The most popular, Sauce Béchamel, is a simple mixture of a butter-flour paste and milk or cream. The other is Velouté Sauce made from a similar butter-flour paste for which the liquid is veal or chicken broth. Both are used interchangeably; however, Béchamel, being the richer of the two, is used where a more substantial cream sauce would be needed.

Some of the most popular uses would be:

- Creamed vegetables (peas, carrots, potatoes, onions are the more popular)
- Creamed main dishes (seafood, fish, poultry, ham, smoked beef, eggs)
- As a base for a cheese sauce (to serve over vegetables such as broccoli, cauliflower, macaroni, ham)
- With herbs (to serve over seafood, poultry, eggs or vegetables)

PREPARATION

There are three secrets to a perfect white sauce. *Combine* the melted butter and flour thoroughly to a smooth paste without lumps. *Gradually add* the liquid about ¼ cup at a time, thoroughly blending to a smooth consistency after each addition. (A wire whisk is of great benefit.) *Stir constantly* while heating to avoid burning.

BASIC WHITE SAUCE
(Sauce Béchamel)

¼ cup margarine or butter
¼ cup flour
½ teaspoon salt
¼ teaspoon pepper
2 cups milk

In medium saucepan, melt margarine. Blend in flour, salt and pepper. Cook until mixture is smooth and bubbly; gradually add milk. Heat until mixture boils and thickens, stirring constantly. 2 cups

NUTRITION INFORMATION PER SERVING

Serving Size: 1/3 cup		Percent U.S. RDA Per Serving	
Calories	140	Protein	5%
Protein	3g	Vitamin A	9%
Carbohydrate	8g	Vitamin C	*
Fat	11g	Thiamin	4%
Sodium	315mg	Riboflavin	9%
Potassium	124mg	Niacin	*
		Calcium	10%
		Iron	*

TIPS: *For THIN WHITE SAUCE, decrease margarine and flour to 2 tablespoons each.*

For THICK WHITE SAUCE, increase margarine and flour to ½ cup each.

For CREAMED EGG SAUCE, add 1 teaspoon dry mustard with flour, salt and pepper. Prepare white sauce. Stir in 2 to 3 chopped or sliced hard-cooked eggs.

For CHEESE SAUCE, decrease margarine and flour to 3 tablespoons each. Prepare white sauce; stir in 2 cups (8 oz.) shredded Cheddar cheese, 2 teaspoons Worcestershire sauce, dash Tabasco sauce and dash cayenne pepper. Heat over low heat and stir until smooth and cheese is melted. 3 cups

For CHEESE-DILL SAUCE, prepare white sauce; stir in ⅓ cup shredded Cheddar cheese and 2 tablespoons crushed dill seed. Heat over low heat and stir until smooth and cheese is melted. 2½ cups

For PIMIENTO CHEESE SAUCE, cook 3 tablespoons green pepper in melted margarine before adding flour. Prepare white sauce; stir in 1 to 2 cups shredded Cheddar cheese, ½ cup canned sliced mushrooms and 2 tablespoons chopped, drained pimiento. Heat over low heat and stir until smooth and cheese is melted. 3 cups

To halve recipe, use half the ingredient amounts.

A light-colored mildly flavored cheese sauce, perfect over seafood, poultry or mild flavored vegetables such as asparagus.

MORNAY SAUCE

3 tablespoons margarine or butter
3 tablespoons flour
1 cube or 1 teaspoon chicken bouillon
¾ cup light cream or milk
¾ cup water
½ cup grated Parmesan cheese
½ cup shredded Swiss cheese

In medium saucepan, melt margarine. Stir in flour and bouillon. Add cream and water. Cook until mixture boils and thickens, stirring constantly. Blend in cheeses. Stir until smooth. 3 cups

NUTRITION INFORMATION PER SERVING

Serving Size: 1/4 cup		Percent U.S. RDA Per Serving	
Calories	102	Protein	6%
Protein	4g	Vitamin A	7%
Carbohydrate	3g	Vitamin C	*
Fat	8g	Thiamin	*
Sodium	186mg	Riboflavin	5%
Potassium	33mg	Niacin	*
		Calcium	11%
		Iron	*

VELOUTÉ SAUCE

2 tablespoons margarine or butter
2 tablespoons flour
1 cube or 1 teaspoon chicken bouillon
1 cup water
1 cup light cream

In small saucepan, melt margarine; stir in flour and bouillon and beat until smooth and bubbly. Add water and cream; cook until mixture boils and thickens, stirring constantly. 1⅓ cups

NUTRITION INFORMATION PER SERVING

Serving Size: 1/4 cup		Percent U.S. RDA Per Serving	
Calories	154	Protein	3%
Protein	2g	Vitamin A	12%
Carbohydrate	4g	Vitamin C	*
Fat	15g	Thiamin	2%
Sodium	269mg	Riboflavin	5%
Potassium	64mg	Niacin	*
		Calcium	5%
		Iron	*

TIP: *For BÉCHAMEL SAUCE, add 1 teaspoon instant minced onion, dash nutmeg and dash thyme.*

ABOUT BROWN SAUCES

SERVING

Actually quite similar to a white sauce, except beef stock is used for the liquid giving the sauce its characteristic warm brown color. As a rich flavorful sauce it is served with stronger flavored meats such as steaks, roast beef, game (especially venison) and sometimes lamb and duck.

PREPARATION

Traditionally the beef stock was made in advance by simmering beef bones, carrots, onions, celery and bouquet garni (a herb and spice mixture) for many hours. The stock is strained and added to a butter-flour paste for thickening. Life is simpler now with canned beef stock and instant beef bouillon at our fingertips. Our basic recipe starts with instant bouillon but if you feel ambitious enough to prepare a homemade concentrated beef stock, it may be substituted in equal amounts for the instant bouillon and water.

BROWN SAUCE

2 tablespoons margarine or butter
2 tablespoons flour
¾ teaspoon salt
⅛ teaspoon pepper
2 cubes or 2 teaspoons beef bouillon
2 cups water

In small saucepan, melt margarine. Add flour and cook until golden brown, stirring constantly. Add remaining ingredients. Cook until mixture boils and thickens, stirring constantly. 2 cups

NUTRITION INFORMATION PER SERVING

Serving Size: 1/4 cup		Percent U.S. RDA Per Serving	
Calories	30	Protein	*
Protein	<1g	Vitamin A	2%
Carbohydrate	1g	Vitamin C	*
Fat	3g	Thiamin	*
Sodium	421mg	Riboflavin	*
Potassium	3mg	Niacin	*
		Calcium	*
		Iron	*

TIPS: *One can (10½ oz.) condensed beef bouillon or consommé added with enough water to make 2 cups liquid may be substituted for instant bouillon and water. If desired, use ½ cup red wine or sherry for part of water.*

For BORDELAISE SAUCE, cook 2 tablespoons minced green onion, 1 garlic clove, 1 finely chopped carrot, 1 small bay leaf and 4 peppercorns in margarine before adding flour. Prepare sauce as directed. Strain to remove vegetables and spices before serving. If desired, stir in ½ teaspoon chopped parsley and dash thyme. Serve warm.

For MADEIRA SAUCE, substitute ½ cup madeira wine for ½ cup of water. 2¼ cups

ABOUT EMULSIFIED SAUCES
(Sauces with oil and egg base)

SERVING

The combining of egg yolks and melted butter or oil will result in a thick light yellow sauce. The 2 most common sauces are hollandaise made from eggs, butter and lemon juice and mayonnaise which is made from eggs, oil and lemon juice. Both sauces being of delicate flavor are used primarily with vegetables, egg dishes and seafood. The hollandaise sauce is cooked and served warm whereas mayonnaise is served cold.

Mayonnaise is the traditional base for a great variety of salad dressings and therefore the basic recipe will be found on page 504. The mayonnaise recipes found in this chapter are generally served with seafood as a dipping sauce.

Hollandaise is most often served over warm vegetables, poached fish and seafood.

Bernaise sauce is a hollandaise sauce to which onion, tarragon leaves and chervil leaves have been added. The extra flavors make it a popular sauce to serve over steak, liver and lamb as well.

PREPARATION

In making an emulsified sauce, tiny oil particles must be suspended in the egg. This takes a little extra time and constant beating. If it is not done properly the sauce will curdle with the addition of the lemon juice. Many cooks have found the blender method to be easier and much more foolproof. If you wish to use that method, specific instructions have been provided.

HOLLANDAISE SAUCE

½ cup margarine or butter
¼ cup hot water
¼ teaspoon salt
Dash pepper
4 egg yolks
1½ tablespoons lemon juice

In small saucepan (or top of double boiler), melt margarine with water, salt and pepper. In small bowl, beat egg yolks slightly. Blend small amount of margarine mixture into beaten egg yolks; add to remaining margarine. Heat over low heat (place top of double boiler over hot, not boiling, water). Beat mixture with rotary beater (or briskly with spoon) until thick and smooth. Blend in lemon juice. Serve immediately. 1 cup

NUTRITION INFORMATION PER SERVING

Serving Size: ¼ cup		Percent U.S. RDA Per Serving	
Calories	264	Protein	5%
Protein	3g	Vitamin A	30%
Carbohydrate	<1g	Vitamin C	6%
Fat	28g	Thiamin	3%
Sodium	415mg	Riboflavin	4%
Potassium	34mg	Niacin	*
		Calcium	3%
		Iron	5%

TIPS: *If sauce curdles, add 1 teaspoon hot water and beat well.*

For BEARNAISE SAUCE, add 1 tablespoon finely chopped onion, 1 teaspoon tarragon leaves and ½ teaspoon chervil leaves to margarine. Add 2 tablespoons white wine with lemon juice.

BLENDER HOLLANDAISE SAUCE

2 egg yolks
¼ teaspoon salt
Dash cayenne pepper
1 tablespoon lemon juice
½ cup margarine or butter

In blender, combine egg yolks, salt, cayenne pepper and lemon juice; blend slightly. Heat margarine until bubbly but not brown. Slowly pour margarine into egg yolk mixture while blending on low speed. Blend just until thickened. Serve immediately. ¾ cup

NUTRITION INFORMATION PER SERVING

Serving Size: 2 tablespoons		Percent U.S. RDA Per Serving	
Calories	155	Protein	*
Protein	<1g	Vitamin A	16%
Carbohydrate	<1g	Vitamin C	*
Fat	17g	Thiamin	*
Sodium	280mg	Riboflavin	*
Potassium	13mg	Niacin	*
		Calcium	*
		Iron	*

You may make your own mayonnaise for either of the following recipes or use a commercially prepared dressing.

CREAMY HERB SAUCE

½ cup mayonnaise or salad dressing
¼ cup dairy sour cream
2 tablespoons minced parsley
¼ teaspoon salt
¼ teaspoon tarragon leaves, crushed
1 garlic clove, crushed
Dash pepper
1 tablespoon lemon juice

In small bowl, combine all ingredients; mix well. Cover and chill. 1 cup

NUTRITION INFORMATION PER SERVING

Serving Size: 1 tablespoon		Percent U.S. RDA Per Serving	
Calories	57	Protein	*
Protein	<1g	Vitamin A	*
Carbohydrate	<1g	Vitamin C	2%
Fat	6g	Thiamin	*
Sodium	77mg	Riboflavin	*
Potassium	8mg	Niacin	*
		Calcium	*
		Iron	*

TARTAR SAUCE

1 cup mayonnaise or salad dressing
¼ cup finely chopped dill pickle or pickle relish
2 tablespoons minced parsley
1 tablespoon chopped pimiento, drained
½ teaspoon grated onion
1 tablespoon lemon juice
¼ teaspoon Worcestershire sauce

In small bowl, combine all ingredients; mix well. Cover and chill. 1⅓ cups

NUTRITION INFORMATION PER SERVING

Serving Size: 1 tablespoon		Percent U.S. RDA Per Serving	
Calories	76	Protein	*
Protein	<1g	Vitamin A	*
Carbohydrate	<1g	Vitamin C	*
Fat	8g	Thiamin	*
Sodium	90mg	Riboflavin	*
Potassium	11mg	Niacin	*
		Calcium	*
		Iron	*

ABOUT SOUR CREAM SAUCES

The tang and smoothness of sour cream gives a pleasant contrast to seafood. And its versatility with a variety of spices makes sour cream sauces popular to prepare.

The mystical flavor of curry is delightful with seafood, especially crab or shrimp.

CURRY-SOUR CREAM SAUCE

1 cup dairy sour cream
1 teaspoon curry powder
¼ teaspoon salt
Dash Tabasco sauce

In small bowl, combine all ingredients; mix well. Cover and chill. 1 cup

NUTRITION INFORMATION PER SERVING

Serving Size: 1 tablespoon		Percent U.S. RDA Per Serving	
Calories	29	Protein	*
Protein	<1g	Vitamin A	2%
Carbohydrate	<1g	Vitamin C	*
Fat	3g	Thiamin	*
Sodium	40mg	Riboflavin	*
Potassium	2mg	Niacin	*
		Calcium	*
		Iron	*

Especially nice with fat fish (see page 264) such as baked or broiled salmon or trout.

CUCUMBER-SOUR CREAM SAUCE

⅔ cup unpeeled shredded cucumber
1 teaspoon grated onion
½ cup dairy sour cream
¼ cup mayonnaise or salad dressing
2 teaspoons minced parsley
¼ teaspoon salt
Dash pepper
2 teaspoons vinegar or lemon juice

Press cucumber and onion in strainer to remove excess juice. In small bowl, combine cucumber and onion with remaining ingredients. Cover and chill. 1 cup

NUTRITION INFORMATION PER SERVING

Serving Size: 1/4 of recipe		Percent U.S. RDA Per Serving	
Calories	160	Protein	*
Protein	1g	Vitamin A	7%
Carbohydrate	2g	Vitamin C	5%
Fat	16g	Thiamin	*
Sodium	231mg	Riboflavin	3%
Potassium	41mg	Niacin	*
		Calcium	4%
		Iron	*

The flavor is similar to sour cream but there are fewer calories.

MOCK SOUR CREAM

1⅓ cups creamed cottage cheese
⅓ cup buttermilk
1 tablespoon lemon juice
½ teaspoon salt

In blender, combine all ingredients. Blend at medium speed until smooth. Use as you would sour cream in sauces, dips and toppings, but not in baking. 2 cups

NUTRITION INFORMATION PER SERVING

Serving Size: 1 tablespoon		Percent U.S. RDA Per Serving	
Calories	10	Protein	*
Protein	1g	Vitamin A	*
Carbohydrate	<1g	Vitamin C	*
Fat	<1g	Thiamin	*
Sodium	57mg	Riboflavin	*
Potassium	12mg	Niacin	*
		Calcium	*
		Iron	*

Since horseradish is such a strong flavor this sauce would go well with beef or game.

HORSERADISH-SOUR CREAM SAUCE

1 cup dairy sour cream
2 tablespoons prepared horseradish
2 tablespoons finely chopped dill pickle
¼ teaspoon salt
⅛ teaspoon paprika

In small bowl, combine all ingredients; mix well. Cover and chill. 1 cup

NUTRITION INFORMATION PER SERVING

Serving Size: 1 tablespoon		Percent U.S. RDA Per Serving	
Calories	29	Protein	*
Protein	<1g	Vitamin A	2%
Carbohydrate	<1g	Vitamin C	*
Fat	3g	Thiamin	*
Sodium	65mg	Riboflavin	*
Potassium	9mg	Niacin	*
		Calcium	*
		Iron	*

TIP: *For MUSTARD-SOUR CREAM SAUCE, decrease horseradish to ½ teaspoon and add 1 tablespoon prepared mustard and 1 chopped green onion or ½ teaspoon chopped chives.*

ABOUT FRUIT SAUCES

Pretty in color and special in flavors, it is no wonder fruit sauces are most often found on the holiday table. These are popularly served with ham, turkey, duck or goose.

CHERRY-ORANGE SAUCE

21-oz. can (2 cups) prepared cherry fruit filling
⅛ teaspoon cloves
½ stick cinnamon
¼ cup orange juice

In medium saucepan, combine all ingredients; mix well. Heat until almost boiling. Simmer 3 to 5 minutes or until flavors are blended. Remove cinnamon stick. Serve warm. 2¼ cups

NUTRITION INFORMATION PER SERVING

Serving Size: 1/4 cup		Percent U.S. RDA Per Serving	
Calories	110	Protein	*
Protein	<1g	Vitamin A	5%
Carbohydrate	28g	Vitamin C	20%
Fat	<1g	Thiamin	*
Sodium	74mg	Riboflavin	*
Potassium	74mg	Niacin	*
		Calcium	*
		Iron	*

SPICY RAISIN SAUCE

½ cup firmly packed brown sugar
1 tablespoon cornstarch
1½ teaspoons dry mustard
⅛ teaspoon cloves
¼ cup raisins
1 tablespoon margarine or butter
1 cup water
2 tablespoons lemon juice

In small saucepan, combine first 4 ingredients. Blend in remaining ingredients; stir until smooth. Heat until mixture boils and thickens, stirring occasionally. Simmer about 10 minutes or until flavors have blended. 1 cup

NUTRITION INFORMATION PER SERVING

Serving Size: 2 tablespoons		Percent U.S. RDA Per Serving	
Calories	83	Protein	*
Protein	<1g	Vitamin A	*
Carbohydrate	18g	Vitamin C	3%
Fat	2g	Thiamin	*
Sodium	23mg	Riboflavin	*
Potassium	89mg	Niacin	*
		Calcium	*
		Iron	4%

WHOLE CRANBERRY SAUCE

2 cups water
2 cups sugar
1 lb. (4 cups) cranberries

In large saucepan, combine all ingredients. Heat to boiling, stirring occasionally until sugar dissolves. Continue simmering until most of berries pop, about 5 minutes. Cover and chill. 2 cups

NUTRITION INFORMATION PER SERVING

Serving Size: 1/4 cup		Percent U.S. RDA Per Serving	
Calories	218	Protein	*
Protein	<1g	Vitamin A	*
Carbohydrate	56g	Vitamin C	10%
Fat	<1g	Thiamin	*
Sodium	2mg	Riboflavin	*
Potassium	46mg	Niacin	*
		Calcium	*
		Iron	*

TIP: *For ORANGE-CRANBERRY SAUCE, substitute 1 cup orange juice for 1 cup of water.*

CUMBERLAND SAUCE

½ cup currant jelly
1 teaspoon grated orange peel
1 teaspoon grated lemon peel
¼ teaspoon dry mustard
Dash ginger
2 tablespoons orange juice
1 teaspoon lemon juice

In small saucepan, heat all ingredients until jelly melts. Serve as a sauce or use to brush over meat during last half hour of roasting; serve remaining sauce with meat.

½ cup

NUTRITION INFORMATION PER SERVING

Serving Size: 1 tablespoon		Percent U.S. RDA Per Serving	
Calories	58	Protein	*
Protein	<1g	Vitamin A	*
Carbohydrate	15g	Vitamin C	9%
Fat	<1g	Thiamin	*
Sodium	3mg	Riboflavin	*
Potassium	42mg	Niacin	*
		Calcium	*
		Iron	*

ABOUT BUTTER SAUCES

Butter sauces add a richness to almost any meat or vegetable. Most are simply creamed butter with seasoning variations. They are served at room temperature as an accompaniment to the vegetable or meat. These special sauces are heated in preparation and served warm.

Try freezing this sauce along with corn. Also nice with fish.

DRAWN BUTTER SAUCE

¼ cup margarine or butter
2 tablespoons flour
½ teaspoon salt
⅛ teaspoon paprika
Dash cayenne pepper
1 cup water

In small saucepan, melt margarine. Stir in flour, salt, paprika and cayenne pepper. Add water and cook until mixture boils and thickens, stirring constantly.

1 cup

NUTRITION INFORMATION PER SERVING

Serving Size: 1 tablespoon		Percent U.S. RDA Per Serving	
Calories	29	Protein	*
Protein	<1g	Vitamin A	2%
Carbohydrate	<1g	Vitamin C	*
Fat	3g	Thiamin	*
Sodium	103mg	Riboflavin	*
Potassium	2mg	Niacin	*
		Calcium	*
		Iron	*

TIP: *If desired, add 1 tablespoon lemon juice and 1 tablespoon chopped parsley or add ¼ cup sliced stuffed olives.*

The standard tradition with lobster. Be careful not to brown the butter when heating.

CLARIFIED BUTTER

In saucepan, slowly melt desired amount of butter. Let stand a few minutes until clear part can be spooned off into serving dish, discarding the milky portion that is left. Serve warm.

NUTRITION INFORMATION PER SERVING

Serving Size: 1 tablespoon		Percent U.S. RDA Per Serving	
Calories	102	Protein	*
Protein	<1g	Vitamin A	9%
Carbohydrate	<1g	Vitamin C	*
Fat	11g	Thiamin	*
Sodium	140mg	Riboflavin	*
Potassium	3mg	Niacin	*
		Calcium	*
		Iron	*

TIP: *If desired, add lemon juice (about 1 to 2 tablespoons) to butter in serving dish.*

Serve as an accompaniment to poached or broiled fish or scallops.

CAPER BUTTER SAUCE

½ cup margarine or butter
2 tablespoons capers
1 tablespoon lemon juice
1 teaspoon grated onion

In small saucepan, melt margarine; stir in remaining ingredients. Heat.

½ cup

NUTRITION INFORMATION PER SERVING

Serving Size: 1 tablespoon (without capers)*		Percent U.S. RDA Per Serving	
Calories	103	Protein	*
Protein	<1g	Vitamin A	9%
Carbohydrate	<1g	Vitamin C	*
Fat	12g	Thiamin	*
Sodium	141mg	Riboflavin	*
Potassium	7mg	Niacin	*
		Calcium	*
		Iron	*

*Insufficient data to give nutritional information with regard to capers.

Just as the title suggests, a rich flavorful topping for a steak or prime rib.

BUTTERY STEAK SAUCE

6 tablespoons margarine or butter, softened
½ teaspoon dry mustard
¼ teaspoon salt
2 teaspoons lemon juice
1 teaspoon Worcestershire sauce
Dash pepper

In small bowl, cream margarine; blend in remaining ingredients, mixing well. Let stand at room temperature until serving time.

½ cup

NUTRITION INFORMATION PER SERVING

Serving Size: 1 tablespoon		Percent U.S. RDA Per Serving	
Calories	78	Protein	*
Protein	<1g	Vitamin A	7%
Carbohydrate	<1g	Vitamin C	*
Fat	9g	Thiamin	*
Sodium	181mg	Riboflavin	*
Potassium	5mg	Niacin	*
		Calcium	*
		Iron	*

Serve as a spread on French bread, as an accompaniment to steak, or as a topper for vegetables such as green beans or potatoes.

GARLIC BUTTER

½ cup margarine or butter, softened
½ to 1 garlic clove, minced

In small bowl, cream margarine until very creamy. Blend in garlic; leave at room temperature until served.

¾ cup

NUTRITION INFORMATION PER SERVING

Serving Size: 1 tablespoon		Percent U.S. RDA Per Serving	
Calories	68	Protein	*
Protein	<1g	Vitamin A	6%
Carbohydrate	<1g	Vitamin C	*
Fat	8g	Thiamin	*
Sodium	93mg	Riboflavin	*
Potassium	3mg	Niacin	*
		Calcium	*
		Iron	*

Delicious on potatoes, carrots or peas.

CHIVE BUTTER

½ cup margarine or butter, softened
3 tablespoons chopped chives
2 tablespoons chopped parsley
¼ teaspoon salt
Dash cayenne pepper, if desired

In small bowl, cream margarine until very creamy; blend in remaining ingredients, mixing well. Leave at room temperature until served.

¾ cup

NUTRITION INFORMATION PER SERVING

Serving Size: 1 tablespoon		Percent U.S. RDA Per Serving	
Calories	68	Protein	*
Protein	<1g	Vitamin A	8%
Carbohydrate	<1g	Vitamin C	2%
Fat	8g	Thiamin	*
Sodium	139mg	Riboflavin	*
Potassium	8mg	Niacin	*
		Calcium	*
		Iron	*

A versatile topper for any green vegetable or beef. See directions for freezing.

SEASONED BUTTER

1 cup margarine or butter, softened
3 tablespoons minced parsley
1 teaspoon garlic or onion salt
½ teaspoon pepper
2 tablespoons lemon juice

In small bowl, cream margarine well. Beat in remaining ingredients. Place in covered container and store in refrigerator up to 1 month or in freezer several months.

1¼ cups

NUTRITION INFORMATION PER SERVING

Serving Size: 1 tablespoon		Percent U.S. RDA Per Serving	
Calories	82	Protein	*
Protein	<1g	Vitamin A	8%
Carbohydrate	<1g	Vitamin C	3%
Fat	9g	Thiamin	*
Sodium	205mg	Riboflavin	*
Potassium	9mg	Niacin	*
		Calcium	*
		Iron	*

ABOUT GRAVIES

Probably the most common sauce in any American household, it is often considered a "must" and the meal is not complete without it. Gravy is made from the meat drippings and is served generally over meat and potatoes.

Two alternative methods are given which may be used either with fried or roasted meats.

PAN GRAVY I

3 tablespoons meat drippings
3 tablespoons flour
2 cups liquid (milk, water, broth)
Salt and pepper

In skillet or roasting pan, add flour to drippings. Blend over low heat until smooth and browned. Add liquid; cook until mixture boils and thickens, stirring constantly. Season with salt and pepper. 2 cups

NUTRITION INFORMATION PER SERVING

Serving Size: 1/4 cup made with milk		Percent U.S. RDA Per Serving	
Calories	65	Protein	4%
Protein	3g	Vitamin A	*
Carbohydrate	5g	Vitamin C	*
Fat	4g	Thiamin	2%
Sodium	87mg	Riboflavin	7%
Potassium	94mg	Niacin	*
		Calcium	7%
		Iron	*

TIPS: *Flour and drippings may be decreased to 2 tablespoons each for thin gravy; increased to 4 tablespoons for thick gravy.*

For MILK GRAVY, use milk for liquid. This is especially good with fried chicken.

PAN GRAVY II

2 cups hot liquid (broth, water, milk)
¼ cup meat or poultry drippings
¼ cup flour
½ cup cold liquid
Salt and pepper

Add hot liquid to drippings in skillet or roasting pan. Combine flour and cold liquid; mix until smooth. Add flour mixture to hot liquid, stirring constantly. Cook until mixture boils and thickens. Season with salt and pepper.
2½ cups

NUTRITION INFORMATION PER SERVING

Serving Size: 1/4 cup		Percent U.S. RDA Per Serving	
Calories	24	Protein	*
Protein	<1g	Vitamin A	*
Carbohydrate	2g	Vitamin C	*
Fat	1g	Thiamin	*
Sodium	55mg	Riboflavin	*
Potassium	7mg	Niacin	*
		Calcium	*
		Iron	*

TIPS: *If gravy lumps, beat with beater or wire whisk, or strain before serving.*

If gravy is too thick, thin with additional liquid. If too thin, thicken with additional flour dissolved in cold water. Heat to boiling.

SANDWICH SAUCE

¼ cup chopped green pepper
1 tablespoon margarine or butter
10¼-oz. can beef gravy
2 teaspoons prepared mustard

In small saucepan, cook green pepper in margarine until tender. Add gravy and mustard. Heat, stirring occasionally.
1⅓ cups

NUTRITION INFORMATION PER SERVING

Serving Size: 1/3 cup		Percent U.S. RDA Per Serving	
Calories	193	Protein	2%
Protein	1g	Vitamin A	3%
Carbohydrate	9g	Vitamin C	12%
Fat	17g	Thiamin	3%
Sodium	785mg	Riboflavin	17%
Potassium	100mg	Niacin	*
		Calcium	*
		Iron	3%

ABOUT BARBECUE SAUCES

Often attributed to American cuisine, the barbecue sauce adds spice to beef, pork or poultry. Most commonly made with a tomato sauce base, a variety of spices are added for flavor interest. A barbecue sauce can be used as a marinade or brushed on during cooking. It is very commonly used when broiling or cooking outdoors to also prevent the meat from drying out.

ZESTY BARBECUE SAUCE

1 medium onion, chopped
1 garlic clove, minced
2 tablespoons oil
¼ cup firmly packed brown sugar
1 teaspoon salt
¼ teaspoon thyme, if desired
1 lemon, thinly sliced
1 cup catsup
½ cup water
3 tablespoons Worcestershire sauce
2 teaspoons prepared mustard
Dash Tabasco sauce

In small saucepan, cook onion and garlic in oil until tender. Stir in remaining ingredients. Simmer covered, 5 to 10 minutes or until flavors have blended.
2 cups

NUTRITION INFORMATION PER SERVING

Serving Size: 1/4 cup		Percent U.S. RDA Per Serving	
Calories	107	Protein	*
Protein	1g	Vitamin A	10%
Carbohydrate	19g	Vitamin C	7%
Fat	4g	Thiamin	3%
Sodium	717mg	Riboflavin	2%
Potassium	194mg	Niacin	3%
		Calcium	2%
		Iron	4%

HOT CATSUP SAUCE

- ½ cup catsup
- 1½ teaspoons vinegar
- ½ teaspoon prepared horseradish
- Dash Tabasco sauce

In small bowl, combine all ingredients; mix well. Cover and chill.

½ cup

NUTRITION INFORMATION PER SERVING

Serving Size: 1 tablespoon		Percent U.S. RDA Per Serving	
Calories	18	Protein	*
Protein	<1g	Vitamin A	5%
Carbohydrate	4g	Vitamin C	4%
Fat	<1g	Thiamin	*
Sodium	178mg	Riboflavin	*
Potassium	64mg	Niacin	*
		Calcium	*
		Iron	*

OTHER SAUCES

Serve as an accompaniment to steaks or prime rib. Also nice as a beef fondue dip.

MUSHROOM SAUCE

- ¼ cup margarine or butter
- 4 oz. (1½ cups) sliced fresh mushrooms
- 1 cup water
- 2 teaspoons cornstarch
- ½ teaspoon salt
- Dash pepper
- 1 teaspoon Worcestershire sauce

In medium saucepan, melt margarine. Add mushrooms and cook until tender. Combine water and cornstarch until smooth; blend into hot mushrooms stirring constantly, until thickened. Add seasonings and Worcestershire sauce.

1½ cups

NUTRITION INFORMATION PER SERVING

Serving Size: 1/4 cup		Percent U.S. RDA Per Serving	
Calories	77	Protein	*
Protein	<1g	Vitamin A	6%
Carbohydrate	2g	Vitamin C	*
Fat	8g	Thiamin	*
Sodium	288mg	Riboflavin	5%
Potassium	75mg	Niacin	4%
		Calcium	*
		Iron	*

A tangy topping on ham, pork or roast beef.

CREAMY MUSTARD SAUCE

- 1 egg, separated
- ¼ cup sugar
- 2 tablespoons dry mustard
- 1 teaspoon flour
- ½ teaspoon salt
- ⅛ teaspoon pepper
- 1 cup light cream
- 2 tablespoons vinegar or lemon juice

In small saucepan, beat egg yolk. Add sugar, mustard, flour, salt, pepper and cream. Blend until smooth. Cook over medium heat until mixture boils and thickens, stirring constantly. Stir in vinegar. In small bowl, beat egg white until soft peaks form; fold into sauce. Serve warm.

2 cups

NUTRITION INFORMATION PER SERVING

Serving Size: 1/4 cup		Percent U.S. RDA Per Serving	
Calories	83	Protein	3%
Protein	2g	Vitamin A	5%
Carbohydrate	9g	Vitamin C	*
Fat	5g	Thiamin	*
Sodium	158mg	Riboflavin	4%
Potassium	59mg	Niacin	*
		Calcium	4%
		Iron	*

Use this sauce and its variations with meats or serve over toast points or party shells.

CREAM SOUP SAUCE

In small saucepan, combine 10¾ oz. can condensed cream soup (any variety) with ¼ to ⅓ cup liquid. Heat through, stirring occasionally.

1½ cups

NUTRITION INFORMATION PER SERVING

Serving Size: 1/4 cup		Percent U.S. RDA Per Serving	
Calories	46	Protein	2%
Protein	2g	Vitamin A	4%
Carbohydrate	4g	Vitamin C	*
Fat	3g	Thiamin	*
Sodium	407mg	Riboflavin	2%
Potassium	47mg	Niacin	*
		Calcium	2%
		Iron	*

TIP: *One of the following may be added: ½ to 1 cup shredded cheese, ½ to 1 teaspoon curry powder, 1 to 2 teaspoons prepared mustard, 2 chopped or sliced hard-cooked eggs, 1 tablespoon minced parsley, ½ teaspoon dill weed or seed, 1 teaspoon prepared horseradish, 1 tablespoon chopped pimiento.*

This sauce is especially nice on shrimp or crab.

SEAFOOD COCKTAIL SAUCE

1 cup chili sauce
1 teaspoon celery seed
¼ cup lemon juice
2 to 3 teaspoons prepared horseradish
1 teaspoon Worcestershire sauce

In small bowl, combine all ingredients; mix well. Cover and chill.

1½ cups

NUTRITION INFORMATION PER SERVING

Serving Size: 1 tablespoon		Percent U.S. RDA Per Serving	
Calories	13	Protein	*
Protein	<1g	Vitamin A	3%
Carbohydrate	3g	Vitamin C	5%
Fat	<1g	Thiamin	*
Sodium	156mg	Riboflavin	*
Potassium	48mg	Niacin	*
		Calcium	*
		Iron	*

SEASONED CRUMBS

½ cup margarine or butter
1 small onion, chopped
2 cups dry bread crumbs
½ cup grated Parmesan cheese
1 teaspoon dry mustard, if desired

In small skillet, cook onion in margarine until tender. Stir in remaining ingredients. Cool. Store in refrigerator up to 1 month, in freezer for several months.

NUTRITION INFORMATION PER SERVING

Serving Size: 1 tablespoon		Percent U.S. RDA Per Serving	
Calories	38	Protein	*
Protein	<1g	Vitamin A	*
Carbohydrate	3g	Vitamin C	*
Fat	2g	Thiamin	*
Sodium	62mg	Riboflavin	*
Potassium	11mg	Niacin	*
		Calcium	*
		Iron	*

VEGETABLES

VEGETABLES

The importance of vegetables in the diet is becoming more apparent as people monitor their daily intake. Concern with calories, cholesterol, sodium, sugar and good nutrition leads more and more people to realize what a good contribution vegetables can offer in their daily menu planning. And what a variety is available! Almost every shape, color, size and taste can be had to tempt even the most finicky of eaters. If one recipe doesn't please, don't give up, try another combination! Many people don't like cooked spinach but how about fresh in a salad. Not sure about steamed squash? Next time try it sautéed with cheese and onions. Relatively low in calories and high in nutrition, vegetables *should* play a major part in everyone's diet.

With each vegetable we have given guides for buying and storage, the peak season, basic preparation and cooking, plus seasoning suggestions for cooking and serving. Also included is the nutritional analysis of one cooked (and where appropriate raw) serving of each vegetable.

BUYING

Vegetables are available in several forms: fresh, frozen, canned and dried. Because of their availability year-round, most of our recipes use frozen vegetables. But please feel free to substitute an equal amount of fresh cooked vegetables when they are available – their flavor and appearance can't be surpassed.

Fresh vegetables are usually least expensive and of best quality during their peak season.

Unlike fruits, most vegetables are shipped at maturity as they will not "ripen" further after harvesting (tomatoes are the exception). Therefore, select vegetables that are in their peak of perfection; they will never improve with age!

Handle with care. The less vegetables are handled, the longer their life. Do not pinch, squeeze or poke them as this only promotes bruising which results in spoilage.

When buying frozen vegetables look for packages that are frost-free and solidly frozen.

Canned vegetables which have bulges or any signs of aging should be avoided. Jars should be vacuum-sealed.

Occasionally you will see vegetables, especially tomatoes and cucumbers, labeled "hydroponic." These vegetables were from plants which were grown in a solution of water and minerals containing all the required nutrients for the plants; no soil is needed. Although hydroponic vegetables do not contain any extra nutritive value, they often have a better flavor and appearance than the off-season vegetables. They can be slightly higher in price, too.

Many vegetables have been commercially waxed. Waxing is done, not to improve the appearance as many think, but as protection against dehydration which causes the shriveling and wilting of vegetables. The wax is completely edible, however, if you wish you may wash it off before preparation.

STORAGE

For each vegetable we have listed an optimum storage time. This does not mean that one cannot keep vegetables any longer, only that there will be a reduction in quality. Also there are variables on how fresh a vegetable is when you buy it because of the conditions under which it has been kept since it was harvested, the time spent in shipping and the time it has been in your local supermarket.

Refrigeration is the most popular and one of the most satisfactory methods of storing vegetables. The object of refrigeration is to prolong storage and maintain quality. The crispers supplied in most refrigerators are especially designed to provide the optimum storage conditions; use it for that purpose! The crisper should be approximately 38 to 42°F. and the relative humidity about 40 to 50 percent. If you do not have a crisper or yours is full, storing in an airtight container will help prevent moisture loss.

Frozen vegetables should remain frozen at 0°F. or lower in your freezer until ready to use. Try to buy them as the last item on your shopping trip.

Canned vegetables should be stored in a cool dry place.

Dried vegetables such as peas, beans and lentils should be kept dry.

BASIC PREPARATION

One of the most serious mistakes a cook can make when preparing vegetables is overcooking. This results in both a nutritional and flavor loss. Some vitamins are water soluble and some are destroyed by heat, so the main rule of thumb is to use as little water as possible and cook only until done, not a moment longer. Here are a few other guides when cooking:

- Use a pan with a tight-fitting lid. This not only prevents loss of nutrients to the air but retains the heat to speed up cooking times.
- Boiling root or tuber vegetables (carrots, beets, potatoes, etc.) with their skins retains more vitamins and minerals than cooking after peeling and cutting.
- Steaming under pressure is quick and satisfactory if carefully timed.
- Holding and reheating cooked vegetables causes additional loss of nutrients, so serve immediately.

There are a variety of ways to cook vegetables:

- baking
- simmering (in a small amount of water)
- steaming (where the vegetable is above the water level)
- stir-frying (cook in a small amount of oil or margarine in a skillet or wok, stirring the vegetables until they are cooked to crisp-tender)
- braising or panning (cook shredded or sliced vegetables in a small amount of fat and water in a covered skillet)

The preferred method will usually be specified in the directions.

VEGETABLE TEMPURA

1 egg, slightly beaten
½ cup cold water
½ cup Pillsbury's Best® All Purpose or Unbleached Flour
1 teaspoon sugar
½ teaspoon salt
Fresh or frozen thawed vegetables*

In large saucepan, heat 2 to 3 inches oil to 400°F. In small bowl, blend first 5 ingredients until dry ingredients are moistened. Dip vegetables* in batter; fry in hot oil (400°F.) for about 3 to 4 minutes or until golden brown. Drain on paper towel. Serve hot. If desired, serve with soy sauce. 4 to 6 servings

Due to variances in the type of vegetable used, the nutritional information cannot be accurately determined.

TIP: **Crisp vegetable slices or pieces such as potato, green beans, green pepper, celery, cauliflower, onions, mushrooms, zucchini, eggplant or summer squash may be used for tempura. Vegetables should be well dried with paper towel before dipping in batter to coat vegetable.*

OVEN-COOKED FROZEN VEGETABLES

Heat oven to 350°F. Place package of frozen vegetables (about 1½ cups) in covered 1 or 1½-quart casserole. Add 1 to 2 tablespoons margarine or butter, ¼ teaspoon salt and other desired seasonings. Bake covered at 350°F. for 45 to 50 minutes or until desired doneness.

3 to 4 servings

TIP: *If using 325°F. oven, bake for 55 to 60 minutes; if using 375°F. oven, bake for 35 to 40 minutes.*

CASHEW BUTTER FOR VEGETABLES

¼ cup margarine or butter
2 tablespoons chopped cashews
½ teaspoon salt
⅛ teaspoon pepper

In small saucepan, melt margarine; add cashews and salt. Stir-fry only until margarine is lightly brown. Add pepper. Serve warm over hot cooked vegetables.

⅓ cup

NUTRITION INFORMATION PER SERVING

Serving Size: 1 tablespoon		Percent U.S. RDA Per Serving	
Calories	121	Protein	2%
Protein	1g	Vitamin A	8%
Carbohydrate	2g	Vitamin C	0%
Fat	14g	Thiamin	2%
Sodium	339mg	Riboflavin	*
Potassium	35mg	Niacin	*
		Calcium	*
		Iron	*

ARTICHOKES (GLOBE OR FRENCH)

The artichoke is the large, unopened flower bud of a thistle-like plant. Grown mainly in California, the artichoke is available year-round. It is cooked in water or steamed under pressure, and served either warm or cold. To eat an artichoke, pluck each leaf and dip into a sauce. After all the leaves have been eaten there is a core center remaining. Cut of the thorny top (if it hasn't already been removed) and pour sauce over the heart; eat with a knife and fork. Whole artichokes are available fresh; artichoke hearts are available bottled, canned and frozen.

NUTRITION INFORMATION PER SERVING

Serving Size: 1 ripened globe artichoke

		Percent U.S. RDA Per Serving	
Calories	67	Protein	5%
Protein	3g	Vitamin A	4%
Carbohydrate	12g	Vitamin C	16%
Fat	<1g	Thiamin	6%
Sodium	36mg	Riboflavin	3%
Potassium	361mg	Niacin	4%
		Calcium	6%
		Iron	7%

BUY: Allow one globe artichoke per person. Select heads which are compact, plump and heavy. The artichoke should yield slightly to pressure and have large, tight fleshy leaves with a good green color. Browning indicates bruising, frost or old age. The size has little to do with quality or flavor.
PEAK SEASON: April and May (available all year).
STORAGE: Refrigerate, without washing, in airtight container 1 to 2 days.
PREPARATION: Wash thoroughly. Cut off 1 inch straight across top, remove any loose leaves around bottom. Remove thorns on each leaf by clipping about ½ inch off leaf tips. Dip artichoke in lemon juice to prevent darkening. Place upright.

Here is a unique serving suggestion.

ARTICHOKES AND DIPPING SAUCES

Allow 1 artichoke per person. Cook artichokes as directed; drain well. Serve hot with hollandaise sauce or drawn butter; serve cold with mayonnaise, Caesar, French or Italian salad dressing.

In center, beneath the tiny pointed leaves, is the artichoke heart. The tiny leaves should be cut off and discarded, and the heart cut into pieces and eaten.

TIP: *If several party snacks are being served, allow ½ artichoke per person.*

ARTICHOKE HEARTS IN SAVORY BUTTER

2 tablespoons margarine or butter
1 teaspoon dry mustard
½ teaspoon salt
Dash pepper
9-oz. pkg. (1 cup) frozen artichoke hearts
1 tablespoon lemon juice

In medium saucepan, melt margarine. Stir in remaining ingredients except lemon juice. Cook covered, 8 to 10 minutes or until tender, stirring occasionally. Before serving, stir in lemon juice.

3 to 4 servings

NUTRITION INFORMATION PER SERVING

Serving Size: 1/4 of recipe

		Percent U.S. RDA Per Serving	
Calories	69	Protein	3%
Protein	2g	Vitamin A	6%
Carbohydrate	4g	Vitamin C	10%
Fat	6g	Thiamin	3%
Sodium	371mg	Riboflavin	6%
Potassium	10mg	Niacin	3%
		Calcium	*
		Iron	*

TANGY ARTICHOKES

9-oz. pkg. (1 cup) frozen artichoke hearts
¼ cup dairy sour cream
2 teaspoons prepared horseradish
1 tablespoon milk
2 tablespoons imitation bacon bits or 2 slices bacon, fried, drained and crumbled

In medium saucepan, prepare artichokes as directed on package. Combine sour cream, horseradish and milk; mix well. Drain artichokes. Add horseradish sauce and bacon bits to artichokes, tossing lightly to coat. 3 to 4 servings

NUTRITION INFORMATION PER SERVING

Serving Size: 1/4 of recipe		Percent U.S. RDA Per Serving	
Calories	112	Protein	11%
Protein	7g	Vitamin A	4%
Carbohydrate	9g	Vitamin C	3%
Fat	6g	Thiamin	3%
Sodium	982mg	Riboflavin	7%
Potassium	13mg	Niacin	3%
		Calcium	2%
		Iron	*

ARTICHOKE KABOBS

2 pkg. (9 oz. each) frozen artichoke hearts
8 oz. (4 cups) fresh mushrooms
¾ cup prepared Italian or French dressing
Cherry tomatoes
Salt and pepper

In medium saucepan, cook artichoke hearts as directed on package; drain. In medium bowl, combine artichoke hearts, mushrooms and dressing. Cover; let stand about 4 hours at room temperature or several hours in refrigerator. Alternately thread artichoke hearts and mushrooms on skewers with cherry tomatoes. Broil or grill 4 to 5 inches from heat for about 5 minutes, turning and basting occasionally with dressing. Season with salt and pepper. Serve immediately with additional dressing. 6 servings

NUTRITION INFORMATION PER SERVING

Serving Size: 1/6 of recipe		Percent U.S. RDA Per Serving	
Calories	209	Protein	6%
Protein	4g	Vitamin A	16%
Carbohydrate	12g	Vitamin C	41%
Fat	18g	Thiamin	10%
Sodium	707mg	Riboflavin	20%
Potassium	346mg	Niacin	15%
		Calcium	*
		Iron	4%

TIPS: *Thinly sliced bacon may be laced over and under vegetables when threading skewers. Broil until bacon is cooked.*

Other vegetables may be used such as green pepper, small onions or drained water chestnuts.

Tomatoes may be done separately (all on one skewer) to prevent overcooking.

ARTICHOKE (JERUSALEM)

The Jerusalem artichoke is not really an artichoke but the root of a variety of sunflower plant. They are sometimes marketed under the name "sunchokes." Similar to the globe artichoke in flavor, it resembles a rather knotted potato. Jerusalem artichokes are prepared similar to a potato and make an excellent substitute. To prepare, peel and slice or leave whole. Cook in small amount of water until tender, about 10 to 15 minutes. They may also be broiled, sautéed or mashed, or added to soups and salads.

NUTRITION INFORMATION PER SERVING

Serving Size: 1/3 lb. Jerusalem artichoke		Percent U.S. RDA Per Serving	
Calories	0	Protein	5%
Protein	3g	Vitamin A	*
Carbohydrate	25g	Vitamin C	10%
Fat	<1g	Thiamin	20%
Sodium	0mg	Riboflavin	5%
Potassium	0mg	Niacin	10%
		Calcium	2%
		Iron	29%

ASPARAGUS

Asparagus is available with both green and white coloring. The green is more common in this country; the white, more common in Europe. White asparagus is a special variety that is grown covered with a mound of dirt. Lack of sunlight keeps the stalks white and gives a slightly milder flavor than the green. Asparagus is available fresh, frozen and canned.

NUTRITION INFORMATION PER SERVING

Serving Size: 1/2 cup cooked asparagus		Percent U.S. RDA Per Serving	
Calories	23	Protein	4%
Protein	3g	Vitamin A	21%
Carbohydrate	4g	Vitamin C	49%
Fat	<1g	Thiamin	12%
Sodium	1mg	Riboflavin	12%
Potassium	209mg	Niacin	8%
		Calcium	2%
		Iron	4%

BUY: Allow 1 lb. for 4 servings. Select green, tender spears with dark green, closed tips. Old asparagus may have woody texture.
PEAK SEASON: Early spring.
STORAGE: Refrigerate, without washing, in airtight container, plastic bag or wrap, 1 to 2 days.
PREPARATION: Wash thoroughly to remove dirt and sand. Snap off base of stalks. (They will snap just between the tender and the tough portion.) Leave top whole or cut or break into 1-inch pieces. Whole stalks may be tied together in a bundle and placed in a deep saucepan or coffee pot.
COOK: Add 1 inch salted water (½ teaspoon salt to 1 cup water) to bundled asparagus spears. Since tips cook faster than spears, only the stalk ends will be in the water. Cover and heat to boiling. Cook until stalk ends are crisp-tender; drain.

To cook cut asparagus, add 1 inch salted water to the lower stalk pieces. Cover and heat to boiling. Cook until crisp-tender; uncover, add tips. Cook until stalk ends are tender; drain.
TIME:

Asparagus	Whole or Butts	Tips
Boiling	*10 to 20 min.*	*5 to 15 min.*
Steaming	*12 to 30 min.*	*7 to 15 min.*
Pressure Saucepan (15 lb. pressure)	*½ to 2 min.*	*½ to 1½ min.*

SEASONING: When cooking add: dill weed, chives, chervil, bacon, equal amount of whole kernel corn, then season with cream and nutmeg.

Before serving add: butter, lemon butter, cheese, creamed egg or hollandaise sauce, toasted almonds, pimiento strips, buttered bread crumbs, Parmesan cheese, sour cream, Caesar or Italian salad dressing. Marinate chilled cooked asparagus in French or vinegar and oil dressing and serve on lettuce as a salad.

ORIENTAL ASPARAGUS

2 tablespoons margarine or butter
2 tablespoons slivered almonds
10-oz. pkg. (1½ cups) frozen cut asparagus
1 stalk celery, sliced
1 tablespoon soy sauce
8-oz. can (⅔ cup) water chestnuts, drained and sliced

In small skillet or shallow saucepan, cook almonds in margarine until golden brown. Remove almonds; set aside. Add remaining ingredients to margarine. Simmer covered, about 10 minutes or until asparagus is tender, stirring occasionally. If necessary, remove lid during last few minutes to allow liquid to evaporate. There should just be a thin glaze on vegetables. Add toasted almonds.

3 to 4 servings

NUTRITION INFORMATION PER SERVING

Serving Size: 1/4 of recipe		Percent U.S. RDA Per Serving	
Calories	106	Protein	6%
Protein	4g	Vitamin A	17%
Carbohydrate	8g	Vitamin C	33%
Fat	8g	Thiamin	9%
Sodium	418mg	Riboflavin	9%
Potassium	290mg	Niacin	6%
		Calcium	4%
		Iron	8%

TIP: *With fresh asparagus, increase cooking time to 10 to 15 minutes. With drained canned asparagus, reduce cooking time to 5 to 10 minutes; stir carefully.*

ASPARAGUS AU GRATIN

10-oz. pkg. frozen spears or cut asparagus
2 tablespoons chopped pimiento, drained
2 tablespoons chopped green pepper
½ cup condensed cream of celery or mushroom soup
1 tablespoon milk
2 tablespoons grated Parmesan cheese

Heat oven to 350°F. In medium saucepan, cook asparagus as directed on package; drain. Arrange asparagus in 1-quart casserole. Combine remaining ingredients except Parmesan cheese.* Bake uncovered at 350°F. for 20 to 25 minutes or until bubbly.

3 to 4 servings

NUTRITION INFORMATION PER SERVING

Serving Size: 1/4 of recipe		Percent U.S. RDA Per Serving	
Calories	50	Protein	5%
Protein	3g	Vitamin A	11%
Carbohydrate	5g	Vitamin C	35%
Fat	2g	Thiamin	7%
Sodium	265mg	Riboflavin	7%
Potassium	180mg	Niacin	4%
		Calcium	6%
		Iron	5%

TIPS: *A 15-oz. can drained asparagus spears or cut asparagus, or 1 lb. (about 15 spears) cooked fresh asparagus may be substituted for frozen asparagus.*

For 6 to 8 servings, double ingredient amounts and bake in 1½-quart casserole for 30 to 35 minutes.

If desired, substitute 1 cup White Sauce (half recipe), page 540, for cream of celery soup.

*To MAKE AHEAD, prepare to *, cover and refrigerate up to 1 day. Bake at 350°F. for 30 to 35 minutes or until heated through.*

BEANS (GREEN AND WAX)

Green and wax beans have tender edible pods. Green beans, sometimes referred to as snap beans, are cut into a variety of shapes for cooking. French-cut beans are cut lengthwise into thin strips. Kitchen-cut are cut diagonally into 1 to 2-inch pieces. Whole green beans are left whole with the stem and tip ends removed. Italian beans are green with a fairly flat pod. Wax beans are yellow in color and are usually cut into about 1-inch pieces. Although there are recipes for each type, they may be used interchangeably or in combination.

NUTRITION INFORMATION PER SERVING

Serving Size: 1/4 lb. cooked green beans — Percent U.S. RDA Per Serving

Calories	16	Protein	*
Protein	1g	Vitamin A	7%
Carbohydrate	3g	Vitamin C	13%
Fat	<1g	Thiamin	3%
Sodium	3mg	Riboflavin	3%
Potassium	95mg	Niacin	*
		Calcium	3%
		Iron	2%

NUTRITION INFORMATION PER SERVING

Serving Size: 1/2 cup cooked wax beans — Percent U.S. RDA Per Serving

Calories	12	Protein	*
Protein	<1g	Vitamin A	3%
Carbohydrate	3g	Vitamin C	12%
Fat	<1g	Thiamin	3%
Sodium	2mg	Riboflavin	3%
Potassium	83mg	Niacin	*
		Calcium	3%
		Iron	*

BUY: Allow 1 lb. for 4 servings. Select beans with firm crisp pods, free of blemishes. If too mature, pods become stringy and tough and the beans are best shelled and pods discarded.
PEAK SEASON: Summer (available all year).
STORAGE: Refrigerate, without washing in airtight container or plastic bag, 3 to 5 days.
PREPARATION: Wash thoroughly and snap off ends. Leave whole, break into pieces, slice lengthwise or slice diagonally.
COOK: Add 1 inch water to beans. Cover and heat to boiling. To avoid toughening beans, salt (½ teaspoon salt to 1 cup water) when cooking is half finished. Cook until tender; drain.

TIME:	**Green Beans Whole or 1-inch Pieces**	**Green Beans Frenched**	**Wax Beans Whole or 1-inch Pieces**
Boiling	*15 to 30 min.*	*10 to 20 min.*	*20 to 35 min.*
Steaming	*20 to 35 min.*	*15 to 25 min.*	*25 to 40 min.*
Pressure Saucepan (15 lb. pressure)	*1½ to 3 min.*	*1 to 2 min.*	*2 to 3½ min.*

SEASONING: When cooking add: sliced bacon, chopped onion, Italian seasoning or savory, 1 to 2 tablespoons onion soup mix, mustard seed, basil leaves, tarragon leaves, oregano leaves, thyme leaves.

Before serving add: cheese sauce, cream soup such as mushroom, sour cream and dill weed, sautéed mushrooms, water chestnuts or almonds. Marinate and chill cooked beans several hours in Italian dressing and serve on lettuce as a salad.

SWEET BUTTERY BEANS

2 pkg. (9 oz. each) frozen cut green beans
1 tablespoon brown sugar
2 tablespoons margarine or butter
1 tablespoon lemon juice

In medium saucepan, cook beans as directed on package; drain. Add remaining ingredients; mix well.

6 servings

NUTRITION INFORMATION PER SERVING

Serving Size: 1/6 of recipe — Percent U.S. RDA Per Serving

Calories	63	Protein	2%
Protein	1g	Vitamin A	12%
Carbohydrate	7g	Vitamin C	8%
Fat	4g	Thiamin	4%
Sodium	48mg	Riboflavin	4%
Potassium	132mg	Niacin	*
		Calcium	3%
		Iron	4%

TIP: *Drained canned or cooked fresh beans may be substituted for frozen beans.*

SAVORY GREEN BEANS

9-oz. pkg. (1¾ cups) frozen cut green beans
1 tablespoon margarine or butter
1 teaspoon vinegar or lemon juice
3 tablespoons grated Parmesan cheese
1 cup herb-seasoned croutons

In medium saucepan, cook beans as directed on package; drain. Add margarine. Place in serving dish; sprinkle with vinegar. Add Parmesan cheese and croutons; toss lightly. 3 to 4 servings

NUTRITION INFORMATION PER SERVING

Serving Size: 1/4 of recipe		Percent U.S. RDA Per Serving	
Calories	100	Protein	5%
Protein	3g	Vitamin A	10%
Carbohydrate	10g	Vitamin C	5%
Fat	5g	Thiamin	3%
Sodium	198mg	Riboflavin	5%
Potassium	97mg	Niacin	*
		Calcium	7%
		Iron	2%

TIP: *A 16-oz. can (2 cups) drained green beans may be substituted for frozen beans.*

HOT BEAN COMPOTE

3 to 4 slices bacon
½ cup sugar
1 tablespoon cornstarch
½ teaspoon salt
¼ teaspoon pepper
⅔ cup vinegar
1 medium onion, sliced
16-oz. can (2 cups) cut green beans, drained
16-oz. can (2 cups) cut wax beans, drained
15½-oz. can (2 cups) red kidney beans, drained

In large saucepan or skillet, fry bacon until crisp; drain on paper towel. Add sugar and cornstarch to bacon drippings; blend well. Stir in salt, pepper and vinegar. Heat until mixture boils and thickens, stirring constantly. Stir in onion and beans. Simmer covered, 20 to 25 minutes, stirring occasionally. Crumble bacon over top.
8 to 10 servings

NUTRITION INFORMATION PER SERVING

Serving Size: 1/10 of recipe		Percent U.S. RDA Per Serving	
Calories	106	Protein	5%
Protein	3g	Vitamin A	3%
Carbohydrate	20g	Vitamin C	6%
Fat	2g	Thiamin	3%
Sodium	271mg	Riboflavin	3%
Potassium	161mg	Niacin	3%
		Calcium	4%
		Iron	9%

TIPS: *To halve recipe, use half the ingredient amounts.*

Cooked lima beans or soy beans may be substituted for kidney beans.

SWEET AND SOUR BEANS

16-oz. can (2 cups) cut green beans, undrained
½ cup sugar
1 teaspoon celery seed
¼ teaspoon dry mustard
½ cup vinegar
1 tablespoon chopped green pepper
1 tablespoon chopped pimiento
1 medium onion, thinly sliced and separated into rings
8-oz. can (1 cup) cut wax beans, drained

In medium saucepan, drain liquid from green beans; stir in sugar, celery seed, mustard and vinegar. Heat to boiling. Place beans and remaining ingredients in 2-quart container. Pour hot vinegar mixture over beans; mix gently. Cover; refrigerate several hours or up to 1 week. 5 to 6 servings

NUTRITION INFORMATION PER SERVING

Serving Size: 1/6 of recipe		Percent U.S. RDA Per Serving	
Calories	94	Protein	2%
Protein	1g	Vitamin A	5%
Carbohydrate	24g	Vitamin C	13%
Fat	<1g	Thiamin	2%
Sodium	182mg	Riboflavin	3%
Potassium	146mg	Niacin	*
		Calcium	5%
		Iron	9%

CONFETTI BEANS

9-oz. pkg. (1¾ cups) frozen wax beans
¼ cup chopped green pepper
2 tablespoons chopped pimiento, drained
3-oz. pkg. cream cheese, cubed

In medium saucepan, cook beans as directed on package; drain. Add remaining ingredients; mix well. Serve immediately. 4 servings

NUTRITION INFORMATION PER SERVING

Serving Size: 1/4 of recipe		Percent U.S. RDA Per Serving	
Calories	99	Protein	4%
Protein	3g	Vitamin A	9%
Carbohydrate	5g	Vitamin C	26%
Fat	8g	Thiamin	4%
Sodium	55mg	Riboflavin	6%
Potassium	132mg	Niacin	*
		Calcium	3%
		Iron	3%

TIPS: *Green beans or combination of wax and green beans may be substituted.*

Drained canned beans may be substituted for cooked frozen beans. Prepare as directed.

To MAKE AHEAD, prepare as directed placing cooked beans in 1-quart casserole. Cover and refrigerate up to 1 day. Bake covered at 350°F. for 20 to 25 minutes or until heated through.

SAUCY ITALIAN BEANS

9-oz. pkg. (1¾ cups) frozen Italian or green beans
1 tablespoon chopped onion
⅛ teaspoon Italian seasoning, oregano leaves or thyme leaves
½ cup tomato sauce
¼ cup shredded Mozzarella cheese

In medium saucepan, cook beans as directed on package; drain. Add remaining ingredients except cheese. Heat through, stirring occasionally. Place in serving dish; top with cheese. Let stand covered a few minutes until cheese melts.

3 to 4 servings

NUTRITION INFORMATION PER SERVING

Serving Size: 1/4 of recipe		Percent U.S. RDA Per Serving	
Calories	85	Protein	3%
Protein	2g	Vitamin A	17%
Carbohydrate	7g	Vitamin C	5%
Fat	6g	Thiamin	4%
Sodium	24mg	Riboflavin	7%
Potassium	99mg	Niacin	2%
		Calcium	8%
		Iron	4%

TIPS: *If desired, 2 tablespoons grated Parmesan cheese may be substituted for Mozzarella.*

To MAKE AHEAD, assemble in 1-quart casserole, cover and refrigerate up to 2 days. Bake at 350°F. for 25 to 30 minutes or until heated through. Top with cheese.

GREEN BEAN CASSEROLE

2 pkg. (9 oz. each) frozen French-style green beans*
10¾-oz. can condensed cream of mushroom soup
3-oz. can (2 cups) French-fried onions

Heat oven to 350°F. In large saucepan, cook beans as directed on package; drain. In 1½-quart casserole, combine beans with mushroom soup. Bake uncovered at 350°F. for 20 to 25 minutes or until bubbly. Top with onions during last 5 minutes of baking.

6 to 8 servings

NUTRITION INFORMATION PER SERVING

Serving Size: 1/6 of recipe		Percent U.S. RDA Per Serving	
Calories	164	Protein	5%
Protein	3g	Vitamin A	9%
Carbohydrate	14g	Vitamin C	6%
Fat	12g	Thiamin	3%
Sodium	465mg	Riboflavin	6%
Potassium	182mg	Niacin	3%
		Calcium	5%
		Iron	5%

TIPS: **A 16-oz. can (2 cups) drained French-style green beans may be substituted for frozen beans.*

4 to 5 servings

For a variation, add 8-oz. can drained and sliced water chestnuts and ¼ teaspoon soy sauce to casserole. Substitute chow mein noodles for onions.

If desired, top with shoestring potatoes, potato chips or crumbled cheese crackers.

To halve recipe, use half the ingredient amounts; bake in 1-quart casserole for 15 to 20 minutes.

LIMA BEANS, BLACK-EYED PEAS, LENTILS, SPLIT PEAS, SOYBEANS AND DRY BEANS

Dried beans belong to the legume family which includes lentils, dry peas and peanuts. These foods are high in protein and can play an important role in the diet by providing protein at a low cost. Although there are individual color and flavor differences, they can often be interchanged in recipes. Some of these peas and beans are available both fresh and dried. When fresh, they may be cooked immediately; when dried they need soaking to rehydrate before cooking. Lentils and split peas are small enough and do not have a skin so they can be rehydrated at the same time they cook.

Some of the types of dried beans and peas include:

BLACK-EYED PEAS: A favorite in the South, these "beans" are oval with a black spot on one side. Yellow-eyed peas have a yellow spot. Both are available fresh or dried.

WHITE BEANS: There are 4 varieties ranging from the small pea bean to the large, round narrow bean. Navy beans are larger than pea beans and often used in pork and beans. Great Northern beans are larger than navy beans and have a delicate flavor that makes them a favorite for baked beans and soups.

NUTRITION INFORMATION PER SERVING

Serving Size: 2/3 cup cooked beans		Percent U.S. RDA Per Serving	
Calories	190	Protein	19%
Protein	12g	Vitamin A	0%
Carbohydrate	34g	Vitamin C	0%
Fat	<1g	Thiamin	24%
Sodium	11mg	Riboflavin	7%
Potassium	670mg	Niacin	7%
		Calcium	8%
		Iron	24%

RED KIDNEY BEANS: Have a bright purple-red skin and are often used in chili, soups or salads. They are available canned and dried.

LIMA BEANS: Have a flat, kidney shape and are available as small "baby limas" or the larger "Fordhook limas." They are available fresh, canned, frozen and dried.

NUTRITION INFORMATION PER SERVING

Serving Size: 1/2 cup cooked lima beans		Percent U.S. RDA Per Serving	
Calories	94	Protein	10%
Protein	6g	Vitamin A	5%
Carbohydrate	17g	Vitamin C	24%
Fat	<1g	Thiamin	10%
Sodium	<1mg	Riboflavin	5%
Potassium	359mg	Niacin	6%
		Calcium	4%
		Iron	12%

SOYBEANS: Their high nutritive value plays an important role in feeding the world's population. When dry, they are about the size of a pea, but look like a bean after soaking and cooking. They have a very distinct flavor that is less noticeable when combined with other flavors. Since they have a noticeable aroma when cooking, it may be advantageous to cook a large amount and freeze the extras for later use. Soy protein is often extracted and used as a protein supplement or substitute in processed foods.

LENTILS: There are 2 varieties of lentils – the French with gray exterior and yellow interior, and the Egyptian, which is smaller, rounder and reddish-yellow in color. Unlike dried beans, they do not need long soaking before cooking, making them convenient for last-minute preparation.

PEAS: Dried peas are available whole and split, yellow and green. They may be used interchangeably, but the whole peas must be soaked before cooking. The split peas have the outer skin removed so rehydrate and cook simultaneously.

BUY: Allow ½ lb. (1 cup) dried peas or beans for 4 servings. For fresh peas or beans, shelled, allow 2 cups. If in the pod, allow 3 lb. for 4 servings.

PEAK SEASON: Summer and fall. Dried peas and beans available all year.
STORAGE: Refrigerate fresh peas and beans in airtight container or plastic bag, 3 to 5 days. Dry peas or beans keep several months in covered container at room temperature.
COOK: For fresh lima beans or black-eyed peas, add 1 inch salted water (½ teaspoon salt to 1 cup water) to beans and peas. Cover and heat to boiling. Cook until tender; drain.
TIME:

	Lima Beans	Black-eyed Peas
Boiling	*25 to 30 min.*	*20 to 25 min.*
Steaming	*25 to 35 min.*	*20 to 30 min.*
Pressure Saucepan (15 lb. pressure)	*1 to 2 min.*	*½ to 1½ min.*

SEASONING: When cooking add: sliced bacon, ham or pork hocks, meat drippings, basil leaves, curry powder. Add tomato mixtures after beans are cooked. The acid can prevent uncooked beans from softening.

Before serving add: margarine or butter, cream, tomato sauce, green pepper, combine with equal amounts of corn and season with margarine or cream.

TO PREPARE: Wash and sort peas or beans. Place in large saucepan; add water. If soaking is necessary, see "To Soak." After soaking, heat beans and soaking water to boiling over high heat. Reduce heat; simmer covered over low heat until tender. Add about 1½ teaspoons salt. Use as desired. Cooked beans freeze well.

TO SOAK: Overnight Method – Let beans stand in cold water overnight or about 12 hours. Use soaking water for cooking.
Quick Method – Combine beans and water; heat to boiling and let boil 2 minutes. Remove from heat, cover and let stand 1 hour. Use soaking water for cooking.

TIP: *One tablespoon oil in water, helps prevent boiling over.*

COOKING CHART FOR DRY BEANS AND PEAS

Type	Amount	Water	Soak	Cook	Yield
Lentils	*½ lb. (1 cup)*	*2 cups*	*No*	*30-35 min.*	*2½ cups*
Split Peas	*½ lb. (1 cup)*	*2 cups*	*No*	*30-45 min.*	*2½ cups*
Whole Peas	*½ lb. (1 cup)*	*2½ to 3 cups*	*Yes*	*1-1¼ hours*	*2½ cups*
Beans or Black-eyed Peas	*½ lb. (1 cup)*	*2½ to 3 cups*	*Yes*	*1½-2 hours*	*2½ cups*
Soybeans	*½ lb. (1 cup)*	*4 cups*	*Yes*	*2-2½ hours*	*2½ cups*

BAKED BEANS

- 2 cups navy or Great Northern beans
- 2 qt. (8 cups) water
- ½ lb. salt pork, cut into ½-inch pieces
- 2 tablespoons firmly packed brown sugar
- ½ teaspoon salt
- ½ teaspoon dry mustard
- 1 small onion, chopped
- ½ cup molasses
- ¼ cup catsup or chili sauce

In large saucepan, cover beans with water. Soak overnight or about 12 hours. Heat beans and soaking water to boiling. Simmer covered, about 1 hour or until beans are almost tender. Drain; reserve liquid. Heat oven to 300°F. In bean pot or large casserole, combine beans and salt pork. Add enough water to reserved bean liquid to measure 2 cups. Stir remaining ingredients into 2 cups bean liquid. Pour over beans; mix gently. Bake covered at 300°F. for 6 to 7 hours, stirring occasionally; adding water if necessary. Remove cover during last hour of baking and bake without stirring.

6 to 8 servings

NUTRITION INFORMATION PER SERVING

Serving Size: 1/8 of recipe		Percent U.S. RDA Per Serving	
Calories	437	Protein	22%
Protein	14g	Vitamin A	2%
Carbohydrate	50g	Vitamin C	4%
Fat	21g	Thiamin	30%
Sodium	437mg	Riboflavin	11%
Potassium	929mg	Niacin	11%
		Calcium	15%
		Iron	32%

TIPS: *Bacon may be substituted for salt pork.*

Other types of beans may be substituted, or use combination of beans. Cook beans before combining with remaining ingredients.

TOMATO-BEAN CASSEROLE

- 10-oz. pkg. (1½ cups) frozen lima beans or black-eyed peas
- 1 small onion, chopped
- 1 teaspoon sugar
- ½ teaspoon salt
- ¼ teaspoon dry or ½ teaspoon prepared mustard
- ⅛ teaspoon pepper
- 16-oz. can (2 cups) tomatoes, undrained and cut up
- 2 slices bacon, cut into 1-inch pieces
- ¼ cup grated Parmesan cheese, if desired

Heat oven to 375°F. In medium saucepan, cook lima beans with onion as directed on package; drain. Combine with remaining ingredients except bacon and cheese, in 1-quart casserole. Top with bacon. Bake uncovered at 375°F. for 1 hour. Sprinkle with Parmesan cheese during last 15 minutes of baking time.

4 to 6 servings

NUTRITION INFORMATION PER SERVING

Serving Size: 1/6 of recipe		Percent U.S. RDA Per Serving	
Calories	150	Protein	10%
Protein	7g	Vitamin A	17%
Carbohydrate	17g	Vitamin C	34%
Fat	6g	Thiamin	8%
Sodium	424mg	Riboflavin	5%
Potassium	410mg	Niacin	7%
		Calcium	7%
		Iron	11%

ZESTY PORK AND BEANS

4 slices bacon
16-oz. can (1¾ cups) pork and beans
¼ cup firmly packed brown sugar
2 tablespoons chopped onion
¼ teaspoon garlic salt
¼ cup catsup or chili sauce

Heat oven to 350°F. In medium skillet, fry bacon until crisp; drain on paper towel, reserving 2 tablespoons drippings. Combine drippings with remaining ingredients in 1-quart casserole. Sprinkle with crumbled bacon. Bake uncovered at 350°F. for 25 to 30 minutes or until bubbly and heated through.

4 servings

NUTRITION INFORMATION PER SERVING

Serving Size: 1/4 of recipe		Percent U.S. RDA Per Serving	
Calories	255	Protein	15%
Protein	10g	Vitamin A	8%
Carbohydrate	40g	Vitamin C	9%
Fat	7g	Thiamin	10%
Sodium	895mg	Riboflavin	5%
Potassium	372mg	Niacin	7%
		Calcium	8%
		Iron	16%

TIPS: *If desired, combine all ingredients in skillet and simmer covered, 10 minutes.*

For additional flavor, add ½ teaspoon dry or prepared mustard, 8-oz. can (1 cup) drained crushed pineapple, 1 chopped apple or 1 to 2 cups sliced wieners, cubed ham or luncheon meat.

BEAN AND POTATO FRY

¼ cup oil, meat drippings or margarine
4 medium potatoes, peeled and coarsely shredded
2 cups cooked beans, peas or lentils
Salt and pepper

In large skillet, heat oil; add potatoes and beans. Cover loosely and cook until tender and browned, about 15 minutes, stirring occasionally. Season with salt and pepper.

4 servings

NUTRITION INFORMATION PER SERVING

Serving Size: 1/4 of recipe		Percent U.S. RDA Per Serving	
Calories	341	Protein	16%
Protein	10g	Vitamin A	0%
Carbohydrate	45g	Vitamin C	35%
Fat	14g	Thiamin	18%
Sodium	79mg	Riboflavin	7%
Potassium	985mg	Niacin	14%
		Calcium	6%
		Iron	19%

TIP: *For additional seasonings, add 1 small chopped onion, ¼ cup chopped green pepper or ½ teaspoon marjoram or thyme. Shredded cheese may be added just before serving.*

GLAZED LIMAS

10-oz. pkg. (1½ cups) frozen lima beans
2 tablespoons margarine or butter
1 small onion, sliced
1 medium cooking apple, peeled and sliced
3 tablespoons firmly packed brown sugar

In medium saucepan, cook beans as directed on package; drain. In same saucepan, cook onion and apple in margarine until tender. Add beans and brown sugar; heat through.

4 to 5 servings

NUTRITION INFORMATION PER SERVING

Serving Size: 1/4 of recipe		Percent U.S. RDA Per Serving	
Calories	212	Protein	10%
Protein	6g	Vitamin A	9%
Carbohydrate	35g	Vitamin C	21%
Fat	6g	Thiamin	6%
Sodium	178mg	Riboflavin	4%
Potassium	428mg	Niacin	5%
		Calcium	5%
		Iron	15%

TIP: *A 16-oz. can (2 cups) drained lima beans or 1 lb. (2 cups shelled) cooked fresh lima beans may be substituted for frozen beans; or substitute cooked beans or lentils for cooked lima beans.*

BAKED LENTILS

1 cup (½ lb.) dry lentils
3 cups water
¼ cup firmly packed brown sugar
1 teaspoon salt
1 teaspoon mustard
2 slices bacon, cut into small pieces
1 small onion, chopped
½ cup water
¼ cup chili sauce or catsup
¼ cup molasses

Sort and wash lentils. In medium saucepan, combine lentils and 3 cups water. Heat to boiling; simmer covered, 20 to 30 minutes or until just about tender. Drain; stir in remaining ingredients. Simmer covered, 20 to 30 minutes, stirring occasionally, adding water if necessary. 5 to 6 servings

NUTRITION INFORMATION PER SERVING

Serving Size: 1/6 of recipe		Percent U.S. RDA Per Serving	
Calories	125	Protein	6%
Protein	4g	Vitamin A	20%
Carbohydrate	25g	Vitamin C	7%
Fat	1g	Thiamin	3%
Sodium	400mg	Riboflavin	4%
Potassium	289mg	Niacin	3%
		Calcium	6%
		Iron	11%

TIPS: *After first cooking, lentils may be combined with remaining ingredients in 2-quart casserole and baked at 350°F. for 30 to 45 minutes.*

These same seasonings may be added to other cooked dry beans. Add just enough water to keep moist.

REFRIED BEANS

2 to 4 tablespoons oil or bacon drippings
2 cups cooked beans, split peas or lentils
¼ cup chopped green chilies, if desired

In medium skillet, heat oil. Add beans and mash with fork or back of spoon. Cook uncovered until bean liquid evaporates and beans are of desired consistency, stirring occasionally. Stir in chilies. If desired, serve topped with sour cream. 3 to 4 servings

NUTRITION INFORMATION PER SERVING

Serving Size: 1/4 of recipe		Percent U.S. RDA Per Serving	
Calories	173	Protein	11%
Protein	7g	Vitamin A	*
Carbohydrate	21g	Vitamin C	42%
Fat	7g	Thiamin	7%
Sodium	3mg	Riboflavin	4%
Potassium	314mg	Niacin	4%
		Calcium	4%
		Iron	13%

TIP: *Other ways to serve refried beans—as taco filling with shredded cheese, chopped tomato and shredded lettuce or as a dip (add sour cream to thin to desired consistency) for taco or corn chips.*

BEETS

NUTRITION INFORMATION PER SERVING

Serving Size: 1/2 cup cooked beets		Percent U.S. RDA Per Serving	
Calories	27	Protein	*
Protein	<1g	Vitamin A	*
Carbohydrate	6g	Vitamin C	8%
Fat	<1g	Thiamin	*
Sodium	37mg	Riboflavin	2%
Potassium	177mg	Niacin	*
		Calcium	*
		Iron	2%

BUY: Allow 1 lb. (4 medium beets) for 4 servings. Select firm round beets with smooth surface and deep red color. Tops wilt quickly but this does not affect quality unless the greens are cooked too. For cooking beet greens, see page 609.
PEAK SEASON: Early summer (available all year).
STORAGE: Cut off all but 2 inches of beet tops; leave root ends attached. Refrigerate beets in airtight container or plastic bag, 1 to 2 weeks.
PREPARATION: Scrub with vegetable brush to remove all dirt. Leave the root ends and 2 inches of beet tops attached.
COOK: Cover with water; add ¾ teaspoon salt. Cover and heat to boiling; cook until tender. Drain; cool by running cold water over beets. Slip off skin and tops. Leave whole, slice, dice or shred.

TIME:

Beets	Young, Whole	Mature, Whole
Boiling	*30 to 45 min.*	*45 to 90 min.*
Steaming	*40 to 60 min.*	*50 to 90 min.*
Pressure Saucepan (15 lb. pressure)	*5 to 10 min.*	*10 to 18 min.*
Baking	*40 to 60 min.*	*40 to 60 min.*

SEASONING: When cooking add cloves.

Before serving add margarine or butter, orange marmalade, sour cream, orange juice concentrate.

(For Pickled Beets, see page 441).

HARVARD BEETS

¼ cup sugar
1 tablespoon cornstarch
1 teaspoon salt
Dash pepper
16-oz. can (2 cups) sliced or diced beets, drained (reserve liquid)
¾ cup liquid (reserved liquid plus water)
3 tablespoons vinegar

In medium saucepan, combine first 4 ingredients. Gradually stir liquid and vinegar into cornstarch mixture; blend until smooth. Heat until mixture boils and thickens, stirring constantly. Add beets; heat through.

4 servings

NUTRITION INFORMATION PER SERVING

Serving Size: 1/4 of recipe		Percent U.S. RDA Per Serving	
Calories	94	Protein	*
Protein	1g	Vitamin A	*
Carbohydrate	24g	Vitamin C	6%
Fat	<1g	Thiamin	*
Sodium	797mg	Riboflavin	*
Potassium	199mg	Niacin	*
		Calcium	2%
		Iron	4%

ORANGE GLAZED BEETS

1 tablespoon chopped onion
2 tablespoons margarine or butter
2 tablespoons cornstarch
1 teaspoon grated orange peel
1 cup orange juice
¼ cup light corn syrup
2 tablespoons lemon juice
Salt and pepper
4 cups cooked, diced or sliced beets, drained

In medium skillet, sauté onion in margarine until tender. Stir in cornstarch; stir in remaining ingredients except beets. Heat to boiling, stirring constantly. Boil and stir 1 minute. Add beets and cook until heated through.

8 servings

NUTRITION INFORMATION PER SERVING

Serving Size: 1/8 of recipe		Percent U.S. RDA Per Serving	
Calories	105	Protein	*
Protein	1g	Vitamin A	4%
Carbohydrate	19g	Vitamin C	25%
Fat	3g	Thiamin	4%
Sodium	80mg	Riboflavin	3%
Potassium	248mg	Niacin	*
		Calcium	2%
		Iron	5%

BROCCOLI

A highly popular vegetable today, broccoli is a member of the cabbage family. Although cultivated in Italy as far back as the 16th century it has only become a frequently served vegetable in the U.S. in recent years. As a first cousin to the cauliflower, it is cooked and served in much the same manner. Broccoli is known for its rather distinct flavor and is highly prized for its nutritional value.

NUTRITION INFORMATION PER SERVING

Serving Size: 1/2 cup cooked broccoli		Percent U.S. RDA Per Serving	
Calories	20	Protein	4%
Protein	2g	Vitamin A	39%
Carbohydrate	4g	Vitamin C	117%
Fat	<1g	Thiamin	5%
Sodium	8mg	Riboflavin	9%
Potassium	208mg	Niacin	3%
		Calcium	7%
		Iron	3%

BUY: Allow 1 lb. for 4 servings. Look for tightly closed dark green flowerets. Stalks should be firm and tender.
PEAK SEASON: All year.
STORAGE: Refrigerate in airtight container, plastic bag or wrap, 3 to 5 days.
PREPARATION: Wash carefully, removing large outer leaves and tough portion of stalk. For uniform cooking, have stalks of similar size, splitting larger ones if necessary. If possible, stand in saucepan with stem end in water (stem takes longer to cook than flowerets).
COOK: Add 1 inch salted water (½ teaspoon salt to 1 cup water) to broccoli. Cover and heat to boiling. Cook until tender; drain.

TIME:

Broccoli	
Boiling	*10 to 15 min.*
Steaming	*15 to 20 min.*
Pressure Saucepan (15 lb. pressure)	*1½ to 3 min.*

SEASONING: When cooking add tarragon or marjoram.

Before serving add: margarine or butter, lemon butter, hollandaise, sour cream, cheese, mushroom or mustard sauce, buttered bread crumbs, horseradish, Parmesan cheese, toasted almonds, sliced lemons, cooked crumbled bacon, shrimp soup, capers.

BROCCOLI WITH LEMON SAUCE

2 pkg. (10 oz. each) frozen broccoli spears
½ cup slivered almonds
1 tablespoon margarine or butter
1 teaspoon grated lemon peel
½ teaspoon ginger
¼ teaspoon salt
⅓ cup milk
1 tablespoon lemon juice
2 pkg. (3 oz. each) cream cheese, softened

In medium saucepan, cook broccoli as directed on package; drain. In small skillet, cook almonds in margarine until golden brown. In small saucepan, combine remaining ingredients; heat until smooth and creamy, stirring occasionally. Pour over broccoli. Garnish with almonds. 6 to 8 servings

NUTRITION INFORMATION PER SERVING

Serving Size: 1/6 of recipe		Percent U.S. RDA Per Serving	
Calories	212	Protein	11%
Protein	7g	Vitamin A	54%
Carbohydrate	7g	Vitamin C	82%
Fat	19g	Thiamin	6%
Sodium	204mg	Riboflavin	16%
Potassium	298mg	Niacin	4%
		Calcium	10%
		Iron	6%

TIP: *To halve recipe, use half the ingredient amounts.*

BROCCOLI WITH POPPY SEED TOPPING

1 tablespoon chopped onion
1 tablespoon margarine or butter
10-oz. pkg. frozen broccoli spears
½ cup dairy sour cream
1 teaspoon sugar
½ teaspoon poppy seed
⅛ teaspoon salt
Toasted almonds, if desired

In medium saucepan, cook onion in margarine until golden brown. Add broccoli. Simmer covered, 8 to 10 minutes or until tender, stirring occasionally. Remove broccoli to serving dish; season with salt. In same saucepan, combine sour cream, sugar, poppy seed and salt. Heat; do not boil. Spoon over broccoli; garnish with almonds.

3 to 4 servings

NUTRITION INFORMATION PER SERVING

Serving Size: 1/4 of recipe		Percent U.S. RDA Per Serving	
Calories	167	Protein	7%
Protein	5g	Vitamin A	39%
Carbohydrate	7g	Vitamin C	60%
Fat	14g	Thiamin	4%
Sodium	144mg	Riboflavin	12%
Potassium	215mg	Niacin	3%
		Calcium	9%
		Iron	5%

BROCCOLI BAKE

2 pkg. (10 oz. each) frozen broccoli spears
2 tablespoons margarine or butter
2 tablespoons flour
½ teaspoon salt
¾ cup milk
1 cup (4 oz.) shredded Cheddar or American cheese
1 large tomato, sliced

Heat oven to 350°F. In medium saucepan, cook broccoli as directed on package; drain. Arrange in 8-inch square pan or 10x6-inch baking dish. In small saucepan, melt margarine; blend in flour and salt. Cook until mixture is smooth and bubbly. Stir in milk; heat until mixture boils and thickens, stirring occasionally. Blend in cheese; pour over broccoli. Bake uncovered at 350°F. for 20 to 25 minutes or until bubbly and heated through. Garnish with tomato slices; return to oven for 5 minutes.

6 to 8 servings

NUTRITION INFORMATION PER SERVING

Serving Size: 1/6 of recipe		Percent U.S. RDA Per Serving	
Calories	168	Protein	14%
Protein	9g	Vitamin A	47%
Carbohydrate	10g	Vitamin C	115%
Fat	11g	Thiamin	7%
Sodium	379mg	Riboflavin	15%
Potassium	328mg	Niacin	4%
		Calcium	22%
		Iron	6%

TIPS: *If desired, 1½ lb. cooked fresh broccoli may be substituted for frozen broccoli.*

To eliminate using oven, cook broccoli, arrange in serving dish, top with hot cheese sauce and garnish with tomato.

BROCCOLI AND ONION CASSEROLE

2 pkg. (10 oz. each) frozen broccoli spears
16-oz. can small whole onions, drained
⅛ teaspoon lemon pepper
⅛ teaspoon salt
2 cups medium White Sauce, page 540
¼ cup (1 oz.) shredded Cheddar cheese
¼ teaspoon lemon pepper
¼ teaspoon Worcestershire sauce
½ cup (2 oz.) shredded Cheddar cheese
Paprika

Cook broccoli as directed on package; drain. Heat oven to 325°F. Alternate layers of broccoli and onions in ungreased 1½ or 2-quart casserole; sprinkle with lemon pepper and salt. Stir ¼ cup cheese, ¼ teaspoon lemon pepper and Worcestershire sauce into white sauce; pour over vegetables. Sprinkle with ½ cup cheese and paprika. Bake at 325°F. for 1 hour.

6 to 8 servings

NUTRITION INFORMATION PER SERVING

Serving Size: 1/6 of recipe		Percent U.S. RDA Per Serving	
Calories	231	Protein	15%
Protein	10g	Vitamin A	38%
Carbohydrate	15g	Vitamin C	53%
Fat	15g	Thiamin	8%
Sodium	473mg	Riboflavin	18%
Potassium	345mg	Niacin	4%
		Calcium	25%
		Iron	6%

BROCCOLI AND ONION CASSEROLE

BROCCOLI AU GRATIN

2 pkg. (10 oz. each) frozen broccoli spears
10¾-oz. can condensed cream of celery or mushroom soup
2 tablespoons chopped pimiento
2 tablespoons chopped green pepper
2 tablespoons grated Parmesan cheese

Heat oven to 350°F. Cook broccoli as directed on package; drain. Place broccoli in shallow 1-quart casserole. In small bowl, combine remaining ingredients except Parmesan cheese; pour over broccoli. Bake uncovered at 350°F. for 20 to 25 minutes or until bubbly.

6 servings

NUTRITION INFORMATION PER SERVING

Serving Size: 1/6 of recipe		Percent U.S. RDA Per Serving	
Calories	66	Protein	6%
Protein	4g	Vitamin A	34%
Carbohydrate	8g	Vitamin C	64%
Fat	3g	Thiamin	4%
Sodium	427mg	Riboflavin	8%
Potassium	236mg	Niacin	3%
		Calcium	7%
		Iron	5%

BRUSSELS SPROUTS

A member of the cabbage family, brussels sprouts look like tiny cabbages. Instead of one large head, the plant produces rows of the small heads at the base of the leaves. Brussels was one of the first areas where this vegetable was grown and some think it may have originated there.

NUTRITION INFORMATION PER SERVING

Serving Size: 1/2 cup cooked brussels sprouts

		Percent U.S. RDA Per Serving	
Calories	28	Protein	5%
Protein	3g	Vitamin A	8%
Carbohydrate	5g	Vitamin C	113%
Fat	<1g	Thiamin	4%
Sodium	8mg	Riboflavin	6%
Potassium	213mg	Niacin	3%
		Calcium	2%
		Iron	5%

BUY: Allow 1 lb. for 4 servings. Look for firm compact heads, bright green in color. Avoid those beginning to yellow.
PEAK SEASON: Fall to early spring.
STORAGE: Refrigerate in airtight container or plastic bag, 1 to 2 days.
PREPARATION: Remove wilted outer leaves and wash thoroughly. Cut off stem.
COOK: Add 1 inch salted water (½ teaspoon salt to 1 cup water) to brussels sprouts. Cover and heat to boiling. Cook until tender; drain.
TIME:

Brussels Sprouts	Whole
Boiling	*10 to 20 min.*
Steaming	*15 to 20 min.*
Pressure Saucepan (15 lb. pressure)	*1 to 2 min.*

SEASONING: When cooking add: curry powder, nutmeg, sage.

Before serving add: margarine or butter, white sauce, cheese, hollandaise or mustard sauce, buttered bread crumbs, Parmesan cheese, celery or mushroom soup, onion dip, lemon juice, hard-boiled egg.

SUNNY SPROUTS

10-oz. pkg. (1½ cups) frozen brussels sprouts
½ teaspoon salt
½ teaspoon sugar
1 medium stalk celery, sliced
1 medium carrot, thinly sliced
½ cup water
2 tablespoons margarine or butter, melted
1 teaspoon prepared or ¼ teaspoon dry mustard
¼ teaspoon salt
Dash pepper

In small saucepan, combine first 6 ingredients. Heat to boiling. Cook loosely covered about 10 minutes or until tender; drain. Combine remaining ingredients; add to vegetables and toss lightly.

4 servings

NUTRITION INFORMATION PER SERVING

Serving Size: 1/4 of recipe

		Percent U.S. RDA Per Serving	
Calories	84	Protein	4%
Protein	3g	Vitamin A	43%
Carbohydrate	7g	Vitamin C	99%
Fat	6g	Thiamin	4%
Sodium	509mg	Riboflavin	5%
Potassium	275mg	Niacin	3%
		Calcium	3%
		Iron	4%

TIP: *If desired, ½ lb. (about 2 cups) cooked fresh brussels sprouts, may be substituted for frozen sprouts.*

SWEET-SOUR BRUSSELS SPROUTS

10-oz. pkg. (1½ cups) frozen brussels sprouts
3 slices bacon
2 tablespoons sugar
1 tablespoon chopped pimiento, if desired
½ teaspoon salt
½ cup water
2 tablespoons vinegar
1½ teaspoons cornstarch

In medium saucepan, cook brussels sprouts as directed on package. Drain; set aside. In same saucepan, fry bacon until crisp; drain on paper towel, reserving 2 tablespoons drippings. To reserved drippings, add sugar, pimiento, salt, ¼ cup water and vinegar. Combine cornstarch with remaining ¼ cup water; add to vinegar mixture in saucepan. Heat mixture until it boils and thickens, stirring constantly. Add brussels sprouts; heat through. Sprinkle with crumbled bacon. 4 servings

NUTRITION INFORMATION PER SERVING

Serving Size: 1/4 of recipe		Percent U.S. RDA Per Serving	
Calories	87	Protein	6%
Protein	4g	Vitamin A	8%
Carbohydrate	12g	Vitamin C	96%
Fat	3g	Thiamin	6%
Sodium	339mg	Riboflavin	5%
Potassium	231mg	Niacin	4%
		Calcium	*
		Iron	5%

BRUSSELS SPROUTS ROYALE

10-oz. pkg. (1½ cups) baby brussels sprouts frozen in butter sauce
½ cup seedless green grapes
2 tablespoons sauterne wine
2 tablespoons blanched slivered almonds

In medium saucepan, cook brussels sprouts according to package directions. Partially open pouch; drain butter sauce into small saucepan. Add grapes to butter sauce; heat through. Remove from heat; add sauterne and almonds. Toss with brussels sprouts. 3 to 4 servings

NUTRITION INFORMATION PER SERVING

Serving Size: 1/3 of recipe		Percent U.S. RDA Per Serving	
Calories	86	Protein	7%
Protein	4g	Vitamin A	11%
Carbohydrate	12g	Vitamin C	130%
Fat	3g	Thiamin	7%
Sodium	15mg	Riboflavin	9%
Potassium	367mg	Niacin	4%
		Calcium	4%
		Iron	6%

CABBAGE

Cabbage is available in 3 types – the familiar smooth-leafed green cabbage, the crinkly-leafed savory cabbage and red cabbage. They can generally be used interchangeably, although red cabbage is more often served with a sweet-tart seasoning and the green cabbage with a butter or cream-type seasoning. Savory cabbage has a slightly milder flavor than green cabbage.

NUTRITION INFORMATION PER SERVING

Serving Size: 1/2 cup shredded raw cabbage		Percent U.S. RDA Per Serving	
Calories	11	Protein	*
Protein	<1g	Vitamin A	*
Carbohydrate	2g	Vitamin C	21%
Fat	<1g	Thiamin	*
Sodium	9mg	Riboflavin	*
Potassium	105mg	Niacin	*
		Calcium	2%
		Iron	*

NUTRITION INFORMATION PER SERVING

Serving Size: 1/2 cup cooked cabbage		Percent U.S. RDA Per Serving	
Calories	15	Protein	*
Protein	<1g	Vitamin A	*
Carbohydrate	3g	Vitamin C	40%
Fat	<1g	Thiamin	*
Sodium	10mg	Riboflavin	*
Potassium	119mg	Niacin	*
		Calcium	3%
		Iron	*

BUY: Allow a small to medium head (about 1½ lb.) for 4 servings. Select heads which are firm and heavy for their size. Leaves should be a dark green, light green or red color, not wilted, yellow or brown.
PEAK SEASON: Green – all year; red – late summer.
STORAGE: Refrigerate in airtight container, plastic bag or wrap, 1 to 2 weeks.
PREPARATION: Wash thoroughly and remove any wilted outer leaves; cut into wedges or shred.
COOK: Add 1 inch salted water (½ teaspoon salt to 1 cup water) to cabbage. Cover and heat to boiling. Cook until crisp-tender. When cooking red cabbage, add a small amount of vinegar or lemon juice (about 2 tablespoons) to retain the red color.

TIME:

Cabbage	Green Quartered	Green Shredded	Red Shredded
Boiling	*10 to 15 min.*	*3 to 10 min.*	*8 to 12 min.*
Steaming	*15 min.*	*8 to 12 min.*	*10 to 15 min.*
Pressure Saucepan (15 lb. pressure	*2 to 3 min.*	*½ to 1½ min.*	*½ to 1½ min.*

SEASONING: When cooking add: caraway, dill seed, onion, nutmeg, oregano leaves, mustard seed.
Before serving add: sour cream, margarine or butter, shredded American cheese, cooked crumbled bacon.

CARAWAY CABBAGE

4 cups (½ medium head) shredded cabbage
½ teaspoon salt
¼ to ½ teaspoon caraway seed
⅛ teaspoon pepper
½ cup dairy sour cream

In medium saucepan, combine cabbage (with water that clings to leaves), salt, caraway seed and pepper. Simmer loosely covered, 10 to 15 minutes or until tender. Stir in sour cream. Cover and let stand 2 to 3 minutes to heat through.

4 to 5 servings

NUTRITION INFORMATION PER SERVING

Serving Size: 1/4 of recipe		Percent U.S. RDA Per Serving	
Calories	75	Protein	3%
Protein	2g	Vitamin A	6%
Carbohydrate	5g	Vitamin C	55%
Fat	6g	Thiamin	3%
Sodium	288mg	Riboflavin	4%
Potassium	163mg	Niacin	*
		Calcium	7%
		Iron	*

SCALLOPED CABBAGE

4 cups (½ medium head) shredded cabbage
½ teaspoon caraway seed or nutmeg
½ teaspoon salt
Dash pepper
2 tablespoons flour
1 cup milk
1 tablespoon margarine or butter

In medium saucepan, combine cabbage (with water that clings to leaves) with caraway seed, salt and pepper. Cook loosely covered, 10 to 15 minutes or until tender. Combine flour with ¼ cup milk; add remaining milk. Stir into cooked cabbage. Heat until mixture boils and thickens, stirring occasionally. Stir in margarine.

4 to 5 servings

NUTRITION INFORMATION PER SERVING

Serving Size: 1/4 of recipe		Percent U.S. RDA Per Serving	
Calories	99	Protein	5%
Protein	4g	Vitamin A	6%
Carbohydrate	10g	Vitamin C	56%
Fat	5g	Thiamin	5%
Sodium	341mg	Riboflavin	9%
Potassium	256mg	Niacin	3%
		Calcium	11%
		Iron	2%

TIP: *Cooked cabbage can be poured into casserole, topped with French-fried onions and baked uncovered at 350°F. for 10 to 15 minutes.*

SWEET-SOUR RED CABBAGE

6 cups (1 medium head) shredded red cabbage
2 tart green apples, peeled and chopped
¼ cup firmly packed brown sugar
1 teaspoon salt
½ teaspoon caraway seed, if desired
Dash pepper
½ cup water
¼ cup vinegar

In medium saucepan, combine all ingredients. Simmer covered, about 1 hour, stirring occasionally.

5 to 6 servings

NUTRITION INFORMATION PER SERVING

Serving Size: 1/6 of recipe		Percent U.S. RDA Per Serving	
Calories	85	Protein	2%
Protein	2g	Vitamin A	*
Carbohydrate	21g	Vitamin C	73%
Fat	<1g	Thiamin	5%
Sodium	377mg	Riboflavin	3%
Potassium	284mg	Niacin	*
		Calcium	4%
		Iron	6%

TIP: *For a more tart flavor, add 2 tablespoons additional vinegar.*

SAUTÉED CABBAGE

3 tablespoons margarine or butter
4 cups (½ medium head) shredded cabbage
½ teaspoon salt
½ teaspoon dill weed
Dash pepper

In medium skillet, melt margarine; stir in remaining ingredients. Cook covered about 10 minutes or until tender, stirring occasionally.

4 servings

NUTRITION INFORMATION PER SERVING

Serving Size: 1/4 of recipe		Percent U.S. RDA Per Serving	
Calories	99	Protein	*
Protein	1g	Vitamin A	9%
Carbohydrate	5g	Vitamin C	71%
Fat	9g	Thiamin	3%
Sodium	385mg	Riboflavin	3%
Potassium	215mg	Niacin	*
		Calcium	5%
		Iron	2%

TIP: *Chinese cabbage may be substituted for cabbage.*

CARROTS

NUTRITION INFORMATION PER SERVING

Serving Size: 1/2 cup raw carrots		Percent U.S. RDA Per Serving	
Calories	23	Protein	*
Protein	<1g	Vitamin A	121%
Carbohydrate	5g	Vitamin C	4%
Fat	<1g	Thiamin	2%
Sodium	26mg	Riboflavin	*
Potassium	188mg	Niacin	*
		Calcium	2%
		Iron	2%

NUTRITION INFORMATION PER SERVING

Serving Size: 1/2 cup cooked carrots		Percent U.S. RDA Per Serving	
Calories	24	Protein	*
Protein	<1g	Vitamin A	164%
Carbohydrate	6g	Vitamin C	8%
Fat	<1g	Thiamin	3%
Sodium	26mg	Riboflavin	2%
Potassium	173mg	Niacin	*
		Calcium	3%
		Iron	3%

BUY: Allow 1 lb. for 4 servings. Look for firm, well-shaped, bright carrots. Young or baby carrots are usually sweeter than mature carrots.
PEAK SEASON: All year.
STORAGE: Refrigerate in airtight container, plastic bag or wrap, 1 to 2 weeks. If they become limp, add a damp paper towel to container.
PREPARATION: Scrape or peel with vegetable peeler to remove thin layer of skin. Cut off tops and tips. Leave whole, slice, dice, shred or cut into strips.
COOK: Add 1 inch salted water (½ teaspoon salt to 1 cup water) to carrots. Cover and heat to boiling. Cook until tender; drain.

SEASONING: When cooking add: raisins, cinnamon, ginger, nutmeg, chives, dill seed, chopped apple.

Before serving add: margarine or butter, mint, parsley, lemon, honey, cooked crumbled bacon, sour cream, savory, marjoram, orange marmalade, peanuts, sherry, brandy, poppy seeds.

CREAMED CARROTS

5 to 6 medium carrots, sliced
½ teaspoon sugar
2 tablespoons water
Milk (about ½ cup)
1 tablespoon flour
⅛ teaspoon nutmeg, if desired
2 tablespoons margarine or butter

In medium saucepan, combine carrots, sugar and water. Simmer covered, 15 to 25 minutes or until tender. Drain juices into measuring cup. Add milk to make ¾ cup; mix with flour and nutmeg until smooth. Add to carrots along with margarine. Cook over medium heat until mixture boils and thickens, stirring constantly. Simmer 1 to 2 minutes. If desired, garnish with parsley. 4 to 5 servings

NUTRITION INFORMATION PER SERVING

Serving Size: 1/4 of recipe		Percent U.S. RDA Per Serving	
Calories	118	Protein	4%
Protein	2g	Vitamin A	204%
Carbohydrate	12g	Vitamin C	13%
Fat	7g	Thiamin	5%
Sodium	128mg	Riboflavin	6%
Potassium	355mg	Niacin	3%
		Calcium	7%
		Iron	4%

TIME:

Carrots	Young Whole	Young Sliced	Mature Whole	Mature Sliced
Boiling	*15 to 20 min.*	*10 to 20 min.*	*20 to 30 min.*	*15 to 25 min.*
Steaming	*20 to 30 min.*	*15 to 25 min.*	*40 to 50 min.*	*25 to 30 min.*
Pressure Saucepan (15 lb. pressure	*3 to 5 min.*	*1½ to 3 min.*	*10 to 15 min.*	*3 min.*
Baking	*35 to 45 min.*	*30 to 40 min.*	*60 min.*	–

GINGERED CARROTS

2 tablespoons margarine or butter
2 tablespoons firmly packed brown sugar or honey
½ teaspoon salt
¼ teaspoon ginger
⅛ teaspoon cinnamon
4 to 5 medium carrots, sliced, diced or cut into strips

In medium saucepan, combine all ingredients. Cook covered, stirring occasionally, 20 to 30 minutes or until carrots are tender.

3 to 4 servings

NUTRITION INFORMATION PER SERVING

Serving Size: 1/4 of recipe		Percent U.S. RDA Per Serving	
Calories	98	Protein	*
Protein	<1g	Vitamin A	163%
Carbohydrate	11g	Vitamin C	5%
Fat	6g	Thiamin	3%
Sodium	377mg	Riboflavin	2%
Potassium	264mg	Niacin	2%
		Calcium	3%
		Iron	4%

TIPS: *If desired, add 1 peeled, chopped or sliced apple. One or 2 tablespoons raisins may also be added.*

For a sherry flavor, add 2 tablespoons dry sherry during last 5 minutes of cooking.

HONEY-GLAZED CARROTS

6 medium carrots, halved, sliced or cut into strips
2 tablespoons firmly packed brown sugar
Dash salt
2 tablespoons margarine or butter
1 tablespoon honey

In medium saucepan, cook carrots as directed; drain. Add remaining ingredients; heat uncovered, 3 to 5 minutes, stirring occasionally to glaze.

3 to 4 servings

NUTRITION INFORMATION PER SERVING

Serving Size: 1/4 of recipe		Percent U.S. RDA Per Serving	
Calories	138	Protein	*
Protein	1g	Vitamin A	243%
Carbohydrate	21g	Vitamin C	15%
Fat	6g	Thiamin	4%
Sodium	181mg	Riboflavin	3%
Potassium	397mg	Niacin	3%
		Calcium	5%
		Iron	6%

TIP: *If desired, ½ teaspoon crushed dried mint leaves may be added, or substitute 2 tablespoons mint jelly and omit brown sugar.*

CARROT NUGGETS EN CASSEROLE

2 pkg. (10 oz. each) carrot nuggets frozen in butter sauce
4 thin orange slices, cut in half
4 thin lemon slices, cut in half
½ cup chopped walnuts
8¾-oz. can (1 cup) pineapple chunks, drained (reserve syrup)
2 tablespoons reserved pineapple syrup
¼ cup firmly packed brown sugar
2 teaspoons cornstarch
¼ cup walnut halves

Cook carrots according to package directions. Heat oven to 350°F. In a 1½-quart casserole, combine carrots, orange and lemon slices, chopped walnuts and pineapple. In small bowl, combine pineapple syrup, brown sugar and cornstarch to thoroughly dissolve cornstarch. Pour over casserole; toss lightly to mix. Sprinkle with walnut halves. Bake at 350°F. for 20 to 25 minutes.
6 to 8 servings

NUTRITION INFORMATION PER SERVING

Serving Size: 1/6 of recipe		Percent U.S. RDA Per Serving	
Calories	218	Protein	5%
Protein	3g	Vitamin A	196%
Carbohydrate	28g	Vitamin C	19%
Fat	12g	Thiamin	8%
Sodium	459mg	Riboflavin	4%
Potassium	302mg	Niacin	3%
		Calcium	6%
		Iron	7%

TIP: *To halve recipe, use half the ingredient amounts; bake in 1-quart casserole for 15 to 20 minutes.*

LEMON-BUTTERED CARROTS

3 tablespoons margarine or butter
6 medium carrots, sliced
1 medium apple, peeled and sliced
1 tablespoon chopped parsley
1 teaspoon grated lemon peel or juice
Salt

In medium saucepan or skillet, combine margarine and carrots. Cook covered, about 10 minutes or until almost tender, stirring occasionally. Add apple; continue cooking about 5 minutes or until tender. Stir in parsley and lemon; season with salt.
4 to 5 servings

NUTRITION INFORMATION PER SERVING

Serving Size: 1/4 of recipe		Percent U.S. RDA Per Serving	
Calories	139	Protein	2%
Protein	1g	Vitamin A	247%
Carbohydrate	15g	Vitamin C	19%
Fat	9g	Thiamin	5%
Sodium	225mg	Riboflavin	4%
Potassium	414mg	Niacin	3%
		Calcium	5%
		Iron	5%

CARROT NUGGET EN CASSEROLE

CAULIFLOWER

NUTRITION INFORMATION PER SERVING

Serving Size: 1/2 cup cooked cauliflower		Percent U.S. RDA Per Serving	
Calories	14	Protein	2%
Protein	1g	Vitamin A	*
Carbohydrate	3g	Vitamin C	35%
Fat	<1g	Thiamin	4%
Sodium	6mg	Riboflavin	3%
Potassium	130mg	Niacin	*
		Calcium	*
		Iron	2%

BUY: Allow 1 small head (about 1 lb.) for 4 servings. Look for clean, compact heavy heads which are white to creamy white in color. Outer leaves should be green, fresh and crisp.

PEAK SEASON: Fall and early winter (available all year).

STORAGE: Refrigerate in airtight container, plastic bag or wrap, 1 week.

PREPARATION: Remove outer leaves and excess part of stem. Wash thoroughly. Leave whole or cut into flowerets. Place whole head, stem-side-down, in saucepan.

COOK: Add 1 inch salted water (½ teaspoon salt to 1 cup water) to cauliflower. Cover and heat to boiling. Cook until tender; drain.

TIME:

Cauliflower	Whole	Flowerets
Boiling	*15 to 25 min.*	*8 to 15 min.*
Steaming	*25 to 30 min.*	*10 to 20 min.*
Pressure Saucepan (15 lb. pressure)	*10 min.*	*1½ to 3 min.*

SEASONING: When cooking add: chicken bouillon, nutmeg, curry powder, rosemary, basil leaves, savory, dill seed, tarragon leaves.

Before serving add: cheese sauce or soup, shrimp soup, hollandaise or mustard sauce, Parmesan cheese, buttered bread crumbs, sour cream, poppy seed.

CURRIED CAULIFLOWER

10-oz. pkg. frozen cauliflower
1 tablespoon margarine or butter
1 tablespoon flour
¼ teaspoon salt
¼ teaspoon curry powder
½ cup milk
Chopped salted peanuts, if desired

In medium saucepan, cook cauliflower as directed on package; drain; set aside. In same saucepan, melt margarine; blend in flour, salt and curry. Cook until mixture is smooth and bubbly. Stir in milk; heat until mixture boils and thickens, stirring constantly. Gently stir in cauliflower; heat through. Garnish with chopped salted peanuts.

3 to 4 servings

NUTRITION INFORMATION PER SERVING

Serving Size: 1/4 of recipe		Percent U.S. RDA Per Serving	
Calories	92	Protein	6%
Protein	4g	Vitamin A	4%
Carbohydrate	6g	Vitamin C	47%
Fat	6g	Thiamin	4%
Sodium	212mg	Riboflavin	6%
Potassium	219mg	Niacin	6%
		Calcium	5%
		Iron	3%

TIP: *Cooked fresh cauliflowerets may be substituted for frozen cauliflower.*

TANGY MUSTARD CAULIFLOWER

1 medium head cauliflower
½ cup mayonnaise, salad dressing or dairy sour cream
1 teaspoon chopped onion
1 teaspoon prepared or dry mustard
½ cup (2 oz.) shredded cheese

Cook cauliflower as directed; drain. Combine mayonnaise with onion and mustard. Spread on hot cauliflower. Sprinkle with cheese. Cover; let stand in saucepan until cheese melts, about 3 minutes. Serve whole, right-side-up in serving dish. 6 servings

NUTRITION INFORMATION PER SERVING

Serving Size: 1/6 of recipe		Percent U.S. RDA Per Serving	
Calories	188	Protein	7%
Protein	5g	Vitamin A	4%
Carbohydrate	5g	Vitamin C	87%
Fat	18g	Thiamin	6%
Sodium	236mg	Riboflavin	7%
Potassium	211mg	Niacin	3%
		Calcium	9%
		Iron	5%

TIP: *If desired, two 10-oz. pkg. frozen cauliflower may be substituted for fresh cauliflower. Cook as directed on package; drain. Toss mayonnaise mixture with cauliflower. Place in serving dish; sprinkle with cheese. Cover and let stand 2 to 3 minutes to melt cheese.*

CAULIFLOWER WITH SHRIMP SAUCE

1 head cauliflower, whole or cut in flowerets
10¾-oz. can condensed cream of mushroom soup
4½-oz. can (¾ cup) tiny or chopped shrimp, drained
¼ cup milk
1 teaspoon prepared mustard

In medium or large saucepan, prepare and cook cauliflower as directed; drain. In small saucepan, combine soup, shrimp, milk and mustard; heat to boiling, stirring occasionally. Place cauliflower in shallow serving dish; pour soup over. Serve immediately.
6 to 8 servings

NUTRITION INFORMATION PER SERVING

Serving Size: 1/6 of recipe		Percent U.S. RDA Per Serving	
Calories	109	Protein	13%
Protein	9g	Vitamin A	2%
Carbohydrate	9g	Vitamin C	52%
Fat	5g	Thiamin	6%
Sodium	428mg	Riboflavin	9%
Potassium	278mg	Niacin	6%
		Calcium	7%
		Iron	8%

TIPS: *Cauliflower and sauce may be kept warm (in ovenproof dish) in 300°F. oven for up to 30 minutes.*

If desired, 2 pkg. (10 oz. each) frozen cauliflower may be substituted for fresh cauliflower.

CAN-CAN CAULIFLOWER

1 small head cauliflower
1½ cups fresh sliced green beans
¼ cup diced pimiento
2 tablespoons sunflower nuts
½ teaspoon salt
6 tablespoons margarine or butter
2 tablespoons sunflower nuts

In large saucepan, cook cauliflower in boiling salted water, 15 minutes or until tender. In medium saucepan, cook beans in small amount of water until tender, about 15 minutes; drain. Add pimiento, 2 tablespoons sunflower nuts, salt and 2 tablespoons margarine; toss lightly. Place whole cauliflower in center of platter. Spoon beans around cauliflower. In small saucepan, heat 4 tablespoons margarine over low heat until lightly browned. Pour browned butter over cauliflower; sprinkle with 2 tablespoons sunflower nuts. Cut into wedges to serve. 6 to 8 servings

NUTRITION INFORMATION PER SERVING

Serving Size: 1/6 of recipe		Percent U.S. RDA Per Serving	
Calories	162	Protein	6%
Protein	4g	Vitamin A	14%
Carbohydrate	6g	Vitamin C	45%
Fat	15g	Thiamin	14%
Sodium	331mg	Riboflavin	6%
Potassium	262mg	Niacin	5%
		Calcium	4%
		Iron	7%

TIP: *One 16-oz. can or 1½ cups frozen sliced green beans may be substituted for fresh. Cook beans only until heated.*

CAN-CAN CAULIFLOWER

CELERIAC OR CELERY ROOT

Celeriac is a bulb-rooted celery and is grown for its bulb rather than the leafy stalk. It is usually cooked and eaten hot or marinated and used as a salad. It also adds a nice flavor to soups and stews.

Insufficient data with regard to celeriac to give nutritional information.

BUY: Allow 1 medium bulb (1½ lb.) for 4 servings. Select celeriac that does not have any sprouts near top as this indicates age and possible woody texture. Celeriac should be firm and heavy and light brown in color. Smaller bulbs are less likely to be woody.
PEAK SEASON: Fall and winter.
STORAGE: Refrigerate in airtight container, plastic bag or wrap, 1 to 2 weeks.
PREPARATION: Peel, leave whole, slice or dice.
COOK: Add salted water (½ teaspoon salt to 1 cup water) to cover whole celeriac. Add 1 inch salted water for sliced or diced celeriac. Add 1 tablespoon vinegar or lemon juice to prevent browning during cooking. Cover and heat to boiling. Cook until tender; drain.

TIME:

Celeriac Root	Whole	Sliced or Diced
Boiling	*40 to 60 min.*	*25 to 30 min.*
Steaming	–	*25 to 35 min.*
Pressure Saucepan (15 lb. pressure)	*7 min.*	*5 min.*

SEASONING: Before serving add: margarine or butter, hollandaise or mustard sauce, sour cream, cream, prepared salad dressings. Marinate and chill cooked celeriac in oil and vinegar or Italian dressing several hours and serve on lettuce as a salad.

CELERY

There are two main varieties of celery grown in this country. The common "Pascal" with its long green stalks and the "Golden Heart," a white variety that is grown under paper to prevent chlorophyll formation which would turn the celery green.

NUTRITION INFORMATION PER SERVING

Serving Size: 1/2 cup raw celery		Percent U.S. RDA Per Serving	
Calories	10	Protein	*
Protein	<1g	Vitamin A	3%
Carbohydrate	2g	Vitamin C	9%
Fat	<1g	Thiamin	*
Sodium	76mg	Riboflavin	*
Potassium	205mg	Niacin	*
		Calcium	2%
		Iron	*

BUY: Allow 1 bunch for 4 servings. Select celery with firm, crisp stalks. Leaves should be fresh and bright green.
PEAK SEASON: All year.
STORAGE: Refrigerate in airtight container, plastic bag or wrap, 1 week.
PREPARATION: Separate stalks and wash thoroughly. Cut off bottom and any blemishes. If outer stalks are especially stringy, remove the larger strings with a vegetable peeler. Cut stalks into slices or about 1-inch pieces.
COOK: Add 1 inch salted water (½ teaspoon salt to 1 cup water) to celery. Cover and heat to boiling. Cook until tender; drain.

TIME:

Celery	Diced
Boiling	*15 to 18 min.*
Steaming	*25 to 30 min.*
Pressure saucepan (15 lb. pressure)	*2 to 3 min.*

SEASONING: When cooking add beef bouillon or onion soup mix.

Before serving add: margarine or butter, softened cream cheese, cheese sauce, cheese soup, toasted almonds, paprika, parsley.

ORIENTAL CELERY

2 tablespoons margarine or butter
2 tablespoons slivered almonds
3 to 4 medium stalks celery, sliced
1 small onion
2 tablespoons soy sauce
8-oz. can (⅔ cup) water chestnuts, drained and sliced
4-oz. can (½ cup) mushroom stems and pieces, drained

In medium skillet or shallow saucepan, combine all ingredients. Simmer covered, 15 minutes or until celery is of desired doneness, stirring occasionally. 4 to 5 servings

NUTRITION INFORMATION PER SERVING

Serving Size: 1/4 of recipe		Percent U.S. RDA Per Serving	
Calories	109	Protein	4%
Protein	2g	Vitamin A	6%
Carbohydrate	9g	Vitamin C	10%
Fat	8g	Thiamin	2%
Sodium	773mg	Riboflavin	8%
Potassium	241mg	Niacin	4%
		Calcium	4%
		Iron	6%

TIP: *About 4 cups thinly sliced celery cabbage may be substituted for celery.*

CREAMED CELERY WITH ALMONDS

2½ cups (5 medium stalks) celery, cut into 1-inch pieces
1 tablespoon chopped onion
1 tablespoon chopped parsley or chives
1 tablespoon chopped pimiento, drained
½ cup milk
10¾-oz. can condensed cream of celery soup
½ cup slivered almonds

Heat oven to 350°F. In 1½-quart casserole, combine all ingredients except slivered almonds. Sprinkle with almonds.* Bake at 350°F. for 50 to 55 minutes or until celery is tender. 4 to 5 servings

NUTRITION INFORMATION PER SERVING

Serving Size: 1/4 of recipe		Percent U.S. RDA Per Serving	
Calories	176	Protein	9%
Protein	6g	Vitamin A	9%
Carbohydrate	13g	Vitamin C	10%
Fat	12g	Thiamin	5%
Sodium	718mg	Riboflavin	14%
Potassium	490mg	Niacin	5%
		Calcium	13%
		Iron	8%

TIPS: *For a main dish, add 2 cups cooked cubed chicken or turkey with soup.*

*To MAKE AHEAD, prepare to *, cover and refrigerate up to 1 day. Bake as directed.*

CHINESE CABBAGE OR CELERY CABBAGE

Chinese cabbage is shaped like a celery bunch with a flavor resembling cabbage, but without the cabbage odor. It is good raw in salads (see Crunchy Cabbage Salad, page 470) or cooked as a vegetable side dish.

BUY: Allow 1 medium bunch for 4 servings. Look for fresh crisp outer leaves that are pale green in color.

NUTRITION INFORMATION PER SERVING

Serving Size: 1/2 cup cooked Chinese cabbage		Percent U.S. RDA Per Serving	
Calories	5	Protein	*
Protein	<1g	Vitamin A	*
Carbohydrate	1g	Vitamin C	16%
Fat	<1g	Thiamin	*
Sodium	<1mg	Riboflavin	*
Potassium	96mg	Niacin	*
		Calcium	*
		Iron	*

CHINESE PEA PODS

Thin pea pods that are often used in Oriental cooking are sometimes available fresh and also available frozen. They differ from regular peas by not having the tough parchment-like lining in the pod. Thus, the pod is as tender and tasty as the tiny peas inside.

Insufficient data with regard to Chinese Pea Pods to give nutritional information.

BUY: Allow ½ lb. for 4 servings. Select crisp pods that are free from blemishes and wilting.
PEAK SEASON: Summer.
STORAGE: Refrigerate in airtight container or plastic bag, 1 to 2 days.
PREPARATION: Wash thoroughly, remove stem and any "string" along top of pod.
COOKING: Add ½ inch salted water (½ teaspoon salt to 1 cup water) to pea pods. Heat to boiling. Cook until crisp-tender; drain.

TIME:

Chinese Pea Pods	Whole
Boiling	*2 to 3 min.*

SEASONING: Before serving add: sautéed mushrooms, sliced water chestnuts, bean sprouts, soy sauce, margarine or butter, combination of drained peach slices and toasted sliced almonds.

CELERY-PEA POD AMANDINE

CELERY-PEA POD AMANDINE

½ cup blanched slivered almonds
2 tablespoons margarine or butter
3 cubes or 3 teaspoons chicken bouillon
1 tablespoon instant minced onion
1 teaspoon monosodium glutamate (MSG), if desired
½ teaspoon sugar
⅛ teaspoon garlic powder
⅛ teaspoon ginger
4 cups (8 medium stalks) diagonally sliced celery
6-oz. pkg. frozen pea pods

In medium skillet, sauté almonds in margarine until golden brown. Stir in bouillon, onion, MSG, sugar, garlic powder and ginger. Add celery and stir-fry just until crisp-tender, about 10 minutes. Stir in pea pods; cook 3 to 4 minutes until pea pods are crisp-tender. Serve immediately.

8 servings

Insufficient data with regard to Chinese Pea Pods to give nutritional information.

CORN

NUTRITION INFORMATION PER SERVING

Serving Size: 1/2 cup cooked corn		Percent U.S. RDA Per Serving	
Calories	69	Protein	4%
Protein	3g	Vitamin A	7%
Carbohydrate	16g	Vitamin C	10%
Fat	<1g	Thiamin	6%
Sodium	0mg	Riboflavin	5%
Potassium	137mg	Niacin	5%
		Calcium	*
		Iron	3%

BUY: Allow 6 to 8 ears of corn for 4 servings. Look for green husks (not decayed or dried ends) and cobs filled with plump juicy kernels that will spurt "milk" when broken.
PEAK SEASON: Summer.
STORAGE: Refrigerate unhusked corn 1 to 2 days. The flavor becomes less sweet as stored because the sugars turn to starch during the aging process. If corn is removed from the cob, refrigerate in airtight covered containter.
PREPARATION: Remove husks and silk; trim ends. Wash thoroughly.
COOK: Heat unsalted water (salt toughens corn) to boiling. Drop corn-on-cob in boiling water to cover. Heat to second boil. Cover and boil gently until tender. Serve corn-on-cob or cut cooked kernels from ears.

TIME:

Corn	On cob
Boiling	*5 to 8 min.*
Steaming	*10 to 15 min.*
Pressure Saucepan (15 lb. pressure)	*½ to 1½ min.*

SEASONING: When cooking add: curry powder, green pepper, pimiento, bacon, pitted ripe olives, 1 tablespoon sugar.

Before serving add: margarine or butter, chive butter, cream, cream cheese, tomato sauce, chili sauce. Combine with lima beans, cooked dry beans or zucchini.

SAUTÉED CORN

2 tablespoons margarine or butter
10-oz. pkg. (1½ cups) frozen cut corn or 2 cups fresh cut corn
2 tablespoons sugar
Salt and pepper

In medium skillet, combine margarine, corn and sugar. Cook about 5 minutes or until tender, stirring occasionally. Season with salt and pepper. 4 servings

NUTRITION INFORMATION PER SERVING

Serving Size: 1/4 of recipe		Percent U.S. RDA Per Serving	
Calories	132	Protein	3%
Protein	2g	Vitamin A	10%
Carbohydrate	20g	Vitamin C	9%
Fat	6g	Thiamin	5%
Sodium	139mg	Riboflavin	3%
Potassium	145mg	Niacin	6%
		Calcium	*
		Iron	3%

TIPS: *If desired, add 2 tablespoons chopped green pepper or pimiento or 1 teaspoon chopped chives.*

Two slices cooked crumbled bacon may be added. Substitute drippings for margarine; garnish cooked corn with crumbled bacon.

CORN CUSTARD SCALLOP

2 slices bacon
¼ cup chopped green pepper
1 tablespoon chopped onion
16-oz. can (2 cups) cream-style corn
½ cup dry bread crumbs
1 teaspoon sugar
½ teaspoon salt
2 eggs, slightly beaten

Heat oven to 375°F. In medium skillet, fry bacon until crisp. Drain on paper towel; crumble. In same skillet, sauté green pepper and onion in bacon drippings until tender. Remove from heat and pour off excess drippings. Add corn, bread crumbs, sugar, salt, eggs and bacon; mix well. Pour into 1½-quart casserole. If desired, sprinkle with paprika. Bake uncovered at 375°F. for 40 to 45 minutes or until set. 5 to 6 servings

NUTRITION INFORMATION PER SERVING

Serving Size: 1/5 of recipe		Percent U.S. RDA Per Serving	
Calories	185	Protein	12%
Protein	8g	Vitamin A	13%
Carbohydrate	23g	Vitamin C	13%
Fat	8g	Thiamin	7%
Sodium	589mg	Riboflavin	9%
Potassium	165mg	Niacin	8%
		Calcium	*
		Iron	8%

ONION CORN-ON-THE-COB

½ cup dry onion soup mix
½ cup margarine or butter, softened
½ teaspoon salt
6 to 8 ears corn

Heat oven to 425°F. In small bowl, combine dry onion soup mix, margarine and salt; blend well. Spread each ear of corn with 1 tablespoon onion mixture. Wrap tightly in foil. Bake at 425°F. or grill over hot coals for 30 to 35 minutes or until tender. Serve with additional margarine, if desired. 6 to 8 servings

NUTRITION INFORMATION PER SERVING

Serving Size: 1/6 of recipe		Percent U.S. RDA Per Serving	
Calories	299	Protein	10%
Protein	6g	Vitamin A	24%
Carbohydrate	35g	Vitamin C	24%
Fat	18g	Thiamin	12%
Sodium	1074mg	Riboflavin	9%
Potassium	338mg	Niacin	10%
		Calcium	*
		Iron	6%

TIP: *Frozen ears of corn may be used. Spread each frozen ear (do not thaw) with 1 tablespoon onion mixture. Wrap tightly in foil and bake as directed above for 35 to 40 minutes.*

EGGPLANT

The first varieties of eggplant were shaped like hen eggs, thus leading to the name. Today it is grown in a variety of sizes and shapes, the most common in this country being the pear-shaped, purple-skinned variety. Eggplant is used in casseroles and Mediterranean cooking, see Moussaka recipe, page **359**.

NUTRITION INFORMATION PER SERVING

Serving Size: 1/2 cup cooked eggplant		Percent U.S. RDA Per Serving	
Calories	19	Protein	*
Protein	1g	Vitamin A	*
Carbohydrate	4g	Vitamin C	5%
Fat	<1g	Thiamin	3%
Sodium	1mg	Riboflavin	2%
Potassium	150mg	Niacin	2%
		Calcium	*
		Iron	3%

BUY: Allow 1 medium eggplant for 4 servings. Look for firm, heavy, smooth eggplants, free from blemishes. The skin should be dark purple and glossy. A dull skin usually indicates an overripe eggplant that may be tough.
PEAK SEASON: Late summer (available all year).
STORAGE: Store in airtight container, plastic bag or wrap at cool room temperature (60°F.) 3 to 4 days.
PREPARATION: Wash and peel if skin is tough. Cut off stem. Slice, dice or cut into strips; dip in lemon juice to prevent darkening.
COOK: Slices are usually fried; (see Fried Eggplant recipe, this page. Add ½ inch salted water (½ teaspoon salt to 1 cup water) to strips or cubed eggplant. Cover and heat to boiling. Cook until tender; drain.

TIME:

Eggplant	Sliced	Strips or Cubes
Boiling	*10 to 20 min.*	*6 to 10 min.*
Steaming	*15 to 20 min.*	*10 to 15 min.*
Fry	*6 to 10 min.*	–

SEASONING: When cooking add: oregano leaves or Italian seasoning, green pepper, tomato sauce, olive oil.

Before serving, add grated Parmesan or Mozzarella cheese.

FRIED EGGPLANT

- **2 eggs, slightly beaten**
- **1 teaspoon salt**
- **2 tablespoons milk**
- **1 eggplant**
- **1¼ to 2 cups dry bread crumbs**
- **½ cup oil or olive oil**

In small bowl, combine eggs, salt and milk. Peel eggplant; slice ¼-inch thick or cut into strips about ½-inch wide. Dip slices into egg mixture, then into bread crumbs. In large skillet, cook eggplant slices in hot oil until tender and golden brown. (Eggplant will absorb oil rapidly; add oil gradually as eggplant is fried.) Drain on paper towel. If necessary, place eggplant slices in warm oven until serving time.

4 to 6 servings

NUTRITION INFORMATION PER SERVING

Serving Size: 1/6 of recipe		Percent U.S. RDA Per Serving	
Calories	237	Protein	7%
Protein	4g	Vitamin A	5%
Carbohydrate	9g	Vitamin C	5%
Fat	21g	Thiamin	6%
Sodium	427mg	Riboflavin	7%
Potassium	194mg	Niacin	4%
		Calcium	4%
		Iron	7%

HOMINY

Hominy is the kernel of hulled dried corn from which the outer germ layer has been removed. Grits are made from the ground hominy. Hominy is available in dry pearl form and canned.

NUTRITION INFORMATION PER SERVING

Serving Size: 1/2 cup		Percent U.S. RDA Per Serving	
Calories	63	Protein	2%
Protein	1g	Vitamin A	*
Carbohydrate	14g	Vitamin C	0%
Fat	<1g	Thiamin	3%
Sodium	*	Riboflavin	2%
Potassium	14mg	Niacin	2%
		Calcium	*
		Iron	2%

SEASONING: When cooking add chili powder or marjoram.

Before serving add: margarine or butter, cheese, cheese sauce, green pepper, cooked crumbled bacon.

KOHLRABI

Kohlrabi is a German word meaning "cabbage turnip" which well describes the turnip shape and cabbage flavor of this vegetable. The bulb grows just above the ground and the leaves sprout from it. The leaves are similar to turnip leaves.

NUTRITION INFORMATION PER SERVING

Serving Size: 1/2 cup cooked kohlrabi		Percent U.S. RDA Per Serving	
Calories	20	Protein	2%
Protein	1g	Vitamin A	*
Carbohydrate	4g	Vitamin C	59%
Fat	<1g	Thiamin	3%
Sodium	5mg	Riboflavin	*
Potassium	216mg	Niacin	*
		Calcium	3%
		Iron	*

BUY: Allow 4 to 6 kohlrabi for 4 servings. Kohlrabi is light green in color and about the size of a large beet. The green tops can be cooked like beet greens. Look for small to medium-sized bulbs with fresh green leaves.
PEAK SEASON: Summer and fall.
STORAGE: Refrigerate in airtight container or plastic bag, 3 to 4 days.
PREPARATION: Remove tops and peel skin from bulb. Wash thoroughly. Slice, cube, dice or cut into strips. Slices or strips are good raw on a relish plate.
COOK: Add 1 inch salted water (½ teaspoon salt to 1 cup water) to kohlrabi. Cover and heat to boiling. Cook until tender; drain.

TIME:

Kohlrabi	Slices or Strips
Boiling	*20 to 25 min.*
Steaming	*30 min.*

SEASONING: When cooking add: nutmeg, marjoram, lemon juice, chives.

Before serving add: margarine or butter, cheese, or lemon juice.

KOHLRABI PARMESAN

2 tablespoons margarine or butter
¼ teaspoon marjoram leaves
4 medium kohlrabi, peeled and sliced
¼ cup grated Parmesan cheese
Salt and pepper

In medium skillet, melt margarine with marjoram; add kohlrabi. Cook loosely covered over medium heat about 20 minutes or until tender, stirring occasionally. Add Parmesan cheese, mixing lightly to combine. Season with salt and pepper.

3 to 4 servings

NUTRITION INFORMATION PER SERVING

Serving Size: 1/3 of recipe		Percent U.S. RDA Per Serving	
Calories	141	Protein	9%
Protein	6g	Vitamin A	9%
Carbohydrate	9g	Vitamin C	91%
Fat	10g	Thiamin	6%
Sodium	346mg	Riboflavin	7%
Potassium	525mg	Niacin	2%
		Calcium	15%
		Iron	4%

MUSHROOMS

Mushrooms are available fresh, canned, frozen and dried. During cooking fresh mushrooms shrink to about half their original size, so if substituting canned for fresh, use half the amount.

NUTRITION INFORMATION PER SERVING

Serving Size: 1 cup raw mushrooms		Percent U.S. RDA Per Serving	
Calories	20	Protein	3%
Protein	2g	Vitamin A	0%
Carbohydrate	3g	Vitamin C	3%
Fat	<1g	Thiamin	5%
Sodium	10mg	Riboflavin	19%
Potassium	290mg	Niacin	15%
		Calcium	*
		Iron	3%

BUY: Allow 1 lb. for 4 servings. Look for plump, firm mushrooms with short stems. Small brown spots or slightly opened caps mean maturity, not inferior quality.
PEAK SEASON: All year.
STORAGE: Refrigerate in airtight container or plastic bag, 3 to 5 days, keeping moist with a damp paper towel.
PREPARATION: Wash, but do not peel. Cut off tips of stems. Leave whole or slice lengthwise.
COOK: Cook in melted margarine or butter until golden brown, stirring occasionally. Broil by brushing mushrooms with margarine or dipping in a batter and broiling 4 to 5 inches from heat until tender.

TIME:

Mushrooms	
Sauté	*4 to 5 min.*
Broil	*8 to 10 min.*

SEASONING: When cooking add: white wine, garlic, green onions, chives, parsley.

Before serving add: toasted almonds, white sauce, lemon juice, dill weed.

MUSHROOMS STUFFED WITH BUTTER AND WALNUTS

32 fresh whole mushrooms
½ cup margarine or butter, softened
2 tablespoons chopped walnuts
4 green onions, finely chopped
¼ teaspoon garlic salt
2½ tablespoons chopped parsley
Dash salt and pepper

Wash and dry mushrooms; remove stems and reserve. Arrange caps in well-greased shallow baking pan. In small skillet, melt 2 tablespoons margarine; add chopped mushroom stems and sauté lightly. In small bowl, combine remaining margarine, walnuts, onion, garlic, parsley, salt and pepper; mix thoroughly. Lightly stir in mushroom stems. Fill each cap with a rounded teaspoonful of mushroom mixture.* Broil mushrooms 3 to 5 minutes until bubbly. Serve immediately.

6 to 8 servings

NUTRITION INFORMATION PER SERVING

Serving Size: 1/6 of recipe		Percent U.S. RDA Per Serving	
Calories	183	Protein	3%
Protein	2g	Vitamin A	15%
Carbohydrate	6g	Vitamin C	6%
Fat	18g	Thiamin	6%
Sodium	196mg	Riboflavin	15%
Potassium	320mg	Niacin	26%
		Calcium	2%
		Iron	7%

TIP: *To MAKE AHEAD, prepare to*. Cover and refrigerate up to 8 hours. Broil as directed.*

OKRA

Okra is grown extensively in the southern states and is popularly known as an ingredient in gumbo. It is available fresh, frozen, canned and pickled.

NUTRITION INFORMATION PER SERVING

Serving Size: 1/2 cup cooked okra		Percent U.S. RDA Per Serving	
Calories	23	Protein	2%
Protein	2g	Vitamin A	8%
Carbohydrate	5g	Vitamin C	27%
Fat	<1g	Thiamin	7%
Sodium	2mg	Riboflavin	8%
Potassium	139mg	Niacin	4%
		Calcium	7%
		Iron	2%

BUY: Allow 1 lb. for 4 servings. Look for bright green, crisp pods, free from blemishes and under 4½ inches long. Small to medium pods are best.
PEAK SEASON: Summer and fall.
STORAGE: Refrigerate in airtight container or plastic bag, 3 to 5 days. Keep moist during storage with a damp paper towel.
PREPARATION: Wash thoroughly and cut off ends. Leave whole or slice.
COOK: Add 1 inch salted water (½ teaspoon salt to 1 cup water) to okra. Cover and heat to boiling. Cook until tender; drain.

TIME:

Okra	**Whole or Sliced**
Boiling	*10 to 15 min.*
Steaming	*20 min.*
Pressure Saucepan (15 lb. pressure)	*3 to 4 min.*

SEASONING: When cooking, add bacon or onion.

Before serving add: margarine or butter, bread crumbs, Parmesan cheese, French dressing, tomato sauce, lemon juice, chili sauce, sour cream.

SOUTHERN STYLE OKRA

3 slices bacon
⅓ cup chopped green pepper
1 medium stalk celery, chopped
1 small onion, sliced
1 teaspoon salt
Dash pepper
1 cup tomatoes, undrained, cut up
10-oz. pkg. frozen cut okra
7-oz. can whole kernel corn or Mexicorn Brand Golden Whole Kernel Corn With Sweet Peppers

In medium skillet, fry bacon until crisp; drain on paper towel; reserve drippings. To reserved bacon drippings, add green pepper, celery and onion. Cook until tender; add remaining ingredients. Simmer covered, 10 to 15 minutes or until okra is tender, stirring occasionally. Sprinkle with crumbled bacon.

4 to 6 servings

NUTRITION INFORMATION PER SERVING

Serving Size: 1/6 of recipe		Percent U.S. RDA Per Serving	
Calories	101	Protein	5%
Protein	3g	Vitamin A	15%
Carbohydrate	14g	Vitamin C	44%
Fat	4g	Thiamin	8%
Sodium	535mg	Riboflavin	7%
Potassium	256mg	Niacin	6%
		Calcium	5%
		Iron	5%

TIP: *A 16-oz. can drained cut okra may be substituted for frozen okra and an 8-oz. can stewed tomatoes may be substituted for cut up tomatoes.*

ONIONS

Green onions are sometimes referred to as scallions. Dry onions are white, yellow or red in color. The white skinned onions are milder in flavor than the yellow skinned. Both are good for cooking. The large flat white Bermuda onion and the large brown or yellow Spanish onion are sweet and mild, making them ideal for salads.

NUTRITION INFORMATION PER SERVING

Serving Size: 1/2 cup sliced cooked onion		Percent U.S. RDA Per Serving	
Calories	30	Protein	*
Protein	1g	Vitamin A	*
Carbohydrate	7g	Vitamin C	12%
Fat	<1g	Thiamin	2%
Sodium	7mg	Riboflavin	*
Potassium	115mg	Niacin	*
		Calcium	3%
		Iron	2%

BUY: Green – allow about ½ bunch per serving. Dry – allow about ¼ lb. or 1 medium onion per serving. Look for green onions with crisp green tops with white portions extending 2 to 3 inches up from root end. Look for dry onions that are firm with small necks and clean dry skins.
PEAK SEASON: Green – summer. Dry – all year.
STORAGE: Green – refrigerate in airtight crisper or plastic bag, 3 to 5 days. Dry – store in cool (room temperature or slightly cooler 60°F. ideal) dry place for several months. Put in loosely woven or open-mesh containers with good circulation of air. Dry onions will decay if air is too humid.
PREPARATION: Green – wash well, cut off green tip about 3 inches above bulb. Dry – peel, leave whole, slice, quarter or chop. To prevent "crying" when peeling fresh onions, keep onions under cold running water while peeling them.
COOK: Green and Dry – cook, loosely covered, in small amount of water until tender.

TIME:

Onions	Green	Dry Whole (small)	Dry Quartered
Boiling	*8 to 10 min.*	*15 to 25 min.*	*10 to 15 min.*
Steaming	*10 to 12 min.*	*30 to 45 min.*	–
Pressure Saucepan (15 lb. pressure)	–	*3 to 5 min.*	–

SEASONING: When cooking add: chicken bouillon, curry, cloves, caraway seed, soy sauce.

Before serving add: white sauce, cheese sauce or soup, buttered bread crumbs, softened cream cheese, peanuts, sherry, Parmesan cheese.

SCALLOPED ONIONS

3 medium onions, thinly sliced or 12 small whole onions
1 cup (half recipe) White Sauce, page 540
2 tablespoons chopped pimiento, drained
1 tablespoon chopped parsley
Dash mace, if desired
½ cup Seasoned Crumbs, page 552 or bread crumbs

Heat oven to 350°F. Cook onions in small amount of water until tender; drain. In 1-quart casserole, combine onions with remaining ingredients except crumbs. Sprinkle with crumbs. Bake uncovered at 350°F. for 20 to 25 minutes or until bubbly and golden brown. 6 servings

NUTRITION INFORMATION PER SERVING

Serving Size: 1/6 of recipe		Percent U.S. RDA Per Serving	
Calories	132	Protein	5%
Protein	4g	Vitamin A	8%
Carbohydrate	11g	Vitamin C	13%
Fat	9g	Thiamin	4%
Sodium	218mg	Riboflavin	7%
Potassium	177mg	Niacin	2%
		Calcium	9%
		Iron	3%

TIP: *One can condensed cream of chicken, celery or mushroom soup may be substituted for white sauce.*

DOUBLE ONION BAKE

3 medium onions, thinly sliced or 12 small whole onions
1 cup (half recipe) White Sauce, page 540
½ cup (2 oz.) shredded Cheddar or American cheese
⅓ cup toasted almonds or chopped peanuts
1 tablespoon chopped parsley
1 cup French-fried onions

Heat oven to 350°F. In medium saucepan, cook onions in small amount of water for 15 to 30 minutes or until tender; drain. Prepare white sauce as directed; stir in cheese, almonds, parsley and onions. Pour into 1 to 1½-quart buttered casserole.* Bake uncovered at 350°F. for 20 to 25 minutes or until bubbly. Top with French-fried onions during last 5 minutes.

4 to 5 servings

NUTRITION INFORMATION PER SERVING

Serving Size: 1/4 of recipe		Percent U.S. RDA Per Serving	
Calories	637	Protein	22%
Protein	14g	Vitamin A	12%
Carbohydrate	37g	Vitamin C	13%
Fat	50g	Thiamin	6%
Sodium	646mg	Riboflavin	20%
Potassium	518mg	Niacin	5%
		Calcium	24%
		Iron	8%

TIPS: *To MAKE AHEAD, prepare to *, cool and refrigerate up to 1 day. Bake as directed.*

Two 10-oz. pkg. frozen creamed onions may be substituted for onions and white sauce. Prepare onions as directed on package and continue by adding cheese and remaining ingredients except French-fried onions. Bake as directed, topping with French-fried onions during last 5 minutes.

PARSNIPS

Parsnips are of the carrot family. They are harvested in late fall after the first frost, which converts the starch to sugar and gives them their sweet flavor. Early settlers thought parsnips poisonous if eaten before the first frost.

NUTRITION INFORMATION PER SERVING

Serving Size: 1/2 cup cooked parsnips		Percent U.S. RDA Per Serving	
Calories	51	Protein	*
Protein	1g	Vitamin A	*
Carbohydrate	12g	Vitamin C	13%
Fat	<1g	Thiamin	4%
Sodium	6mg	Riboflavin	4%
Potassium	296mg	Niacin	*
		Calcium	4%
		Iron	3%

BUY: Allow 1¼ lb. (5 medium parsnips) for 4 servings. Select smooth, firm, well shaped parsnips. The small to medium-size usually have the best flavor as the larger ones may have a woody core.
PEAK SEASON: Winter and early spring (available all year).
STORAGE: Refrigerate in airtight container or plastic bag, 1 to 2 weeks, keeping moist with a damp paper towel.
PREPARATION: Peel or scrape to remove outer skin. Leave whole or cut in halves, quarters, slices or cubes.
COOK: Add 1 inch salted water (½ teaspoon salt to 1 cup water) to parsnips. Cover and heat to boiling. Cook until tender; drain.

TIME:

Parsnips	Whole	Quartered
Boiling	*20 to 40 min.*	*8 to 15 min.*
Steaming	*30 to 45 min.*	*30 to 40 min.*
Pressure Saucepan (15 lb. pressure)	*9 to 10 min.*	*4 to 8 min.*
Baking	*30 to 45 min.*	–

SEASONING: Before serving add: margarine or butter, bacon drippings, brown sugar, honey, jelly, orange marmalade, cheese sauce, parsley, paprika.

PEAS

NUTRITION INFORMATION PER SERVING

Serving Size: 1/2 cup cooked shelled peas		Percent U.S. RDA Per Serving	
Calories	57	Protein	7%
Protein	4g	Vitamin A	9%
Carbohydrate	10g	Vitamin C	27%
Fat	<1g	Thiamin	15%
Sodium	<1mg	Riboflavin	5%
Potassium	157mg	Niacin	9%
		Calcium	*
		Iron	8%

BUY: Allow 3 lb. unshelled peas for 4 servings. Allow 2 cups shelled peas for 4 servings. Select bright green, plump pods, free from blemishes.
PEAK SEASON: Early summer.
STORAGE: Refrigerate peas in pods in uncovered container, 1 to 2 days. Store shelled peas in airtight container or plastic bag, 1 to 2 days. The sugar in peas turns to starch upon storage, so use as soon as possible.
PREPARATION: Shell peas by pressing the pod between thumb and forefinger to split open. Remove peas and wash thoroughly.
COOK: Add 1 inch salted water (½ teaspoon salt to 1 cup water) to peas. Cover and heat to boiling. Cook until peas are bright green and tender; drain.

TIME:

Green peas	
Boiling	*12 to 16 min.*
Steaming	*10 to 20 min.*
Pressure Saucepan (15 lb. pressure)	*0 to 1 min.*

SEASONING: When cooking add: ½ teaspoon sugar, marjoram, savory, dill, chicken bouillon, green onions, poppy seed, basil, rosemary, sage.
Before serving add: margarine or butter, sour cream, sautéed mushrooms or almonds, orange marmalade, jelly, mint leaves, sherry, lemon pepper, cooked crumbled bacon, onion dip, pimiento cheese spread.

FRENCH PEAS

4 to 6 large lettuce leaves
2 pkg. (10 oz. each) frozen peas or 3 cups fresh peas
1 teaspoon sugar
½ teaspoon salt
2 tablespoons margarine or butter

Line bottom and sides of medium saucepan with lettuce, leaving 1 leaf for top. Place peas and remaining ingredients in lettuce-lined pan. Top with remaining lettuce leaf. Simmer covered over low heat, 20 to 25 minutes for frozen peas and 10 to 15 minutes for fresh peas or until peas are tender. Remove lettuce leaves before serving. 5 to 6 servings

NUTRITION INFORMATION PER SERVING

Serving Size: 1/6 of recipe		Percent U.S. RDA Per Serving	
Calories	94	Protein	7%
Protein	4g	Vitamin A	13%
Carbohydrate	11g	Vitamin C	18%
Fat	4g	Thiamin	15%
Sodium	318mg	Riboflavin	4%
Potassium	115mg	Niacin	7%
		Calcium	*
		Iron	9%

PEAS WITH ONIONS AND MUSHROOMS

10-oz. pkg. (1½ cups) frozen peas
¼ cup chopped onion
4-oz. can (½ cup) mushroom stems and pieces, drained
2 tablespoons margarine or butter
¼ teaspoon salt
Dash pepper
Dash allspice

In medium saucepan, cook peas as directed on package; drain and set aside. In same saucepan, cook onions and mushrooms in margarine until tender. Add peas and seasonings; heat through. 4 servings

NUTRITION INFORMATION PER SERVING

Serving Size: 1/4 of recipe		Percent U.S. RDA Per Serving	
Calories	101	Protein	6%
Protein	4g	Vitamin A	12%
Carbohydrate	9g	Vitamin C	16%
Fat	6g	Thiamin	12%
Sodium	281mg	Riboflavin	6%
Potassium	140mg	Niacin	7%
		Calcium	*
		Iron	7%

PEPPERS

There are 2 general types – the sweet bell-shaped peppers that are green at maturity and turn red as they mature further, and the smaller, hotter and more pungent red and yellow which are often pickled or dried to make chili powder, paprika or cayenne pepper.

Pimiento is a member of the sweet pepper family, but is heart-shaped and especially sweet flavored. Peppers are available fresh, frozen, canned and dehydrated.

NUTRITION INFORMATION PER SERVING

Serving Size: 1 medium raw green pepper		Percent U.S. RDA Per Serving	
Calories	16	Protein	*
Protein	<1g	Vitamin A	6%
Carbohydrate	3g	Vitamin C	156%
Fat	<1g	Thiamin	4%
Sodium	9mg	Riboflavin	3%
Potassium	155mg	Niacin	*
		Calcium	*
		Iron	3%

NUTRITION INFORMATION PER SERVING

Serving Size: 1 medium cooked green pepper		Percent U.S. RDA Per Serving	
Calories	13	Protein	*
Protein	<1g	Vitamin A	6%
Carbohydrate	3g	Vitamin C	117%
Fat	<1g	Thiamin	3%
Sodium	7mg	Riboflavin	3%
Potassium	109mg	Niacin	*
		Calcium	*
		Iron	2%

BUY: Allow 4 peppers for 4 servings. Select firm peppers that are bright in color with a glossy sheen.
PEAK SEASON: Summer and fall (available all year).
STORAGE: Refrigerate in airtight container, plastic bag or wrap, 5 to 7 days.
PREPARATION: Wash thoroughly; remove stem and membrane with the seeds. Leave whole, cut in half, rings, strips or chop.
COOK: Parboil whole peppers (covered with boiling water) before stuffing or baking. (For Stuffed Pepper, see page 322.) Pepper strips or rings may be cooked in small amount of margarine or butter until tender; drain.

TIME:

Green peppers	Whole	Slices or rings
Parboil	*3 to 5 min.*	–
Steam	*10 to 15 min.*	–
Fry	–	*3 to 5 min.*

SEASONING: When cooking add: margarine or butter, corn, basil leaves, oregano leaves, marjoram.

PEPPERS AND SQUASH

¼ cup oil or margarine
2 medium green peppers, cut into 1-inch squares
1 medium yellow summer squash or zucchini, cut into 1-inch cubes
3 tablespoons capers, if desired
½ teaspoon sugar
¼ teaspoon oregano leaves
¼ teaspoon basil leaves
¼ teaspoon salt
2 tomatoes, cut up
Dash pepper
1 teaspoon vinegar or lemon juice

In medium skillet, cook green peppers and squash in oil for 5 minutes or until tender. Add remaining ingredients; mix lightly. Simmer covered, 5 minutes or until tender.

6 to 8 servings

NUTRITION INFORMATION PER SERVING

Serving Size: 1/6 of recipe		Percent U.S. RDA Per Serving	
Calories	110	Protein	2%
Protein	2g	Vitamin A	16%
Carbohydrate	7g	Vitamin C	145%
Fat	9g	Thiamin	6%
Sodium	99mg	Riboflavin	5%
Potassium	294mg	Niacin	4%
		Calcium	2%
		Iron	4%

POTATOES

Preparation and cooking times for both white and sweet potatoes are similar. Potatoes are available throughout the year, although the type varies according to the season. In summer, early potatoes are usually available. They have very thin red or light brown skin and are a sweeter, more moist potato. In fall, the winter potatoes are harvested and are available throughout fall and winter. These potatoes have brown skin and a mealy texture which makes them ideal for baking, salads and all-purpose cooking.

Sweet potatoes and yams are native to this country and vary in sweetness, shape and texture according to variety. In the following sweet potato recipes, yams and sweet potatoes may be used interchangeably.

Potatoes are available fresh, canned, frozen and dehydrated.

NUTRITION INFORMATION PER SERVING

Serving Size: 1 medium boiled potato		Percent U.S. RDA Per Serving	
Calories	126	Protein	5%
Protein	4g	Vitamin A	0%
Carbohydrate	29g	Vitamin C	45%
Fat	<1g	Thiamin	9%
Sodium	5mg	Riboflavin	3%
Potassium	684mg	Niacin	12%
		Calcium	*
		Iron	5%

NUTRITION INFORMATION PER SERVING

Serving Size: 1 cooked sweet potato		Percent U.S. RDA Per Serving	
Calories	139	Protein	3%
Protein	2g	Vitamin A	193%
Carbohydrate	32g	Vitamin C	35%
Fat	<1g	Thiamin	7%
Sodium	12mg	Riboflavin	4%
Potassium	296mg	Niacin	4%
		Calcium	4%
		Iron	5%

BUY: Allow about ½ lb. or 1 medium potato per serving. Look for reasonably smooth, well-shaped, firm potatoes free from blemishes, sunburn (a green discoloration under the skin) and decay. Soft spots indicate spoilage and inferior quality.

PEAK SEASON: All year.
STORAGE: Store white potatoes in cool, dry place several months; store sweet potatoes in cool place several weeks. Too cool temperatures (near freezing) may change the potato texture.
PREPARATION: Wash and scrub with brush or plastic scouring pad. Peel or leave skins on. Leave whole or cut in pieces, cubes or slices. For Baked Potatoes, see page 600. Sweet potatoes hold their shape best if cooked before peeled.
COOK: Simmer, tightly covered in small amount of water. Bake at 350° to 400°F.

TIME:

Potatoes	Whole (medium)	Whole (large)	Quartered
Boiling	*25 to 40 min.*	–	*20 to 25 min.*
Steaming	*30 to 45 min.*	–	*20 to 30 min.*
Pressure Saucepan (15 lb. pressure)	*8 to 11 min.*	–	*3 to 5 min.*
Baking (400°F.)	*45 to 60 min.*	*60 to 75 min.*	–

SEASONING: When cooking add: chives, green onions, garlic, caraway seed, rosemary.

Before serving add: softened cream cheese, sour cream, grated cheese, cheese sauce, mushrooms, poppy or sesame seed, paprika, dill weed. (See salad chapter for Potato Salad recipes.)

MASHED POTATOES

4 medium potatoes, peeled, cooked and drained
½ teaspoon salt
2 tablespoons margarine or butter
2 to 3 tablespoons milk

Mash hot potatoes. Add remaining ingredients except milk; gradually add milk, beating until light and fluffy. If desired, top with additional margarine and sprinkle with pepper or paprika. 4 servings

NUTRITION INFORMATION PER SERVING

Serving Size: 1/4 of recipe		Percent U.S. RDA Per Serving	
Calories	144	Protein	4%
Protein	3g	Vitamin A	5%
Carbohydrate	20g	Vitamin C	36%
Fat	6g	Thiamin	8%
Sodium	348mg	Riboflavin	3%
Potassium	398mg	Niacin	8%
		Calcium	2%
		Iron	4%

TIP: *If desired, add 2 to 4 tablespoons sour cream and omit milk, or add 3-oz. pkg. cream cheese with milk.*

BAKED POTATOES

Heat oven to 350°F to 400°F. Select medium or large size (uniform for same baking time) white baking potatoes. Scrub potatoes and if desired, rub with small amount of shortening to soften skins. Prick with fork to allow steam to escape. Bake at 350°F. for 1 to 1½ hours, at 400°F. for 45 minutes to 1¼ hours or until tender. Using paper towels to protect hands from heat, roll potatoes between hands to make inside potato mixture light and mealy. Cut crisscross slit in tops; gently squeeze lower part of potato to force potato up through slit. Top with margarine or butter, salt and pepper and/or one of these toppings:

Sour cream and chives
Cooked crumbled bacon
Sliced green onions
Crumbled blue cheese or shredded Cheddar cheese
Whipped cream cheese
Garlic or onion salt
One-half cup margarine or butter, whipped with 2 teaspoons lemon juice and 2 teaspoons chopped parsley
One chopped onion cooked in ½ cup margarine or butter
Cheese sauce

NUTRITION INFORMATION PER SERVING

Serving Size: 1 potato		Percent U.S. RDA Per Serving	
Calories	139	Protein	6%
Protein	4g	Vitamin A	0%
Carbohydrate	32g	Vitamin C	50%
Fat	<1g	Thiamin	10%
Sodium	6mg	Riboflavin	4%
Potassium	754mg	Niacin	13%
		Calcium	*
		Iron	6%

HASH BROWNS

6 cups (6 medium) shredded raw or cooked potato
6 tablespoons margarine or butter
1 tablespoon finely chopped onion
Salt and pepper

Drain raw potatoes well. In large skillet, melt margarine. In medium bowl, lightly toss potatoes, onion, salt and pepper. Firmly pack potato mixture in skillet leaving ½-inch space around edge. Fry, partially covered over low heat until bottom has a crisp golden crust and potatoes are tender. Turn and brown on other side. 6 servings

NUTRITION INFORMATION PER SERVING

Serving Size: 1/6 of recipe		Percent U.S. RDA Per Serving	
Calories	217	Protein	5%
Protein	3g	Vitamin A	9%
Carbohydrate	26g	Vitamin C	35%
Fat	12g	Thiamin	10%
Sodium	190mg	Riboflavin	4%
Potassium	617mg	Niacin	11%
		Calcium	*
		Iron	5%

FRENCH FRIED POTATOES

In deep saucepan or deep fat fryer, heat oil or shortening (fill pan half full) to 375°F. Prepare 4 medium potatoes as directed, page 599. Cut into thin strips ¼ to ⅜ inch wide. Fill basket ¼ full; lower slowly into hot oil (375°F.). Raise and lower a couple times if fat bubbles excessively. Fry 5 to 8 minutes or until golden. Drain on paper towel; salt to taste. Repeat. 4 servings

NUTRITION INFORMATION PER SERVING

Serving Size: 10 (1-2-inch) strips, unsalted		Percent U.S. RDA Per Serving	
Calories	96	Protein	*
Protein	1g	Vitamin A	*
Carbohydrate	13g	Vitamin C	12%
Fat	5g	Thiamin	3%
Sodium	2mg	Riboflavin	*
Potassium	299mg	Niacin	5%
		Calcium	*
		Iron	3%

BOILED POTATOES

After boiling 4 medium potatoes as directed on page 599, drain (add liquid to gravy or sauces). Serve plain or add seasonings to make one of these:

PARSLIED POTATOES: Melt ¼ cup margarine or butter with 2 to 4 tablespoons minced parsley and ¼ teaspoon dill weed or celery seed. Drizzle over cooked potatoes, turning to coat with margarine.

CREAMED POTATOES: Cut cooked potatoes into pieces or slices and add to white sauce or cheese sauce. Heat through.

CALORIE WATCHER'S POTATOES: Add 1 or 2 slices onion and 2 cubes or 2 teaspoons beef or chicken bouillon with water when boiling quartered or sliced potatoes. They have a hearty flavor without the addition of margarine or gravy.

POTATO PATTIES

1½ cups cold mashed potatoes
2 tablespoons flour
1 teaspoon chopped chives
Salt and pepper
¼ teaspoon Worcestershire sauce
1 egg
2 to 3 tablespoons margarine, oil or bacon drippings

In medium bowl, combine all ingredients except margarine; mix with fork until well blended. Shape into 4 or 5 patties. Coat with additional flour or bread crumbs.* In medium skillet, fry in hot margarine until golden brown, turn and fry other side. 4 to 5 servings

NUTRITION INFORMATION PER SERVING

Serving Size: 1/4 of recipe		Percent U.S. RDA Per Serving	
Calories	139	Protein	6%
Protein	4g	Vitamin A	9%
Carbohydrate	13g	Vitamin C	13%
Fat	8g	Thiamin	7%
Sodium	396mg	Riboflavin	6%
Potassium	229mg	Niacin	5%
		Calcium	3%
		Iron	4%

TIPS: *If desired, one of the following may be added to potato mixture:*
2 tablespoons dry sour cream or cheese sauce mix
2 slices bacon, cooked and crumbled
¼ cup shredded cheese

To MAKE AHEAD, prepare to, refrigerate up to 2 days or freeze up to 2 months, wrapping separately. To serve, fry over low heat, partially covered, until golden brown and heated through.*

STUFFED BAKED POTATOES

6 medium baking potatoes
1 teaspoon salt
⅛ teaspoon pepper
¼ cup margarine or butter
¼ cup milk
1 cup (4 oz.) shredded American or Cheddar cheese

Heat oven to 400°F. Prepare and bake as directed for Baked Potatoes, page 600. Cut potatoes in half lengthwise. Scoop potato out of shells into bowl; mash. Add remaining ingredients except cheese. Beat until light and fluffy. Spoon back into shells and place in 13x9-inch pan; top with cheese.* Bake at 400°F. for 20 to 25 minutes or until cheese is light golden brown.
6 servings

NUTRITION INFORMATION PER SERVING

Serving Size: 1/6 of recipe		Percent U.S. RDA Per Serving	
Calories	285	Protein	13%
Protein	9g	Vitamin A	11%
Carbohydrate	33g	Vitamin C	51%
Fat	14g	Thiamin	11%
Sodium	674mg	Riboflavin	9%
Potassium	793mg	Niacin	13%
		Calcium	16%
		Iron	7%

TIPS: *One of the following may be added to potato mixture before spooning into shells:*
¼ to ½ cup sour cream (omit milk)
2 to 3 tablespoons dry sour cream or cheese sauce mix
Dry soup or salad dressing mix
1 to 2 tablespoons chopped chives or parsley
2 to 3 slices cooked and crumbled bacon
2 to 4 tablespoons imitation bacon bits

To MAKE AHEAD, prepare to, cool and refrigerate up to 2 days or wrap individually in foil and freeze up to 3 months. Cook refrigerated potatoes as directed. Bake frozen foil-wrapped potatoes at 350°F. for 30 minutes; unwrap, add cheese and bake 20 to 30 minutes or until heated through and cheese is light golden brown.*

AU GRATIN POTATOES

¼ cup margarine or butter
¼ cup flour
½ teaspoon salt
2 cups milk
1 cup (4 oz.) shredded American or Cheddar cheese
½ cup grated Parmesan cheese
5 cups (5 medium) peeled, sliced raw potatoes
¼ cup dry bread crumbs
1 tablespoon margarine or butter, melted

Heat oven to 350°F. In medium saucepan, melt margarine; stir in flour and salt. Add milk; cook until mixture boils and thickens, stirring constantly. Stir in cheeses and potatoes. Pour into 2-quart casserole or individual casserole dishes. Combine crumbs with melted margarine; sprinkle over potatoes. Bake covered at 350°F. for 1 to 1½ hours or until bubbly. If desired, garnish with chopped chives.

6 servings

NUTRITION INFORMATION PER SERVING

Serving Size: 1/6 of recipe		Percent U.S. RDA Per Serving	
Calories	355	Protein	20%
Protein	13g	Vitamin A	16%
Carbohydrate	31g	Vitamin C	30%
Fat	20g	Thiamin	13%
Sodium	614mg	Riboflavin	20%
Potassium	661mg	Niacin	12%
		Calcium	32%
		Iron	6%

TIP: *Potatoes may be cooked before combining with other ingredients. Reduce baking time to 30 to 35 minutes.*

SCALLOPED POTATOES

4 medium potatoes, thinly sliced
1 small onion, sliced, if desired
2 tablespoons flour
1 teaspoon salt
⅛ teaspoon pepper
2 tablespoons margarine or butter
1½ to 1¾ cups hot milk

Heat oven to 350°F. Layer ⅓ of potatoes and ½ of onion slices in greased 1½ to 2-quart casserole. Sprinkle with 1 tablespoon flour, ½ teaspoon salt and dash pepper; dot with 1 tablespoon margarine. Repeat layering, ending with potatoes on top. Pour milk over potatoes to barely cover. Bake uncovered at 350°F. for 1½ to 2 hours or until tender. If desired, garnish with crumbled bacon.

5 to 6 servings

NUTRITION INFORMATION PER SERVING

Serving Size: 1/6 of recipe		Percent U.S. RDA Per Serving	
Calories	165	Protein	7%
Protein	5g	Vitamin A	5%
Carbohydrate	23g	Vitamin C	26%
Fat	6g	Thiamin	9%
Sodium	437mg	Riboflavin	9%
Potassium	522mg	Niacin	9%
		Calcium	9%
		Iron	4%

TIP: *Scalloped potatoes may also be prepared with 1 recipe White Sauce, page 540, prepared as directed. One can of condensed cream of mushroom or celery soup combined with ½ cup milk may be substituted for the white sauce. Cover potatoes with white sauce or soup mixture. Bake as directed.*

POTATOES AMANDINE

1 lb. potatoes, peeled
3 egg yolks
2 tablespoons minced onion
Salt and white pepper
2 eggs
2 tablespoons cold water
2 tablespoons oil
¼ teaspoon salt
1 cup finely chopped almonds

In medium saucepan, boil potatoes in salted water until tender; drain. Mash potatoes. Add egg yolks and onion and whip until fluffy. Salt and pepper to taste. In small bowl, combine eggs, water, oil and salt; beat well. Drop potato mixture by rounded heaping tablespoonfuls into egg mixture. Roll potato balls in almonds, coating evenly. In large saucepan, heat 2 inches of oil to 350°F. Fry a few at a time in hot oil for 5 to 6 minutes or until golden brown. Sprinkle with additional salt and pepper. Serve hot.

4 servings

NUTRITION INFORMATION PER SERVING

Serving Size: 1/4 of recipe		Percent U.S. RDA Per Serving	
Calories	425	Protein	22%
Protein	14g	Vitamin A	16%
Carbohydrate	24g	Vitamin C	17%
Fat	32g	Thiamin	16%
Sodium	318mg	Riboflavin	28%
Potassium	628mg	Niacin	12%
		Calcium	13%
		Iron	20%

CREAMED GARDEN POTATOES AND PEAS

1 lb. small early red-skinned potatoes
10-oz. pkg. (1½ cups) frozen peas
2 tablespoons margarine or butter
1 tablespoon chopped onion
2 tablespoons flour
1¼ teaspoons salt
½ teaspoon dill weed
⅛ teaspoon pepper
1½ cups milk

In medium saucepan, cook unpeeled potatoes in boiling water for 20 to 25 minutes or until tender. Drain; peel if desired. Set aside. In same saucepan, cook peas as directed on package; drain. In medium saucepan, cook onion in margarine until tender. Blend in flour, salt, dill and pepper. Stir in milk; heat until mixture boils and thickens, stirring constantly. Add potatoes and peas. Heat through.

4 to 5 servings

NUTRITION INFORMATION PER SERVING

Serving Size: 1/4 of recipe		Percent U.S. RDA Per Serving	
Calories	247	Protein	14%
Protein	9g	Vitamin A	15%
Carbohydrate	33g	Vitamin C	43%
Fat	9g	Thiamin	21%
Sodium	861mg	Riboflavin	16%
Potassium	645mg	Niacin	15%
		Calcium	14%
		Iron	11%

TIPS: *When early potatoes are not available, substitute about 4 medium potatoes. Cook as directed and cut into pieces before adding to sauce.*

Mixture may be assembled a few hours ahead in casserole, then reheated, covered at 350°F. for 30 to 45 minutes or until bubbly.

DANISH BROWNED POTATOES

1 tablespoon margarine or butter
1 to 2 tablespoons sugar
8 to 10 small potatoes, cooked and peeled
½ teaspoon salt

In small skillet, melt margarine; add sugar. Cook and stir until mixture is browned; add potatoes and stir constantly until lightly browned. Sprinkle with salt. 4 servings

NUTRITION INFORMATION PER SERVING

Serving Size: 1/4 of recipe		Percent U.S. RDA Per Serving	
Calories	125	Protein	4%
Protein	3g	Vitamin A	2%
Carbohydrate	23g	Vitamin C	22%
Fat	3g	Thiamin	8%
Sodium	309mg	Riboflavin	2%
Potassium	386mg	Niacin	8%
		Calcium	*
		Iron	4%

DANISH BROWNED POTATOES

SPUDS AND ONIONS

4 medium potatoes, peeled
2 medium onions, thinly sliced and cut in half
6 tablespoons margarine or butter, softened
1 teaspoon salt or seasoned salt
Paprika, parsley, chives or Parmesan cheese

Heat oven to 425°F. Cut potatoes almost through crosswise in ¼-inch slices. Place each on square of foil. Insert ½ onion slice (straight edge down) between potato slices. Spread top of each potato with 1½ tablespoons margarine; season with salt and other choice of seasonings. Bring up edges of foil; fold in double fold and seal potato inside. Bake at 425°F. for 40 to 50 minutes or until tender. 4 servings

NUTRITION INFORMATION PER SERVING

Serving Size: 1/4 of recipe		Percent U.S. RDA Per Serving	
Calories	321	Protein	8%
Protein	5g	Vitamin A	15%
Carbohydrate	38g	Vitamin C	44%
Fat	17g	Thiamin	12%
Sodium	757mg	Riboflavin	5%
Potassium	878mg	Niacin	13%
		Calcium	4%
		Iron	8%

TIP: *To cook over coals, use heavy duty foil; lay foil packets on bed of hot coals. Cook 20 minutes, turn and cook 20 minutes longer or until tender.*

SOMETHING SPECIAL SWEET POTATOES

23-oz. can sweet potatoes, drained
½ cup firmly packed brown sugar
½ cup well-drained crushed pineapple
½ cup quartered pitted prunes
¼ teaspoon salt
1 teaspoon grated orange peel, if desired
2 tablespoons margarine or butter
¼ to ½ cup slivered almonds

Heat oven to 350°F. Drain sweet potatoes; blot on paper towels. In small bowl, combine brown sugar, pineapple, prunes, salt and orange peel. Place sweet potatoes in 1-quart casserole. Spread fruit mixture over top; dot with margarine and sprinkle with almonds. Bake at 350°F. for 40 to 45 minutes. 6 servings

NUTRITION INFORMATION PER SERVING

Serving Size: 1/6 of recipe		Percent U.S. RDA Per Serving	
Calories	297	Protein	4%
Protein	2g	Vitamin A	113%
Carbohydrate	60g	Vitamin C	11%
Fat	7g	Thiamin	5%
Sodium	195mg	Riboflavin	6%
Potassium	329mg	Niacin	5%
		Calcium	5%
		Iron	11%

GLAZED SWEET POTATOES

4 medium sweet potatoes, cooked
¼ cup firmly packed brown sugar
¼ teaspoon salt
¼ cup margarine or butter, melted

Heat oven to 350°F. Peel cooked potatoes; cut into quarters or slice. Arrange in shallow baking dish. Combine remaining ingredients; drizzle over potatoes.* Bake uncovered at 350°F. for 20 to 30 minutes or until glazed and heated through. 4 to 5 servings

NUTRITION INFORMATION PER SERVING

Serving Size: 1/4 of recipe		Percent U.S. RDA Per Serving	
Calories	314	Protein	4%
Protein	2g	Vitamin A	194%
Carbohydrate	50g	Vitamin C	42%
Fat	12g	Thiamin	7%
Sodium	293mg	Riboflavin	5%
Potassium	393mg	Niacin	4%
		Calcium	6%
		Iron	8%

TIPS: *A 16-oz. can drained sweet potatoes may be substituted for fresh sweet potatoes.*

To MAKE AHEAD, prepare to and refrigerate up to 2 days. Increase baking time to 30 to 45 minutes.*

If desired, omit brown sugar and add ⅓ cup maple-flavored syrup.

For variations add: ½ teaspoon grated orange peel, ⅛ teaspoon cinnamon or nutmeg, ½ cup well-drained crushed pineapple, ¼ cup orange juice or other fruit juice, 2 tablespoons rum or brandy. Garnish with coconut, salted peanuts, macadamia nuts or miniature marshmallows.

MASHED SWEET POTATOES

4 medium sweet potatoes, cooked
½ teaspoon salt
⅓ cup milk or orange juice
¼ cup margarine or butter

Peel potatoes and mash well. Mix in remaining ingredients; beat until light and fluffy. Serve immediately or spoon into buttered 1½-quart casserole and bake at 350°F. for 20 to 30 minutes. 5 servings

NUTRITION INFORMATION PER SERVING

Serving Size: 1/5 of recipe		Percent U.S. RDA Per Serving	
Calories	256	Protein	5%
Protein	3g	Vitamin A	235%
Carbohydrate	39g	Vitamin C	41%
Fat	10g	Thiamin	9%
Sodium	352mg	Riboflavin	7%
Potassium	376mg	Niacin	4%
		Calcium	7%
		Iron	6%

TIPS: *A 16-oz. can drained sweet potatoes may be substituted for fresh sweet potatoes.*

Variations: Stir in ½ cup drained crushed pineapple; top casserole with marshmallows, coconut, brown sugar or nuts before baking.

RUTABAGAS

Rutabagas are of the turnip family and are sometimes referred to as a Swedish turnip. The yellow variety is the most common although a white variety is also available. Turnips and rutabagas can normally be used interchangeably in recipes.

NUTRITION INFORMATION PER SERVING

Serving Size: 1/2 cup diced cooked rutabaga		Percent U.S. RDA Per Serving	
Calories	30	Protein	*
Protein	<1g	Vitamin A	9%
Carbohydrate	7g	Vitamin C	37%
Fat	<1g	Thiamin	3%
Sodium	3mg	Riboflavin	3%
Potassium	142mg	Niacin	3%
		Calcium	5%
		Iron	*

BUY: Allow 2 lb. (1 large or 2 medium rutabagas) for 4 servings. Select heavy, firm, smooth-skinned rutabagas.
PEAK SEASON: Fall through early spring.
STORAGE: Store in cool dry place or in refrigerator several weeks.
PREPARATION: Peel and slice, cube or cut into strips.
COOK: Add 1 inch salted water (½ teaspoon salt to 1 cup water) to rutabaga. Cover and heat to boiling. Cook 20 to 30 minutes or until tender; drain.

TIME:

Rutabagas	2-inch pieces	Diced
Boiling	*30 to 40 min.*	*20 to 25 min.*
Steaming	*40 to 60 min.*	*35 to 40 min.*
Pressure Saucepan (15 lb. pressure)	*6 to 10 min.*	*5 to 8 min.*

SEASONING: Before serving add: margarine or butter, lemon juice, parsley.

MASHED RUTABAGAS

2 to 3 medium rutabagas, peeled
½ teaspoon salt
⅛ teaspoon pepper
Dash nutmeg, if desired
¼ cup hot milk
¼ cup margarine or butter

In medium saucepan, cook rutabagas as directed. Drain well and mash. Add remaining ingredients; beat until light and fluffy.

6 servings

NUTRITION INFORMATION PER SERVING

Serving Size: 1/6 of recipe		Percent U.S. RDA Per Serving	
Calories	116	Protein	2%
Protein	1g	Vitamin A	19%
Carbohydrate	10g	Vitamin C	51%
Fat	8g	Thiamin	5%
Sodium	277mg	Riboflavin	5%
Potassium	212mg	Niacin	5%
		Calcium	8%
		Iron	2%

SPINACH AND OTHER GREENS (Including beet and turnip greens, Swiss chard and kale)

NUTRITION INFORMATION PER SERVING

Serving Size: 1/8 lb. raw spinach		Percent U.S. RDA Per Serving	
Calories	15	Protein	3%
Protein	2g	Vitamin A	92%
Carbohydrate	2g	Vitamin C	48%
Fat	<1g	Thiamin	4%
Sodium	40mg	Riboflavin	7%
Potassium	268mg	Niacin	*
		Calcium	5%
		Iron	10%

NUTRITION INFORMATION PER SERVING

Serving Size: 1/2 cup cooked spinach		Percent U.S. RDA Per Serving	
Calories	21	Protein	4%
Protein	3g	Vitamin A	146%
Carbohydrate	3g	Vitamin C	42%
Fat	<1g	Thiamin	4%
Sodium	45mg	Riboflavin	7%
Potassium	292mg	Niacin	2%
		Calcium	8%
		Iron	11%

BUY: Allow 1½ lb. (about 4 cups) for 4 servings. Select fresh, tender, bright green leaves. Avoid yellow or wilted leaves.
PEAK SEASON: Spring and summer (available all year).
STORAGE: Wash and drain leaves; refrigerate in airtight container, plastic bag or wrap, 2 to 3 days.
PREPARATION: Wash and drain leaves several times, removing tough stems or ribs and wilted leaves. Chop kale.
COOK: Cover and cook greens in water which clings to leaves from washing, (cover kale with water) until tender.

TIME:

	Spinach	Swiss Chard	Kale	Beet Greens	Turnip Greens
Boiling	*3 to 10 min.*	*10 to 20 min.*	*10 to 15 min.*	*5 to 15 min.*	*10 to 15 min.*
Steaming	*5 to 12 min.*	*15 to 25 min.*	–	–	–
Pressure Saucepan (15 lb. pressure)	*0 to 1½ min.*	*1½ to 3 min.*	–	–	–

SEASONING: Before serving add: cooked crumbled bacon, hard-cooked egg, vinegar, lemon juice, white sauce, soy sauce, toasted sesame seed, sour cream, horseradish, French dressing.

SWISS SPINACH BAKE

10-oz. pkg. (1¼ cups) frozen chopped spinach
1 egg
⅓ cup milk
½ cup (2 oz.) shredded Swiss cheese
½ teaspoon salt
½ teaspoon instant minced onion
Dash pepper

Heat oven to 325°F. In medium saucepan, cook spinach (without salt) as directed on package. Drain well, pressing with fork to remove excess water. In 1-quart casserole, beat egg. Stir in remaining ingredients and spinach.* Bake uncovered at 325°F. for 30 to 35 minutes or until center is set.

3 to 4 servings

NUTRITION INFORMATION PER SERVING

Serving Size: 1/4 of recipe		Percent U.S. RDA Per Serving	
Calories	102	Protein	12%
Protein	8g	Vitamin A	94%
Carbohydrate	4g	Vitamin C	13%
Fat	6g	Thiamin	4%
Sodium	427mg	Riboflavin	13%
Potassium	249mg	Niacin	*
		Calcium	23%
		Iron	9%

TIPS: *To double recipe, double the ingredient amounts; bake in 1½-quart casserole for 45 to 50 minutes.*

To MAKE AHEAD, prepare to, cool and refrigerate up to 1 day. If mixture is cold, increase baking time 5 to 10 minutes.*

SPINACH DELISH

10- oz. pkg. (1¼ cups) frozen chopped spinach
1 tablespoon dry onion soup mix
1 tablespoon water
½ cup dairy sour cream

In medium saucepan, combine spinach, soup mix and water. Simmer over low heat, about 10 minutes or until tender. Stir in sour cream. Let stand covered 2 minutes to heat through. 3 to 4 servings

NUTRITION INFORMATION PER SERVING

Serving Size: 1/3 of recipe		Percent U.S. RDA Per Serving	
Calories	53	Protein	3%
Protein	2g	Vitamin A	61%
Carbohydrate	3g	Vitamin C	12%
Fat	4g	Thiamin	2%
Sodium	149mg	Riboflavin	5%
Potassium	132mg	Niacin	*
		Calcium	6%
		Iron	4%

CHEESY CREAMED SPINACH

2 pkg. (10 oz. each) frozen chopped spinach
10¾- oz. can condensed cream of mushroom soup
1 cup (4 oz.) shredded cheese

Heat oven to 375°F. In medium saucepan, cook spinach as directed on package; drain. Pour into 1½-quart casserole; top with soup. Sprinkle with cheese. Bake uncovered at 375°F. for 15 to 20 minutes or until bubbly.

6 to 8 servings

NUTRITION INFORMATION PER SERVING

Serving Size: 1/6 of recipe		Percent U.S. RDA Per Serving	
Calories	147	Protein	12%
Protein	8g	Vitamin A	121%
Carbohydrate	7g	Vitamin C	23%
Fat	10g	Thiamin	4%
Sodium	565mg	Riboflavin	14%
Potassium	300mg	Niacin	3%
		Calcium	24%
		Iron	10%

TIP: *For a luncheon dish, arrange sliced hard-cooked eggs over spinach before topping with soup.*

SPINACH SOUFFLÉ

10- oz. pkg. (1¼ cups) frozen chopped spinach
¼ cup margarine or butter
¼ cup flour
½ teaspoon salt
⅛ teaspoon pepper
1 cup milk
3 eggs, separated

In medium saucepan, cook spinach as directed on package; drain well. Heat oven to 350°F. In small saucepan, melt margarine; blend in flour, salt and pepper. Cook until mixture is smooth and bubbly. Stir in milk; heat until mixture boils and thickens, stirring occasionally. Remove from heat.

In small bowl, beat egg yolks until thick and lemon-colored. Stir yolks into white sauce; stir in spinach. In large bowl, beat egg whites until stiff. Stir ¼ of beaten egg whites into sauce mixture. Gently fold sauce mixture into remaining egg whites. Pour into buttered 1½-quart casserole. Set casserole in pan of water (1-inch deep). Bake at 350°F. for 40 to 50 minutes or until a knife inserted in the center comes out clean. Serve immediately.

4 to 5 servings

NUTRITION INFORMATION PER SERVING

Serving Size: 1/4 of recipe		Percent U.S. RDA Per Serving	
Calories	247	Protein	15%
Protein	10g	Vitamin A	107%
Carbohydrate	12g	Vitamin C	18%
Fat	18g	Thiamin	10%
Sodium	507mg	Riboflavin	20%
Potassium	331mg	Niacin	4%
		Calcium	16%
		Iron	13%

TIP: *For ASPARAGUS SOUFFLÉ, substitute 16-oz. can (2 cups) drained cut asparagus for spinach; decrease salt to ¼ teaspoon. If desired, liquid drained from asparagus may be used for part of milk.*

SQUASH – SUMMER

SUMMER VARIETIES: Include zucchini, patty pan, straight neck yellow, crooked neck yellow and cocozelle. They are quick-growing types with thin, tender skins.

NUTRITION INFORMATION PER SERVING

Serving Size: 1/2 cup cooked squash		Percent U.S. RDA Per Serving	
Calories	15	Protein	*
Protein	<1g	Vitamin A	8%
Carbohydrate	3g	Vitamin C	17%
Fat	<1g	Thiamin	3%
Sodium	1mg	Riboflavin	5%
Potassium	148mg	Niacin	4%
		Calcium	3%
		Iron	2%

BUY: Allow 2 lb. for 4 servings. Select squash with smooth, brightly colored skin that feel heavy for their size. Skin should be firm but soft enough to puncture easily with fingernail.

PEAK SEASON: Summer.

STORAGE: Store in vegetable crisper drawer several days.

PREPARATION: Wash, but do not peel. Cut off stem, blossom end and if necessary, remove seeds and fibers. Slice or cube.

COOK: Add 1 inch salted water (½ teaspoon salt to 1 cup water) to squash. Cover and heat to boiling. Cook 8 to 15 minutes for slices, 7 to 8 minutes for cubes; drain.

TIME:

Summer Squash	½-inch Slices or Cubes
Boiling	*8 to 15 min.*
Steaming	*15 to 20 min.*
Pressure Saucepan (15 lb. pressure)	*1½ to 3 min.*
Baking	*30 min.*

SEASONINGS: When cooking add: oregano leaves, basil leaves, dill seed, nutmeg, bacon.

Before serving add margarine, butter or Parmesan cheese.

CROOKED NECK

STRAIGHT NECK

ZUCCHINI

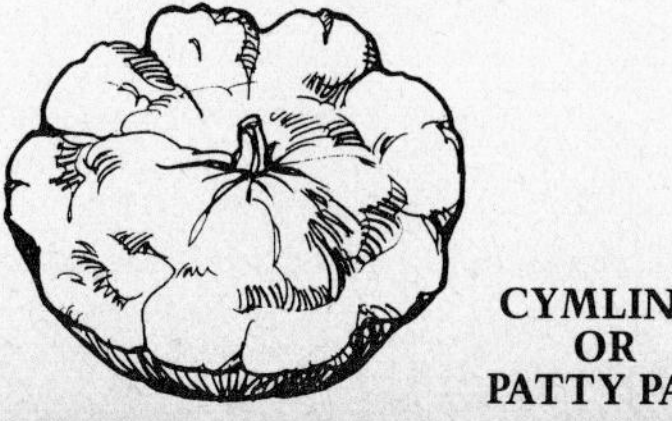

CYMLING OR PATTY PAN

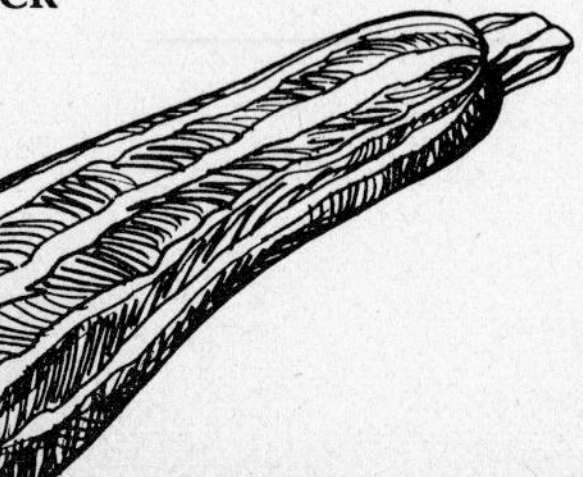

COCOZELLE

STUFFED ZUCCHINI BOATS

4 medium zucchini
1 lb. ground beef or lamb
1 small onion, chopped
1 garlic clove, minced
1 teaspoon oregano leaves
½ teaspoon salt
¼ teaspoon pepper
¼ cup grated Parmesan cheese
10¾-oz. can condensed tomato soup
1 cup (4 oz.) grated Mozzarella cheese

Heat oven to 375°F. Cut off stem end of zucchini. Cut zucchini in half lengthwise; scoop out seeds and pulp (reserve pulp) leaving ¼-inch shell. In medium skillet, brown ground beef, onion, garlic and oregano; drain excess fat. Add chopped zucchini pulp, Parmesan cheese, ¼ of soup, salt and pepper. Arrange zucchini shells in 13x9-inch pan. Spoon meat mixture into shells. Spoon remaining soup over top; sprinkle with additional Parmesan cheese.* Bake covered with foil at 375°F. for 35 minutes or until zucchini are tender. Sprinkle grated Mozzarella cheese over zucchini. Return to oven and bake 5 minutes.

6 to 8 servings

NUTRITION INFORMATION PER SERVING

Serving Size: 1/8 of recipe		Percent U.S. RDA Per Serving	
Calories	233	Protein	21%
Protein	14g	Vitamin A	14%
Carbohydrate	9g	Vitamin C	31%
Fat	16g	Thiamin	7%
Sodium	527mg	Riboflavin	17%
Potassium	436mg	Niacin	16%
		Calcium	18%
		Iron	13%

TIP: *To MAKE AHEAD, prepare to* * *Refrigerate up to 1 day. Bake as directed.*

GARDEN FRESH COMBO

4 tablespoons margarine, butter or oil
4 cups (3 medium) sliced zucchini or summer squash
8 oz. (3 cups) sliced fresh mushrooms
1 medium onion, sliced
1 stalk celery, sliced
½ teaspoon salt
½ teaspoon thyme leaves
2 medium tomatoes, quartered
¼ cup grated Parmesan cheese

In large skillet, combine all ingredients except tomatoes and cheese. Cover loosely and cook about 10 minutes or until tender, stirring occasionally. Add tomatoes and cheese; cook 1 to 2 minutes or until heated through. Serve immediately.

5 to 6 servings

NUTRITION INFORMATION PER SERVING

Serving Size: 1/6 of recipe		Percent U.S. RDA Per Serving	
Calories	121	Protein	6%
Protein	4g	Vitamin A	19%
Carbohydrate	8g	Vitamin C	47%
Fat	9g	Thiamin	6%
Sodium	315mg	Riboflavin	14%
Potassium	425mg	Niacin	11%
		Calcium	9%
		Iron	7%

TIP: *Corn or shredded cabbage may be substituted for one of vegetables above.*

STUFFED TOMATOES,
GARDEN FRESH COMBO,
CREAMED GARDEN POTATOES AND PEAS,
ONION CORN-ON-THE-COB

CHEESE-FRIED ZUCCHINI

¼ cup dry bread crumbs
2 tablespoons grated Parmesan cheese
2 tablespoons flour
1 teaspoon salt
2 medium zucchini, thinly sliced
1 egg, beaten
2 to 4 tablespoons oil or olive oil

In plastic bag or shallow bowl, combine first 4 ingredients. Dip zucchini in egg; coat with crumb mixture. In medium skillet, fry in hot oil until golden brown and crisp, turning occasionally. Drain on paper towel. Serve immediately.

3 to 4 servings

NUTRITION INFORMATION PER SERVING

Serving Size: 1/4 of recipe		Percent U.S. RDA Per Serving	
Calories	125	Protein	6%
Protein	4g	Vitamin A	8%
Carbohydrate	7g	Vitamin C	21%
Fat	9g	Thiamin	5%
Sodium	581mg	Riboflavin	8%
Potassium	159mg	Niacin	5%
		Calcium	6%
		Iron	4%

SAUCY ITALIAN ZUCCHINI

3 medium zucchini, thinly sliced
½ teaspoon salt
⅛ teaspoon pepper
⅛ to ¼ teaspoon Italian seasoning, oregano or basil leaves
1 tablespoon margarine or butter
8-oz. can (1 cup) tomato sauce
1 cup (4 oz.) shredded Mozzarella cheese or ¼ cup grated Parmesan cheese

Heat oven to 375°F. In 1½-quart casserole, combine all ingredients except cheese. Sprinkle with cheese. Bake uncovered at 375°F. for 30 to 40 minutes or until tender.

4 to 6 servings

NUTRITION INFORMATION PER SERVING

Serving Size: 1/6 of recipe		Percent U.S. RDA Per Serving	
Calories	163	Protein	5%
Protein	3g	Vitamin A	21%
Carbohydrate	8g	Vitamin C	19%
Fat	14g	Thiamin	5%
Sodium	259mg	Riboflavin	13%
Potassium	190mg	Niacin	6%
		Calcium	17%
		Iron	4%

ZUCCHINI STUFFED TOMATOES

6 firm ripe tomatoes
¼ cup margarine or butter
2 cups thinly sliced zucchini
2 tablespoons finely chopped onion
1½ teaspoons garlic salt
½ teaspoon dill weed
1 tablespoon flour
7-oz. can (1 cup) whole kernel corn, drained

Wash and dry tomatoes; cut ¼-inch slice from stem end. With spoon scoop out inside of tomatoes; reserve pulp. In large skillet, melt margarine. Stir in zucchini, onion, garlic salt and dill weed. Cook uncovered over low heat 5 minutes or until zucchini is crisp-tender, stirring occasionally. Stir in flour, corn and ½ cup tomato pulp. Cook over low heat, stirring frequently 3 to 5 minutes or until mixture is thickened. Lightly salt tomato shells; fill each with ⅓ cup zucchini mixture. Place in ungreased 9-inch square baking dish or shallow casserole. Bake at 350°F. for 12 to 15 minutes or until tomatoes are heated through but firm.

6 servings

NUTRITION INFORMATION PER SERVING

Serving Size: 1/6 of recipe		Percent U.S. RDA Per Serving	
Calories	122	Protein	3%
Protein	2g	Vitamin A	23%
Carbohydrate	12g	Vitamin C	21%
Fat	8g	Thiamin	5%
Sodium	637mg	Riboflavin	4%
Potassium	260mg	Niacin	6%
		Calcium	2%
		Iron	4%

ZUCCHINI STUFFED TOMATOES

SQUASH – WINTER

WINTER VARIETIES: Include banana, butternut, hubbard, buttercup and acorn. They have hard tough rinds with deep orange flesh.

NUTRITION INFORMATION PER SERVING

Serving Size: 1/2 cup cooked squash		Percent U.S. RDA Per Serving	
Calories	57	Protein	3%
Protein	2g	Vitamin A	29%
Carbohydrate	14g	Vitamin C	22%
Fat	<1g	Thiamin	3%
Sodium	1mg	Riboflavin	8%
Potassium	494mg	Niacin	4%
		Calcium	4%
		Iron	6%

BUY: Allow 3 lb. for 4 servings. Select squash with full maturity, indicated by a hard tough rind. Look for squash that is heavy for its size (meaning a thick wall and more edible flesh). Slight variations in skin color do not affect flavor.
PEAK SEASON: Fall and winter. Acorn squash is available all year.

STORAGE: Store whole squash in cool (about 60°F.) dry place for several months. Refrigerate cut pieces in airtight container, plastic bag or wrap, 2 to 3 days.
PREPARATION: Large squash; cut into serving-size pieces. Remove seeds and fibers. Medium squash; (acorn and buttercup) cut in half and remove seeds and fiber, or leave whole and remove seeds and fiber after cooking as directed for Baked Winter Squash, page 616.

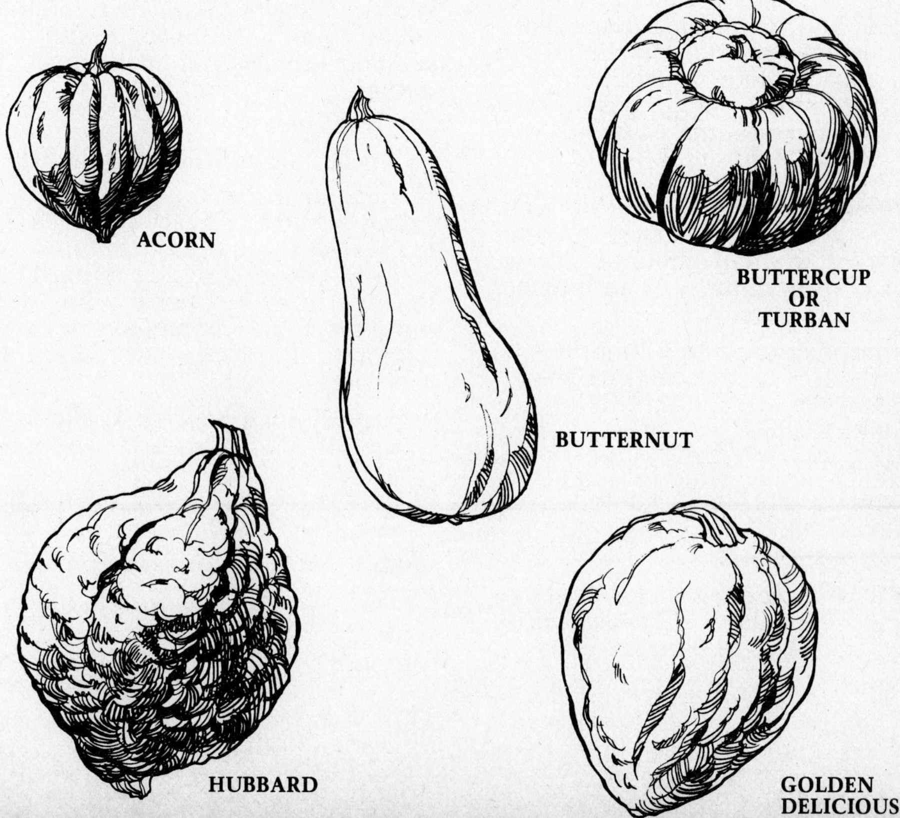

COOKING: Medium squash are usually cooked by baking. Large squash can be boiled. Add 1 inch salted water (½ teaspoon salt to 1 cup water) to squash pieces. Cover and heat to boiling. Cook until tender; drain. See recipes for Baked, Sautéed and Simmered Winter Squash.

TIME:

Squash	Hubbard or Butternut, 2-inch Pieces	Banana, 2-inch Pieces	Acorn or Buttercup
Boiling	*15 to 20 min.*	*7 to 10 min.*	–
Steaming	*25 to 40 min.*	*15 to 20 min.*	–
Pressure Saucepan (15 lb. pressure)	*6 to 12 min.*	*2 to 5 min.*	–
Baking			
Pieces	*40 to 60 min.*	*30 min.*	–
Halved	–	–	*40 to 60 min.*
Whole	–	–	*60 to 90 min.*

SEASONING: Before serving add: margarine or butter, cinnamon, nutmeg, ginger, brown sugar, honey, maple-flavored syrup, cooked crumbled bacon, peanuts, cashews.

SIMMERED WINTER SQUASH

Cook peeled 2-inch pieces squash, covered, in small amount of water for 15 to 20 minutes or until tender. Season to taste.

NUTRITION INFORMATION PER SERVING

Serving Size: 1/2 lb. squash		Percent U.S. RDA Per Serving	
Calories	115	Protein	5%
Protein	3g	Vitamin A	149%
Carbohydrate	28g	Vitamin C	24%
Fat	<1g	Thiamin	6%
Sodium	2mg	Riboflavin	14%
Potassium	839mg	Niacin	6%
		Calcium	5%
		Iron	8%

TIP: *For steaming, increase time to 25 to 40 minutes. For pressure cooking, cook 6 to 12 minutes.*

BAKED WINTER SQUASH

Heat oven to 400°F. Prepare squash as directed. Place serving-size pieces of unpeeled squash cut-side-up, in pan with small amount of water (about ¼-inch). Season with salt and pepper; dot with margarine or butter. Cover with foil. Bake acorn, hubbard, butternut and buttercup at 400°F. for 30 to 50 minutes or until tender; bake banana squash 20 to 30 minutes. Squash may be served as is or removed from skin and mashed with additional seasonings.

NUTRITION INFORMATION PER SERVING

Serving Size: 1/2 lb. squash		Percent U.S. RDA Per Serving	
Calories	218	Protein	5%
Protein	3g	Vitamin A	159%
Carbohydrate	28g	Vitamin C	24%
Fat	12g	Thiamin	6%
Sodium	685mg	Riboflavin	14%
Potassium	842mg	Niacin	6%
		Calcium	6%
		Iron	8%

TIP: *If planning an oven meal, small squash such as buttercup or acorn may be baked like a baked potato. Wash and prick well. Bake at 350° to 375°F. for 1 to 1½ hours. Halve and remove seeds and fiber before serving.*

SAUTÉED WINTER SQUASH

In medium skillet, melt ¼ cup margarine or butter; add about 4 cups (2 lb.) peeled, sliced squash. Simmer covered, 15 to 20 minutes or until tender, stirring occasionally. Remove cover last few minutes to evaporate excess moisture. Season as desired.

NUTRITION INFORMATION PER SERVING

Serving Size: 1/4 of recipe		Percent U.S. RDA Per Serving	
Calories	216	Protein	6%
Protein	4g	Vitamin A	68%
Carbohydrate	29g	Vitamin C	32%
Fat	12g	Thiamin	7%
Sodium	142mg	Riboflavin	16%
Potassium	1002mg	Niacin	7%
		Calcium	8%
		Iron	13%

ACORN SQUASH GLAZES AND FILLINGS

Heat oven to 400°F. Bake squash as directed (omitting margarine) for 30 minutes or until just about tender. Fill each half with one of glazes. (Glaze and filling amounts are for each squash half.) Return to oven, bake uncovered for 10 to 15 minutes longer.

BASIC GLAZE: Add ½ tablespoon margarine or butter and 1 tablespoon firmly packed brown sugar, honey or maple syrup.

BRANDY GLAZE: Add ½ tablespoon margarine or butter, 1 tablespoon firmly packed brown sugar and 1 to 2 tablespoons brandy or fruit-flavored brandy.

ORANGE GLAZE: Add ½ tablespoon grated orange peel to Basic Glaze, or use 1 tablespoon margarine or butter and 1 tablespoon orange marmalade.

VERMONT GLAZE: Add 1 tablespoon margarine or butter, 1 tablespoon firmly packed brown sugar or maple-flavored syrup and 1 slice uncooked bacon, cut into 3 pieces. Bake 10 to 12 minutes or until bacon is cooked.

APPLE FILLING: Add ½ peeled and sliced apple or ¼ cup applesauce, ½ tablespoon raisins, 2 tablespoons firmly packed brown sugar, 1 tablespoon margarine or butter and dash of cinnamon. Bake 15 minutes or until apple is tender.

MINCEMEAT FILLING: Add ¼ peeled and chopped apple, 3 tablespoons mincemeat, ½ tablespoon margarine or butter and dash of nutmeg.

CRAN-APPLE FILLING: Substitute prepared cranberry sauce for mincemeat in Mincemeat Filling.

HONEY-GLAZED SQUASH

4 cups (about 2 lb.) peeled, cubed winter squash
¼ cup margarine or butter, melted
¼ cup honey
1 teaspoon salt

Heat oven to 350°F. Arrange squash in shallow 10x6-inch (1½-quart) baking dish. Combine remaining ingredients; pour over squash. Bake covered at 350°F. for 40 to 45 minutes or until tender. Uncover and continue baking 10 minutes.

4 servings

NUTRITION INFORMATION PER SERVING

Serving Size: 1/4 of recipe		Percent U.S. RDA Per Serving	
Calories	310	Protein	7%
Protein	4g	Vitamin A	196%
Carbohydrate	52g	Vitamin C	50%
Fat	12g	Thiamin	8%
Sodium	677mg	Riboflavin	18%
Potassium	1061mg	Niacin	8%
		Calcium	7%
		Iron	11%

TOMATOES

There are 3 basic types of tomatoes – the large red tomatoes used for slicing, salads and canning; cherry tomatoes used for eating raw, cooking, preserves and pickles; and the Italian type of pear-shaped red or yellow tomatoes used in tomato paste, canning, pickles or eating raw.

NUTRITION INFORMATION PER SERVING

Serving Size: 1 medium tomato		Percent U.S. RDA Per Serving	
Calories	27	Protein	2%
Protein	1g	Vitamin A	22%
Carbohydrate	6g	Vitamin C	47%
Fat	<1g	Thiamin	5%
Sodium	4mg	Riboflavin	3%
Potassium	300mg	Niacin	4%
		Calcium	*
		Iron	3%

NUTRITION INFORMATION PER SERVING

Serving Size: 1/2 cup cooked tomato		Percent U.S. RDA Per Serving	
Calories	32	Protein	2%
Protein	2g	Vitamin A	25%
Carbohydrate	7g	Vitamin C	49%
Fat	<1g	Thiamin	6%
Sodium	5mg	Riboflavin	4%
Potassium	353mg	Niacin	5%
		Calcium	*
		Iron	4%

BUY: Allow 1½ lb. (5 medium tomatoes) for 4 servings. Select slightly soft tomatoes, bright red in color and well-shaped. Deep red soft tomatoes may be overripe.
PEAK SEASON: Summer and fall (available all year).
STORAGE: Leave underripe tomatoes at room temperature to ripen. Store tomatoes in cool place or refrigerator, 3 to 5 days.
PREPARATION: Wash and cut out stem. Peel, if desired. To remove skin easily, dip tomato into boiling water ½ minute, remove and dip into cold water. Leave whole, quarter or slice.
COOK: Simmer covered without additional liquid (juice from the tomatoes makes the liquid). Cook until tender.

TIME:

Tomatoes	
Boiling	*7 to 15 min.*
Pressure Saucepan (15 lb. pressure)	*½ to 1 min.*
Baking	*15 to 30 min.*

SEASONING: When cooking add: basil leaves, oregano leaves, thyme, green pepper, parsley, bay leaves, celery seed, sesame seed, tarragon leaves.

Before serving add: mayonnaise, sour cream, Parmesan cheese.

SPLIT PEAS WITH TOMATOES

¼ cup chopped salt pork with 2 slices bacon, cut up
2 cups water
1 cup dry green or yellow split peas or lentils
½ teaspoon salt
1 small onion, chopped
1 teaspoon sugar, if desired
Dash pepper
8-oz. can (1 cup) stewed tomatoes or tomato sauce

In large saucepan or skillet, fry salt pork and bacon until brown and crisp. Add water, heat to boiling. Add peas and boil 2 minutes. Remove from heat; cover and let stand 30 minutes. Add salt and onion; heat to boiling. Simmer covered, 25 minutes or until peas are tender, stirring occasionally. Stir in remaining ingredients and heat through.

6 servings

NUTRITION INFORMATION PER SERVING

Serving Size: 1/6 of recipe		Percent U.S. RDA Per Serving	
Calories	208	Protein	15%
Protein	10g	Vitamin A	8%
Carbohydrate	25g	Vitamin C	14%
Fat	8g	Thiamin	21%
Sodium	325mg	Riboflavin	7%
Potassium	424mg	Niacin	8%
		Calcium	2%
		Iron	12%

TIP: *If desired, add ½ cup cubed cheese with tomatoes. Heat through.*

BROILED TOMATOES

Cut 6 medium tomatoes in half and arrange on broiler pan or shallow pan. Season with salt and pepper. Broil tomatoes cut-side-up, 3 to 5 inches from heat for 5 minutes. Top with desired topping. Return to oven, broil 2 to 5 minutes longer. Crumb toppings brown quickly so watch closely.

MAYONNAISE TOPPING: Combine ⅓ cup mayonnaise or salad dressing with 3 tablespoons prepared mustard and 2 tablespoons finely chopped onion.

NUTRITION INFORMATION PER SERVING

Serving Size: 2 tomato halves		Percent U.S. RDA Per Serving	
Calories	122	Protein	3%
Protein	2g	Vitamin A	23%
Carbohydrate	7g	Vitamin C	33%
Fat	10g	Thiamin	5%
Sodium	261mg	Riboflavin	3%
Potassium	319mg	Niacin	4%
		Calcium	3%
		Iron	5%

SAVORY CRUMB TOPPING: Cook 1 tablespoon finely chopped onion in 2 tablespoons margarine or butter. Stir in ½ cup dry bread crumbs, 1 tablespoon minced parsley and ⅛ teaspoon thyme.

NUTRITION INFORMATION PER SERVING

Serving Size: 2 tomato halves		Percent U.S. RDA Per Serving	
Calories	95	Protein	4%
Protein	2g	Vitamin A	26%
Carbohydrate	12g	Vitamin C	33%
Fat	4g	Thiamin	6%
Sodium	202mg	Riboflavin	4%
Potassium	321mg	Niacin	6%
		Calcium	3%
		Iron	6%

CHEESE TOPPING: Combine 2 tablespoons melted margarine or butter with ¼ cup grated Parmesan cheese and 1 teaspoon chopped chives.

NUTRITION INFORMATION PER SERVING

Serving Size: 2 tomato halves		Percent U.S. RDA Per Serving	
Calories	78	Protein	4%
Protein	3g	Vitamin A	26%
Carbohydrate	6g	Vitamin C	33%
Fat	5g	Thiamin	5%
Sodium	171mg	Riboflavin	5%
Potassium	307mg	Niacin	4%
		Calcium	7%
		Iron	4%

CHEESE-CRUMB TOPPING: Combine 2 tablespoons melted margarine or butter, ½ cup dry bread crumbs, 2 tablespoons grated Parmesan cheese and ¼ teaspoon basil leaves. If desired, cook 3 slices bacon, using drippings for margarine. Garnish broiled tomatoes with crumbled bacon.

NUTRITION INFORMATION PER SERVING

Serving Size: 2 tomato halves		Percent U.S. RDA Per Serving	
Calories	101	Protein	5%
Protein	3g	Vitamin A	26%
Carbohydrate	12g	Vitamin C	33%
Fat	5g	Thiamin	6%
Sodium	214mg	Riboflavin	5%
Potassium	318mg	Niacin	6%
		Calcium	5%
		Iron	5%

STEWED TOMATOES and CORN CUSTARD SCALLOP

STEWED TOMATOES

1 cup herb-seasoned bread stuffing cubes
¼ cup margarine or butter, melted
28-oz. can (3½ cups) tomatoes, undrained and cut up
1 tablespoon sugar
½ teaspoon salt
⅛ teaspoon pepper
⅛ teaspoon basil leaves

Heat oven to 350°F. In small bowl, toss bread stuffing with margarine. In 2-quart casserole, combine tomatoes, sugar, salt, pepper and basil. Sprinkle with bread stuffing cubes. Bake uncovered at 350°F. for 20 to 30 minutes or until heated through.

6 servings

NUTRITION INFORMATION PER SERVING

Serving Size: 1/6 of recipe		Percent U.S. RDA Per Serving	
Calories	122	Protein	3%
Protein	2g	Vitamin A	30%
Carbohydrate	11g	Vitamin C	38%
Fat	8g	Thiamin	5%
Sodium	506mg	Riboflavin	3%
Potassium	299mg	Niacin	5%
		Calcium	*
		Iron	5%

BAKED STUFFED TOMATOES

Heat oven to 350°F. Cut off thin slice from stem end of each tomato; remove pulp. Sprinkle inside of tomatoes with salt and pepper; invert to drain. Fill with one of the prepared vegetables below. Place in shallow pan. Bake at 350°F. for 15 to 20 minutes or until tomatoes are hot. toes are hot.

TIP: *Prepared vegetables that make attractive and tasty fillings for stuffed tomatoes:*

Spinach Delish, page 610 (3 tomatoes)
Double Onion Bake, page 596 (5 tomatoes)
Scalloped Onions, page 595 (5 tomatoes)
Caraway Cabbage, page 577 (4 tomatoes)
Scalloped Cabbage, page 578 (4 tomatoes)
Creamed Celery with Almonds, page 586 (5 tomatoes)
Peas with Onions and Mushrooms, page 597 (4 tomatoes)

BACON AND CREAM-TOPPED TOMATOES

4 slices bacon
½ cup dairy sour cream
½ teaspoon salt
4 medium tomatoes

In large skillet, fry bacon until crisp; remove. Crumble bacon and blend with sour cream and salt. Cut ends off tomatoes and cut tomatoes in half. Sauté cut-side of tomatoes in bacon drippings; turn over. Top with sour cream mixture. Cover; sauté 2 minutes or until heated through. 4 servings

NUTRITION INFORMATION PER SERVING

Serving Size: 1/4 of recipe		Percent U.S. RDA Per Serving	
Calories	169	Protein	10%
Protein	6g	Vitamin A	21%
Carbohydrate	6g	Vitamin C	21%
Fat	13g	Thiamin	9%
Sodium	434mg	Riboflavin	7%
Potassium	257mg	Niacin	7%
		Calcium	5%
		Iron	5%

BACON AND CREAM TOPPED TOMATOES

TURNIPS

Turnips are white in color with green tops that are not only edible, but very nutritious. Yellow turnips are of the turnip family, but are usually known as rutabagas.

NUTRITION INFORMATION PER SERVING

Serving Size: 1/2 cup cubed cooked turnip		Percent U.S. RDA Per Serving	
Calories	18	Protein	*
Protein	<1g	Vitamin A	0%
Carbohydrate	4g	Vitamin C	29%
Fat	<1g	Thiamin	2%
Sodium	27mg	Riboflavin	2%
Potassium	147mg	Niacin	*
		Calcium	3%
		Iron	*

BUY: Allow ¼ lb. or 1 small turnip per serving. Select smooth, heavy turnips with fresh green tops.
PEAK SEASON: Winter.
STORAGE: Store in cool, moist area or in vegetable crisper drawer of refrigerator up to several weeks.
PREPARATION: Peel off the thick layer of skin. Wash and slice or cube. Tops may be removed and cooked as greens.
COOKING: Add 1 inch salted water (½ teaspoon salt to 1 cup water) to turnips. Cover loosely and heat to boiling. Simmer 15 to 20 minutes or until tender; drain.
TIME:

Turnips	Sliced
Boiling	*15 to 20 min.*
Steaming	*20 to 25 min.*
Pressure Saucepan (15 lb. pressure)	*1 to 2 min.*

SEASONING: Before serving add: margarine or butter, lemon juice, parsley.

A

B

E

F

G

M

P

T

U

V

W

Y

Z